12 Rules for Life

JORDAN B. PETERSON

12 Rules For Life

An Antidote to Chaos

Foreword by Norman Doidge

Illustrations by Ethan Van Sciver

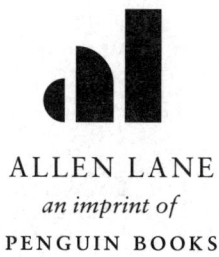

ALLEN LANE
an imprint of
PENGUIN BOOKS

ALLEN LANE

UK | USA | Canada | Ireland | Australia
India | New Zealand | South Africa

Allen Lane is part of the Penguin Random House group of companies
whose addresses can be found at global.penguinrandomhouse.com.

First published in Canada by Random House Canada 2018
First published in Great Britain by Allen Lane 2018

034

Copyright © Luminate Psychological Services, Ltd., 2018
Foreword copyright © Norman Doidge, 2018
Illustrations copyright © Luminate Psychological Services, Ltd., 2018

The moral right of the author has been asserted

Printed and bound in Great Britain by Clays Ltd, Elcograf S.p.A.

A CIP catalogue record for this book is available from the British Library

HARDBACK ISBN: 978–0–241–35163–5
TRADE PAPERBACK ISBN: 978–0–241–35164–2

www.greenpenguin.co.uk

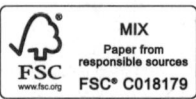

Penguin Random House is committed to a
sustainable future for our business, our readers
and our planet. This book is made from Forest
Stewardship Council® certified paper.

TABLE OF CONTENTS

Foreword by Norman Doidge **vii**

Overture **xxv**

RULE 1 / Stand up straight with your shoulders back **1**

RULE 2 / Treat yourself like someone you are responsible for helping **31**

RULE 3 / Make friends with people who want the best for you **67**

RULE 4 / Compare yourself to who you were yesterday,
not to who someone else is today **85**

RULE 5 / Do not let your children do anything that
makes you dislike them **113**

RULE 6 / Set your house in perfect order
before you criticize the world **147**

RULE 7 / Pursue what is meaningful (not what is expedient) **161**

RULE 8 / Tell the truth—or, at least, don't lie **203**

RULE 9 / Assume that the person you are listening
to might know something you don't **233**

RULE 10 / Be precise in your speech **259**

RULE 11 / Do not bother children when they are skateboarding **285**

RULE 12 / Pet a cat when you encounter one on the street **335**

Coda **355**

Acknowledgements **369** / Endnotes **371** / Index **390**

FOREWORD

RULES? MORE RULES? REALLY? Isn't life complicated enough, restricting enough, without abstract rules that don't take our unique, individual situations into account? And given that our brains are plastic, and all develop differently based on our life experiences, why even expect that a few rules might be helpful to us all?

People don't clamour for rules, even in the Bible . . . as when Moses comes down the mountain, after a long absence, bearing the tablets inscribed with ten commandments, and finds the Children of Israel in revelry. They'd been Pharaoh's slaves and subject to his tyrannical regulations for four hundred years, and after that Moses subjected them to the harsh desert wilderness for another forty years, to purify them of their slavishness. Now, free at last, they are unbridled, and have lost all control as they dance wildly around an idol, a golden calf, displaying all manner of corporeal corruption.

"I've got some good news . . . and I've got some bad news," the lawgiver yells to them. "Which do you want first?"

"The good news!" the hedonists reply.

"I got Him from fifteen commandments down to ten!"

"Hallelujah!" cries the unruly crowd. "And the bad?"

"Adultery is still in."

So rules there will be—but, please, not too many. We are ambivalent about rules, even when we know they are good for us. If we are spirited souls, if we have character, rules seem restrictive, an affront to our sense of agency and our pride in working out our own lives. Why should we be judged according to another's rule?

And judged we are. After all, God didn't give Moses "The Ten Suggestions," he gave Commandments; and if I'm a free agent, my first reaction to a command might just be that nobody, not even God, tells me what to do, even if it's good for me. But the story of the golden calf also reminds us that without rules we quickly become slaves to our passions—and there's nothing freeing about that.

And the story suggests something more: unchaperoned, and left to our own untutored judgment, we are quick to aim low and worship qualities that are beneath us—in this case, an artificial animal that brings out our own animal instincts in a completely unregulated way. The old Hebrew story makes it clear how the ancients felt about our prospects for civilized behaviour in the absence of rules that seek to elevate our gaze and raise our standards.

One neat thing about the Bible story is that it doesn't simply list its rules, as lawyers or legislators or administrators might; it embeds them in a dramatic tale that illustrates why we need them, thereby making them easier to understand. Similarly, in this book Professor Peterson doesn't just propose his twelve rules, he tells stories, too, bringing to bear his knowledge of many fields as he illustrates and explains why the best rules do not ultimately restrict us but instead facilitate our goals and make for fuller, freer lives.

The first time I met Jordan Peterson was on September 12, 2004, at the home of two mutual friends, TV producer Wodek Szemberg and medical internist Estera Bekier. It was Wodek's birthday party. Wodek and Estera are Polish émigrés who grew up within the Soviet empire, where it was understood that many topics were off limits, and that casually questioning certain social arrangements and philosophical ideas (not to mention the regime itself) could mean big trouble.

But now, host and hostess luxuriated in easygoing, honest talk, by having elegant parties devoted to the pleasure of saying what you *really* thought and hearing others do the same, in an uninhibited give-and-take. Here, the rule was "Speak your mind." If the conversation turned to politics, people of different political persuasions spoke to each other—indeed, looked forward to it—in a manner that is increasingly rare. Sometimes Wodek's own opinions, or truths, exploded out of him, as did his laugh. Then he'd hug whoever had made him laugh or provoked him to speak his mind with greater intensity than even he might have intended. This was the best part of the parties, and this frankness, and his warm embraces, made it worth provoking him. Meanwhile, Estera's voice lilted across the room on a very precise path towards its intended listener. Truth explosions didn't make the atmosphere any less easygoing for the company—they made for more truth explosions!—liberating us, and more laughs, and making the whole evening more pleasant, because with de-repressing Eastern Europeans like the Szemberg-Bekiers, you always knew with what and with whom you were dealing, and that frankness was enlivening. Honoré de Balzac, the novelist, once described the balls and parties in his native France, observing that what appeared to be a single party was always really two. In the first hours, the gathering was suffused with bored people posing and posturing, and attendees who came to meet perhaps one special person who would confirm them in their beauty and status. Then, only in the very late hours, after most of the guests had left, would the second party, the real party, begin. Here the conversation was shared by each person present, and open-hearted laughter replaced the starchy airs. At Estera and Wodek's parties, this kind of wee-hours-of-the-morning disclosure and intimacy often began as soon as we entered the room.

Wodek is a silver-haired, lion-maned hunter, always on the lookout for potential public intellectuals, who knows how to spot people who can *really* talk in front of a TV camera and who look authentic because they are (the camera picks up on that). He often invites such people to these salons. That day Wodek brought a psychology professor, from my own University of Toronto, who fit the bill: intellect and emotion in tandem. Wodek was the first to put Jordan Peterson in front of a camera, and thought of him as a teacher in search of students—because he was always ready to explain. And it helped that he liked the camera and that the camera liked him back.

That afternoon there was a large table set outside in the Szemberg-Bekiers' garden; around it was gathered the usual collection of lips and ears, and loquacious virtuosos. We seemed, however, to be plagued by a buzzing paparazzi of bees, and here was this new fellow at the table, with an Albertan accent, in cowboy boots, who was ignoring them, and kept on talking. He kept talking while the rest of us were playing musical chairs to keep away from the pests, yet also trying to remain at the table because this new addition to our gatherings was so interesting.

He had this odd habit of speaking about the deepest questions to whoever was at this table—most of them new acquaintances—as though he were just making small talk. Or, if he did do small talk, the interval between "How do you know Wodek and Estera?" or "I was a beekeeper once, so I'm used to them" and more serious topics would be nanoseconds.

One might hear such questions discussed at parties where professors and professionals gather, but usually the conversation would remain between two specialists in the topic, off in a corner, or if shared with the whole group it was often not without someone preening. But this Peterson, though erudite, didn't come across as a pedant. He had the enthusiasm of a kid who had just learned something new and had to share it. He seemed to be assuming, as a child would—before learning how dulled adults can become—that if he thought something was interesting, then so might others. There was something boyish in the cowboy, in his broaching of subjects as though we had all grown up together in the same small town, or family, and had all been thinking about the very same problems of human existence all along.

Peterson wasn't really an "eccentric"; he had sufficient conventional chops, had been a Harvard professor, was a gentleman (as cowboys can be) though he did say *damn* and *bloody* a lot, in a rural 1950s sort of way. But everyone listened, with fascination on their faces, because he was in fact addressing questions of concern to everyone at the table.

There was something freeing about being with a person so learned yet speaking in such an unedited way. His thinking was motoric; it seemed he needed to think *aloud*, to use his motor cortex to think, but that motor also had to run fast to work properly. To get to liftoff. Not quite manic, but his idling speed revved high. Spirited thoughts were tumbling out. But unlike many academics who take the floor and hold it, if someone challenged or corrected him he really seemed to *like* it. He didn't rear up and neigh. He'd say, in a kind of folksy way, "Yeah," and bow his head involuntarily, wag it if he had overlooked something, laughing at himself for overgeneralizing. He appreciated being shown another side of an issue, and it became clear that thinking through a problem was, for him, a dialogic process.

One could not but be struck by another unusual thing about him: for an egghead Peterson was extremely practical. His examples were filled with applications to everyday life: business management, how to make furniture (he made much of his own), designing a simple house, making a room beautiful (now an internet meme) or in another, specific case related to education, creating an online writing project that kept minority students from dropping out of school by getting them to do a kind of psychoanalytic exercise on themselves, in which they would free-associate about their past, present and future (now known as the Self-Authoring Program).

I was always especially fond of mid-Western, Prairie types who come from a farm (where they learned all about nature), or from a very small town, and who have worked with their hands to make things, spent long periods outside in the harsh elements, and are often self-educated and go to university against the odds. I found them quite unlike their sophisticated but somewhat denatured urban counterparts, for whom higher education was pre-ordained, and for that reason sometimes taken for granted, or thought of not as an end in itself but simply as a life stage in the service of career advancement. These Westerners were different: self-made, unentitled, hands on, neighbourly and less precious than many of their big-city peers, who increasingly spend their lives indoors, manipulating symbols on computers. This cowboy psychologist seemed to care about a thought only if it might, in some way, be helpful to someone.

We became friends. As a psychiatrist and psychoanalyst who loves literature, I was drawn to him because here was a clinician who also had given himself a great books education, and who not only loved soulful Russian novels, philosophy and ancient mythology, but who also seemed to treat them as his most treasured inheritance. But he also did illuminating statistical research on personality and temperament, and had studied neuroscience. Though trained as a behaviourist, he was powerfully drawn to psychoanalysis with its focus on dreams, archetypes, the persistence of childhood conflicts in the adult, and the role of defences and rationalization in everyday life. He was also an outlier in being the only member of the research-oriented Department of Psychology at the University of Toronto who also kept a clinical practice.

On my visits, our conversations began with banter and laughter— that was the small-town Peterson from the Alberta hinterland—his teenage years right out of the movie *FUBAR*—welcoming you into his home. The house had been gutted by Tammy, his wife, and himself, and turned into perhaps the most fascinating and shocking middle-class home I had seen. They had art, some carved masks, and abstract portraits, but they were overwhelmed by a huge collection of original Socialist Realist paintings of Lenin and the early Communists commissioned by the USSR. Not long after the Soviet Union fell, and most of the world breathed a sigh of relief, Peterson began purchasing this propaganda for a song online. Paintings lionizing the Soviet revolutionary spirit completely filled every single wall, the ceilings, even the bathrooms. The paintings were not there because Jordan had any totalitarian sympathies, but because he wanted to remind himself of something he knew he and everyone would rather forget: that over a hundred million people were murdered in the name of utopia.

It took getting used to, this semi-haunted house "decorated" by a delusion that had practically destroyed mankind. But it was eased by his wonderful and unique spouse, Tammy, who was all in, who embraced and encouraged this unusual need for expression! These paintings provided a visitor with the first window onto the full extent of Jordan's concern about our human capacity for evil in the name of good, and the psychological mystery of self-deception (how can a person deceive himself and get away with it?)—an interest we share. And then there were also the hours we'd spend discussing what I might call a lesser problem (lesser because rarer), the human capacity for evil for the sake of evil, the joy some people take in destroying others, captured famously by the seventeenth-century English poet John Milton in *Paradise Lost*.

And so we'd chat and have our tea in his kitchen-underworld, walled by this odd art collection, a visual marker of his earnest quest to move beyond simplistic ideology, left or right, and not repeat mistakes of the past. After a while, there was nothing peculiar about taking tea in the kitchen, discussing family issues, one's latest reading, with those ominous pictures hovering. It was just living in the world as it was, or in some places, is.

In Jordan's first and only book before this one, *Maps of Meaning*, he shares his profound insights into universal themes of world mythology, and explains how all cultures have created stories to help us grapple with, and ultimately map, the chaos into which we are thrown at birth; this chaos is everything that is unknown to us, and any unexplored territory that we must traverse, be it in the world outside or the psyche within.

Combining evolution, the neuroscience of emotion, some of the best of Jung, some of Freud, much of the great works of Nietzsche, Dostoevsky, Solzhenitsyn, Eliade, Neumann, Piaget, Frye and Frankl, *Maps of Meaning*, published nearly two decades ago, shows Jordan's wide-ranging approach to understanding how human beings and the human brain deal with the archetypal situation that arises whenever we, in our daily lives, must face something we do not understand. The brilliance of the book is in his demonstration of how rooted this situation is in evolution, our DNA, our brains and our most ancient stories. And he shows that these stories have survived because they still provide guidance in dealing with uncertainty, and the unavoidable unknown.

One of the many virtues of the book you are reading now is that it provides an entry point into *Maps of Meaning,* which is a highly complex work because Jordan was working out his approach to psychology as he wrote it. But it was foundational, because no matter how different our genes or life experiences may be, or how differently our plastic brains are wired by our experience, we all have to deal with the unknown, and we all attempt to move from chaos to order. And this is why many of the rules in this book, being based on *Maps of Meaning,* have an element of universality to them.

Maps of Meaning was sparked by Jordan's agonized awareness, as a teenager growing up in the midst of the Cold War, that much of mankind seemed on the verge of blowing up the planet to defend their various identities. He felt he had to understand how it could be that people would sacrifice everything for an "identity," whatever that was. And he felt he had to understand the ideologies that drove totalitarian regimes to a variant of that same behaviour: killing their own citizens. In *Maps of Meaning,* and again in this book, one of the matters he cautions readers to be most wary of is ideology, no matter who is peddling it or to what end.

Ideologies are simple ideas, disguised as science or philosophy, that purport to explain the complexity of the world and offer remedies that will perfect it. Ideologues are people who pretend they know how to "make the world a better place" before they've taken care of their own chaos within. (The warrior identity that their ideology gives them covers over that chaos.) That's hubris, of course, and one of the most important themes of this book, is "set your house in order" first, and Jordan provides practical advice on how to do this.

Ideologies are substitutes for true knowledge, and ideologues are always dangerous when they come to power, because a simple-minded I-know-it-all approach is no match for the complexity of existence. Furthermore, when their social contraptions fail to fly, ideologues blame not themselves but all who see through the simplifications. Another great U of T professor, Lewis Feuer, in his book *Ideology and the Ideologists*, observed that ideologies retool the very religious stories they purport to have supplanted, but eliminate the narrative and psychological richness. Communism borrowed from the story of the Children of Israel in Egypt, with an enslaved class, rich persecutors, a leader, like Lenin, who goes abroad, lives among the enslavers, and then leads the enslaved to the promised land (the utopia; the dictatorship of the proletariat).

To understand ideology, Jordan read extensively about not only the Soviet gulag, but also the Holocaust and the rise of Nazism. I had never before met a person, born Christian and of my generation, who was so utterly tormented by what happened in Europe to the Jews, and who had worked so hard to understand how it could have occurred. I too had studied this in depth. My own father survived Auschwitz. My grandmother was middle-aged when she stood face to face with Dr. Josef Mengele, the Nazi physician who conducted unspeakably cruel experiments on his victims, and she survived Auschwitz by disobeying his order to join the line with the elderly, the grey and the weak, and instead slipping into a line with younger people. She avoided the gas chambers a second time by trading food for hair dye so she wouldn't be murdered for looking too old. My grandfather, her husband, survived the Mauthausen concentration camp, but choked to death on the first piece of solid food he was given just before liberation day. I relate this, because years after we became friends, when Jordan would take a classical liberal stand for free speech, he would be accused by left-wing extremists as being a right-wing bigot.

Let me say, with all the moderation I can summon: *at best*, those accusers have simply not done their due diligence. I have; with a family history such as mine, one develops not only radar, but underwater sonar for right-wing bigotry; but even more important, one learns to recognize the kind of person with the comprehension, tools, good will and courage to combat it, and Jordan Peterson is *that* person.

My own dissatisfaction with modern political science's attempts to understand the rise of Nazism, totalitarianism and prejudice was a major factor in my decision to supplement my studies of political science with the study of the unconscious, projection, psychoanalysis, the regressive potential of group psychology, psychiatry and the brain. Jordan switched out of political science for similar reasons. With these important parallel interests, we didn't always agree on "the answers" (thank God), but we almost always agreed on the questions.

Our friendship wasn't all doom and gloom. I have made a habit of attending my fellow professors' classes at our university, and so attended his, which were always packed, and I saw what now millions have seen online: a brilliant, often dazzling public speaker who was at his best riffing like a jazz artist; at times he resembled an ardent Prairie preacher (not in evangelizing, but in his passion, in his ability to tell stories that convey the life-stakes that go with believing or disbelieving various ideas). Then he'd just as easily switch to do a breathtakingly systematic summary of a series of scientific studies. He was a master at helping students become more reflective, and take themselves and their futures seriously. He taught them to respect many of the greatest books ever written. He gave vivid examples from clinical practice, was (appropriately) self-revealing, even of his own vulnerabilities, and made fascinating links between evolution, the brain and religious stories. In a world where students are taught to see evolution and religion as simply opposed (by thinkers like Richard Dawkins), Jordan showed his students how evolution, of all things, helps to explain the profound psychological appeal and wisdom of many ancient stories, from Gilgamesh to the life of the Buddha, Egyptian mythology and the Bible. He showed, for instance, how stories about journeying voluntarily into the unknown—the hero's quest—mirror universal tasks for which the brain evolved. He respected the stories, was not reductionist, and never claimed to exhaust their wisdom. If he discussed a topic such as prejudice, or its emotional relatives fear and disgust, or the differences between the sexes on average, he was able to show how these traits evolved and why they survived.

Above all, he alerted his students to topics rarely discussed in university, such as the simple fact that all the ancients, from Buddha to the biblical authors, knew what every slightly worn-out adult knows, that life is suffering. If you are suffering, or someone close to you is, that's sad. But alas, it's not particularly special. We don't suffer only because "politicians are dimwitted," or "the system is corrupt," or because you and I, like almost everyone else, can *legitimately* describe ourselves, in some way, as a victim of something or someone. It is because we are born human that we are guaranteed a good dose of suffering. And chances are, if you or someone you love is not suffering now, they will be within five years, unless you are freakishly lucky. Rearing kids is hard, work is hard, aging, sickness and death are hard, and Jordan emphasized that doing all that totally on your own, without the benefit of a loving relationship, or wisdom, or the psychological insights of the greatest psychologists, only makes it harder. He wasn't scaring the students; in fact, they found this frank talk reassuring, because in the depths of their psyches, most of them knew what he said was true, even if there was never a forum to discuss it—perhaps because the adults in their lives had become so naively overprotective that they deluded themselves into thinking that not talking about suffering would in some way magically protect their children from it.

Here he would relate the myth of the hero, a cross-cultural theme explored psychoanalytically by Otto Rank, who noted, following Freud, that hero myths are similar in many cultures, a theme that was picked up by Carl Jung, Joseph Campbell and Erich Neumann, among others. Where Freud made great contributions in explaining neuroses by, among other things, focusing on understanding what we might call a failed-hero story (that of Oedipus), Jordan focused on triumphant heroes. In all these triumph stories, the hero has to go into the unknown, into an unexplored territory, and deal with a new great challenge and take great risks. In the process, something of himself has to die, or be given up, so he can be reborn and meet the challenge. This requires courage, something rarely discussed in a psychology class or textbook. During his recent public stand for free speech and against what I call "forced speech" (because it involves a government forcing citizens to voice political views), the stakes were very high; he had much to lose, and knew it. Nonetheless, I saw him (and Tammy, for that matter) not only display such courage, but also continue to live by many of the rules in this book, some of which can be very demanding.

I saw him grow, from the remarkable person he was, into someone even more able and assured—through living by these rules. In fact, it was the process of writing this book, and developing these rules, that led him to take the stand he did against forced or compelled speech. And that is why, during those events, he started posting some of his thoughts about life and these rules on the internet. Now, over 100 million YouTube hits later, we know they have struck a chord.

Given our distaste for rules, how do we explain the extraordinary response to his lectures, which give rules? In Jordan's case, it was of course his charisma and a rare willingness to stand for a principle that got him a wide hearing online initially; views of his first YouTube statements quickly numbered in the hundreds of thousands. But people have kept listening because what he is saying meets a deep and unarticulated need. And that is because alongside our wish to be free of rules, we all search for structure.

The hunger among many younger people for rules, or at least guidelines, is greater today for good reason. In the West at least, millennials are living through a unique historical situation. They are, I believe, the first generation to have been so thoroughly taught two seemingly contradictory ideas about morality, simultaneously—at their schools, colleges and universities, by many in my own generation. This contradiction has left them at times disoriented and uncertain, without guidance and, more tragically, deprived of riches they don't even know exist.

The first idea or teaching is that morality is relative, at best a personal "value judgment." *Relative* means that there is no absolute right or wrong in anything; instead, morality and the rules associated with it are just a matter of personal opinion or happenstance, "relative to" or "related to" a particular framework, such as one's ethnicity, one's upbringing, or the culture or historical moment one is born into. It's nothing but an accident of birth. According to this argument (now a creed), history teaches that religions, tribes, nations and ethnic groups tend to disagree about fundamental matters, and always have. Today, the postmodernist left makes the additional claim that one group's morality is *nothing but* its attempt to exercise power over another group. So, the decent thing to do—once it becomes apparent how arbitrary your, and your society's, "moral values" are—is to show tolerance for people who think differently, and who come from different (diverse) backgrounds. That emphasis on tolerance is so paramount that for many people one of the worst character flaws a person can have is to be "judgmental."* And, since we don't know right from wrong, or what is good, just about *the most inappropriate thing an adult can do is give a young person advice* about how to live.

And so a generation has been raised untutored in what was once called, aptly, "practical wisdom," which guided previous generations. Millennials, often told they have received the finest education available anywhere, have actually suffered a form of serious intellectual and moral neglect. The relativists of my generation and Jordan's, many of whom became their professors, chose to devalue thousands of years of human knowledge about how to acquire virtue, dismissing it as passé, "not relevant" or even "oppressive." They were so successful at it that the very word "virtue" sounds out of date, and someone using it appears anachronistically moralistic and self-righteous.

---

* Some argue—mistakenly—that Freud (often mentioned in these pages) contributed to our current longing for a culture, schools and institutions that are "non-judgmental." It is true that he recommended that when psychoanalysts listen to their patients in therapy, they be tolerant, empathic, and not voice critical, moralistic judgments. But this was for the express purposes of helping patients feel comfortable in being totally honest, and not diminish their problems. This encouraged self-reflection, and allowed them to explore warded off feelings, wishes, even shameful anti-social urges. It also—and this was the masterstroke—allowed them to discover their own unconscious conscience (and its judgments), and their own harsh self-criticism of their "lapses," and their own unconscious guilt which they had often hidden from themselves, but which often formed the basis of their low self-esteem, depression and anxiety. If anything, Freud showed that we are both more immoral and more moral than we are aware of. This kind of "non-judgmentalism," *in therapy*, is a powerful and liberating technique or tactic—an ideal attitude when you want to better understand yourself. But Freud never argued (as do some who want all culture to become one huge group therapy session) that one can live one's *entire life* without *ever* making judgments, or without morality. In fact, his point in *Civilization and its Discontents* is that civilization only arises when some restraining rules and morality are in place.

The study of virtue is not quite the same as the study of morals (right and wrong, good and evil). Aristotle defined the virtues simply as the ways of behaving that are most conducive to happiness in life. Vice was defined as the ways of behaving least conducive to happiness. He observed that the virtues always aim for balance and avoid the extremes of the vices. Aristotle studied the virtues and the vices in his *Nicomachean Ethics*. It was a book based on experience and observation, not conjecture, about the kind of happiness that was possible for human beings. Cultivating *judgment* about the difference between virtue and vice is the beginning of wisdom, something that can never be out of date.

By contrast, our modern relativism begins by asserting that making judgments about how to live is impossible, because there is no *real* good, and no *true* virtue (as these too are relative). Thus relativism's closest approximation to "virtue" is "tolerance." Only tolerance will provide social cohesion between different groups, and save us from harming each other. On Facebook and other forms of social media, therefore, you signal your so-called virtue, telling everyone how tolerant, open and compassionate you are, and wait for likes to accumulate. (Leave aside that telling people you're virtuous isn't a virtue, it's self-promotion. Virtue signalling is not virtue. Virtue signalling is, quite possibly, our commonest vice.)

Intolerance of others' views (no matter how ignorant or incoherent they may be) is not simply wrong; in a world where there is no right or wrong, it is worse: it is a sign you are embarrassingly unsophisticated or, possibly, dangerous.

But it turns out that many people cannot tolerate the vacuum—the chaos—which is inherent in life, but made worse by this moral relativism; they cannot live without a moral compass, without an ideal at which to aim in their lives. (For relativists, ideals are values too, and like all values, they are merely "relative" and hardly worth sacrificing for.) So, right alongside relativism, we find the spread of nihilism and despair, and also the opposite of moral relativism: the blind certainty offered by ideologies that claim to have an answer for everything.

And so we arrive at the second teaching that millennials have been bombarded with. They sign up for a humanities course, to study greatest books ever written. But they're not assigned the books; instead they are given ideological attacks on them, based on some appalling simplification. Where the relativist is filled with uncertainty, the ideologue is the very opposite. He or she is hyper-judgmental and censorious, always knows what's wrong about others, and what to do about it. Sometimes it seems the only people willing to give advice in a relativistic society are those with the least to offer.

Modern moral relativism has many sources. As we in the West learned more history, we understood that different epochs had different moral codes. As we travelled the seas and explored the globe, we learned of far-flung tribes on different continents whose different moral codes made sense relative to, or within the framework of, their societies. Science played a role, too, by attacking the religious view of the world, and thus undermining the religious grounds for ethics and rules. Materialist social science implied that we could divide the world into facts (which all could observe, and were objective and "real") and values (which were subjective and personal). Then we could first agree on the facts, and, maybe, one day, develop a scientific code of ethics (which has yet to arrive). Moreover, by implying that values had a lesser reality than facts, science contributed in yet another way to moral relativism, for it treated "value" as secondary. (But the idea that we can easily separate facts and values was and remains naive; to some extent, one's values determine what one will pay attention to, and what will count as a fact.)

The idea that different societies had different rules and morals was known to the ancient world too, and it is interesting to compare its response to this realization with the modern response (relativism, nihilism and ideology). When the ancient Greeks sailed to India and elsewhere, they too discovered that rules, morals and customs differed from place to place, and saw that the explanation for what was right and wrong was often rooted in some ancestral authority. The Greek response was not despair, but a new invention: philosophy.

Socrates, reacting to the uncertainty bred by awareness of these conflicting moral codes, decided that instead of becoming a nihilist, a relativist or an ideologue, he would devote his life to the search for wisdom that could reason about these differences, i.e., he helped invent philosophy. He spent his life asking perplexing, foundational questions, such as "What is virtue?" and "How can one live the good life?" and "What is justice?" and he looked at different approaches, asking which seemed most coherent and most in accord with human nature. These are the kinds of questions that I believe animate this book.

For the ancients, the discovery that different people have different ideas about how, practically, to live, did not paralyze them; it deepened their understanding of humanity and led to some of the most satisfying conversations human beings have ever had, about how life might be lived.

Likewise, Aristotle. Instead of despairing about these differences in moral codes, Aristotle argued that though specific rules, laws and customs differed from place to place, what does not differ is that in all places human beings, by their nature, have a proclivity to make rules, laws and customs. To put this in modern terms, it seems that all human beings are, by some kind of biological endowment, so ineradicably concerned with morality that we create a structure of laws and rules wherever we are. The idea that human life can be free of moral concerns is a fantasy.

We are rule generators. And given that we are moral animals, what must be the effect of our simplistic modern relativism upon us? It means we are hobbling ourselves by pretending to be something we are not. It is a mask, but a strange one, for it mostly deceives the one who wears it. *Sccccccratcch* the most clever postmodern-relativist professor's Mercedes with a key, and you will see how fast the mask of relativism (with its pretense that there can be neither right nor wrong) and the cloak of radical tolerance come off.

Because we do not yet have an ethics based on modern science, Jordan is not trying to develop his rules by wiping the slate clean—by dismissing thousands of years of wisdom as mere superstition and ignoring our greatest moral achievements. Far better to integrate the best of what we are now learning with the books human beings saw fit to preserve over millennia, and with the stories that have survived, against all odds, time's tendency to obliterate.

He is doing what reasonable guides have always done: he makes no claim that human wisdom begins with himself, but, rather, turns first to his own guides. And although the topics in this book are serious, Jordan often has great fun addressing them with a light touch, as the chapter headings convey. He makes no claim to be exhaustive, and sometimes the chapters consist of wide-ranging discussions of our psychology as he understands it.

So why not call this a book of "guidelines," a far more relaxed, user-friendly and less rigid sounding term than "rules"?

Because these really are rules. And the foremost rule is that you must take responsibility for your own life. Period.

One might think that a generation that has heard endlessly, from their more ideological teachers, about the rights, rights, rights that belong to them, would object to being told that they would do better to focus instead on taking responsibility. Yet this generation, many of whom were raised in small families by hyper-protective parents, on soft-surface playgrounds, and then taught in universities with "safe spaces" where they don't have to hear things they don't want to—schooled to be risk-averse—has among it, now, millions who feel stultified by this underestimation of their potential resilience and who have embraced Jordan's message that each individual has ultimate responsibility to bear; that if one wants to live a full life, one first sets one's own house in order; and only then can one sensibly aim to take on bigger responsibilities. The extent of this reaction has often moved both of us to the brink of tears.

Sometimes these rules are demanding. They require you to undertake an incremental process that over time will stretch you to a new limit. That requires, as I've said, venturing into the unknown. Stretching yourself beyond the boundaries of your current self requires carefully choosing and then pursuing ideals: ideals that are up there, above you, superior to you—and that you can't always be sure you will reach.

But if it's uncertain that our ideals are attainable, why do we bother reaching in the first place? Because if you don't reach for them, it is certain you will never feel that your life has meaning.

And perhaps because, as unfamiliar and strange as it sounds, in the deepest part of our psyche, we all want to be judged.

Dr. Norman Doidge, MD, is the author
of *The Brain That Changes Itself*

OVERTURE

THIS BOOK HAS A SHORT history and a long history. We'll begin with the short history.

In 2012, I started contributing to a website called Quora. On Quora, anyone can ask a question, of any sort—and anyone can answer. Readers upvote those answers they like, and downvote those they don't. In this manner, the most useful answers rise to the top, while the others sink into oblivion. I was curious about the site. I liked its free-for-all nature. The discussion was often compelling, and it was interesting to see the diverse range of opinions generated by the same question.

When I was taking a break (or avoiding work), I often turned to Quora, looking for questions to engage with. I considered, and eventually answered, such questions as "What's the difference between being happy and being content?", "What things get better as you age?" and "What makes life more meaningful?"

Quora tells you how many people have viewed your answer and how many upvotes you received. Thus, you can determine your reach, and see what people think of your ideas. Only a small minority of those who view an answer upvote it. As of July 2017, as I write this—and five years after I addressed "What makes life more meaningful?"—my answer to that question has received a relatively small audience (14,000 views, and 133 upvotes), while my response to the question about aging has been viewed by 7,200 people and received 36 upvotes. Not exactly home runs. However, it's to be expected. On such sites, most answers receive very little attention, while a tiny minority become disproportionately popular.

Soon after, I answered another question: "What are the most valuable things everyone should know?" I wrote a list of rules, or maxims; some dead serious, some tongue-in-cheek—"Be grateful in spite of your suffering," "Do not do things that you hate," "Do not hide things in the fog," and so on. The Quora readers appeared pleased with this list. They commented on and shared it. They said such things as "I'm definitely printing this list out and keeping it as a reference. Simply phenomenal," and "You win Quora. We can just close the site now." Students at the University of Toronto, where I teach, came up to me and told me how much they liked it. To date, my answer to "What are the most valuable things . . ." has been viewed by a hundred and twenty thousand people and been upvoted twenty-three hundred times. Only a few hundred of the roughly six hundred thousand questions on Quora have cracked the two-thousand-upvote barrier. My procrastination-induced musings hit a nerve. I had written a 99.9 percentile answer.

It was not obvious to me when I wrote the list of rules for living that it was going to perform so well. I had put a fair bit of care into all the sixty or so answers I submitted in the few months surrounding that post. Nonetheless, Quora provides market research at its finest. The respondents are anonymous. They're disinterested, in the best sense. Their opinions are spontaneous and unbiased. So, I paid attention to the results, and thought about the reasons for that answer's disproportionate success. Perhaps I struck the right balance between the familiar and the unfamiliar while formulating the rules. Perhaps people were drawn to the structure that such rules imply. Perhaps people just like lists.

A few months earlier, in March of 2012, I had received an email from a literary agent. She had heard me speak on CBC radio during a show entitled *Just Say No to Happiness*, where I had criticized the idea that happiness was the proper goal for life. Over the previous decades

I had read more than my share of dark books about the twentieth century, focusing particularly on Nazi Germany and the Soviet Union. Aleksandr Solzhenitsyn, the great documenter of the slave-labour-camp horrors of the latter, once wrote that the "pitiful ideology" holding that "human beings are created for happiness" was an ideology "done in by the first blow of the work assigner's cudgel."[1] In a crisis, the inevitable suffering that life entails can rapidly make a mockery of the idea that happiness is the proper pursuit of the individual. On the radio show, I suggested, instead, that a deeper meaning was required. I noted that the nature of such meaning was constantly re-presented in the great stories of the past, and that it had more to do with developing character in the face of suffering than with happiness. This is part of the long history of the present work.

From 1985 until 1999 I worked for about three hours a day on the only other book I have ever published: *Maps of Meaning: The Architecture of Belief.* During that time, and in the years since, I also taught a course on the material in that book, first at Harvard, and now at the University of Toronto. In 2013, observing the rise of YouTube, and because of the popularity of some work I had done with TVO, a Canadian public TV station, I decided to film my university and public lectures and place them online. They attracted an increasingly large audience—more than a million views by April 2016. The number of views has risen very dramatically since then (up to eighteen million as I write this), but that is in part because I became embroiled in a political controversy that drew an inordinate amount of attention.

That's another story. Maybe even another book.

I proposed in *Maps of Meaning* that the great myths and religious stories of the past, particularly those derived from an earlier, oral tradition, were *moral* in their intent, rather than descriptive. Thus, they did not concern themselves with what the world was, as a scientist might have it, but with how a human being should act. I suggested that our ancestors portrayed the world as a stage—a drama—instead of a place of objects. I described how I had come to believe that the constituent elements of the world as drama were order and chaos, and not material things.

Order is where the people around you act according to well-understood social norms, and remain predictable and cooperative. It's the world of social structure, explored territory, and familiarity. The state of Order is typically portrayed, symbolically—imaginatively—as masculine. It's the Wise King and the Tyrant, forever bound together, as society is simultaneously structure and oppression.

Chaos, by contrast, is where—or when—something unexpected happens. Chaos emerges, in trivial form, when you tell a joke at a party with people you think you know and a silent and embarrassing chill falls over the gathering. Chaos is what emerges more catastrophically when you suddenly find yourself without employment, or are betrayed by a lover. As the antithesis of symbolically masculine order, it's presented imaginatively as feminine. It's the new and unpredictable suddenly emerging in the midst of the commonplace familiar. It's Creation and Destruction, the source of new things and the destination of the dead (as nature, as opposed to culture, is simultaneously birth and demise).

Order and chaos are the yang and yin of the famous Taoist symbol: two serpents, head to tail.* Order is the white, masculine serpent; Chaos, its black, feminine counterpart. The black dot in the white—and the white in the black—indicate the possibility of transformation: just when things seem secure, the unknown can loom, unexpectedly and large. Conversely, just when everything seems lost, new order can emerge from catastrophe and chaos.

For the Taoists, meaning is to be found on the border between the ever-entwined pair. To walk that border is to stay on the path of life, the divine Way.

And that's much better than happiness.

The literary agent I referred to listened to the CBC radio broadcast where I discussed such issues. It left her asking herself deeper questions. She emailed me, asking if I had considered writing a book for a

---

* The yin/yang symbol is the second part of the more comprehensive five-part *tajitu*, a diagram representing both the original absolute unity and its division into the multiplicity of the observed world. This is discussed in more detail in Rule 2, below, as well as elsewhere in the book.

general audience. I had previously attempted to produce a more accessible version of *Maps of Meaning*, which is a very dense book. But I found that the spirit was neither in me during that attempt nor in the resultant manuscript. I think this was because I was imitating my former self, and my previous book, instead of occupying the place between order and chaos and producing something new. I suggested that she watch four of the lectures I had done for a TVO program called *Big Ideas* on my YouTube channel. I thought if she did that we could have a more informed and thorough discussion about what kind of topics I might address in a more publicly accessible book.

She contacted me a few weeks later, after watching all four lectures and discussing them with a colleague. Her interest had been further heightened, as had her commitment to the project. That was promising—and unexpected. I'm always surprised when people respond positively to what I am saying, given its seriousness and strange nature. I'm amazed I have been allowed (even encouraged) to teach what I taught first in Boston and now in Toronto. I've always thought that if people really noticed what I was teaching there would be Hell to pay. You can decide for yourself what truth there might be in that concern after reading this book. :)

She suggested that I write a guide of sorts to what a person needs "to live well"—whatever that might mean. I thought immediately about my Quora list. I had in the meantime written some further thoughts about of the rules I had posted. People had responded positively toward those new ideas, as well. It seemed to me, therefore, that there might be a nice fit between the Quora list and my new agent's ideas. So, I sent her the list. She liked it.

At about the same time, a friend and former student of mine—the novelist and screenwriter Gregg Hurwitz—was considering a new book, which would become the bestselling thriller *Orphan X*. He liked the rules, too. He had Mia, the book's female lead, post a selection of them, one by one, on her fridge, at points in the story where they seemed apropos. That was another piece of evidence supporting my supposition of their attractiveness. I suggested to my agent that I write a brief chapter on each of the rules. She agreed, so I wrote a book proposal suggesting as much. When I started writing the actual chapters, how-ever, they weren't at all brief. I had much more to say about each rule than I originally envisioned.

This was partly because I had spent a very long time researching my first book: studying history, mythology, neuroscience, psychoanal-ysis, child psychology, poetry, and large sections of the Bible. I read and perhaps even understood much of Milton's *Paradise Lost*, Goethe's *Faust* and Dante's *Inferno*. I integrated all of that, for better or worse, trying to address a perplexing problem: the reason or reasons for the nuclear standoff of the Cold War. I couldn't understand how belief systems could be so important to people that they were willing to risk the destruction of the world to protect them. I came to realize that shared belief systems made people intelligible to one another—and that the systems weren't just about belief.

People who live by the same code are rendered mutually predict-able to one another. They act in keeping with each other's expectations and desires. They can cooperate. They can even compete peacefully, because everyone knows what to expect from everyone else. A shared belief system, partly psychological, partly acted out, simplifies every-one—in their own eyes, and in the eyes of others. Shared beliefs sim-plify the world, as well, because people who know what to expect from one another can act together to tame the world. There is perhaps nothing more important than the maintenance of this organization—this simplification. If it's threatened, the great ship of state rocks.

It isn't precisely that people will fight for what they believe. They will fight, instead, to maintain *the match between* what they believe, what they expect, and what they desire. They will fight to maintain the match between what they expect and how everyone is acting. It is precisely the maintenance of that match that enables everyone to live together peacefully, predictably and productively. It reduces uncer-tainty and the chaotic mix of intolerable emotions that uncertainty inevitably produces.

Imagine someone betrayed by a trusted lover. The sacred social contract obtaining between the two has been violated. Actions speak louder than words, and an act of betrayal disrupts the fragile and carefully negotiated peace of an intimate relationship. In the aftermath of disloyalty, people are seized by terrible emotions: disgust, contempt (for self and traitor), guilt, anxiety, rage and dread. Conflict is inevitable, sometimes with deadly results. Shared belief systems—shared systems of agreed-upon conduct and expectation—regulate and control all those powerful forces. It's no wonder that people will fight to protect something that saves them from being possessed by emotions of chaos and terror (and after that from degeneration into strife and combat).

There's more to it, too. A shared cultural system stabilizes human interaction, but is also a system of value—a hierarchy of value, where some things are given priority and importance and others are not. In the absence of such a system of value, people simply cannot act. In fact, they can't even perceive, because both action and perception require a goal, and a valid goal is, by necessity, something valued. We experience much of our positive emotion in relation to goals. We are not happy, technically speaking, unless we see ourselves progressing—and the very idea of progression implies value. Worse yet is the fact that the meaning of life without positive value is not simply neutral. Because we are vulnerable and mortal, pain and anxiety are an integral part of human existence. We must have something to set against the suffering that is intrinsic to Being.* We must have the meaning inherent in a profound system of value or the horror of existence rapidly becomes paramount. Then, nihilism beckons, with its hopelessness and despair.

So: no value, no meaning. Between value systems, however, there is the possibility of conflict. We are thus eternally caught between the

---

* I use the term Being (with a capital "B") in part because of my exposure to the ideas of the 20th-century German philosopher Martin Heidegger. Heidegger tried to distinguish between reality, as conceived objectively, and the totality of human experience (which is his "Being"). Being (with a capital "B") is what each of us experiences, subjectively, personally and individually, as well as what we each experience jointly with others. As such, it includes emotions, drives, dreams, visions and revelations, as well as our private thoughts and perceptions. Being is also, finally, something that is brought into existence by action, so its nature is to an indeterminate degree a consequence of our decisions and choices—something shaped by our hypothetically free will. Construed in this manner, Being is (1) not something easily and directly reducible to the material and objective and (2) something that most definitely requires its own term, as Heidegger labored for decades to indicate.

most diamantine rock and the hardest of places: loss of group-centred belief renders life chaotic, miserable, intolerable; presence of group-centred belief makes conflict with other groups inevitable. In the West, we have been withdrawing from our tradition-, religion- and even nation-centred cultures, partly to decrease the danger of group conflict. But we are increasingly falling prey to the desperation of meaninglessness, and that is no improvement at all.

While writing *Maps of Meaning*, I was (also) driven by the realization that we can no longer afford conflict—certainly not on the scale of the world conflagrations of the twentieth century. Our technologies of destruction have become too powerful. The potential consequences of war are literally apocalyptic. But we cannot simply abandon our systems of value, our beliefs, our cultures, either. I agonized over this apparently intractable problem for months. Was there a third way, invisible to me? I dreamt one night during this period that I was suspended in mid-air, clinging to a chandelier, many stories above the ground, directly under the dome of a massive cathedral. The people on the floor below were distant and tiny. There was a great expanse between me and any wall—and even the peak of the dome itself.

I have learned to pay attention to dreams, not least because of my training as a clinical psychologist. Dreams shed light on the dim places where reason itself has yet to voyage. I have studied Christianity a fair bit, too (more than other religious traditions, although I am always trying to redress this lack). Like others, therefore, I must and do draw more from what I do know than from what I do not. I knew that cathedrals were constructed in the shape of a cross, and that the point under the dome was the centre of the cross. I knew that the cross was simultaneously, the point of greatest suffering, the point of death and transformation, and the symbolic centre of the world. That was not somewhere I wanted to be. I managed to get down, out of the heights—out of the symbolic sky—back to safe, familiar, anonymous ground. I don't know how. Then, still in my dream, I returned to my bedroom and my bed and tried to return to sleep and the peace of unconsciousness. As I relaxed, however, I could feel my body transported. A great wind was dissolving me, preparing to propel me back to the cathedral, to place me once again at that central point. There was no escape. It was a true nightmare. I forced myself awake. The curtains behind me were blowing in over my pillows. Half asleep, I looked at the foot of the bed. I saw the great cathedral doors. I shook myself completely awake and they disappeared.

My dream placed me at the centre of Being itself, and there was no escape. It took me months to understand what this meant. During this time, I came to a more complete, personal realization of what the great stories of the past continually insist upon: the centre is occupied by the individual. The centre is marked by the cross, as X marks the spot. Existence at that cross is suffering and transformation—and that fact, above all, needs to be voluntarily accepted. It is possible to transcend slavish adherence to the group and its doctrines and, simultaneously, to avoid the pitfalls of its opposite extreme, nihilism. It is possible, instead, to find sufficient meaning in individual consciousness and experience.

How could the world be freed from the terrible dilemma of conflict, on the one hand, and psychological and social dissolution, on the other? The answer was this: through the elevation and development of the individual, and through the willingness of everyone to shoulder the burden of Being and to take the heroic path. We must each adopt as much responsibility as possible for individual life, society and the world. We must each tell the truth and repair what is in disrepair and break down and recreate what is old and outdated. It is in this manner that we can and must reduce the suffering that poisons the world. It's asking a lot. It's asking for everything. But the alternative—the horror of authoritarian belief, the chaos of the collapsed state, the tragic catastrophe of the unbridled natural world, the existential angst and weakness of the purposeless individual—is clearly worse.

I have been thinking and lecturing about such ideas for decades. I have built up a large corpus of stories and concepts pertaining to them. I am not for a moment claiming, however, that I am entirely correct or complete in my thinking. Being is far more complicated than one person can know, and I don't have the whole story. I'm simply offering the best I can manage.

In any case, the consequence of all that previous research and thinking was the new essays which eventually became this book. My initial idea was to write a short essay on all forty of the answers I had provided to Quora. That proposal was accepted by Penguin Random House Canada. While writing, however, I cut the essay number to twenty-five and then to sixteen and then finally, to the current twelve. I've been editing that remainder, with the help and care of my official editor (and with the vicious and horribly accurate criticism of Hurwitz, mentioned previously) for the past three years.

It took a long time to settle on a title: *12 Rules for Life: An Antidote to Chaos*. Why did that one rise up above all others? First and foremost, because of its simplicity. It indicates clearly that people need ordering principles, and that chaos otherwise beckons. We require rules, standards, values—alone and together. We're pack animals, beasts of burden. We must bear a load, to justify our miserable existence. We require routine and tradition. That's order. Order can become excessive, and that's not good, but chaos can swamp us, so we drown—and that is also not good. We need to stay on the straight and narrow path. Each of the twelve rules of this book—and their accompanying essays—therefore provide a guide to being there. "There" is the dividing line between order and chaos. That's where we are simultaneously stable enough, exploring enough, transforming enough, repairing enough, and cooperating enough. It's there we find the meaning that justifies life and its inevitable suffering. Perhaps, if we lived properly, we would be able to tolerate the weight of our own self-consciousness. Perhaps, if we lived properly, we could withstand the knowledge of our own fragility and mortality, without the sense of aggrieved victimhood that produces, first, resentment, then envy, and then the desire for vengeance and destruction. Perhaps, if we lived properly, we wouldn't have to turn to totalitarian certainty to shield ourselves from the knowledge of our own insufficiency and ignorance. Perhaps we could come to avoid those pathways to Hell—and we have seen in the terrible twentieth century just how real Hell can be.

I hope that these rules and their accompanying essays will help people understand what they already know: that the soul of the individual eternally hungers for the heroism of genuine Being, and that the willingness to take on that responsibility is identical to the decision to live a meaningful life.

If we each live properly, we will collectively flourish.

Best wishes to you all, as you proceed through these pages.

Dr. Jordan B. Peterson
Clinical Psychologist and Professor of Psychology

RULE 1

STAND UP STRAIGHT
WITH YOUR SHOULDERS BACK

LOBSTERS—AND TERRITORY

IF YOU ARE LIKE MOST PEOPLE, you don't often think about lobsters[2]—
unless you're eating one. However, these interesting and delicious
crustaceans are very much worth considering. Their nervous systems
are comparatively simple, with large, easily observable neurons, the
magic cells of the brain. Because of this, scientists have been able to
map the neural circuitry of lobsters very accurately. This has helped
us understand the structure and function of the brain and behaviour
of more complex animals, including human beings. Lobsters have
more in common with you than you might think (particularly when
you are feeling crabby—ha ha).

Lobsters live on the ocean floor. They need a home base down
there, a range within which they hunt for prey and scavenge around
for stray edible bits and pieces of whatever rains down from the continual chaos of carnage and death far above. They want somewhere
secure, where the hunting and the gathering is good. They want a home.

This can present a problem, since there are many lobsters. What if two of them occupy the same territory, at the bottom of the ocean, at the same time, and both want to live there? What if there are hundreds of lobsters, all trying to make a living and raise a family, in the same crowded patch of sand and refuse?

Other creatures have this problem, too. When songbirds come north in the spring, for example, they engage in ferocious territorial disputes. The songs they sing, so peaceful and beautiful to human ears, are siren calls and cries of domination. A brilliantly musical bird is a small warrior proclaiming his sovereignty. Take the wren, for example, a small, feisty, insect-eating songbird common in North America. A newly arrived wren wants a sheltered place to build a nest, away from the wind and rain. He wants it close to food, and attractive to potential mates. He also wants to convince competitors for that space to keep their distance.

Birds—and Territory

My dad and I designed a house for a wren family when I was ten years old. It looked like a Conestoga wagon, and had a front entrance about the size of a quarter. This made it a good house for wrens, who are tiny, and not so good for other, larger birds, who couldn't get in. My elderly neighbour had a birdhouse, too, which we built for her at the same time, from an old rubber boot. It had an opening large enough for a bird the size of a robin. She was looking forward to the day it was occupied.

A wren soon discovered our birdhouse, and made himself at home there. We could hear his lengthy, trilling song, repeated over and over, during the early spring. Once he'd built his nest in the covered wagon, however, our new avian tenant started carrying small sticks to our neighbour's nearby boot. He packed it so full that no other bird, large or small, could possibly get in. Our neighbour was not pleased by this pre-emptive strike, but there was nothing to be done about it. "If we take it down," said my dad, "clean it up, and put it back in the tree, the wren will just pack it full of sticks again." Wrens are small, and they're cute, but they're merciless.

I had broken my leg skiing the previous winter—first time down the hill—and had received some money from a school insurance policy designed to reward unfortunate, clumsy children. I purchased a cassette recorder (a high-tech novelty at the time) with the proceeds. My dad suggested that I sit on the back lawn, record the wren's song, play it back, and watch what happened. So, I went out into the bright spring sunlight and taped a few minutes of the wren laying furious claim to his territory with song. Then I let him hear his own voice. That little bird, one-third the size of a sparrow, began to dive-bomb me and my cassette recorder, swooping back and forth, inches from the speaker. We saw a lot of that sort of behaviour, even in the absence of the tape recorder. If a larger bird ever dared to sit and rest in any of the trees near our birdhouse there was a good chance he would get knocked off his perch by a kamikaze wren.

Now, wrens and lobsters are very different. Lobsters do not fly, sing or perch in trees. Wrens have feathers, not hard shells. Wrens can't breathe underwater, and are seldom served with butter. However, they are also similar in important ways. Both are obsessed with status and position, for example, like a great many creatures. The Norwegian zoologist and comparative psychologist Thorlief Schjelderup-Ebbe observed (back in 1921) that even common barnyard chickens establish a "pecking order."[3]

The determination of Who's Who in the chicken world has important implications for each individual bird's survival, particularly in times of scarcity. The birds that always have priority access to whatever food is sprinkled out in the yard in the morning are the celebrity chickens. After them come the second-stringers, the hangers-on and wannabes. Then the third-rate chickens have their turn, and so on, down to the bedraggled, partially-feathered and badly-pecked wretches who occupy the lowest, untouchable stratum of the chicken hierarchy.

Chickens, like suburbanites, live communally. Songbirds, such as wrens, do not, but they still inhabit a dominance hierarchy. It's just spread out over more territory. The wiliest, strongest, healthiest and most fortunate birds occupy prime territory, and defend it. Because of this, they are more likely to attract high-quality mates, and to hatch

chicks who survive and thrive. Protection from wind, rain and predators, as well as easy access to superior food, makes for a much less
stressed existence. Territory matters, and there is little difference
between territorial rights and social status. It is often a matter of life
and death.

If a contagious avian disease sweeps through a neighbourhood of
well-stratified songbirds, it is the least dominant and most stressed
birds, occupying the lowest rungs of the bird world, who are most likely
to sicken and die.[4] This is equally true of human neighbourhoods,
when bird flu viruses and other illnesses sweep across the planet. The
poor and stressed always die first, and in greater numbers. They are
also much more susceptible to non-infectious diseases, such as cancer,
diabetes and heart disease. When the aristocracy catches a cold, as it
is said, the working class dies of pneumonia.

Because territory matters, and because the best locales are always
in short supply, territory-seeking among animals produces conflict.
Conflict, in turn, produces another problem: how to win or lose without the disagreeing parties incurring too great a cost. This latter point
is particularly important. Imagine that two birds engage in a squabble
about a desirable nesting area. The interaction can easily degenerate
into outright physical combat. Under such circumstances, one bird,
usually the largest, will eventually win—but even the victor may be
hurt by the fight. That means a third bird, an undamaged, canny
bystander, can move in, opportunistically, and defeat the now-crippled
victor. That is not at all a good deal for the first two birds.

Conflict—and Territory

Over the millennia, animals who must co-habit with others in the
same territories have in consequence learned many tricks to establish
dominance, while risking the least amount of possible damage. A
defeated wolf, for example, will roll over on its back, exposing its throat
to the victor, who will not then deign to tear it out. The now-dominant
wolf may still require a future hunting partner, after all, even one as
pathetic as his now-defeated foe. Bearded dragons, remarkable social

lizards, wave their front legs peaceably at one another to indicate their wish for continued social harmony. Dolphins produce specialized sound pulses while hunting and during other times of high excitement to reduce potential conflict among dominant and subordinate group members. Such behavior is endemic in the community of living things.

Lobsters, scuttling around on the ocean floor, are no exception.[5] If you catch a few dozen, and transport them to a new location, you can observe their status-forming rituals and techniques. Each lobster will first begin to explore the new territory, partly to map its details, and partly to find a good place for shelter. Lobsters learn a lot about where they live, and they remember what they learn. If you startle one near its nest, it will quickly zip back and hide there. If you startle it some distance away, however, it will immediately dart towards the nearest suitable shelter, previously identified and now remembered.

A lobster needs a safe hiding place to rest, free from predators and the forces of nature. Furthermore, as lobsters grow, they moult, or shed their shells, which leaves them soft and vulnerable for extended periods of time. A burrow under a rock makes a good lobster home, particularly if it is located where shells and other detritus can be dragged into place to cover the entrance, once the lobster is snugly ensconced inside. However, there may be only a small number of high-quality shelters or hiding places in each new territory. They are scarce and valuable. Other lobsters continually seek them out.

This means that lobsters often encounter one another when out exploring. Researchers have demonstrated that even a lobster raised in isolation knows what to do when such a thing happens.[6] It has complex defensive and aggressive behaviours built right into its nervous system. It begins to dance around, like a boxer, opening and raising its claws, moving backward, forward, and side to side, mirroring its opponent, waving its opened claws back and forth. At the same time, it employs special jets under its eyes to direct streams of liquid at its opponent. The liquid spray contains a mix of chemicals that tell the other lobster about its size, sex, health, and mood.

Sometimes one lobster can tell immediately from the display of claw size that it is much smaller than its opponent, and will back down without a fight. The chemical information exchanged in the spray can have the same effect, convincing a less healthy or less aggressive lobster to retreat. That's dispute resolution Level 1.[7] If the two lobsters are very close in size and apparent ability, however, or if the exchange of liquid has been insufficiently informative, they will proceed to dispute resolution Level 2. With antennae whipping madly and claws folded downward, one will advance, and the other retreat. Then the defender will advance, and the aggressor retreat. After a couple of rounds of this behaviour, the more nervous of the lobsters may feel that continuing is not in his best interest. He will flick his tail reflexively, dart backwards, and vanish, to try his luck elsewhere. If neither blinks, however, the lobsters move to Level 3, which involves genuine combat.

This time, the now enraged lobsters come at each other viciously, with their claws extended, to grapple. Each tries to flip the other on its back. A successfully flipped lobster will conclude that its opponent is capable of inflicting serious damage. It generally gives up and leaves (although it harbours intense resentment and gossips endlessly about the victor behind its back). If neither can overturn the other—or if one will not quit despite being flipped—the lobsters move to Level 4. Doing so involves extreme risk, and is not something to be engaged in without forethought: one or both lobsters will emerge damaged from the ensuing fray, perhaps fatally.

The animals advance on each other with increasing speed. Their claws are open, so they can grab a leg, or antenna, or an eye-stalk, or anything else exposed and vulnerable. Once a body part has been successfully grabbed, the grabber will tail-flick backwards, sharply, with claw clamped firmly shut, and try to tear it off. Disputes that have escalated to this point typically create a clear winner and loser. The loser is unlikely to survive, particularly if he or she remains in the territory occupied by the winner, now a mortal enemy.

In the aftermath of a losing battle, regardless of how aggressively a lobster has behaved, it becomes unwilling to fight further, even against another, previously defeated opponent. A vanquished competitor loses confidence, sometimes for days. Sometimes the defeat can have even more severe consequences. If a dominant lobster is badly defeated, its brain basically dissolves. Then it grows a new, subordinate's brain—one more appropriate to its new, lowly position.[8] Its original brain just isn't sophisticated enough to manage the transformation from king to bottom dog without virtually complete dissolution and regrowth. Anyone who has experienced a painful transformation after a serious defeat in romance or career may feel some sense of kinship with the once successful crustacean.

The Neurochemistry of Defeat and Victory

A lobster loser's brain chemistry differs importantly from that of a lobster winner. This is reflected in their relative postures. Whether a lobster is confident or cringing depends on the ratio of two chemicals that modulate communication between lobster neurons: serotonin and octopamine. Winning increases the ratio of the former to the latter.

A lobster with high levels of serotonin and low levels of octopamine is a cocky, strutting sort of shellfish, much less likely to back down when challenged. This is because serotonin helps regulate postural flexion. A flexed lobster extends its appendages so that it can look tall and dangerous, like Clint Eastwood in a spaghetti Western. When a lobster that has just lost a battle is exposed to serotonin, it will stretch itself out, advance even on former victors, and fight longer and harder.[9] The drugs prescribed to depressed human beings, which are selective serotonin reuptake inhibitors, have much the same chemical and behavioural effect. In one of the more staggering demonstrations of the evolutionary continuity of life on Earth, Prozac even cheers up lobsters.[10]

High serotonin/low octopamine characterizes the victor. The opposite neurochemical configuration, a high ratio of octopamine to serotonin, produces a defeated-looking, scrunched-up, inhibited, drooping, skulking sort of lobster, very likely to hang around street corners, and to vanish at the first hint of trouble. Serotonin and octopamine also regulate the tail-flick reflex, which serves to propel a lobster rapidly backwards when it needs to escape. Less provocation is necessary to trigger that reflex in a defeated lobster. You can see an echo of that in the heightened startle reflex characteristic of the soldier or battered child with post-traumatic stress disorder.

The Principle of Unequal Distribution

When a defeated lobster regains its courage and dares to fight again it is more likely to lose again than you would predict, statistically, from a tally of its previous fights. Its victorious opponent, on the other hand, is more likely to win. It's winner-take-all in the lobster world, just as it is in human societies, where the top 1 percent have as much loot as the bottom 50 percent[11]—and where the richest eighty-five people have as much as the bottom three and a half billion.

That same brutal principle of unequal distribution applies outside the financial domain—indeed, anywhere that creative production is required. The majority of scientific papers are published by a very small group of scientists. A tiny proportion of musicians produces almost all the recorded commercial music. Just a handful of authors sell all the books. A million and a half separately titled books (!) sell each year in the US. However, only five hundred of these sell more than a hundred thousand copies.[12] Similarly, just four classical composers (Bach, Beethoven, Mozart, and Tchaikovsky) wrote almost all the music played by modern orchestras. Bach, for his part, composed so prolifically that it would take decades of work merely to hand-copy his scores, yet only a small fraction of this prodigious output is commonly performed. The same thing applies to the output of the other three members of this group of hyper-dominant composers: only a small fraction of their work is still widely played. Thus, a small fraction of the music composed by a small fraction of all the classical composers who have ever composed makes up almost all the classical music that the world knows and loves.

This principle is sometimes known as Price's law, after Derek J. de Solla Price,[13] the researcher who discovered its application in science in 1963. It can be modelled using an approximately L-shaped graph, with number of people on the vertical axis, and productivity or resources on the horizontal. The basic principle had been discovered much earlier. Vilfredo Pareto (1848–1923), an Italian polymath, noticed its applicability to wealth distribution in the early twentieth century, and it appears true for every society ever studied, regardless of governmental form. It also applies to the population of cities (a very small number have almost all the people), the mass of heavenly bodies (a very small number hoard all the matter), and the frequency of words in a language (90 percent of communication occurs using just 500 words), among many other things. Sometimes it is known as the Matthew Principle (Matthew 25:29), derived from what might be the harshest statement ever attributed to Christ: "to those who have everything, more will be given; from those who have nothing, everything will be taken."

You truly know you are the Son of God when your dicta apply even to crustaceans.

Back to the fractious shellfish: it doesn't take that long before lobsters, testing each other out, learn who can be messed with and who should be given a wide berth—and once they have learned, the resultant hierarchy is exceedingly stable. All a victor needs to do, once he has won, is to wiggle his antennae in a threatening manner, and a previous opponent will vanish in a puff of sand before him. A weaker lobster will quit trying, accept his lowly status, and keep his legs attached to his body. The top lobster, by contrast—occupying the best shelter, getting some good rest, finishing a good meal—parades his dominance around his territory, rousting subordinate lobsters from their shelters at night, just to remind them who's their daddy.

All the Girls

The female lobsters (who also fight hard for territory during the explicitly maternal stages of their existence[14]) identify the top guy quickly, and become irresistibly attracted to him. This is brilliant strategy, in my estimation. It's also one used by females of many different species, including humans. Instead of undertaking the computationally difficult task of identifying the best man, the females outsource the problem to the machine-like calculations of the dominance hierarchy.

They let the males fight it out and peel their paramours from the top. This is very much what happens with stock-market pricing, where the value of any particular enterprise is determined through the competition of all.

When the females are ready to shed their shells and soften up a bit, they become interested in mating. They start hanging around the dominant lobster's pad, spraying attractive scents and aphrodisiacs towards him, trying to seduce him. His aggression has made him successful, so he's likely to react in a dominant, irritable manner. Furthermore, he's large, healthy and powerful. It's no easy task to switch his attention from fighting to mating. (If properly charmed, however, he will change his behaviour towards the female. This is the lobster equivalent of *Fifty Shades of Grey*, the fastest-selling paperback of all time, and the eternal Beauty-and-the-Beast plot of archetypal romance. This is the pattern of behaviour continually represented in the sexually explicit literary fantasies that are as popular among women as provocative images of naked women are among men.)

It should be pointed out, however, that sheer physical power is an unstable basis on which to found lasting dominance, as the Dutch primatologist Frans de Waal[15] has taken pains to demonstrate. Among the chimp troupes he studied, males who were successful in the longer term had to buttress their physical prowess with more sophisticated attributes. Even the most brutal chimp despot can be taken down, after all, by two opponents, each three-quarters as mean. In consequence, males who stay on top longer are those who form reciprocal coalitions with their lower-status compatriots, and who pay careful attention to the troupe's females and their infants. The political ploy of baby-kissing is literally millions of years old. But lobsters are still comparatively primitive, so the bare plot elements of Beast and Beauty suffice for them.

Once the Beast has been successfully charmed, the successful female (lobster) will disrobe, shedding her shell, making herself dangerously soft, vulnerable, and ready to mate. At the right moment, the male, now converted into a careful lover, deposits a packet of sperm into the appropriate receptacle. Afterward, the female hangs around, and hardens up for a couple of weeks (another phenomenon not entirely unknown among human beings). At her leisure, she returns to her own domicile, laden with fertilized eggs. At this point another female will attempt the same thing—and so on. The dominant male, with his upright and confident posture, not only gets the prime real estate and easiest access to the best hunting grounds. He also gets all the girls. It is exponentially more worthwhile to be successful, if you are a lobster, and male.

Why is all this relevant? For an amazing number of reasons, apart from those that are comically obvious. First, we know that lobsters have been around, in one form or another, for more than 350 million years.[16] This is a very long time. Sixty-five million years ago, there were still dinosaurs. That is the unimaginably distant past to us. To the lobsters, however, dinosaurs were the *nouveau riche*, who appeared and disappeared in the flow of near-eternal time. This means that dominance hierarchies have been an essentially permanent feature of the environment to which all complex life has adapted. A third of a billion years ago, brains and nervous systems were comparatively simple. Nonetheless, they already had the structure and neurochemistry necessary to process information about status and society. The importance of this fact can hardly be overstated.

The Nature of Nature

It is a truism of biology that evolution is conservative. When something evolves, it must build upon what nature has already produced. New features may be added, and old features may undergo some alteration, but most things remain the same. It is for this reason that the wings of bats, the hands of human beings, and the fins of whales look astonishingly alike in their skeletal form. They even have the same number of bones. Evolution laid down the cornerstones for basic physiology long ago.

Evolution works, in large part, through variation and natural selection. Variation exists for many reasons, including gene-shuffling (to put it simply) and random mutation. Individuals vary within a species for such reasons. Nature chooses from among them, across time. That theory, as stated, appears to account for the continual alteration of life-forms over the eons. But there's an additional question lurking under the surface: what exactly is the "nature" in "natural selection"? What exactly is "the environment" to which animals adapt? We make many assumptions about nature—about the environment— and these have consequences. Mark Twain once said, "It's not what we don't know that gets us in trouble. It's what we know for sure that just ain't so."

First, it is easy to assume that "nature" is something with a nature— something static. But it's not: at least not in any simple sense. It's static and dynamic, at the same time. The environment—the nature that selects—itself transforms. The famous yin and yang symbols of the Taoists capture this beautifully. Being, for the Taoists—reality itself— is composed of two opposing principles, often translated as feminine and masculine, or even more narrowly as female and male. However, yin and yang are more accurately understood as chaos and order. The Taoist symbol is a circle enclosing twin serpents, head to tail. The black serpent, chaos, has a white dot in its head. The white serpent, order, has a black dot in its head. This is because chaos and order are interchangeable, as well as eternally juxtaposed. There is nothing so certain that it cannot vary. Even the sun itself has its cycles of insta- bility. Likewise, there is nothing so mutable that it cannot be fixed. Every revolution produces a new order. Every death is, simultaneously, a metamorphosis.

Considering nature as purely static produces serious errors of apprehension. Nature "selects." The idea of *selects* contains implic- itly nested within it the idea of *fitness*. It is "fitness" that is "selected." Fitness, roughly speaking, is the probability that a given organism will leave offspring (will propagate its genes through time). The "fit" in "fitness" is therefore the matching of organismal attributes to envi- ronmental demand. If that demand is conceptualized as static—if nature is conceptualized as eternal and unchanging—then evolution is a never-ending series of linear improvements, and fitness is some- thing that can be ever more closely approximated across time. The still-powerful Victorian idea of evolutionary progress, with man at the pinnacle, is a partial consequence of this model of nature. It produces the erroneous notion that there is a destination of natural selection (increasing fitness to the environment), and that it can be conceptualized as a fixed point.

But nature, the selecting agent, is not a static selector—not in any simple sense. Nature dresses differently for each occasion. Nature varies like a musical score—and that, in part, explains why music produces its deep intimations of meaning. As the environment supporting a species transforms and changes, the features that make a given individual successful in surviving and reproducing also transform and change. Thus, the theory of natural selection does not posit creatures matching themselves ever more precisely to a template specified by the world. It is more that creatures are in a dance with nature, albeit one that is deadly. "In my kingdom," as the Red Queen tells Alice in Wonderland, "you have to run as fast as you can just to stay in the same place." No one standing still can triumph, no matter how well constituted.

Nature is not simply dynamic, either. Some things change quickly, but they are nested within other things that change less quickly (music frequently models this, too). Leaves change more quickly than trees, and trees more quickly than forests. Weather changes faster than climate. If it wasn't this way, then the conservatism of evolution would not work, as the basic morphology of arms and hands would have to change as fast as the length of arm bones and the function of fingers. It's chaos, within order, within chaos, within higher order. The order that is most real is the order that is most unchanging—and that is not necessarily the order that is most easily seen. The leaf, when perceived, might blind the observer to the tree. The tree can blind him to the forest. And some things that are most real (such as the ever-present dominance hierarchy) cannot be "seen" at all.

It is also a mistake to conceptualize nature romantically. Rich, modern city-dwellers, surrounded by hot, baking concrete, imagine the environment as something pristine and paradisal, like a French impressionist landscape. Eco-activists, even more idealistic in their viewpoint, envision nature as harmoniously balanced and perfect, absent the disruptions and depredations of mankind. Unfortunately, "the environment" is also elephantiasis and guinea worms (don't ask), anopheles mosquitoes and malaria, starvation-level droughts, AIDS and the Black Plague. We don't fantasize about the beauty of these aspects of nature, although they are just as real as their Edenic counterparts. It is because of the existence of such things, of course, that we attempt to modify our surroundings, protecting our children, building cities and transportation systems and growing food and generating power. If Mother Nature wasn't so hell-bent on our destruction, it would be easier for us to exist in simple harmony with her dictates.

And this brings us to a third erroneous concept: that nature is something strictly segregated from the cultural constructs that have emerged within it. The order within the chaos and order of Being is all the more "natural" the longer it has lasted. This is because "nature" is "what selects," and the longer a feature has existed the more time it has had to be selected—and to shape life. It does not matter whether that feature is physical and biological, or social and cultural. All that matters, from a Darwinian perspective, is permanence—and the dominance hierarchy, however social or cultural it might appear, has been around for some half a billion years. It's permanent. It's real. The dominance hierarchy is not capitalism. It's not communism, either, for that matter. It's not the military-industrial complex. It's not the patriarchy—that disposable, malleable, arbitrary cultural artefact. It's not even a human creation; not in the most profound sense. It is instead a near-eternal aspect of the environment, and much of what is blamed on these more ephemeral manifestations is a consequence of its unchanging existence. We (the sovereign *we*, the *we* that has been around since the beginning of life) have lived in a dominance hierarchy for a long, long time. We were struggling for position before we had skin, or hands, or lungs, or bones. There is little more natural than culture. Dominance hierarchies are older than trees.

The part of our brain that keeps track of our position in the dominance hierarchy is therefore exceptionally ancient and fundamental.[17] It is a master control system, modulating our perceptions, values, emotions, thoughts and actions. It powerfully affects every aspect of our Being, conscious and unconscious alike. This is why, when we are defeated, we act very much like lobsters who have lost a fight. Our posture droops. We face the ground. We feel threatened, hurt, anxious and weak. If things do not improve, we become chronically depressed. Under such conditions, we can't easily put up the kind of fight that life demands, and we become easy targets for harder-shelled bullies. And it is not only the behavioural and experiential similarities that are striking. Much of the basic neurochemistry is the same.

Consider serotonin, the chemical that governs posture and escape in the lobster. Low-ranking lobsters produce comparatively low levels of serotonin. This is also true of low-ranking human beings (and those low levels decrease more with each defeat). Low serotonin means decreased confidence. Low serotonin means more response to stress and costlier physical preparedness for emergency—as anything what-soever may happen, at any time, at the bottom of the dominance hier-archy (and rarely something good). Low serotonin means less happiness, more pain and anxiety, more illness, and a shorter lifespan—among humans, just as among crustaceans. Higher spots in the dominance hierarchy, and the higher serotonin levels typical of those who inhabit them, are characterized by less illness, misery and death, even when factors such as absolute income—or number of decaying food scraps—are held constant. The importance of this can hardly be overstated.

Top and Bottom

There is an unspeakably primordial calculator, deep within you, at the very foundation of your brain, far below your thoughts and feelings. It monitors exactly where you are positioned in society—on a scale of one to ten, for the sake of argument. If you're a number one, the highest level of status, you're an overwhelming success. If you're male, you have preferential access to the best places to live and the highest-quality food. People compete to do you favours. You have limitless opportunity for romantic and sexual contact. You are a successful lobster, and the most desirable females line up and vie for your attention.[18]

If you're female, you have access to many high-quality suitors: tall, strong and symmetrical; creative, reliable, honest and generous. And, like your dominant male counterpart, you will compete ferociously, even pitilessly, to maintain or improve your position in the equally competitive female mating hierarchy. Although you are less likely to use physical aggression to do so, there are many effective verbal tricks and strategies at your disposal, including the disparaging of opponents, and you may well be expert at their use.

If you are a low-status ten, by contrast, male or female, you have nowhere to live (or nowhere good). Your food is terrible, when you're not going hungry. You're in poor physical and mental condition. You're of minimal romantic interest to anyone, unless they are as desperate as you. You are more likely to fall ill, age rapidly, and die young, with few, if any, to mourn you.[19] Even money itself may prove of little use. You won't know how to use it, because it is difficult to use money properly, particularly if you are unfamiliar with it. Money will make you liable to the dangerous temptations of drugs and alcohol, which are much more rewarding if you have been deprived of pleasure for a long period. Money will also make you a target for predators and psychopaths, who thrive on exploiting those who exist on the lower rungs of society. The bottom of the dominance hierarchy is a terrible, dangerous place to be.

The ancient part of your brain specialized for assessing dominance watches how you are treated by other people. On that evidence, it renders a determination of your value and assigns you a status. If you are judged by your peers as of little worth, the counter restricts serotonin availability. That makes you much more physically and psychologically reactive to any circumstance or event that might produce emotion, particularly if it is negative. You need that reactivity. Emergencies are common at the bottom, and you must be ready to survive.

Unfortunately, that physical hyper-response, that constant alertness, burns up a lot of precious energy and physical resources. This response is really what everyone calls stress, and it is by no means only or even primarily psychological. It's a reflection of the genuine constraints of unfortunate circumstances. When operating at the bottom, the ancient brain counter assumes that even the smallest unexpected impediment might produce an uncontrollable chain of negative events, which will have to be handled alone as useful friends are rare indeed on society's fringes. You will therefore continually sacrifice what you could otherwise physically store for the future, using it up on heightened readiness and immediate panicked action in the present. When you don't know what to do, you must be prepared to do anything and everything, in case it becomes necessary. You're sitting in your car with the gas and brake pedals both punched to the mat. Too much of that and everything falls apart. The ancient counter will even shut down your immune system, expending the energy and resources required for future health now, during the crises of the present. It will render you impulsive,[20] so that you will jump, for example, at any short-term mating opportunities, or any possibilities of pleasure, no matter how sub-par, disgraceful or illegal. It will leave you far more likely to live, or die, carelessly, for a rare opportunity at pleasure, when it manifests itself. The physical demands of emergency preparedness will wear you down in every way.[21]

If you have a high status, on the other hand, the counter's cold, pre-reptilian mechanics assume that your niche is secure, productive and safe, and that you are well buttressed with social support. It thinks the chance that something will damage you is low and can be safely discounted. Change might be opportunity, instead of disaster. The serotonin flows plentifully. This renders you confident and calm, standing tall and straight, and much less on constant alert. Because your position is secure, the future is likely to be good for you. It's worthwhile to think in the long term and plan for a better tomorrow. You don't need to grasp impulsively at whatever crumbs come your way, because you can realistically expect good things to remain available. You can delay gratification, without forgoing it forever. You can afford to be a reliable and thoughtful citizen.

Malfunction

Sometimes, however, the counter mechanism can go wrong. Erratic habits of sleeping and eating can interfere with its function. Uncertainty can throw it for a loop. The body, with its various parts, needs to function like a well-rehearsed orchestra. Every system must play its role properly, and at exactly the right time, or noise and chaos ensue. It is for this reason that routine is so necessary. The acts of life we repeat every day need to be automatized. They must be turned into stable and reliable habits, so they lose their complexity and gain predictability and simplicity. This can be perceived most clearly in the case of small children, who are delightful and comical and playful when their sleeping and eating schedules are stable, and horrible and whiny and nasty when they are not.

It is for such reasons that I always ask my clinical clients first about sleep. Do they wake up in the morning at approximately the time the typical person wakes up, and at the same time every day? If the answer is no, fixing that is the first thing I recommend. It doesn't matter so much if they go to bed at the same time each evening, but waking up at a consistent hour is a necessity. Anxiety and depression cannot be easily treated if the sufferer has unpredictable daily routines. The systems that mediate negative emotion are tightly tied to the properly cyclical circadian rhythms.

The next thing I ask about is breakfast. I counsel my clients to eat a fat and protein-heavy breakfast as soon as possible after they awaken (no simple carbohydrates, no sugars, as they are digested too rapidly, and produce a blood-sugar spike and rapid dip). This is because anxious and depressed people are already stressed, particularly if their lives have not been under control for a good while. Their bodies are therefore primed to hypersecrete insulin, if they engage in any complex or demanding activity. If they do so after fasting all night and before eating, the excess insulin in their bloodstream will mop up all their blood sugar. Then they become hypoglycemic and psychophysiologically unstable.[22] All day. Their systems cannot be reset until after more sleep. I have had many clients whose anxiety was reduced to subclinical levels merely because they started to sleep on a predictable schedule and eat breakfast.

Other bad habits can also interfere with the counter's accuracy. Sometimes this happens directly, for poorly understood biological reasons, and sometimes it happens because those habits initiate a complex positive feedback loop. A positive feedback loop requires an input detector, an amplifier, and some form of output. Imagine a signal picked up by the input detector, amplified, and then emitted, in amplified form. So far, so good. The trouble starts when the input detector detects that output, and runs it through the system again, amplifying and emitting it again. A few rounds of intensification and things get dangerously out of control.

Most people have been subject to the deafening howling of feedback at a concert when the sound system squeals painfully. The microphone sends a signal to the speakers. The speakers emit the signal. The signal can be picked up by the microphone and sent through the system again, if it's too loud or too close to the speakers. The sound rapidly amplifies to unbearable levels, sufficient to destroy the speakers, if it continues.

The same destructive loop happens within people's lives. Much of the time, when it happens, we label it mental illness, even though it's not only or even at all occurring inside people's psyches. Addiction to alcohol or another mood-altering drug is a common positive-feedback process. Imagine a person who enjoys alcohol, perhaps a bit too much. He has a quick three or four drinks. His blood alcohol level spikes sharply. This can be extremely exhilarating, particularly for someone who has a genetic predisposition to alcoholism.[23] But it only occurs while blood alcohol levels are actively rising, and that only continues if the drinker keeps drinking. When he stops, not only does his blood alcohol level plateau and then start to sink, but his body begins to produce a variety of toxins, as it metabolizes the ethanol already consumed. He also starts to experience alcohol withdrawal, as the anxiety systems that were suppressed during intoxication start to hyper-respond. A hangover is alcohol withdrawal (which quite frequently kills withdrawing alcoholics), and it starts all too soon after drinking ceases. To continue the warm glow, and stave off the unpleasant aftermath, the drinker may just continue to drink, until all the liquor in his house is consumed, the bars are closed and his money is spent.

The next day, the drinker wakes up, badly hungover. So far, this is just unfortunate. The real trouble starts when he discovers that his hangover can be "cured" with a few more drinks the morning after. Such a cure is, of course, temporary. It merely pushes the withdrawal symptoms a bit further into the future. But that might be what is required, in the short term, if the misery is sufficiently acute. So now he has learned to drink to cure his hangover. When the medication causes the disease, a positive feedback loop has been established. Alcoholism can quickly emerge under such conditions.

Something similar often happens to people who develop an anxiety disorder, such as agoraphobia. People with agoraphobia can become so overwhelmed with fear that they will no longer leave their homes. Agoraphobia is the consequence of a positive feedback loop. The first event that precipitates the disorder is often a panic attack. The sufferer is typically a middle-aged woman who has been too dependent on other people. Perhaps she went immediately from over-reliance on her father to a relationship with an older and comparatively dominant boyfriend or husband, with little or no break for independent existence.

In the weeks leading up to the emergence of her agoraphobia, such a woman typically experiences something unexpected and anomalous. It might be something physiological, such as heart palpitations, which are common in any case, and whose likelihood is increased during menopause, when the hormonal processes regulating a women's psychological experience fluctuate unpredictably. Any perceptible alteration in heart-rate can trigger thoughts both of heart attack and an all-too-public and embarrassing display of post-heart attack distress and suffering (death and social humiliation constituting the two most basic fears). The unexpected occurrence might instead be conflict in the sufferer's marriage, or the illness or death of a spouse. It might be a close friend's divorce or hospitalization. Some real event typically precipitates the initial increase in fear of mortality and social judgment.[24]

After the shock, perhaps, the pre-agoraphobic woman leaves her house, and makes her way to the shopping mall. It's busy and difficult to park. This makes her even more stressed. The thoughts of vulnerability occupying her mind since her recent unpleasant experience rise close to the surface. They trigger anxiety. Her heart rate rises. She begins to breathe shallowly and quickly. She feels her heart racing and begins to wonder if she is suffering a heart attack. This thought triggers more anxiety. She breathes even more shallowly, increasing the levels of carbon dioxide in her blood. Her heart rate increases again, because of her additional fear. She detects that, and her heart rate rises again.

Poof! Positive feedback loop. Soon the anxiety transforms into panic, regulated by a different brain system, designed for the severest of threats, which can be triggered by too much fear. She is overwhelmed by her symptoms, and heads for the emergency room, where after an anxious wait her heart function is checked. There is nothing wrong. But she is not reassured.

It takes an additional feedback loop to transform even that unpleasant experience into full-blown agoraphobia. The next time she needs to go to the mall, the pre-agoraphobic becomes anxious, remembering what happened last time. But she goes, anyway. On the way, she can feel her heart pounding. That triggers another cycle of anxiety and concern. To forestall panic, she avoids the stress of the mall and returns home. But now the anxiety systems in her brain note that she ran away from the mall, and conclude that the journey there was truly dangerous. Our anxiety systems are very practical. They assume that anything you run away from is dangerous. The proof of that is, of course, the fact you ran away.

So now the mall is tagged "too dangerous to approach" (or the budding agoraphobic has labelled herself, "too fragile to approach the mall"). Perhaps that is not yet taking things far enough to cause her real trouble. There are other places to shop. But maybe the nearby supermarket is mall-like enough to trigger a similar response, when she visits it instead, and then retreats. Now the supermarket occupies the same category. Then it's the corner store. Then it's buses and taxis and subways. Soon it's everywhere. The agoraphobic will even eventually become afraid of her house, and would run away from that if she could. But she can't. Soon she's stuck in her home. Anxiety-induced retreat makes everything retreated from more anxiety-inducing. Anxiety-induced retreat makes the self smaller and the ever-more-dangerous world larger.

There are many systems of interaction between brain, body and social world that can get caught in positive feedback loops. Depressed people, for example, can start feeling useless and burdensome, as well as grief-stricken and pained. This makes them withdraw from contact with friends and family. Then the withdrawal makes them more lonesome and isolated, and more likely to feel useless and burdensome. Then they withdraw more. In this manner, depression spirals and amplifies.

If someone is badly hurt at some point in life—traumatized—the dominance counter can transform in a manner that makes additional hurt more rather than less likely. This often happens in the case of people, now adults, who were viciously bullied during childhood or adolescence. They become anxious and easily upset. They shield themselves with a defensive crouch, and avoid the direct eye contact interpretable as a dominance challenge.

This means that the damage caused by the bullying (the lowering of status and confidence) can continue, even after the bullying has ended.[25] In the simplest of cases, the formerly lowly persons have matured and moved to new and more successful places in their lives. But they don't fully notice. Their now-counterproductive physiological adaptations to earlier reality remain, and they are more stressed and uncertain than is necessary. In more complex cases, a habitual assumption of subordination renders the person more stressed and uncertain than necessary, *and* their habitually submissive posturing continues to attract genuine negative attention from one or more of the fewer and generally less successful bullies still extant in the adult world. In such situations, the psychological consequence of the previous bullying increases the likelihood of continued bullying in the present (even though, strictly speaking, it wouldn't have to, because of maturation, or geographical relocation, or continued education, or improvement in objective status).

Rising Up

Sometimes people are bullied because they *can't* fight back. This can happen to people who are weaker, physically, than their opponents. This is one of the most common reasons for the bullying experienced by children. Even the toughest of six-year-olds is no match for someone who is nine. A lot of that power differential disappears in adulthood, however, with the rough stabilization and matching of physical size (with the exception of that pertaining to men and women, with the former typically larger and stronger, particularly in the upper body) as well as the increased penalties generally applied in adulthood to those who insist upon continuing with physical intimidation.

But just as often, people are bullied because they *won't* fight back. This happens not infrequently to people who are by temperament compassionate and self-sacrificing—particularly if they are also high in negative emotion, and make a lot of gratifying noises of suffering when someone sadistic confronts them (children who cry more easily, for example, are more frequently bullied).[26] It also happens to people who have decided, for one reason or another, that all forms of aggression, including even feelings of anger, are morally wrong. I have seen people with a particularly acute sensitivity to petty tyranny and over-aggressive competitiveness restrict within themselves all the emotions that might give rise to such things. Often they are people whose fathers were excessively angry and controlling. Psychological forces are never unidimensional in their value, however, and the truly appalling potential of anger and aggression to produce cruelty and mayhem are balanced by the ability of those primordial forces to push back against oppression, speak truth, and motivate resolute movement forward in times of strife, uncertainty and danger.

With their capacity for aggression strait-jacketed within a too-narrow morality, those who are only or merely compassionate and self-sacrificing (and naïve and exploitable) cannot call forth the genuinely righteous and appropriately self-protective anger necessary to defend themselves. If you *can* bite, you generally don't *have to*. When skillfully integrated, the ability to respond with aggression and violence decreases rather than increases the probability that actual aggression will become necessary. If you say no, early in the cycle of oppression, and you mean what you say (which means you state your refusal in no uncertain terms and stand behind it) then the scope for oppression on the part of oppressor will remain properly bounded and limited. The forces of tyranny expand inexorably to fill the space made available for their existence. People who refuse to muster appropriately self-protective territorial responses are laid open to exploitation as much as those who genuinely can't stand up for their own rights because of a more essential inability or a true imbalance in power.

Naive, harmless people usually guide their perceptions and actions with a few simple axioms: people are basically good; no one really wants to hurt anyone else; the threat (and, certainly, the use) of force, physical or otherwise, is wrong. These axioms collapse, or worse, in the presence of individuals who are genuinely malevolent.[27] *Worse* means that naive beliefs can become a positive invitation to abuse, because those who aim to harm have become specialized to prey on people who think precisely such things. Under such conditions, the axioms of harmlessness must be retooled. In my clinical practice I often draw the attention of my clients who think that good people never become angry to the stark realities of their own resentments.

No one likes to be pushed around, but people often put up with it for too long. So, I get them to see their resentment, first, as anger, and then as an indication that something needs to be said, if not done (not least because honesty demands it). Then I get them to see such action as part of the force that holds tyranny at bay—at the social level, as much as the individual. Many bureaucracies have petty authoritarians within them, generating unnecessary rules and procedures simply to express and cement power. Such people produce powerful undercurrents of resentment around them which, if expressed, would limit their expression of pathological power. It is in this manner that the willingness of the individual to stand up for him- or herself protects everyone from the corruption of society.

When naive people discover the capacity for anger within themselves, they are shocked, sometimes severely. A profound example of that can be found in the susceptibility of new soldiers to post-traumatic stress disorder, which often occurs because of something they watch themselves doing, rather than because of something that has happened to them. They react like the monsters they can truly be in extreme battlefield conditions, and the revelation of that capacity undoes their world. And no wonder. Perhaps they assumed that all of history's terrible perpetrators were people totally unlike themselves. Perhaps they were never able to see within themselves the capacity for oppression and bullying (and perhaps not their capacity for assertion and success, as well). I have had clients who were terrified into literally years of daily hysterical convulsions by the sheer look of malevolence on their attackers' faces. Such individuals typically come from hyper-sheltered families, where nothing terrible is allowed to exist, and everything is fairyland wonderful (or else).

When the wakening occurs—when once-naïve people recognize in themselves the seeds of evil and monstrosity, and see themselves as dangerous (at least potentially) their fear decreases. They develop more self-respect. Then, perhaps, they begin to resist oppression. They see that they have the ability to withstand, because they are terrible too. They see they can and must stand up, because they begin to understand how genuinely monstrous they will become, otherwise, feeding on their resentment, transforming it into the most destructive of wishes. To say it again: There is very little difference between the capacity for mayhem and destruction, integrated, and strength of character. This is one of the most difficult lessons of life.

Maybe you are a loser. And maybe you're not—but if you are, you don't have to continue in that mode. Maybe you just have a bad habit. Maybe you're even just a collection of bad habits. Nonetheless, even if you came by your poor posture honestly—even if you were unpopular or bullied at home or in grade school[28]—it's not necessarily appropriate now. Circumstances change. If you slump around, with the same bearing that characterizes a defeated lobster, people will assign you a lower status, and the old counter that you share with crustaceans, sitting at the very base of your brain, will assign you a low dominance number. Then your brain will not produce as much serotonin. This will make you less happy, and more anxious and sad, and more likely to back down when you should stand up for yourself. It will also decrease the probability that you will get to live in a good neighbourhood, have access to the highest quality resources, and obtain a healthy, desirable mate. It will render you more likely to abuse cocaine and alcohol, as you live for the present in a world full of uncertain futures. It will increase your susceptibility to heart disease, cancer and dementia. All in all, it's just not good.

Circumstances change, and so can you. Positive feedback loops, adding effect to effect, can spiral counterproductively in a negative direction, but can also work to get you ahead. That's the other, far more optimistic lesson of Price's law and the Pareto distribution: those who start to have will probably get more. Some of these upwardly moving loops can occur in your own private, subjective space. Alterations in body language offer an important example. If you are asked by a researcher to move your facial muscles, one at a time, into a position that would look sad to an observer, you will report feeling sadder. If you are asked to move the muscles one by one into a position that looks happy, you will report feeling happier. Emotion is partly bodily expression, and can be amplified (or dampened) by that expression.[29]

Some of the positive feedback loops instantiated by body language can occur beyond the private confines of subjective experience, in the social space you share with other people. If your posture is poor, for example—if you slump, shoulders forward and rounded, chest tucked in, head down, looking small, defeated and ineffectual (protected, in theory, against attack from behind)—then you will feel small, defeated and ineffectual. The reactions of others will amplify that. People, like lobsters, size each other up, partly in consequence of stance. If you present yourself as defeated, then people will react to you as if you are losing. If you start to straighten up, then people will look at and treat you differently.

You might object: the bottom is real. Being at the bottom is equally real. A mere transformation of posture is insufficient to change anything that fixed. If you're in number ten position, then standing up straight and appearing dominant might only attract the attention of those who want, once again, to put you down. And fair enough. But standing up straight with your shoulders back is not something that is only physical, because you're not only a body. You're a spirit, so to speak—a psyche—as well. Standing up physically also implies and invokes and demands standing up metaphysically. Standing up means voluntarily accepting the burden of Being. Your nervous system responds in an entirely different manner when you face the demands of life voluntarily. You respond to a challenge, instead of bracing for a catastrophe. You see the gold the dragon hoards, instead of shrinking in terror from the all-too-real fact of the dragon. You step forward to take your place in the dominance hierarchy, and occupy your territory, manifesting your willingness to defend, expand and transform it. That can all occur practically or symbolically, as a physical or as a conceptual restructuring.

To stand up straight with your shoulders back is to accept the terrible responsibility of life, with eyes wide open. It means deciding to voluntarily transform the chaos of potential into the realities of habitable order. It means adopting the burden of self-conscious vulnerability, and accepting the end of the unconscious paradise of childhood, where finitude and mortality are only dimly comprehended. It means willingly undertaking the sacrifices necessary to generate a productive and meaningful reality (it means acting to please God, in the ancient language).

To stand up straight with your shoulders back means building the ark that protects the world from the flood, guiding your people through the desert after they have escaped tyranny, making your way away from comfortable home and country, and speaking the prophetic word to those who ignore the widows and children. It means shouldering the cross that marks the X, the place where you and Being intersect so terribly. It means casting dead, rigid and too tyrannical order back into the chaos in which it was generated; it means withstanding the ensuing uncertainty, and establishing, in consequence, a better, more meaningful and more productive order.

So, attend carefully to your posture. Quit drooping and hunching around. Speak your mind. Put your desires forward, as if you had a right to them—at least the same right as others. Walk tall and gaze forthrightly ahead. Dare to be dangerous. Encourage the serotonin to flow plentifully through the neural pathways desperate for its calming influence.

People, including yourself, will start to assume that you are competent and able (or at least they will not immediately conclude the reverse). Emboldened by the positive responses you are now receiving, you will begin to be less anxious. You will then find it easier to pay attention to the subtle social clues that people exchange when they are communicating. Your conversations will flow better, with fewer awkward pauses. This will make you more likely to meet people, interact with them, and impress them. Doing so will not only genuinely increase the probability that good things will happen to you—it will also make those good things feel better when they do happen.

Thus strengthened and emboldened, you may choose to embrace Being, and work for its furtherance and improvement. Thus strengthened, you may be able to stand, even during the illness of a loved one, even during the death of a parent, and allow others to find strength alongside you when they would otherwise be overwhelmed with despair. Thus emboldened, you will embark on the voyage of your life, let your light shine, so to speak, on the heavenly hill, and pursue your rightful destiny. Then the meaning of your life may be sufficient to keep the corrupting influence of mortal despair at bay.

Then you may be able to accept the terrible burden of the World, and find joy.

Look for your inspiration to the victorious lobster, with its 350 million years of practical wisdom. Stand up straight, with your shoulders back.

RULE 2

TREAT YOURSELF LIKE SOMEONE
YOU ARE RESPONSIBLE FOR HELPING

WHY WON'T YOU JUST TAKE YOUR DAMN PILLS?

IMAGINE THAT A HUNDRED PEOPLE are prescribed a drug. Consider what happens next. One-third of them won't fill the prescription.[30] Half of the remaining sixty-seven will fill it, but won't take the medication correctly. They'll miss doses. They'll quit taking it early. They might not even take it at all.

Physicians and pharmacists tend to blame such patients for their noncompliance, inaction and error. You can lead a horse to water, they reason. Psychologists tend to take a dim view of such judgments. We are trained to assume that the failure of patients to follow professional advice is the fault of the practitioner, not the patient. We believe the health-care provider has a responsibility to proffer advice that will be followed, offer interventions that will be respected, plan with the patient or client until the desired result is achieved, and follow up to ensure that everything is going correctly. This is just one of the many things that make psychologists so wonderful – :). Of course, we have the luxury of time with our clients, unlike other more beleaguered professionals, who wonder why sick people won't take their medication. What's wrong with them? Don't they want to get better?

Here's something worse. Imagine that someone receives an organ transplant. Imagine it's a kidney. A transplant typically occurs only after a long period of anxious waiting on the part of the recipient. Only a minority of people donate organs when they die (and even fewer when they are still alive). Only a small number of donated organs are a good match for any hopeful recipient. This means that the typical kidney transplantee has been undergoing dialysis, the only alternative, for years. Dialysis involves passing all the patient's blood out of his or her body, through a machine, and back in. It is an unlikely and miraculous treatment, so that's all good, but it's not pleasant. It must happen five to seven times a week, for eight hours a time. It should happen every time the patient sleeps. That's too much. No one wants to stay on dialysis.

Now, one of the complications of transplantation is rejection. Your body does not like it when parts of someone else's body are stitched into it. Your immune system will attack and destroy such foreign elements, even when they are crucial to your survival. To stop this from happening, you must take anti-rejection drugs, which weaken immunity, increasing your susceptibility to infectious disease. Most people are happy to accept the trade-off. Recipients of transplants still suffer the effects of organ rejection, despite the existence and utility of these drugs. It's not because the drugs fail (although they sometimes do). It's more often because those prescribed the drugs do not take them. This beggars belief. It is seriously not good to have your kidneys fail. Dialysis is no picnic. Transplantation surgery occurs after long waiting, at high risk and great expense. To lose all that because you don't take your medication? How could people do that to themselves? How could this possibly be?

It's complicated, to be fair. Many people who receive a transplanted organ are isolated, or beset by multiple physical health problems (to say nothing of problems associated with unemployment or family crisis). They may be cognitively impaired or depressed. They may not entirely trust their doctor, or understand the necessity of the medication. Maybe they can barely afford the drugs, and ration them, desperately and unproductively.

But—and this is the amazing thing—imagine that it isn't you who feels sick. It's your dog. So, you take him to the vet. The vet gives you a prescription. What happens then? You have just as many reasons to distrust a vet as a doctor. Furthermore, if you cared so little for your pet that you weren't concerned with what improper, substandard or error-ridden prescription he might be given, you wouldn't have taken him to the vet in the first place. Thus, you care. Your actions prove it. In fact, on average, you care *more*. People are better at filling and properly administering prescription medication to their pets than to themselves. That's not good. Even from your pet's perspective, it's not good. Your pet (probably) loves you, and would be happier if you took your medication.

It is difficult to conclude anything from this set of facts except that people appear to love their dogs, cats, ferrets and birds (and maybe even their lizards) more than themselves. How horrible is that? How much shame must exist, for something like that to be true? What could it be about people that makes them prefer their pets to themselves?

It was an ancient story in the Book of Genesis—the first book in the Old Testament—that helped me find an answer to that perplexing question.

The Oldest Story and the Nature of the World

Two stories of Creation from two different Middle Eastern sources appear to be woven together in the Genesis account. In the chronologically first but historically more recent account—known as the "Priestly"—God created the cosmos, using His divine Word, speaking light, water and land into existence, following that with the plants and the heavenly bodies. Then He created birds and animals and fish (again, employing speech)—and ended with man, male and female, both somehow formed in his image. That all happens in Genesis 1. In the second, older, "Jawhist" version, we find another origin account, involving Adam and Eve (where the details of creation differ some-what), as well as the stories of Cain and Abel, Noah and the Tower of Babel. That is Genesis 2 to 11. To understand Genesis 1, the Priestly story, with its insistence on speech as the fundamental creative force, it is first necessary to review a few fundamental, ancient assumptions (these are markedly different in type and intent from the assumptions of science, which are, historically speaking, quite novel).

Scientific truths were made explicit a mere five hundred years ago, with the work of Francis Bacon, René Descartes and Isaac Newton. In whatever manner our forebears viewed the world prior to that, it was not through a scientific lens (any more than they could view the moon and the stars through the glass lenses of the equally recent telescope). Because we are so scientific now—and so determinedly materialistic—it is very difficult for us even to understand that other ways of seeing can and do exist. But those who existed during the distant time in which the foundational epics of our culture emerged were much more concerned with the actions that dictated survival (and with interpreting the world in a manner commensurate with that goal) than with anything approximating what we now understand as objective truth.

Before the dawn of the scientific worldview, reality was construed differently. Being was understood as a place of action, not a place of things.[31] It was understood as something more akin to story or drama. That story or drama was lived, subjective experience, as it manifested itself moment to moment in the consciousness of every living person. It was something similar to the stories we tell each other about our lives and their personal significance; something similar to the happen-ings that novelists describe when they capture existence in the pages of their books. Subjective experience—that includes familiar objects such as trees and clouds, primarily objective in their existence, but also (and more importantly) such things as emotions and dreams as well as hunger, thirst and pain. It is such things, experienced person-ally, that are the most fundamental elements of human life, from the archaic, dramatic perspective, and they are not easily reducible to the detached and objective—even by the modern reductionist, materialist mind. Take pain, for example—subjective pain. That's something so real no argument can stand against it. Everyone acts as if their pain is real—ultimately, finally real. Pain matters, more than matter matters. It is for this reason, I believe, that so many of the world's traditions regard the suffering attendant upon existence as the irreducible truth of Being.

In any case, *that which we subjectively experience* can be likened much more to a novel or a movie than to a scientific description of physical reality. It is the drama of lived experience—the unique, tragic, personal death of your father, compared to the objective death listed in the hospital records; the pain of your first love; the despair of dashed hopes; the joy attendant upon a child's success.

The Domain, Not of Matter, but of What Matters

The scientific world of matter can be reduced, in some sense, to its fundamental constituent elements: molecules, atoms, even quarks. However, the world of experience has primal constituents, as well. These are the necessary elements whose interactions define drama and fiction. One of these is chaos. Another is order. The third (as there are three) is the process that mediates between the two, which appears identical to what modern people call consciousness. It is our eternal subjugation to the first two that makes us doubt the validity of existence—that makes us throw up our hands in despair, and fail to care for ourselves properly. It is proper understanding of the third that allows us the only real way out.

Chaos is the domain of ignorance itself. It's *unexplored territory*. Chaos is what extends, eternally and without limit, beyond the boundaries of all states, all ideas, and all disciplines. It's the foreigner, the stranger, the member of another gang, the rustle in the bushes in the night-time, the monster under the bed, the hidden anger of your mother, and the sickness of your child. Chaos is the despair and horror you feel when you have been profoundly betrayed. It's the place you end up when things fall apart; when your dreams die, your career collapses, or your marriage ends. It's the underworld of fairytale and myth, where the dragon and the gold it guards eternally co-exist. Chaos is where we are when we don't know where we are, and what we are doing when we don't know what we are doing. It is, in short, all those things and situations we neither know nor understand.

Chaos is also the formless potential from which the God of Genesis 1 called forth order using language at the beginning of time. It's the same potential from which we, made in that Image, call forth the novel and ever-changing moments of our lives. And Chaos is freedom, dreadful freedom, too.

Order, by contrast, is *explored territory*. That's the hundreds-of-millions-of-years-old hierarchy of place, position and authority. That's the structure of society. It's the structure provided by biology, too—particularly insofar as you are adapted, as you are, to the structure of society. Order is tribe, religion, hearth, home and country. It's the warm, secure living-room where the fireplace glows and the children play. It's the flag of the nation. It's the value of the currency. Order is the floor beneath your feet, and your plan for the day. It's the greatness of tradition, the rows of desks in a school classroom, the trains that leave on time, the calendar, and the clock. Order is the public façade we're called upon to wear, the politeness of a gathering of civilized strangers, and the thin ice on which we all skate. Order is the place where the behavior of the world matches our expectations and our desires; the place where all things turn out the way we want them to. But order is sometimes tyranny and stultification, as well, when the demand for certainty and uniformity and purity becomes too one-sided.

Where everything is certain, we're in order. We're there when things are going according to plan and nothing is new and disturbing. In the domain of order, things behave as God intended. We like to be there. Familiar environments are congenial. In order, we're able to think about things in the long term. There, things work, and we're stable, calm and competent. We seldom leave places we understand—geographical or conceptual—for that reason, and we certainly do not like it when we are compelled to or when it happens accidentally.

You're in order, when you have a loyal friend, a trustworthy ally.

When the same person betrays you, sells you out, you move from the daytime world of clarity and light to the dark underworld of chaos, confusion and despair. That's the same move you make, and the same place you visit, when the company you work starts to fail and your job is placed in doubt. When your tax return has been filed, that's order. When you're audited, that's chaos. Most people would rather be mugged than audited. Before the Twin Towers fell—that was order. Chaos manifested itself afterward. Everyone felt it. The very air became uncertain. What exactly was it that fell? Wrong question. What exactly remained standing? That was the issue at hand.

When the ice you're skating on is solid, that's order. When the bottom drops out, and things fall apart, and you plunge through the ice, that's chaos. Order is the Shire of Tolkien's hobbits: peaceful, productive and safely inhabitable, even by the naive. Chaos is the underground kingdom of the dwarves, usurped by Smaug, the treasure-hoarding serpent. Chaos is the deep ocean bottom to which Pinocchio voyaged to rescue his father from Monstro, whale and fire-breathing dragon. That journey into darkness and rescue is the most difficult thing a puppet must do, if he wants to be real; if he wants to extract himself from the temptations of deceit and acting and victimization and impulsive pleasure and totalitarian subjugation; if he wants to take his place as a genuine Being in the world.

Order is the stability of your marriage. It's buttressed by the traditions of the past and by your expectations—grounded, often invisibly, in those traditions. Chaos is that stability crumbling under your feet when you discover your partner's infidelity. Chaos is the experience of reeling unbound and unsupported through space when your guiding routines and traditions collapse.

Order is the place and time where the oft-invisible axioms you live by organize your experience and your actions so that what should happen does happen. Chaos is the new place and time that emerges when tragedy strikes suddenly, or malevolence reveals its paralyzing visage, even in the confines of your own home. Something unexpected or undesired can always make its appearance, when a plan is being laid out, regardless of how familiar the circumstances. When that happens, the territory has shifted. Make no mistake about it: the space, the apparent space, may be the same. But we live in time, as well as space. In consequence, even the oldest and most familiar places retain an ineradicable capacity to surprise you. You may be cruising happily down the road in the automobile you have known and loved for years. But time is passing. The brakes could fail. You might be walking down the road in the body you have always relied on. If your heart malfunctions, even momentarily, everything changes. Friendly old dogs can still bite. Old and trusted friends can still deceive. New ideas can destroy old and comfortable certainties. Such things matter. They're real.

Our brains respond instantly when chaos appears, with simple, hyper-fast circuits maintained from the ancient days, when our ancestors dwelled in trees, and snakes struck in a flash.[32] After that nigh-instantaneous, deeply reflexive bodily response comes the later-evolving, more complex but slower responses of emotions—and, after that, comes thinking, of the higher order, which can extend over seconds, minutes or years. All that response is instinctive, in some sense—but the faster the response, the more instinctive.

Chaos and Order: Personality, Female and Male

Chaos and order are two of the most fundamental elements of lived experience—two of the most basic subdivisions of Being itself. But they're not things, or objects, and they're not experienced as such. Things or objects are part of the objective world. They're inanimate; spiritless. They're dead. This is not true of chaos and order. Those are perceived, experienced and understood (to the degree that they are understood at all) as personalities—and that is just as true of the perceptions, experiences and understanding of modern people as their ancient forebears. It's just that moderners don't notice.

Order and chaos are not understood first, objectively (as things or objects), and *then* personified. That would only be the case if we perceived objective reality *first*, and *then* inferred intent and purpose. But that isn't how perception operates, despite our preconceptions.

12 RULES FOR LIFE

Perception of things as tools, for example, occurs before or in concert with perception of things as objects. We see what things mean just as fast or faster than we see what they are.[33] Perception of things as entities with personality also occurs before perception of things as things. This is particularly true of the action of others,[34] living others, but we also see the non-living "objective world" as animated, with purpose and intent. This is because of the operation of what psychologists have called "the hyperactive agency detector" within us.[35] We evolved, over millennia, within intensely social circumstances. This means that the most significant elements of our environment of origin were personalities, not things, objects or situations.

The personalities we have evolved to perceive have been around, in predictable form, and in typical, hierarchical configurations, forever, for all intents and purposes. They have been male or female, for example, for a billion years. That's a long time. The division of life into its twin sexes occurred before the evolution of multi-cellular animals. It was in a still-respectable one-fifth of that time that mammals, who take extensive care of their young, emerged. Thus, the category of "parent" and/or "child" has been around for 200 million years. That's longer than birds have existed. That's longer than flowers have grown. It's not a billion years, but it's still a very long time. It's plenty long enough for male and female and parent and child to serve as vital and fundamental parts of the environment to which we have adapted. This means that male and female and parent and child are categories, for us—natural categories, deeply embedded in our perceptual, emotional and motivational structures.

Our brains are deeply social. Other creatures (particularly, other humans) were crucially important to us as we lived, mated and evolved. Those creatures were literally our natural habitat—our environment. From a Darwinian perspective, nature—reality itself; the environment, itself—is *what selects*. The environment cannot be defined in any more fundamental manner. It is not mere inert matter. Reality itself is whatever we contend with when we are striving to survive and reproduce. A lot of that is other beings, their opinions of us, and their communities. And that's that.

Over the millennia, as our brain capacity increased and we developed curiosity to spare, we became increasingly aware of and curious about the nature of the world—what we eventually conceptualized as the objective world—outside the personalities of family and troupe. And "outside" is not merely unexplored physical territory. *Outside* is outside of what we currently understand—and understanding is *dealing with* and *coping with* and not merely *representing objectively*. But our brains had been long concentrating on other people. Thus, it appears that we first began to perceive the unknown, chaotic, non-human world with the innate categories of our social brain.[36] And even this is a misstatement: when we first began to perceive the unknown, chaotic, non-animal world, we used categories that had originally evolved to represent the *pre-human animal social world*. Our minds are far older than mere humanity. Our categories are far older than our species. Our most basic category—as old, in some sense, as the sexual act itself—appears to be that of sex, male and female. We appear to have taken that primordial knowledge of structured, creative opposition and begun to interpret everything through its lens.[37]

Order, the known, appears symbolically associated with masculinity (as illustrated in the aforementioned *yang* of the Taoist yin-yang symbol). This is perhaps because the primary hierarchical structure of human society is masculine, as it is among most animals, including the chimpanzees who are our closest genetic and, arguably, behavioural match. It is because men are and throughout history have been the builders of towns and cities, the engineers, stonemasons, bricklayers, and lumberjacks, the operators of heavy machinery.[38] Order is God the Father, the eternal Judge, ledger-keeper and dispenser of rewards and punishments. Order is the peacetime army of policemen and soldiers. It's the political culture, the corporate environment, and the system. It's the "they" in "you know what they say." It's credit cards, classrooms, supermarket checkout lineups, turn-taking, traffic lights, and the familiar routes of daily commuters. Order, when pushed too far, when imbalanced, can also manifest itself destructively and terribly. It does so as the forced migration, the concentration camp, and the soul-devouring uniformity of the goose-step.

Chaos—the unknown—is symbolically associated with the feminine. This is partly because all the things we have come to know were born, originally, of the unknown, just as all beings we encounter were born of mothers. Chaos is *mater*, origin, source, mother; *materia*, the substance from which all things are made. It is also *what matters*, or *what is the matter*—the very subject matter of thought and communication. In its positive guise, chaos is possibility itself, the source of ideas, the mysterious realm of gestation and birth. As a negative force, it's the impenetrable darkness of a cave and the accident by the side of the road. It's the mother grizzly, all compassion to her cubs, who marks you as potential predator and tears you to pieces.

Chaos, the eternal feminine, is also the crushing force of sexual selection. Women are choosy maters (unlike female chimps, their closest animal counterparts[39]). Most men do not meet female human standards. It is for this reason that women on dating sites rate 85 percent of men as below average in attractiveness.[40] It is for this reason that we all have twice as many female ancestors as male (imagine that all the women who have ever lived have averaged one child. Now imagine that half the men who have ever lived have fathered two children, if they had any, while the other half fathered none).[41] It is Woman as Nature who looks at half of all men and says, "No!" For the men, that's a direct encounter with chaos, and it occurs with devastating force every time they are turned down for a date. Human female choosiness is also why we are very different from the common ancestor we shared with our chimpanzee cousins, while the latter are very much the same. Women's proclivity to say no, more than any other force, has shaped our evolution into the creative, industrious, upright, large-brained (competitive, aggressive, domineering) creatures that we are.[42] It is Nature as Woman who says, "Well, bucko, you're good enough for a friend, but my experience of you so far has not indicated the suitability of your genetic material for continued propagation."

The most profound religious symbols rely for their power in large part on this underlying fundamentally bipartisan conceptual subdivision. The Star of David is, for example, the downward pointing triangle of femininity and the upward pointing triangle of the male.* It's the same for the *yoni* and *lingam* of Hinduism (which come covered with snakes, our ancient adversaries and provocateurs: the Shiva Linga is depicted with snake deities called the Nagas). The ancient Egyptians represented Osiris, god of the state, and Isis, goddess of the underworld, as twin cobras with their tails knotted together. The same symbol was used in China to portray Fuxi and Nuwa, creators of humanity and of writing. The representations in Christianity are less abstract, more like personalities, but the familiar Western images of the Virgin Mary with the Christ Child and the Pietà both express the female/male dual unity, as does the traditional insistence on the androgyny of Christ.[43]

It should also be noted, finally, that the structure of the brain itself at a gross morphological level appears to reflect this duality. This, to me, indicates the fundamental, beyond-the-metaphorical reality of this symbolically feminine/masculine divide, since the brain is adapted, by definition, to reality itself (that is, reality conceptualized in this quasi-Darwinian manner). Elkhonon Goldberg, student of the great Russian neuropsychologist Alexander Luria, has proposed quite lucidly and directly that the very hemispheric structure of the cortex reflects the fundamental division between novelty (the unknown, or chaos) and routinization (the known, order).[44] He doesn't make reference to the symbols representing the structure of the world in reference to this theory, but that's all the better: an idea is more credible when it emerges as a consequence of investigations in different realms.[45]

We already know all this, but we don't know we know it. But we immediately comprehend it when it's articulated in a manner such as

---

* It is of great interest, in this regard, that the five-part *taijitu* (referred to in Chapter 1 and the source of the simpler yin/yang symbol) expresses the origin of the cosmos as, first, originating in the undifferentiated absolute, then dividing into yin and yang (chaos/order, feminine/masculine), and then into the five agents (wood, fire, earth, metal, water) and then, simply put, "the ten thousand things." The Star of David (chaos/order, feminine/masculine) gives rise in the same way to the four basic elements: fire, air, water and earth (out of which everything else is built). A similar hexagram is used by the Hindus. The downward triangle symbolizes Shakti, the feminine; the upward triangle, Shiva, the masculine. The two components are known as *om* and *hrim* in Sanskrit. Remarkable examples of conceptual parallelism.

this. Everyone understands order and chaos, world and underworld, when it's explained using these terms. We all have a palpable sense of the chaos lurking under everything familiar. That's why we understand the strange, surreal stories of *Pinocchio*, and *Sleeping Beauty*, and *The Lion King*, and *The Little Mermaid*, and *Beauty and the Beast*, with their eternal landscapes of known and unknown, world and underworld. We've all been in both places, many times: sometimes by happenstance, sometimes by choice.

Many things begin to fall into place when you begin to consciously understand the world in this manner. It's as if the knowledge of your body and soul falls into alignment with the knowledge of your intellect. And there's more: such knowledge is prescriptive, as well as descriptive. This is the kind of knowing *what* that helps you know *how*. This is the kind of *is* from which you can derive an *ought*. The Taoist juxtaposition of yin and yang, for example, doesn't simply portray chaos and order as the fundamental elements of Being—it also tells you how to act. The Way, the Taoist path of life, is represented by (or exists on) the border between the twin serpents. The Way is the path of proper Being. It's the same Way as that referred to by Christ in John 14:6: *I am the way, and the truth and the life.* The same idea is expressed in Matthew 7:14: *Because strait is the gate, and narrow is the way, which leadeth unto life, and few there be that find it.*

We eternally inhabit order, surrounded by chaos. We eternally occupy known territory, surrounded by the unknown. We experience meaningful engagement when we mediate appropriately between them. We are adapted, in the deepest Darwinian sense, not to the world of objects, but to the meta-realities of order and chaos, yang and yin. Chaos and order make up the eternal, transcendent environment of the living.

To straddle that fundamental duality is to be balanced: to have one foot firmly planted in order and security, and the other in chaos, possibility, growth and adventure. When life suddenly reveals itself as intense, gripping and meaningful; when time passes and you're so engrossed in what you're doing you don't notice—it is there and then that you are located precisely on the border between order and chaos.

The subjective meaning that we encounter there is the reaction of our deepest being, our neurologically and evolutionarily grounded instinctive self, indicating that we are ensuring the stability but also the expansion of habitable, productive territory, of space that is personal, social and natural. It's the right place to be, in every sense. You are there when—and where—it matters. That's what music is telling you, too, when you're listening—even more, perhaps, when you're dancing—when its harmonious layered patterns of predictability and unpredictability make meaning itself well up from the most profound depths of your Being.

Chaos and order are fundamental elements because every lived situation (even every conceivable lived situation) is made up of both. No matter where we are, there are some things we can identify, make use of, and predict, and some things we neither know nor understand. No matter who we are, Kalahari Desert–dweller or Wall Street banker, some things are under our control, and some things are not. That's why both can understand the same stories, and dwell within the confines of the same eternal truths. Finally, the fundamental reality of chaos and order is true for everything alive, not only for us. Living things are always to be found in places they can master, surrounded by things and situations that make them vulnerable.

Order is not enough. You can't just be stable, and secure, and unchanging, because there are still vital and important new things to be learned. Nonetheless, chaos can be too much. You can't long tolerate being swamped and overwhelmed beyond your capacity to cope while you are learning what you still need to know. Thus, you need to place one foot in what you have mastered and understood and the other in what you are currently exploring and mastering. Then you have positioned yourself where the terror of existence is under control and you are secure, but where you are also alert and engaged. That is where there is something new to master and some way that you can be improved. That is where meaning is to be found.

The Garden of Eden

Remember, as discussed earlier, that the Genesis stories were amalgamated from several sources. After the newer Priestly story (Genesis 1), recounting the emergence of order from chaos, comes the second, even more ancient, "Jahwist" part, beginning, essentially, with Genesis 2. The Jahwist account, which uses the name YHWH or Jahweh to represent God, contains the story of Adam and Eve, along with a much fuller explication of the events of the sixth day alluded to in the previous "Priestly" story. The continuity between the stories appears to be the result of careful editing by the person or persons known singly to biblical scholars as the "Redactor," who wove the stories together. This may have occurred when the peoples of two traditions united, for one reason or another, and the subsequent illogic of their melded stories, growing together over time in an ungainly fashion, bothered someone conscious, courageous, and obsessed with coherence.

According to the Jahwist creation story, God first created a bounded space, known as Eden (which, in Aramaic—Jesus's putative language—means well-watered place) or Paradise (*pairidaeza* in old Iranian or Avestan, which means walled or protected enclosure or garden). God placed Adam in there, along with all manner of fruit-bearing trees, two of which were marked out. One of these was the Tree of Life; the other, the Tree of Knowledge of Good and Evil. God then told Adam to have his fill of fruit, as he wished, but added that the fruit of the Tree of the Knowledge of Good and Evil was forbidden. After that, He created Eve as a partner for Adam.*

Adam and Eve don't seem very conscious, at the beginning, when they are first placed in Paradise, and they were certainly not self-conscious. As the story insists, the original parents were naked, but not ashamed. Such phrasing implies first that it's perfectly natural and normal for people to be ashamed of their nakedness (otherwise nothing

---

* Or, in another interpretation, He split the original androgynous individual into two parts, male and female. According to this line of thinking, Christ, the "second Adam," is also the original Man, before the sexual subdivision. The symbolic meaning of this should be clear to those who have followed the argument thus far.

would have to be said about its absence) and second that there was something amiss, for better or worse, with our first parents. Although there are exceptions, the only people around now who would be unashamed if suddenly dropped naked into a public place—excepting the odd exhibitionist—are those younger than three years of age. In fact, a common nightmare involves the sudden appearance of the dreamer, naked, on a stage in front of a packed house.

In the third verse of Genesis, a serpent appears—first, apparently, in legged form. God only knows why He allowed—or placed—such a creature in the garden. I have long puzzled over the meaning of this. It seems to be a reflection, in part, of the order/chaos dichotomy characterizing all of experience, with Paradise serving as habitable order and the serpent playing the role of chaos. The serpent in Eden therefore means the same thing as the black dot in the yin side of the Taoist yin/yang symbol of totality—that is, the possibility of the unknown and revolutionary suddenly manifesting itself where everything appears calm.

It just does not appear possible, even for God himself, to make a bounded space completely protected from the outside—not in the real world, with its necessary limitations, surrounded by the transcendent. The outside, chaos, always sneaks into the inside, because nothing can be completely walled off from the rest of reality. So even the ultimate in safe spaces inevitably harbours a snake. There were—forever—genuine, quotidian, reptilian snakes in the grass and in the trees of our original African paradise.[46] Even had all of those been banished, however (in some inconceivable manner, by some primordial St. George) snakes would have still remained in the form of our primordial human rivals (at least when they were acting like enemies, from our limited, in-group, kin-bonded perspectives). There was, after all, no shortage of conflict and warfare among our ancestors, tribal and otherwise.[47]

And even if we had defeated all the snakes that beset us from without, reptilian and human alike, we would still not have been safe. Nor are we now. We have seen the enemy, after all, and he is us. The snake inhabits each of our souls. This is the reason, as far as I can tell, for the strange Christian insistence, made most explicit by John Milton, that the snake in the Garden of Eden was also Satan, the Spirit of Evil itself. The importance of this symbolic identification—its staggering brilliance—can hardly be overstated. It is through such millennia-long exercise of the imagination that the idea of abstracted moral concepts themselves, with all they entail, developed. Work beyond comprehension was invested into the idea of Good and Evil, and its surrounding, dream-like metaphor. *The worst of all possible snakes is the eternal human proclivity for evil.* The worst of all possible snakes is *psychological, spiritual, personal, internal.* No walls, however tall, will keep that out. Even if the fortress were thick enough, in principle, to keep everything bad whatsoever outside, it would immediately appear again within. As the great Russian writer Aleksandr Solzhenitsyn insisted, the line dividing good and evil cuts through the heart of every human being.[48]

There is simply no way to wall off some isolated portion of the greater surrounding reality and make everything permanently predictable and safe within it. Some of what has been no-matter-how-carefully excluded will always sneak back in. A serpent, metaphorically speaking, will inevitably appear. Even the most assiduous of parents cannot fully protect their children, even if they lock them in the basement, safely away from drugs, alcohol and internet porn. In that extreme case, the too-cautious, too-caring parent merely substitutes him or herself for the other terrible problems of life. This is the great Freudian Oedipal nightmare.[49] *It is far better to render Beings in your care competent than to protect them.*

And even if it were possible to permanently banish everything threatening—everything dangerous (and, therefore, everything challenging and interesting), that would mean only that another danger would emerge: that of permanent human infantilism and absolute uselessness. How could the nature of man ever reach its full potential without challenge and danger? How dull and contemptible would we become if there was no longer reason to pay attention? Maybe God thought His new creation would be able to handle the serpent, and considered its presence the lesser of two evils.

Question for parents: do you want to make your children safe, or strong?

In any case, there's a serpent in the Garden, and he's a "subtil" beast, according to the ancient story (difficult to see, vaporous, cunning, deceitful and treacherous). It therefore comes as no surprise when he decides to play a trick on Eve. Why Eve, instead of Adam? It could just be chance. It was fifty-fifty for Eve, statistically speaking, and those are pretty high odds. But I have learned that these old stories contain nothing superfluous. Anything accidental—anything that does not serve the plot—has long been forgotten in the telling. As the Russian playwright Anton Chekhov advised, "If there is a rifle hanging on the wall in act one, it must be fired in the next act. Otherwise it has no business being there."[50] Perhaps primordial Eve had more reason to attend to serpents than Adam. Maybe they were more likely, for example, to prey on her tree-dwelling infants. Perhaps it is for this reason that Eve's daughters are more protective, self-conscious, fearful and nervous, to this day (even, and especially, in the most egalitarian of modern human societies[51]). In any case, the serpent tells Eve that if she eats the forbidden fruit, she won't die. Instead, her eyes will be opened. She will become like God, knowing good from evil. Of course, the serpent doesn't let her know she will be like God in only that one way. But he is a serpent, after all. Being human, and wanting to know more, Eve decides to eat the fruit. Poof! She wakes up: she's conscious, or perhaps self-conscious, for the first time.

Now, no clear-seeing, conscious woman is going to tolerate an unawakened man. So, Eve immediately shares the fruit with Adam. That makes *him* self-conscious. Little has changed. Women have been making men self-conscious since the beginning of time. They do this primarily by rejecting them—but they also do it by shaming them, if men do not take responsibility. Since women bear the primary burden of reproduction, it's no wonder. It is very hard to see how it could be otherwise. But the capacity of women to shame men and render them self-conscious is still a primal force of nature.

Now, you may ask: what in the world have snakes got to do with vision? Well, first, it's clearly of some importance to *see* them, because they might prey on you (particularly when you're little and live in trees, like our arboreal ancestors). Dr. Lynn Isbell, professor of anthropology and animal behaviour at the University of California, has suggested that the stunningly acute vision almost uniquely possessed by human beings was an adaptation forced on us tens of millions of years ago by the necessity of detecting and avoiding the terrible danger of snakes, with whom our ancestors co-evolved.[52] This is perhaps one of the reasons the snake features in the garden of Paradise as the creature who gave us the vision of God (in addition to serving as the primordial and eternal enemy of mankind). This is perhaps one of the reasons why Mary, the eternal, archetypal mother—Eve perfected—is so commonly shown in medieval and Renaissance iconography holding the Christ Child in the air, as far away as possible from a predatory reptile, which she has firmly pinned under her foot.[53] And there's more. It's fruit that the snake offers, and fruit is also associated with a transformation of vision, in that our ability to see colour is an adaptation that allows us to rapidly detect the ripe and therefore edible bounty of trees.[54]

Our primordial parents hearkened to the snake. They ate the fruit. Their eyes opened. They both awoke. You might think, as Eve did initially, that this would be a good thing. Sometimes, however, half a gift is worse than none. Adam and Eve wake up, all right, but only enough to discover some terrible things. First, they notice that they're naked.

The Naked Ape

My son figured out that he was naked well before he was three. He wanted to dress himself. He kept the washroom door firmly shut. He didn't appear in public without his clothes. I couldn't for the life of me see how this had anything to do with his upbringing. It was his own discovery, his own realization, and his own choice of reactions. It looked built in, to me.

What does it mean to know yourself naked—or, potentially worse, to know yourself and your partner naked? All manner of terrible things—expressed in the rather horrifying manner, for example, of the Renaissance painter Hans Baldung Grien, whose painting inspired the illustration that begins this chapter. Naked means vulnerable and easily damaged. Naked means subject to judgment for beauty and health. Naked means unprotected and unarmed in the jungle of nature and man. This is why Adam and Eve became ashamed, immediately after their eyes were opened. They could see—and what they first saw was themselves. Their faults stood out. Their vulnerability was on display. Unlike other mammals, whose delicate abdomens are protected by the armour-like expanse of their backs, they were upright creatures, with the most vulnerable parts of their body presented to the world. And worse was to come. Adam and Eve made themselves loincloths (in the International Standard Version; aprons in the King James Version) right away, to cover up their fragile bodies—and to protect their egos. Then they promptly skittered off and hid. In their vulnerability, now fully realized, they felt unworthy to stand before God.

If you can't identify with that sentiment, you're just not thinking. Beauty shames the ugly. Strength shames the weak. Death shames the living—and the Ideal shames us all. Thus we fear it, resent it—even hate it (and, of course, that's the theme next examined in Genesis, in the story of Cain and Abel). What are we to do about that? Abandon all ideals of beauty, health, brilliance and strength? That's not a good solution. That would merely ensure that we would feel ashamed, all the time—and that we would even more justly deserve it. I don't want women who can stun by their mere presence to disappear just so that others can feel unselfconscious. I don't want intellects such as John von Neumann's to vanish, just because of my barely-grade-twelve grasp of mathematics. By the time he was nineteen, he had redefined numbers.[55] Numbers! Thank God for John von Neumann! Thank God for Grace Kelly and Anita Ekberg and Monica Bellucci! I'm proud to feel unworthy in the presence of people like that. It's the price we all pay for aim, achievement and ambition. But it's also no wonder that Adam and Eve covered themselves up.

The next part of the story is downright farcical, in my opinion, although it's also tragic and terrible. That evening, when Eden cools down, God goes out for His evening stroll. But Adam is absent. This puzzles God, who is accustomed to walking with him. "Adam," calls God, apparently forgetting that He can see through bushes, "Where are you?" Adam immediately reveals himself, but badly: first as a neurotic; then, as a ratfink. The creator of all the universe calls, and Adam replies: "I heard you, God. But I was naked, and hid." What does this mean? It means that people, unsettled by their vulnerability, eternally fear to tell the truth, to mediate between chaos and order, and to manifest their destiny. In other words, they are afraid to walk with God. That's not particularly admirable, perhaps, but it's certainly understandable. God's a judgmental father. His standards are high. He's hard to please.

God says, "Who told you that you were naked? Did you eat something you weren't supposed to?" And Adam, in his wretchedness, points right at Eve, his love, his partner, his soul-mate, and snitches on her. And then he blames God. He says, "The woman, whom you gave to me, she gave it to me (and then I ate it)." How pathetic—and how accurate. The first woman made the first man self-conscious and resentful. Then the first man blamed the woman. And then the first man blamed God. This is exactly how every spurned male feels, to this day. First, he feels small, in front of the potential object of his love, after she denigrates his reproductive suitability. Then he curses God for making her so bitchy, himself so useless (if he has any sense) and Being itself so deeply flawed. Then he turns to thoughts of revenge. How thoroughly contemptible (and how utterly understandable). At least the woman had the serpent to blame, and it later turns out that snake is Satan himself, unlikely as that seems. Thus, we can understand and sympathize with Eve's error. She was deceived by the best. But Adam! No one forced his words from his mouth.

Unfortunately, the worst isn't over—for Man or Beast. First, God curses the serpent, telling him that he will now have to slither around, legless, forever in peril of being stomped on by angry humans. Second, He tells the woman that she will now bring forth children in sorrow, and desire an unworthy, sometimes resentful man, who will in consequence lord her biological fate over her, permanently. What might this mean? It could just mean that God is a patriarchal tyrant, as politically motivated interpretations of the ancient story insist. I think it's— merely descriptive. Merely. And here is why: As human beings evolved, the brains that eventually gave rise to self-consciousness expanded tremendously. This produced an evolutionary arms race between fetal head and female pelvis.[56] The female graciously widened her hips, almost to the point where running would no longer be possible. The baby, for his part, allowed himself to be born more than a year early, compared to other mammals of his size, and evolved a semi-collapsible head.[57] This was and is a painful adjustment for both. The essentially fetal baby is almost completely dependent on his mother for everything during that first year. The programmability of his massive brain means that he must be trained until he is eighteen (or thirty) before being pushed out of the nest. This is to say nothing of the woman's consequential pain in childbirth, and high risk of death for mother and infant alike. This all means that women pay a high price for pregnancy and child-rearing, particularly in the early stages, and that one of the inevitable consequences is increased dependence upon the sometimes unreliable and always problematic good graces of men.

After God tells Eve what is going to happen, now that she has awakened, He turns to Adam—who, along with his male descendants, doesn't get off any easier. God says something akin to this: "Man, because you attended to the woman, your eyes have been opened. Your godlike vision, granted to you by snake, fruit and lover, allows you to see far, even into the future. But those who see into the future can also eternally see trouble coming, and must then prepare for all contingencies and possibilities. To do that, you will have to eternally sacrifice the present for the future. You must put aside pleasure for security. In short: you will have to work. And it's going to be difficult. I hope you're fond of thorns and thistles, because you're going to grow a lot of them."

And then God banishes the first man and the first woman from Paradise, out of infancy, out of the unconscious animal world, into the horrors of history itself. And then He puts cherubim and a flaming sword at the gate of Eden, just to stop them from eating the Fruit of the Tree of Life. That, in particular, appears rather mean-spirited. Why not just make the poor humans immortal, right away? Particularly if that is your plan for the ultimate future, anyway, as the story goes? But who would dare to question God?

Perhaps Heaven is something you must build, and immortality something you must earn.

And so we return to our original query: Why would someone buy prescription medication for his dog, and then so carefully administer it, when he would not do the same for himself? Now you have the answer, derived from one of the foundational texts of mankind. Why should anyone take care of anything as naked, ugly, ashamed, frightened, worthless, cowardly, resentful, defensive and accusatory as a descendant of Adam? Even if that thing, that being, is himself? And I do not mean at all to exclude women with this phrasing.

All the reasons we have discussed so far for taking a dim view of humanity are applicable to others, as much as to the self. They're generalizations about human nature; nothing more specific. But you know so much more about yourself. You're bad enough, as other people know you. But only you know the full range of your secret transgressions, insufficiencies and inadequacies. No one is more familiar than you with all the ways your mind and body are flawed. No one has more reason to hold you in contempt, to see you as pathetic—and by withholding something that might do you good, you can punish yourself for all your failings. A dog, a harmless, innocent, unselfconscious dog, is clearly more deserving.

But if you are not yet convinced, let us consider another vital issue. Order, chaos, life, death, sin, vision, work and suffering: that is not enough for the authors of Genesis, nor for humanity itself. The story continues, in all its catastrophe and tragedy, and the people involved (that's us) must contend with yet another painful awakening. We are next fated to contemplate morality itself.

Good and Evil

When their eyes are opened, Adam and Eve realize more than just their nakedness and the necessity of toil. They also come to know Good and Evil (the serpent says, referring to the fruit, "For God doth know that in the day ye eat thereof, then your eyes shall be opened, and ye shall be as gods, knowing good and evil"). What could that possibly mean?

What could be left to explore and relate, after the vast ground already covered? Well, simple context indicates that it must have something to do with gardens, snakes, disobedience, fruit, sexuality and nakedness. It was the last item—nakedness—that finally clued me in. It took years.

Dogs are predators. So are cats. They kill things and eat them. It's not pretty. But we'll take them as pets and care for them, and give them their medication when they're sick, regardless. Why? They're predators, but it's just their nature. They do not bear responsibility for it. They're hungry, not evil. They don't have the presence of mind, the creativity—and, above all, the self-consciousness—necessary for the inspired cruelty of man.

Why not? It's simple. Unlike us, predators have no comprehension of their fundamental weakness, their fundamental vulnerability, their own subjugation to pain and death. But we know exactly how and where we can be hurt, and why. That is as good a definition as any of self-consciousness. We are aware of our own defencelessness, finitude and mortality. We can feel pain, and self-disgust, and shame, and horror, and we know it. We know what makes us suffer. We know how dread and pain can be inflicted on us—and that means we know exactly how to inflict it on others. We know how we are naked, and how that nakedness can be exploited—and that means we know how others are naked, and how they can be exploited.

We can terrify other people, consciously. We can hurt and humiliate them for faults we understand only too well. We can torture them—literally—slowly, artfully and terribly. That's far more than predation. That's a qualitative shift in understanding. That's a cataclysm as large as the development of self-consciousness itself. That's the entry of the knowledge of Good and Evil into the world. That's a second as-yet-unhealed fracture in the structure of Existence. That's the transformation of Being itself into a moral endeavour—all attendant on the development of sophisticated self-consciousness.

Only man could conceive of the rack, the iron maiden and the thumbscrew. Only man will inflict suffering for the sake of suffering. That is the best definition of evil I have been able to formulate. Animals can't manage that, but humans, with their excruciating, semi-divine capacities, most certainly can. And with this realization we have well-nigh full legitimization of the idea, very unpopular in modern intellectual circles, of Original Sin. And who would dare to say that there was no element of voluntary choice in our evolutionary, individual and theological transformation? Our ancestors chose their sexual partners, and they selected for—consciousness? And self-consciousness? And moral knowledge? And who can deny the sense of existential guilt that pervades human experience? And who could avoid noting that without that guilt—that sense of inbuilt corruption and capacity for wrongdoing—a man is one step from psychopathy?

Human beings have a great capacity for wrongdoing. It's an attribute that is unique in the world of life. We can and do make things worse, voluntarily, with full knowledge of what we are doing (as well as accidentally, and carelessly, and in a manner that is willfully blind). Given that terrible capacity, that proclivity for malevolent actions, is it any wonder we have a hard time taking care of ourselves, or others— or even that we doubt the value of the entire human enterprise? And we've suspected ourselves, for good reason, for a very long time. Thousands of years ago, the ancient Mesopotamians believed, for example, that mankind itself was made from the blood of Kingu, the single most terrible monster that the great Goddess of Chaos could produce, in her most vengeful and destructive moments.[58] After drawing conclusions such as that, how could we not question the value of our being, and even of Being itself? Who then could be faced with illness, in himself or another, without doubting the moral utility of prescribing a healing medicament? And no one understands the darkness of the individual better than the individual himself. Who, then, when ill, is going to be fully committed to his own care?

Perhaps Man is something that should never have been. Perhaps the world should even be cleansed of all human presence, so that Being and consciousness could return to the innocent brutality of the animal. I believe that the person who claims never to have wished for such a thing has neither consulted his memory nor confronted his darkest fantasies.

What then is to be done?

A Spark of the Divine

In Genesis 1, God creates the world with the divine, truthful Word, generating habitable, paradisal order from the precosmogonic chaos. He then creates Man and Woman in His Image, imbuing them with the capacity to do the same—to create order from chaos, and continue His work. At each stage of creation, including that involving the formation of the first couple, God reflects upon what has come to be, and pronounces it Good.

The juxtaposition of Genesis 1 with Genesis 2 & 3 (the latter two chapters outlining the fall of man, describing why our lot is so tragedy-ridden and ethically torturous) produces a narrative sequence almost unbearable in its profundity. The moral of Genesis 1 is that Being brought into existence through true speech is Good. This is true even of man himself, prior to his separation from God. This goodness is terribly disrupted by the events of the fall (and of Cain and Abel and the Flood and the Tower of Babel), but we retain an intimation of the prelapsarian state. We remember, so to speak. We remain eternally nostalgic for the innocence of childhood, the divine, unconscious Being of the animal, and the untouched cathedral-like old-growth forest. We find respite in such things. We worship them, even if we are self-proclaimed atheistic environmentalists of the most anti-human sort. The original state of Nature, conceived in this manner, is paradisal. But we are no longer one with God and Nature, and there is no simple turning back.

The original Man and Woman, existing in unbroken unity with their Creator, did not appear conscious (and certainly not self-conscious). Their eyes were not open. But, in their perfection, they were also less, not more, than their post-Fall counterparts. Their goodness was something bestowed, rather than deserved or earned. They exercised no choice. God knows, that's easier. But maybe it's not better than, for example, goodness genuinely earned. Maybe, even in some cosmic sense (assuming that consciousness itself is a phenomenon of cosmic significance), free choice matters. Who can speak with certainty about such things? I am unwilling to take these questions off the table, however, merely because they are difficult. So, here's a proposition: perhaps it is not simply the emergence of self-consciousness and the rise of our moral knowledge of Death and the Fall that besets us and makes us doubt our own worth. Perhaps it is instead our unwillingness—reflected in Adam's shamed hiding—to walk with God, despite our fragility and propensity for evil.

The entire Bible is structured so that everything after the Fall—the history of Israel, the prophets, the coming of Christ—is presented as a remedy for that Fall, a way out of evil. The beginning of conscious history, the rise of the state and all its pathologies of pride and rigidity, the emergence of great moral figures who try to set things right, culminating in the Messiah Himself—that is all part of humanity's attempt, God willing, to set itself right. And what would that mean?

And this is an amazing thing: the answer is already implicit in Genesis 1: to embody the Image of God—to speak out of chaos the Being that is Good—but to do so consciously, of our own free choice. *Back* is the way forward—as T. S. Eliot so rightly insisted—but back as awake beings, exercising the proper choice of awake beings, instead of back to sleep:

> *We shall not cease from exploration*
> *And the end of all our exploring*
> *Will be to arrive where we started*
> *And know the place for the first time.*
> *Through the unknown, remembered gate*
> *When the last of earth left to discover*
> *Is that which was the beginning;*
> *At the source of the longest river*
> *The voice of the hidden waterfall*
> *And the children in the apple-tree*
>
> *Not known, because not looked for*
> *But heard, half-heard, in the stillness*
> *Between two waves of the sea.*
> *Quick now, here, now, always—*

A condition of complete simplicity
(Costing not less than everything)
And all shall be well and
All manner of things shall be well
When the tongues of flames are in-folded
Into the crowned knot of fire
And the fire and the rose are one.
("Little Gidding," *Four Quartets*, 1943)

If we wish to take care of ourselves properly, we would have to respect ourselves—but we don't, because we are—not least in our own eyes—fallen creatures. If we lived in Truth; if we spoke the Truth—then we could walk with God once again, and respect ourselves, and others, and the world. Then we might treat ourselves like people we cared for. We might strive to set the world straight. We might orient it toward Heaven, where we would want people we cared for to dwell, instead of Hell, where our resentment and hatred would eternally sentence everyone.

In the areas where Christianity emerged two thousand years ago, people were much more barbaric than they are today. Conflict was everywhere. Human sacrifice, including that of children, was a common occurrence even in technologically sophisticated societies, such as that of ancient Carthage.[59] In Rome, arena sports were competitions to the death, and the spilling of blood was a commonplace. The probability that a modern person, in a functional democratic country, will now kill or be killed is infinitesimally low compared to what it was in previous societies (and still is, in the unorganized and anarchic parts of the world).[60] Then, the primary moral issue confronting society was control of violent, impulsive selfishness and the mindless greed and brutality that accompanies it. People with those aggressive tendencies still exist. At least now they know that such behaviour is sub-optimal, and either try to control it or encounter major social obstacles if they don't.

But now, also, another problem has arisen, which was perhaps less common in our harsher past. It is easy to believe that people are arrogant, and egotistical, and always looking out for themselves. The cynicism that makes that opinion a universal truism is widespread and fashionable. But such an orientation to the world is not at all characteristic of many people. They have the opposite problem: they shoulder intolerable burdens of self-disgust, self-contempt, shame and self-consciousness. Thus, instead of narcissistically inflating their own importance, they don't value themselves at all, and they don't take care of themselves with attention and skill. It seems that people often don't really believe that they deserve the best care, personally speaking. They are excruciatingly aware of their own faults and inadequacies, real and exaggerated, and ashamed and doubtful of their own value. They believe that other people shouldn't suffer, and they will work diligently and altruistically to help them alleviate it. They extend the same courtesy even to the animals they are acquainted with—but not so easily to themselves.

It is true that the idea of virtuous self-sacrifice is deeply embedded in Western culture (at least insofar as the West has been influenced by Christianity, which is based on the imitation of someone who performed the ultimate act of self-sacrifice). Any claim that the Golden Rule does not mean "sacrifice yourself for others" might therefore appear dubious. But Christ's archetypal death exists as an example of how to accept finitude, betrayal and tyranny heroically—how to walk with God despite the tragedy of self-conscious knowledge—and not as a directive to victimize ourselves in the service of others. To sacrifice ourselves to God (to the highest good, if you like) does not mean to suffer silently and willingly when some person or organization demands more from us, consistently, than is offered in return. That means we are supporting tyranny, and allowing ourselves to be treated like slaves. It is not virtuous to be victimized by a bully, even if that bully is oneself.

I learned two very important lessons from Carl Jung, the famous Swiss depth psychologist, about "doing unto others as you would have them do unto you" or "loving your neighbour as yourself." The first lesson was that neither of these statements has anything to do with being nice. The second was that both are equations, rather than injunctions. If I am someone's friend, family member, or lover, then I am morally obliged to bargain as hard on my own behalf as they are on theirs. If I fail to do so, I will end up a slave, and the other person a tyrant. What good is that? It is much better for any relationship when both partners are strong. Furthermore, there is little difference between standing up and speaking for yourself, when you are being bullied or otherwise tormented and enslaved, and standing up and speaking for someone else. As Jung points out, this means embracing and loving the sinner who is yourself, as much as forgiving and aiding someone else who is stumbling and imperfect.

As God himself claims (so goes the story), "Vengeance is mine; I will repay, saith the Lord." According to this philosophy, you do not simply belong to yourself. You are not simply your own possession to torture and mistreat. This is partly because your Being is inexorably tied up with that of others, and your mistreatment of yourself can have catastrophic consequences for others. This is most clearly evident, perhaps, in the aftermath of suicide, when those left behind are often both bereft and traumatized. But, metaphorically speaking, there is also this: you have a spark of the divine in you, which belongs not to you, but to God. We are, after all—according to Genesis—made in His image. We have the semi-divine capacity for consciousness. Our consciousness participates in the speaking forth of Being. We are low-resolution ("kenotic") versions of God. We can make order from chaos—and vice versa—in our way, with our words. So, we may not exactly be God, but we're not exactly nothing, either.

In my own periods of darkness, in the underworld of the soul, I find myself frequently overcome and amazed by the ability of people to befriend each other, to love their intimate partners and parents and children, and to do what they must do to keep the machinery of the world running. I knew a man, injured and disabled by a car accident, who was employed by a local utility. For years after the crash he worked side by side with another man, who for his part suffered with a degenerative neurological disease. They cooperated while repairing the lines, each making up for the other's inadequacy. This sort of everyday heroism is the rule, I believe, rather than the exception.

Most individuals are dealing with one or more serious health problems while going productively and uncomplainingly about their business. If anyone is fortunate enough to be in a rare period of grace and health, personally, then he or she typically has at least one close family member in crisis. Yet people prevail and continue to do difficult and effortful tasks to hold themselves and their families and society together. To me this is miraculous—so much so that a dumbfounded gratitude is the only appropriate response. There are so many ways that things can fall apart, or fail to work altogether, and it is always wounded people who are holding it together. They deserve some genuine and heartfelt admiration for that. It's an ongoing miracle of fortitude and perseverance.

In my clinical practice I encourage people to credit themselves and those around them for acting productively and with care, as well as for the genuine concern and thoughtfulness they manifest towards others. People are so tortured by the limitations and constraint of Being that I am amazed they ever act properly or look beyond themselves at all. But enough do so that we have central heat and running water and infinite computational power and electricity and enough for everyone to eat and even the capacity to contemplate the fate of broader society and nature, terrible nature, itself. All that complex machinery that protects us from freezing and starving and dying from lack of water tends unceasingly towards malfunction through entropy, and it is only the constant attention of careful people that keeps it working so unbelievably well. Some people degenerate into the hell of resentment and the hatred of Being, but most refuse to do so, despite their suffering and disappointments and losses and inadequacies and ugliness, and again that is a miracle for those with the eyes to see it.

Humanity, in toto, and those who compose it as identifiable people deserve some sympathy for the appalling burden under which the human individual genuinely staggers; some sympathy for subjugation to mortal vulnerability, tyranny of the state, and the depredations of nature. It is an existential situation that no mere animal encounters or endures, and one of severity such that it would take a God to fully bear it. It is this sympathy that should be the proper medicament for self-conscious self-contempt, which has its justification, but is only half the full and proper story. Hatred for self and mankind must be balanced with gratefulness for tradition and the state and astonishment at what normal, everyday people accomplish—to say nothing of the staggering achievements of the truly remarkable.

We deserve some respect. You deserve some respect. You are important to other people, as much as to yourself. You have some vital role to play in the unfolding destiny of the world. You are, therefore, morally obliged to take care of yourself. You should take care of, help and be good to yourself the same way you would take care of, help and be good to someone you loved and valued. You may therefore have to conduct yourself habitually in a manner that allows you some respect for your own Being—and fair enough. But every person is deeply flawed. Everyone falls short of the glory of God. If that stark fact meant, however, that we had no responsibility to care, for ourselves as much as others, everyone would be brutally punished all the time. That would not be good. That would make the shortcomings of the world, which can make everyone who thinks honestly question the very propriety of the world, worse in every way. That simply cannot be the proper path forward.

To treat yourself as if you were someone you are responsible for helping is, instead, to consider what would be truly good for you. This is not "what you want." It is also not "what would make you happy." Every time you give a child something sweet, you make that child happy. That does not mean that you should do nothing for children except feed them candy. "Happy" is by no means synonymous with "good." You must get children to brush their teeth. They must put on their snowsuits when they go outside in the cold, even though they might object strenuously. You must help a child become a virtuous, responsible, awake being, capable of full reciprocity—able to take care of himself and others, and to thrive while doing so. Why would you think it acceptable to do anything less for yourself?

You need to consider the future and think, "What might my life look like if I were caring for myself properly? What career would challenge me and render me productive and helpful, so that I could shoulder my share of the load, and enjoy the consequences? What should I be doing, when I have some freedom, to improve my health, expand my knowledge, and strengthen my body?" You need to know where you are, so you can start to chart your course. You need to know who you are, so that you understand your armament and bolster yourself in respect to your limitations. You need to know where you are going, so that you can limit the extent of chaos in your life, restructure order, and bring the divine force of Hope to bear on the world.

You must determine where you are going, so that you can bargain for yourself, so that you don't end up resentful, vengeful and cruel. You have to articulate your own principles, so that you can defend yourself against others' taking inappropriate advantage of you, and so that you are secure and safe while you work and play. You must discipline yourself carefully. You must keep the promises you make to yourself, and reward yourself, so that you can trust and motivate yourself. You need to determine how to act toward yourself so that you are most likely to become and to stay a good person. It would be good to make the world a better place. Heaven, after all, will not arrive of its own accord. We will have to work to bring it about, and strengthen ourselves, so that we can withstand the deadly angels and flaming sword of judgment that God used to bar its entrance.

Don't underestimate the power of vision and direction. These are irresistible forces, able to transform what might appear to be unconquerable obstacles into traversable pathways and expanding opportunities. Strengthen the individual. Start with yourself. Take care with yourself. Define who you are. Refine your personality. Choose your destination and articulate your Being. As the great nineteenth-century German philosopher Friedrich Nietzsche so brilliantly noted, "He whose life has a why can bear almost any how."[61]

You could help direct the world, on its careening trajectory, a bit more toward Heaven and a bit more away from Hell. Once having understood Hell, researched it, so to speak—particularly your own individual Hell—you could decide against going there or creating that. You could aim elsewhere. You could, in fact, devote your life to this. That would give you a Meaning, with a capital M. That would justify your miserable existence. That would atone for your sinful nature, and replace your shame and self-consciousness with the natural pride and forthright confidence of someone who has learned once again to walk with God in the Garden.

You could begin by treating yourself as if you were someone you were responsible for helping.

RULE 3

MAKE FRIENDS WITH PEOPLE
WHO WANT THE BEST FOR YOU

THE OLD HOMETOWN

THE TOWN I GREW UP IN had been scraped only fifty years earlier out of the endless flat Northern prairie. Fairview, Alberta, was part of the frontier, and had the cowboy bars to prove it. The Hudson's Bay Co. department store on Main Street still bought beaver, wolf and coyote furs directly from the local trappers. Three thousand people lived there, four hundred miles away from the nearest city. Cable TV, video games and internet did not exist. It was no easy matter to stay innocently amused in Fairview, particularly during the five months of winter, when long stretches of forty-below days and even colder nights were the norm.

The world is a different place when it's cold like that. The drunks in our town ended their sad lives early. They passed out in snowbanks at three in the morning and froze to death. You don't go outside casually when it's forty below. On first breath, the arid desert air constricts your lungs. Ice forms on your eyelashes and they stick together. Long hair, wet from the shower, freezes solid and then stands on end wraith-like of its own accord later in a warm house, when it thaws bone dry, charged with electricity. Children only put their tongues on steel playground equipment once. Smoke from house chimneys doesn't rise. Defeated by the cold, it drifts downwards, and collects like fog on snow-covered rooftops and yards. Cars must be plugged in at night, their engines warmed by block heaters, or oil will not flow through them in the morning, and they won't start. Sometimes they won't anyway. Then you turn the engine over pointlessly until the starter clatters and falls silent. Then you remove the frozen battery from the car, loosening bolts with stiffening fingers in the intense cold, and bring it into the house. It sits there, sweating for hours, until it warms enough to hold a decent charge. You are not going to see out of the back window of your car, either. It frosts over in November and stays that way until May. Scraping it off just dampens the upholstery. Then it's frozen, too. Late one night going to visit a friend I sat for two hours on the edge of the passenger seat in a 1970 Dodge Challenger, jammed up against the stick-shift, using a vodka-soaked rag to keep the inside of the front windshield clear in front of the driver because the car heater had quit. Stopping wasn't an option. There was nowhere to stop.

And it was hell on house cats. Felines in Fairview had short ears and tails because they had lost the tips of both to frostbite. They came to resemble Arctic foxes, which evolved those features to deal proactively with the intense cold. One day our cat got outside and no one noticed. We found him, later, fur frozen fast to the cold hard backdoor cement steps where he sat. We carefully separated cat from concrete, with no lasting damage—except to his pride. Fairview cats were also at great risk in the winter from cars, but not for the reasons you think. It wasn't automobiles sliding on icy roads and running them over. Only loser cats died that way. It was cars parked immediately after being driven that were dangerous. A frigid cat might think highly of climbing up under such a vehicle and sitting on its still-warm engine block. But what if the driver decided to use the car again, before the engine cooled down and cat departed? Let's just say that heat-seeking house-pets and rapidly rotating radiator fans do not coexist happily.

Because we were so far north, the bitterly cold winters were also very dark. By December, the sun didn't rise until 9:30 a.m. We trudged to school in the pitch black. It wasn't much lighter when we walked home, just before the early sunset. There wasn't much for young people to do in Fairview, even in the summer. But the winters were worse. Then your friends mattered. More than anything.

My Friend Chris and His Cousin

I had a friend at that time. We'll call him Chris. He was a smart guy. He read a lot. He liked science fiction of the kind I was attracted to (Bradbury, Heinlein, Clarke). He was inventive. He was interested in electronic kits and gears and motors. He was a natural engineer. All this was overshadowed, however, by something that had gone wrong in his family. I don't know what it was. His sisters were smart and his father was soft-spoken and his mother was kind. The girls seemed OK. But Chris had been left unattended to in some important way. Despite his intelligence and curiosity he was angry, resentful and without hope.

All this manifested itself in material form in the shape of his 1972 blue Ford pickup truck. That notorious vehicle had at least one dent in every quarter panel of its damaged external body. Worse, it had an equivalent number of dents inside. Those were produced by the impact of the body parts of friends against the internal surfaces during the continual accidents that resulted in the outer dents. Chris's truck was the exoskeleton of a nihilist. It had the perfect bumper sticker: *Be Alert—The World Needs More Lerts*. The irony it produced in combination with the dents elevated it nicely to theatre of the absurd. Very little of that was (so to speak) accidental.

Every time Chris crashed his truck, his father would fix it, and buy him something else. He had a motorbike and a van for selling ice cream. He did not care for his motorbike. He sold no ice cream. He often expressed dissatisfaction with his father and their relationship. But his dad was older and unwell, diagnosed with an illness only after many years. He didn't have the energy he should have. Maybe he couldn't pay enough attention to his son. Maybe that's all it took to fracture their relationship.

Chris had a cousin, Ed, who was about two years younger. I liked him, as much as you can like the younger cousin of a teenage friend. He was a tall, smart, charming, good-looking kid. He was witty, too. You would have predicted a good future for him, had you met him when he was twelve. But Ed drifted slowly downhill, into a dropout, semi-drifting mode of existence. He didn't get as angry as Chris, but he was just as confused. If you knew Ed's friends, you might say that it was peer pressure that set him on his downward path. But his peers weren't obviously any more lost or delinquent than he was, although they were generally somewhat less bright. It was also the case that Ed's—and Chris's—situation did not appear particularly improved by their discovery of marijuana. Marijuana isn't bad for everyone any more than alcohol is bad for everyone. Sometimes it even appears to improve people. But it didn't improve Ed. It didn't improve Chris, either.

To amuse ourselves in the long nights, Chris and I and Ed and the rest of the teenagers drove around and around in our 1970s cars and pickup trucks. We cruised down Main Street, along Railroad Avenue, up past the high school, around the north end of town, over to the west—or up Main Street, around the north end of town, over to the east—and so on, endlessly repeating the theme. If we weren't driving in town, we were driving in the countryside. A century earlier, survey-ors had laid out a vast grid across the entire three-hundred-thousand-square-mile expanse of the great western prairie. Every two miles north, a plowed gravel road stretched forever, east to west. Every mile west, another travelled north and south. We never ran out of roads.

Teenage Wasteland

If we weren't circling around town and countryside we were at a party. Some relatively young adult (or some relatively creepy older adult) would open his house to friends. It would then become temporary home to all manner of party crashers, many of whom started out seri-ously undesirable or quickly become that way when drinking. A party might also happen accidentally, when some teenager's unwitting par-ents had left town. In that case, the occupants of the cars or trucks always cruising around would notice house lights on, but household car absent. This was not good. Things could get seriously out of hand.

I did not like teenage parties. I do not remember them nostalgically. They were dismal affairs. The lights were kept low. That kept self-consciousness to a minimum. The over-loud music made conversation impossible. There was little to talk about in any case. There were always a couple of the town psychopaths attending. Everybody drank and smoked too much. A dreary and oppressive sense of aimlessness hung over such occasions, and nothing ever happened (unless you count the time my too-quiet classmate drunkenly began to brandish his fully-loaded 12-gauge shotgun, or the time the girl I later married contemptuously insulted someone while he threatened her with a knife, or the time another friend climbed a large tree, swung out on a branch, and crashed flat onto his back, half dead right beside the campfire we had started at its base, followed precisely one minute later by his halfwit sidekick).

No one knew what the hell they were doing at those parties. Hoping for a cheerleader? Waiting for Godot? Although the former would have been immediately preferred (although cheerleading squads were scarce in our town), the latter was closer to the truth. It would be more romantic, I suppose, to suggest that we would have all jumped at the chance for something more productive, bored out of our skulls as we were. But it's not true. We were all too prematurely cynical and world-weary and leery of responsibility to stick to the debating clubs and Air Cadets and school sports that the adults around us tried to organize. Doing *anything* wasn't cool. I don't know what teenage life was like before the revolutionaries of the late sixties advised everyone young to tune in, turn on and drop out. Was it OK for a teenager to belong wholeheartedly to a club in 1955? Because it certainly wasn't twenty years later. Plenty of us turned on and dropped out. But not so many tuned in.

I wanted to be elsewhere. I wasn't the only one. Everyone who eventually left the Fairview I grew up in knew they were leaving by the age of twelve. I knew. My wife, who grew up with me on the street our families shared, knew. The friends I had who did and didn't leave also knew, regardless of which track they were on. There was an unspoken expectation in the families of those who were college-bound that such a thing was a matter of course. For those from less-educated families, a future that included university was simply not part of the conceptual realm. It wasn't for lack of money, either. Tuition for advanced education was very low at that time, and jobs in Alberta were plentiful and high-paying. I earned more money in 1980 working at a plywood mill than I would again doing anything else for twenty years. No one missed out on university because of financial need in oil-rich Alberta in the 1970s.

Some Different Friends—and Some More of the Same

In high school, after my first group of cronies had all dropped out, I made friends with a couple of newcomers. They came to Fairview as boarders. There was no school after ninth grade in their even more remote and aptly named hometown, Bear Canyon. They were an ambitious duo, comparatively speaking; straightforward and reliable, but also cool and very amusing. When I left town to attend Grande Prairie Regional College, ninety miles away, one of them became my roommate. The other went off elsewhere to pursue further education. Both were aiming upward. Their decisions to do so bolstered mine.

I was a happy clam when I arrived at college. I found another, expanded group of like-minded companions, whom my Bear Canyon comrade also joined. We were all captivated by literature and philosophy. We ran the Student Union. We made it profitable, for the first time in its history, hosting college dances. How can you lose money selling beer to college kids? We started a newspaper. We got to know our professors of political science and biology and English literature in the tiny seminars that characterized even our first year. The instructors were thankful for our enthusiasm and taught us well. We were building a better life.

I sloughed off a lot of my past. In a small town, everyone knows who you are. You drag your years behind you like a running dog with tin cans tied to its tail. You can't escape who you have been. Everything wasn't online then, and thank God for that, but it was stored equally indelibly in everyone's spoken and unspoken expectations and memory.

When you move, everything is up in the air, at least for a while. It's stressful, but in the chaos there are new possibilities. People, including you, can't hem you in with their old notions. You get shaken out of your ruts. You can make new, better ruts, with people aiming at better things. I thought this was just a natural development. I thought that every person who moved would have—and want—the same phoenix-like experience. But that wasn't always the case.

One time, when I was about fifteen, I went with Chris and another friend, Carl, to Edmonton, a city of six hundred thousand. Carl had never been to a city. This was not uncommon. Fairview to Edmonton was an eight-hundred-mile round trip. I had done it many times, sometimes with my parents, sometimes without. I liked the anonymity that the city provided. I liked the new beginnings. I liked the escape from the dismal, cramped adolescent culture of my home town. So, I convinced my two friends to make the journey. But they did not have the same experience. As soon as we arrived, Chris and Carl wanted to buy some pot. We headed for the parts of Edmonton that were exactly like the worst of Fairview. We found the same furtive street-vending marijuana providers. We spent the weekend drinking in the hotel room. Although we had travelled a long distance, we had gone nowhere at all.

I saw an even more egregious example of this a few years later. I had moved to Edmonton to finish my undergraduate degree. I took an apartment with my sister, who was studying to be a nurse. She was also an up-and-out-of-there person. (Not too many years later she would plant strawberries in Norway and run safaris through Africa and smuggle trucks across the Tuareg-menaced Sahara Desert, and babysit orphan gorillas in the Congo.) We had a nice place in a new high-rise, overlooking the broad valley of the North Saskatchewan River. We had a view of the city skyline in the background. I bought a beautiful new Yamaha upright piano, in a fit of enthusiasm. The place looked good.

I heard through the grapevine that Ed—Chris's younger cousin— had moved to the city. I thought that was a good thing. One day he called. I invited him over. I wanted to see how he was faring. I hoped he was achieving some of the potential I once saw in him. That is not what happened. Ed showed up, older, balder and stooped. He was a lot more not-doing-so-well young adult and a lot less youthful possibility. His eyes were the telltale red slits of the practised stoner. Ed had taken some job—lawn-mowing and casual landscaping—which would have been fine for a part-time university student or for someone who could not do better but which was wretchedly low-end as a career for an intelligent person.

He was accompanied by a friend.

It was his friend I really remember. He was spaced. He was baked. He was stoned out of his gourd. His head and our nice, civilized apartment did not easily occupy the same universe. My sister was there. She knew Ed. She'd seen this sort of thing before. But I still wasn't happy that Ed had brought this character into our place. Ed sat down. His friend sat down, too, although it wasn't clear he noticed. It was tragicomedy. Stoned as he was, Ed still had the sense to be embarrassed. We sipped our beer. Ed's friend looked upwards. "My particles are scattered all over the ceiling," he managed. Truer words were never spoken.

I took Ed aside and told him politely that he had to leave. I said that he shouldn't have brought his useless bastard of a companion. He nodded. He understood. That made it even worse. His older cousin Chris wrote me a letter much later about such things. I included it in my first book, *Maps of Meaning: The Architecture of Belief*, published in 1999: "I had friends," he said.[62] "Before. Anyone with enough self-contempt that they could forgive me mine."

What was it that made Chris and Carl and Ed unable (or, worse, perhaps, unwilling) to move or to change their friendships and improve the circumstances of their lives? Was it inevitable—a consequence of their own limitations, nascent illnesses and traumas of the past? After all, people vary significantly, in ways that seem both structural and deterministic. People differ in intelligence, which is in large part the ability to learn and transform. People have very different personalities, as well. Some are active, and some passive. Others are anxious or calm. For every individual driven to achieve, there is another who is indolent. The degree to which these differences are immutably part and parcel of someone is greater than an optimist might presume or desire. And then there is illness, mental and physical, diagnosed or invisible, further limiting or shaping our lives.

Chris had a psychotic break in his thirties, after flirting with insanity for many years. Not long afterward, he committed suicide. Did his heavy marijuana use play a magnifying role, or was it understandable self-medication? Use of physician-prescribed drugs for pain has, after all, decreased in marijuana-legal states such as Colorado.[63] Maybe the pot made things better for Chris, not worse. Maybe it eased his suffering, instead of exacerbating his instability. Was it the nihilistic philosophy he nurtured that paved the way to his eventual breakdown? Was that nihilism, in turn, a consequence of genuine ill health, or just an intellectual rationalization of his unwillingness to dive responsibly into life? Why did he—like his cousin, like my other friends—continually choose people who, and places that, were not good for him?

Sometimes, when people have a low opinion of their own worth—or, perhaps, when they refuse responsibility for their lives—they choose a new acquaintance, of precisely the type who proved troublesome in the past. Such people don't believe that they deserve any better—so they don't go looking for it. Or, perhaps, they don't want the trouble of better. Freud called this a "repetition compulsion." He thought of it as an unconscious drive to repeat the horrors of the past—sometimes, perhaps, to formulate those horrors more precisely, sometimes to attempt more active mastery and sometimes, perhaps, because no alternatives beckon. People create their worlds with the tools they have directly at hand. Faulty tools produce faulty results. Repeated use of the same faulty tools produces the same faulty results. It is in this manner that those who fail to learn from the past doom themselves to repeat it. It's partly fate. It's partly inability. It's partly . . . unwillingness to learn? Refusal to learn? *Motivated* refusal to learn?

Rescuing the Damned

People choose friends who aren't good for them for other reasons, too. Sometimes it's because they want to rescue someone. This is more typical of young people, although the impetus still exists among older folks who are too agreeable or have remained naive or who are willfully blind. Someone might object, "It is only right to see the best in people. The highest virtue is the desire to help." But not everyone who is failing is a victim, and not everyone at the bottom wishes to rise, although many do, and many manage it. Nonetheless, people will often accept or even amplify their own suffering, as well as that of others, if they can brandish it as evidence of the world's injustice. There is no shortage of oppressors among the downtrodden, even if, given their lowly positions, many of them are only tyrannical wannabes. It's the easiest path to choose, moment to moment, although it's nothing but hell in the long run.

Imagine someone not doing well. He needs help. He might even want it. But it is not easy to distinguish between someone truly wanting and needing help and someone who is merely exploiting a willing helper. The distinction is difficult even for the person who is wanting and needing and possibly exploiting. The person who tries and fails, and is forgiven, and then tries again and fails, and is forgiven, is also too often the person who wants everyone to believe in the authenticity of all that trying.

When it's not just naïveté, the attempt to rescue someone is often fuelled by vanity and narcissism. Something like this is detailed in the incomparable Russian author Fyodor Dostoevsky's bitter classic, *Notes from Underground*, which begins with these famous lines: "I am a sick man . . . I am a spiteful man. I am an unattractive man. I believe my liver is diseased." It is the confession of a miserable, arrogant sojourner in the underworld of chaos and despair. He analyzes himself mercilessly, but only pays in this manner for a hundred sins, despite committing a thousand. Then, imagining himself redeemed, the underground man commits the worst transgression of the lot. He offers aid to a genuinely unfortunate person, Liza, a woman on the desperate nineteenth-century road to prostitution. He invites her for a visit, promising to set her life back on the proper course. While waiting for her to appear, his fantasies spin increasingly messianic:

> One day passed, however, another and another; she did not come and I began to grow calmer. I felt particularly bold and cheerful after nine o'clock, I even sometimes began dreaming, and rather sweetly: I, for instance, became the salvation of Liza, simply through her coming to me and my talking to her. . . . I develop her, educate her. Finally, I notice that she loves me, loves me passionately. I pretend not to understand (I don't know, however, why I pretend, just for effect, perhaps). At last all confusion, transfigured, trembling and sobbing, she flings herself at my feet and says that I am her savior, and that she loves me better than anything in the world.

Nothing but the narcissism of the underground man is nourished by such fantasies. Liza herself is demolished by them. The salvation he offers to her demands far more in the way of commitment and maturity than the underground man is willing or able to offer. He simply does not have the character to see it through—something he quickly realizes, and equally quickly rationalizes. Liza eventually arrives at his shabby apartment, hoping desperately for a way out, staking everything she has on the visit. She tells the underground man that she wants to leave her current life. His response?

> "Why have you come to me, tell me that, please?" I began, gasping for breath and regardless of logical connection in my words. I longed to have it all out at once, at one burst; I did not even trouble how to begin. "Why have you come? Answer, answer," I cried, hardly knowing what I was doing. "I'll tell you, my good girl, why you have come. You've come because I talked sentimental stuff to you then. So now you are soft as butter and longing for fine sentiments again. So you may as well know that I was laughing at you then. And I am laughing at you now. Why are you shuddering? Yes, I was laughing at you! I had been insulted just before, at dinner, by the fellows who came that evening before me. I came to you, meaning to thrash one of

them, an officer; but I didn't succeed, I didn't find him; I had to avenge the insult on someone to get back my own again; you turned up, I vented my spleen on you and laughed at you. I had been humiliated, so I wanted to humiliate; I had been treated like a rag, so I wanted to show my power. . . . That's what it was, and you imagined I had come there on purpose to save you. Yes? You imagined that? You imagined that?"

I knew that she would perhaps be muddled and not take it all in exactly, but I knew, too, that she would grasp the gist of it, very well indeed. And so, indeed, she did. She turned white as a handkerchief, tried to say something, and her lips worked painfully; but she sank on a chair as though she had been felled by an axe. And all the time afterwards she listened to me with her lips parted and her eyes wide open, shuddering with awful terror. The cynicism, the cynicism of my words overwhelmed her. . . .

The inflated self-importance, carelessness and sheer malevolence of the underground man dashes Liza's last hopes. He understands this well. Worse: something in him was aiming at this all along. And he knows that too. But a villain who despairs of his villainy has not become a hero. A hero is something positive, not just the absence of evil.

But Christ himself, you might object, befriended tax-collectors and prostitutes. How dare I cast aspersions on the motives of those who are trying to help? But Christ was the archetypal perfect man. And you're you. How do you know that your attempts to pull someone up won't instead bring them—or you—further down? Imagine the case of someone supervising an exceptional team of workers, all of them striving towards a collectively held goal; imagine them hardworking, brilliant, creative and unified. But the person supervising is also responsible for someone troubled, who is performing poorly, elsewhere. In a fit of inspiration, the well-meaning manager moves that problematic person into the midst of his stellar team, hoping to improve him by example. What happens?—and the psychological literature is clear on this point.[64] Does the errant interloper immediately straighten up and fly right? No. Instead, the entire team degenerates.

The newcomer remains cynical, arrogant and neurotic. He complains. He shirks. He misses important meetings. His low-quality work causes delays, and must be redone by others. He still gets paid, however, just like his teammates. The hard workers who surround him start to feel betrayed. "Why am I breaking myself into pieces striving to finish this project," each thinks, "when my new team member never breaks a sweat?" The same thing happens when well-meaning counsellors place a delinquent teen among comparatively civilized peers. The delinquency spreads, not the stability.[65] Down is a lot easier than up.

Maybe you are saving someone because you're a strong, generous, well-put-together person who wants to do the right thing. But it's also possible—and, perhaps, more likely—that you just want to draw attention to your inexhaustible reserves of compassion and good-will. Or maybe you're saving someone because you want to convince yourself that the strength of your character is more than just a side effect of your luck and birthplace. Or maybe it's because it's easier to look virtuous when standing alongside someone utterly irresponsible.

Assume first that you are doing the easiest thing, and not the most difficult.

Your raging alcoholism makes my binge drinking appear trivial. My long serious talks with you about your badly failing marriage convince both of us that you are doing everything possible and that I am helping you to my utmost. It looks like effort. It looks like progress. But real improvement would require far more from both of you. Are you so sure the person crying out to be saved has not decided a thousand times to accept his lot of pointless and worsening suffering, simply because it is easier than shouldering any true responsibility? Are you enabling a delusion? Is it possible that your contempt would be more salutary than your pity?

Or maybe you have no plan, genuine or otherwise, to rescue anybody. You're associating with people who are bad for you not because it's better for anyone, but because it's easier. You know it. Your friends know it. You're all bound by an implicit contract—one aimed at nihilism, and failure, and suffering of the stupidest sort. You've all decided to sacrifice the future to the present. You don't talk about it. You don't all get together and say, "Let's take the easier path. Let's indulge in whatever the moment might bring. And let's agree, further, not to call each other on it. That way, we can more easily forget what we are doing." You don't mention any of that. But you all know what's really going on.

Before you help someone, you should find out why that person is in trouble. You shouldn't merely assume that he or she is a noble victim of unjust circumstances and exploitation. It's the most unlikely explanation, not the most probable. In my experience—clinical and otherwise—it's just never been that simple. Besides, if you buy the story that everything terrible just happened on its own, with no personal responsibility on the part of the victim, you deny that person all agency in the past (and, by implication, in the present and future, as well). In this manner, you strip him or her of all power.

It is far more likely that a given individual has just decided to reject the path upward, because of its difficulty. Perhaps that should even be your default assumption, when faced with such a situation. That's too harsh, you think. You might be right. Maybe that's a step too far. But consider this: failure is easy to understand. No explanation for its existence is required. In the same manner, fear, hatred, addiction, promiscuity, betrayal and deception require no explanation. It's not the existence of vice, or the indulgence in it, that requires explanation. Vice is easy. Failure is easy, too. It's easier not to shoulder a burden. It's easier not to think, and not to do, and not to care. It's easier to put off until tomorrow what needs to be done today, and drown the upcoming months and years in today's cheap pleasures. As the infamous father of the Simpson clan puts it, immediately prior to downing a jar of mayonnaise and vodka, "That's a problem for Future Homer. Man, I don't envy that guy!"[66]

How do I know that your suffering is not the demand of martyrdom for my resources, so that you can oh-so-momentarily stave off the inevitable? Maybe you have even moved beyond caring about the impending collapse, but don't yet want to admit it. Maybe my help won't rectify anything—can't rectify anything—but it does keep that too-terrible, too-personal realization temporarily at bay. Maybe your misery is a demand placed on me so that I fail too, so that the gap you so painfully feel between us can be reduced, while you degenerate and sink. How do I know that you would refuse to play such a game? How do I know that I am not myself merely pretending to be responsible, while pointlessly "helping" you, so that *I* don't have to do something truly difficult—and genuinely possible?

Maybe your misery is the weapon you brandish in your hatred for those who rose upward while you waited and sank. Maybe your misery is your attempt to prove the world's injustice, instead of the evidence of your own sin, your own missing of the mark, your conscious refusal to strive and to live. Maybe your willingness to suffer in failure is inexhaustible, given what you use that suffering to prove. Maybe it's your revenge on Being. How exactly should I befriend you when you're in such a place? How exactly could I?

Success: that's the mystery. Virtue: that's what's inexplicable. To fail, you merely have to cultivate a few bad habits. You just have to bide your time. And once someone has spent enough time cultivating bad habits and biding their time, they are much diminished. Much of what they could have been has dissipated, and much of the less that they have become is now real. Things fall apart, of their own accord, but the sins of men speed their degeneration. And then comes the flood.

I am not saying that there is no hope of redemption. But it is much harder to extract someone from a chasm than to lift him from a ditch. And some chasms are very deep. And there's not much left of the body at the bottom.

Maybe I should at least wait, to help you, until it's clear that you want to be helped. Carl Rogers, the famous humanistic psychologist, believed it was impossible to start a therapeutic relationship if the person seeking help did not want to improve.[67] Rogers believed it was impossible to convince someone to change for the better. The desire to improve was, instead, the precondition for progress. I've had court-mandated psychotherapy clients. They did not want my help. They were forced to seek it. It did not work. It was a travesty.

If I stay in an unhealthy relationship with you, perhaps it's because I'm too weak-willed and indecisive to leave, but I don't want to know it. Thus, I continue helping you, and console myself with my point-less martyrdom. Maybe I can then conclude, about myself, "Someone that self-sacrificing, that willing to help someone—that has to be a good person." Not so. It might be just a person trying to look good pretend-ing to solve what appears to be a difficult problem instead of actually being good and addressing something real.

Maybe instead of continuing our friendship I should just go off somewhere, get my act together, and lead by example.

And none of this is a justification for abandoning those in real need to pursue your narrow, blind ambition, in case it has to be said.

A Reciprocal Arrangement

Here's something to consider: If you have a friend whose friendship you wouldn't recommend to your sister, or your father, or your son, why would you have such a friend for yourself? You might say: out of loyalty. Well, loyalty is not identical to stupidity. Loyalty must be nego-tiated, fairly and honestly. Friendship is a reciprocal arrangement. You are not morally obliged to support someone who is making the world a worse place. Quite the opposite. You should choose people who want things to be better, not worse. It's a good thing, not a selfish thing, to choose people who are good for you. It's appropriate and praiseworthy to associate with people whose lives would be improved if they saw your life improve.

If you surround yourself with people who support your upward aim, they will not tolerate your cynicism and destructiveness. They will instead encourage you when you do good for yourself and others and punish you carefully when you do not. This will help bolster your resolve to do what you should do, in the most appropriate and careful manner. People who are not aiming up will do the opposite. They will offer a former smoker a cigarette and a former alcoholic a beer. They will become jealous when you succeed, or do something pristine. They will withdraw their presence or support, or actively punish you for it. They will over-ride your accomplishment with a past action, real or imaginary, of their own. Maybe they are trying to test you, to see if your resolve is real, to see if you are genuine. But mostly they are dragging you down because your new improvements cast their faults in an even dimmer light.

It is for this reason that every good example is a fateful challenge, and every hero, a judge. Michelangelo's great perfect marble David cries out to its observer: "You could be more than you are." When you dare aspire upward, you reveal the inadequacy of the present and the promise of the future. Then you disturb others, in the depths of their souls, where they understand that their cynicism and immobility are unjustifiable. You play Abel to their Cain. You remind them that they ceased caring not because of life's horrors, which are undeniable, but because they do not want to lift the world up on to their shoulders, where it belongs.

Don't think that it is easier to surround yourself with good healthy people than with bad unhealthy people. It's not. A good, healthy person is an ideal. It requires strength and daring to stand up near such a person. Have some humility. Have some courage. Use your judgment, and protect yourself from too-uncritical compassion and pity.

Make friends with people who want the best for you.

RULE 4

COMPARE YOURSELF TO WHO YOU WERE YESTERDAY, NOT TO WHO SOMEONE ELSE IS TODAY

THE INTERNAL CRITIC

IT WAS EASIER FOR PEOPLE to be good at something when more of us lived in small, rural communities. Someone could be homecoming queen. Someone else could be spelling-bee champ, math whiz or basketball star. There were only one or two mechanics and a couple of teachers. In each of their domains, these local heroes had the opportunity to enjoy the serotonin-fuelled confidence of the victor. It may be for that reason that people who were born in small towns are statistically overrepresented among the eminent.[68] If you're one in a million now, but originated in modern New York, there's twenty of you—and most of us now live in cities. What's more, we have become digitally connected to the entire seven billion. Our hierarchies of accomplishment are now dizzyingly vertical.

No matter how good you are at something, or how you rank your accomplishments, there is someone out there who makes you look incompetent. You're a decent guitar player, but you're not Jimmy Page or Jack White. You're almost certainly not even going to rock your local pub. You're a good cook, but there are many great chefs. Your mother's recipe for fish heads and rice, no matter how celebrated in her village of origin, doesn't cut it in these days of grapefruit foam and Scotch/tobacco ice-cream. Some Mafia don has a tackier yacht. Some obsessive CEO has a more complicated self-winding watch, kept in his more valuable mechanical hardwood-and-steel automatic self-winding watch case. Even the most stunning Hollywood actress eventually transforms into the Evil Queen, on eternal, paranoid watch for the new Snow White. And you? Your career is boring and pointless, your housekeeping skills are second-rate, your taste is appalling, you're fatter than your friends, and everyone dreads your parties. Who cares if you are prime minister of Canada when someone else is the president of the United States?

Inside us dwells a critical internal voice and spirit that knows all this. It's predisposed to make its noisy case. It condemns our mediocre efforts. It can be very difficult to quell. Worse, critics of its sort are necessary. There is no shortage of tasteless artists, tuneless musicians, poisonous cooks, bureaucratically-personality-disordered middle managers, hack novelists and tedious, ideology-ridden professors. Things and people differ importantly in their qualities. Awful music torments listeners everywhere. Poorly designed buildings crumble in earthquakes. Substandard automobiles kill their drivers when they crash. Failure is the price we pay for standards and, because mediocrity has consequences both real and harsh, standards are necessary.

We are not equal in ability or outcome, and never will be. A very small number of people produce very much of everything. The winners don't take all, but they take most, and the bottom is not a good place to be. People are unhappy at the bottom. They get sick there, and remain unknown and unloved. They waste their lives there. They die there. In consequence, the self-denigrating voice in the minds of people weaves a devastating tale. Life is a zero-sum game. Worthlessness is the default condition. What but willful blindness could possibly shelter people from such withering criticism? It is for such reasons that a whole generation of social psychologists recommended "positive illusions" as the only reliable route to mental health.[69] Their credo? Let a lie be your umbrella. A more dismal, wretched, pessimistic philosophy can hardly be imagined: things are so terrible that only delusion can save you.

Here is an alternative approach (and one that requires no illusions). If the cards are always stacked against you, perhaps the game you are playing is somehow rigged (perhaps by you, unbeknownst to yourself). If the internal voice makes you doubt the value of your endeavours—or your life, or life itself—perhaps you should stop listening. If the critical voice within says the same denigrating things about everyone, no matter how successful, how reliable can it be? Maybe its comments are chatter, not wisdom. *There will always be people better than you*—that's a cliché of nihilism, like the phrase, *In a million years, who's going to know the difference?* The proper response to that statement is not, *Well, then, everything is meaningless.* It's, *Any idiot can choose a frame of time within which nothing matters.* Talking yourself into irrelevance is not a profound critique of Being. It's a cheap trick of the rational mind.

Many Good Games

Standards of better or worse are not illusory or unnecessary. If you hadn't decided that what you are doing right now was better than the alternatives, you wouldn't be doing it. The idea of a value-free choice is a contradiction in terms. Value judgments are a precondition for action. Furthermore, every activity, once chosen, comes with its own internal standards of accomplishment. If something can be done at all, it can be done better or worse. To do anything at all is therefore to play a game with a defined and valued end, which can always be reached more or less efficiently and elegantly. Every game comes with its chance of success or failure. Differentials in quality are omnipresent. Furthermore, if there was no better and worse, nothing would be worth doing. There would be no value and, therefore, no meaning. Why make an effort if it doesn't improve anything? Meaning itself requires the difference between better and worse. How, then, can the voice of critical self-consciousness be stilled? Where are the flaws in the apparently impeccable logic of its message?

We might start by considering the all-too-black-and-white words themselves: "success" or "failure." You are either a success, a comprehensive, singular, over-all good thing, or its opposite, a failure, a comprehensive, singular, irredeemably bad thing. The words imply no alternative and no middle ground. However, in a world as complex as ours, such generalizations (really, such failure to differentiate) are a sign of naive, unsophisticated or even malevolent analysis. There are vital degrees and gradations of value obliterated by this binary system, and the consequences are not good.

To begin with, there is not just one game at which to succeed or fail. There are many games and, more specifically, many good games— games that match your talents, involve you productively with other people, and sustain and even improve themselves across time. Lawyer is a good game. So is plumber, physician, carpenter, or schoolteacher. The world allows for many ways of Being. If you don't succeed at one, you can try another. You can pick something better matched to your unique mix of strengths, weaknesses and situation. Furthermore, if changing games does not work, you can invent a new one. I recently watched a talent show featuring a mime who taped his mouth shut and did something ridiculous with oven mitts. That was unexpected. That was original. It seemed to be working for him.

It's also unlikely that you're playing only one game. You have a career and friends and family members and personal projects and artistic endeavors and athletic pursuits. You might consider judging your success across all the games you play. Imagine that you are very good at some, middling at others, and terrible at the remainder. Perhaps that's how it should be. You might object: I should be winning at everything! But winning at everything might only mean that you're not doing anything new or difficult. You might be winning but you're not growing, and growing might be the most important form of winning. Should victory in the present always take precedence over trajectory across time?

Finally, you might come to realize that the specifics of the many games you are playing are so unique to you, so individual, that comparison to others is simply inappropriate. Perhaps you are over-valuing what you don't have and undervaluing what you do. There's some real utility in gratitude. It's also good protection against the dangers of victimhood and resentment. Your colleague outperforms you at work. His wife, however, is having an affair, while your marriage is stable and happy. Who has it better? The celebrity you admire is a chronic drunk driver and bigot. Is his life truly preferable to yours?

When the internal critic puts you down using such comparisons, here's how it operates: First, it selects a single, arbitrary domain of comparison (fame, maybe, or power). Then it acts as if that domain is the only one that is relevant. Then it contrasts you unfavourably with someone truly stellar, within that domain. It can take that final step even further, using the unbridgeable gap between you and its target of comparison as evidence for the fundamental injustice of life. That way your motivation to do anything at all can be most effectively under-mined. Those who accept such an approach to self-evaluation cer-tainly can't be accused of making things too easy for themselves. But it's just as big a problem to make things too difficult.

When we are very young we are neither individual nor informed. We have not had the time nor gained the wisdom to develop our own standards. In consequence, we must compare ourselves to others, because standards are necessary. Without them, there is nowhere to go and nothing to do. As we mature we become, by contrast, increas-ingly individual and unique. The conditions of our lives become more and more personal and less and less comparable with those of others. Symbolically speaking, this means we must leave the house ruled by our father, and confront the chaos of our individual Being. We must take note of our disarray, without completely abandoning that father in the process. We must then rediscover the values of our culture—veiled from us by our ignorance, hidden in the dusty treasure-trove of the past—rescue them, and integrate them into our own lives. This is what gives existence its full and necessary meaning.

Who are you? You think you know, but maybe you don't. You are, for example, neither your own master, nor your own slave. You cannot easily tell yourself what to do and compel your own obedience (any more than you can easily tell your husband, wife, son or daughter what to do, and compel theirs). You are interested in some things and not in others. You can shape that interest, but there are limits. Some activities will always engage you, and others simply will not.

You have a nature. You can play the tyrant to it, but you will certainly rebel. How hard can you force yourself to work and sustain your desire to work? How much can you sacrifice to your partner before generosity turns to resentment? What is it that you actually love? What is it that you genuinely want? Before you can articulate your own standards of value, you must see yourself as a stranger—and then you must get to know yourself. What do you find valuable or pleasurable? How much leisure, enjoyment, and reward do you require, so that you feel like more than a beast of burden? How must you treat yourself, so you won't kick over the traces and smash up your corral? You could force yourself through your daily grind and kick your dog in frustration when you come home. You could watch the precious days tick by. Or you could learn how to entice yourself into sustainable, productive activity. Do you ask yourself what you want? Do you negotiate fairly with yourself? Or are you a tyrant, with yourself as slave?

When do you dislike your parents, your spouse, or your children, and why? What might be done about that? What do you need and want from your friends and your business partners? This is not a mere matter of what you *should* want. I'm not talking about what other people require from you, or your duties to them. I'm talking about determining the nature of your moral obligation, to yourself. *Should* might enter into it, because you are nested within a network of social obligations. *Should* is your responsibility, and you should live up to it. But this does not mean you must take the role of lap-dog, obedient and harmless. That's how a dictator wants his slaves.

Dare, instead, to be dangerous. Dare to be truthful. Dare to articulate yourself, and express (or at least become aware of) what would really justify your life. If you allowed your dark and unspoken desires for your partner, for example, to manifest themselves—if you were even willing to consider them—you might discover that they were not so dark, given the light of day. You might discover, instead, that you were just afraid and, so, pretending to be moral. You might find that getting what you actually desire would stop you from being tempted and straying. Are you so sure that your partner would be unhappy if more of you rose to the surface? The femme fatale and the anti-hero are sexually attractive for a reason. . . .

How do you need to be spoken to? What do you need to take from people? What are you putting up with, or pretending to like, from duty or obligation? Consult your resentment. It's a revelatory emotion, for all its pathology. It's part of an evil triad: arrogance, deceit, and resentment. Nothing causes more harm than this underworld Trinity. But resentment always means one of two things. Either the resentful person is immature, in which case he or she should shut up, quit whining, and get on with it, or there is tyranny afoot—in which case the person subjugated has a moral obligation to speak up. Why? Because the consequence of remaining silent is worse. Of course, it's easier in the moment to stay silent and avoid conflict. But in the long term, that's deadly. When you have something to say, silence is a lie—and tyranny feeds on lies. When should you push back against oppression, despite the danger? When you start nursing secret fantasies of revenge; when your life is being poisoned and your imagination fills with the wish to devour and destroy.

I had a client decades ago who suffered from severe obsessive-compulsive disorder. He had to line up his pyjamas just right before he could go to sleep at night. Then he had to fluff his pillow. Then he had to adjust the bedsheets. Over and over and over and over. I said, "Maybe that part of you, that insanely persistent part, wants something, inarticulate though it may be. Let it have its say. What could it be?" He said, "Control." I said, "Close your eyes and let it tell you what it wants. Don't let fear stop you. You don't have to act it out, just because you're thinking it." He said, "It wants me to take my stepfather by the collar, put him up against the door, and shake him like a rat." Maybe it was time to shake someone like a rat, although I suggested something a bit less primal. But God only knows what battles must be fought, forthrightly, voluntarily, on the road to peace. What do you do to avoid conflict, necessary though it may be? What are you inclined to lie about, assuming that the truth might be intolerable? What do you fake?

The infant is dependent on his parents for almost everything he needs. The child—the successful child—can leave his parents, at least temporarily, and make friends. He gives up a little of himself to do that, but gains much in return. The successful adolescent must take that process to its logical conclusion. He has to leave his parents and become like everyone else. He has to integrate with the group so he can transcend his childhood dependency. Once integrated, the successful adult then must learn how to be just the right amount different from everyone else.

Be cautious when you're comparing yourself to others. You're a singular being, once you're an adult. You have your own particular, specific problems—financial, intimate, psychological, and otherwise. Those are embedded in the unique broader context of your existence. Your career or job works for you in a personal manner, or it does not, and it does so in a unique interplay with the other specifics of your life. You must decide how much of your time to spend on this, and how much on that. You must decide what to let go, and what to pursue.

The Point of Our Eyes (or, Take Stock)

Our eyes are always pointing at things we are interested in approaching, or investigating, or looking for, or having. We must see, but to see, we must aim, so we are always aiming. Our minds are built on the hunting-and-gathering platforms of our bodies. To hunt is to specify a target, track it, and throw at it. To gather is to specify and to grasp. We fling stones, and spears, and boomerangs. We toss balls through hoops, and hit pucks into nets, and curl carved granite rocks down the ice onto horizontal bull's-eyes. We launch projectiles at targets with bows, guns, rifles and rockets. We hurl insults, launch plans, and pitch ideas. We succeed when we score a goal or hit a target. We fail, or sin, when we do not (as the word *sin* means to miss the mark[70]). We cannot navigate, without something to aim at and, while we are in this world, we must always navigate.[71]

We are always and simultaneously *at* point "a" (which is less desirable than it could be), *moving towards* point "b" (which we deem better, in accordance with our explicit and implicit values). We always encounter the world in a state of insufficiency and seek its correction. We can imagine new ways that things could be set right, and improved, even if we have everything we thought we needed. Even when satisfied, temporarily, we remain curious. We live within a framework that defines the present as eternally lacking and the future as eternally better. If we did not see things this way, we would not act at all. We wouldn't even be able to see, because to see we must focus, and to focus we must pick one thing above all else on which to focus.

But we can see. We can even see things that aren't there. We can envision new ways that things could be better. We can construct new, hypothetical worlds, where problems we weren't even aware of can now show themselves and be addressed. The advantages of this are obvious: we can change the world so that the intolerable state of the present can be rectified in the future. The disadvantage to all this foresight and creativity is chronic unease and discomfort. Because we always contrast what is with what could be, we have to aim at what could be. But we can aim too high. Or too low. Or too chaotically. So we fail and live in disappointment, even when we appear to others to be living well. How can we benefit from our imaginativeness, our ability to improve the future, without continually denigrating our current, insufficiently successful and worthless lives?

The first step, perhaps, is to take stock. Who are you? When you buy a house and prepare to live in it, you hire an inspector to list all its faults—as it is, in reality, now, not as you wish it could be. You'll even pay him for the bad news. You need to know. You need to discover the home's hidden flaws. You need to know whether they are cosmetic imperfections or structural inadequacies. You need to know because you can't fix something if you don't know it's broken—and you're broken. You need an inspector. The internal critic—it could play that role, if you could get it on track; if you and it could cooperate. It could help you take stock. But you must walk through your psychological house with it and listen judiciously to what it says. Maybe you're a handy-man's dream, a real fixer-upper. How can you start your renovations without being demoralized, even crushed, by your internal critic's lengthy and painful report of your inadequacies?

Here's a hint. The future is like the past. But there's a crucial difference. The past is fixed, but the future—it could be better. It could be better, some precise amount—the amount that can be achieved, perhaps, in a day, with some minimal engagement. The present is eternally flawed. But where you start might not be as important as the direction you are heading. *Perhaps happiness is always to be found in the journey uphill, and not in the fleeting sense of satisfaction awaiting at the next peak.* Much of happiness is hope, no matter how deep the underworld in which that hope was conceived.

Called upon properly, the internal critic will suggest something to set in order, which you *could* set in order, which you *would* set in order—voluntarily, without resentment, even with pleasure. Ask yourself: is there one thing that exists in disarray in your life or your situation that you could, and would, set straight? Could you, and would you, fix that one thing that announces itself humbly in need of repair? Could you do it now? Imagine that you are someone with whom you must negotiate. Imagine further that you are lazy, touchy, resentful and hard to get along with. With that attitude, it's not going to be easy to get you moving. You might have to use a little charm and playfulness. "Excuse me," you might say to yourself, without irony or sarcasm. "I'm trying to reduce some of the unnecessary suffering around here. I could use some help." Keep the derision at bay. "I'm wondering if there is anything that you would be willing to do? I'd be very grateful for your service." Ask honestly and with humility. That's no simple matter.

You might have to negotiate further, depending on your state of mind. Maybe you don't trust yourself. You think that you'll ask yourself for one thing and, having delivered, immediately demand more. And you'll be punitive and hurtful about it. And you'll denigrate what was already offered. Who wants to work for a tyrant like that? Not you. That's why you don't do what you want yourself to do. You're a bad employee—but a worse boss. Maybe you need to say to yourself, "OK.

I know we haven't gotten along very well in the past. I'm sorry about that. I'm trying to improve. I'll probably make some more mistakes along the way, but I'll try to listen if you object. I'll try to learn. I noticed, just now, today, that you weren't really jumping at the opportunity to help when I asked. Is there something I could offer in return for your cooperation? Maybe if you did the dishes, we could go for coffee. You like espresso. How about an espresso—maybe a double shot? Or is there something else you want?" Then you could listen. Maybe you'll hear a voice inside (maybe it's even the voice of a long-lost child). Maybe it will reply, "Really? You really want to do something nice for me? You'll really do it? It's not a trick?"

This is where you must be careful.

That little voice—that's the voice of someone once burnt and twice shy. So, you could say, very carefully, "Really. I might not do it very well, and I might not be great company, but I will do something nice for you. I promise." A little careful kindness goes a long way, and judicious reward is a powerful motivator. Then you could take that small bit of yourself by the hand and do the damn dishes. And then you better not go clean the bathroom and forget about the coffee or the movie or the beer or it will be even harder to call those forgotten parts of yourself forth from the nooks and crannies of the underworld.

You might ask yourself, "What could I say to someone else—my friend, my brother, my boss, my assistant—that would set things a bit more right between us tomorrow? What bit of chaos might I eradicate at home, on my desk, in my kitchen, tonight, so that the stage could be set for a better play? What snakes might I banish from my closet—and my mind?" Five hundred small decisions, five hundred tiny actions, compose your day, today, and every day. Could you aim one or two of these at a better result? Better, in your own private opinion, by your own individual standards? Could you compare your specific personal tomorrow with your specific personal yesterday? Could you use your own judgment, and ask yourself what that better tomorrow might be?

Aim small. You don't want to shoulder too much to begin with, given your limited talents, tendency to deceive, burden of resentment, and ability to shirk responsibility. Thus, you set the following goal: by the end of the day, I want things in my life to be a tiny bit better than they were this morning. Then you ask yourself, "What could I do, that I would do, that would accomplish that, and what small thing would I like as a reward?" Then you do what you have decided to do, even if you do it badly. Then you give yourself that damn coffee, in triumph. Maybe you feel a bit stupid about it, but you do it anyway. And you do the same thing tomorrow, and the next day, and the next. And, with each day, your baseline of comparison gets a little higher, and that's magic. That's compound interest. Do that for three years, and your life will be entirely different. Now you're aiming for something higher. Now you're wishing on a star. Now the beam is disappearing from your eye, and you're learning to see. And what you aim at determines what you see. That's worth repeating. *What you aim at determines what you see.*

What You Want and What You See

The dependency of sight on aim (and, therefore, on value—because you aim at what you value) was demonstrated unforgettably by the cognitive psychologist Daniel Simons more than fifteen years ago.[72] Simons was investigating something called "sustained inattentional blindness." He would sit his research subjects in front of a video monitor and show them, for example, a field of wheat. Then he would transform the photo slowly, secretly, while they watched. He would slowly fade in a road cutting through the wheat. He didn't insert some little easy-to-miss footpath, either. It was a major trail, occupying a good third of the image. Remarkably, the observers would frequently fail to take notice.

The demonstration that made Dr. Simons famous was of the same kind, but more dramatic—even unbelievable. First, he produced a video of two teams of three people.[73] One team was wearing white shirts, the other, black. (The two teams were not off in the distance, either, or in any way difficult to see. The six of them filled much of the video screen, and their facial features were close enough to see clearly.) Each team had its own ball, which they bounced or threw to their other team members, as they moved and feinted in the small space in front of the elevators where the game was filmed. Once Dan had his video, he showed it to his study participants. He asked each of them to count the number of times the white shirts threw the ball back and forth to one another. After a few minutes, his subjects were asked to report the number of passes. Most answered "15." That was the correct answer. Most felt pretty good about that. Ha! They passed the test! But then Dr. Simons asked, "Did you see the gorilla?"

Was this a joke? What gorilla?

So, he said, "Watch the video again. But this time, don't count." Sure enough, a minute or so in, a man dressed in a gorilla suit waltzes right into the middle of the game for a few long seconds, stops, and then beats his chest in the manner of stereotyped gorillas everywhere. Right in the middle of the screen. Large as life. Painfully and irrefutably evident. But one out of every two of his research subjects missed it, the first time they saw the video. It gets worse. Dr. Simons did another study. This time, he showed his subjects a video of someone being served at a counter. The server dips behind the counter to retrieve something, and pops back up. So what? Most of his participants don't detect anything amiss. But it was a different person who stood up in the original server's place! "No way," you think. "I'd notice." But it's "yes way." There's a high probability you wouldn't detect the change, even if the gender or race of the person is switched at the same time. You're blind too.

This is partly because vision is expensive—psychophysiologically expensive; neurologically expensive. Very little of your retina is high-resolution fovea—the very central, high-resolution part of the eye, used to do such things as identify faces. Each of the scarce foveal cells needs 10,000 cells in the visual cortex merely to manage the first part of the multi-stage processing of seeing.[74] Then each of those 10,000 requires 10,000 more just to get to stage two. If all your retina was fovea you would require the skull of a B-movie alien to house your brain. In consequence, we triage, when we see. Most of our vision is peripheral, and low resolution. We save the fovea for things of importance. We point our high-resolution capacities at the few specific things we are aiming at. And we let everything else—which is almost everything—fade, unnoticed, into the background.

If something you're not attending to pops its ugly head up in a manner that directly interferes with your narrowly focused current activity, you will see it. Otherwise, it's just not there. The ball on which Simons's research subjects were focused was never obscured by the gorilla or by any of the six players. Because of that—because the gorilla did not interfere with the ongoing, narrowly defined task—it was indistinguishable from everything else the participants didn't see, when they were looking at that ball. The big ape could be safely ignored. That's how you deal with the overwhelming complexity of the world: you ignore it, while you concentrate minutely on your private concerns. You see things that facilitate your movement forward, toward your desired goals. You detect obstacles, when they pop up in your path. You're blind to everything else (and there's a lot of everything else—so you're very blind). And it has to be that way, because there is much more of the world than there is of you. You must shepherd your limited resources carefully. Seeing is very difficult, so you must choose what to see, and let the rest go.

There's a profound idea in the ancient Vedic texts (the oldest scriptures of Hinduism, and part of the bedrock of Indian culture): the world, as perceived, is *maya*—appearance or illusion. This means, in part, that people are blinded by their desires (as well as merely incapable of seeing things as they truly are). This is true, in a sense that transcends the metaphorical. Your eyes are tools. They are there to help you get what you want. The price you pay for that utility, that specific, focused direction, is blindness to everything else. This doesn't matter so much when things are going well, and we are getting what we want (although it can be a problem, even then, because getting what we currently want can make us blind to higher callings). But all that ignored world presents a truly terrible problem when we're in crisis, and nothing whatsoever is turning out the way we want it to. Then, there can be far too much to deal with. Happily, however, that problem contains within it the seeds of its own solution. Since you've ignored so much, there is plenty of possibility left where you have not yet looked.

Imagine that you're unhappy. You're not getting what you need. Perversely, this may be because of what you want. You are blind, because of what you desire. Perhaps what you really need is right in front of your eyes, but you cannot see it because of what you are currently aiming for. And that brings us to something else: the price that must be paid before you, or anyone, can get what they want (or, better yet, what they need). Think about it this way. You look at the world in your particular, idiosyncratic manner. You use a set of tools to screen most things out and let some things in. You have spent a lot of time building those tools. They've become habitual. They're not mere abstract thoughts. They're built right into you. They orient you in the world. They're your deepest and often implicit and unconscious values. They've become part of your biological structure. They're alive. And they don't want to disappear, or transform, or die. But sometimes their time has come, and new things need to be born. For this reason (although not only for this reason) it is necessary to let things go during the journey uphill. If things are not going well for you—well, that might be because, as the most cynical of aphorisms has it, life sucks, and then you die. Before your crisis impels you to that hideous conclusion, however, you might consider the following: *life doesn't have the problem. You do.* At least that realization leaves you with some options. If your life is not going well, perhaps it is your current knowledge that is insufficient, not life itself. Perhaps your value structure needs some serious retooling. Perhaps what you want is blinding you to what else could be. Perhaps you are holding on to your desires, in the present, so tightly that you cannot see anything else—even what you truly need.

Imagine that you are thinking, enviously, "I should have my boss's job." If your boss sticks to his post, stubbornly and competently, thoughts like that will lead you into in a state of irritation, unhappiness and disgust. You might realize this. You think, "I am unhappy. However, I could be cured of this unhappiness if I could just fulfill my ambition." But then you might think further. "Wait," you think. "Maybe I'm not unhappy because I don't have my boss's job. Maybe I'm unhappy because I can't stop wanting that job." That doesn't mean you can just simply and magically tell yourself to stop wanting that job, and then listen and transform. You won't—can't, in fact—just change yourself that easily. You have to dig deeper. You must change what you are after more profoundly.

So, you might think, "I don't know what to do about this stupid suffering. I can't just abandon my ambitions. That would leave me nowhere to go. But my longing for a job that I can't have isn't working." You might decide to take a different tack. You might ask, instead, for the revelation of a different plan: one that would fulfill your desires and gratify your ambitions in a real sense, but that would remove from your life the bitterness and resentment with which you are currently affected. You might think, "I will make a different plan. I will try to want whatever it is *that would make my life better*—whatever that might be—and I will start working on it now. If that turns out to mean something other than chasing my boss's job, I will accept that and I will move forward."

Now you're on a whole different kind of trajectory. Before, what was right, desirable, and worthy of pursuit was something narrow and concrete. But you became stuck there, tightly jammed and unhappy. So you let go. You make the necessary sacrifice, and allow a whole new world of possibility, hidden from you because of your previous ambition, to reveal itself. And there's a lot there. What would your life look like, *if it were better*? What would Life Itself look like? What does "better" even mean? You don't know. And it doesn't matter that you don't know, exactly, right away, because you will start to slowly see what is "better," once you have truly decided to want it. You will start to perceive what remained hidden from you by your presuppositions and preconceptions—by the previous mechanisms of your vision. You will begin to learn.

This will only work, however, if you genuinely want your life to improve. You can't fool your implicit perceptual structures. Not even a bit. They aim where you point them. To retool, to take stock, to aim somewhere better, you have to think it through, bottom to top. You have to scour your psyche. You have to clean the damned thing up. And you must be cautious, because making your life better means adopting a lot of responsibility, and that takes more effort and care than living stupidly in pain and remaining arrogant, deceitful and resentful.

What if it was the case that the world revealed whatever goodness it contains in precise proportion to your desire for the best? What if the more your conception of the best has been elevated, expanded and rendered sophisticated the more possibility and benefit you could perceive? This doesn't mean that you can have what you want merely by wishing it, or that everything is interpretation, or that there is no reality. The world is still there, with its structures and limits. As you move along with it, it cooperates or objects. But you can dance with it, if your aim is to dance—and maybe you can even lead, if you have enough skill and enough grace. This is not theology. It's not mysticism. It's empirical knowledge. There is nothing magical here—or nothing more than the already-present magic of consciousness. We only see what we aim at. The rest of the world (and that's most of it) is hidden. If we start aiming at something different—something like "I want my life to be better"—our minds will start presenting us with new information, derived from the previously hidden world, to aid us in that pursuit. Then we can put that information to use and move, and act, and observe, and improve. And, after doing so, after improving, we might pursue something different, or higher—something like, "I want whatever might be better than just my life being better." And then we enter a more elevated and more complete reality.

In that place, what might we focus on? What might we see?

Think about it like this. Start from the observation that we indeed desire things—even that we need them. That's human nature. We share the experience of hunger, loneliness, thirst, sexual desire, aggression, fear and pain. Such things are elements of Being—primordial, axiomatic elements of Being. But we must sort and organize these primordial desires, because the world is a complex and obstinately real place. We can't just get the one particular thing we especially just want now, along with everything else we usually want, because our desires can produce conflict with our other desires, as well as with other people, and with the world. Thus, we must become conscious of our desires, and articulate them, and prioritize them, and arrange them into hierarchies. That makes them sophisticated. That makes them work with each other, and with the desires of other people, and with the world. It is in that manner that our desires elevate themselves. It is in that manner that they organize themselves into values and become moral. Our values, our morality—they are indicators of our sophistication.

The philosophical study of morality—of right and wrong—is ethics. Such study can render us more sophisticated in our choices. Even older and deeper than ethics, however, is religion. Religion concerns itself not with (mere) right and wrong but with good and evil themselves—with the archetypes of right and wrong. Religion concerns itself with domains of value, ultimate value. That is not the scientific domain. It's not the territory of empirical description. The people who wrote and edited the Bible, for example, weren't scientists. They couldn't have been scientists, even if they had wanted to be. The viewpoints, methods and practices of science hadn't been formulated when the Bible was written.

Religion is instead *about proper behaviour*. It's about what Plato called "the Good." A genuine religious acolyte isn't trying to formulate accurate ideas about the objective nature of the world (although he may be trying to do that too). He's striving, instead, to be a "good person." It may be the case that to him "good" means nothing but "obedient"—even blindly obedient. Hence the classic liberal Western enlightenment objection to religious belief: obedience is not enough. But it's at least a start (and we have forgotten this): *You cannot aim yourself at anything if you are completely undisciplined and untutored.* You will not know what to target, and you won't fly straight, even if you somehow get your aim right. And then you will conclude, "There is nothing to aim for." And then you will be lost.

It is therefore necessary and desirable for religions to have a dogmatic element. What good is a value system that does not provide a stable structure? What good is a value system that does not point the way to a higher order? And what good can you possibly be if you cannot or do not internalize that structure, or accept that order—not as a final destination, necessarily, but at least as a starting point? Without that, you're nothing but an adult two-year-old, without the charm or the potential. That is not to say (to say it again) that obedience is sufficient. But a person capable of obedience—let's say, instead, a properly disciplined person—is at least a well-forged tool. At least that (and that is not nothing). Of course, there must be vision, beyond discipline; beyond dogma. A tool still needs a purpose. It is for such reasons that Christ said, in the Gospel of Thomas, "The Kingdom of the Father is spread out upon the earth, but men do not see it."[75]

Does that mean that what we see is dependent on our religious beliefs? Yes! And what we don't see, as well! You might object, "But I'm an atheist." No, you're *not* (and if you want to understand this, you could read Dostoevsky's *Crime and Punishment*, perhaps the greatest novel ever written, in which the main character, Raskolnikov, decides to take his atheism with true seriousness, commits what he has rationalized as a benevolent murder, and pays the price). You're simply not an atheist in your actions, and it is your actions that most accurately reflect your deepest beliefs—those that are implicit, embedded in your being, underneath your conscious apprehensions and articulable attitudes and surface-level self-knowledge. You can only find out what you actually believe (rather than what you think you believe) by watching how you act. You simply don't know what you believe, before that. You are too complex to understand yourself.

It takes careful observation, and education, and reflection, and communication with others, just to scratch the surface of your beliefs. Everything you value is a product of unimaginably lengthy developmental processes, personal, cultural and biological. You don't understand how what you want—and, therefore, what you see—is conditioned by the immense, abysmal, profound past. You simply don't understand how every neural circuit through which you peer at the world has been shaped (and painfully) by the ethical aims of millions of years of human ancestors and all of the life that was lived for the billions of years before that.

You don't understand anything.

You didn't even know that you were blind.

Some of our knowledge of our beliefs has been documented. We have been watching ourselves act, reflecting on that watching, and telling stories distilled through that reflection, for tens and perhaps hundreds of thousands of years. That is all part of our attempts, individual and collective, to discover and articulate what it is that we believe. Part of the knowledge so generated is what is encapsulated in the fundamental teachings of our cultures, in ancient writings such as the Tao Te Ching, or the aforementioned Vedic scriptures, or the Biblical stories. The Bible is, for better or worse, the foundational document of Western civilization (of Western values, Western morality, and Western conceptions of good and evil). It's the product of processes that remain fundamentally beyond our comprehension. The Bible is a library composed of many books, each written and edited by many people. It's a truly emergent document—a selected, sequenced and finally coherent story written by no one and everyone over many thousands of years. The Bible has been thrown up, out of the deep, by the collective human imagination, which is itself a product of unimaginable forces operating over unfathomable spans of time. Its careful, respectful study can reveal things to us about what we believe and how we do and should act that can be discovered in almost no other manner.

Old Testament God and New Testament God

The God of the Old Testament can appear harsh, judgmental, unpredictable and dangerous, particularly on cursory reading. The degree to which this is true has arguably been exaggerated by Christian commentators, intent on magnifying the distinction between the older and newer divisions of the Bible. There has been a price paid, however, for such plotting (and I mean that in both senses of the word): the tendency for modern people to think, when confronted with Jehovah, "I would never believe in a God like that." But Old Testament God doesn't much care what modern people think. He often didn't care what Old Testament people thought, either (although He could be bargained with, to a surprising degree, as is particularly evident in the Abrahamic stories). Nonetheless, when His people strayed from the path—when they disobeyed His injunctions, violated His covenants, and broke His commandments—trouble was certain to follow. If you did not do what

Old Testament God demanded—whatever that might have been and however you might have tried to hide from it—you and your children and your children's children were in terrible, serious trouble.

It was realists who created, or noticed, Old Testament God. When the denizens of those ancient societies wandered carelessly down the wrong path, they ended up enslaved and miserable—sometimes for centuries—when they were not obliterated completely. Was that reasonable? Was that just? Was that fair? The authors of the Old Testament asked such questions with extreme caution and under very limited conditions. They assumed, instead, that the Creator of Being knew what he was doing, that all power was essentially with Him, and that His dictates should be carefully followed. They were wise. He was a Force of Nature. Is a hungry lion reasonable, fair or just? What kind of nonsensical question is that? The Old Testament Israelites and their forebears knew that God was not to be trifled with, and that whatever Hell the angry Deity might allow to be engendered if he was crossed was real. Having recently passed through a century defined by the bottomless horrors of Hitler, Stalin, and Mao, we might realize the same thing.

New Testament God is often presented as a different character (although the Book of Revelation, with its Final Judgment, warns against any excessively naïve complacency). He is more the kindly Geppetto, master craftsman and benevolent father. He wants nothing for us but the best. He is all-loving and all-forgiving. Sure, He'll send you to Hell, if you misbehave badly enough. Fundamentally, however, he's the God of Love. That seems more optimistic, more naively welcoming, but (in precise proportion to that) less believable. In a world such as this—this hothouse of doom—who could buy such a story? The all-good God, in a post-Auschwitz world? It was for such reasons that the philosopher Nietzsche, perhaps the most astute critic ever to confront Christianity, considered New Testament God the worst literary crime in Western history. In *Beyond Good and Evil*, he wrote:[76]

In the Jewish 'Old Testament', the book of divine justice, there are men, things and speeches on such a grand style that Greek and

Indian literature has nothing to compare with it. One stands with fear and reverence before those stupendous remains of what man was formerly, and one has sad thoughts about old Asia and its little out-pushed peninsula Europe. . . . To have bound up this New Testament (a kind of ROCOCO of taste in every respect) along with the Old Testament into one book, as the "Bible," as "The Book in Itself" is perhaps the greatest audacity and "sin against the spirit" which literary Europe has on its conscience.

Who but the most naive among us could posit that such an all-good, merciful Being ruled this so-terrible world? But something that seems incomprehensible to someone unseeing might be perfectly evident to someone who had opened his eyes.

Let's return to the situation where your aim is being determined by something petty—your aforementioned envy of your boss. Because of that envy, the world you inhabit reveals itself as a place of bitterness, disappointment and spite. Imagine that you come to notice, and contemplate, and reconsider your unhappiness. Further, you determine to accept responsibility for it, and dare to posit that it might be something at least partly under your control. You crack open one eye, for a moment, and look. You ask for something better. You sacrifice your pettiness, repent of your envy, and open your heart. Instead of cursing the darkness, you let in a little light. You decide to aim for a better life—instead of a better office.

But you don't stop there. You realize that it's a mistake to aim for a better life, if it comes at the cost of worsening someone else's. So, you get creative. You decide to play a more difficult game. You decide that you want a better life, in a manner that will also make the life of your family better. Or the life of your family, and your friends. Or the life of your family, and your friends, and the strangers who surround them. What about your enemies? Do you want to include them, too? You bloody well don't know how to manage that. But you've read some history. You know how enmity compounds. So, you start to wish even your enemies well, at least in principle, although you are by no means yet a master of such sentiments.

And the direction of your sight changes. You see past the limitations that hemmed you in, unknowingly. New possibilities for your life emerge, and you work toward their realization. Your life indeed improves. And then you start to think, further: "Better? Perhaps that means better for me, and my family, and my friends—even for my enemies. But that's not all it means. It means better today, in a manner that makes everything better tomorrow, and next week, and next year, and a decade from now, and a hundred years from now. And a thousand years from now. And forever."

And then "better" means to aim at the Improvement of Being, with a capital "I" and a capital "B." Thinking all of this—realizing all of this—you take a risk. You decide that you will start treating Old Testament God, with all His terrible and oft-arbitrary-seeming power, as if He could also be New Testament God (even though you understand the many ways in which that is absurd). In other words, you decide to act as if existence might be justified by its goodness—if only you behaved properly. And it is that decision, that declaration of existential faith, that allows you to overcome nihilism, and resentment, and arrogance. It is that declaration of faith that keeps hatred of Being, with all its attendant evils, at bay. And, as for such faith: it is not at all the will to believe things that you know perfectly well to be false. Faith is not the childish belief in magic. That is ignorance or even willful blindness. It is instead the realization that the tragic irrationalities of life must be counterbalanced by an equally irrational commitment to the essential goodness of Being. It is simultaneously the will to dare set your sights at the unachievable, and to sacrifice everything, including (and most importantly) your life. You realize that you have, literally, nothing better to do. But how can you do all this?—assuming you are foolish enough to try.

You might start by *not thinking*—or, more accurately, but less trenchantly, by refusing to subjugate your faith to your current rationality, and its narrowness of view. This doesn't mean "make yourself stupid." It means the opposite. It means instead that you must quit manoeuvring and calculating and conniving and scheming and enforcing and demanding and avoiding and ignoring and punishing. It means you must place your old strategies aside. It means, instead, that you must pay attention, as you may never have paid attention before.

Pay Attention

Pay attention. Focus on your surroundings, physical and psychological. Notice something that bothers you, that concerns you, that will not let you be, which you *could* fix, that you *would* fix. You can find such somethings by asking yourself (as if you genuinely want to know) three questions: "What is it that is bothering me?" "Is that something I could fix?" and "Would I actually be willing to fix it?" If you find that the answer is "no," to any or all of the questions, then look elsewhere. Aim lower. Search until you find something that bothers you, that you could fix, that you would fix, and then fix it. That might be enough for the day.

Maybe there is a stack of paper on your desk, and you have been avoiding it. You won't even really look at it, when you walk into your room. There are terrible things lurking there: tax forms, and bills and letters from people wanting things you aren't sure you can deliver. Notice your fear, and have some sympathy for it. Maybe there are snakes in that pile of paper. Maybe you'll get bitten. Maybe there are even hydras lurking there. You'll cut off one head, and seven more will grow. How could you possibly cope with that?

You could ask yourself, "Is there anything at all that I might be willing to do about that pile of paper? Would I look, maybe, at one part of it? For twenty minutes?" Maybe the answer will be, "No!" But you might look for ten, or even for five (and if not that, for one). Start there. You will soon find that the entire pile shrinks in significance, merely because you have looked at part of it. And you'll find that the whole thing is made of parts. What if you allowed yourself a glass of wine with dinner, or curled up on the sofa and read, or watched a stupid movie, as a reward? What if you instructed your wife, or your husband, to say "good job" after you fixed whatever you fixed? Would that motivate you? The people from whom you want thanks might not be very proficient in offering it, to begin with, but that shouldn't stop you.

People can learn, even if they are very unskilled at the beginning. Ask yourself what you would require to be motivated to undertake the job, honestly, and listen to the answer. Don't tell yourself, "I shouldn't need to do that to motivate myself." What do you know about yourself? You are, on the one hand, the most complex thing in the entire universe, and on the other, someone who can't even set the clock on your microwave. Don't over-estimate your self-knowledge.

Let the tasks for the day announce themselves for your contemplation. Maybe you can do this in the morning, as you sit on the edge of your bed. Maybe you can try, the night before, when you are preparing to sleep. Ask yourself for a voluntary contribution. If you ask nicely, and listen carefully, and don't try any treachery, you might be offered one. Do this every day, for a while. Then do it for the rest of your life. Soon you will find yourself in a different situation. Now you will be asking yourself, habitually, "What could I do, that I would do, to make Life a little better?" You are not dictating to yourself what "better" must be. You are not being a totalitarian, or a utopian, even to yourself, because you have learned from the Nazis and the Soviets and the Maoists and from your own experience that being a totalitarian is a bad thing. Aim high. Set your sights on the betterment of Being. Align yourself, in your soul, with Truth and the Highest Good. There is habitable order to establish and beauty to bring into existence. There is evil to overcome, suffering to ameliorate, and yourself to better.

It is this, in my reading, that is the culminating ethic of the canon of the West. It is this, furthermore, that is communicated by those eternally confusing, glowing stanzas from Christ's Sermon on the Mount, the essence, in some sense, of the wisdom of the New Testament. This is the attempt of the Spirit of Mankind to transform the understanding of ethics from the initial, necessary Thou Shalt Not of the child and the Ten Commandments into the fully articulated, positive vision of the true individual. This is the expression not merely of admirable self-control and self-mastery but of the fundamental desire to set the world right. This is not the cessation of sin, but sin's opposite, good itself. The Sermon on the Mount outlines the true nature of man, and the proper aim of mankind: concentrate on the day, so that you can live in the present, and attend completely and properly to what is right in front of you—but do that only after you have decided to let what is within shine forth, so that it can justify Being and illuminate the world. Do that only after you have determined to sacrifice whatever it is that must be sacrificed so that you can pursue the highest good.

> Consider the lilies of the field, how they grow; they toil not, neither do they spin:
> And yet I say unto you, That even Solomon in all his glory was not arrayed like one of these.
> Wherefore, if God so clothe the grass of the field, which to day is, and to morrow is cast into the oven, shall he not much more clothe you, O ye of little faith?
> Therefore take no thought, saying, What shall we eat? or, What shall we drink? or, Wherewithal shall we be clothed?
> (For after all these things do the Gentiles seek:) for your heavenly Father knoweth that ye have need of all these things.
> But seek ye first the kingdom of God, and his righteousness; and all these things shall be added unto you.
> Take therefore no thought for the morrow: for the morrow shall take thought for the things of itself. Sufficient unto the day is the evil thereof. (Luke 12: 22–34)

Realization is dawning. Instead of playing the tyrant, therefore, you are paying attention. You are telling the truth, instead of manipulating the world. You are negotiating, instead of playing the martyr or the tyrant. You no longer have to be envious, because you no longer know that someone else truly has it better. You no longer have to be frustrated, because you have learned to aim low, and to be patient. You are discovering who you are, and what you want, and what you are willing to do. You are finding that the solutions to your particular problems have to be tailored to you, personally and precisely. You are less concerned with the actions of other people, because you have plenty to do yourself.

Attend to the day, but aim at the highest good.

Now, your trajectory is heavenward. That makes you hopeful. Even a man on a sinking ship can be happy when he clambers aboard a lifeboat! And who knows where he might go, in the future. To journey happily may well be better than to arrive successfully. . . .

Ask, and ye shall receive. Knock, and the door will open. If you ask, as if you want, and knock, as if you want to enter, you may be offered the chance to improve your life, a little; a lot; completely—and with that improvement, some progress will be made in Being itself.

Compare yourself to who you were yesterday, not to who someone else is today.

THE COMMON LAW

HERE THE COMMON LAW OF ENGLAND WAS ESTABLISHED
ON THIS CONTINENT WITH THE ARRIVAL OF THE FIRST
SETTLERS ON MAY 13, 1607. THE FIRST CHARTER GRANTED
BY JAMES I TO THE VIRGINIA COMPANY IN 1606 DECLARED
THAT THE INHABITANTS OF THE COLONY "...SHALL HAVE
AND ENJOY ALL LIBERTIES, FRANCHISES AND IMMUNITIES...
AS IF THEY HAD BEEN ABIDING AND BORNE WITHIN THIS
OUR REALME OF ENGLANDE...". SINCE MAGNA CARTA THE
COMMON LAW HAS BEEN THE CORNERSTONE OF INDIVIDUAL
LIBERTIES, EVEN AS AGAINST THE CROWN. SUMMARIZED
LATER IN THE BILL OF RIGHTS ITS PRINCIPLES HAVE
INSPIRED THE DEVELOPMENT OF OUR SYSTEM OF FREEDOM
UNDER LAW, WHICH IS AT ONCE OUR DEAREST
POSSESSION AND PROUDEST ACHIEVEMENT.

PRESENTED BY THE VIRGINIA STATE BAR MAY 17, 1959

DO NOT LET YOUR CHILDREN DO
ANYTHING THAT MAKES YOU DISLIKE THEM

ACTUALLY, IT'S NOT OK

RECENTLY, I WATCHED A THREE-YEAR-OLD boy trail his mother and father slowly through a crowded airport. He was screaming violently at five-second intervals—and, more important, he was doing it voluntarily. He wasn't at the end of his tether. As a parent, I could tell from the tone. He was irritating his parents and hundreds of other people to gain attention. Maybe he needed something. But that was no way to get it, and his parents should have let him know that. You might object that "perhaps they were worn out, and jet-lagged, after a long trip." But thirty seconds of carefully directed problem-solving would have brought the shameful episode to a halt. More thoughtful parents would not have let someone they truly cared for become the object of a crowd's contempt.

I have also watched a couple, unable or unwilling to say no to their two-year-old, obliged to follow closely behind him everywhere he went, every moment of what was supposed to be an enjoyable social visit, because he misbehaved so badly when not micro-managed that he could not be given a second of genuine freedom without risk. The desire of his parents to let their child act without correction on every impulse perversely produced precisely the opposite effect: they deprived him instead of every opportunity to engage in independent action. Because they did not dare to teach him what "No" means, he had no conception of the reasonable limits enabling maximal toddler autonomy. It was a classic example of too much chaos breeding too much order (and the inevitable reversal). I have, similarly, seen parents rendered unable to engage in adult conversation at a dinner party because their children, four and five, dominated the social scene, eating the centres out of all the sliced bread, subjecting everyone to their juvenile tyranny, while mom and dad watched, embarrassed and bereft of the ability to intervene.

When my now-adult daughter was a child, another child once hit her on the head with a metal toy truck. I watched that same child, one year later, viciously push his younger sister backwards over a fragile glass-surfaced coffee table. His mother picked him up, immediately afterward (but not her frightened daughter), and told him in hushed tones not to do such things, while she patted him comfortingly in a manner clearly indicative of approval. She was out to produce a little God-Emperor of the Universe. That's the unstated goal of many a mother, including many who consider themselves advocates for full gender equality. Such women will object vociferously to any command uttered by an adult male, but will trot off in seconds to make their progeny a peanut-butter sandwich if he demands it while immersed self-importantly in a video game. The future mates of such boys have every reason to hate their mothers-in-law. Respect for women? That's for other boys, other men—not for their dear sons.

Something of the same sort may underlie, in part, the preference for male children seen most particularly in places such as India, Pakistan and China, where sex-selective abortion is widely practised. The Wikipedia entry for that practice attributes its existence to "cultural norms" favouring male over female children. (I cite Wikipedia because it is collectively written and edited and, therefore, the perfect place to find accepted wisdom.) But there's no evidence that such ideas are strictly cultural. There are plausible psycho-biological reasons for the evolution of such an attitude, and they're not pretty, from a modern, egalitarian perspective. If circumstances force you to put all your eggs into one basket, so to speak, a son is a better bet, by the strict standards of evolutionary logic, where the proliferation of your genes is all that matters. Why?

Well, a reproductively successful daughter might gain you eight or nine children. The Holocaust survivor Yitta Schwartz, a star in this regard, had three generations of direct descendants who matched such performance. She was the ancestor of almost two thousand people by the time of her death in 2010.[77] But the sky is truly the limit with a reproductively successful son. Sex with multiple female partners is his ticket to exponential reproduction (given our species' practical limitation to single births). Rumour has it that the actor Warren Beatty and the athlete Wilt Chamberlain each bedded multiple thousands of women (something not unknown, as well, among rock stars). They didn't produce children in those numbers. Modern birth control limits that. But similar celebrity types in the past have done so. The forefather of the Qing dynasty, Giocangga (circa 1550), for example, is the male-line ancestor of a million and a half people in northeastern China.[78] The medieval Uí Néill dynasty produced up to three million male descendants, localized mainly in northwestern Ireland and the US, through Irish emigration.[79] And the king of them all, Genghis Khan, conqueror of much of Asia, is forefather of 8 percent of the men in Central Asia—sixteen million male descendants, 34 generations later.[80] So, from a deep, biological perspective there are reasons why parents might favour sons sufficiently to eliminate female fetuses, although I am not claiming direct causality, nor suggesting a lack of other, more culturally-dependent reasons.

Preferential treatment awarded a son during development might even help produce an attractive, well-rounded, confident man. This happened in the case of the father of psychoanalysis, Sigmund Freud, by his own account: "A man who has been the indisputable favorite of his mother keeps for life the feeling of a conqueror, that confidence of success that often induces real success."[81] Fair enough. But "feeling of a conqueror" can all too easily become "actual conqueror." Genghis Khan's outstanding reproductive success certainly came at the cost of any success whatsoever for others (including the dead millions of Chinese, Persians, Russians and Hungarians). Spoiling a son might therefore work well from the standpoint of the "selfish gene" (allowing the favoured child's genes to replicate themselves in innumerable off-spring), to use the evolutionary biologist Richard Dawkins' famous expression. But it can make for a dark, painful spectacle in the here and now, and mutate into something indescribably dangerous.

None of this means that all mothers favour all sons over their daughters (or that daughters are not sometimes favoured over sons, or that fathers don't sometimes favor their sons). Other factors can clearly dominate. Sometimes, for example, unconscious hatred (sometimes not-so-unconscious, either) overrides any concern a parent might have for any child, regardless of gender or personality or situation. I saw a four-year old boy allowed to go hungry on a regular basis. His nanny had been injured, and he was being cycled through the neighbours for temporary care. When his mother dropped him off at our house, she indicated that he wouldn't eat at all, all day. "That's OK," she said. It wasn't OK (in case that's not obvious). This was the same four-year-old boy who clung to my wife for hours in absolute desperation and total commitment, when she tenaciously, persistently and mercifully managed to feed him an entire lunch-time meal, rewarding him throughout for his cooperation, and refusing to let him fail. He started out with a closed mouth, sitting with all of us at the dining room table, my wife and I, our two kids, and two neighbourhood kids we looked after during the day. She put the spoon in front of him, waiting patiently, persistently, while he moved his head back and forth, refusing it entry, using defensive methods typical of a recalcitrant and none-too-well-attended two-year old.

She didn't let him fail. She patted him on the head every time he managed a mouthful, telling him sincerely that he was a "good boy" when he did so. She did think he was a good boy. He was a cute, damaged kid. Ten not-too-painful minutes later he finished his meal. We were all watching intently. It was a drama of life and death.

"Look," she said, holding up his bowl. "You finished all of it." This boy, who was standing in the corner, voluntarily and unhappily, when I first saw him; who wouldn't interact with the other kids, who frowned chronically, who wouldn't respond to me when I tickled and prodded him, trying to get him to play—this boy broke immediately into a wide, radiant smile. It brought joy to everyone at the table. Twenty years later, writing it down today, it still brings me to tears. Afterward, he followed my wife around like a puppy for the rest of the day, refusing to let her out of his sight. When she sat down, he jumped in her lap, cuddling in, opening himself back up to the world, searching desperately for the love he had been continually denied. Later in the day, but far too soon, his mother reappeared. She came down the stairs into the room we all occupied. "Oh, SuperMom," she uttered, resentfully, seeing her son curled up in my wife's lap. Then she departed, black, murderous heart unchanged, doomed child in hand. She was a psychologist. The things you can see, with even a single open eye. It's no wonder that people want to stay blind.

Everybody Hates Arithmetic

My clinical clients frequently come to me to discuss their day-to-day familial problems. Such quotidian concerns are insidious. Their habitual and predictable occurrence makes them appear trivial. But that appearance of triviality is deceptive: it is the things that occur every single day that truly make up our lives, and time spent the same way over and again adds up at an alarming rate. One father recently spoke with me about the trouble he was having putting his son to sleep at night*—a ritual that typically involved about three-quarters of an hour of fighting. We did the arithmetic. Forty-five minutes a day, seven days a week—that's three hundred minutes, or five hours, a week. Five hours for each of the four weeks of a month—that's twenty hours per

---

* I draw here and will many times again in the course of this book on my clinical experience (as I have, already, on my personal history). I have tried to keep the moral of the stories intact, while disguising the details for the sake of the privacy of those involved. I hope I got the balance right.

month. Twenty hours a month for twelve months is two hundred and forty hours a year. That's a month and a half of standard forty-hour work weeks.

My client was spending a month and a half of work weeks per year fighting ineffectually and miserably with his son. Needless to say, both were suffering for it. No matter how good your intentions, or how sweet and tolerant your temperament, you will not maintain good relations with someone you fight with for a month and a half of work weeks per year. Resentment will inevitably build. Even if it doesn't, all that wasted, unpleasant time could clearly be spent in more productive and useful and less stressful and more enjoyable activity. How are such situations to be understood? Where does the fault lie, in child or in parent? In nature or society? And what, if anything, is to be done?

Some localize all such problems in the adult, whether in the parent or broader society. "There are no bad children," such people think, "only bad parents." When the idealized image of an unsullied child is brought to mind, this notion appears fully justified. The beauty, openness, joy, trust and capacity for love characterizing children makes it easy to attribute full culpability to the adults on the scene. But such an attitude is dangerously and naively romantic. It's too one-sided, in the case of parents granted a particularly difficult son or daughter. It's also not for the best that all human corruption is uncritically laid at society's feet. That conclusion merely displaces the problem, back in time. It explains nothing, and solves no problems. If society is corrupt, but not the individuals within it, then where did the corruption originate? How is it propagated? It's a one-sided, deeply ideological theory.

Even more problematic is the insistence logically stemming from this presumption of social corruption that all individual problems, no matter how rare, must be solved by cultural restructuring, no matter how radical. Our society faces the increasing call to deconstruct its stabilizing traditions to include smaller and smaller numbers of people who do not or will not fit into the categories upon which even our perceptions are based. This is not a good thing. Each person's private trouble cannot be solved by a social revolution, because revolutions are destabilizing and dangerous. We have learned to live together and organize our complex societies slowly and incrementally, over vast stretches of time, and we do not understand with sufficient exactitude why what we are doing works. Thus, altering our ways of social being carelessly in the name of some ideological shibboleth (diversity springs to mind) is likely to produce far more trouble than good, given the suffering that even small revolutions generally produce.

Was it really a good thing, for example, to so dramatically liberalize the divorce laws in the 1960s? It's not clear to me that the children whose lives were destabilized by the hypothetical freedom this attempt at liberation introduced would say so. Horror and terror lurk behind the walls provided so wisely by our ancestors. We tear them down at our peril. We skate, unconsciously, on thin ice, with deep, cold waters below, where unimaginable monsters lurk.

I see today's parents as terrified by their children, not least because they have been deemed the proximal agents of this hypothetical social tyranny, and simultaneously denied credit for their role as benevolent and necessary agents of discipline, order and conventionality. They dwell uncomfortably and self-consciously in the all-too-powerful shadow of the adolescent ethos of the 1960s, a decade whose excesses led to a general denigration of adulthood, an unthinking disbelief in the existence of competent power, and the inability to distinguish between the chaos of immaturity and responsible freedom. This has increased parental sensitivity to the short-term emotional suffering of their children, while heightening their fear of damaging their children to a painful and counterproductive degree. Better this than the reverse, you might argue—but there are catastrophes lurking at the extremes of every moral continuum.

The Ignoble Savage

It has been said that every individual is the conscious or unconscious follower of some influential philosopher. The belief that children have an intrinsically unsullied spirit, damaged only by culture and society, is derived in no small part from the eighteenth-century Genevan French philosopher Jean-Jacques Rousseau.[82] Rousseau was a fervent believer in the corrupting influence of human society and private ownership alike. He claimed that nothing was so gentle and wonderful as man in his pre-civilized state. At precisely the same time, noting his inability as a father, he abandoned five of his children to the tender and fatal mercies of the orphanages of the time.

The noble savage Rousseau described, however, was an ideal—an abstraction, archetypal and religious—and not the flesh-and-blood reality he supposed. The mythologically perfect Divine Child permanently inhabits our imagination. He's the potential of youth, the newborn hero, the wronged innocent, and the long-lost son of the rightful king. He's the intimations of immortality that accompany our earliest experiences. He's Adam, the perfect man, walking without sin with God in the Garden before the Fall. But human beings are evil, as well as good, and the darkness that dwells forever in our souls is also there in no small part in our younger selves. In general, people improve with age, rather than worsening, becoming kinder, more conscientious, and more emotionally stable as they mature.[83] Bullying at the sheer and often terrible intensity of the schoolyard[84] rarely manifests itself in grown-up society. William Golding's dark and anarchistic *Lord of the Flies* is a classic for a reason.

Furthermore, there is plenty of direct evidence that the horrors of human behaviour cannot be so easily attributed to history and society. This was discovered most painfully, perhaps, by the primatologist Jane Goodall, beginning in 1974, when she learned that her beloved chimpanzees were capable of and willing to murder each other (to use the terminology appropriate to humans).[85] Because of its shocking nature and great anthropological significance, she kept her observations secret for years, fearing that her contact with the animals had led them to manifest unnatural behaviour. Even after she published her account, many refused to believe it. It soon became obvious, however, that what she observed was by no means rare.

Bluntly put: chimpanzees conduct inter-tribal warfare. Furthermore, they do it with almost unimaginable brutality. The typical full-grown chimp is more than twice as strong as a comparable human being, despite their smaller size.[86] Goodall reported with some terror the proclivity of the chimps she studied to snap strong steel cables and levers.[87] Chimps can literally tear each other to pieces—and they do. Human societies and their complex technologies cannot be blamed for that.[88] "Often when I woke in the night," she wrote, "horrific pictures sprang unbidden to my mind—Satan [a long-observed chimp] cupping his hand below Sniff's chin to drink the blood that welled from a great wound in his face . . . Jomeo tearing a strip of skin from Dé's thigh; Figan, charging and hitting, again and again, the stricken, quivering body of Goliath, one of his childhood heroes."[89] Small gangs of adolescent chimps, mostly male, roam the borders of their territory. If they encounter foreigners (even chimps they once knew, who had broken away from the now-too-large group) and, if they outnumber them, the gang will mob and destroy them, without mercy. Chimps don't have much of a super-ego, and it is prudent to remember that the human capacity for self-control may also be overestimated. Careful perusal of a book as shocking and horrific as Iris Chang's *The Rape of Nanking*,[90] which describes the brutal decimation of that Chinese city by the invading Japanese, will disenchant even a committed romantic. And the less said about Unit 731, a covert Japanese biological warfare research unit established at that time, the better. Read about it at your peril. You have been warned.

Hunter-gatherers, too, are much more murderous than their urban, industrialized counterparts, despite their communal lives and localized cultures. The yearly rate of homicide in the modern UK is about 1 per 100,000.[91] It's four to five times higher in the US, and about ninety times higher in Honduras, which has the highest rate recorded of any modern nation. But the evidence strongly suggests that human beings have become more peaceful, rather than less so, as time has progressed and societies became larger and more organized. The !Kung bushmen of Africa, romanticized in the 1950s by Elizabeth Marshall Thomas as "the harmless people,"[92] had a yearly murder rate of 40 per 100,000, which declined by more than 30% once they became subject to state authority.[93] This is a very instructive example of complex social structures serving to reduce, not exacerbate, the violent tendencies of human beings. Yearly rates of 300 per 100,000 have been reported for the Yanomami of Brazil, famed for their aggression—but the stats don't max out there. The denizens of Papua, New Guinea, kill each other at yearly rates ranging from 140 to 1000 per 100,000.[94] However, the record appears to be held by the Kato, an indigeneous people of California, 1450 of whom per 100,000 met a violent death circa 1840.[95]

Because children, like other human beings, are not only good, they cannot simply be left to their own devices, untouched by society, and bloom into perfection. Even dogs must be socialized if they are to become acceptable members of the pack—and children are much more complex than dogs. This means that they are much more likely to go complexly astray if they are not trained, disciplined and properly encouraged. This means that it is not just wrong to attribute all the violent tendencies of human beings to the pathologies of social structure. It's wrong enough to be virtually backward. The vital process of socialization prevents much harm and fosters much good. Children must be shaped and informed, or they cannot thrive. This fact is reflected starkly in their behavior: kids are utterly desperate for attention from both peers and adults because such attention, which renders them effective and sophisticated communal players, is vitally necessary.

Children can be damaged as much or more by a lack of incisive attention as they are by abuse, mental or physical. This is damage by omission, rather than commission, but it is no less severe and long-lasting. Children are damaged when their "mercifully" inattentive parents fail to make them sharp and observant and awake and leave them, instead, in an unconscious and undifferentiated state. Children are damaged when those charged with their care, afraid of any conflict or upset, no longer dare to correct them, and leave them without guidance. I can recognize such children on the street. They are doughy and unfocused and vague. They are leaden and dull instead of golden and bright. They are uncarved blocks, trapped in a perpetual state of waiting-to-be.

Such children are chronically ignored by their peers. This is because they are not fun to play with. Adults tend to manifest the same attitude (although they will deny it desperately when pressed). When I worked in daycare centres, early in my career, the comparatively neglected children would come to me desperately, in their fumbling, half-formed manner, with no sense of proper distance and no attentive playfulness. They would flop, nearby—or directly on my lap, no matter what I was doing—driven inexorably by the powerful desire for adult attention, the necessary catalyst for further development. It was very difficult not to react with annoyance, even disgust, to such children and their too-prolonged infantilism—difficult not to literally push them aside—even though I felt very badly for them, and understood their predicament well. I believe that response, harsh and terrible though it may be, was an almost universally-experienced internal warning signal indicating the comparative danger of establishing a relationship with a poorly socialized child: the likelihood of immediate and inappropriate dependence (which should have been the responsibility of the parent) and the tremendous demand of time and resources that accepting such dependence would necessitate. Confronted with such a situation, potentially friendly peers and interested adults are much more likely to turn their attention to interacting with other children whose cost/benefit ratio, to speak bluntly, would be much lower.

Parent or Friend

The neglect and mistreatment that is part and parcel of poorly structured or even entirely absent disciplinary approaches can be deliberate—motivated by explicit, conscious (if misguided) parental motives. But more often than not, modern parents are simply paralyzed by the fear that they will no longer be liked or even loved by their children if they chastise them for any reason. They want their children's friendship above all, and are willing to sacrifice respect to get it. This is not good. A child will have many friends, but only two parents—if that—and parents are more, not less, than friends. Friends have very limited authority to correct. Every parent therefore needs to learn to tolerate the momentary anger or even hatred directed towards them by their children, after necessary corrective action has been taken, as the capacity of children to perceive or care about long-term consequences is very limited. Parents are the arbiters of society. They teach children how to behave so that other people will be able to interact meaningfully and productively with them.

It is an act of responsibility to discipline a child. It is not anger at misbehavior. It is not revenge for a misdeed. It is instead a careful combination of mercy and long-term judgment. Proper discipline requires effort—indeed, is virtually synonymous with effort. It is difficult to pay careful attention to children. It is difficult to figure out what is wrong and what is right and why. It is difficult to formulate just and compassionate strategies of discipline, and to negotiate their application with others deeply involved in a child's care. Because of this combination of responsibility and difficulty, any suggestion that all constraints placed on children are damaging can be perversely welcome. Such a notion, once accepted, allows adults who should know better to abandon their duty to serve as agents of enculturation and pretend that doing so is good for children. It's a deep and pernicious act of self-deception. It's lazy, cruel and inexcusable. And our proclivity to rationalize does not end there.

We assume that rules will irremediably inhibit what would otherwise be the boundless and intrinsic creativity of our children, even though the scientific literature clearly indicates, first, that creativity beyond the trivial is shockingly rare[96] and, second, that strict limitations facilitate rather than inhibit creative achievement.[97] Belief in the purely destructive element of rules and structure is frequently conjoined with the idea that children will make good choices about when to sleep and what to eat, if their perfect natures are merely allowed to manifest themselves. These are equally ungrounded assumptions. Children are perfectly capable of attempting to subsist on hot dogs, chicken fingers and Froot Loops if doing so will attract attention, provide power, or shield them from trying anything new. Instead of going to bed wisely and peacefully, children will fight night-time unconsciousness until they are staggered by fatigue. They are also perfectly willing to provoke adults, while exploring the complex contours of the social environment, just like juvenile chimps harassing the adults in their troupes.[98] Observing the consequences of teasing and taunting enables chimp and child alike to discover the limits of what might otherwise be a too-unstructured and terrifying freedom. Such limits, when discovered, provide security, even if their detection causes momentary disappointment or frustration.

I remember taking my daughter to the playground once when she was about two. She was playing on the monkey bars, hanging in mid-air. A particularly provocative little monster of about the same age was standing above her on the same bar she was gripping. I watched him move towards her. Our eyes locked. He slowly and deliberately stepped on her hands, with increasing force, over and over, as he stared me down. He knew exactly what he was doing. Up yours, Daddy-O— that was his philosophy. He had already concluded that adults were contemptible, and that he could safely defy them. (Too bad, then, that he was destined to become one.) That was the hopeless future his parents had saddled him with. To his great and salutary shock, I picked him bodily off the playground structure, and threw him thirty feet down the field.

No, I didn't. I just took my daughter somewhere else. But it would have been better for him if I had.

Imagine a toddler repeatedly striking his mother in the face. Why would he do such a thing? It's a stupid question. It's unacceptably naive. The answer is obvious. To dominate his mother. To see if he can get away with it. Violence, after all, is no mystery. It's peace that's the mystery. Violence is the default. It's easy. It's peace that is difficult: learned, inculcated, earned. (People often get basic psychological questions backwards. Why do people take drugs? Not a mystery. It's why they don't take them all the time that's the mystery. Why do people suffer from anxiety? That's not a mystery. How is that people can ever be calm? There's the mystery. We're breakable and mortal. A million things can go wrong, in a million ways. We should be terrified out of our skulls at every second. But we're not. The same can be said for depression, laziness and criminality.)

If I can hurt and overpower you, then I can do exactly what I want, when I want, even when you're around. I can torment you, to appease my curiosity. I can take the attention away from you, and dominate you. I can steal your toy. Children hit first because aggression is innate, although more dominant in some individuals and less in others, and, second, because aggression facilitates desire. It's foolish to assume that such behaviour must be learned. A snake does not have to be taught to strike. It's in the nature of the beast. Two-year-olds, statistically speaking, are the most violent of people.[99] They kick, hit and bite, and they steal the property of others. They do so to explore, to express outrage and frustration, and to gratify their impulsive desires. More importantly, for our purposes, they do so to discover the true limits of permissible behaviour. How else are they ever going to puzzle out what is acceptable? Infants are like blind people, searching for a wall. They have to push forward, and test, to see where the actual boundaries lie (and those are too seldom where they are said to be).

Consistent correction of such action indicates the limits of acceptable aggression to the child. Its absence merely heightens curiosity—so the child will hit and bite and kick, if he is aggressive and dominant, until something indicates a limit. How hard can I hit Mommy? Until she objects. Given that, correction is better sooner than later (if the desired end result of the parent is not to be hit). Correction also helps the child learn that hitting others is a sub-optimal social strategy. Without that correction, no child is going to undergo the effortful process of organizing and regulating their impulses, so that those impulses can coexist, without conflict, within the psyche of the child, and in the broader social world. It is no simple matter to organize a mind.

My son was particularly ornery when he was a toddler. When my daughter was little, I could paralyze her into immobility with an evil glance. Such an intervention had no effect at all on my son. He had my wife (who is no pushover) stymied at the dinner table by the time he was nine months of age. He fought her for control over the spoon. "Good!" we thought. We didn't want to feed him one more minute than necessary anyway. But the little blighter would only eat three or four mouthfuls. Then he would play. He would stir his food around in his bowl. He would drop bits of it over the high chair table top, and watch as it fell on the floor below. No problem. He was exploring. But then he wasn't eating enough. Then, because he wasn't eating enough, he wasn't sleeping enough. Then his midnight crying was waking his parents. Then they were getting grumpy and out of sorts. He was frustrating his mother, and she was taking it out on me. The trajectory wasn't good.

After a few days of this degeneration, I decided to take the spoon back. I prepared for war. I set aside sufficient time. A patient adult can defeat a two-year-old, hard as that is to believe. As the saying goes: "Old age and treachery can always overcome youth and skill." This is partly because time lasts forever, when you're two. Half an hour for me was a week for my son. I assured myself of victory. He was stubborn and horrible. But I could be worse. We sat down, face to face, bowl in front of him. It was *High Noon*. He knew it, and I knew it. He picked up the spoon. I took it from him, and spooned up a delicious mouthful of mush. I moved it deliberately towards his mouth. He eyed me in precisely the same manner as the playground foot monster. He curled his lips downward into a tight frown, rejecting all entry. I chased his mouth around with the spoon as he twisted his head around in tight circles.

But I had more tricks up my sleeve. I poked him in the chest, with my free hand, in a manner calculated to annoy. He didn't budge. I did it again. And again. And again. Not hard—but not in a manner to be ignored, either. Ten or so pokes later, he opened his mouth, planning to emit a sound of outrage. Hah! His mistake. I deftly inserted the spoon. He tried, gamely, to force out the offending food with his tongue. But I know how to deal with that, too. I just placed my forefinger horizontally across his lips. Some came out. But some was swallowed, too. Score one for Dad. I gave him a pat on the head, and told him that he was a good boy. And I meant it. When someone does something you are trying to get them to do, reward them. No grudge after victory. An hour later, it was all over. There was outrage. There was some wailing. My wife had to leave the room. The stress was too much. But food was eaten by child. My son collapsed, exhausted, on my chest. We had a nap together. And he liked me a lot better when he woke up than he had before he was disciplined.

This was something I commonly observed when we went head to head—and not only with him. A little later we entered into a babysitting swap with another couple. All the kids would get together at one house. Then one pair of parents would go out to dinner, or a movie, and leave the other pair to watch the children, who were all under three. One evening, another set of parents joined us. I was unfamiliar with their son, a large, strong boy of two.

"He won't sleep," said his father. "After you put him to bed, he will crawl out of his bed, and come downstairs. We usually put on an Elmo video and let him watch it."

"There's no damn way I'm rewarding a recalcitrant child for unacceptable behaviour," I thought, "and I'm certainly not showing anyone any Elmo video." I always hated that creepy, whiny puppet. He was a disgrace to Jim Henson's legacy. So reward-by-Elmo was not on the table. I didn't say anything, of course. There is just no talking to parents about their children—until they are ready to listen.

Two hours later, we put the kids to bed. Four of the five went promptly to sleep—but not the Muppet aficionado. I had placed him in a crib, however, so he couldn't escape. But he could still howl, and that's exactly what he did. That was tricky. It was good strategy on his part. It was annoying, and it threatened to wake up all the other kids, who would then also start to howl. Score one for the kid. So, I journeyed into the bedroom. "Lie down," I said. That produced no effect. "Lie down," I said, "or I will lay you down." Reasoning with kids isn't often of too much use, particularly under such circumstances, but I believe in fair warning. Of course, he didn't lie down. He howled again, for effect.

Kids do this frequently. Scared parents think that a crying child is always sad or hurt. This is simply not true. Anger is one of the most common reasons for crying. Careful analysis of the musculature patterns of crying children has confirmed this.[100] Anger-crying and fear-or-sadness crying do not look the same. They also don't sound the same, and can be distinguished with careful attention. Anger-crying is often an act of dominance, and should be dealt with as such. I lifted him up, and laid him down. Gently. Patiently. But firmly. He got up.

I laid him down. He got up. I laid him down. He got up. This time, I laid him down, and kept my hand on his back. He struggled, mightily, but ineffectually. He was, after all, only one-tenth my size. I could take him with one hand. So, I kept him down and spoke calmly to him and told him he was a good boy and that he should relax. I gave him a soother and pounded gently on his back. He started to relax. His eyes began to close. I removed my hand.

He promptly got to his feet. I was impressed. The kid had spirit! I lifted him up, and laid him down, again. "Lie down, monster," I said. I pounded his back gently some more. Some kids find that soothing. He was getting tired. He was ready to capitulate. He closed his eyes. I got to my feet, and headed quietly and quickly to the door. I glanced back, to check his position, one last time. He was back on his feet. I pointed my finger at him. "Down, monster," I said, and I meant it. He went down like a shot. I closed the door. We liked each other. Neither my wife nor I heard a peep out of him for the rest of the night.

"How was the kid?" his father asked me when he got home, much later that night. "Good," I said. "No problem at all. He's asleep right now."

"Did he get up?" said his father.

"No," I said. "He slept the whole time."

Dad looked at me. He wanted to know. But he didn't ask. And I didn't tell.

Don't cast pearls before swine, as the old saying goes. And you might think that's harsh. But training your child not to sleep, and rewarding him with the antics of a creepy puppet? That's harsh too. You pick your poison, and I'll pick mine.

Discipline and Punish

Modern parents are terrified of two frequently juxtaposed words: discipline and punish. They evoke images of prisons, soldiers and jackboots. The distance between disciplinarian and tyrant or punishment and torture is, indeed, easily traversed. *Discipline* and *punish* must be handled with care. The fear is unsurprising. But both are necessary.

They can be applied unconsciously or consciously, badly or well, but there is no escaping their use.

It's not that it's impossible to discipline with reward. In fact, rewarding good behaviour can be very effective. The most famous of all behavioural psychologists, B.F. Skinner, was a great advocate of this approach. He was expert at it. He taught pigeons to play ping-pong, although they only rolled the ball back and forth by pecking it with their beaks.[101] But they were pigeons. So even though they played badly, it was still pretty good. Skinner even taught his birds to pilot missiles during the Second World War, in Project Pigeon (later Orcon).[102] He got a long way, before the invention of electronic guidance systems rendered his efforts obsolete.

Skinner observed the animals he was training to perform such acts with exceptional care. Any actions that approximated what he was aiming at were immediately followed by a reward of just the right size: not small enough to be inconsequential, and not so large that it devalued future rewards. Such an approach can be used with children, and works very well. Imagine that you would like your toddler to help set the table. It's a useful skill. You'd like him better if he could do it. It would be good for his (shudder) self-esteem. So, you break the target behaviour down into its component parts. One element of setting the table is carrying a plate from the cupboard to the table. Even that might be too complex. Perhaps your child has only been walking a few months. He's still wobbly and unreliable. So, you start his training by handing him a plate and having him hand it back. A pat on the head could follow. You might turn it into a game. Pass with your left. Switch to your right. Circle around your back. Then you might give him a plate and take a few steps backward so that he has to traverse a few steps before giving it back. Train him to become a plate-handling virtuoso. Don't leave him trapped in his klutz-dom.

You can teach virtually anyone anything with such an approach. First, figure out what you want. Then, watch the people around you like a hawk. Finally, whenever you see anything a bit more like what you want, swoop in (hawk, remember) and deliver a reward. Your daughter has been very reserved since she became a teenager. You wish she would talk more. That's the target: more communicative daughter. One morning, over breakfast, she shares an anecdote about school. That's an excellent time to pay attention. That's the reward. Stop texting and listen. Unless you don't want her to tell you anything ever again.

Parental interventions that make children happy clearly can and should be used to shape behaviour. The same goes for husbands, wives, co-workers and parents. Skinner, however, was a realist. He noted that use of reward was very difficult: the observer had to attend patiently until the target spontaneously manifested the desired behaviour, and then reinforce. This required a lot of time, and a lot of waiting, and that's a problem. He also had to starve his animals down to three-quarters of their normal body weight before they would become interested enough in food reward to truly pay attention. But these are not the only shortcomings of the purely positive approach.

Negative emotions, like their positive counterparts, help us learn. We need to learn, because we're stupid and easily damaged. We can die. That's not good, and we don't feel good about it. If we did, we would seek death, and then we would die. We don't even feel good about dying if it only *might* happen. And that's all the time. In that manner, negative emotions, for all their unpleasantness, protect us. We feel hurt and scared and ashamed and disgusted so we can avoid damage. And we're susceptible to feeling such things a lot. In fact, we feel more negative about a loss of a given size than we feel good about the same-sized gain. Pain is more potent than pleasure, and anxiety more than hope.

Emotions, positive and negative, come in two usefully differentiated variants. Satisfaction (technically, satiation) tells us that what we did was good, while hope (technically, incentive reward) indicates that something pleasurable is on the way. Pain hurts us, so we won't repeat actions that produced personal damage or social isolation (as loneliness is also, technically, a form of pain). Anxiety makes us stay away from hurtful people and bad places so we don't have to feel pain. All these emotions must be balanced against each other, and carefully judged in context, but they're all required to keep us alive and thriving. We therefore do our children a disservice by failing to use whatever is available to help them learn, including negative emotions, even though such use should occur in the most merciful possible manner.

Skinner knew that threats and punishments could stop unwanted behaviours, just as reward reinforces what is desirable. In a world paralyzed at the thought of interfering with the hypothetically pristine path of natural child development, it can be difficult even to discuss the former techniques. However, children would not have such a lengthy period of natural development, prior to maturity, if their behaviour did not have to be shaped. They would just leap out of the womb, ready to trade stocks. Children also cannot be fully sheltered from fear and pain. They are small and vulnerable. They don't know much about the world. Even when they are doing something as natural as learning to walk, they're constantly being walloped by the world. And this is to say nothing of the frustration and rejection they inevitably experience when dealing with siblings and peers and uncooperative, stubborn adults. Given this, the fundamental moral question is not how to shelter children completely from misadventure and failure, so they never experience any fear or pain, but how to maximize their learning so that useful knowledge may be gained with minimal cost.

In the Disney movie *Sleeping Beauty*, the King and Queen have a daughter, the princess Aurora, after a long wait. They plan a great christening, to introduce her to the world. They welcome everyone who loves and honours their new daughter. But they fail to invite Maleficent (malicious, malevolent), who is essentially Queen of the Underworld, or Nature in her negative guise. This means, symbolically, that the two monarchs are overprotecting their beloved daughter, by setting up a world around her that has nothing negative in it. But this does not protect her. It makes her weak. Maleficent curses the princess, sentencing her to death at the age of sixteen, caused by the prick of a spinning wheel's needle. The spinning wheel is the wheel of fate; the prick, which produces blood, symbolizes the loss of virginity, a sign of the emergence of the woman from the child.

Fortunately, a good fairy (the positive element of Nature) reduces the punishment to unconsciousness, redeemable with love's first kiss.

The panicked King and Queen get rid of all the spinning wheels in the land, and turn their daughter over to the much-too-nice good fairies, of whom there are three. They continue with their strategy of removing all dangerous things—but in doing so they leave their daughter naïve, immature and weak. One day, just before Aurora's sixteenth birthday, she meets a prince in the forest, and falls in love, the same day. By any reasonable standard, that's a bit much. Then she loudly bemoans the fact that she is to be wed to Prince Philip, to whom she was betrothed as a child, and collapses emotionally when she is brought back to her parents' castle for her birthday. It is at that moment that Maleficent's curse manifests itself. A portal opens up in the castle, a spinning wheel appears, and Aurora pricks her finger and falls unconscious. She becomes Sleeping Beauty. In doing so (again, symbolically speaking) she chooses unconsciousness over the terror of adult life. Something existentially similar to this occurs very frequently with overprotected children, who can be brought low—and then desire the bliss of unconsciousness—by their first real contact with failure or, worse, genuine malevolence, which they do not or will not understand and against which they have no defence.

Take the case of the three-year-old who has not learned to share. She displays her selfish behaviour in the presence of her parents, but they're too nice to intervene. More truthfully, they refuse to pay attention, admit to what is happening, and teach her how to act properly. They're annoyed, of course, when she won't share with her sister, but they pretend everything is OK. It's not OK. They'll snap at her later, for something totally unrelated. She will be hurt by that, and confused, but learn nothing. Worse: when she tries to make friends, it won't go well, because of her lack of social sophistication. Children her own age will be put off by her inability to cooperate. They'll fight with her, or wander off and find someone else to play with. The parents of those children will observe her awkwardness and misbehaviour, and won't invite her back to play with their kids. She will be lonely and rejected. That will produce anxiety, depression and resentment. That will produce the turning from life that is equivalent to the wish for unconsciousness.

Parents who refuse to adopt the responsibility for disciplining their children think they can just opt out of the conflict necessary for proper child-rearing. They avoid being the bad guy (in the short term). But they do not at all rescue or protect their children from fear and pain. Quite the contrary: the judgmental and uncaring broader social world will mete out conflict and punishment far greater than that which would have been delivered by an awake parent. You can discipline your children, or you can turn that responsibility over to the harsh, uncaring judgmental world—and the motivation for the latter decision should never be confused with love.

You might object, as modern parents sometimes do: why should a child even *be* subject to the arbitrary dictates of a parent? In fact, there is a new variant of politically correct thinking that presumes that such an idea is "adultism:"[103] a form of prejudice and oppression analogous to, say, sexism or racism. The question of adult authority must be answered with care. That requires a thorough examination of the question itself. Accepting an objection as formulated is halfway to accepting its validity, and that can be dangerous if the question is ill-posed. Let's break it down.

First, why should a child be *subject*? That's easy. Every child must listen to and obey adults because he or she is dependent on the care that one or more imperfect grown-ups is willing to bestow. Given this, it is better for the child to act in a manner that invites genuine affection and goodwill. Something even better might be imagined. The child could act in a manner that simultaneously ensures optimal adult attention, in a manner that benefits his or her present state of being and future development. That's a very high standard, but it's in the best interests of the child, so there is every reason to aspire to it.

Every child should also be taught to comply gracefully with the expectations of civil society. This does not mean crushed into mindless ideological conformity. It means instead that parents must reward those attitudes and actions that will bring their child success in the world outside the family, and use threat and punishment when necessary to eliminate behaviours that will lead to misery and failure. There's a tight window of opportunity for this, as well, so getting it right quickly matters. If a child has not been taught to behave properly by the age of four, it will forever be difficult for him or her to make friends. The research literature is quite clear on this. This matters, because peers are the primary source of socialization after the age of four. Rejected children cease to develop, because they are alienated from their peers. They fall further and further behind, as the other children continue to progress. Thus, the friendless child too often becomes the lonely, antisocial or depressed teenager and adult. This is not good. Much more of our sanity than we commonly realize is a consequence of our fortunate immersion in a social community. We must be continually reminded to think and act properly. When we drift, people that care for and love us nudge us in small ways and large back on track. So, we better have some of those people around.

It's also not the case (back to the question) that adult dictates are all arbitrary. That's only true in a dysfunctional totalitarian state. But in civilized, open societies, the majority abide by a functional social contract, aimed at mutual betterment—or at least at existence in close proximity without too much violence. Even a system of rules that allows for only that minimum contract is by no means arbitrary, given the alternatives. If a society does not adequately reward productive, pro-social behavior, insists upon distributing resources in a markedly arbitrary and unfair manner, and allows for theft and exploitation, it will not remain conflict-free for long. If its hierarchies are based only (or even primarily) on power, instead of the competence necessary to get important and difficult things done, it will be prone to collapse, as well. This is even true, in simpler form, of the hierarchies of chimpanzees, which is an indication of its fundamental, biological and non-arbitrary emergent truth.[104]

Poorly socialized children have terrible lives. Thus, it is better to socialize them optimally. Some of this can be done with reward, but not all of it. The issue is therefore not whether to use punishment and threat. The issue is whether to do it consciously and thoughtfully. How, then, should children be disciplined? This is a very difficult question, because children (and parents) differ vastly in their temperaments. Some children are agreeable. They deeply want to please, but pay for that with a tendency to be conflict-averse and dependent. Others are tougher-minded and more independent. Those kids want to do what they want, when they want, all the time. They can be challenging, non-compliant and stubborn. Some children are desperate for rules and structure, and are content even in rigid environments. Others, with little regard for predictability and routine, are immune to demands for even minimal necessary order. Some are wildly imaginative and creative, and others more concrete and conservative. These are all deep, important differences, heavily influenced by biological factors and difficult to modify socially. It is fortunate indeed that in the face of such variability we are the beneficiaries of much thoughtful meditation on the proper use of social control.

Minimum Necessary Force

Here's a straightforward initial idea: rules should not be multiplied beyond necessity. Alternatively stated, bad laws drive out respect for good laws. This is the ethical—even legal—equivalent of Occam's razor, the scientist's conceptual guillotine, which states that the simplest possible hypothesis is preferable. So, don't encumber children—or their disciplinarians—with too many rules. That path leads to frustration.

Limit the rules. Then, figure out what to do when one of them gets broken. A general, context-independent rule for punishment severity is hard to establish. However, a helpful norm has already been enshrined in English common law, one of the great products of Western civilization. Its analysis can help us establish a second useful principle.

English common law allows you to defend your rights, but only in a reasonable manner. Someone breaks into your house. You have a loaded pistol. You have a right to defend yourself, but it's better to do it in stages. What if it's a drunk and confused neighbour? "Shoot 'em!" you think. But it's not that simple. So, you say, instead, "Stop! I have a gun." If that produces neither explanation nor retreat, you might consider a warning shot. Then, if the perpetrator still advances, you might take aim at his leg. (Don't mistake any of this for legal advice. It's an example.) A single brilliantly practical principle can be used to generate all these incrementally more severe reactions: that of minimum necessary force. So now we have two general principles of discipline. The first: limit the rules. The second: Use the least force necessary to enforce those rules.

About the first principle, you might ask, "Limit the rules to what, exactly?" Here are some suggestions. Do not bite, kick or hit, except in self-defence. Do not torture and bully other children, so you don't end up in jail. Eat in a civilized and thankful manner, so that people are happy to have you at their house, and pleased to feed you. Learn to share, so other kids will play with you. Pay attention when spoken to by adults, so they don't hate you and might therefore deign to teach you something. Go to sleep properly, and peaceably, so that your parents can have a private life and not resent your existence. Take care of your belongings, because you need to learn how and because you're lucky to have them. Be good company when something fun is happening, so that you're invited for the fun. Act so that other people are happy you're around, so that people will want you around. A child who knows these rules will be welcome everywhere.

About the second, equally important principle, your question might be: What is minimum necessary force? This must be established experimentally, starting with the smallest possible intervention. Some children will be turned to stone by a glare. A verbal command will stop another. A thumb-cocked flick of the index finger on a small hand might be necessary for some. Such a strategy is particularly useful in public places such as restaurants. It can be administered suddenly, quietly and effectively, without risking escalation. What's the alternative? A child who is crying angrily, demanding attention, is not making himself popular. A child who is running from table to table and disrupting everyone's peace is bringing disgrace (an old word, but a good one) on himself and his parents. Such outcomes are far from optimal, and children will definitely misbehave more in public, because they are experimenting: trying to establish if the same old rules also apply in the new place. They don't sort that out verbally, not when they are under three.

When our children were little and we took them to restaurants, they attracted smiles. They sat nicely and ate politely. They couldn't keep it up for long, but we didn't keep them there too long. When they started to get antsy, after sitting for forty-five minutes, we knew it was time to go. That was part of the deal. Nearby diners would tell us how nice it was to see a happy family. We weren't always happy, and our children weren't always properly behaved. But they were most of the time, and it was wonderful to see people responding so positively to their presence. It was truly good for the kids. They could see that people liked them. This also reinforced their good behaviour. That was the reward.

People will really like your kids if you give them the chance. This is something I learned as soon as we had our first baby, our daughter, Mikhaila. When we took her down the street in her little foldup stroller in our French Montreal working-class neighbourhood, rough-looking heavy-drinking lumberjack types would stop in their tracks and smile at her. They would coo and giggle and make stupid faces. Watching people respond to children restores your faith in human nature. All that's multiplied when your kids behave in public. To ensure that such things happen, you have to discipline your children carefully and effectively—and to do that, you have to know something about reward, and about punishment, instead of shying away from the knowledge.

Part of establishing a relationship with your son or daughter is learning how that small person responds to disciplinary intervention— and then intervening effectively. It's very easy to mouth clichés instead, such as: "There is no excuse for physical punishment," or, "Hitting children merely teaches them to hit." Let's start with the former claim: *there is no excuse for physical punishment.* First, we should note the widespread consensus around the idea that some forms of misbehavior, particularly those associated with theft and assault, are both wrong and should be subject to sanction. Second, we should note that almost all those sanctions involve punishment in its many psychological and more directly physical forms. Deprivation of liberty causes pain in a manner essentially similar to that of physical trauma. The same can be said of the use of social isolation (including time out). We know this neurobiologically. The same brain areas mediate response to all three, and all are ameliorated by the same class of drugs, opiates.[105] Jail is clearly physical punishment—particularly solitary confinement—even when nothing violent happens. Third, we should note that some misbegotten actions must be brought to a halt both effectively and immediately, not least so that something worse doesn't happen. What's the proper punishment for someone who will not stop poking a fork into an electrical socket? Or who runs away laughing in a crowded supermarket parking lot? The answer is simple: whatever will stop it fastest, within reason. Because the alternative could be fatal.

That's pretty obvious, in the case of parking lot or outlet. But the same thing applies in the social realm, and that brings us to the fourth point regarding excuses for physical punishment. The penalties for misbehavior (of the sort that could have been effectively halted in childhood) become increasingly severe as children get older—and it is disproportionately those who remain unsocialized effectively by age four who end up punished explicitly by society in their later youth and early adulthood. Those unconstrained four-year-olds, in turn, are often those who were unduly aggressive, by nature, at age two. They were statistically more likely than their peers to kick, hit, bite and take away toys (later known as stealing). They comprise about five per cent of boys, and a much smaller percentage of girls.[106] To unthinkingly parrot the magic line "There is no excuse for physical punishment" is also to foster the delusion that teenage devils magically emerge from once-innocent little child-angels. You're not doing your child any favors by overlooking any misbehavior (particularly if he or she is temperamentally more aggressive).

To hold the *no excuse for physical punishment* theory is also (fifth) to assume that the word *no* can be effectively uttered to another person in the absence of the threat of punishment. A woman can say *no* to a powerful, narcissistic man only because she has social norms, the law and the state backing her up. A parent can only say *no* to a child who wants a third piece of cake because he or she is larger, stronger and more capable than the child (and is additionally backed up in his authority by law and state). What *no* means, in the final analysis, is always "If you continue to do that, something you do not like will happen to you." Otherwise it means nothing. Or, worse, it means "another nonsensical nothing muttered by ignorable adults." Or, worse still, it means, "all adults are ineffectual and weak." This is a particularly bad lesson, when every child's destiny is to become an adult, and when most things that are learned without undue personal pain are modelled or explicitly taught by adults). What does a child who ignores adults and holds them in contempt have to look forward to? Why grow up at all? And that's the story of Peter Pan, who thinks all adults are variants of Captain Hook, tyrannical and terrified of his own mortality (think hungry crocodile with clock in his stomach). The only time *no* ever means *no* in the absence of violence is when it is uttered by one civilized person to another.

And what about the idea that *hitting a child merely teaches them to hit*? First: *No. Wrong.* Too simple. For starters, "hitting" is a very unsophisticated word to describe the disciplinary act of an effective parent. If "hitting" accurately described the entire range of physical force, then there would be no difference between rain droplets and atom bombs. Magnitude matters—and so does context, if we're not being wilfully blind and naïve about the issue. Every child knows the difference between being bitten by a mean, unprovoked dog and being nipped by his own pet when he tries playfully but too carelessly to take its bone. How hard someone is hit, and why they are hit, cannot merely be ignored when speaking of hitting. Timing, part of context, is also of crucial importance. If you flick your two-year-old with your finger just after he smacks the baby on the head with a wooden block, he will get the connection, and be at least somewhat less willing to smack her again in the future. That seems like a good outcome. He certainly won't conclude that he should hit her more, using the flick of his mother's finger as an example. He's not stupid. He's just jealous, impulsive and not very sophisticated. And how else are you going to protect his younger sibling? If you discipline ineffectively, then the baby will suffer. Maybe for years. The bullying will continue, because you won't do a damn thing to stop it. You'll avoid the conflict that's necessary to establish peace. You'll turn a blind eye. And then later, when the younger child confronts you (maybe even in adulthood), you'll say, "I never knew it was like that." You just didn't want to know. So, you didn't. You just rejected the responsibility of discipline, and justified it with a continual show of your niceness. Every gingerbread house has a witch inside it that devours children.

So where does all that leave us? With the decision to discipline effectively, or to discipline ineffectively (but never the decision to forego discipline altogether, because nature and society will punish in a draconian manner whatever errors of childhood behavior remain uncorrected). So here are a few practical hints: time out can be an extremely effective form of punishment, particularly if the misbehaving child is welcome as soon as he controls his temper. An angry child should sit by himself until he calms down. Then he should be allowed to return to normal life. That means the child wins—instead of his anger. The rule is "Come be with us as soon as you can behave properly." This is a very good deal for child, parent and society. You'll be able to tell if your child has really regained control. You'll like him again, despite his earlier misbehaviour. If you're still mad, maybe he hasn't completely repented—or maybe you should do something about your tendency to hold a grudge.

If your child is the kind of determined varmint who simply runs away, laughing, when placed on the steps or in his room, physical restraint might have to be added to the time out routine. A child can be held carefully but firmly by the upper arms, until he or she stops squirming and pays attention. If that fails, being turned over a parent's knee might be required. For the child who is pushing the limits in a spectacularly inspired way, a swat across the backside can indicate requisite seriousness on the part of a responsible adult. There are some situations in which even that will not suffice, partly because some children are very determined, exploratory, and tough, or because the offending behaviour is truly severe. And if you're not thinking such things through, then you're not acting responsibly as a parent. You're leaving the dirty work to someone else, who will be much dirtier doing it.

A Summary of Principles

Disciplinary principle 1: *limit the rules*. Principle 2: *use minimum necessary force*. Here's a third: *parents should come in pairs*.[107] Raising young children is demanding and exhausting. Because of this, it's easy for a parent to make a mistake. Insomnia, hunger, the aftermath of an argument, a hangover, a bad day at work—any of these things singly can make a person unreasonable, while in combination they can produce someone dangerous. Under such circumstances, it is necessary to have someone else around, to observe, and step in, and discuss. This will make it less likely that a whiny provocative child and her fed-up cranky parent will excite each other to the point of no return. Parents should come in pairs so the father of a newborn can watch the new mother so she won't get worn out and do something desperate after hearing her colicky baby wail from eleven in the evening until five in the morning for thirty nights in a row. I am not saying we should be mean to single mothers, many of whom struggle impossibly and courageously—and a proportion of whom have had to escape, singly, from a brutal relationship—but that doesn't mean we should pretend that all family forms are equally viable. They're not. Period.

Here's a fourth principle, one that is more particularly psychological: *parents should understand their own capacity to be harsh, vengeful, arrogant, resentful, angry and deceitful*. Very few people set out, consciously, to do a terrible job as father or mother, but bad parenting happens all the time. This is because people have a great capacity for evil, as well as good—and because they remain willfully blind to that fact. People are aggressive and selfish, as well as kind and thoughtful. For this reason, no adult human being—no hierarchical, predatory ape—can truly tolerate being dominated by an upstart child. Revenge will come. Ten minutes after a pair of all-too-nice-and-patient parents have failed to prevent a public tantrum at the local supermarket, they will pay their toddler back with the cold shoulder when he runs up, excited, to show mom and dad his newest accomplishment. Enough embarrassment, disobedience, and dominance challenge, and even the most hypothetically selfless parent will become resentful. And then the real punishment will begin. Resentment breeds the desire for vengeance. Fewer spontaneous offers of love will be offered, with more rationalizations for their absence. Fewer opportunities for the personal development of the child will be sought out. A subtle turning away will begin. And this is only the beginning of the road to total familial warfare, conducted mostly in the underworld, underneath the false façade of normality and love.

This frequently-travelled path is much better avoided. A parent who is seriously aware of his or her limited tolerance and capacity for misbehaviour when provoked can therefore seriously plan a proper disciplinary strategy—particularly if monitored by an equally awake partner—and never let things degenerate to the point where genuine hatred emerges. Beware. There are toxic families everywhere. They make no rules and limit no misbehaviour. The parents lash out randomly and unpredictably. The children live in that chaos and are crushed, if they're timid, or rebel, counterproductively, if they're tough. It's not good. It can get murderous.

Here's a fifth and final and most general principle. Parents have a duty to act as proxies for the real world—merciful proxies, caring proxies—but proxies, nonetheless. This obligation supersedes any responsibility to ensure happiness, foster creativity, or boost self-esteem. It is the primary duty of parents to make their children socially desirable. That will provide the child with opportunity, self-regard, and security. It's more important even than fostering individual identity. That Holy Grail can only be pursued, in any case, after a high degree of social sophistication has been established.

The Good Child—and the Responsible Parent

A properly socialized three-year-old is polite and engaging. She's also no pushover. She evokes interest from other children and appreciation from adults. She exists in a world where other kids welcome her and compete for her attention, and where adults are happy to see her, instead of hiding behind false smiles. She will be introduced to the world by people who are pleased to do so. This will do more for her eventual individuality than any cowardly parental attempt to avoid day-to-day conflict and discipline.

Discuss your likes and dislikes with regards to your children with your partner or, failing that, a friend. But do not be afraid to have likes and dislikes. You can judge suitable from unsuitable, and wheat from chaff. You realize the difference between good and evil. Having clarified your stance—having assessed yourself for pettiness, arrogance and resentment—you take the next step, and you make your children behave. You take responsibility for their discipline. You take responsibility for the mistakes you will inevitably make while disciplining. You can apologize, when you're wrong, and learn to do better.

You love your kids, after all. If their actions make you dislike them, think what an effect they will have on other people, who care much less about them than you. Those other people will punish them, severely, by omission or commission. Don't allow that to happen. Better to let your little monsters know what is desirable and what is not, so they become sophisticated denizens of the world outside the family.

A child who pays attention, instead of drifting, and can play, and does not whine, and is comical, but not annoying, and is trustworthy—that child will have friends wherever he goes. His teachers will like him, and so will his parents. If he attends politely to adults, he will be attended to, smiled at and happily instructed. He will thrive, in what can so easily be a cold, unforgiving and hostile world. Clear rules make for secure children and calm, rational parents. Clear principles of discipline and punishment balance mercy and justice so that social development and psychological maturity can be optimally promoted. Clear rules and proper discipline help the child, and the family, and society, establish, maintain and expand the order that is all that protects us from chaos and the terrors of the underworld, where everything is uncertain, anxiety-provoking, hopeless and depressing. There are no greater gifts that a committed and courageous parent can bestow.

Do not let your children do anything that makes you dislike them.

SET YOUR HOUSE IN PERFECT ORDER

BEFORE YOU CRITICIZE THE WORLD

A RELIGIOUS PROBLEM

IT DOES NOT SEEM REASONABLE to describe the young man who shot twenty children and six staff members at Sandy Hook Elementary School in Newtown, Connecticut, in 2012 as a religious person. This is equally true for the Colorado theatre gunman and the Columbine High School killers. But these murderous individuals had a problem with reality that existed at a religious depth. As one of the members of the Columbine duo wrote:[108]

> The human race isn't worth fighting for, only worth killing. Give the Earth back to the animals. They deserve it infinitely more than we do. Nothing means anything anymore.

People who think such things view Being itself as inequitable and harsh to the point of corruption, and *human* Being, in particular, as contemptible. They appoint themselves supreme adjudicators of reality and find it wanting. They are the ultimate critics. The deeply cynical writer continues:

> If you recall your history, the Nazis came up with a "final solution" to the Jewish problem. . . . Kill them all. Well, in case you haven't figured it out, I say "KILL MANKIND." No one should survive.

For such individuals, the world of experience is insufficient and evil—so to hell with everything!

What is happening when someone comes to think in this manner? A great German play, *Faust: A Tragedy*, written by Johann Wolfgang von Goethe, addresses that issue. The play's main character, a scholar named Heinrich Faust, trades his immortal soul to the devil, Mephistopheles. In return, he receives whatever he desires while still alive on Earth. In Goethe's play, Mephistopheles is the eternal adversary of Being. He has a central, defining credo:[109]

> *I am the spirit who negates*
> *and rightly so, for all that comes to be*
> *deserves to perish, wretchedly.*
> *It were better nothing would begin!*
> *Thus everything that your terms sin,*
> *destruction, evil represent—*
> *that is my proper element.*

Goethe considered this hateful sentiment so important—so key to the central element of vengeful human destructiveness—that he had Mephistopheles say it a second time, phrased somewhat differently, in Part II of the play, written many years later.[110]

People think often in the Mephistophelean manner, although they seldom act upon their thoughts as brutally as the mass murderers of school, college and theatre. Whenever we experience injustice, real or imagined; whenever we encounter tragedy or fall prey to the machinations of others; whenever we experience the horror and pain of our own apparently arbitrary limitations—the temptation to question

Being and then to curse it rises foully from the darkness. Why must innocent people suffer so terribly? What kind of bloody, horrible planet is this, anyway?

Life is in truth very hard. Everyone is destined for pain and slated for destruction. Sometimes suffering is clearly the result of a personal fault such as willful blindness, poor decision-making or malevolence. In such cases, when it appears to be self-inflicted, it may even seem just. People get what they deserve, you might contend. That's cold comfort, however, even when true. Sometimes, if those who are suffering changed their behaviour, then their lives would unfold less tragically. But human control is limited. Susceptibility to despair, disease, aging and death is universal. In the final analysis, we do not appear to be the architects of our own fragility. Whose fault is it, then?

People who are very ill (or, worse, who have a sick child) will inevitably find themselves asking this question, whether they are religious believers or not. The same is true of someone who finds his shirtsleeve caught in the gears of a giant bureaucracy—who is suffering through a tax audit, or fighting an interminable lawsuit or divorce. And it's not only the obviously suffering who are tormented by the need to blame someone or something for the intolerable state of their Being. At the height of his fame, influence and creative power, for example, the towering Leo Tolstoy himself began to question the value of human existence.[III] He reasoned in this way:

> My position was terrible. I knew that I could find nothing in the way of rational knowledge except a denial of life; and in faith I could find nothing except a denial of reason, and this was even more impossible than a denial of life. According to rational knowledge, it followed that life is evil, and people know it. They do not have to live, yet they have lived and they do live, just as I myself had lived, even though I had known for a long time that life is meaningless and evil.

Try as he might, Tolstoy could identify only four means of escaping from such thoughts. One was retreating into childlike ignorance of the problem. Another was pursuing mindless pleasure. The third was "continuing to drag out a life that is evil and meaningless, knowing beforehand that nothing can come of it." He identified that particular form of escape with weakness: "The people in this category know that death is better than life, but they do not have the strength to act rationally and quickly put an end to the delusion by killing themselves. . . ."

Only the fourth and final mode of escape involved "strength and energy. It consists of destroying life, once one has realized that life is evil and meaningless." Tolstoy relentlessly followed his thoughts:

> Only unusually strong and logically consistent people act in this manner. Having realized all the stupidity of the joke that is being played on us and seeing that the blessings of the dead are greater than those of the living and that it is better not to exist, they act and put an end to this stupid joke; and they use any means of doing it: a rope around the neck, water, a knife in the heart, a train.

Tolstoy wasn't pessimistic enough. The stupidity of the joke being played on us does not merely motivate suicide. It motivates murder—mass murder, often followed by suicide. That is a far more effective existential protest. By June of 2016, unbelievable as it may seem, there had been one thousand mass killings (defined as four or more people shot in a single incident, excluding the shooter) in the US in twelve hundred and sixty days.[112] That's one such event on five of every six days for more than three years. Everyone says, "We don't understand." How can we still pretend that? Tolstoy understood, more than a century ago. The ancient authors of the biblical story of Cain and Abel understood, as well, more than twenty centuries ago. They described murder as the first act of post-Edenic history: and not just murder, but fratricidal murder—murder not only of someone innocent but of someone ideal and good, and murder done consciously to spite the creator of the universe. Today's killers tell us the same thing, in their own words. Who would dare say that this is not the worm at the core of the apple? But we will not listen, because the truth cuts too close to the bone. Even for a mind as profound as that of the celebrated Russian author, there was no way out. How can the rest of us manage, when a man of Tolstoy's stature admits defeat? For years, he hid his guns from himself and would not walk with a rope in hand, in case he hanged himself.

How can a person who is awake avoid outrage at the world?

Vengeance or Transformation

A religious man might shake his fist in desperation at the apparent injustice and blindness of God. Even Christ Himself felt abandoned before the cross, or so the story goes. A more agnostic or atheistic individual might blame fate, or meditate bitterly on the brutality of chance. Another might tear himself apart, searching for the character flaws underlying his suffering and deterioration. These are all variations on a theme. The name of the target changes, but the underlying psychology remains constant. Why? Why is there so much suffering and cruelty?

Well, perhaps it really is God's doing—or the fault of blind, pointless fate, if you are inclined to think that way. And there appears to be every reason to think that way. But, what happens if you do? Mass murderers believe that the suffering attendant upon existence justifies judgment and revenge, as the Columbine boys so clearly indicated:[113]

> I will sooner die than betray my own thoughts. Before I leave this worthless place, I will kill who ever I deem unfit for anything, especially life. If you pissed me off in the past, you will die if I see you. You might be able to piss off others, and have it eventually all blow over, but not me. I don't forget people who wronged me.

One of the most vengeful murderers of the twentieth century, the terrible Carl Panzram, was raped, brutalized and betrayed in the Minnesota institution responsible for his "rehabilitation" when he was a delinquent juvenile. He emerged, enraged beyond measure, as burglar, arsonist, rapist and serial killer. He aimed consciously and consistently at destruction, even keeping track of the dollar value of the property he burned. He started by hating the individuals who had hurt him. His resentment grew, until his hatred encompassed all of mankind, and he didn't stop there. His destructiveness was aimed in some fundamental manner at God Himself. There is no other way of phrasing it. Panzram raped, murdered and burned to express his outrage at Being. He acted as if Someone was responsible. The same thing happens in the story of Cain and Abel. Cain's sacrifices are rejected. He exists in suffering. He calls out God and challenges the Being He created. God refuses his plea. He tells Cain that his trouble is self-induced. Cain, in his rage, kills Abel, God's favourite (and, truth be known, Cain's idol). Cain is jealous, of course, of his successful brother. But he destroys Abel primarily to spite God. This is the truest version of what happens when people take their vengeance to the ultimate extreme.

Panzram's response was (and this is what was so terrible) perfectly understandable. The details of his autobiography reveal that he was one of Tolstoy's strong and logically consistent people. He was a powerful, consistent, fearless actor. He had the courage of his convictions. How could someone like him be expected to forgive and forget, given what had happened to him? Truly terrible things happen to people. It's no wonder they're out for revenge. Under such conditions, vengeance seems a moral necessity. How can it be distinguished from the demand for justice? After the experience of terrible atrocity, isn't forgiveness just cowardice, or lack of willpower? Such questions torment me. But people emerge from terrible pasts to do good, and not evil, although such an accomplishment can seem superhuman.

I have met people who managed to do it. I know a man, a great artist, who emerged from just such a "school" as the one described by Panzram—only this man was thrown into it as an innocent five-year-old, fresh from a long stretch in a hospital, where he had suffered measles, mumps and chicken pox, simultaneously. Incapable of speaking the language of the school, deliberately isolated from his family, abused, starved and otherwise tormented, he emerged an angry, broken young man. He hurt himself badly in the aftermath with drugs and alcohol and other forms of self-destructive behaviour. He detested everyone—God, himself and blind fate included. But he put an end to all of that. He stopped drinking. He stopped hating (although it still emerges in flashes). He revitalized the artistic culture of his Native tradition, and trained young men to continue in his footsteps. He produced a fifty-foot totem pole memorializing the events of his life, and a canoe, forty feet long, from a single log, of a kind rarely if ever produced now. He brought his family together, and held a great pot-latch, with sixteen hours of dancing and hundreds of people in attendance, to express his grief, and make peace with the past. He decided to be a good person, and then did the impossible things required to live that way.

I had a client who did not have good parents. Her mother died when she was very young. Her grandmother, who raised her, was a harridan, bitter and over-concerned with appearances. She mistreated her granddaughter, punishing her for her virtues: creativity, sensitivity, intelligence—unable to resist acting out her resentment for an admittedly hard life on her granddaughter. She had a better relationship with her father, but he was an addict who died, badly, while she cared for him. My client had a son. She perpetuated none of this with him. He grew up truthful, and independent, and hard-working, and smart. Instead of widening the tear in the cultural fabric she inherited, and transmitting it, she sewed it up. She rejected the sins of her forefathers. Such things can be done.

> Distress, whether psychic, physical, or intellectual, need not at all produce nihilism (that is, the radical rejection of value, meaning and desirability). Such distress always permits a variety of interpretations.

Nietzsche wrote those words.[114] What he meant was this: people who experience evil may certainly desire to perpetuate it, to pay it forward. But it is also possible to learn good by experiencing evil. A bullied boy can mimic his tormentors. But he can also learn from his own abuse that it is wrong to push people around and make their lives miserable. Someone tormented by her mother can learn from her terrible experiences how important it is to be a good parent. Many, perhaps even most, of the adults who abuse children were abused themselves as children. However, the majority of people who were abused as children do not abuse their own children. This is a well-established fact, which can be demonstrated, simply, arithmetically, in this way: if one parent abused three children, and each of those children had three children, and so on, then there would be three abusers the first generation, nine the second, twenty-seven the third, eighty-one the fourth—and so on exponentially. After twenty generations, more than ten billion would have suffered childhood abuse: more people than currently inhabit the planet. But instead, abuse disappears across generations. People constrain its spread. That's a testament to the genuine dominance of good over evil in the human heart.

The desire for vengeance, however justified, also bars the way to other productive thoughts. The American/English poet T. S. Eliot explained why, in his play, *The Cocktail Party*. One of his characters is not having a good time of it. She speaks of her profound unhappiness to a psychiatrist. She says she hopes that all her suffering is her own fault. The psychiatrist is taken aback. He asks why. She has thought long and hard about this, she says, and has come to the following conclusion: if it's her fault, she might be able to do something about it. If it's God's fault, however—if reality itself is flawed, hell-bent on ensuring her misery—then she is doomed. She couldn't change the structure of reality itself. But maybe she could change her own life.

Aleksandr Solzhenitsyn had every reason to question the structure of existence when he was imprisoned in a Soviet labour camp, in the middle of the terrible twentieth century. He had served as a soldier on the ill-prepared Russian front lines in the face of a Nazi invasion. He had been arrested, beaten and thrown into prison by his own people. Then he was struck by cancer. He could have become resentful and bitter. His life had been rendered miserable by both Stalin and Hitler, two of the worst tyrants in history. He lived in brutal conditions. Vast stretches of his precious time were stolen from him and squandered. He witnessed the pointless and degrading suffering and death of his friends and acquaintances. Then he contracted an extremely serious disease. Solzhenitsyn had cause to curse God. Job himself barely had it as hard.

But the great writer, the profound, spirited defender of truth, did not allow his mind to turn towards vengeance and destruction. He opened his eyes, instead. During his many trials, Solzhenitsyn encountered people who comported themselves nobly, under horrific circumstances. He contemplated their behaviour deeply. Then he asked himself the most difficult of questions: had he personally contributed to the catastrophe of his life? If so, how? He remembered his unquestioning support of the Communist Party in his early years. He reconsidered his whole life. He had plenty of time in the camps. How had he missed the mark, in the past? How many times had he acted against his own conscience, engaging in actions that he knew to be wrong? How many times had he betrayed himself, and lied? Was there any way that the sins of his past could be rectified, atoned for, in the muddy hell of a Soviet gulag?

Solzhenitsyn pored over the details of his life, with a fine-toothed comb. He asked himself a second question, and a third. Can I stop making such mistakes, now? Can I repair the damage done by my past failures, now? He learned to watch and to listen. He found people he admired; who were honest, despite everything. He took himself apart, piece by piece, let what was unnecessary and harmful die, and resurrected himself. Then he wrote *The Gulag Archipelago*, a history of the Soviet prison camp system.[115] It's a forceful, terrible book, written with the overwhelming moral force of unvarnished truth. Its sheer outrage screamed unbearably across hundreds of pages. Banned (and for good reason) in the USSR, it was smuggled to the West in the 1970s, and burst upon the world. Solzhenitsyn's writing utterly and finally demolished the intellectual credibility of communism, as ideology or society. He took an axe to the trunk of the tree whose bitter fruits had nourished him so poorly—and whose planting he had witnessed and supported.

One man's decision to change his life, instead of cursing fate, shook the whole pathological system of communist tyranny to its core. It crumbled entirely, not so many years later, and Solzhenitsyn's courage was not the least of the reasons why. He was not the only such person to perform such a miracle. Václav Havel, the persecuted writer who later, impossibly, became the president of Czechoslovakia, then of the new Czech Republic, comes to mind, as does Mahatma Gandhi.

Things Fall Apart

Whole peoples have adamantly refused to judge reality, to criticize Being, to blame God. It's interesting to consider the Old Testament Hebrews in this regard. Their travails followed a consistent pattern. The stories of Adam and Eve and Cain and Abel and Noah and the Tower of Babel are truly ancient. Their origins vanish into the mysteries of time. It's not until after the flood story in Genesis that something like history, as we understand it, truly starts. It starts with Abraham. Abraham's descendants become the Hebrew people of the Old Testament, also known as the Hebrew Bible. They enter a covenant with Yahweh—with God—and begin their recognizably historical adventures.

Under the leadership of a great man, the Hebrews organize themselves into a society, and then an empire. As their fortunes rise, success breeds pride and arrogance. Corruption raises its ugly head. The increasingly hubristic state becomes obsessed with power, begins to forget its duty to the widows and orphans, and deviates from its age-old agreement with God. A prophet arises. He brazenly and publicly reviles the authoritarian king and faithless country for their failures before God—an act of blind courage—telling them of the terrible judgment to come. When his wise words are not completely ignored, they are heeded too late. God smites his wayward people, dooming them to abject defeat in battle and generations of subjugation. The Hebrews repent, at length, blaming their misfortune on their own failure to adhere to God's word. They insist to themselves that they could have done better. They rebuild their state, and the cycle begins again.

This is life. We build structures to live in. We build families, and states, and countries. We abstract the principles upon which those structures are founded and formulate systems of belief. At first we inhabit those structures and beliefs like Adam and Eve in Paradise. But success makes us complacent. We forget to pay attention. We take what we have for granted. We turn a blind eye. We fail to notice that things are changing, or that corruption is taking root. And everything falls apart. Is that the fault of reality—of God? Or do things fall apart because we have not paid sufficient attention?

When the hurricane hit New Orleans, and the town sank under the waves, was that a natural disaster? The Dutch prepare their dikes for the worst storm in ten thousand years. Had New Orleans followed that example, no tragedy would have occurred. It's not that no one knew. The Flood Control Act of 1965 mandated improvements in the levee system that held back Lake Pontchartrain. The system was to be completed by 1978. Forty years later, only 60 percent of the work had been done. Willful blindness and corruption took the city down.

A hurricane is an act of God. But failure to prepare, when the necessity for preparation is well known—that's sin. That's failure to hit the mark. And the wages of sin is death (Romans 6:23). The ancient Jews always blamed themselves when things fell apart. They acted as if God's goodness—the goodness of reality—was axiomatic, and took responsibility for their own failure. That's insanely responsible. But the alternative is to judge reality as insufficient, to criticize Being itself, and to sink into resentment and the desire for revenge.

If you are suffering—well, that's the norm. People are limited and life is tragic. If your suffering is unbearable, however, and you are starting to become corrupted, here's something to think about.

Clean Up Your Life

Consider your circumstances. Start small. Have you taken full advantage of the opportunities offered to you? Are you working hard on your career, or even your job, or are you letting bitterness and resentment hold you back and drag you down? Have you made peace with your brother? Are you treating your spouse and your children with dignity and respect? Do you have habits that are destroying your health and well-being? Are you truly shouldering your responsibilities? Have you said what you need to say to your friends and family members? Are there things that you could do, that you know you could do, that would make things around you better?

Have you cleaned up your life?

If the answer is no, here's something to try: *Start to stop doing what you know to be wrong.* Start stopping today. Don't waste time questioning how you know that what you're doing is wrong, if you are certain that it is. Inopportune questioning can confuse, without enlightening, as well as deflecting you from action. You can know that something is wrong or right without knowing why. Your entire Being can tell you something that you can neither explain nor articulate. Every person is too complex to know themselves completely, and we all contain wisdom that we cannot comprehend.

So, simply stop, when you apprehend, however dimly, that you should stop. Stop acting in that particular, despicable manner. Stop saying those things that make you weak and ashamed. Say only those things that make you strong. Do only those things that you could speak of with honour.

You can use your own standards of judgment. You can rely on yourself for guidance. You don't have to adhere to some external, arbitrary code of behaviour (although you should not overlook the guidelines of your culture. Life is short, and you don't have time to figure everything out on your own. The wisdom of the past was hard-earned, and your dead ancestors may have something useful to tell you).

Don't blame capitalism, the radical left, or the iniquity of your enemies. Don't reorganize the state until you have ordered your own experience. Have some humility. If you cannot bring peace to your household, how dare you try to rule a city? Let your own soul guide you. Watch what happens over the days and weeks. When you are at work you will begin to say what you really think. You will start to tell your wife, or your husband, or your children, or your parents, what you really want and need. When you know that you have left something undone, you will act to correct the omission. Your head will start to clear up, as you stop filling it with lies. Your experience will improve, as you stop distorting it with inauthentic actions. You will then begin to discover new, more subtle things that you are doing wrong. Stop doing those, too. After some months and years of diligent effort, your life will become simpler and less complicated. Your judgment will improve. You will untangle your past. You will become stronger and less bitter. You will move more confidently into the future. You will stop making your life unnecessarily difficult. You will then be left with the inevitable bare tragedies of life, but they will no longer be compounded with bitterness and deceit.

Perhaps you will discover that your now less-corrupted soul, much stronger than it might otherwise have been, is now able to bear those remaining, necessary, minimal, inescapable tragedies. Perhaps you will even learn to encounter them so that they stay tragic—merely tragic—instead of degenerating into outright hellishness. Maybe your anxiety, and hopelessness, and resentment, and anger—however murderous, initially—will recede. Perhaps your uncorrupted soul will then see its existence as a genuine good, as something to celebrate, even in the face of your own vulnerability. Perhaps you will become an ever-more-powerful force for peace and whatever is good.

Perhaps you will then see that if all people did this, in their own lives, the world might stop being an evil place. After that, with continued effort, perhaps it could even stop being a tragic place. Who knows what existence might be like if we all decided to strive for the best? Who knows what eternal heavens might be established by our spirits, purified by truth, aiming skyward, right here on the fallen Earth?

Set your house in perfect order before you criticize the world.

RULE 7

PURSUE WHAT IS MEANINGFUL

(NOT WHAT IS EXPEDIENT)

GET WHILE THE GETTING'S GOOD

LIFE IS SUFFERING. THAT'S CLEAR. There is no more basic, irrefutable truth. It's basically what God tells Adam and Eve, immediately before he kicks them out of Paradise.

> Unto the woman he said, I will greatly multiply thy sorrow and thy conception; in sorrow thou shalt bring forth children; and thy desire shall be to thy husband, and he shall rule over thee.
>
> And unto Adam he said, Because thou hast hearkened unto the voice of thy wife, and hast eaten of the tree, of which I commanded thee, saying, Thou shalt not eat of it: cursed is the ground for thy sake; in sorrow shalt thou eat of it all the days of thy life;
>
> Thorns also and thistles shall it bring forth to thee; and thou shalt eat the herb of the field;
>
> By the sweat of your brow you will eat your food until you return to the ground, since from it you were taken; for dust you are and to dust you will return. (Genesis 3:16-19. KJV)

What in the world should be done about that?

The simplest, most obvious, and most direct answer? Pursue pleasure. Follow your impulses. Live for the moment. Do what's expedient. Lie, cheat, steal, deceive, manipulate—but don't get caught. In an ultimately meaningless universe, what possible difference could it make? And this is by no means a new idea. The fact of life's tragedy and the suffering that is part of it has been used to justify the pursuit of immediate selfish gratification for a very long time.

> Short and sorrowful is our life, and there is no remedy when a man comes to his end, and no one has been known to return from Hades.
>
> Because we were born by mere chance, and hereafter we shall be as though we had never been; because the breath in our nostrils is smoke, and reason is a spark kindled by the beating of our hearts.
>
> When it is extinguished, the body will turn to ashes, and the spirit will dissolve like empty air. Our name will be forgotten in time and no one will remember our works; our life will pass away like the traces of a cloud, and be scattered like mist that is chased by the rays of the sun and overcome by its heat.
>
> For our allotted time is the passing of a shadow, and there is no return from our death, because it is sealed up and no one turns back.
>
> Come, therefore, let us enjoy the good things that exist, and make use of the creation to the full as in youth.
>
> Let us take our fill of costly wine and perfumes, and let no flower of spring pass by us.
>
> Let us crown ourselves with rosebuds before they wither.
>
> Let none of us fail to share in our revelry, everywhere let us leave signs of enjoyment, because this is our portion, and this our lot.
>
> Let us oppress the righteous poor man; let us not spare the widow nor regard the gray hairs of the aged.
>
> But let our might be our law of right, for what is weak proves itself to be useless. (Wisdom 2:1-11, RSV).

The pleasure of expediency may be fleeting, but it's pleasure, none-theless, and that's something to stack up against the terror and pain of existence. Every man for himself, and the devil take the hindmost, as the old proverb has it. Why not simply take everything you can get, whenever the opportunity arises? Why not determine to live in that manner?

Or is there an alternative, more powerful and more compelling?

Our ancestors worked out very sophisticated answers to such questions, but we still don't understand them very well. This is because they are in large part still implicit—manifest primarily in ritual and myth and, as of yet, incompletely articulated. We act them out and represent them in stories, but we're not yet wise enough to formulate them explicitly. We're still chimps in a troupe, or wolves in a pack. We know how to behave. We know who's who, and why. We've learned that through experience. Our knowledge has been shaped by our interaction with others. We've established predictable routines and patterns of behavior—but we don't really understand them, or know where they originated. They've evolved over great expanses of time. No one was formulating them explicitly (at least not in the dimmest reaches of the past), even though we've been telling each other how to act forever. One day, however, not so long ago, we woke up. We were already doing, but we started *noticing* what we were doing. We started using our bodies as devices to represent their own actions. We started imitating and dramatizing. We invented ritual. We started acting out our own experiences. Then we started to tell stories. We coded our observations of our own drama in these stories. In this manner, the information that was first only embedded in our behaviour became represented in our stories. But we didn't and still don't understand what it all means.

The Biblical narrative of Paradise and the Fall is one such story, fabricated by our collective imagination, working over the centuries. It provides a profound account of the nature of Being, and points the way to a mode of conceptualization and action well-matched to that nature. In the Garden of Eden, prior to the dawn of self-consciousness—so goes the story—human beings were sinless. Our primordial parents, Adam and Eve, walked with God. Then, tempted by the snake, the first couple ate from the tree of the knowledge of good and evil, discovered

Death and vulnerability, and turned away from God. Mankind was exiled from Paradise, and began its effortful mortal existence. The idea of sacrifice enters soon afterward, beginning with the account of Cain and Abel, and developing through the Abrahamic adventures and the Exodus: After much contemplation, struggling humanity learns that God's favour could be gained, and his wrath averted, through proper sacrifice—and, also, that bloody murder might be motivated among those unwilling or unable to succeed in this manner.

The Delay of Gratification

When engaging in sacrifice, our forefathers began to act out what would be considered a proposition, if it were stated in words: *that something better might be attained in the future by giving up something of value in the present.* Recall, if you will, that the necessity for work is one of the curses placed by God upon Adam and his descendants in consequence of Original Sin. Adam's waking to the fundamental constraints of his Being—his vulnerability, his eventual death—is equivalent to his discovery of the future. The future: that's where you go to die (hopefully, not too soon). Your demise might be staved off through work; through the sacrifice of the *now* to gain benefit *later*. It is for this reason—among others, no doubt—that the concept of sacrifice is introduced in the Biblical chapter immediately following the drama of the Fall. There is little difference between sacrifice and work. They are also both uniquely human. Sometimes, animals act as if they are working, but they are really only following the dictates of their nature. Beavers build dams. They do so because they are beavers, and beavers build dams. They don't think, "Yeah, but I'd rather be on a beach in Mexico with my girlfriend," while they're doing it.

Prosaically, such sacrifice—work—is delay of gratification, but that's a very mundane phrase to describe something of such profound significance. The discovery that gratification could be delayed was simultaneously the discovery of time and, with it, causality (at least the causal force of voluntary human action). Long ago, in the dim mists of time, *we began to realize that reality was structured as if it could be bargained with.* We learned that behaving properly now, in the present—regulating our impulses, considering the plight of others—could bring rewards in the future, in a time and place that did not yet exist. We began to inhibit, control and organize our immediate impulses, so that we could stop interfering with other people and our future selves. Doing so was indistinguishable from organizing society: the discovery of the causal relationship between our efforts today and the quality of tomorrow motivated the social contract—the organization that enables today's work to be stored, reliably (mostly in the form of promises from others).

Understanding is often acted out before it can be articulated (just as a child acts out what it means to be "mother" or "father" before being able to give a spoken account of what those roles mean).[116] The act of making a ritual sacrifice to God was an early and sophisticated enactment of the idea of the usefulness of delay. There is a long conceptual journey between merely feasting hungrily and learning to set aside some extra meat, smoked by the fire, for the end of the day, or for someone who isn't present. It takes a long time to learn to keep anything later for yourself, or to share it with someone else (and those are very much the same thing as, in the former case, you are sharing with your future self). It is much easier and far more likely to selfishly and immediately wolf down everything in sight. There are similar long journeys between every leap in sophistication with regard to delay and its conceptualization: short-term sharing, storing away for the future, representation of that storage in the form of records and, later, in the form of currency—and, ultimately, the saving of money in a bank or other social institution. Some conceptualizations had to serve as intermediaries, or the full range of our practices and ideas surrounding sacrifice and work and their representation could have never emerged.

Our ancestors acted out a drama, a fiction: they personified the force that governs fate as a spirit that can be bargained with, traded with, as if it were another human being. And the amazing thing is *that it worked*. This was in part because the future is largely composed of other human beings—often precisely those who have watched and evaluated and appraised the tiniest details of your past behavior. It's not very far from that to God, sitting above on high, tracking your every move and writing it down for further reference in a big book. Here's a productive symbolic idea: *the future is a judgmental father.* That's a good start. But two additional, archetypal, foundational questions arose, because of the discovery of sacrifice, of work. Both have to do with the ultimate extension of the logic of work—which is *sacrifice now, to gain later.*

First question. What must be sacrificed? Small sacrifices may be sufficient to solve small, singular problems. But it is possible that larger, more comprehensive sacrifices might solve an array of large and complex problems, all at the same time. That's harder, but it might be better. Adapting to the necessary discipline of medical school will, for example, fatally interfere with the licentious lifestyle of a hardcore undergraduate party animal. Giving that up is a sacrifice. But a physician can—to paraphrase George W.—really put food on his family. That's a lot of trouble dispensed with, over a very long period of time. So, sacrifices are necessary, to improve the future, and larger sacrifices can be better.

Second question (set of related questions, really): We've already established the basic principle—*sacrifice will improve the future.* But a principle, once established, has to be fleshed out. Its full extension or significance has to be understood. What is implied by the idea that sacrifice will improve the future, in the most extreme and final of cases? Where does that basic principle find its limits? We must ask, to begin, "What would be the largest, most effective—most pleasing—of all possible sacrifices?" and then "How good might the best possible future be, if the most effective sacrifice could be made?"

The biblical story of Cain and Abel, Adam and Eve's sons, immediately follows the story of the expulsion from Paradise, as mentioned previously. Cain and Abel are really the first humans, since their parents were made directly by God, and not born in the standard manner. Cain and Abel live *in history*, not in Eden. They must work. They must make sacrifices, to please God, and they do so, with altar and proper ritual. But things get complicated. Abel's offerings please God, but

Cain's do not. Abel is rewarded, many times over, but Cain is not. It's not precisely clear why (although the text strongly hints that Cain's heart is just not in it). Maybe the quality of what Cain put forward was low. Maybe his spirit was begrudging. Or maybe God was vexed, for some secret reasons of His own. And all of this is realistic, including the text's vagueness of explanation. Not all sacrifices are of equal quality. Furthermore, it often appears that sacrifices of apparently high quality are not rewarded with a better future—and it's not clear why. Why isn't God happy? What would have to change to make Him so? Those are difficult questions—and everyone asks them, all the time, even if they don't notice.

Asking such questions is indistinguishable from thinking.

The realization that pleasure could be usefully forestalled dawned on us with great difficulty. It runs absolutely contrary to our ancient, fundamental animal instincts, which demand immediate satisfaction (particularly under conditions of deprivation, which are both inevitable and commonplace). And, to complicate the matter, such delay only becomes useful when civilization has stabilized itself enough to guarantee the existence of the delayed reward, in the future. If everything you save will be destroyed or, worse, stolen, there is no point in saving. It is for this reason that a wolf will down twenty pounds of raw meat in a single meal. He isn't thinking, "Man, I hate it when I binge. I should save some of this for next week." So how was it that those two impossible and necessarily simultaneous accomplishments (delay and the stabilization of society into the future) could possibly have manifested themselves?

Here is a developmental progression, from animal to human. It's wrong, no doubt, in the details. But it's sufficiently correct, for our purposes, in theme: First, there is excess food. Large carcasses, mammoths or other massive herbivores, might provide that. (We ate a lot of mammoths. Maybe all of them.) After a kill, with a large animal, there is some left for later. That's accidental, at first—but, eventually, the utility of "for later" starts to be appreciated. Some provisional notion of sacrifice develops at the same time: "If I leave some, even if I want it now, I won't have to be hungry later." That provisional notion develops, to the next level ("If I leave some for later, I won't have to go hungry, and neither will those I care for") and then to the next ("I can't possibly eat all of this mammoth, but I can't store the rest for too long, either. Maybe I should feed some to other people. Maybe they'll remember, and feed me some of their mammoth, when they have some and I have none. Then I'll get some mammoth now, *and* some mammoth later. That's a good deal. And maybe those I'm sharing with will come to trust me, more generally. Maybe then we could trade forever"). In such a manner, "mammoth" becomes "future mammoth," and "future mammoth" becomes "personal reputation." That's the emergence of the social contract.

To share does not mean to give away something you value, and get nothing back. That is instead only what every child who refuses to share fears it means. To share means, properly, to initiate the process of trade. A child who can't share—who can't trade—can't have any friends, because having friends is a form of trade. Benjamin Franklin once suggested that a newcomer to a neighbourhood ask a new neighbour to do him or her a favour, citing an old maxim: *He that has once done you a kindness will be more ready to do you another than he whom you yourself have obliged.*[117] In Franklin's opinion, asking someone for something (not too extreme, obviously) was the most useful and immediate invitation to social interaction. Such asking on the part of the newcomer provided the neighbour with an opportunity to show him- or herself as a good person, at first encounter. It also meant that the latter could now ask the former for a favour, in return, because of the debt incurred, increasing their mutual familiarity and trust. In that manner both parties could overcome their natural hesitancy and mutual fear of the stranger.

It is better to have something than nothing. It's better yet to share generously the something you have. It's even better than that, however, to become widely known for generous sharing. That's something that lasts. That's something that's reliable. And, at this point of abstraction, we can observe how the groundwork for the conceptions *reliable*, *honest* and *generous* has been laid. The basis for an articulated morality has been put in place. The productive, truthful sharer is the prototype for the good citizen, and the good man. We can see in this manner how from the simple notion that "leftovers are a good idea" the highest moral principles might emerge.

It's as if something like the following happened as humanity developed. First were the endless tens or hundreds of thousands of years prior to the emergence of written history and drama. During this time, the twin practices of delay and exchange begin to emerge, slowly and painfully. Then they become represented, in metaphorical abstraction, as rituals and tales of sacrifice, told in a manner such as this: "It's *as if* there is a powerful Figure in the Sky, who sees all, and is judging you. Giving up something you value seems to make Him happy—and you want to make Him happy, because all Hell breaks loose if you don't. So, practise sacrificing, and sharing, until you become expert at it, and things will go well for you."* No one said any of this, at least not so plainly and directly. But it was implicit in the practice and then in the stories.

Action came first (as it had to, as the animals we once were could act but could not think). *Implicit, unrecognized value came first* (as the actions that preceded thought embodied value, but did not make that value explicit). People watched the successful succeed and the unsuccessful fail for thousands and thousands of years. We thought it over, and drew a conclusion: *The successful among us delay gratification. The successful among us bargain with the future.* A great idea begins to emerge, taking ever-more-clearly-articulated form, in ever more-clearly-articulated stories: What's the difference between the successful and the unsuccessful? *The successful sacrifice.* Things get better, as the successful practise their sacrifices. The questions become increasingly precise and, simultaneously, broader: What is the greatest possible sacrifice? For the greatest possible good? And the answers become increasingly deeper and profound.

The God of Western tradition, like so many gods, requires sacrifice. We have already examined why. But sometimes He goes even

---

* And this is all true, note, whether there is—or is not—*actually* such a powerful figure, "in the sky" :)

further. He demands not only sacrifice, but the sacrifice of precisely what is loved best. This is most starkly portrayed (and most confusingly evident) in the story of Abraham and Isaac. Abraham, beloved of God, long wanted a son—and God promised him exactly that, after many delays, and under the apparently impossible conditions of old age and a long-barren wife. But not so long afterward, when the miraculously-borne Isaac is still a child, God turns around and in unreasonable and apparently barbaric fashion demands that His faithful servant offer his son as a sacrifice. The story ends happily: God sends an angel to stay Abraham's obedient hand and accepts a ram in Isaac's stead. That's a good thing, but it doesn't really address the issue at hand: Why is God's going further necessary? Why does He—why does life—impose such demands?

We'll start our analysis with a truism, stark, self-evident and under-stated: *Sometimes things do not go well*. That seems to have much to do with the terrible nature of the world, with its plagues and famines and tyrannies and betrayals. But here's the rub: *sometimes, when things are not going well, it's not the world that's the cause. The cause is instead that which is currently most valued, subjectively and personally.* Why? Because the world is revealed, to an indeterminate degree, through the template of your values (much more on this in Rule 10). If the world you are seeing is not the world you want, therefore, it's time to examine your values. It's time to rid yourself of your current presuppositions. It's time to let go. It might even be time to sacrifice what you love best, so that you can become who you might become, instead of staying who you are.

There's an old and possibly apocryphal story about how to catch a monkey that illustrates this set of ideas very well. First, you must find a large, narrow-necked jar, just barely wide enough in diameter at the top for a monkey to put its hand inside. Then you must fill the jar part way with rocks, so it is too heavy for a monkey to carry. Then you must scatter some treats, attractive to monkeys, near the jar, to attract one, and put some more inside the jar. A monkey will come along, reach into the narrow opening, and grab while the grabbing's good. But now he won't be able to extract his fist, now full of treats, from the too-narrow opening of the jar. Not without unclenching his hand. Not without relinquishing what he already has. And that's just what he won't do. The monkey-catcher can just walk over to the jar and pick up the monkey. The animal will not sacrifice the part to preserve the whole.

Something valuable, given up, ensures future prosperity. Something valuable, sacrificed, pleases the Lord. What is most valuable, and best sacrificed?—or, what is at least *emblematic of that*? A choice cut of meat. The best animal in a flock. A most valued possession. What's above even that? Something intensely personal and painful to give up. That's symbolized, perhaps, in God's insistence on circumcision as part of Abraham's sacrificial routine, where the part is offered, symbolically, to redeem the whole. What's beyond that? What pertains more closely to the whole person, rather than the part? What constitutes the ultimate sacrifice—for the gain of the ultimate prize?

It's a close race between child and self. The sacrifice of the mother, offering her child to the world, is exemplified profoundly by Michelangelo's great sculpture, the *Pietà*, illustrated at the beginning of this chapter. Michelangelo crafted Mary contemplating her Son, crucified and ruined. It's *her fault*. It was through her that He entered the world and its great drama of Being. *Is it right to bring a baby into this terrible world?* Every woman asks herself that question. Some say no, and they have their reasons. Mary answers yes, voluntarily, knowing full well what's to come—as do all mothers, if they allow themselves to see. It's an act of supreme courage, when undertaken voluntarily.

In turn, Mary's son, Christ, offers Himself to God and the world, to betrayal, torture and death—to the very point of despair on the cross, where he cries out those terrible words: *my God, my God, why hast thou forsaken me?* (Matthew 27:46). That is the archetypal story of the man who gives his all for the sake of the better—who offers up his life for the advancement of Being—who allows God's will to become manifest fully within the confines of a single, mortal life. That is the model for the honourable man. In Christ's case, however—as He sacrifices Himself—God, His Father, is simultaneously sacrificing *His* son. It is for this reason that the Christian sacrificial drama of Son and Self is archetypal. It's a story at the limit, where nothing more extreme—nothing greater—can be imagined. That's the very definition of "archetypal." That's the core of what constitutes "religious."

Pain and suffering define the world. Of that, there can be no doubt. Sacrifice can hold pain and suffering in abeyance, to a greater or lesser degree—and greater sacrifices can do that more effectively than lesser. Of that, there can be no doubt. Everyone holds this knowledge in their soul. Thus, the person who wishes to alleviate suffering—who wishes to rectify the flaws in Being; who wants to bring about the best of all possible futures; who wants to create Heaven on Earth—will make the greatest of sacrifices, of self and child, of everything that is loved, to live a life aimed at the Good. He will forego expediency. He will pursue the path of ultimate meaning. And he will in that manner bring salvation to the ever-desperate world.

But is such a thing even possible? Is this simply not asking too much of the individual? It's all well and good for Christ, it might be objected—but He was the veritable Son of God. But we do have other examples, some much less mythologized and archetypal. Consider, for example, the case of Socrates, the ancient Greek philosopher. After a lifetime of seeking the truth and educating his countrymen, Socrates faced a trial for crimes against the city-state of Athens, his hometown. His accusers provided him with plenty of opportunity to simply leave, and avoid the trouble.[118] But the great sage had already considered and rejected this course of action. His companion Hermogenes observed him at this time discussing "any and every subject"[119] other than his trial, and asked him why he appeared so unconcerned. Socrates first answered that he had been preparing his whole life to defend himself,[120] but then said something more mysterious and significant: When he attempted specifically to consider strategies that would produce acquittal "by fair means or foul"[121]—or even when merely considering his potential actions at the trial[122]—he found himself interrupted by his divine sign: his internal spirit, voice or *daemon*. Socrates discussed this voice at the trial itself.[123] He said that one of the factors distinguishing him from other men[124] was his absolute willingness to listen to its warnings—to *stop speaking* and *cease acting* when it objected. The Gods themselves had deemed him wise above other men, not least for this reason, according to the Delphic Oracle herself, held to be a reliable judge of such things.[125]

Because his ever-reliable internal voice objected to fleeing (or even to defending himself) Socrates radically altered his view of the significance of his trial. He began to consider that it might be a blessing, rather than a curse. He told Hermogenes of his realization that the spirit to whom he had always listened might be offering him a way out of life, in a manner "easiest but also the least irksome to one's friends,"[126] with "sound body and a spirit capable of showing kindliness"[127] and absent the "throes of illness" and vexations of extreme old age.[128] Socrates' decision to accept his fate allowed him to put away mortal terror in the face of death itself, prior to and during the trial, after the sentence was handed down,[129] and even later, during his execution.[130] He saw that his life had been so rich and full that he could let it go, gracefully. He was given the opportunity to put his affairs in order. He saw that he could escape the terrible slow degeneration of the advancing years. He came to understand all that was happening to him as a gift from the gods. He was not therefore required to defend himself against his accusers—at least not with the aim of pronouncing his innocence, and escaping his fate. Instead, he turned the tables, addressing his judges in a manner that makes the reader understand precisely why the town council wanted this man dead. Then he took his poison, like a man.

Socrates rejected expediency, and the necessity for manipulation that accompanied it. He chose instead, under the direst of conditions, to maintain his pursuit of the meaningful and the true. Twenty-five hundred years later, we remember his decision and take comfort from it. What can we learn from this? If you cease to utter falsehoods and live according to the dictates of your conscience, you can maintain your nobility, even when facing the ultimate threat; if you abide, truthfully and courageously, by the highest of ideals, you will be provided with more security and strength than will be offered by any short-sighted concentration on your own safety; if you live properly, fully, you can discover meaning so profound that it protects you even from the fear of death.

Could all that possibly be true?

Death, Toil and Evil

The tragedy of self-conscious Being produces suffering, inevitable suffering. That suffering in turn motivates the desire for selfish, immediate gratification—for expediency. But sacrifice—and work—serves far more effectively than short-term impulsive pleasure at keeping suffering at bay. However, tragedy itself (conceived of as the arbitrary harshness of society and nature, set against the vulnerability of the individual) is not the only—and perhaps not even the primary—source of suffering. There is also the problem of evil to consider. The world is set hard against us, of a certainty, but man's inhumanity to man is something even worse. Thus, the problem of sacrifice is compounded in its complexity: it is not only privation and mortal limitation that must be addressed by work—by the willingness to offer, and to give up. It is the problem of evil as well.

Consider, once again, the story of Adam and Eve. Life becomes very hard for their children (that's us) after the fall and awakening of our archetypal parents. First is the terrible fate awaiting us in the post-Paradisal world—in the world of history. Not the least of this is what Goethe called "our creative, endless toil."[131] Humans work, as we have seen. We work because we have awakened to the truth of our own vulnerability, our subjugation to disease and death, and wish to protect ourselves for as long as possible. Once we can see the future, we must prepare for it, or live in denial and terror. We therefore sacrifice the pleasures of today for the sake of a better tomorrow. But the realization of mortality and the necessity of work is not the only revelation to Adam and Eve when they eat the forbidden Fruit, wake up, and open their eyes. They were also granted (or cursed by) the knowledge of Good and Evil.

It took me decades to understand what that means (to understand even part of what that means). It's this: once you become consciously aware that you, yourself, are vulnerable, you understand the nature of human vulnerability, in general. You understand what it's like to be fearful, and angry, and resentful, and bitter. You understand what pain means. And once you truly understand such feelings in yourself, and how they're produced, *you understand how to produce them in others*. It is in this manner that the self-conscious beings that we are become voluntarily and exquisitely capable of tormenting others (and ourselves, of course—but it's the others we are concerned about right now). We see the consequences of this new knowledge manifest themselves when we meet Cain and Abel, the sons of Adam and Eve.

By the time of their appearance, mankind has learned to make sacrifices to God. On altars of stone, designed for that purpose, a communal ritual is performed: the immolation of something valuable, a choice animal or portion thereof, and its transformation through fire to the smoke (to the spirit) that rises to Heaven above. In this manner, the idea of delay is dramatized, so that the future might improve. Abel's sacrifices are accepted by God, and he flourishes. Cain's, however, are rejected. He becomes jealous and bitter—and it's no wonder. If someone fails and is rejected because he refused to make any sacrifices at all—well, that's at least understandable. He may still feel resentful and vengeful, but knows in his heart that he is personally to blame. That knowledge generally places a limit on his outrage. It's much worse, however, if he had actually foregone the pleasures of the moment—if he had strived and toiled and things still didn't work out—if he was rejected, despite his efforts. Then he's lost the present *and* the future. Then his work—his sacrifice—has been pointless. Under such conditions, the world darkens, and the soul rebels.

Cain is outraged by his rejection. He confronts God, accuses Him, and curses His creation. That proves to be a very poor decision. God responds, in no uncertain terms, that the fault is all with Cain—and worse: that Cain has knowingly and creatively dallied with sin,[132] and reaped the consequences. This is not at all what Cain wanted to hear. It's by no means an apology on God's part. Instead, it's insult, added to injury. Cain, embittered to the core by God's response, plots revenge. He defies the creator, audaciously. It's daring. Cain knows how to hurt. He's self-conscious, after all—and has become even more so, in his suffering and shame. So, he murders Abel in cold blood. He kills his brother, his own ideal (as Abel is everything Cain wishes to be). He commits this most terrible of crimes to spite himself, all of mankind, and God Himself, all at once. He does it to wreak havoc and gain his vengeance. He does it to register his fundamental opposition to existence—to protest the intolerable vagaries of Being itself. And Cain's children—the offspring, as it were of both his body and his decision—are worse. In his existential fury, Cain kills once. Lamech, his descendant, goes much further. "I have slain a man to my wounding," says Lamech, "and a young man to my hurt. If Cain shall be avenged sevenfold, truly Lamech seventy and sevenfold" (Genesis 4:23-24). Tubulcain, an instructor of "every artificer in brass and iron" (Genesis 4:22), is by tradition seven generations from Cain—and the first creator of weapons of war. And next, in the Genesis stories, comes the flood. The juxtaposition is by no means accidental.

Evil enters the world with self-consciousness. The toil with which God curses Adam—that's bad enough. The trouble in childbirth with which Eve is burdened and her consequent dependence on her husband are no trivial matters, either. They are indicative of the implicit and oft-agonizing tragedies of insufficiency, privation, brute necessity and subjugation to illness and death that simultaneously define and plague existence. Their mere factual reality is sometimes sufficient to turn even a courageous person against life. It has been my experience, however, that human beings are strong enough to tolerate the implicit tragedies of Being without faltering—without breaking or, worse, breaking bad. I have seen evidence of this repeatedly in my private life, in my work as a professor, and in my role as a clinical practitioner. Earthquakes, floods, poverty, cancer—we're tough enough to take on all of that. But human evil adds a whole new dimension of misery to the world. It is for this reason that the rise of self-consciousness and its attendant realization of mortality and knowledge of Good and Evil is presented in the early chapters of Genesis (and in the vast tradition that surrounds them) as a cataclysm of cosmic magnitude.

Conscious human malevolence can break the spirit even tragedy could not shake. I remember discovering (with her) that one of my clients had been shocked into years of serious post-traumatic stress disorder—daily physical shaking and terror, and chronic nightly insomnia—by the mere expression on her enraged, drunken boy-friend's face. His "fallen countenance" (Genesis 4:5) indicated his clear and conscious desire to do her harm. She was more naïve than she should have been, and that predisposed her to the trauma, but that's not the point: the voluntary evil we do one another can be profoundly and permanently damaging, even to the strong. And what is it, precisely, that motivates such evil?

It doesn't make itself manifest merely in consequence of the hard lot of life. It doesn't even emerge, simply, because of failure itself, or because of the disappointment and bitterness that failure often and understandably engenders. But the hard lot of life, magnified by the consequence of continually rejected sacrifices (however poorly conceptualized; however half-heartedly executed)? That will bend and twist people into the truly monstrous forms who then begin, consciously, to work evil; who then begin to generate for themselves and others little besides pain and suffering (and who do it for the sake of that pain and suffering). In that manner, a truly vicious circle takes hold: begrudging sacrifice, half-heartedly undertaken; rejection of that sacrifice by God or by reality (take your pick); angry resentment, generated by that rejection; descent into bitterness and the desire for revenge; sacrifice undertaken even more begrudgingly, or refused altogether. And it's Hell itself that serves as the destination place of that downward spiral.

Life is indeed "nasty, brutish and short," as the English philosopher Thomas Hobbes so memorably remarked. But man's capacity for evil makes it worse. This means that the central problem of life—the dealing with its brute facts—is not merely what and how to sacrifice to diminish suffering, but what and how to sacrifice to diminish suffering *and evil—the conscious and voluntary and vengeful source of the worst suffering.* The story of Cain and Abel is one manifestation of the archetypal tale of the hostile brothers, hero and adversary: the two elements of the individual human psyche, one aimed up, at the Good, and the other, down, at Hell itself. Abel is a hero, true: but a hero who is ultimately defeated by Cain. Abel could please God—a non-trivial and unlikely accomplishment—but he could not overcome human evil. For this reason, Abel is archetypally incomplete. Perhaps he was naive, although a vengeful brother can be inconceivably treacherous and *subtil,* like the snake in Genesis 3:1. But excuses—even reasons—even understandable reasons—don't matter; not in the final analysis. The problem of evil remained unsolved even by the divinely acceptable sacrifices of Abel. It took thousands of additional years for humanity to come up with anything else resembling a solution. The same issue emerges again, in its culminating form, in the story of Christ and his temptation by Satan. But this time it's expressed more comprehensively—and the hero wins.

Evil, Confronted

Jesus was led into the wilderness, according to the story, "to be tempted by the Devil" (Matthew 4:1), prior to his crucifixion. This is the story of Cain, restated abstractly. Cain is neither content nor happy, as we have seen. He's working hard, or so he thinks, but God is not pleased. Meanwhile, Abel is, by all appearances, dancing his way through life. His crops flourish. Women love him. Worst of all, he's a genuinely good man. Everyone knows it. He deserves his good fortune. All the more reason to envy and hate him. Things do not progress well for Cain, by contrast, and he broods on his misfortune, like a vulture on an egg. He strives, in his misery, to give birth to something hellish and, in doing so, enters the desert wilderness of his own mind. He obsesses over his ill fortune; his betrayal by God. He nourishes his resentment. He indulges in ever more elaborate fantasies of revenge. And as he does so, his arrogance grows to Luciferian proportions. "I'm ill-used and oppressed," he thinks. "This is a stupid bloody planet. As far as I'm concerned, it can go to Hell." And with that, Cain encounters Satan in the wilderness, for all intents and purposes, and falls prey to his temptations. And he does what he can to make things as bad as possible, motivated by (in John Milton's imperishable words):

So deep a malice, to confound the Race
Of Mankind in one Root, and Earth with Hell

to mingle and involve—done all to spite
the Great Creator . . .[133]

Cain turns to Evil to obtain what Good denied him, and he does it voluntarily, self-consciously and with malice aforethought.

Christ takes a different path. His sojourn in the desert is the dark night of the soul—a deeply human and universal human experience. It's the journey to that place each of us goes when things fall apart, friends and family are distant, hopelessness and despair reign, and black nihilism beckons. And, let us suggest, in testament to the exactitude of the story: forty days and nights starving alone in the wilderness might take you exactly to that place. It is in such a manner that the objective and subjective worlds come crashing, synchronistically, together. Forty days is a deeply symbolic period of time, echoing the forty years the Israelites spent wandering in the desert after escaping the tyranny of Pharaoh and Egypt. Forty days is a long time in the underworld of dark assumptions, confusion and fear—long enough to journey to the very center, which is Hell itself. A journey there to see the sights can be undertaken by anyone—anyone, that is, who is willing to take the evil of self and Man with sufficient seriousness. A bit of familiarity with history can help. A sojourn through the totalitarian horrors of the twentieth century, with its concentration camps, forced labor and murderous ideological pathologies is as good a place as any to start—that, and some consideration of the fact that the worst of the concentration camp guards were human, all-too-human, too. That's all part of making the desert story real again; part of updating it, for the modern mind.

"After Auschwitz," said Theodor Adorno, student of authoritarianism, "there should be no poetry." He was wrong. But the poetry should be about Auschwitz. In the grim wake of the last ten decades of the previous millennium, the terrible destructiveness of man has become a problem whose seriousness self-evidently dwarfs even the problem of unredeemed suffering. And neither one of those problems is going to be solved in the absence of a solution to the other. This is where the idea of Christ's taking on the sins of mankind as if they were

His own becomes key, opening the door to deep understanding of the desert encounter with the devil himself. *"Homo sum, humani nihil a me alienum puto,"* said the Roman playwright Terence: nothing human is alien to me.

"No tree can grow to Heaven," adds the ever-terrifying Carl Gustav Jung, psychoanalyst extraordinaire, "unless its roots reach down to Hell."[134] Such a statement should give everyone who encounters it pause. There was no possibility for movement upward, in that great psychiatrist's deeply considered opinion, without a corresponding move down. It is for this reason that enlightenment is so rare. Who is willing to do that? Do you really want to meet who's in charge, at the very bottom of the most wicked thoughts? What did Eric Harris, mass murderer of the Columbine high school, write so incomprehensibly the very day prior to massacring his classmates? *It's interesting, when I'm in my human form, knowing I'm going to die. Everything has a touch of triviality to it.*[135] Who would dare explain such a missive?—or, worse, explain it away?

In the desert, Christ encounters Satan (see Luke 4:1–13 and Matthew 4:1–11). This story has a clear psychological meaning—a metaphorical meaning—in addition to whatever else material and metaphysical alike it might signify. It means that Christ *is forever He who determines to take personal responsibility for the full depth of human depravity.* It means that Christ is eternally He who is willing to confront and deeply consider and risk the temptations posed by the most malevolent elements of human nature. It means that Christ is always he who is willing to confront evil—consciously, fully and voluntarily— in the form that dwelt simultaneously within Him and in the world. This is nothing merely abstract (although it is abstract); nothing to be brushed over. It's no merely intellectual matter.

Soldiers who develop post-traumatic stress disorder frequently develop it not because of something they saw, but because of something they did.[136] There are many demons, so to speak, on the battle-field. Involvement in warfare is something that can open a gateway to Hell. Now and then something climbs through and possesses some naive farm-boy from Iowa, and he turns monstrous. He does something terrible. He rapes and kills the women and massacres the infants of My Lai. And he watches himself do it. And some dark part of him enjoys it—and that is the part that is most unforgettable. And, later, he will not know how to reconcile himself with the reality about himself and the world that was then revealed. And no wonder.

In the great and fundamental myths of ancient Egypt, the god Horus—often regarded as a precursor to Christ, historically and conceptually speaking[137]—experienced the same thing, when he confronted his evil uncle Set,* usurper of the throne of Osiris, Horus's father. Horus, the all-seeing Egyptian falcon god, the Egyptian eye of supreme, eternal attention itself, has the courage to contend with Set's true nature, meeting him in direct combat. In the struggle with his dread uncle, however, his consciousness is damaged. He loses an eye. This is despite his godly stature and his unparalleled capacity for vision. What would a mere man lose, who attempted the same thing? But perhaps he might gain in internal vision and understanding something proportional to what he loses in perception of the outside world.

Satan embodies the refusal of sacrifice; he is arrogance, incarnate; spite, deceit, and cruel, conscious malevolence. He is pure hatred of Man, God and Being. He will not humble himself, even when he knows full well that he should. Furthermore, he knows exactly what he is doing, obsessed with the desire for destruction, and does it deliberately, thoughtfully and completely. It has to be him, therefore—the very archetype of Evil—who confronts and tempts Christ, the archetype of Good. It must be him who offers to the Savior of Mankind, under the most trying of conditions, what all men most ardently desire.

Satan first tempts the starving Christ to quell His hunger by transforming the desert rocks into bread. Then he suggests that He throw Himself off a cliff, calling on God and the angels to break His fall. Christ responds to the first temptation by saying, "One does not live by bread alone, but by every word that proceeds from the mouth of God." What does this answer mean? It means that even under conditions of

---

* In keeping with this observation is the fact that the word Set is an etymological precursor to the word Satan. See Murdock, D.M. (2009). *Christ in Egypt: the Horus-Jesus connection*. Seattle, WA: Stellar House, p. 75.

extreme privation, there are more important things than food. To put it another way: Bread is of little use to the man who has betrayed his soul, even if he is currently starving.* Christ could clearly use his near-infinite power, as Satan indicates, to gain bread, now—to break his fast—even, in the broader sense, to gain wealth, in the world (which would theoretically solve the problem of bread, more permanently). But at what cost? And to what gain? Gluttony, in the midst of moral desolation? That's the poorest and most miserable of feasts. Christ aims, therefore, at something higher: at the description of a mode of Being that would finally and forever solve the problem of hunger. If we all chose instead of expedience to dine on the Word of God? That would require each and every person to live, and produce, and sacrifice, and speak, and share in a manner that would permanently render the privation of hunger a thing of the past. And that's how the problem of hunger in the privations of the desert is most truly and finally addressed.

There are other indications of this in the gospels, in dramatic, enacted form. Christ is continually portrayed as the purveyor of endless sustenance. He miraculously multiplies bread and fish. He turns water into wine. What does this mean? It's a call to the pursuit of higher meaning as the mode of living that is simultaneously most practical and of highest quality. It's a call portrayed in dramatic/literary form: live as the archetypal Saviour lives, and you and those around you will hunger no more. The beneficence of the world manifests itself to those who live properly. That's better than bread. That's better than the money that will buy bread. Thus Christ, the symbolically perfect individual, overcomes the first temptation. Two more follow.

"Throw yourself off that cliff," Satan says, offering the next temptation. "If God exists, He will surely save you. If you are in fact his Son, God will surely save you." Why would God not make Himself manifest, to rescue His only begotten Child from hunger and isolation

---

* For anyone who thinks this is somehow unrealistic, given the concrete material reality and genuine suffering that is associated with privation, I would once again recommend Solzhenitsyn's *Gulag Archipelago*, which contains a series of exceptionally profound discussions about proper ethical behavior and its exaggerated rather than diminished importance in situations of extreme want and suffering.

and the presence of great evil? But that establishes no pattern for life. It doesn't even work as literature. The *deus ex machina*—the emergence of a divine force that magically rescues the hero from his predicament—is the cheapest trick in the hack writer's playbook. It makes a mockery of independence, and courage, and destiny, and free will, and responsibility. Furthermore, God is in no wise a safety net for the blind. He's not someone to be commanded to perform magic tricks, or forced into Self-revelation—not even by His own Son.

"Do not put the Lord your God to the test" (Matthew 4:7)—this answer, though rather brief, dispenses with the second temptation. Christ does not casually order or even dare ask God to intervene on his behalf. He refuses to dispense with His responsibility for the events of His own life. He refuses to demand that God prove His presence. He refuses, as well, to solve the problems of mortal vulnerability in a merely personal manner—by compelling God to save Him—because that would not solve the problem for everyone else and for all time. There is also the echo of the rejection of the comforts of insanity in this forgone temptation. Easy but psychotic self-identification as the merely magical Messiah might well have been a genuine temptation under the harsh conditions of Christ's sojourn in the desert. Instead He rejects the idea that salvation—or even survival, in the shorter term—depends on narcissistic displays of superiority and the commanding of God, even by His Son.

Finally comes the third temptation, the most compelling of all. Christ sees the kingdoms of the world laid before Him for the taking. That's the siren call of earthly power: the opportunity to control and order everyone and everything. Christ is offered the pinnacle of the dominance hierarchy, the animalistic desire of every naked ape: the obedience of all, the most wondrous of estates, the power to build and to increase, the possibility of unlimited sensual gratification. That's expedience, writ large. But that's not all. Such expansion of status also provides unlimited opportunity for the inner darkness to reveal itself. The lust for blood, rape and destruction is very much part of power's attraction. It is not only that men desire power so that they will no longer suffer. It is not only that they desire power so that they can overcome subjugation to want, disease and death. Power also means the capacity to take vengeance, ensure submission, and crush enemies. Grant Cain enough power and he will not only kill Abel. He will torture him, first, imaginatively and endlessly. Then and only then will he kill him. Then he will come after everyone else.

There's something above even the pinnacle of the highest of dominance hierarchies, access to which should not be sacrificed for mere proximal success. It's a real place, too, although not to be conceptualized in the standard geographical sense of place we typically use to orient ourselves. I had a vision, once, of an immense landscape, spread for miles out to the horizon before me. I was high in the air, granted a bird's-eye view. Everywhere I could see great stratified multi-storied pyramids of glass, some small, some large, some overlapping, some separate—all akin to modern skyscrapers; all full of people striving to reach each pyramid's very pinnacle. But there was something above that pinnacle, a domain outside each pyramid, in which all were nested. That was the privileged position of the eye that could or perhaps chose to soar freely above the fray; that chose not to dominate any specific group or cause but instead to somehow simultaneously transcend all. That was attention, itself, pure and untrammeled: detached, alert, watchful attention, waiting to act when the time was right and the place had been established. As the Tao te Ching has it:

> *He who contrives, defeats his purpose;*
> *and he who is grasping, loses.*
> *The sage does not contrive to win,*
> *and therefore is not defeated;*
> *he is not grasping, so does not lose.*[138]

There is a powerful call to proper Being in the story of the third temptation. To obtain the greatest possible prize—the establishment of the Kingdom of God on Earth, the resurrection of Paradise—the individual must conduct his or her life in a manner that requires the rejection of immediate gratification, of natural and perverse desires alike, no matter how powerfully and convincingly and realistically those are offered, and dispense, as well with the temptations of evil. Evil amplifies the catastrophe of life, increasing dramatically the motivation for expediency already there because of the essential tragedy of Being. Sacrifice of the more prosaic sort can keep that tragedy at bay, more or less successfully, but it takes a special kind of sacrifice to defeat evil. It is the description of that special sacrifice that has preoccupied the Christian (and more than Christian) imagination for centuries. Why has it not had the desired effect? Why do we remain unconvinced that there is no better plan than lifting our eyes skyward, aiming at the Good, and sacrificing everything to that ambition? Have we merely failed to understand, or have we fallen, wilfully or otherwise, off the path?

Christianity and its Problems

Carl Jung hypothesized that the European mind found itself motivated to develop the cognitive technologies of science—to investigate the material world—after implicitly concluding that Christianity, with its laser-like emphasis on spiritual salvation, had failed to sufficiently address the problem of suffering in the here-and-now. This realization became unbearably acute in the three or four centuries before the Renaissance. In consequence, a strange, profound, compensatory fantasy began to emerge, deep in the collective Western psyche, manifesting itself first in the strange musings of alchemy, and developing only after many centuries into the fully articulated form of science.[139] It was the alchemists who first seriously began to examine the transformations of matter, hoping to discover the secrets of health, wealth and longevity. These great dreamers (Newton foremost among them[140]) intuited and then imagined that the material world, damned by the Church, held secrets the revelation of which could free humanity from its earthly pain and limitations. It was that vision, driven by doubt, that provided the tremendous collective and individual motivational power necessary for the development of science, with its extreme demands on individual thinkers for concentration and delay of gratification.

This is not to say that Christianity, even in its incompletely realized form, was a failure. Quite the contrary: Christianity achieved the well-nigh impossible. The Christian doctrine elevated the individual soul, placing slave and master and commoner and nobleman alike on the same metaphysical footing, rendering them equal before God and the law. Christianity insisted that even the king was only one among many. For something so contrary to all apparent evidence to find its footing, the idea that worldly power and prominence were indicators of God's particular favor had to be radically de-emphasized. This was partly accomplished through the strange Christian insistence that salvation could not be obtained through effort or worth—through "works."[141] Whatever its limitations, the development of such doctrine prevented king, aristocrat and wealthy merchant alike from lording it morally over the commoner. In consequence, the metaphysical conception of the implicit transcendent worth of each and every soul established itself against impossible odds as the fundamental presupposition of Western law and society. That was not the case in the world of the past, and is not the case yet in most places in the world of the present. It is in fact nothing short of a miracle (and we should keep this fact firmly before our eyes) that the hierarchical slave-based societies of our ancestors reorganized themselves, under the sway of an ethical/religious revelation, such that the ownership and absolute domination of another person came to be viewed as wrong.

It would do us well to remember, as well, that the immediate utility of slavery is obvious, and that the argument that the strong should dominate the weak is compelling, convenient and eminently practical (at least for the strong). This means that a revolutionary critique of everything slave-owning societies valued was necessary before the practice could be even questioned, let alone halted (including the idea that wielding power and authority made the slave-owner noble; including the even more fundamental idea that the power wielded by the slave-owner was valid and even virtuous). Christianity made explicit the surprising claim that even the lowliest person had rights, genuine rights—and that sovereign and state were morally charged, at a fundamental level, to recognize those rights. Christianity put forward, explicitly, the even more incomprehensible idea that the act of human ownership degraded the slaver (previously viewed as admirable nobility) as much or even more than the slave. We fail to understand how difficult such an idea is to grasp. We forget that the opposite was self-evident throughout most of human history. We think that it is the desire to enslave and dominate that requires explanation. We have it backwards, yet again.

This is not to say that Christianity was without its problems. But it is more appropriate to note that they were the sort of problems that emerge only after an entirely different set of more serious problems has been solved. The society produced by Christianity was far less barbaric than the pagan—even the Roman—ones it replaced. Christian society at least recognized that feeding slaves to ravenous lions for the entertainment of the populace was wrong, even if many barbaric practices still existed. It objected to infanticide, to prostitution, and to the principle that might means right. It insisted that women were as valuable as men (even though we are still working out how to manifest that insistence politically). It demanded that even a society's enemies be regarded as human. Finally, it separated church from state, so that all-too-human emperors could no longer claim the veneration due to gods. All of this was asking the impossible: but it happened.

As the Christian revolution progressed, however, the impossible problems it had solved disappeared from view. That's what happens to problems that are solved. And after the solution was implemented, *even the fact that such problems had ever existed disappeared from view.* Then and only then could the problems that remained, less amenable to quick solution by Christian doctrine, come to occupy a central place in the consciousness of the West—come to motivate, for example, the development of science, aimed at resolving the corporeal, material suffering that was still all-too-painfully extant within successfully Christianized societies. The fact that automobiles pollute only becomes a problem of sufficient magnitude to attract public attention when the far worse problems that the internal combustion engine solves has vanished from view. People stricken with poverty don't care about carbon dioxide. It's not precisely that CO_2 levels are irrelevant. It's that they're irrelevant when you're working yourself to death, starving, scraping a bare living from the stony, unyielding, thorn-and-thistle-infested ground. It's that they're irrelevant until after the tractor is invented and hundreds of millions stop starving. In any case, by the time Nietzsche entered the picture, in the late nineteenth century, the problems Christianity had left unsolved had become paramount.

Nietzsche described himself, with no serious overstatement, as philosophizing with a hammer.[142] His devastating critique of Christianity—already weakened by its conflict with the very science to which it had given rise—involved two main lines of attack. Nietzsche claimed, first, that it was precisely the sense of truth developed in the highest sense by Christianity itself that ultimately came to question and then to undermine the fundamental presuppositions of the faith. That was partly because the difference between moral or narrative truth and objective truth had not yet been fully comprehended (and so an opposition was presumed where none necessarily exists)—but that does not bely the point. Even when the modern atheists opposed to Christianity belittle fundamentalists for insisting, for example, that the creation account in Genesis is objectively true, they are using their sense of truth, highly developed over the centuries of Christian culture, to engage in such argumentation. Carl Jung continued to develop Nietzsche's arguments decades later, pointing out that Europe awoke, during the Enlightenment, as if from a Christian dream, noticing that everything it had heretofore taken for granted could and should be questioned. "God is dead," said Nietzsche. "God remains dead. And we have killed him. How shall we, murderers of all murderers, console ourselves? That which was the holiest and mightiest of all that the world has yet possessed has bled to death under our knives. Who will wipe this blood off us?"[143]

The central dogmas of the Western faith were no longer credible, according to Nietzsche, given what the Western mind now considered truth. But it was his second attack—on the removal of the true moral burden of Christianity during the development of the Church—that was most devastating. The hammer-wielding philosopher mounted an assault on an early-established and then highly influential line of

Christian thinking: *that Christianity meant accepting the proposition that Christ's sacrifice, and only that sacrifice, had redeemed humanity*. This did not mean, absolutely, that a Christian who believed that Christ died on the cross for the salvation of mankind was thereby freed from any and all personal moral obligation. But it did strongly imply that the primary responsibility for redemption had already been borne by the Saviour, and that nothing too important to do remained for all-too-fallen human individuals.

Nietzsche believed that Paul, and later the Protestants following Luther, had removed moral responsibility from Christ's followers. They had watered down the idea of *the imitation of Christ*. This imitation was the sacred duty of the believer not to adhere (or merely to mouth) a set of statements about abstract belief but instead to actually manifest the spirit of the Saviour in the particular, specific conditions of his or her life—to realize or incarnate the archetype, as Jung had it; to clothe the eternal pattern in flesh. Nietzsche writes, "The Christians have never practiced the actions Jesus prescribed them; and the impudent garrulous talk about the 'justification by faith' and its supreme and sole significance is only the consequence of the Church's lack of courage and will to profess the works Jesus demanded."[144] Nietzsche was, indeed, a critic without parallel.

Dogmatic belief in the central axioms of Christianity (that Christ's crucifixion redeemed the world; that salvation was reserved for the hereafter; that salvation could not be achieved through works) had three mutually reinforcing consequences: First, *devaluation of the significance of earthly life, as only the hereafter mattered*. This also meant that it had become acceptable to overlook and shirk responsibility for the suffering that existed in the here-and-now; Second, *passive acceptance of the status quo, because salvation could not be earned in any case through effort in this life* (a consequence that Marx also derided, with his proposition that religion was the opiate of the masses); and, finally, third, *the right of the believer to reject any real moral burden* (outside of the stated belief in salvation through Christ), *because the Son of God had already done all the important work*. It was for such reasons that Dostoevsky, who was a great influence on Nietzsche, also criticized institutional Christianity (although he arguably managed it in a more ambiguous but also more sophisticated manner). In his masterwork, *The Brothers Karamazov*, Dostoevsky has his atheist superman, Ivan, tell a little story, "The Grand Inquisitor."[145] A brief review is in order.

Ivan speaks to his brother Alyosha—whose pursuits as a monastic novitiate he holds in contempt—of Christ returning to Earth at the time of the Spanish Inquisition. The returning Savior makes quite a ruckus, as would be expected. He heals the sick. He raises the dead. His antics soon attract attention from the Grand Inquisitor himself, who promptly has Christ arrested and thrown into a prison cell. Later, the Inquisitor pays Him a visit. He informs Christ that he is no longer needed. His return is simply too great a threat to the Church. The Inquisitor tells Christ that the burden He laid on mankind—the burden of existence in faith and truth—was simply too great for mere mortals to bear. The Inquisitor claims that the Church, in its mercy, diluted that message, lifting the demand for perfect Being from the shoulders of its followers, providing them instead with the simple and merciful escapes of faith and the afterlife. That work took centuries, says the Inquisitor, and the last thing the Church needs after all that effort is the return of the Man who insisted that people bear all the weight in the first place. Christ listens in silence. Then, as the Inquisitor turns to leave, Christ embraces him, and kisses him on the lips. The Inquisitor turns white, in shock. Then he goes out, leaving the cell door open.

The profundity of this story and the greatness of spirit necessary to produce it can hardly be exaggerated. Dostoevsky, one of the great literary geniuses of all time, confronted the most serious existential problems in all his great writings, and he did so courageously, head-long, and heedless of the consequences. Clearly Christian, he nonetheless adamantly refuses to make a straw man of his rationalist and atheistic opponents. Quite the contrary: In *The Brothers Karamazov*, for example, Dostoevsky's atheist, Ivan, argues against the presuppositions of Christianity with unsurpassable clarity and passion. Alyosha, aligned with the Church by temperament and decision, cannot undermine a single one of his brother's arguments (although his faith remains unshakeable). Dostoevsky knew and admitted that Christianity had been defeated by the rational faculty—by the intellect, even—but (and this is of primary importance) *he did not hide from that fact*. He didn't attempt through denial or deceit or even satire to weaken the position that opposed what he believed to be most true and valuable. He instead placed action above words, and addressed the problem successfully. By the novel's end, Dostoevsky has the great embodied moral goodness of Alyosha—the novitiate's courageous imitation of Christ— attain victory over the spectacular but ultimately nihilistic critical intelligence of Ivan.

The Christian church described by the Grand Inquisitor is the same church pilloried by Nietzsche. Childish, sanctimonious, patriarchal, servant of the state, that church is everything rotten still objected to by modern critics of Christianity. Nietzsche, for all his brilliance, allows himself anger, but does not perhaps sufficiently temper it with judgement. This is where Dostoevsky truly transcends Nietzsche, in my estimation—where Dostoevsky's great literature transcends Nietzsche's mere philosophy. The Russian writer's Inquisitor is the genuine article, in every sense. He is an opportunistic, cynical, manipulative and cruel interrogator, willing to persecute heretics—even to torture and kill them. He is the purveyor of a dogma he knows to be false. But Dostoevsky has Christ, the archetypal perfect man, kiss him anyway. Equally importantly, in the aftermath of the kiss, the Grand Inquisitor leaves the door ajar so Christ can escape his pending execution. Dostoevsky saw that the great, corrupt edifice of Christianity still managed to make room for the spirit of its Founder. That's the gratitude of a wise and profound soul for the enduring wisdom of the West, despite its faults.

It's not as if Nietzsche was unwilling to give the faith—and, more particularly, Catholicism—its due. Nietzsche believed that the long tradition of "unfreedom" characterizing dogmatic Christianity—its insistence that everything be explained within the confines of a single, coherent metaphysical theory—was a necessary precondition for the emergence of the disciplined but free modern mind. As he stated in *Beyond Good and Evil*:

The long bondage of the spirit . . . the persistent spiritual will to interpret everything that happened according to a Christian scheme, and in every occurrence to rediscover and justify the Christian God in every accident:—all this violence, arbitrariness, severity, dreadfulness, and unreasonableness, has proved itself the disciplinary means whereby the European spirit has attained its strength, its remorseless curiosity and subtle mobility; granted also that much irrecoverable strength and spirit had to be stifled, suffocated and spoiled in the process.[146]

For Nietzsche and Dostoevsky alike, freedom—even the ability to act—requires constraint. For this reason, they both recognized the vital necessity of the dogma of the Church. The individual must be constrained, moulded—even brought close to destruction—by a restrictive, coherent disciplinary structure, before he or she can act freely and competently. Dostoevsky, with his great generosity of spirit, granted to the church, corrupt as it might be, a certain element of mercy, a certain pragmatism. He admitted that the spirit of Christ, the world-engendering Logos, had historically and might still find its resting place—even its sovereignty—within that dogmatic structure.

If a father disciplines his son properly, he obviously interferes with his freedom, particularly in the here-and-now. He puts limits on the voluntary expression of his son's Being, forcing him to take his place as a socialized member of the world. Such a father requires that all that childish potential be funneled down a single pathway. In placing such limitations on his son, he might be considered a destructive force, acting as he does to replace the miraculous plurality of childhood with a single narrow actuality. But if the father does not take such action, he merely lets his son remain Peter Pan, the eternal Boy, King of the Lost Boys, Ruler of the non-existent Neverland. That is not a morally acceptable alternative.

The dogma of the Church was undermined by the spirit of truth strongly developed by the Church itself. That undermining culminated in the death of God. But the dogmatic structure of the Church was a necessary disciplinary structure. A long period of unfreedom—

adherence to a singular interpretive structure—is necessary for the development of a free mind. Christian dogma provided that unfreedom. But the dogma is dead, at least to the modern Western mind. It perished along with God. What has emerged from behind its corpse, however—and this is an issue of central importance—is something even more dead; something that was never alive, even in the past: *nihilism, as well as an equally dangerous susceptibility to new, totalizing, utopian ideas.* It was in the aftermath of God's death that the great collective horrors of Communism and Fascism sprang forth (as both Dostoevsky and Nietzsche predicted they would). Nietzsche, for his part, posited that individual human beings would have to invent their own values in the aftermath of God's death. But this is the element of his thinking that appears weakest, psychologically: *we cannot invent our own values, because we cannot merely impose what we believe on our souls.* This was Carl Jung's great discovery—made in no little part because of his intense study of the problems posed by Nietzsche.

We rebel against our own totalitarianism, as much as that of others. I cannot merely order myself to action, and neither can you. "I will stop procrastinating," I say, but I don't. "I will eat properly," I say, but I don't. "I will end my drunken misbehavior," I say, but I don't. I cannot merely make myself over in the image constructed by my intellect (particularly if that intellect is possessed by an ideology). I have a nature, and so do you, and so do we all. We must discover that nature, and contend with it, before making peace with ourselves. What is it, that we most truly are? What is it that we could most truly become, knowing who we most truly are? We must get to the very bottom of things before such questions can be truly answered.

Doubt, Past Mere Nihilism

Three hundred years before Nietzsche, the great French philosopher René Descartes set out on an intellectual mission to take his doubt seriously, to break things apart, to get to what was essential—to see if he could establish, or discover, a single proposition impervious to his skepticism. He was searching for the foundation stone on which proper

Being could be established. Descartes found it, as far as he was concerned, in the "I" who thinks—the "I" who was aware—as expressed in his famous dictum, *cogito ergo sum* (I think, therefore I am). But that "I" had been conceptualized long before. Thousands of years ago, the aware "I" was the all-seeing eye of Horus, the great Egyptian son-and-sun-god, who renewed the state by attending to and then confronting its inevitable corruption. Before that, it was the creator-God Marduk of the Mesopotamians, whose eyes encircled his head and who spoke forth words of world-engendering magic. During the Christian epoch, the "I" transformed into the Logos, the Word that speaks order into Being at the beginning of time. It might be said that Descartes merely secularized the Logos, turning it, more explicitly, into "that which is aware and thinks." That's the modern self, simply put. But what exactly is that self?

We can understand, to some degree, its horrors, if we wish to, but its goodness remains more difficult to define. The self is the great actor of evil who strode about the stage of Being as Nazi and Stalinist alike; who produced Auschwitz, Buchenwald, Dachau, and the multiplicity of the Soviet gulags. And all of that must be considered with dread seriousness. But what is its opposite? What is the good that is the necessary counterpart of that evil; that is made more corporeal and comprehensible by the very existence of that evil? And here we can state with conviction and clarity that even the rational intellect—that faculty so beloved of those who hold traditional wisdom in contempt—is at minimum something closely and necessarily akin to the archetypal dying and eternally resurrected god, the eternal savior of humanity, the Logos itself. The philosopher of science Karl Popper, certainly no mystic, regarded thinking itself as a logical extension of the Darwinian process. A creature that cannot think must solely embody its Being. It can merely act out its nature, concretely, in the here-and-now. If it cannot manifest in its behavior what the environment demands while doing so, it will simply die. But that is not true of human beings. We can produce abstracted representations of potential modes of Being. We can produce an idea in the theatre of the imagination. We can test it out against our other ideas, the ideas of others, or the world itself. If it falls short, we can let it go. We can, in Popper's formulation, let our ideas die in our stead.[147] Then the essential part, the creator of those ideas, can continue onward, now untrammeled, by comparison, with error. *Faith in the part of us that continues across those deaths is a prerequisite to thinking itself.*

Now, an idea is not the same thing as a fact. A fact is something that is dead, in and of itself. It has no consciousness, no will to power, no motivation, no action. There are billions of dead facts. The internet is a graveyard of dead facts. But an idea that grips a person is alive. It wants to express itself, to live in the world. It is for this reason that the depth psychologists—Freud and Jung paramount among them—insisted that the human psyche was a battleground for ideas. *An idea has an aim. It wants something. It posits a value structure.* An idea believes that what it is aiming for is better than what it has now. It reduces the world to those things that aid or impede its realization, and it reduces everything else to irrelevance. An idea defines figure against ground. *An idea is a personality, not a fact.* When it manifests itself within a person, it has a strong proclivity to make of that person its avatar: to impel that person to act it out. Sometimes, that impulsion (possession is another word) can be so strong that the person will die, rather than allowing the idea to perish. This is, generally speaking, a bad decision, given that it is often the case that only the idea need die, and that the person with the idea can stop being its avatar, change his or her ways, and continue.

To use the dramatic conceptualization of our ancestors: It is the most fundamental convictions that must die—must be sacrificed—when the relationship with God has been disrupted (when the presence of undue and often intolerable suffering, for example, indicates that something has to change). This is to say nothing other than that the future can be made better if the proper sacrifices take place in the present. No other animal has ever figured this out, and it took us untold hundreds of thousands of years to do it. It took further eons of observation and hero-worship, and then millennia of study, to distill that idea into a story. It then took additional vast stretches of time to assess that story, to incorporate it, so that we now can simply say, "If you are disciplined and privilege the future over the present you can change the structure of reality in your favour."

But how best to do that?

In 1984, I started down the same road as Descartes. I did not know it was the same road at the time, and I am not claiming kinship with Descartes, who is rightly regarded as one of the greatest philosophers of all time. But I was truly plagued with doubt. I had outgrown the shallow Christianity of my youth by the time I could understand the fundamentals of Darwinian theory. After that, I could not distinguish the basic elements of Christian belief from wishful thinking. The socialism that soon afterward became so attractive to me as an alternative proved equally insubstantial; with time, I came to understand, through the great George Orwell, that much of such thinking found its motivation in hatred of the rich and successful, instead of true regard for the poor. Besides, the socialists were more intrinsically capitalist than the capitalists. They believed just as strongly in money. They just thought that if different people had the money, the problems plaguing humanity would vanish. This is simply untrue. There are many problems that money does not solve, and others that it makes worse. Rich people still divorce each other, and alienate themselves from their children, and suffer from existential angst, and develop cancer and dementia, and die alone and unloved. Recovering addicts cursed with money blow it all in a frenzy of snorting and drunkenness. And boredom weighs heavily on people who have nothing to do.

I was simultaneously tormented by the fact of the Cold War. It obsessed me. It gave me nightmares. It drove me into the desert, into the long night of the human soul. I could not understand how it had come to pass that the world's two great factions aimed mutual assured destruction at each other. Was one system just as arbitrary and corrupt as the other? Was it a mere matter of opinion? Were all value structures merely the clothing of power?

Was everyone crazy?

Just exactly what happened in the twentieth century, anyway? How was it that so many tens of millions had to die, sacrificed to the new dogmas and ideologies? How was it that we discovered something worse, much worse, than the aristocracy and corrupt religious beliefs that communism and fascism sought so rationally to supplant? No one had answered those questions, as far as I could tell. Like Descartes, I was plagued with doubt. I searched for one thing—anything—I could regard as indisputable. I wanted a rock upon which to build my house. It was doubt that led me to it.

I once read of a particularly insidious practice at Auschwitz. A guard would force an inmate to carry a hundred-pound sack of wet salt from one side of the large compound to the other—and then to carry it back. *Arbeit macht frei*, said the sign over the camp entrance— "Work will set you free"—and the freedom was death. Carrying the salt was an act of pointless torment. It was a piece of malevolent art. It allowed me to realize with certainty that some actions are wrong.

Aleksandr Solzhenitsyn wrote, definitively and profoundly, about the horrors of the twentieth century, the tens of millions who were stripped of employment, family, identity and life. In his *Gulag Archipelago*, in the second part of the second volume, he discussed the Nuremburg trials, which he considered the most significant event of the twentieth century. The conclusion of those trials? *There are some actions that are so intrinsically terrible that they run counter to the proper nature of human Being.* This is true essentially, cross-culturally—across time and place. *These are evil actions. No excuses are available for engaging in them.* To dehumanize a fellow being, to reduce him or her to the status of a parasite, to torture and to slaughter with no consideration of individual innocence or guilt, to make an art form of pain—that is wrong.

What can I not doubt? The reality of suffering. It brooks no arguments. Nihilists cannot undermine it with skepticism. Totalitarians cannot banish it. Cynics cannot escape from its reality. Suffering is real, and the artful infliction of suffering on another, for its own sake, is wrong. That became the cornerstone of my belief. Searching through the lowest reaches of human thought and action, understanding my own capacity to act like a Nazi prison guard or a gulag archipelago trustee or a torturer of children in a dungeon, I grasped what it meant to "take the sins of the world onto oneself." Each human being has an immense capacity for evil. Each human being understands, *a priori*, perhaps not what is good, but certainly what is not. And if there is something that *is not good*, then there is something that *is good*. If the worst sin is the torment of others, merely for the sake of the suffering produced—then the good is whatever is diametrically opposed to that. The good is whatever stops such things from happening.

Meaning as the Higher Good

It was from this that I drew my fundamental moral conclusions. Aim up. Pay attention. Fix what you can fix. Don't be arrogant in your knowledge. Strive for humility, because totalitarian pride manifests itself in intolerance, oppression, torture and death. Become aware of your own insufficiency—your cowardice, malevolence, resentment and hatred. Consider the murderousness of your own spirit before you dare accuse others, and before you attempt to repair the fabric of the world. Maybe it's not the world that's at fault. Maybe it's you. You've failed to make the mark. You've missed the target. You've fallen short of the glory of God. You've sinned. And all of that is your contribution to the insufficiency and evil of the world. And, above all, don't lie. Don't lie about anything, ever. Lying leads to Hell. It was the great and the small lies of the Nazi and Communist states that produced the deaths of millions of people.

Consider then that the alleviation of unnecessary pain and suffering is a good. Make that an axiom: to the best of my ability I will act in a manner that leads to the alleviation of unnecessary pain and suffering. You have now placed at the pinnacle of your moral hierarchy a set of presuppositions and actions aimed at the betterment of Being. Why? Because we know the alternative. The alternative was the twentieth century. The alternative was so close to Hell that the difference is not worth discussing. And the opposite of Hell is Heaven. To place the alleviation of unnecessary pain and suffering at the pinnacle of your hierarchy of value is to work to bring about the Kingdom of God on Earth. That's a state, and a state of mind, at the same time.

Jung observed that the construction of such a moral hierarchy was inevitable—although it could remain poorly arranged and internally self-contradictory. For Jung, whatever was at the top of an individual's moral hierarchy was, for all intents and purposes, that person's ultimate value, that person's god. It was what the person acted out. It was what the person believed most deeply. Something enacted is not a fact, or even a set of facts. Instead, it's a personality—or, more precisely, a choice between two opposing personalities. It's Sherlock Holmes or Moriarty. It's Batman or the Joker. It's Superman or Lex Luthor, Charles Francis Xavier or Magneto, and Thor or Loki. It's Abel or Cain—and it's Christ or Satan. If it's working for the ennobling of Being, for the establishment of Paradise, then it's Christ. If it's working for the destruction of Being, for the generation and propagation of unnecessary suffering and pain, then it's Satan. That's the inescapable, archetypal reality.

Expedience is the following of blind impulse. It's short-term gain. It's narrow, and selfish. It lies to get its way. It takes nothing into account. It's immature and irresponsible. Meaning is its mature replacement. Meaning emerges when impulses are regulated, organized and unified. Meaning emerges from the interplay between the possibilities of the world and the value structure operating within that world. If the value structure is aimed at the betterment of Being, the meaning revealed will be life-sustaining. It will provide the antidote for chaos and suffering. It will make everything matter. It will make everything better.

If you act properly, your actions allow you to be psychologically integrated now, and tomorrow, and into the future, while you benefit yourself, your family, and the broader world around you. Everything will stack up and align along a single axis. Everything will come together. This produces maximal meaning. This stacking up is a place in space and time whose existence we can detect with our ability to experience more than is simply revealed here and now by our senses, which are obviously limited to their information-gathering and representational capacity. Meaning trumps expedience. Meaning gratifies all impulses, now and forever. That's why we can detect it.

If you decide that you are not justified in your resentment of Being, despite its inequity and pain, you may come to notice things you could fix to reduce even by a bit some unnecessary pain and suffering. You may come to ask yourself, "What should I do today?" in a manner that means "How could I use my time to make things better, instead of worse?" Such tasks may announce themselves as the pile of undone paperwork that you could attend to, the room that you could make a bit more welcoming, or the meal that could be a bit more delicious and more gratefully delivered to your family.

You may find that if you attend to these moral obligations, once you have placed "make the world better" at the top of your value hierarchy, you experience ever-deepening meaning. It's not bliss. It's not happiness. It is something more like atonement for the criminal fact of your fractured and damaged Being. It's payment of the debt you owe for the insane and horrible miracle of your existence. It's how you remember the Holocaust. It's how you make amends for the pathology of history. It's adoption of the responsibility for being a potential denizen of Hell. It is willingness to serve as an angel of Paradise.

Expedience—that's hiding all the skeletons in the closet. That's covering the blood you just spilled with a carpet. That's avoiding responsibility. It's cowardly, and shallow, and wrong. It's wrong because mere expedience, multiplied by many repetitions, produces the character of a demon. It's wrong because expedience merely transfers the curse on your head to someone else, or to your future self, in a manner that will make your future, and the future generally, worse instead of better.

There is no faith and no courage and no sacrifice in doing what is expedient. There is no careful observation that actions and presuppositions matter, or that the world is made of what matters. To have meaning in your life is better than to have what you want, because you may neither know what you want, nor what you truly need. Meaning is something that comes upon you, of its own accord. You can set up the preconditions, you can follow meaning, when it manifests itself, but you cannot simply produce it, as an act of will. Meaning signifies that you are in the right place, at the right time, properly balanced between order and chaos, where everything lines up as best it can at that moment.

What is expedient works only for the moment. It's immediate, impulsive and limited. What is meaningful, by contrast, is the organization of what would otherwise merely be expedient into a symphony of Being. Meaning is what is put forth more powerfully than mere words can express by Beethoven's "Ode to Joy," a triumphant bringing forth from the void of pattern after pattern upon beautiful pattern, every instrument playing its part, disciplined voices layered on top of that, spanning the entire breadth of human emotion from despair to exhilaration.

Meaning is what manifests itself when the many levels of Being arrange themselves into a perfectly functioning harmony, from atomic microcosm to cell to organ to individual to society to nature to cosmos, so that action at each level beautifully and perfectly facilitates action at all, such that past, present and future are all at once redeemed and reconciled. Meaning is what emerges beautifully and profoundly like a newly formed rosebud opening itself out of nothingness into the light of sun and God. Meaning is the lotus striving upward through the dark lake depths through the ever-clearing water, blooming forth on the very surface, revealing within itself the Golden Buddha, himself perfectly integrated, such that the revelation of the Divine Will can make itself manifest in his every word and gesture.

Meaning is when everything there is comes together in an ecstatic dance of single purpose—the glorification of a reality so that no matter how good it has suddenly become, it can get better and better and better more and more deeply forever into the future. Meaning happens when that dance has become so intense that all the horrors of the past, all the terrible struggle engaged in by all of life and all of humanity to that moment becomes a necessary and worthwhile part of the increasingly successful attempt to build something truly Mighty and Good.

Meaning is the ultimate balance between, on the one hand, the chaos of transformation and possibility and on the other, the discipline of pristine order, whose purpose is to produce out of the attendant chaos a new order that will be even more immaculate, and capable of bringing forth a still more balanced and productive chaos and order. Meaning is the Way, the path of life more abundant, the place you live when you are guided by Love and speaking Truth and when nothing you want or could possibly want takes any precedence over precisely that.

Do what is meaningful, not what is expedient.

TELL THE TRUTH—
OR, AT LEAST, DON'T LIE

TRUTH IN NO-MAN'S-LAND

I TRAINED TO BECOME A clinical psychologist at McGill University, in Montreal. While doing so, I sometimes met my classmates on the grounds of Montreal's Douglas Hospital, where we had our first direct experiences with the mentally ill. The Douglas occupies acres of land and dozens of buildings. Many are connected by underground tunnels to protect workers and patients from the interminable Montreal winters. The hospital once sheltered hundreds of long-term in-house patients. This was before anti-psychotic drugs and the large scale deinstitutionalization movements of the late sixties all but closed down the residential asylums, most often dooming the now "freed" patients to a much harder life on the streets. By the early eighties, when I first visited the grounds, all but the most seriously afflicted residents had been discharged. Those who remained were strange, much-damaged people. They clustered around the vending machines scattered throughout the hospital's tunnels. They looked as if they had been photographed by Diane Arbus or painted by Hieronymus Bosch.

One day my classmates and I were all standing in line. We were awaiting further instruction from the strait-laced German psychologist who ran the Douglas clinical training program. A long-term inpatient, fragile and vulnerable, approached one of the other students, a sheltered, conservative young woman. The patient spoke to her in a friendly, childlike manner, and asked, "Why are you all standing here? What are you doing? Can I come along with you?" My classmate turned to me and asked uncertainly, "What should I say to her?" She was taken aback, just as I was, by this request coming from someone so isolated and hurt. Neither of us wanted to say anything that might be construed as a rejection or reprimand.

We had temporarily entered a kind of no-man's-land, in which society offers no ground rules or guidance. We were new clinical students, unprepared to be confronted on the grounds of a mental hospital by a schizophrenic patient asking a naive, friendly question about the possibility of social belonging. The natural conversational give-and-take between people attentive to contextual cues was not happening here, either. What exactly were the rules, in such a situation, far outside the boundaries of normal social interaction? What exactly were the options?

There were only two, as far as I could quickly surmise. I could tell the patient a story designed to save everyone's face, or I could answer truthfully. "We can only take eight people in our group," would have fallen into the first category, as would have, "We are just leaving the hospital now." Neither of these answers would have bruised any feelings, at least on the surface, and the presence of the status differences that divided us from her would have gone unremarked. But neither answer would have been exactly true. So, I didn't offer either.

I told the patient as simply and directly as I could that we were new students, training to be psychologists, and that she couldn't join us for that reason. The answer highlighted the distinction between her situation and ours, making the gap between us greater and more evident. The answer was harsher than a well-crafted white lie. But I already had an inkling that untruth, however well-meant, can produce unintended consequences. She looked crestfallen, and hurt, but only for a moment. Then she understood, and it was all right. That was just how it was.

I had had a strange set of experiences a few years before embarking upon my clinical training.[148] I found myself subject to some rather violent compulsions (none acted upon), and developed the conviction, in consequence, that I really knew rather little about who I was and what I was up to. So, I began paying much closer attention to what I was doing—and saying. The experience was disconcerting, to say the least. I soon divided myself into two parts: one that spoke, and one, more detached, that paid attention and judged. I soon came to realize that almost everything I said was untrue. I had motives for saying these things: I wanted to win arguments and gain status and impress people and get what I wanted. I was using language to bend and twist the world into delivering what I thought was necessary. But I was a fake. Realizing this, I started to practise only saying things that the internal voice would not object to. I started to practise telling the truth—or, at least, not lying. I soon learned that such a skill came in very handy when I didn't know what to do. What should you do, when you don't know what to do? Tell the truth. So, that's what I did my first day at the Douglas Hospital.

Later, I had a client who was paranoid and dangerous. Working with paranoid people is challenging. They believe they have been targeted by mysterious conspiratorial forces, working malevolently behind the scenes. Paranoid people are hyper-alert and hyper-focused. They are attending to non-verbal cues with an intentness never manifest during ordinary human interactions. They make mistakes in interpretation (that's the paranoia) but they are still almost uncanny in their ability to detect mixed motives, judgment and falsehood. You have to listen very carefully and tell the truth if you are going to get a paranoid person to open up to you.

I listened carefully and spoke truthfully to my client. Now and then, he would describe blood-curdling fantasies of flaying people for revenge. I would watch how I was reacting. I paid attention to what thoughts and images emerged in the theatre of my imagination while he spoke, and I told him what I observed. I was not trying to control or direct his thoughts or actions (or mine). I was only trying to let him know as transparently as I could how what he was doing was directly affecting at least one person—me. My careful attention and frank responses did not mean at all that I remained unperturbed, let alone approved. I told him when he scared me (often), that his words and behaviour were misguided, and that he was going to get into serious trouble.

He talked to me, nonetheless, because I listened and responded honestly, even though I was not encouraging in my responses. He trusted me, despite (or, more accurately, because of) my objections. He was paranoid, not stupid. He knew his behaviour was socially unacceptable. He knew that any decent person was likely to react with horror to his insane fantasies. He trusted me and would talk to me because that's how I reacted. There was no chance of understanding him without that trust.

Trouble for him generally started in a bureaucracy, such as a bank. He would enter an institution and attempt some simple task. He was looking to open an account, or pay a bill, or fix some mistake. Now and then he encountered the kind of non-helpful person that everyone encounters now and then in such a place. That person would reject the ID he offered, or require some information that was unnecessary and difficult to obtain. Sometimes, I suppose, the bureaucratic runaround was unavoidable—but sometimes it was unnecessarily complicated by petty misuses of bureaucratic power. My client was very attuned to such things. He was obsessed with honour. It was more important to him than safety, freedom or belonging. Following that logic (because paranoid people are impeccably logical), he could never allow himself to be demeaned, insulted or put down, even a little bit, by anyone. Water did not roll off his back. Because of his rigid and inflexible attitude, my client's actions had already been subjected to several restraining orders. Restraining orders work best, however, with the sort of person who would never require a restraining order.

"I will be your worst nightmare," was his phrase of choice, in such situations. I have wished intensely that I could say something like that, after encountering unnecessary bureaucratic obstacles, but it's generally best to let such things go. My client meant what he said, however, and sometimes he really did become someone's nightmare. He was the bad guy in *No Country for Old Men*. He was the person you meet in the wrong place, at the wrong time. If you messed with him, even accidentally, he was going to stalk you, remind you what you had done, and scare the living daylights out of you. He was no one to lie to. I told him the truth and that cooled him off.

My Landlord

I had a landlord around that time who had been president of a local biker gang. My wife, Tammy, and I lived next door to him in his parents' small apartment building. His girlfriend bore the marks of self-inflicted injuries characteristic of borderline personality disorder. She killed herself while we lived there.

Denis, large, strong, French-Canadian, with a grey beard, was a gifted amateur electrician. He had some artistic talent, too, and was supporting himself making laminated wood posters with custom neon lights. He was trying to stay sober, after being released from jail. Still, every month or so, he would disappear on a days-long bender. He was one of those men who have a miraculous capacity for alcohol; he could drink fifty or sixty beers in a two-day binge and remain standing the whole time. This may seem hard to believe, but it's true. I was doing research on familial alcoholism at the time, and it was not rare for my subjects to report their fathers' habitual consumption of forty ounces of vodka a day. These patriarchs would buy one bottle every afternoon, Monday through Friday, and then two on Saturday, to tide them over through the Sunday liquor-store closure.

Denis had a little dog. Sometimes Tammy and I would hear Denis and the dog out in the backyard at four in the morning, during one of Denis's marathon drinking sessions, both of them howling madly at the moon. Now and then, on occasions like that, Denis would drink up every cent he had saved. Then he would show up at our apartment. We would hear a knock at night. Denis would be at the door, swaying precipitously, upright, and miraculously conscious.

He would be standing there, toaster, microwave, or poster in hand. He wanted to sell these to me so he could keep on drinking. I bought a few things like this, pretending that I was being charitable. Eventually, Tammy convinced me that I couldn't do it anymore. It made her nervous, and it was bad for Denis, whom she liked. Reasonable and even necessary as her request was, it still placed me in a tricky position.

What do you say to a severely intoxicated, violence-prone ex-biker-gang-president with patchy English when he tries to sell his microwave to you at your open door at two in the morning? This was a question even more difficult than those presented by the institutionalized patient or the paranoid flayer. But the answer was the same: the truth. But you'd bloody well better know what the truth is.

Denis knocked again soon after my wife and I had talked. He looked at me in the direct skeptical narrow-eyed manner characteristic of the tough, heavy-drinking man who is no stranger to trouble. That look means, "Prove your innocence." Weaving slightly back and forth, he asked—politely—if I might be interested in purchasing his toaster. I rid myself, to the bottom of my soul, of primate-dominance motivations and moral superiority. I told him as directly and carefully as I could that I would not. I was playing no tricks. In that moment I wasn't an educated, anglophone, fortunate, upwardly-mobile young man. He wasn't an ex-con Québécois biker with a blood alcohol level of .24. No, we were two men of good will trying to help each other out in our common struggle to do the right thing. I said that he had told me he was trying to quit drinking. I said that it would not be good for him if I provided him with more money. I said that he made Tammy, whom he respected, nervous when he came over so drunk and so late and tried to sell me things.

He glared seriously at me without speaking for about fifteen seconds. That was plenty long enough. He was watching, I knew, for any micro-expression revealing sarcasm, deceit, contempt or self-congratulation. But I had thought it through, carefully, and I had only said things I truly meant. I had chosen my words, carefully, traversing a treacherous swamp, feeling out a partially submerged stone path. Denis turned and left. Not only that, he remembered our conversation, despite his state of professional-level intoxication. He didn't try to sell me anything again. Our relationship, which was quite good, given the great cultural gaps between us, became even more solid.

Taking the easy way out or telling the truth—those are not merely two different choices. They are different pathways through life. They are utterly different ways of existing.

Manipulate the World

You can use words to manipulate the world into delivering what you want. This is what it means to "act politically." This is spin. It's the specialty of unscrupulous marketers, salesmen, advertisers, pickup artists, slogan-possessed utopians and psychopaths. It's the speech people engage in when they attempt to influence and manipulate others. It's what university students do when they write an essay to please the professor, instead of articulating and clarifying their own ideas. It's what everyone does when they want something, and decide to falsify themselves to please and flatter. It's scheming and sloganeering and propaganda.

To conduct life like this is to become possessed by some ill-formed desire, and then to craft speech and action in a manner that appears likely, rationally, to bring about that end. Typical calculated ends might include "to impose my ideological beliefs," "to prove that I am (or was) right," "to appear competent," "to ratchet myself up the dominance hierarchy," "to avoid responsibility" (or its twin, "to garner credit for others' actions"), "to be promoted," "to attract the lion's share of attention," "to ensure that everyone likes me," "to garner the benefits of martyrdom," "to justify my cynicism," "to rationalize my antisocial outlook," "to minimize immediate conflict," "to maintain my naïveté," "to capitalize on my vulnerability," "to always appear as the sainted one," or (this one is particularly evil) "to ensure that it is always my unloved child's fault." These are all examples of what Sigmund Freud's compatriot, the lesser-known Austrian psychologist Alfred Adler, called "life-lies."[149]

Someone living a life-lie is attempting to manipulate reality with perception, thought and action, so that only some narrowly desired and pre-defined outcome is allowed to exist. A life lived in this manner is based, consciously or unconsciously, on two premises. The first is that current knowledge is sufficient to define what is good, unquestioningly, far into the future. The second is that reality would be unbearable if left to its own devices. The first presumption is philosophically unjustifiable. What you are currently aiming at might not be worth attaining, just as what you are currently doing might be an error. The second is even worse. It is valid only if reality is intrinsically intolerable and, simultaneously, something that can be successfully manipulated and distorted. Such speaking and thinking requires the arrogance and certainty that the English poet John Milton's genius identified with Satan, God's highest angel gone most spectacularly wrong. The faculty of rationality inclines dangerously to pride: *all I know is all that needs to be known.* Pride falls in love with its own creations, and tries to make them absolute.

I have seen people define their utopia and then bend their lives into knots trying to make it reality. A left-leaning student adopts a trendy, anti-authority stance and spends the next twenty years working resentfully to topple the windmills of his imagination. An eighteen-year-old decides, arbitrarily, that she wants to retire at fifty-two. She works for three decades to make that happen, failing to notice that she made that decision when she was little more than a child. What did she know about her fifty-two-year-old self, when still a teenager? Even now, many years later, she has only the vaguest, lowest-resolution idea of her post-work Eden. She refuses to notice. What did her life mean, if that initial goal was wrong? She's afraid of opening Pandora's box, where all the troubles of the world reside. But hope is in there, too. Instead, she warps her life to fit the fantasies of a sheltered adolescent.

A naively formulated goal transmutes, with time, into the sinister form of the life-lie. One forty-something client told me his vision, formulated by his younger self: "I see myself retired, sitting on a tropical beach, drinking margaritas in the sunshine." That's not a plan. That's a travel poster. After eight margaritas, you're fit only to await the hangover. After three weeks of margarita-filled days, if you have any sense, you're bored stiff and self-disgusted. In a year, or less, you're pathetic. It's just not a sustainable approach to later life. This kind of oversimplification and falsification is particularly typical of ideologues. They adopt a single axiom: government is bad, immigration is bad, capitalism is bad, patriarchy is bad. Then they filter and screen their experiences and insist ever more narrowly that everything can be explained by that axiom. They believe, narcissistically, underneath all that bad theory, that the world could be put right, if only they held the controls.

There is another fundamental problem, too, with the life-lie, particularly when it is based on avoidance. A sin of commission occurs when you do something you know to be wrong. A sin of omission occurs when you let something bad happen when you could do something to stop it. The former is regarded, classically, as more serious than the latter—than avoidance. I'm not so sure.

Consider the person who insists that everything is right in her life. She avoids conflict, and smiles, and does what she is asked to do. She finds a niche and hides in it. She does not question authority or put her own ideas forward, and does not complain when mistreated. She strives for invisibility, like a fish in the centre of a swarming school. But a secret unrest gnaws at her heart. She is still suffering, because life is suffering. She is lonesome and isolated and unfulfilled. But her obedience and self-obliteration eliminate all the meaning from her life. She has become nothing but a slave, a tool for others to exploit. She does not get what she wants, or needs, because doing so would mean speaking her mind. So, there is nothing of value in her existence to counter-balance life's troubles. And that makes her sick.

It might be the noisy troublemakers who disappear, first, when the institution you serve falters and shrinks. But it's the invisible who will be sacrificed next. Someone hiding is not someone vital. Vitality requires original contribution. Hiding also does not save the conforming and conventional from disease, insanity, death and taxes. And hiding from others also means suppressing and hiding the potentialities of the unrealized self. And that's the problem.

If you will not reveal yourself to others, you cannot reveal yourself to yourself. That does not only mean that you suppress who you are, although it also means that. It means that so much of what you could be will never be forced by necessity to come forward. This is a biological truth, as well as a conceptual truth. When you explore boldly, when you voluntarily confront the unknown, you gather information and build your renewed self out of that information. That is the conceptual element. However, researchers have recently discovered that new genes in the central nervous system turn themselves on when an organism is placed (or places itself) in a new situation. These genes code for new proteins. These proteins are the building blocks for new structures in the brain. This means that a lot of you is still nascent, in the most physical of senses, and will not be called forth by stasis. You have to say something, go somewhere and do things to get turned on. And, if not . . . you remain incomplete, and life is too hard for anyone incomplete.

If you say no to your boss, or your spouse, or your mother, when it needs to be said, then you transform yourself into someone who *can* say no when it needs to be said. If you say yes when no needs to be said, however, you transform yourself into someone who can only say yes, even when it is very clearly time to say no. If you ever wonder how perfectly ordinary, decent people could find themselves doing the terrible things the gulag camp guards did, you now have your answer. By the time *no* seriously needed to be said, there was no one left capable of saying it.

If you betray yourself, if you say untrue things, if you act out a lie, you weaken your character. If you have a weak character, then adversity will mow you down when it appears, as it will, inevitably. You will hide, but there will be no place left to hide. And then you will find yourself doing terrible things.

Only the most cynical, hopeless philosophy insists that reality could be improved through falsification. Such a philosophy judges Being and becoming alike, and deems them flawed. It denounces truth as insufficient and the honest man as deluded. It is a philosophy that both brings about and then justifies the endemic corruption of the world.

It is not vision as such, and not a plan devised to achieve a vision, that is at fault under such circumstances. A vision of the future, the desirable future, is necessary. Such a vision links action taken now with important, long-term, foundational values. It lends actions in the present significance and importance. It provides a frame limiting uncertainty and anxiety.

It's not vision. It is instead willful blindness. It's the worst sort of lie. It's subtle. It avails itself of easy rationalizations. Willful blindness is the refusal to know something that could be known. It's refusal to admit that the knocking sound means someone at the door. It's refusal to acknowledge the eight-hundred-pound gorilla in the room, the elephant under the carpet, the skeleton in the closet. It's refusal to admit to error while pursuing the plan. Every game has rules. Some of the most important rules are implicit. You accept them merely by deciding to play the game. The first of these rules is that the game is important. If it wasn't important, you wouldn't be playing it. Playing a game defines it as important. The second is that moves undertaken during the game are valid if they help you win. If you make a move and it isn't helping you win, then, by definition, it's a bad move. You need to try something different. You remember the old joke: insanity is doing the same thing over and over while expecting different results.

If you're lucky, and you fail, and you try something new, you move ahead. If that doesn't work, you try something different again. A minor modification will suffice in fortunate circumstances. It is therefore prudent to begin with small changes, and see if they help. Sometimes, however, the entire hierarchy of values is faulty, and the whole edifice has to be abandoned. The whole game must be changed. That's a revolution, with all the chaos and terror of a revolution. It's not something to be engaged in lightly, but it's sometimes necessary. Error necessitates sacrifice to correct it, and serious error necessitates serious sacrifice. To accept the truth means to sacrifice—and if you have rejected the truth for a long time, then you've run up a dangerously large sacrificial debt. Forest fires burn out deadwood and return trapped elements to the soil. Sometimes, however, fires are suppressed, artificially. That does not stop the deadwood from accumulating.

Sooner or later, a fire will start. When it does, it will burn so hot that everything will be destroyed—even the soil in which the forest grows.

The prideful, rational mind, comfortable with its certainty, enamoured of its own brilliance, is easily tempted to ignore error, and to sweep dirt under the rug. Literary, existential philosophers, beginning with Søren Kierkegaard, conceived of this mode of Being as "inauthentic." An inauthentic person continues to perceive and act in ways his own experience has demonstrated false. He does not speak with his own voice.

"Did what I want happen? No. Then my aim or my methods were wrong. I still have something to learn." That is the voice of authenticity.

"Did what I want happen? No. Then the world is unfair. People are jealous, and too stupid to understand. It is the fault of something or someone else." That is the voice of inauthenticity. It is not too far from there to "they should be stopped" or "they must be hurt" or "they must be destroyed." Whenever you hear about something incomprehensibly brutal, such ideas have manifested themselves.

There is no blaming any of this on unconsciousness, either, or repression. When the individual lies, he knows it. He may blind himself to the consequences of his actions. He may fail to analyze and articulate his past, so that he does not understand. He may even forget that he lied and so be unconscious of that fact. But he was conscious, in the present, during the commission of each error, and the omission of each responsibility. At that moment, he knew what he was up to. And the sins of the inauthentic individual compound and corrupt the state.

Someone power-hungry makes a new rule at your workplace. It's unnecessary. It's counterproductive. It's an irritant. It removes some of the pleasure and meaning from your work. But you tell yourself it's all right. It's not worth complaining about. Then it happens again. You've already trained yourself to allow such things, by failing to react the first time. You're a little less courageous. Your opponent, unopposed, is a little bit stronger. The institution is a little bit more corrupt. The process of bureaucratic stagnation and oppression is underway, and you've contributed, by pretending that it was OK. Why not complain? Why not take a stand? If you do, other people, equally afraid to speak up, may come to your defence. And if not—maybe it's time for a revolution. Maybe you should find a job somewhere else, where your soul is less in danger from corruption.

For what shall it profit a man if he gain the whole world and forfeit his soul? (Mark 8:36)

One of the major contributions of Aleksandr Solzhenitsyn's masterwork, *The Gulag Archipelago*, was his analysis of the direct causal relationship between the pathology of the Soviet prison-work-camp dependent state (where millions suffered and died) and the almost universal proclivity of the Soviet citizen to falsify his own day-to-day personal experience, deny his own state-induced suffering, and thereby prop up the dictates of the rational, ideology-possessed communist system. It was this bad faith, this denial, that in Solzhenitsyn's opinion aided and abetted that great paranoid mass-murderer, Joseph Stalin, in his crimes. Solzhenitsyn wrote the truth, his truth, hard-learned through his own experiences in the camps, exposing the lies of the Soviet state. No educated person dared defend that ideology again after Solzhenitsyn published *The Gulag Archipelago*. No one could ever say again, "What Stalin did, that was not true communism."

Viktor Frankl, the psychiatrist and Nazi concentration camp survivor who wrote the classic *Man's Search for Meaning*, drew a similar social-psychological conclusion: *deceitful, inauthentic individual existence is the precursor to social totalitarianism*. Sigmund Freud, for his part, analogously believed that "repression" contributed in a non-trivial manner to the development of mental illness (and the difference between repression of truth and a lie is a matter of degree, not kind). Alfred Adler knew it was lies that bred sickness. C.G. Jung knew that moral problems plagued his patients, and that such problems were caused by untruth. All these thinkers, all centrally concerned with pathology both individual and cultural, came to the same conclusion: lies warp the structure of Being. Untruth corrupts the soul and the state alike, and one form of corruption feeds the other.

I have repeatedly observed the transformation of mere existential misery into outright hell by betrayal and deceit. The barely manageable crisis of a parent's terminal illness can be turned, for example, into something awful beyond description by the unseemly and petty squabbling of the sufferer's adult children. Obsessed by the unresolved past, they gather like ghouls around the deathbed, forcing tragedy into an unholy dalliance with cowardice and resentment.

The inability of a son to thrive independently is exploited by a mother bent on shielding her child from all disappointment and pain. He never leaves, and she is never lonely. It's an evil conspiracy, forged slowly, as the pathology unfolds, by thousands of knowing winks and nods. She plays the martyr, doomed to support her son, and garners nourishing sympathy, like a vampire, from supporting friends. He broods in his basement, imagining himself oppressed. He fantasizes with delight about the havoc he might wreak on the world that rejected him for his cowardice, awkwardness and inability. And sometimes he wreaks precisely that havoc. And everyone asks, "Why?" They could know, but refuse to.

Even well-lived lives can, of course, be warped and hurt and twisted by illness and infirmity and uncontrollable catastrophe. Depression, bipolar disorder and schizophrenia, like cancer, all involve biological factors beyond the individual's immediate control. The difficulties intrinsic to life itself are sufficient to weaken and overwhelm each of us, pushing us beyond our limits, breaking us at our weakest point. Not even the best-lived life provides an absolute defence against vulnerability. But the family that fights in the ruins of their earthquake-devastated dwelling place is much less likely to rebuild than the family made strong by mutual trust and devotion. Any natural weakness or existential challenge, no matter how minor, can be magnified into a serious crisis with enough deceit in the individual, family or culture.

The honest human spirit may continually fail in its attempts to bring about Paradise on Earth. It may manage, however, to reduce the suffering attendant on existence to bearable levels. The tragedy of Being is the consequence of our limitations and the vulnerability defining human experience. It may even be the price we pay for Being itself—since existence must be limited, to be at all.

I have seen a husband adapt honestly and courageously while his wife descended into terminal dementia. He made the necessary adjustments, step by step. He accepted help when he needed it. He refused to deny her sad deterioration and in that manner adapted gracefully to it. I saw the family of that same woman come together in a supporting and sustaining manner as she lay dying, and gain newfound connections with each other—brother, sisters, grandchildren and father—as partial but genuine compensation for their loss. I have seen my teenage daughter live through the destruction of her hip and her ankle and survive two years of continual, intense pain and emerge with her spirit intact. I watched her younger brother voluntarily and without resentment sacrifice many opportunities for friendship and social engagement to stand by her and us while she suffered. With love, encouragement, and character intact, a human being can be resilient beyond imagining. What cannot be borne, however, is the absolute ruin produced by tragedy and deception.

The capacity of the rational mind to deceive, manipulate, scheme, trick, falsify, minimize, mislead, betray, prevaricate, deny, omit, rationalize, bias, exaggerate and obscure is so endless, so remarkable, that centuries of pre-scientific thought, concentrating on clarifying the nature of moral endeavour, regarded it as positively demonic. This is not because of rationality itself, as a process. That process can produce clarity and progress. It is because rationality is subject to the single worst temptation—to raise what it knows now to the status of an absolute.

We can turn to the great poet John Milton, once again, to clarify just what this means. Over thousands of years of history, the Western world wrapped a dream-like fantasy about the nature of evil around its central religious core. That fantasy had a protagonist, an adversarial personality, absolutely dedicated to the corruption of Being. Milton took it upon himself to organize, dramatize and articulate the essence of this collective dream, and gave it life, in the figure of Satan—Lucifer, the "light bearer." He writes of Lucifer's primal temptation, and its immediate consequences:[150]

> He trusted to have equaled the most High,
> If he opposed; and with ambitious aim
> Against the Throne and Monarchy of God

Raised impious War in Heaven and Battel proud
With vain attempt. Him the Almighty Power
Hurled headlong flaming from the Ethereal Sky
With hideous ruin and combustion down
To bottomless perdition, there to dwell
In Adamantine Chains and penal Fire . . .

Lucifer, in Milton's eyes—the spirit of reason—was the most wondrous angel brought forth from the void by God. This can be read psychologically. Reason is something alive. It lives in all of us. It's older than any of us. It's best understood as a personality, not a faculty. It has its aims, and its temptations, and its weaknesses. It flies higher and sees farther than any other spirit. But reason falls in love with itself, and worse. It falls in love with its own productions. It elevates them, and worships them as absolutes. Lucifer is, therefore, the spirit of totalitarianism. He is flung from Heaven into Hell because such elevation, such rebellion against the Highest and Incomprehensible, inevitably produces Hell.

To say it again: it is the greatest temptation of the rational faculty to glorify its own capacity and its own productions and to claim that in the face of its theories nothing transcendent or outside its domain need exist. This means that all important facts have been discovered. This means that nothing important remains unknown. But most importantly, it means denial of the necessity for courageous individual confrontation with Being. What is going to save you? The totalitarian says, in essence, "You must rely on faith in what you already know." But that is not what saves. *What saves is the willingness to learn from what you don't know.* That is faith in the possibility of human transformation. That is faith in the sacrifice of the current self for the self that could be. The totalitarian denies the necessity for the individual to take ultimate responsibility for Being.

That denial is the meaning of rebellion against "the most High." That is what *totalitarian* means: Everything that needs to be discovered has been discovered. Everything will unfold precisely as planned. All problems will vanish, forever, once the perfect system is accepted.

Milton's great poem was a prophecy. As rationality rose ascendant from the ashes of Christianity, the great threat of total systems accompanied it. Communism, in particular, was attractive not so much to oppressed workers, its hypothetical beneficiaries, but to intellectuals—to those whose arrogant pride in intellect assured them they were always right. But the promised utopia never emerged. Instead humanity experienced the inferno of Stalinist Russia and Mao's China and Pol Pot's Cambodia, and the citizens of those states were required to betray their own experience, turn against their fellow citizens, and die in the tens of millions.

There is an old Soviet joke. An American dies and goes to hell. Satan himself shows him around. They pass a large cauldron. The American peers in. It's full of suffering souls, burning in hot pitch. As they struggle to leave the pot, low-ranking devils, sitting on the rim, pitchfork them back in. The American is properly shocked. Satan says, "That's where we put sinful Englishmen." The tour continues. Soon the duo approaches a second cauldron. It's slightly larger, and slightly hotter. The American peers in. It is also full of suffering souls, all wearing berets. Devils are pitchforking would-be escapees back into this cauldron, as well. "That's where we put sinful Frenchmen," Satan says. In the distance is a third cauldron. It's much bigger, and is glowing, white hot. The American can barely get near it. Nonetheless, at Satan's insistence, he approaches it and peers in. It is absolutely packed with souls, barely visible, under the surface of the boiling liquid. Now and then, however, one clambers out of the pitch and desperately reaches for the rim. Oddly, there are no devils sitting on the edge of this giant pot, but the clamberer disappears back under the surface anyway. The American asks, "Why are there no demons here to keep everyone from escaping?" Satan replies, "This is where we put the Russians. If one tries to escape, the others pull him back in."

Milton believed that stubborn refusal to change in the face of error not only meant ejection from heaven, and subsequent degeneration into an ever-deepening hell, but the rejection of redemption itself. Satan knows full well that even if he was willing to seek reconciliation, and God willing to grant it, he would only rebel again, because he will not change. Perhaps it is this prideful stubbornness that constitutes the mysterious unforgivable sin against the Holy Ghost:

> . . . *Farewell happy Fields*
> *Where Joy for ever dwells: Hail horrors, hail*
> *Infernal world, and thou profoundest Hell*
> *Receive thy new Possessor: One who brings*
> *A mind not to be changed by Place or Time.*[151]

This is no afterlife fantasy. This is no perverse realm of post-existence torture for political enemies. This is an abstract idea, and abstractions are often more real than what they represent. The idea that hell exists in some metaphysical manner is not only ancient, and pervasive; it's true. Hell is eternal. It has always existed. It exists now. It's the most barren, hopeless and malevolent subdivision of the underworld of chaos, where disappointed and resentful people forever dwell.

> *The mind is its own place, and in itself*
> *Can make a Heav'n of Hell, a Hell of Heav'n.*[152]
> . . .
> *Here we may reign secure, and in my choice*
> *To reign is worth ambition though in Hell:*
> *Better to reign in Hell, than serve in Heav'n.*[153]

Those who have lied enough, in word and action, live there, in hell—now. Take a walk down any busy urban street. Keep your eyes open and pay attention. You will see people who are there, now. These are the people to whom you instinctively give a wide berth. These are the people who are immediately angered if you direct your gaze toward them, although sometimes they will instead turn away in shame. I saw a horribly damaged street alcoholic do exactly that in the presence of my young daughter. He wanted above all to avoid seeing his degraded state incontrovertibly reflected in her eyes.

It is deceit that makes people miserable beyond what they can bear. It is deceit that fills human souls with resentment and vengefulness. It is deceit that produces the terrible suffering of mankind: the death camps of the Nazis; the torture chambers and genocides of Stalin and that even greater monster, Mao. It was deceit that killed hundreds of millions of people in the twentieth century. It was deceit that almost doomed civilization itself. It is deceit that still threatens us, most profoundly, today.

The Truth, Instead

What happens if, instead, we decide to stop lying? What does this even mean? We are limited in our knowledge, after all. We must make decisions, here and now, even though the best means and the best goals can never be discerned with certainty. An aim, an ambition, provides the structure necessary for action. An aim provides a destination, a point of contrast against the present, and a framework, within which all things can be evaluated. An aim defines progress and makes such progress exciting. An aim reduces anxiety, because if you have no aim everything can mean anything or nothing, and neither of those two options makes for a tranquil spirit. Thus, we have to think, and plan, and limit, and posit, in order to live at all. How then to envision the future, and establish our direction, without falling prey to the temptation of totalitarian certainty?

Some reliance on tradition can help us establish our aims. It is reasonable to do what other people have always done, unless we have a very good reason not to. It is reasonable to become educated and work and find love and have a family. That is how culture maintains itself. But it is necessary to aim at your target, however traditional, with your eyes wide open. You have a direction, but it might be wrong. You have a plan, but it might be ill-formed. You may have been led astray by your own ignorance—and, worse, by your own unrevealed corruption. You must make friends, therefore, with what you don't know, instead of what you know. You must remain awake to catch yourself in the act. You must remove the beam in your own eye, before you concern yourself with the mote in your brother's. And in this way, you strengthen your own spirit, so it can tolerate the burden of existence, and you rejuvenate the state.

The ancient Egyptians had already figured this out thousands of years ago, although their knowledge remained embodied in dramatic form.[154] They worshipped Osiris, mythological founder of the state and the god of tradition. Osiris, however, was vulnerable to overthrow and banishment to the underworld by Set, his evil, scheming brother. The Egyptians represented in story the fact that social organizations ossify with time, and tend towards willful blindness. Osiris would not see his brother's true character, even though he could have. Set waits and, at an opportune moment, attacks. He hacks Osiris into pieces, and scatters the divine remains through the kingdom. He sends his brother's spirit to the underworld. He makes it very difficult for Osiris to pull himself back together.

Fortunately, the great king did not have to deal with Set on his own. The Egyptians also worshipped Horus, the son of Osiris. Horus took the twin forms of a falcon, the most visually acute of all creatures, and the still-famous hieroglyphic single Egyptian eye (as alluded to in Rule 7). Osiris is tradition, aged and willfully blind. Horus, his son, could and would, by contrast, see. Horus was the god of attention. That is not the same as rationality. Because he paid attention, Horus could perceive and triumph against the evils of Set, his uncle, albeit at great cost. When Horus confronts Set, they have a terrible battle. Before Set's defeat and banishment from the kingdom, he tears out one of his nephew's eyes. But the eventually victorious Horus takes back the eye. Then he does something truly unexpected: *he journeys voluntarily to the underworld and gives the eye to his father.*

What does this mean? First, that the encounter with malevolence and evil is of sufficient terror to damage even the vision of a god; second, *that the attentive son can restore the vision of his father.* Culture is always in a near-dead state, even though it was established by the spirit of great people in the past. But the present is not the past. The wisdom of the past thus deteriorates, or becomes outdated, in proportion to the genuine difference between the conditions of the present and the past. That is a mere consequence of the passage of time, and the change that passage inevitably brings. But it is also the case that culture and its wisdom is additionally vulnerable to corruption—to voluntary, willful blindness and Mephistophelean intrigue. Thus, the inevitable functional decline of the institutions granted to us by our ancestors is sped along by our misbehavior—our missing of the mark—in the present.

It is our responsibility to see what is before our eyes, courageously, and to learn from it, even if it seems horrible—even if the horror of seeing it damages our consciousness, and half-blinds us. The act of seeing is particularly important when it challenges what we know and rely on, upsetting and destabilizing us. It is the act of seeing that informs the individual and updates the state. It was for this reason that Nietzsche said that a man's worth was determined by how much truth he could tolerate. You are by no means only what you already know. You are also all that which you could know, if you only would. Thus, you should never sacrifice what you could be for what you are. You should never give up the better that resides within for the security you already have—and certainly not when you have already caught a glimpse, an undeniable glimpse, of something beyond.

In the Christian tradition, Christ is identified with the Logos. The Logos is the Word of God. That Word transformed chaos into order at the beginning of time. In His human form, Christ sacrificed himself voluntarily to the truth, to the good, to God. In consequence, He died and was reborn. The Word that produces order from Chaos sacrifices everything, even itself, to God. That single sentence, wise beyond comprehension, sums up Christianity. Every bit of learning is a little death. Every bit of new information challenges a previous conception, forcing it to dissolve into chaos before it can be reborn as something better. Sometimes such deaths virtually destroy us. In such cases, we might never recover or, if we do, we change a lot. A good friend of mine discovered that his wife of decades was having an affair. He didn't see it coming. It plunged him into a deep depression. He descended into the underworld. He told me, at one point, "I always thought that people who were depressed should just shake it off. I didn't have any idea what I was talking about." Eventually, he returned from the depths. In many ways, he's a new man—and, perhaps, a wiser and better man. He lost forty pounds. He ran a marathon. He travelled to Africa and climbed Mount Kilimanjaro. He chose rebirth over descent into Hell.

Set your ambitions, even if you are uncertain about what they should be. The better ambitions have to do with the development of character and ability, rather than status and power. Status you can lose. You carry character with you wherever you go, and it allows you to prevail against adversity. Knowing this, tie a rope to a boulder. Pick up the great stone, heave it in front of you, and pull yourself towards it. Watch and observe while you move forward. Articulate your experience as clearly and carefully to yourself and others as you possibly can. In this manner, you will learn to proceed more effectively and efficiently towards your goal. And, while you are doing this, do not lie. Especially to yourself.

If you pay attention to what you do and say, you can learn to feel a state of internal division and weakness when you are misbehaving and misspeaking. It's an embodied sensation, not a thought. I experience an internal sensation of sinking and division, rather than solidity and strength, when I am incautious with my acts and words. It seems to be centred in my solar plexus, where a large knot of nervous tissue resides. I learned to recognize when I was lying, in fact, by noticing this sinking and division, and then inferring the presence of a lie. It often took me a long time to ferret out the deception. Sometimes I was using words for appearance. Sometimes I was trying to disguise my own true ignorance of the topic at hand. Sometimes I was using the words of others to avoid the responsibility of thinking for myself.

If you pay attention, when you are seeking something, you will move towards your goal. More importantly, however, you will acquire the information that allows your goal itself to transform. A totalitarian never asks, "What if my current ambition is in error?" He treats it, instead, as the Absolute. It becomes his God, for all intents and purposes. It constitutes his highest value. It regulates his emotions and motivational states, and determines his thoughts. All people serve their ambition. In that matter, there are no atheists. There are only people who know, and don't know, what God they serve.

If you bend everything totally, blindly and willfully towards the attainment of a goal, and only that goal, you will never be able to discover if another goal would serve you, and the world, better. It is this that you sacrifice if you do not tell the truth. If, instead, you tell the truth, your values transform as you progress. If you allow yourself to be informed by the reality manifesting itself, as you struggle forward, your notions of what is important will change. You will reorient yourself, sometimes gradually, and sometimes suddenly and radically.

Imagine: you go to engineering school, because that is what your parents desire—but it is not what you want. Working at cross-purposes to your own wishes, you will find yourself unmotivated, and failing. You will struggle to concentrate and discipline yourself, but it will not work. Your soul will reject the tyranny of your will (how else could that be said?). Why are you complying? You may not want to disappoint your parents (although if you fail you will do exactly that). You may lack the courage for the conflict necessary to free yourself. You may not want to sacrifice your childish belief in parental omniscience, wishing devoutly to continue believing that there is someone who knows you better than you know yourself, and who also knows all about the world. You want to be shielded in this manner from the stark existential aloneness of individual Being and its attendant responsibility. This is all very common and understandable. But you suffer because you are truly not meant to be an engineer.

One day you have had enough. You drop out. You disappoint your parents. You learn to live with that. You consult only yourself, even though that means you must rely on your own decisions. You take a philosophy degree. You accept the burden of your own mistakes. You become your own person. By rejecting your father's vision, you develop your own. And then, as your parents age, you've become adult enough to be there for them, when they come to need you. They win, too. But both victories had to be purchased at the cost of the conflict engendered by your truth. As Matthew 10:34 has it, citing Christ— emphasizing the role of the spoken Truth: "Think not that I have come to send peace on earth: I came not to send peace, but a sword."

As you continue to live in accordance with the truth, as it reveals itself to you, you will have to accept and deal with the conflicts that mode of Being will generate. If you do so, you will continue to mature and become more responsible, in small ways (don't underestimate their importance) and in large. You will ever more closely approach your newer and more wisely formulated goals, and become even wiser in their formulation, when you discover and rectify your inevitable errors. Your conception of what is important will become more and more appropriate, as you incorporate the wisdom of your experience. You will quit wildly oscillating and walk ever more directly towards the good—a good you could never have comprehended if you had insisted despite all evidence that you were right, absolutely right, at the beginning.

If existence is good, then the clearest and cleanest and most correct relationship with it is also good. If existence is not good, by contrast, you're lost. Nothing will save you—certainly not the petty rebellions, murky thinking and obscurantist blindness that constitute deceit. Is existence good? You have to take a terrible risk to find out. Live in truth, or live in deceit, face the consequences, and draw your conclusions.

This is the "act of faith" whose necessity was insisted upon by the Danish philosopher Kierkegaard. You cannot know ahead of time. Even a good example is insufficient for proof, given the differences between individuals. The success of a good example can always be attributed to luck. Thus, you have to risk your particular, individual life to find out. It is this risk that the ancients described as the sacrifice of personal will to the will of God. It is not an act of submission (at least as submission is currently understood). It is an act of courage. It is faith that the wind will blow your ship to a new and better port. It is the faith that Being can be corrected by becoming. It is the spirit of exploration itself.

Perhaps it is better to conceptualize it this way: Everyone needs a concrete, specific goal—an ambition, and a purpose—to limit chaos and make intelligible sense of his or her life. But all such concrete goals can and should be subordinated to what might be considered a meta-goal, which is a way of approaching and formulating goals themselves. The meta-goal could be "live in truth." This means, "Act diligently towards some well-articulated, defined and temporary end. Make your criteria for failure and success timely and clear, at least for yourself (and even better if others can understand what you are doing and evaluate it with you). While doing so, however, allow the world and your spirit to unfold as they will, while you act out and articulate the truth." This is both pragmatic ambition and the most courageous of faiths.

Life is suffering. The Buddha stated that, explicitly. Christians portray the same sentiment imagistically, with the divine crucifix. The Jewish faith is saturated with its remembrance. The equivalence of life and limitation is the primary and unavoidable fact of existence. The vulnerability of our Being renders us susceptible to the pains of social judgement and contempt and the inevitable breakdown of our bodies. But even all those ways of suffering, terrible as they are, are not sufficient to corrupt the world, to transform it into Hell, the way the Nazis and the Maoists and the Stalinists corrupted the world and turned it into Hell. For that, as Hitler stated so clearly, you need the lie:[155]

> [I]n the big lie there is always a certain force of credibility; because the broad masses of a nation are always more easily corrupted in the deeper strata of their emotional nature than consciously or voluntarily; and thus in the primitive simplicity of their minds they more readily fall victims to the big lie than the small lie, since they themselves often tell small lies in little matters but would be ashamed to resort to large-scale falsehoods. It would never come into their heads to fabricate colossal untruths, and they would not believe that others could have the impudence to distort the truth so infamously. Even though the facts which prove this to be so may be brought clearly to their minds, they will still doubt and waver and will continue to think that there may be some other explanation.

For the big lie, you first need the little lie. The little lie is, metaphorically speaking, the bait used by the Father of Lies to hook his victims. The human capacity for imagination makes us capable of dreaming up and creating alternative worlds. This is the ultimate source of our creativity. With that singular capacity, however, comes the counterpart, the opposite side of the coin: we can deceive ourselves and others into believing and acting as if things are other than we know they are.

And why not lie? Why not twist and distort things to obtain a small gain, or to smooth things over, or to keep the peace, or to avoid hurt feelings? Reality has its terrible aspect: do we really need to confront its snake-headed face in every moment of our waking consciousness, and at every turn in our lives? Why not turn away, at least, when looking is simply too painful?

The reason is simple. *Things fall apart.* What worked yesterday will not necessarily work today. We have inherited the great machinery of state and culture from our forefathers, but they are dead, and cannot deal with the changes of the day. *The living can.* We can open our eyes and modify what we have where necessary and keep the machinery running smoothly. Or we can pretend that everything is alright, fail to make the necessary repairs, and then curse fate when nothing goes our way.

Things fall apart: this is one of the great discoveries of humanity. And we speed the natural deterioration of great things through blindness, inaction and deceit. Without attention, culture degenerates and dies, and evil prevails.

What you see of a lie when you act it out (and most lies are acted out, rather than told) is very little of what it actually is. A lie is connected to everything else. It produces the same effect on the world that a single drop of sewage produces in even the largest crystal magnum of champagne. It is something best considered live and growing.

When the lies get big enough, the whole world spoils. But if you look close enough, the biggest of lies is composed of smaller lies, and those are composed of still smaller lies—and the smallest of lies is where the big lie starts. It is not the mere misstatement of fact. It is instead an act that has the aspect of the most serious conspiracy ever to possess the race of man. Its seeming innocuousness, its trivial meanness, the feeble arrogance that gives rise to it, the apparently trivial circumventing of responsibility that it aims at—these all work effectively to camouflage its true nature, its genuine dangerousness, and its equivalence with the great acts of evil that man perpetrates and often enjoys. Lies corrupt the world. Worse, that is their intent.

First, a little lie; then, several little lies to prop it up. After that, distorted thinking to avoid the shame that those lies produce, then a few more lies to cover up the consequences of the distorted thinking. Then, most terribly, the transformation of those now necessary lies through practice into automatized, specialized, structural, neurologically instantiated "unconscious" belief and action. Then the sickening of experience itself as action predicated on falsehood fails to produce the results intended. If you don't believe in brick walls, you will still be injured when you run headlong into one. Then you will curse reality itself for producing the wall.

After that comes the arrogance and sense of superiority that inevitably accompanies the production of successful lies (*hypothetically* successful lies—and that is one of the greatest dangers: apparently everyone is fooled, so everyone is stupid, except me. Everyone is stupid and fooled, *by* me—so I can get away with whatever I want). Finally, there is the proposition: "Being itself is susceptible to my manipulations. Thus, it deserves no respect."

That's things falling apart, like Osiris, severed into pieces. That's the structure of the person or the state disintegrating under the influence of a malign force. That's the chaos of the underworld emerging, like a flood, to subsume familiar ground. But it's not yet Hell.

Hell comes later. Hell comes when lies have destroyed the relationship between individual or state and reality itself. Things fall apart. Life degenerates. Everything becomes frustration and disappointment. Hope consistently betrays. The deceitful individual desperately gestures at sacrifice, like Cain, but fails to please God. Then the drama enters its final act.

Tortured by constant failure, the individual becomes bitter. Disappointment and failure amalgamate, and produce a fantasy: *the world is bent on my personal suffering, my particular undoing, my destruction.* I need, I deserve, I must have—my revenge. That's the gateway to Hell. That's when the underworld, a terrifying and unfamiliar place, becomes misery itself.

At the beginning of time, according to the great Western tradition, the Word of God transformed chaos into Being through the act of speech. It is axiomatic, within that tradition, that man and woman alike are made in the image of that God. We also transform chaos into Being, through speech. We transform the manifold possibilities of the future into the actualities of past and present.

To tell the truth is to bring the most habitable reality into Being. Truth builds edifices that can stand a thousand years. Truth feeds and clothes the poor, and makes nations wealthy and safe. Truth reduces the terrible complexity of a man to the simplicity of his word, so that he can become a partner, rather than an enemy. Truth makes the past truly past, and makes the best use of the future's possibilities. Truth is the ultimate, inexhaustible natural resource. It's the light in the darkness.

See the truth. Tell the truth.

Truth will not come in the guise of opinions shared by others, as the truth is neither a collection of slogans nor an ideology. It will instead be personal. Your truth is something only you can tell, based as it is on the unique circumstances of your life. Apprehend your personal truth. Communicate it carefully, in an articulate manner, to yourself and others. This will ensure your security and your life more abundantly now, while you inhabit the structure of your current beliefs. This will ensure the benevolence of the future, diverging as it might from the certainties of the past.

The truth springs forth ever anew from the most profound wellsprings of Being. It will keep your soul from withering and dying while you encounter the inevitable tragedy of life. It will help you avoid the terrible desire to seek vengeance for that tragedy—part of the terrible sin of Being, which everything must bear gracefully, just so it can exist.

If your life is not what it could be, try telling the truth. If you cling desperately to an ideology, or wallow in nihilism, try telling the truth. If you feel weak and rejected, and desperate, and confused, try telling the truth. In Paradise, everyone speaks the truth. That is what makes it Paradise.

Tell the truth. Or, at least, don't lie.

RULE 9

ASSUME THAT THE PERSON
YOU ARE LISTENING TO MIGHT
KNOW SOMETHING YOU DON'T

NOT ADVICE

PSYCHOTHERAPY IS NOT ADVICE. Advice is what you get when the
person you're talking with about something horrible and complicated
wishes you would just shut up and go away. Advice is what you get
when the person you are talking to wants to revel in the superiority
of his or her own intelligence. If you weren't so stupid, after all, you
wouldn't have your stupid problems.

Psychotherapy is genuine conversation. Genuine conversation is
exploration, articulation and strategizing. When you're involved in a
genuine conversation, you're listening, and talking—but mostly listening. Listening is paying attention. It's amazing what people will tell
you if you listen. Sometimes if you listen to people they will even tell
you what's wrong with them. Sometimes they will even tell you how
they plan to fix it. Sometimes that helps you fix something wrong with
yourself. One surprising time (and this is only one occasion of many

when such things happened), I was listening to someone very carefully, and she told me within minutes (a) that she was a witch and (b) that her witch coven spent a lot of its time visualizing world peace together. She was a long-time lower-level functionary in some bureaucratic job. I would never have guessed that she was a witch. I also didn't know that witch covens spent any of their time visualizing world peace. I didn't know what to make of any of it, either, but it wasn't boring, and that's something.

In my clinical practice, I talk and I listen. I talk more to some people, and listen more to others. Many of the people I listen to have no one else to talk to. Some of them are truly alone in the world. There are far more people like that than you think. You don't meet them, because they are alone. Others are surrounded by tyrants or narcissists or drunks or traumatized people or professional victims. Some are not good at articulating themselves. They go off on tangents. They repeat themselves. They say vague and contradictory things. They're hard to listen to. Others have terrible things happening around them. They have parents with Alzheimer's or sick children. There's not much time left over for their personal concerns.

One time a client who I had been seeing for a few months came into my office* for her scheduled appointment and, after some brief preliminaries, she announced "I think I was raped." It is not easy to know how to respond to a statement like that, although there is frequently some mystery around such events. Often alcohol is involved, as it is in most sexual assault cases. Alcohol can cause ambiguity. That's partly why people drink. Alcohol temporarily lifts the terrible burden of self-consciousness from people. Drunk people know about the future, but they don't care about it. That's exciting. That's exhilarating. Drunk people can party like there's no tomorrow. But, because there is a tomorrow—most of the time—drunk people also get in trouble. They black out. They go to dangerous places with careless people. They have fun. But they also get raped. So, I immediately thought

---

* Here, again, I have disguised many of the details of this case, to maintain the privacy of those involved, while attempting to maintain the central meaning of the events.

something like that might be involved. How else to understand "I think"? But that wasn't the end of the story. She added an extra detail: "Five times." The first sentence was awful enough, but the second produced something unfathomable. Five times? What could that possibly mean?

My client told me that she would go to a bar and have a few drinks. Someone would start to talk with her. She would end up at his place or her place with him. The evening would proceed, inevitably, to its sexual climax. The next day she would wake up, uncertain about what happened—uncertain about her motives, uncertain about his motives, and uncertain about the world. Miss S, we'll call her, was vague to the point of non-existence. She was a ghost of a person. She dressed, however, like a professional. She knew how to present herself, for first appearances. In consequence, she had finagled her way onto a government advisory board considering the construction of a major piece of transportation infrastructure (even though she knew nothing about government, advising or construction). She also hosted a local public-access radio show dedicated to small business, even though she had never held a real job, and knew nothing about being an entrepreneur. She had been receiving welfare payments for the entirety of her adulthood.

Her parents had never provided her with a minute of attention. She had four brothers and they were not at all good to her. She had no friends now, and none in the past. She had no partner. She had no one to talk to, and she didn't know how to think on her own (that's not rare). She had no self. She was, instead, a walking cacophony of unintegrated experiences. I had tried previously to help her find a job. I asked her if she had a CV. She said yes. I asked her to bring it to me. She brought it to our next session. It was fifty pages long. It was in a file folder box, divided into sections, with manila tag separators—the ones with the little colorful index-markers on the sides. The sections included such topics as "My Dreams" and "Books I Have Read." She had written down dozens of her night-time dreams in the "My Dreams" section, and provided brief summaries and reviews of her reading material. This was what she proposed to send to prospective employers (or perhaps already had: who really knew?). It is impossible to understand how much someone has to be no one at all to exist in a world where a file folder box containing fifty indexed pages listing dreams and novels constitutes a CV. Miss S knew nothing about herself. She knew nothing about other individuals. She knew nothing about the world. She was a movie played out of focus. And she was desperately waiting for a story about herself to make it all make sense.

If you add some sugar to cold water, and stir it, the sugar will dissolve. If you heat up that water, you can dissolve more. If you heat the water to boiling, you can add a lot more sugar and get that to dissolve too. Then, if you take that boiling sugar water, and slowly cool it, and don't bump it or jar it, you can trick it (I don't know how else to phrase this) into holding a lot more dissolved sugar than it would have it if it had remained cold all along. That's called a super-saturated solution. If you drop a single crystal of sugar into that super-saturated solution, all the excess sugar will suddenly and dramatically crystallize. It's as if it were crying out for order. That was my client. People like her are the reason that the many forms of psychotherapy currently practised all work. People can be so confused that their psyches will be ordered and their lives improved by the adoption of any reasonably orderly system of interpretation. This is the bringing together of the disparate elements of their lives in a disciplined manner—any disciplined manner. So, if you have come apart at the seams (or if you never have been together at all) you can restructure your life on Freudian, Jungian, Adlerian, Rogerian or behavioural principles. At least then you make sense. At least then you're coherent. At least then you might be good for something, if not good yet for everything. You can't fix a car with an axe, but you can cut down a tree. That's still something.

At about the same time I was seeing this client, the media was all afire with stories of recovered memories—particularly of sexual assault. The dispute raged apace: were these genuine accounts of past trauma? Or were they post-hoc constructs, dreamed up as a consequence of pressure wittingly or unwittingly applied by incautious therapists, grasped onto desperately by clinical clients all-too-eager to find a simple cause for all their trouble? Sometimes, it was the former, perhaps; and sometimes the latter. I understood much more clearly and precisely, however, how easy it might be to instill a false memory into the mental landscape as soon as my client revealed her uncertainty about her sexual experiences. The past appears fixed, but it's not—not in an important psychological sense. There is an awful lot to the past, after all, and the way we organize it can be subject to drastic revision.

Imagine, for example, a movie where nothing but terrible things happen. But, in the end, everything works out. Everything is resolved. A sufficiently happy ending can change the meaning of all the previous events. They can all be viewed as worthwhile, given that ending. Now imagine another movie. A lot of things are happening. They're all exciting and interesting. But there are a lot of them. Ninety minutes in, you start to worry. "This is a great movie," you think, "but there are a lot of things going on. I sure hope the filmmaker can pull it all together." But that doesn't happen. Instead, the story ends, abruptly, unresolved, or something facile and clichéd occurs. You leave deeply annoyed and unsatisfied—failing to notice that you were fully engaged and enjoying the movie almost the whole time you were in the theatre. The present can change the past, and the future can change the present.

When you are remembering the past, as well, you remember some parts of it and forget others. You have clear memories of some things that happened, but not others, of potentially equal import—just as in the present you are aware of some aspects of your surroundings and unconscious of others. You categorize your experience, grouping some elements together, and separating them from the rest. There is a mysterious arbitrariness about all of this. You don't form a comprehensive, objective record. You can't. You just don't know enough. You just can't perceive enough. You're not objective, either. You're alive. You're subjective. You have vested interests—at least in yourself, at least usually. What exactly should be included in the story? Where exactly is the border between events?

The sexual abuse of children is distressingly common.[156] However, it's not as common as poorly trained psychotherapists think, and it also does not always produce terribly damaged adults.[157] People vary in their resilience. An event that will wipe one person out can be shrugged off by another. But therapists with a little second-hand knowledge of Freud often axiomatically assume that a distressed adult in their practice must have been subject to childhood sexual abuse. Why else would they be distressed? So, they dig, and infer, and intimate, and suggest, and overreact, and bias and tilt. They exaggerate the importance of some events, and downplay the importance of others. They trim the facts to fit their theory.[158] And they convince their clients that they were sexually abused—if they could only remember. And then the clients start to remember. And then they start to accuse. And sometimes what they remember never happened, and the people accused are innocent. The good news? At least the therapist's theory remains intact. That's good—for the therapist. But there's no shortage of collateral damage. However, people are often willing to produce a lot of collateral damage if they can retain their theory.

I knew about all this when Miss S came to talk to me about her sexual experiences. When she recounted her trips to the singles bars, and their recurring aftermath, I thought a bunch of things at once. I thought, "You're so vague and so non-existent. You're a denizen of chaos and the underworld. You are going ten different places at the same time. Anyone can take you by the hand and guide you down the road of their choosing." After all, if you're not the leading man in your own drama, you're a bit player in someone else's—and you might well be assigned to play a dismal, lonely and tragic part. After Miss S recounted her story, we sat there. I thought, "You have normal sexual desires. You're extremely lonely. You're unfulfilled sexually. You're afraid of men and ignorant of the world and know nothing of yourself. You wander around like an accident waiting to happen and the accident happens and that's your life."

I thought, "Part of you wants to be taken. Part of you wants to be a child. You were abused by your brothers and ignored by your father and so part of you wants revenge upon men. Part of you is guilty. Another part is ashamed. Another part is thrilled and excited. Who are you? What did you do? What happened?" What was the objective truth? There was no way of knowing the objective truth. And there never would be. There was no objective observer, and there never would be. There was no complete and accurate story. Such a thing did not and could not exist. There were, and are, only partial accounts and fragmentary viewpoints. But some are still better than others. Memory is not a description of the objective past. *Memory is a tool.* Memory is the past's guide to the future. If you remember that something bad happened, and you can figure out why, then you can try to avoid that bad thing happening again. That's the purpose of memory. It's not "to remember the past." It's to stop the same damn thing from happening over and over.

I thought, "I could simplify Miss S's life. I could say that her suspicions of rape were fully justified, and that her doubt about the events was nothing but additional evidence of her thorough and long-term victimization. I could insist that her sexual partners had a legal obligation to ensure that she was not too impaired by alcohol to give consent. I could tell her that she had indisputably been subject to violent and illicit acts, unless she had consented to each sexual move explicitly and verbally. I could tell her that she was an innocent victim." I could have told her all that. And it would have been true. And she would have accepted it as true, and remembered it for the rest of her life. She would have been a new person, with a new history, and a new destiny.

But I also thought, "I could tell Miss S that she is a walking disaster. I could tell her that she wanders into a bar like a courtesan in a coma, that she is a danger to herself and others, that she needs to wake up, and that if she goes to singles bars and drinks too much and is taken home and has rough violent sex (or even tender caring sex), then what the hell does she expect?" In other words, I could have told her, in more philosophical terms, that she was Nietzsche's "pale criminal"—the person who at one moment dares to break the sacred law and at the next shrinks from paying the price. And that would have been true, too, and she would have accepted it as such, and remembered it.

If I had been the adherent of a left-wing, social-justice ideology, I would have told her the first story. If I had been the adherent of a conservative ideology, I would have told her the second. And her responses after having been told either the first or the second story would have proved to my satisfaction and hers that the story I had told her was true—completely, irrefutably true. And that would have been advice.

Figure It Out for Yourself

I decided instead to listen. I have learned not to steal my clients' problems from them. I don't want to be the redeeming hero or the *deus ex machina*—not in someone else's story. I don't want their lives. So, I asked her to tell me what she thought, and I listened. She talked a lot. When we were finished, she still didn't know if she had been raped, and neither did I. Life is very complicated.

Sometimes you have to change the way you understand everything to properly understand a single something. "Was I raped?" can be a very complicated question. The mere fact that the question would present itself in that form indicates the existence of infinite layers of complexity—to say nothing of "five times." There are a myriad of questions hidden inside "Was I raped?": What is rape? What is consent? What constitutes appropriate sexual caution? How should a person defend herself? Where does the fault lie? "Was I raped?" is a hydra. If you cut off the head of a hydra, seven more grow. That's life. Miss S would have had to talk for twenty years to figure out whether she had been raped. And someone would have had to be there to listen. I started the process, but circumstances made it impossible for me to finish. She left therapy with me only somewhat less ill-formed and vague than when she first met me. But at least she didn't leave as the living embodiment of my damned ideology.

The people I listen to need to talk, because that's how people think. People need to think. Otherwise they wander blindly into pits. When people think, they simulate the world, and plan how to act in it. If they do a good job of simulating, they can figure out what stupid things they shouldn't do. Then they can not do them. Then they don't have to suffer the consequences. That's the purpose of thinking. But we can't do it alone. We simulate the world, and plan our actions in it. Only human beings do this. That's how brilliant we are. We make little avatars of ourselves. We place those avatars in fictional worlds. Then we watch what happens. If our avatar thrives, then we act like he does, in the real world. Then we thrive (we hope). If our avatar fails, we don't go there, if we have any sense. We let him die in the fictional world, so that we don't have to really die in the present.

Imagine two children talking. The younger one says, "Wouldn't it be fun to climb up on the roof?" He has just placed a little avatar of himself in a fictional world. But his older sister objects. She chimes in. "That's stupid," she says. "What if you fall off the roof? What if Dad catches you?" The younger child can then modify the original simulation, draw the appropriate conclusion, and let the whole fictional world wither on the vine. Or not. Maybe the risk is worth it. But at least now it can be factored in. The fictional world is a bit more complete, and the avatar a bit wiser.

People think they think, but it's not true. It's mostly self-criticism that passes for thinking. True thinking is rare—just like true listening. Thinking is listening to yourself. It's difficult. To think, you have to be at least two people at the same time. Then you have to let those people disagree. Thinking is an internal dialogue between two or more different views of the world. Viewpoint One is an avatar in a simulated world. It has its own representations of past, present and future, and its own ideas about how to act. So do Viewpoints Two, and Three, and Four. Thinking is the process by which these internal avatars imagine and articulate their worlds to one another. You can't set straw men against one another when you're thinking, either, because then you're not thinking. You're rationalizing, post-hoc. You're matching what you want against a weak opponent so that you don't have to change your mind. You're propagandizing. You're using double-speak. You're using your conclusions to justify your proofs. You're hiding from the truth.

True thinking is complex and demanding. It requires you to be articulate speaker and careful, judicious listener, at the same time. It involves conflict. So, you have to tolerate conflict. Conflict involves negotiation and compromise. So, you have to learn to give and take and to modify your premises and adjust your thoughts—even your perceptions of the world. Sometimes it results in the defeat and elimination of one or more internal avatar. They don't like to be defeated or eliminated, either. They're hard to build. They're valuable. They're alive. They like to stay alive. They'll fight to stay alive. You better listen to them. If you don't they'll go underground and turn into devils and torture you. In consequence, thinking is emotionally painful, as well as physiologically demanding; more so than anything else—except not thinking. But you have to be very articulate and sophisticated to have all of this occur inside your own head. What are you to do, then, if you aren't very good at thinking, at being two people at one time? That's easy. You talk. But you need someone to listen. A listening person is your collaborator and your opponent.

A listening person tests your talking (and your thinking) without having to say anything. A listening person is a representative of common humanity. He stands for the crowd. Now the crowd is by no means always right, but it's *commonly* right. It's *typically* right. If you say something that takes everyone aback, therefore, you should reconsider what you said. I say that, knowing full well that controversial opinions are sometimes correct—sometimes so much so that the crowd will perish if it refuses to listen. It is for this reason, among others, that the individual is morally obliged to stand up and tell the truth of his or her own experience. But something new and radical is still almost always wrong. You need good, even great, reasons to ignore or defy general, public opinion. That's your culture. It's a mighty oak. You perch on one of its branches. If the branch breaks, it's a long way down—farther, perhaps, than you think. If you're reading this book, there's a strong probability that you're a privileged person. You can read. You have time to read. You're perched high in the clouds. It took untold generations to get you where you are. A little gratitude might be in order. If you're going to insist on bending the world to your way, you better have your reasons. If you're going to stand your ground, you better have your reasons. You better have thought them through. You might otherwise be in for a very hard landing. You should do what other people do, unless you have a very good reason not to. If you're in a rut, at least you know that other people have travelled that path.

Out of the rut is too often off the road. And in the desert that awaits off the road there are highwaymen and monsters.

So speaks wisdom.

A Listening Person

A listening person can reflect the crowd. He can do that without talking. He can do that merely by letting the talking person listen to himself. That is what Freud recommended. He had his patients lay on a couch, look at the ceiling, let their minds wander, and say whatever wandered in. That's his method of *free association*. That's the way the Freudian psychoanalyst avoids transferring his or her own personal biases and opinions into the internal landscape of the patient. It was for such reasons that Freud did not face his patients. He did not want their spontaneous meditations to be altered by his emotional expressions, no matter how slight. He was properly concerned that his own opinions—and, worse, his own unresolved problems—would find themselves uncontrollably reflected in his responses and reactions, conscious and unconscious alike. He was afraid that he would in such a manner detrimentally affect the development of his patients. It was for such reasons, as well, that Freud insisted that psychoanalysts be analyzed themselves. He wanted those who practiced his method to uncover and eliminate some of their own worst blind spots and prejudices, so they would not practise corruptly. Freud had a point. He was, after all, a genius. You can tell that because people still hate him. But there are disadvantages to the detached and somewhat distant approach recommended by Freud. Many of those who seek therapy desire and need a closer, more personal relationship (although that also has its dangers). This is in part why I have opted in my practice for the conversation, instead of the Freudian method—as have most clinical psychologists.

It can be worthwhile for my clients to see my reactions. To protect them from the undue influence that might produce, I attempt to set my aim properly, so that my responses emerge from the appropriate motivation. I do what I can to want the best for them (whatever that might be). I do my best to want the best, period, as well (because that is part of wanting the best for my clients). I try to clear my mind, and to leave my own concerns aside. That way I am concentrating on what is best for my clients, while I am simultaneously alert to any cues that I might be misunderstanding what that best is. That's something that has to be negotiated, not assumed on my part. It's something that has to be managed very carefully, to mitigate the risks of close, personal interaction. My clients talk. I listen. Sometimes I respond. Often the response is subtle. It's not even verbal. My clients and I face each other. We make eye contact. We can see each other's expressions. They can observe the effects of their words on me, and I can observe the effects of mine on them. They can respond to my responses.

A client of mine might say, "I hate my wife." It's out there, once said. It's hanging in the air. It has emerged from the underworld, materialized from chaos, and manifested itself. It is perceptible and concrete and no longer easily ignored. It's become real. The speaker has even startled himself. He sees the same thing reflected in my eyes. He notes that, and continues on the road to sanity. "Hold it," he says. "Back up. That's too harsh. *Sometimes* I hate my wife. I hate her when she won't tell me what she wants. My mom did that all the time, too. It drove Dad crazy. It drove all of us crazy, to tell you the truth. It even drove Mom crazy! She was a nice person, but she was very resentful. Well, at least my wife isn't as bad as my mother. Not at all. Wait! I guess my wife is actually pretty good at telling me what she wants, but I get really bothered when she doesn't, because Mom tortured us all half to death being a martyr. That really affected me. Maybe I overreact now when it happens even a bit. Hey! I'm acting just like Dad did when Mom upset him! That isn't me. That doesn't have anything to do with my wife! I better let her know." I observe from all this that my client had failed previously to properly distinguish his wife from his mother. And I see that he was possessed, unconsciously, by the spirit of his father. He sees all of that too. Now he is a bit more differentiated, a bit less an uncarved block, a bit less hidden in the fog. He has sewed up a small tear in the fabric of his culture. He says, "That was a good session, Dr. Peterson." I nod. You can be pretty smart if you can just shut up.

I'm a collaborator and opponent even when I'm not talking. I can't help it. My expressions broadcast my response, even when they're subtle. So, I'm communicating, as Freud so rightly stressed, even when silent. But I also talk in my clinical sessions. How do I know when to say something? First, as I said, I put myself in the proper frame of mind. I aim properly. I want things to be better. My mind orients itself, given this goal. It tries to produce responses to the therapeutic dialogue that furthers that aim. I watch what happens, internally. I reveal my responses. That's the first rule. Sometimes, for example, a client will say something, and a thought will occur to me, or a fantasy flit through my mind. Frequently it's about something that was said by the same client earlier that day, or during a previous session. Then I tell my client that thought or fantasy. Disinterestedly. I say, "You said this and I noticed that I then became aware of this." Then we discuss it. We try to determine the relevance of meaning of my reaction. Sometimes, perhaps, it's about me. That was Freud's point. But sometimes it is just the reaction of a detached but positively inclined human being to a personally revealing statement by another human being. It's meaningful—sometimes, even, corrective. Sometimes, however, it's me that gets corrected.

You have to get along with other people. A therapist is one of those other people. A good therapist will tell you the truth about what he thinks. (That is not the same thing as telling you that what he thinks is the truth.) Then at least you have the honest opinion of at least one person. That's not so easy to get. That's not nothing. That's key to the psychotherapeutic process: two people tell each other the truth—and both listen.

How Should You Listen?

Carl Rogers, one of the twentieth century's great psychotherapists, knew something about listening. He wrote, "The great majority of us cannot listen; we find ourselves compelled to evaluate, because listening is too dangerous. The first requirement is courage, and we do not always have it."[159] He knew that listening could transform people. On that, Rogers commented, "Some of you may be feeling that you listen well to people, and that you have never seen such results. The chances are very great indeed that your listening has not been of the type I have described." He suggested that his readers conduct a short experiment when they next found themselves in a dispute: "Stop the discussion for a moment, and institute this rule: 'Each person can speak up for himself only after he has first restated the ideas and feelings of the previous speaker accurately, and to that speaker's satisfaction.'" I have found this technique very useful, in my private life and in my practice. I routinely summarize what people have said to me, and ask them if I have understood properly. Sometimes they accept my summary. Sometimes I am offered a small correction. Now and then I am wrong completely. All of that is good to know.

There are several primary advantages to this process of summary. The first advantage is that I genuinely come to understand what the person is saying. Of this, Rogers notes, "Sounds simple, doesn't it? But if you try it you will discover it is one of the most difficult things you have ever tried to do. If you really understand a person in this way, if you are willing to enter his private world and see the way life appears to him, you run the risk of being changed yourself. You might see it his way, you might find yourself influenced in your attitudes or personality. This risk of being changed is one of the most frightening prospects most of us can face." More salutary words have rarely been written.

The second advantage to the act of summary is that it aids the person in consolidation and utility of memory. Consider the following situation: A client in my practice recounts a long, meandering, emotion-laden account of a difficult period in his or her life. We summarize, back and forth. The account becomes shorter. It is now summed up, in the client's memory (and in mine) in the form we discussed. It is now a different memory, in many ways—with luck, a *better* memory. It is now less weighty. It has been distilled; reduced to the gist. We have extracted the moral of the story. It becomes a description of the cause and the result of what happened, formulated such that repetition of the tragedy and pain becomes less likely in the future. "*This* is what happened. *This* is why. *This* is what I have to do to avoid such things from now on": That's a successful memory. That's the purpose of memory. You remember the past not so that it is "accurately recorded," to say it again, but so that you are prepared for the future.

The third advantage to employing the Rogerian method is the difficulty it poses to the careless construction of straw-man arguments. When someone opposes you, it is very tempting to oversimplify, parody, or distort his or her position. This is a counterproductive game, designed both to harm the dissenter and to unjustly raise your personal status. By contrast, if you are called upon to summarize someone's position, so that the speaking person agrees with that summary, you may have to state the argument even more clearly and succinctly than the speaker has even yet managed. If you first give the devil his due, looking at his arguments from his perspective, you can (1) find the value in them, and learn something in the process, or (2) hone your positions against them (if you still believe they are wrong) and strengthen your arguments further against challenge. This will make you much stronger. Then you will no longer have to misrepresent your opponent's position (and may well have bridged at least part of the gap between the two of you). You will also be much better at withstanding your own doubts.

Sometimes it takes a long time to figure out what someone genuinely means when they are talking. This is because often they are articulating their ideas for the first time. They can't do it without wandering down blind alleys or making contradictory or even nonsensical claims. This is partly because talking (and thinking) is often more about forgetting than about remembering. To discuss an event, particularly something emotional, like a death or serious illness, is to slowly choose what to leave behind. To begin, however, much that is not necessary must be put into words. The emotion-laden speaker must recount the whole experience, in detail. Only then can the central narrative, cause and consequence, come into focus or consolidate itself. Only then can the moral of the story be derived.

Imagine that someone holds a stack of hundred-dollar bills, some of which are counterfeit. All the bills might have to be spread on a table, so that each can be seen, and any differences noted, before the genuine can be distinguished from the false. This is the sort of method-ical approach you have to take when really listening to someone trying to solve a problem or communicate something important. If upon learning that some of the bills are counterfeit you too casually dismiss all of them (as you would if you were in a hurry, or otherwise unwill-ing to put in the effort), the person will never learn to separate wheat from chaff.

If you listen, instead, without premature judgment, people will generally tell you everything they are thinking—and with very little deceit. People will tell you the most amazing, absurd, interesting things. Very few of your conversations will be boring. (You can in fact tell whether or not you are actually listening in this manner. If the conversation is boring, you probably aren't.)

Primate Dominance–Hierarchy Manoeuvres—and Wit

Not all talking is thinking. Nor does all listening foster transformation. There are other motives for both, some of which produce much less valuable, counterproductive and even dangerous outcomes. There is the conversation, for example, where one participant is speaking merely to establish or confirm his place in the dominance hierarchy. One person begins by telling a story about some interesting occur-rence, recent or past, that involved something good, bad or surprising enough to make the listening worthwhile. The other person, now con-cerned with his or her potentially substandard status as less-interesting individual, immediately thinks of something better, worse, or more surprising to relate. This isn't one of those situations where two con-versational participants are genuinely playing off each other, riffing on the same themes, for the mutual enjoyment of both (and everyone else). This is jockeying for position, pure and simple. You can tell when one of those conversations is occurring. They are accompanied by a feeling of embarrassment among speakers and alike, all who know that something false and exaggerated has just been said.

There is another, closely allied form of conversation, where neither speaker is listening in the least to the other. Instead, each is using the time occupied by the current speaker to conjure up what he or she will say next, which will often be something off-topic, because the person anxiously waiting to speak has not been listening. This can and will bring the whole conversational train to a shuddering halt. At this point, it is usual for those who were on board during the crash to remain silent, and look occasionally and in a somewhat embarrassed manner at each other, until everyone leaves, or someone thinks of something witty and puts Humpty Dumpty together again.

Then there is the conversation where one participant is trying to attain victory for his point of view. This is yet another variant of the dominance-hierarchy conversation. During such a conversation, which often tends toward the ideological, the speaker endeavours to (1) denigrate or ridicule the viewpoint of anyone holding a contrary position, (2) use selective evidence while doing so and, finally, (3) impress the listeners (many of whom are already occupying the same ideological space) with the validity of his assertions. The goal is to gain support for a comprehensive, unitary, oversimplified world-view. Thus, the purpose of the conversation is to make the case that *not* thinking is the correct tack. The person who is speaking in this manner believes that winning the argument makes him right, and that doing so necessarily validates the assumption-structure of the dominance hierarchy he most identifies with. This is often—and unsurprisingly—the hierarchy within which he has achieved the most success, or the one with which he is most temperamentally aligned. Almost all discussions involving politics or economics unfold in this manner, with each participant attempting to justify fixed, *a priori* positions instead of trying to learn something or to adopt a different frame (even for the novelty). It is for this reason that conservatives and liberals alike believe their positions to be self-evident, particularly as they become more extreme. Given certain temperamentally-based assumptions, a predictable conclusion emerges—but only when you ignore the fact that the assumptions themselves are mutable.

These conversations are very different from the listening type. When a genuine listening conversation is taking place, one person at a time has the floor, and everyone else is listening. The person speaking is granted the opportunity to seriously discuss some event, usually unhappy or even tragic. Everyone else responds sympathetically. These conversations are important because the speaker is organizing the troublesome event in his or her mind, while recounting the story. The fact is important enough to bear repeating: people organize their brains with conversation. If they don't have anyone to tell their story to, they lose their minds. Like hoarders, they cannot unclutter themselves. The input of the community is required for the integrity of the individual psyche. To put it another way: It takes a village to organize a mind.

Much of what we consider healthy mental function is the result of our ability to use the reactions of others to keep our complex selves functional. *We outsource the problem of our sanity.* This is why it is the fundamental responsibility of parents to render their children socially acceptable. If a person's behaviour is such that other people can tolerate him, then all he has to do is place himself in a social context. Then people will indicate—by being interested in or bored by what he says, or laughing or not laughing at his jokes, or teasing or ridiculing, or even by lifting an eyebrow—whether his actions and statements are what they should be. Everyone is always broadcasting to everyone else their desire to encounter the ideal. We punish and reward each other precisely to the degree that each of us behaves in keeping with that desire—except, of course, when we are looking for trouble.

The sympathetic responses offered during a genuine conversation indicate that the teller is valued, and that the story being told is important, serious, deserving of consideration, and understandable. Men and women often misunderstand each other when these conversations are focused on a specified problem. Men are often accused of wanting to "fix things" too early on in a discussion. This frustrates men, who like to solve problems and to do it efficiently and who are in fact called upon frequently by women for precisely that purpose. It might be easier for my male readers to understand why this does not work, however, if they could realize and then remember that before a problem can be solved it must be formulated precisely. Women are often intent on formulating the problem when they are discussing something, and they need to be listened to—even questioned—to help ensure clarity in the formulation. Then, whatever problem is left, if any, can be helpfully solved. (It should also be noted first that too-early problem-solving may also merely indicate a desire to escape from the effort of the problem-formulating conversation.)

Another conversational variant is the lecture. A lecture is—somewhat surprisingly—a conversation. The lecturer speaks, but the audience communicates with him or her non-verbally. A surprising amount of human interaction—much of the delivery of emotional information, for example—takes place in this manner, through postural display and facial emotion (as we noted in our discussion of Freud). A good lecturer is not only delivering facts (which is perhaps the least important part of a lecture), but also telling stories about those facts, pitching them precisely to the level of the audience's comprehension, gauging that by the interest they are showing. The story he or she is telling conveys to the members of the audience not only what the facts are, but *why* they are relevant—why it is important to know certain things about which they are currently ignorant. To demonstrate the importance of some set of facts is to tell those audience members how such knowledge could change their behaviour, or influence the way they interpret the world, so that they will now be able to avoid some obstacles and progress more rapidly to some better goals.

A good lecturer is thus talking *with* and not *at* or even *to* his or her listeners. To manage this, the lecturer needs to be closely attending to the audience's every move, gesture and sound. Perversely, *this cannot be done by watching the audience, as such*. A good lecturer speaks directly to and watches the response of single, identifiable people,* instead of doing something clichéd, such as "presenting a talk" to an audience. Everything about that phrase is wrong. You don't present. You talk.

---

* The strategy of speaking to individuals is not only vital to the delivery of any message, it's a useful antidote to fear of public speaking. No one wants to be stared at by hundreds of unfriendly, judgmental eyes. However, almost everybody can talk to just one attentive person. So, if you have to deliver a speech (another terrible phrase) then do that. Talk to the individuals in the audience—and don't hide: not behind the podium, not with downcast eyes, not by speaking too quietly or mumbling, not by apologizing for your lack of brilliance or preparedness, not behind ideas that are not yours, and not behind clichés.

There is no such thing as "a talk," unless it's canned, and it shouldn't be. There is also no "audience." There are *individuals*, who need to be included in the conversation. A well-practised and competent public speaker addresses a single, identifiable person, watches that individual nod, shake his head, frown, or look confused, and responds appropriately and directly to those gestures and expressions. Then, after a few phrases, rounding out some idea, he switches to another audience member, and does the same thing. In this manner, he infers and reacts to the attitude of the entire group (insofar as such a thing exists).

There are still other conversations that work primarily as demonstrations of wit. These also have a dominance element, but the goal is to be the most entertaining speaker (which is an accomplishment that everyone participating will also enjoy). The purpose of these conversations, as a witty friend of mine once observed, was to say "anything that was either true or funny." As truth and humour are often close allies, that combination worked fine. I think that this might be the intelligent blue-collar worker's conversation. I participated in many fine bouts of sarcasm, satire, insult and generally over-the-top comedic exchange among people I grew up with in Northern Alberta and, later, among some Navy SEALs I met in California, who were friends of an author I know who writes somewhat horrifying popular fiction. They were all perfectly happy to say anything, no matter how appalling, as long it was funny.

I attended this writer's fortieth birthday celebration not too long ago in LA. He had invited one of the aforementioned SEALs. A few months beforehand, however, his wife had been diagnosed with a serious medical condition, necessitating brain surgery. He called up his SEAL friend, informed him of the circumstances, and indicated that the event might have to be cancelled. "You think you guys have a problem," responded his friend. "I just bought non-refundable airline tickets to your party!" It's not clear what percentage of the world's population would find that response amusing. I retold the story recently to a group of newer acquaintances and they were more shocked and appalled than amused. I tried to defend the joke as an indication of the SEAL's respect for the couple's ability to withstand and transcend tragedy, but I wasn't particularly successful. Nonetheless, I believe that he did intend exactly that respect, and I think he was terrifyingly witty. His joke was daring, anarchic to the point of recklessness, which is exactly the point where serious funny occurs. My friend and his wife recognized the compliment. They saw that their friend knew they were tough enough to withstand that level of—well, let's call it competitive humour. It was a test of character, which they passed with flying colours.

I found that such conversations occurred less and less frequently as I moved from university to university, up the educational and social ladder. Maybe it wasn't a class thing, although I have my suspicions it was. Maybe it's just that I'm older, or that the friends a person makes later in life, after adolescence, lack the insane competitive closeness and perverse playfulness of those early tribal bonds. When I went back up north to my hometown for my fiftieth birthday party, however, my old friends made me laugh so hard I had to duck into a different room several times to catch my breath. Those conversations are the most fun, and I miss them. You have to keep up, or risk severe humiliation, but there is nothing more rewarding than topping the last comedian's story, joke, insult or curse. Only one rule really applies: do not be boring (although it is also very bad form to *actually* put someone down, when you are only *pretending* to put them down).

Conversation on the Way

The final type of conversation, akin to listening, is a form of mutual exploration. It requires true reciprocity on the part of those listening and speaking. It allows all participants to express and organize their thoughts. A conversation of mutual exploration has a topic, generally complex, of genuine interest to the participants. Everyone participating is trying to solve a problem, instead of insisting on the *a priori* validity of their own positions. All are acting on the premise that they have something to learn. This kind of conversation constitutes active philosophy, the highest form of thought, and the best preparation for proper living.

The people involved in such a conversation must be discussing ideas they genuinely use to structure their perceptions and guide their actions and words. They must be existentially involved with their philosophy: that is, they must be living it, not merely believing or understanding it. They also must have inverted, at least temporarily, the typical human preference for order over chaos (and I don't mean the chaos typical of mindless antisocial rebellion). Other conversational types—except for the listening type—all attempt to buttress some existing order. The conversation of mutual exploration, by contrast, requires people who have decided that the unknown makes a better friend than the known.

You already know what you know, after all—and, unless your life is perfect, what you know is not enough. You remain threatened by disease, and self-deception, and unhappiness, and malevolence, and betrayal, and corruption, and pain, and limitation. You are subject to all these things, in the final analysis, because you are just too ignorant to protect yourself. If you just knew enough, you could be healthier and more honest. You would suffer less. You could recognize, resist and even triumph over malevolence and evil. You would neither betray a friend, nor deal falsely and deceitfully in business, politics or love. However, your current knowledge has neither made you perfect nor kept you safe. So, it is insufficient, by definition—radically, fatally insufficient.

You must accept this before you can converse philosophically, instead of convincing, oppressing, dominating or even amusing. You must accept this before you can tolerate a conversation where the Word that eternally mediates between order and chaos is operating, psychologically speaking. To have this kind of conversation, it is necessary to respect the personal experience of your conversational partners. You must assume that they have reached careful, thoughtful, genuine conclusions (and, perhaps, they must have done the work that justifies this assumption). You must believe that if they shared their conclusions with you, you could bypass at least some of the pain of personally learning the same things (as learning from the experience of others can be quicker and much less dangerous). You must meditate, too, instead of strategizing towards victory. If you fail, or refuse, to do so, then you merely and automatically repeat what you already believe, seeking its validation and insisting on its rightness. But if you are meditating as you converse, then you listen to the other person, and say the new and original things that can rise from deep within of their own accord.

It's as if you are listening to yourself during such a conversation, just as you are listening to the other person. You are describing how you are responding to the new information imparted by the speaker. You are reporting what that information has done to you—what new things it made appear within you, how it has changed your presuppositions, how it has made you think of new questions. You tell the speaker these things, directly. Then they have the same effect on him. In this manner, you both move towards somewhere newer and broader and better. You both change, as you let your old presuppositions die—as you shed your skins and emerge renewed.

A conversation such as this is one where it is the desire for truth itself—on the part of both participants—that is truly listening and speaking. That's why it's engaging, vital, interesting and meaningful. That sense of meaning is a signal from the deep, ancient parts of your Being. You're where you should be, with one foot in order, and the other tentatively extended into chaos and the unknown. You're immersed in the Tao, following the great Way of Life. There, you're stable enough to be secure, but flexible enough to transform. There, you're allowing new information to *inform* you—to permeate your stability, to repair and improve its structure, and expand its domain. There the constituent elements of your Being can find their more elegant formation. A conversation like that places you in the same place that listening to great music places you, and for much the same reason. A conversation like that puts you in the realm where souls connect, and that's a real place. It leaves you thinking, "That was really worthwhile. We really got to know each other." The masks came off, and the searchers were revealed.

So, listen, to yourself and to those with whom you are speaking. Your wisdom then consists not of the knowledge you already have, but the continual search for knowledge, which is the highest form of wisdom. It is for this reason that the priestess of the Delphic Oracle in ancient Greece spoke most highly of Socrates, who always sought the truth. She described him as the wisest living man, because he knew that what he knew was nothing.

Assume that the person you are listening to might know something you don't.

RULE 10

BE PRECISE IN YOUR SPEECH

WHY IS MY LAPTOP OBSOLETE?

WHAT DO YOU SEE, when you look at a computer—at your own laptop, more precisely? You see a flat, thin, grey-and-black box. Less evidently, you see something to type on and look at. Nonetheless, even with the second perceptions included, what are you seeing is hardly the computer at all. That grey and black box happens to be a computer right now, right here and now, and maybe even an expensive computer. Nevertheless, it will soon be something so unlike a computer that it will be difficult even to give away.

We will all discard our laptops within the next five years, even though they may still work perfectly—even though the screens, keyboards, mice and internet connections may still flawlessly perform their tasks. Fifty years from now, early twenty-first-century laptops will be oddities like the brass scientific tools of the late nineteenth century. The latter now appear more like the arcane accoutrements of alchemy, designed to measure phenomena whose existence we no longer even recognize. How can high-tech machines, each possessing more computing power than the entire Apollo space program, lose their value in such a short period of time? How can they transform so quickly from exciting, useful and status-enhancing machines to complex pieces of junk? It's because of the nature of our perceptions themselves, and the oft-invisible interaction between those perceptions and the underlying complexity of the world.

Your laptop is a note in a symphony currently being played by an orchestra of incalculable size. It's a very small part of a much greater whole. Most of its capacity resides beyond its hard shell. It maintains its function only because a vast array of other technologies are currently and harmoniously at play. It is fed, for example, by a power grid whose function is invisibly dependent on the stability of a myriad of complex physical, biological, economic and interpersonal systems. The factories that make its parts are still in operation. The operating system that enables its function is based on those parts, and not on others yet to be created. Its video hardware runs the technology expected by the creative people who post their content on the web. Your laptop is in communication with a certain, specified ecosystem of other devices and web servers.

And, finally, all this is made possible by an even less visible element: the social contract of trust—the interconnected and fundamentally honest political and economic systems that make the reliable electrical grid a reality. This interdependency of part on whole, invisible in systems that work, becomes starkly evident in systems that don't. The higher-order, surrounding systems that enable personal computing hardly exist at all in corrupt, third-world countries, so that the power lines, electrical switches, outlets, and all the other entities so hopefully and concretely indicative of such a grid are absent or compromised, and in fact make little contribution to the practical delivery of electricity to people's homes and factories. This makes perceiving the electronic and other devices that electricity theoretically enables as separate, functional units frustrating, at minimum, and impossible, at worst. This is partly because of technical insufficiency: the systems simply don't work. But it is also in no small part because of the lack of trust characteristic of systemically corrupt societies.

To put it another way: What you perceive as your computer is like a single leaf, on a tree, in a forest—or, even more accurately, like your fingers rubbing briefly across that leaf. A single leaf can be plucked from a branch. It can be perceived, briefly, as a single, self-contained entity—but that perception misleads more than clarifies. In a few weeks, the leaf will crumble and dissolve. It would not have been there at all, without the tree. It cannot continue to exist, in the absence of the tree. This is the position of our laptops in relation to the world. So much of what they are resides outside their boundaries that the screened devices we hold on our laps can only maintain their computer-like façade for a few short years.

Almost everything we see and hold is like that, although often not so evidently.

Tools, Obstacles and Extension into the World

We assume that we see objects or things when we look at the world, but that's not really how it is. Our evolved perceptual systems transform the interconnected, complex multi-level world that we inhabit not so much into *things* per se as into *useful* things (or their nemeses, things that get in the way). This is the necessary, practical reduction of the world. This is the transformation of the near-infinite complexity of things through the narrow specification of our purpose. This is how precision makes the world sensibly manifest. That is not at all the same as perceiving *objects*.

We don't see valueless entities and then attribute meaning to them. We perceive the meaning directly.[160] We see floors, to walk on, and doors, to duck through, and chairs, to sit on. It's for this reason that a beanbag and a stump both fall into the latter category, despite having little objectively in common. We see rocks, because we can throw them, and clouds, because they can rain on us, and apples, to eat, and the automobiles of other people, to get in our way and annoy us. We see tools and obstacles, not objects or things. Furthermore, we see tools and obstacles at the "handy" level of analysis that makes them most useful (or dangerous), given our needs, abilities and perceptual limitations. The world reveals itself to us as something to utilize and something to navigate through—not as something that merely is.

We see the faces of the people we are talking to, because we need to communicate with those people and cooperate with them. We don't see their microcosmic substructures, their cells, or the subcellular organelles, molecules and atoms that make up those cells. We don't see, as well, the macrocosm that surrounds them: the family members and friends that make up their immediate social circles, the economies they are embedded within, or the ecology that contains all of them. Finally, and equally importantly, we don't see them across time. We see them in the narrow, immediate, overwhelming now, instead of surrounded by the yesterdays and tomorrows that may be a more important part of them than whatever is currently and obviously manifest. And we have to see in this way, or be overwhelmed.

When we look at the world, we perceive only what is enough for our plans and actions to work and for us to get by. What we inhabit, then, is this "enough." That is a radical, functional, unconscious simplification of the world—and it's almost impossible for us not to mistake it for the world itself. But the objects we see are not simply there, in the world, for our simple, direct perceiving.* They exist in a complex, multi-dimensional relationship to one another, not as self-evidently separate, bounded, independent objects. We perceive not them, but their functional utility and, in doing so, we make them sufficiently simple for sufficient understanding. *It is for this reason that we must be precise in our aim.* Absent that, we drown in the complexity of the world.

This is true even for our perceptions of ourselves, of our individual persons. We assume that we end at the surface of our skin, because of the way that we perceive. But we can understand with a little thought the provisional nature of that boundary. We shift what is inside our skin, so to speak, as the context we inhabit changes. Even when we do

___

* This is why, for example, it has taken us far longer than we originally assumed to make robots that could function autonomously in the world. The problem of perception is far more difficult than our immediate effortless access to our own perceptions predisposes us to infer. In fact, the problem of perception is so difficult that it stalled the early progress of artificial intelligence almost fatally (from the perspective of that time), as we discovered that disembodied abstract reason could not solve even simple real-world problems. Pioneers such as Rodney Brooks proposed in the late 1980s and early '90s that bodies in action were necessary preconditions to the parsing of the world into manageable things, and the AI revolution regained its confidence and momentum.

something as apparently simple as picking up a screwdriver, our brain automatically adjusts what it considers body to include the tool.[161] We can literally feel things with the end of the screwdriver. When we extend a hand, holding the screwdriver, we automatically take the length of the latter into account. We can probe nooks and crannies with its extended end, and comprehend what we are exploring. Furthermore, we instantly regard the screwdriver we are holding as "our" screwdriver, and get possessive about it. We do the same with the much more complex tools we use, in much more complex situations. The cars we pilot instantaneously and automatically become ourselves. Because of this, when someone bangs his fist on our car's hood after we have irritated him at a crosswalk, we take it personally. This is not always reasonable. Nonetheless, without the extension of self into machine, it would be impossible to drive.

The extensible boundaries of our selves also expand to include other people—family members, lovers and friends. A mother will sacrifice herself for her children. Is our father or son or wife or husband more or less integral to us than an arm or a leg? We can answer, in part, by asking: Which would we rather lose? Which loss would we sacrifice more to avoid? We practice for such permanent extension— such permanent commitment—by identifying with the fictional characters of books and movies. Their tragedies and triumphs rapidly and convincingly become ours. Sitting still in our seats, we nonetheless act out a multitude of alternate realities, extending ourselves experimentally, testing multiple potential paths, before specifying the one we will actually take. Engrossed in a fictional world, we can even become things that don't "really" exist. In the blink of an eye, in the magic hall of a movie theatre, we can become fantastical creatures. We sit in the dark before rapidly flickering images and become witches, superheroes, aliens, vampires, lions, elves or wooden marionettes. We feel everything they feel, and are peculiarly happy to pay for the privilege, even when what we experience is sorrow, fear or horror.

Something similar, but more extreme, happens when we identify, not with a character in a fictional drama, but with a whole group, in a competition. Think of what happens when a favourite team wins or loses an important game against an arch-rival. The winning goal will bring the whole network of fans to their feet, before they think, in unscripted unison. It is as if their many nervous systems are directly wired to the game unfolding in front of them. Fans take the victories and defeats of their teams very personally, even wearing the jerseys of their heroes, often celebrating their wins and losses more than any such events that "actually" occur in their day-to-day lives. This identification manifests itself deeply—even biochemically and neurologically. Vicarious experiences of winning and losing, for example, raise and lower testosterone levels among fans "participating" in the contest.[162] Our capacity for identification is something that manifests itself at every level of our Being.

To the degree that we are patriotic, similarly, our country is not just *important* to us. It *is* us. We might even sacrifice our entire smaller individual selves, in battle, to maintain the integrity of our country. For much of history, such willingness to die has been regarded as something admirable and courageous, as a part of human duty. Paradoxically, that is a direct consequence not of our aggression but of our extreme sociability and willingness to cooperate. If we can become not only ourselves, but our families, teams and countries, cooperation comes easily to us, relying on the same deeply innate mechanisms that drive us (and other creatures) to protect our very bodies.

The World Is Simple Only When It Behaves

It is very difficult to make sense of the interconnected chaos of reality, just by looking at it. It's a very complicated act, requiring, perhaps, half our brains. Everything shifts and changes in the real world. Each hypothetically separate thing is made up of smaller hypothetically separate things, and is simultaneously part of larger hypothetically separate things. The boundaries between the levels—and between different things themselves at a given level—are neither clear nor self-evident, objectively. They must be established practically, pragmatically, and they retain their validity only under very narrow and specified conditions. The conscious illusion of complete and sufficient perception only sustains itself, for example—only remains sufficient for our purposes—when everything goes according to plan. Under such circumstances, what we see is accurate enough, so that there is no utility in looking farther. To drive successfully, we don't have to understand, or even perceive, the complex machinery of our automobiles. The hidden complexities of our private cars only intrude on our consciousness when that machinery fails, or when we collide unexpectedly with something (or something with us). Even in the case of mere mechanical failure (to say nothing of a serious accident) such intrusion is always felt, at least initially, as anxiety-provoking. That's a consequence of emergent uncertainty.

A car, as we perceive it, is not a thing, or an object. It is instead something that takes us somewhere we want to go. It is only when it stops taking us and going, in fact, that we perceive it much at all. It is only when a car quits, suddenly—or is involved in an accident and must be pulled over to the side of the road—that we are forced to apprehend and analyze the myriad of parts that "car as thing that goes" depends on. When our car fails, our incompetence with regards to its complexity is instantly revealed. That has practical consequences (we don't get to go to where we were going), as well as psychological: our peace of mind disappears along with our functioning vehicle. We must generally turn to the experts who inhabit garages and workshops to restore both functionality to our vehicle and simplicity to our perceptions. That's mechanic-as-psychologist.

It is precisely then that we can understand, although we seldom deeply consider, the staggeringly low-resolution quality of our vision and the inadequacy of our corresponding understanding. In a crisis, when our thing no longer goes, we turn to those whose expertise far transcends ours to restore the match between our expectant desire and what actually happens. This all means that the failure of our car can also force us to confront the uncertainty of the broader social context, which is usually invisible to us, in which the machine (and mechanic) are mere parts. Betrayed by our car, we come up against all the things we don't know. Is it time for a new vehicle? Did I err in my original purchase? Is the mechanic competent, honest and reliable? Is the garage he works for trustworthy? Sometimes, too, we must contemplate something worse, something broader and deeper: Have the roads now become too dangerous? Have I become (or always been) too incompetent? Too scattered and inattentive? Too old? The limitations of all our perceptions of things and selves manifest themselves when something we can usually depend on in our simplified world breaks down. Then the more complex world that was always there, invisible and conveniently ignored, makes its presence known. It is then that the walled garden we archetypally inhabit reveals its hidden but ever-present snakes.

You and I Are Simple Only When the World Behaves

When things break down, what has been ignored rushes in. When things are no longer specified, with precision, the walls crumble, and chaos makes its presence known. When we've been careless, and let things slide, what we have refused to attend to gathers itself up, adopts a serpentine form, and strikes—often at the worst possible moment. It is then that we see what focused intent, precision of aim and careful attention protect us from.

Imagine a loyal and honest wife suddenly confronted by evidence of her husband's infidelity. She has lived alongside him for years. She saw him as she assumes he is: reliable, hard-working, loving, dependable. In her marriage, she is standing on a rock, or so she believes. But he becomes less attentive and more distracted. He begins, in the cli-chéd manner, to work longer hours. Small things she says and does irritate him unjustifiably. One day she sees him in a downtown café with another woman, interacting with her in a manner difficult to rationalize and ignore. The limitations and inaccuracy of her former perceptions become immediately and painfully obvious.

Her theory of her husband collapses. What happens, in consequence? First, something—someone—emerges in his stead: a complex, frightening stranger. That's bad enough. But it's only half the problem. Her theory of herself collapses, too, in the aftermath of the betrayal, so that it's not one stranger that's the problem: it's two. Her husband is not who she perceived him to be—but neither is she, the betrayed wife. She is no longer the "well-loved, secure wife, and valued partner." Strangely enough, despite our belief in the permanent immutability of the past, she may never have been.

The past is not necessarily what it was, even though it has already been. The present is chaotic and indeterminate. The ground shifts continually around her feet, and ours. Equally, the future, not yet here, changes into something it was not supposed to be. Is the once reasonably content wife now a "deceived innocent"—or a "gullible fool"? Should she view herself as victim, or as co-conspirator in a shared delusion? Her husband is—what? An unsatisfied lover? A target of seduction? A psychopathic liar? The very Devil himself? *How could he be so cruel?* How could anyone? What is this home she has been living in? How could she be so naïve? How could anyone? She looks in the mirror. *Who is she? What's going on?* Are any of her relationships real? Have any of them ever been? What has happened to the future? Everything is up for grabs, when the deeper realities of the world unexpectedly manifest themselves.

Everything is intricate beyond imagining. Everything is affected by everything else. We perceive a very narrow slice of a causally interconnected matrix, although we strive with all our might to avoid being confronted by knowledge of that narrowness. The thin veneer of perceptual sufficiency cracks, however, when something fundamental goes wrong. The dreadful inadequacy of our senses reveals itself. Everything we hold dear crumbles to dust. We freeze. We turn to stone. What then do we see? Where can we look, when it is precisely what we see that has been insufficient?

What Do We See When We Don't Know What We're Looking At?

What is it, that is the world, after the Twin Towers disintegrate? What, if anything, is left standing? What dread beast rises from the ruins when the invisible pillars supporting the world's financial system tremble and fall? What do we see when we are swept up in the fire and drama of a National Socialist rally, or cower, paralyzed with fear, in the midst of a massacre in Rwanda? What is it that we see, when we cannot understand what is happening to us, cannot determine where we are, know no longer who we are, and no longer understand what surrounds us? What we *don't* see is the well-known and comforting world of tools—of useful objects—of personalities. We don't even see familiar obstacles—sufficiently troubling though they are in normal times, already mastered—that we can simply step around.

What we perceive, when things fall apart, is no longer the stage and settings of habitable order. It's the eternal watery *tohu va bohu*, formless emptiness, and the *tehom*, the abyss, to speak biblically—the chaos forever lurking beneath our thin surfaces of security. It's from that chaos that the Holy Word of God Himself extracted order at the beginning of time, according to the oldest opinions expressed by mankind (and it is in the image of that same Word that we were made, male and female, according to the same opinions). It's from that chaos that whatever stability we had the good fortune to experience emerged, originally—for some limited time—when we first learned to perceive. It's chaos that we see, when things fall apart (even though we cannot truly see it). What does all this mean?

Emergency—emergence(y). This is the sudden manifestation from somewhere unknown of some previously unknown phenomenon (from the Greek *phainesthai*, to "shine forth"). This is the reappearance of the eternal dragon, from its eternal cavern, from its now-disrupted slumber. This is the underworld, with its monsters rising from the depths. How do we prepare for an emergency, when we do not know what has emerged, or from where? How do we prepare for catastrophe, when we do not know what to expect, or how to act? We turn from our minds, so to speak—too slow, too ponderous—to our bodies. Our bodies react much faster than our minds.

When things collapse around us our perception disappears, and we act. Ancient reflexive responses, rendered automatic and efficient over hundreds of millions of years, protect us in those dire moments when not only thought but perception itself fails. Under such circumstances, our bodies ready themselves for all possible eventualities.[163] First, we freeze. The reflexes of the body then shade into emotion, the next stage of perception. Is this something scary? Something useful? Something that must be fought? Something that can be ignored? How will we determine this—and when? We don't know. Now we are in a costly and demanding state of readiness. Our bodies are flooded with cortisol and adrenaline. Our hearts beat faster. Our breath quickens. We realize, painfully, that our sense of competence and completeness is gone; it was just a dream. We draw on physical and psychological resources saved carefully for just this moment (if we are fortunate enough to have them). We prepare for the worst—or the best. We push the gas pedal furiously to the floor, and slam on the brakes at the same time. We scream, or laugh. We look disgusted, or terrified. We cry. And then we begin to parse apart the chaos.

And so, the deceived wife, increasingly unhinged, feels the motivation to reveal all—to herself, her sister, her best friend, to a stranger on a bus—or retreats into silence, and ruminates obsessively, to the same end. *What went wrong? What did she do that was so unforgivable? Who is this person she has been living with? What kind of world is this, where such things can happen? What kind of God would make such a place?* What conversation could she possibly initiate with this new, infuriating person, inhabiting the shell of her former husband? What forms of revenge might satisfy her anger? Who could she seduce, in return for this insult? She is by turns enraged, terrified, struck down by pain, and exhilarated by the possibilities of her new-found freedom.

Her last place of bedrock security was in fact not stable, not certain—not bedrock at all. Her house was built on a foundation of sand. The ice she was skating on was simply too thin. She fell through, into the water below, and is drowning. She has been hit so hard that her anger, terror and grief consume her. Her sense of betrayal widens, until the whole world caves in. Where is she? *In the underworld, with all its terrors.* How did she get there? This experience, this voyage into the substructure of things—this is all perception, too, in its nascent form; this preparation; this consideration of what-might-have-been and what-could-still-be; this emotion and fantasy. This is all the deep perception now necessary before the familiar objects that she once knew reappear, if they ever do, in their simplified and comfortable form. This is perception before the chaos of possibility is re-articulated into the functional realities of order.

"Was it really so unexpected?" she asks herself—she asks others—thinking back. Should she now feel guilty about ignoring the warning signs, subtle though they may have been, encouraged though she was to avoid them? She remembers when she first married, eagerly joining her husband, every single night, to make love. Perhaps that was too much to expect—or even too much to cope with—but once, in the last six months? Once every two or three months, for years, before that? Would anyone she could truly respect—including herself—put up with such a situation?

There is a story for children, *There's No Such Thing as a Dragon*, by Jack Kent, that I really like. It's a very simple tale, at least on the surface. I once read its few pages to a group of retired University of Toronto alumni, and explained its symbolic meaning.* It's about a small boy, Billy Bixbee, who spies a dragon sitting on his bed one morning. It's about the size of a house cat, and friendly. He tells his mother about it, but she tells him that there's no such thing as a dragon. So, it starts to grow. It eats all of Billy's pancakes. Soon it fills the whole house. Mom tries to vacuum, but she has to go in and out of the house through the windows because of the dragon everywhere. It takes her forever. Then, the dragon runs off with the house. Billy's dad comes home—and there's just an empty space, where he used to live. The mailman tells him where the house went. He chases after it, climbs up the dragon's head and neck (now sprawling out into the street) and rejoins his wife and son. Mom still insists that the dragon does not exist, but Billy, who's pretty much had it by now, insists, "There is a dragon, Mom." Instantly, it starts to shrink. Soon, it's cat-sized again. Everyone agrees that dragons of that size (1) exist and (2) are much preferable to their gigantic counterparts. Mom, eyes reluctantly opened by this point, asks somewhat plaintively why it had to get so big. Billy quietly suggests: "maybe it wanted to be noticed."

* The recording is available at Peterson, J.B. (2002). Slaying the Dragon Within Us. Lecture, originally broadcast by TVO: available at https://www.youtube.com/watch?v=REjUkEj1O_o

Maybe! That's the moral of many, many stories. Chaos emerges in a household, bit by bit. Mutual unhappiness and resentment pile up. Everything untidy is swept under the rug, where the dragon feasts on the crumbs. But no one says anything, as the shared society and negotiated order of the household reveals itself as inadequate, or disintegrates, in the face of the unexpected and threatening. Everybody whistles in the dark, instead. Communication would require admission of terrible emotions: resentment, terror, loneliness, despair, jealousy, frustration, hatred, boredom. Moment by moment, it's easier to keep the peace. But in the background, in Billy Bixbee's house, and in all that are like it, the dragon grows. One day it bursts forth, in a form that no one can ignore. It lifts the very household from its foundations. Then it's an affair, or a decades-long custody dispute of ruinous economic and psychological proportions. Then it's the concentrated version of the acrimony that could have been spread out, tolerably, issue by issue, over the years of the pseudo-paradise of the marriage. Every one of the three hundred thousand unrevealed issues, which have been lied about, avoided, rationalized away, hidden like an army of skeletons in some great horrific closet, bursts forth like Noah's flood, drowning everything. There's no ark, because no one built one, even though everyone felt the storm gathering.

Don't ever underestimate the destructive power of sins of omission.

Maybe the demolished couple could have had a conversation, or two, or two hundred, about their sex lives. Maybe the physical intimacy they undoubtedly shared should have been matched, as it often is not, *by a corresponding psychological intimacy*. Maybe they could have fought through their roles. In many households, in recent decades, the traditional household division of labour has been demolished, not least in the name of liberation and freedom. That demolition, however, has not left so much glorious lack of restriction in its wake as chaos, conflict and indeterminacy. The escape from tyranny is often followed not by Paradise, but by a sojourn in the desert, aimless, confused and deprived. Furthermore, in the absence of agreed-upon tradition (and the constraints—often uncomfortable; often even unreasonable—that it imposes) there exist only three difficult options: slavery, tyranny or negotiation. The slave merely does what he or she is told—happy, perhaps, to shed the responsibility—and solves the problem of complexity in that manner. But it's a temporary solution. The spirit of the slave rebels. The tyrant merely tells the slave what to do, and solves the problem of complexity in that manner. But it's a temporary solution. The tyrant tires of the slave. There's nothing and no one there, except for predictable and sullen obedience. Who can live forever with that? But negotiation—that requires forthright admission on the part of both players that the dragon exists. That's a reality difficult to face, even when it's still too small to simply devour the knight who dares confront it.

Maybe the demolished couple could have more precisely specified their desired manner of Being. Maybe in that manner they could have jointly prevented the waters of chaos from springing uncontrollably forth and drowning them. Maybe they could have done that instead of saying, in the agreeable, lazy and cowardly way: "It's OK. It's not worth fighting about." There is little, in a marriage, that is so little that it is not worth fighting about. You're stuck in a marriage like the two proverbial cats in a barrel, bound by the oath that lasts in theory until one or both of you die. That oath is there to make you take the damn situation seriously. Do you really want the same petty annoyance tormenting you every single day of your marriage, for the decades of its existence?

"Oh, I can put up with it," you think. And maybe you should. You're no paragon of genuine tolerance. And maybe if you brought up how your partner's giddy laugh is beginning to sound like nails on a blackboard he (or she) would tell you, quite properly, to go to hell. And maybe the fault is with you, and you should grow up, get yourself together and keep quiet. But perhaps braying like a donkey in the midst of a social gathering is not reflecting well on your partner, and you should stick to your guns. Under such circumstances, there is nothing but a fight—a fight with peace as the goal—that will reveal the truth. But you remain silent, and you convince yourself it's because you are a good, peace-loving, patient person (and nothing could be further from the truth). And the monster under the rug gains a few more pounds.

Maybe a forthright conversation about sexual dissatisfaction might have been the proverbial stitch in time—not that it would be easy. Perhaps *madame* desired the death of intimacy, clandestinely, because she was deeply and secretly ambivalent about sex. God knows there's reason to be. Perhaps *monsieur* was a terrible, selfish lover. Maybe they both were. Sorting that out is worth a fight, isn't it? That's a big part of life, isn't it? Perhaps addressing that and (you never know) solving the problem would be worth two months of pure misery just telling each other the truth (not with intent to destroy, or attain victory, because that's not the truth: that's just all-out war).

Maybe it wasn't sex. Maybe every conversation between husband and wife had deteriorated into boring routine, as no shared adventure animated the couple. Maybe that deterioration was easier, moment by moment, day by day, than bearing the responsibility of keeping the relationship alive. Living things die, after all, without attention. Life is indistinguishable from effortful maintenance. No one finds a match so perfect that the need for continued attention and work vanishes (and, besides, if you found the perfect person, he or she would run away from ever-so-imperfect you in justifiable horror). In truth, what you need—what you deserve, after all—is someone exactly as imperfect as you.

Maybe the husband who betrayed his wife was appallingly imma-ture and selfish. Maybe that selfishness got the upper hand. Maybe she did not oppose this tendency with enough force and vigour. Maybe she could not agree with him on the proper disciplinary approach to the children, and shut him out of their lives, in consequence. Maybe that allowed him to circumvent what he saw as an unpleasant respon-sibility. Maybe hatred brewed in the hearts of the children, watching this underground battle, punished by the resentment of their mother and alienated, bit by bit, from good old Dad. Maybe the dinners she prepared for him—or he for her—were cold and bitterly eaten. Maybe all that unaddressed conflict left both resentful, in a manner unspo-ken, but effectively enacted. Maybe all that unspoken trouble started to undermine the invisible networks that supported the marriage. Maybe respect slowly turned into contempt, and no one deigned to notice. Maybe love slowly turned into hate, without mention.

Everything clarified and articulated becomes visible; maybe neither wife nor husband wished to see or understand. Maybe they left things purposefully in the fog. Maybe they generated the fog, to hide what they did not want to see. What did missus gain, when she turned from mistress to maid or mother? Was it a relief when her sex life disappeared? Could she complain more profitably to the neighbours and her mother when her husband turned away? Maybe that was more gratifying, secretly, than anything good that could be derived from any marriage, no matter how perfect. What can possibly compare to the pleasures of sophisticated and well-practised martyrdom? "She's such a saint, and married to such a terrible man. She deserved much better." That's a gratifying myth to live by, even if unconsciously chosen (the truth of the situation be damned). Maybe she never really liked her husband. Maybe she never really liked men, and still doesn't. Maybe that was her mother's fault—or her grandmother's. Maybe she mimicked their behaviour, acting out their trouble, transmitted unconsciously, implicitly, down the generations. Maybe she was taking revenge on her father, or her brother, or society.

What did her husband gain, for his part, when his sex life at home died? Did he willingly play along, as martyr, and complain bitterly to his friends? Did he use it as the excuse he wanted anyway to search for a new lover? Did he use it to justify the resentment he still felt towards women, in general, for the rejections he had faced so continuously before falling into his marriage? Did he seize the opportunity to get effortlessly fat and lazy because he wasn't desired, in any case?

Maybe both, wife and husband alike, used the opportunity to mess up their marriage to take revenge upon God (perhaps the one Being who could have sorted through the mess).

Here's the terrible truth about such matters: every single voluntarily unprocessed and uncomprehended and ignored reason for marital failure will compound and conspire and will then plague that betrayed and self-betrayed woman for the rest of her life. The same goes for her husband. All she—he—they—or we—must do to ensure such an outcome *is nothing*: *don't notice, don't react, don't attend, don't discuss, don't consider, don't work for peace, don't take responsibility.* Don't confront the chaos and turn it into order—just wait, anything but naïve and innocent, for the chaos to rise up and engulf you instead.

Why avoid, when avoidance necessarily and inevitably poisons the future? Because the possibility of a monster lurks underneath all disagreements and errors. Maybe the fight you are having (or not having) with your wife or your husband signifies the beginning of the end of your relationship. Maybe your relationship is ending *because you are a bad person*. It's likely, at least in part. Isn't it? Having the argument necessary to solve a real problem therefore necessitates willingness to confront two forms of miserable and dangerous potential simultaneously: chaos (the potential fragility of the relationship—of all relationships—of life itself) and Hell (the fact that you—and your partner—could each be the person bad enough to ruin everything with your laziness and spite). There's every motivation to avoid. But it doesn't help.

Why remain vague, when it renders life stagnant and murky? Well, if you don't know who you are, you can hide in doubt. Maybe you're *not* a bad, careless, worthless person. Who knows? Not you. Particularly if you refuse to think about it—and you have every reason not to. But not thinking about something you don't want to know about doesn't make it go away. You are merely trading specific, particular, pointed knowledge of the likely finite list of your real faults and flaws for a much longer list of undefined potential inadequacies and insufficiencies.

Why refuse to investigate, when knowledge of reality enables mastery of reality (and if not mastery, at least the stature of an honest amateur)? Well, what if there truly is something rotten in the state of Denmark? Then what? Isn't it better under such conditions to live in willful blindness and enjoy the bliss of ignorance? Well, not if the monster is real! Do you truly think it is a good idea to retreat, to abandon the possibility of arming yourself against the rising sea of troubles, and to thereby diminish yourself in your own eyes? Do you truly think it wise to let the catastrophe grow in the shadows, while you shrink and decrease and become ever more afraid? Isn't it better to prepare, to sharpen your sword, to peer into the darkness, and then to beard the lion in its den? Maybe you'll get hurt. *Probably* you'll get hurt. Life, after all, is suffering. But maybe the wound won't be fatal.

If you wait instead until what you are refusing to investigate comes a-knocking at your door, things will certainly not go so well for you. What you least want will inevitably happen—and when you are least prepared. What you least want to encounter will make itself manifest when you are weakest and it is strongest. And you will be defeated.

> *Turning and turning in the widening gyre*
> *The falcon cannot hear the falconer;*
> *Things fall apart; the centre cannot hold;*
> *Mere anarchy is loosed upon the world,*
> *The blood-dimmed tide is loosed, and everywhere*
> *The ceremony of innocence is drowned;*
> *The best lack all conviction, while the worst*
> *Are full of passionate intensity.*[164]
> (William Butler Yeats,"The Second Coming")

Why refuse to specify, when specifying the problem would enable its solution? Because to specify the problem is to admit that it exists. Because to specify the problem is to allow yourself to know what you want, say, from friend or lover—and then you will know, precisely and cleanly, when you don't get it, and that will hurt, sharply and specifically. But you will learn something from that, and use what you learn in the future—and the alternative to that single sharp pain is the dull ache of continued hopelessness and vague failure and the sense that time, precious time, is slipping by.

Why refuse to specify? Because while you are failing to define success (and thereby rendering it impossible) you are also refusing to define failure, to yourself, so that if and when you fail you won't notice, and it won't hurt. But that won't work! You cannot be fooled so easily—unless you have gone very far down the road! You will instead carry with you a continual sense of disappointment in your own Being and the self-contempt that comes along with that and the increasing hatred for the world that all of that generates (or degenerates).

Surely some revelation is at hand;
Surely the Second Coming is at hand.
The Second Coming! Hardly are those words out
When a vast image out of Spiritus Mundi
Troubles my sight: somewhere in sands of the desert
A shape with lion body and the head of a man,
A gaze blank and pitiless as the sun,
Is moving its slow thighs, while all about it
Reel shadows of the indignant desert birds.
The darkness drops again; but now I know
That twenty centuries of stony sleep
Were vexed to nightmare by a rocking cradle,
And what rough beast, its hour come round at last,
Slouches towards Bethlehem to be born?

What if she who has been betrayed, now driven by desperation, is now determined to face all the incoherence of past, present and future? What if she decided to sort through the mess, even though she has avoided doing so until now, and is all the weaker and more confused for it? Perhaps the effort will nearly kill her (but she is now on a path worse than death in any case). To re-emerge, to escape, to be reborn, she must thoughtfully articulate the reality she comfortably but dangerously left hidden behind a veil of ignorance and the pretence of peace. She must separate the particular details of her specific catastrophe from the intolerable general condition of Being, in a world where everything has fallen apart. Everything—that's far too much. It was *specific* things that fell apart, not everything; *identifiable beliefs* failed; *particular actions* were false and inauthentic. What were they? How can they be fixed, now? How can she be better, in the future? She will never return to dry land if she refuses or is unable to figure it all out. She can put the world back together by some precision of thought, some precision of speech, some reliance on her word, some reliance on the Word. But perhaps it's better to leave things in the fog. Perhaps by now there just isn't enough left of her—perhaps too much of her has been left unrevealed, undeveloped. Maybe she simply no longer has the energy. . . .

Some earlier care and courage and honesty in expression might have saved her from all this trouble. What if she had communicated her unhappiness with the decline of her romantic life, right when it started to decline? Precisely, exactly, when that decline first bothered her? Or, if it didn't bother her—what if she had instead communicated the fact it didn't bother her as much as it perhaps should have? What if she had clearly and carefully confronted the fact of her husband's contempt for her household efforts? Would she have discovered her resentment of her father and society itself (and the consequent contamination of her relationships)? What if she had fixed all that? How much stronger would she then have become? How much less likely to avoid facing up to difficulties, in consequence? How might she then have served herself, her family, and the world?

What if she had continually and honestly risked conflict in the present, in the service of longer-term truth and peace? What if she had treated the micro-collapses of her marriage as evidence of an underlying instability, eminently worthy of attention, instead of ignoring them, putting up with them, or smiling through them, in such a nice, agreeable manner? Maybe she would be different, and her husband, different too. Maybe they would still be married, formally and in spirit. Maybe they would both be much younger, physically and mentally, than they are now. Maybe her house would have been founded more on rock and less on sand.

When things fall apart, and chaos re-emerges, we can give structure to it, and re-establish order, through our speech. If we speak carefully and precisely, we can sort things out, and put them in their proper place, and set a new goal, and navigate to it—often communally, if we negotiate; if we reach consensus. If we speak carelessly and imprecisely, however, things remain vague. The destination remains unproclaimed. The fog of uncertainty does not lift, and there is no negotiating through the world.

The Construction of Soul and World

The psyche (the soul) and the world are both organized, at the highest levels of human existence, with language, through communication. Things are not as they appear when the outcome has been neither intended nor desired. Being has not been sorted into its proper categories, when it is not behaving. When something goes wrong, even perception itself must be questioned, along with evaluation, thought and action. When error announces itself, undifferentiated chaos is at hand. Its reptilian form paralyzes and confuses. But dragons, which do exist (perhaps more than anything else exists) also hoard gold. In that collapse into the terrible mess of uncomprehended Being lurks the possibility of new and benevolent order. Clarity of thought—courageous clarity of thought—is necessary to call it forth.

The problem itself must be admitted to, as close to the time of its emergence as possible. "I'm unhappy," is a good start (not "I have a right to be unhappy," because that is still questionable, at the beginning of the problem-solving process). Perhaps your unhappiness is justified, under the current circumstances. Perhaps any reasonable person would be displeased and miserable to be where you are. Alternatively, perhaps, you are just whiny and immature? Consider both at least equally probable, as terrible as such consideration might appear. Just exactly how immature might you be? There's a potentially bottomless pit. But at least you might rectify it, if you can admit to it.

We parse the complex, tangled chaos, and specify the nature of things, including ourselves. It is in this way that our creative, communicative exploration continually generates and regenerates the world. We are shaped and informed by what we voluntarily encounter, and we shape what we inhabit, as well, in that encounter. This is difficult, but the difficulty is not relevant, because the alternative is worse.

Maybe our errant husband ignored the dinner conversation of his wife because he hated his job and was tired and resentful. Maybe he hated his job because his career was forced on him by his father and he was too weak or "loyal" to object. Maybe she put up with his lack of attention because she believed that forthright objection itself was rude and immoral. Maybe she hated her own father's anger and decided, when very young, that all aggression and assertiveness were morally wrong. Maybe she thought her husband wouldn't love her if she had any opinions of her own. It is very difficult to put such things in order—but damaged machinery will continue to malfunction if its problems are neither diagnosed nor fixed.

Wheat from Chaff

Precision specifies. When something terrible happens, it is precision that separates the unique terrible thing that has actually happened from all the other, equally terrible things that might have happened—but did not. If you wake up in pain, you might be dying. You might be dying slowly and terribly from one of a diverse number of painful, horrible diseases. If you refuse to tell your doctor about your pain, then what you have is unspecified: it could be *any* of those diseases—and it certainly (since you have avoided the diagnostic conversation—the act of articulation) is something unspeakable. But if you talk to your doctor, all those terrible possible diseases will collapse, with luck, into just one terrible (or not so terrible) disease, or even into nothing. Then you can laugh at your previous fears, and if something really is wrong, well, you're prepared. Precision may leave the tragedy intact, but it chases away the ghouls and the demons.

What you hear in the forest but cannot see might be a tiger. It might even be a conspiracy of tigers, each hungrier and more vicious than the other, led by a crocodile. But it might not be, too. If you turn and look, perhaps you'll see that it's just a squirrel. (I know someone who was actually chased by a squirrel.) Something is out there in the woods. You know that with certainty. But often it's only a squirrel. If you refuse to look, however, then it's a dragon, and you're no knight: you're a mouse confronting a lion; a rabbit, paralyzed by the gaze of a wolf. And I am not saying that it's always a squirrel. Often it's something truly terrible. But even what is terrible in actuality often pales in significance compared to what is terrible in imagination. And often what cannot be confronted because of its horror in imagination can in fact be confronted when reduced to its-still-admittedly-terrible actuality.

If you shirk the responsibility of confronting the unexpected, even when it appears in manageable doses, reality itself will become unsustainably disorganized and chaotic. Then it will grow bigger and swallow all order, all sense, and all predictability. Ignored reality transforms itself (reverts back) into the great Goddess of Chaos, the great reptilian Monster of the Unknown—the great predatory beast against which mankind has struggled since the dawn of time. If the gap between pretence and reality goes unmentioned, it will widen, you will fall into it, and the consequences will not be good. Ignored reality manifests itself in an abyss of confusion and suffering.

Be careful with what you tell yourself and others about what you have done, what you are doing, and where you are going. Search for the correct words. Organize those words into the correct sentences, and those sentences into the correct paragraphs. The past can be redeemed, when reduced by precise language to its essence. The present can flow by without robbing the future if its realities are spoken out clearly. With careful thought and language, the singular, stellar destiny that justifies existence can be extracted from the multitude of murky and unpleasant futures that are far more likely to manifest themselves of their own accord. This is how the Eye and the Word make habitable order.

Don't hide baby monsters under the carpet. They will flourish. They will grow large in the dark. Then, when you least expect it, they will jump out and devour you. You will descend into an indeterminate, confusing hell, instead of ascending into the heaven of virtue and clarity. Courageous and truthful words will render your reality simple, pristine, well-defined and habitable.

If you identify things, with careful attention and language, you bring them forward as viable, obedient objects, detaching them from their underlying near-universal interconnectedness. You simplify them. You make them specific and useful, and reduce their complexity. You make it possible to live with them and use them without dying from that complexity, with its attendant uncertainty and anxiety. If you leave things vague, then you'll never know what is one thing and what is another. Everything will bleed into everything else. This makes the world too complex to be managed.

You have to consciously define the topic of a conversation, particularly when it is difficult—or it becomes about everything, and everything is too much. This is so frequently why couples cease communicating. Every argument degenerates into every problem that ever emerged in the past, every problem that exists now, and every terrible thing that is likely to happen in the future. No one can have a discussion about "everything." Instead, you can say, "This exact, precise thing—that is what is making me unhappy. This exact, precise thing— that is what I want, as an alternative (although I am open to suggestions, if they are specific). This exact, precise thing—that is what you could deliver, so that I will stop making your life and mine miserable." But to do that, you have to *think*: What is wrong, *exactly*? What do I want, *exactly*? You must speak forthrightly and call forth the habitable world from chaos. You must use honest precise speech to do that. If instead you shrink away and hide, what you are hiding from will transform itself into the giant dragon that lurks under your bed and in your forest and in the dark recesses of your mind—and it will devour you.

You must determine where you have been in your life, so that you can know where you are now. If you don't know where you are, precisely, then you could be anywhere. Anywhere is too many places to be, and some of those places are very bad. You must determine where you have been in your life, because otherwise you can't get to where you're going. You can't get from point A to point B unless you are already at point A, and if you're just "anywhere" the chances you are at point A are very small indeed.

You must determine where you are going in your life, because you cannot get there unless you move in that direction. Random wandering will not move you forward. It will instead disappoint and frustrate you and make you anxious and unhappy and hard to get along with (and then resentful, and then vengeful, and then worse).

Say what you mean, so that you can find out what you mean. Act out what you say, so you can find out what happens. Then pay attention.

Note your errors. Articulate them. Strive to correct them. That is how you discover the meaning of your life. That will protect you from the tragedy of your life. How could it be otherwise?

Confront the chaos of Being. Take aim against a sea of troubles. Specify your destination, and chart your course. Admit to what you want. Tell those around you who you are. Narrow, and gaze attentively, and move forward, forthrightly.

Be precise in your speech.

RULE 11

DO NOT BOTHER CHILDREN
WHEN THEY ARE SKATEBOARDING

DANGER AND MASTERY

THERE WAS A TIME WHEN KIDS skateboarded on the west side of Sidney Smith Hall, at the University of Toronto, where I work. Sometimes I stood there and watched them. There are rough, wide, shallow concrete steps there, leading up from the street to the front entrance, accompanied by tubular iron handrails, about two and a half inches in diameter and twenty feet long. The crazy kids, almost always boys, would pull back about fifteen yards from the top of the steps. Then they would place a foot on their boards, and skate like mad to get up some speed. Just before they collided with the handrail, they would reach down, grab their board with a single hand and jump onto the top of the rail, boardsliding their way down its length, propelling themselves off and landing—sometimes, gracefully, still atop their boards, sometimes, painfully, off them. Either way, they were soon back at it.

Some might call that stupid. Maybe it was. But it was brave, too. I thought those kids were amazing. I thought they deserved a pat on the back and some honest admiration. Of course it was dangerous. Danger was the point. They wanted to triumph over danger. They would have been safer in protective equipment, but that would have ruined it. They weren't trying to be safe. They were trying to become competent—and it's competence that makes people as safe as they can truly be.

I wouldn't dare do what those kids were doing. Not only that, I couldn't. I certainly couldn't climb a construction crane, like a certain type of modern daredevil, evident on YouTube (and, of course, people who work on construction cranes). I don't like heights, although the twenty-five thousand feet to which airliners ascend is so high that it doesn't bother me. I have flown several times in a carbon fibre stunt plane—even doing a hammerhead roll—and that was OK, although it's very physically and mentally demanding. (To perform a hammerhead roll, you pilot the plane straight up vertically, until the force of gravity makes it stall. Then it falls backwards, corkscrewing, until eventually it flips and noses straight down, after which you pull out of the dive. Or you don't do another hammerhead roll.) But I can't skateboard—especially down handrails—and I can't climb cranes.

Sidney Smith Hall faces another street on the east side. Along that street, named St. George—ironically enough—the university installed a series of rough, hard-edged, concrete plant boxes, sloping down to the roadway. The kids used to go out there, too, and boardslide along the box edges, as they did along the concrete surround of a sculpture adjacent to the building. That didn't last very long. Little steel brackets known as "skatestoppers" soon appeared, every two or three feet, along those edges. When I first saw them, I remembered something that happened in Toronto several years previously. Two weeks before elementary school classes started, throughout the city, all the playground equipment disappeared. The legislation governing such things had changed, and there was a panic about insurability. The playgrounds were hastily removed, even though they were sufficiently safe, grandfathered re their insurability, and often paid for (and quite recently) by parents. This meant no playgrounds at all for more than a year. During this time, I often saw bored but admirable kids charging around on the roof of our local school. It was that or scrounge about in the dirt with the cats and the less adventurous children.

I say "sufficiently safe" about the demolished playgrounds because when playgrounds are made too safe, kids either stop playing in them or start playing in unintended ways. Kids need playgrounds dangerous enough to remain challenging. People, including children (who are people too, after all) don't seek to minimize risk. They seek to optimize it. They drive and walk and love and play so that they achieve what they desire, but they push themselves a bit at the same time, too, so they continue to develop. Thus, if things are made too safe, people (including children) start to figure out ways to make them dangerous again.[165]

When untrammeled—and encouraged—we prefer to live on the edge. There, we can still be both confident in our experience and confronting the chaos that helps us develop. We're hard-wired, for that reason, to enjoy risk (some of us more than others). We feel invigorated and excited when we work to optimize our future performance, while playing in the present. Otherwise we lumber around, sloth-like, unconscious, unformed and careless. Overprotected, we will fail when something dangerous, unexpected and full of opportunity suddenly makes its appearance, as it inevitably will.

The skatestoppers are unattractive. The surround of the nearby sculpture would have to have been badly damaged by diligent board-sliders before it would look as mean as it does now, studded with metal like a pit bull's collar. The large plant boxes have metal guards placed at irregular intervals across their tops, and this, in addition to the wear caused by the skateboarders, produces a dismal impression of poor design, resentment and badly executed afterthoughts. It gives the area, which was supposed to be beautified by the sculpture and vegetation, a generic industrial/prison/mental institution/work-camp look of the kind that appears when builders and public officials do not like or trust the people they serve.

The sheer harsh ugliness of the solution makes a lie of the reasons for its implementation.

Success and Resentment

If you read the depth psychologists—Freud and Jung, for example, as well as their precursor, Friedrich Nietzsche—you learn that there is a dark side to everything. Freud delved deeply into the latent, implicit content of dreams, which were often aimed, in his opinion, at the expression of some improper wish. Jung believed that every act of social propriety was accompanied by its evil twin, its unconscious shadow. Nietzsche investigated the role played by what he termed *ressentiment* in motivating what were ostensibly selfless actions—and, often, exhibited all too publicly.[166]

> For that man be delivered from revenge—that is for me the bridge to the highest hope, and a rainbow after long storms. The tarantulas, of course, would have it otherwise. "What justice means to us is precisely that the world be filled with the storms of our revenge"—thus they speak to each other. "We shall wreak vengeance and abuse on all whose equals we are not"—thus do the tarantula-hearts vow. "And 'will to equality' shall henceforth be the name for virtue; and against all that has power we want to raise our clamor!" You preachers of equality, the tyrant-mania of impotence clamors thus out of you for equality: your most secret ambitions to be tyrants thus shroud themselves in words of virtue.

The incomparable English essayist George Orwell knew this sort of thing well. In 1937, he wrote *The Road to Wigan Pier*, which was in part a scathing attack on upper-class British socialists (this, despite being inclined towards socialism himself). In the first half of this book, Orwell portrays the appalling conditions faced by UK miners in the 1930s:[167]

> Several dentists have told me that in industrial districts a person over thirty with any of his or her own teeth is coming to be an abnormality. In Wigan various people gave me their opinion that it is best to get shut of your teeth as early in life as possible. 'Teeth is just a misery,' one woman said to me.

A Wigan Pier coal miner had to walk—crawl would be a better word, given the height of the mine shafts—up to three miles, underground, in the dark, banging his head and scraping his back, just to get to his seven-and-a-half-hour shift of backbreaking work. After that, he crawled back. "It is comparable, perhaps, to climbing a smallish mountain before and after your day's work," stated Orwell. None of the time spent crawling was paid.

Orwell wrote *The Road to Wigan Pier* for the Left Book Club, a socialist publishing group that released a select volume every month. After reading the first half of his book, which deals directly with the miners' personal circumstances, it is impossible not to feel sympathy for the working poor. Only a monster could keep his heart hardened through the accounts of the lives Orwell describes:

> It is not long since conditions in the mines were worse than they are now. There are still living a few very old women who in their youth have worked underground, crawling on all fours and dragging tubs of coal. They used to go on doing this even when they were pregnant.

In book's second half, however, Orwell turned his gaze to a different problem: the comparative unpopularity of socialism in the UK at the time, despite the clear and painful inequity observable everywhere. He concluded that the tweed-wearing, armchair-philosophizing, victim-identifying, pity-and-contempt-dispensing social-reformer types frequently did not like the poor, as they claimed. *Instead, they just hated the rich.* They disguised their resentment and jealousy with piety, sanctimony and self-righteousness. Things in the unconscious— or on the social justice–dispensing leftist front—haven't changed much, today. It is because of Freud, Jung, Nietzsche—and Orwell— that I always wonder, "What, then, do you stand against?" whenever I hear someone say, too loudly, "I stand for this!" The question seems particularly relevant if the same someone is complaining, criticizing, or trying to change someone else's behaviour.

I believe it was Jung who developed the most surgically wicked of psychoanalytic dicta: *if you cannot understand why someone did something, look at the consequences—and infer the motivation.* This is a psychological scalpel. It's not always a suitable instrument. It can cut too deeply, or in the wrong places. It is, perhaps, a last-resort option. Nonetheless, there are times when its application proves enlightening.

If the consequences of placing skatestoppers on plant-boxes and sculpture bases, for example, is unhappy adolescent males and brutalist aesthetic disregard of beauty then, perhaps, that was the aim. When someone claims to be acting from the highest principles, for the good of others, there is no reason to assume that the person's motives are genuine. People motivated to make things better usually aren't concerned with changing other people—or, if they are, they take responsibility for making the same changes to themselves (and first). Beneath the production of rules stopping the skateboarders from doing highly skilled, courageous and dangerous things I see the operation of an insidious and profoundly anti-human spirit.

More about Chris

My friend Chris, whom I wrote about earlier, was possessed by such a spirit—to the serious detriment of his mental health. Part of what plagued him was guilt. He attended elementary and junior high school in a number of towns, up in the frigid expanses of the northernmost Alberta prairie, prior to ending up in the Fairview I wrote about earlier. Fights with Native kids were a too-common part of his experience, during those moves. It's no overstatement to point out that such kids were, on average, rougher than the white kids, or that they were touchier (and they had their reasons). I knew this well from my own experience.

I had a rocky friendship with a Métis kid, Rene Heck,[*] when I was in elementary school. It was rocky because the situation was complex. There was a large cultural divide between Rene and me. His clothes were dirtier. He was rougher in speech and attitude. I had skipped a grade in school, and was, in addition, small for my age. Rene was a big, smart, good-looking kid, and he was tough. We were in grade six

---

[*] Names and other details have been changed for the sake of privacy.

together, in a class taught by my father. Rene was caught chewing gum. "Rene," said my father, "spit that gum out. You look like a cow." "Ha, ha," I laughed, under my breath. "Rene the cow." Rene might have been a cow, but there was nothing wrong with his hearing. "Peterson," he said, "after school—you're dead."

Earlier in the morning, Rene and I had arranged to see a movie that night at the local movie theatre, the Gem. It looked like that was off. In any case, the rest of the day passed, quickly and unpleasantly, as it does when threat and pain lurk. Rene was more than capable of giving me a good pounding. After school, I took off for the bike stands outside the school as fast as I could, but Rene beat me there. We circled around the bikes, him on one side, me on the other. We were characters in a "Keystone Cops" short. As long as I kept circling, he couldn't catch me, but my strategy couldn't work forever. I yelled out that I was sorry, but he wasn't mollified. His pride was hurt, and he wanted me to pay.

I crouched down and hid behind some bikes, keeping an eye on Rene. "Rene," I yelled, "I'm sorry I called you a cow. Let's quit fighting." He started to approach me again. I said, "Rene, I am sorry I said that. Really. And I still want to go to the movie with you." This wasn't just a tactic. I meant it. Otherwise what happened next would not have happened. Rene stopped circling. Then he stared at me. Then he broke into tears. Then he ran off. That was Native-white relationships in a nutshell, in our hard little town. We never did go to a movie together.

When my friend Chris got into it with Native kids, he wouldn't fight back. He didn't feel that his self-defence was morally justified, so he took his beatings. "We took their land," he later wrote. "That was wrong. No wonder they're angry." Over time, step by step, Chris withdrew from the world. It was partly his guilt. He developed a deep hatred for masculinity and masculine activity. He saw going to school or working or finding a girlfriend as part of the same process that had led to the colonization of North America, the horrible nuclear stalemate of the cold war, and the despoiling of the planet. He had read some books about Buddhism, and felt that negation of his own Being was ethically required, in the light of the current world situation. He came to believe that the same applied to others.

When I was an undergraduate, Chris was, for a while, one of my roommates. One late night we went to a local bar. We walked home, afterward. He started to snap the side-view mirrors off parked cars, one after the other. I said, "Quit that, Chris. What possible good is it going to do to make the people who own these cars miserable?" He told me that they were all part of the frenetic human activity that was ruining everything, and that they deserved whatever they got. I said that taking revenge on people who were just living normal lives was not going to help anything.

Years later, when I was in graduate school in Montreal, Chris showed up, for what was supposed to be a visit. He was aimless, however, and lost. He asked if I could help. He ended up moving in. I was married by then, living with my wife, Tammy, and our year-old daughter, Mikhaila. Chris had also been friends with Tammy back in Fairview (and held out hopes of more than friendship). That complicated the situation even more—but not precisely in the manner you might think. Chris started by hating men, but he ended by hating women. He wanted them, but he had rejected education, and career, and desire. He smoked heavily, and was unemployed. Unsurprisingly, therefore, he was not of much interest to women. That made him bitter. I tried to convince him that the path he had chosen was only going to lead to further ruin. He needed to develop some humility. He needed to get a life.

One evening, it was Chris's turn to make dinner. When my wife came home, the apartment was filled with smoke. Hamburgers were burning furiously in the frying pan. Chris was on his hands and knees, attempting to repair something that had come loose on the legs of the stove. My wife knew his tricks. She knew he was burning dinner on purpose. He resented having to make it. He resented the feminine role (even though the household duties were split in a reasonable manner; even though he knew that perfectly well). He was fixing the stove to provide a plausible, even creditable excuse for burning the food. When she pointed out what he was doing, he played the victim, but he was deeply and dangerously furious. Part of him, and not the good part, was convinced that he was smarter than anyone else. It was a blow to his pride that she could see through his tricks. It was an ugly situation.

Tammy and I took a walk up towards a local park the next day. We needed to get away from the apartment, although it was thirty-five below—bitterly, frigidly cold, humid and foggy. It was windy. It was hostile to life. Living with Chris was too much, Tammy said. We entered the park. The trees forked their bare branches upward through the damp grey air. A black squirrel, tail hairless from mange, gripped a leafless branch, shivered violently, struggling to hold on against the wind. What was it doing out there in the cold? Squirrels are partial hibernators. They only come out in the winter when it's warm. Then we saw another, and another, and another, and another, and another. There were squirrels all around us in the park, all partially hairless, tails and bodies alike, all windblown on their branches, all shaking and freezing in the deathly cold. No one else was around. It was impossible. It was inexplicable. It was exactly appropriate. We were on the stage of an absurdist play. It was directed by God. Tammy left soon after with our daughter for a few days elsewhere.

Near Christmas time, that same year, my younger brother and his new wife came out to visit from western Canada. My brother also knew Chris. They all put on their winter clothes in preparation for a walk around downtown Montreal. Chris put on a long dark winter coat. He pulled a black toque, a brimless knitted cap, far down over his head. His coat was black, as were his pants and boots. He was very tall, and thin, and somewhat stooped. "Chris," I joked. "You look like a serial killer." Ha bloody ha. The three came back from their walk. Chris was out of sorts. There were strangers in his territory. Another happy couple. It was salt in his wounds.

We had dinner, pleasantly enough. We talked, and ended the evening. But I couldn't sleep. Something wasn't right. It was in the air. At four in the morning, I had had enough. I crawled out of bed. I knocked quietly on Chris's door and went without waiting for an answer into his room. He was awake on the bed, staring at the ceiling, as I knew he would be. I sat down beside him. I knew him very well. I talked him down from his murderous rage. Then I went back to bed, and slept. The next morning my brother pulled me aside. He wanted to speak with me. We sat down. He said, "What the hell was going on last night? I couldn't sleep at all. Was something wrong?" I told my brother that Chris wasn't doing so well. I didn't tell him that he was lucky to be alive—that we all were. The spirit of Cain had visited our house, but we were left unscathed.

Maybe I picked up some change in scent that night, when death hung in the air. Chris had a very bitter odour. He showered frequently, but the towels and the sheets picked up the smell. It was impossible to get them clean. It was the product of a psyche and a body that did not operate harmoniously. A social worker I knew, who also knew Chris, told me of her familiarity with that odour. Everyone at her workplace knew of it, although they only discussed it in hushed tones. They called it the smell of the unemployable.

Soon after this I finished my post-doctoral studies. Tammy and I moved away from Montreal to Boston. We had our second baby. Now and then, Chris and I talked on the phone. He came to visit once. It went well. He had found a job at an auto-parts place. He was trying to make things better. He was OK at that point. But it didn't last. I didn't see him in Boston again. Almost ten years later—the night before Chris's fortieth birthday, as it happened—he called me again. By this time, I had moved my family to Toronto. He had some news. A story he had written was going to be published in a collection put together by a small but legitimate press. He wanted to tell me that. He wrote good short stories. I had read them all. We had discussed them at length. He was a good photographer, too. He had a good, creative eye. The next day, Chris drove his old pickup—the same battered beast from Fairview—into the bush. He ran a hose from the exhaust pipe into the front cab. I can see him there, looking through the cracked windshield, smoking, waiting. They found his body a few weeks later. I called his dad. "My beautiful boy," he sobbed.

Recently, I was invited to give a TEDx talk at a nearby university. Another professor talked first. He had been invited to speak because of his work—his genuinely fascinating, technical work—with computationally intelligent surfaces (like computer touchscreens, but capable of being placed everywhere). He spoke instead about the threat human beings posed to the survival of the planet. Like Chris—like far too many people—he had become anti-human, to the core. He had not walked as far down that road as my friend, but the same dread spirit animated them both.

He stood in front of a screen displaying an endless slow pan of a blocks-long Chinese high-tech factory. Hundreds of white-suited workers stood like sterile, inhuman robots behind their assembly lines, soundlessly inserting piece A into slot B. He told the audience—filled with bright young people—of the decision he and his wife had made to limit their number of children to one. He told them it was something they should all consider, if they wanted to regard themselves as ethical people. I felt that such a decision was properly considered—but only in his particular case (where less than one might have been even better). The many Chinese students in attendance sat stolidly through his moralizing. They thought, perhaps, of their parents' escape from the horrors of Mao's Cultural Revolution and its one-child policy. They thought, perhaps, of the vast improvement in living standard and freedom provided by the very same factories. A couple of them said as much in the question period that followed.

Would the professor have reconsidered his opinions, if he knew where such ideas can lead? I would like to say yes, but I don't believe it. I think he could have known, but refused to. Worse, perhaps: he knew, but didn't care—or knew, and was headed there, voluntarily, in any case.

Self-Appointed Judges of the Human Race

It has not been long since the Earth seemed infinitely larger than the people who inhabited it. It was only in the late 1800s that the brilliant biologist Thomas Huxley (1825-95)—staunch defender of Darwin and Aldous Huxley's grandfather—told the British Parliament that it was literally impossible for mankind to exhaust the oceans. Their power of generation was simply too great, as far as he could determine, compared to even the most assiduous human predations. It's been an even shorter fifty years since Rachel Carson's *Silent Spring* ignited the environmental movement.[168] Fifty years! That's nothing! That's not even yesterday.

We've only just developed the conceptual tools and technologies that allow us to understand the web of life, however imperfectly. We deserve a bit of sympathy, in consequence, for the hypothetical outrage of our destructive behaviour. Sometimes we don't know any better. Sometimes we do know better, but haven't yet formulated any practical alternatives. It's not as if life is easy for human beings, after all, even now—and it's only a few decades ago that the majority of human beings were starving, diseased and illiterate.[169] Wealthy as we are (increasingly, everywhere) we still only live decades that can be counted on our fingers. Even at present, it is the rare and fortunate family that does not contain at least one member with a serious illness—and all will face that problem eventually. We do what we can to make the best of things, in our vulnerability and fragility, and the planet is harder on us than we are on it. We could cut ourselves some slack.

Human beings are, after all, seriously remarkable creatures. We have no peers, and it's not clear that we have any real limits. Things happen now that appeared humanly impossible even at the same time in the recent past when we began to wake up to our planet-sized responsibilities. A few weeks before writing this I happened across two videos juxtaposed on YouTube. One showed the Olympic gold medal vault from 1956; the other, the Olympic silver medal vault from 2012. It didn't even look like the same sport—or the same animal. What McKayla Maroney did in 2012 would have been considered super-human in the fifties. Parkour, a sport derived from French military obstacle course training, is amazing, as is free running. I watch compilations of such performances with unabashed admiration. Some of the kids jump off three-storey buildings without injury. It's dangerous—and amazing. Crane climbers are so brave it rattles the mind. The same goes for extreme mountain bikers, freestyle snowboarders, surfers of fifty-foot waves, and skateboarders.

The boys who shot up Columbine High School, whom we discussed earlier, had appointed themselves judges of the human race—like the TEDx professor, although much more extreme; like Chris, my doomed friend. For Eric Harris, the more literate of the two killers, human beings were a failed and corrupt species. Once a presupposition such as that is accepted, its inner logic will inevitably manifest itself. If something is a plague, as David Attenborough has it,[170] or a cancer, as the Club of Rome claimed,[171] the person who eradicates it is a hero—a veritable planetary saviour, in this case. A real messiah might follow through with his rigorous moral logic, and eliminate himself, as well. This is what mass murderers, driven by near-infinite resentment, typically do. Even their own Being does not justify the existence of humanity. In fact, they kill themselves precisely to demonstrate the purity of their commitment to annihilation. No one in the modern world may without objection express the opinion that existence would be bettered by the absence of Jews, blacks, Muslims, or Englishmen. Why, then, is it virtuous to propose that the planet might be better off, if there were fewer people on it? I can't help but see a skeletal, grinning face, gleeful at the possibility of the apocalypse, hiding not so very far behind such statements. And why does it so often seem to be the very people standing so visibly against prejudice who so often appear to feel obligated to denounce humanity itself?

I have seen university students, particularly those in the humanities, suffer genuine declines in their mental health from being philosophically berated by such defenders of the planet for their existence as members of the human species. It's worse, I think, for young men. As privileged beneficiaries of the patriarchy, their accomplishments are considered unearned. As possible adherents of rape culture, they're sexually suspect. Their ambitions make them plunderers of the planet. They're not welcome. At the junior high, high school and university level, they're falling behind educationally. When my son was fourteen, we discussed his grades. He was doing very well, he said, matter-of-factly, for a boy. I inquired further. Everyone knew, he said, that girls do better in school than boys. His intonation indicated surprise at my ignorance of something so self-evident. While writing this, I received the latest edition of *The Economist*. The cover story? "The Weaker Sex"— meaning males. In modern universities women now make up more than 50 percent of the students in more than two-thirds of all disciplines.

Boys are suffering, in the modern world. They are more disobedient—negatively—or more independent—positively—than girls, and they suffer for this, throughout their pre-university educational career. They are less agreeable (agreeableness being a personality trait associated with compassion, empathy and avoidance of conflict) and less susceptible to anxiety and depression,[172] at least after both sexes hit puberty.[173] Boys' interests tilt towards things; girls' interests tilt towards people.[174] Strikingly, these differences, strongly influenced by biological factors, are most pronounced in the Scandinavian societies where gender-equality has been pushed hardest: this is the opposite of what would be expected by those who insist, ever more loudly, that gender is a social construct. It isn't. This isn't a debate. The data are in.[175]

Boys like competition, and they don't like to obey, particularly when they are adolescents. During that time, they are driven to escape their families, and establish their own independent existence. There is little difference between doing that and challenging authority. Schools, which were set up in the late 1800s precisely to inculcate obedience,[176] do not take kindly to provocative and daring behaviour, no matter how tough-minded and competent it might show a boy (or a girl) to be. Other factors play their role in the decline of boys. Girls will, for example, play boys' games, but boys are much more reluctant to play girls' games. This is in part because it is admirable for a girl to win when competing with a boy. It is also OK for her to lose to a boy. For a boy to beat a girl, however, it is often not OK—and just as often, it is even less OK for him to lose. Imagine that a boy and a girl, aged nine, get into a fight. Just for engaging, the boy is highly suspect. If he wins, he's pathetic. If he loses—well, his life might as well be over. Beat up by a girl.

Girls can win by winning in their own hierarchy—by being good at what girls value, as girls. They can add to this victory by winning in the boys' hierarchy. Boys, however, can only win by winning in the male hierarchy. They will lose status, among girls *and* boys, by being good at what girls value. It costs them in reputation among the boys, and in attractiveness among the girls. Girls aren't attracted to boys who are their friends, even though they might like them, whatever that means. They are attracted to boys who win status contests with other

12 RULES FOR LIFE

boys. If you're male, however, you just can't hammer a female as hard as you would a male. Boys can't (won't) play truly competitive games with girls. It isn't clear how they can win. As the game turns into a girls' game, therefore, the boys leave. Are the universities—particularly the humanities—about to become a girls' game? Is this what we want?

The situation in the universities (and in educational institutions in general) is far more problematic than the basic statistics indicate.[177] If you eliminate the so-called STEM (science, technology, engineering and mathematics) programs (excluding psychology), the female/male ratio is even more skewed.[178] Almost 80 percent of students majoring in the fields of healthcare, public administration, psychology and education, which comprise one-quarter of all degrees, are female. The disparity is still rapidly increasing. At this rate, there will be very few men in most university disciplines in fifteen years. This is not good news for men. It might even be catastrophic news for men. But it's also not good news for women.

Career and Marriage

The women at female-dominated institutes of higher education are finding it increasingly difficult to arrange a dating relationship of even moderate duration. In consequence, they must settle, if inclined, for a hook-up, or sequential hook-ups. Perhaps this is a move forward, in terms of sexual liberation, but I doubt it. I think it's terrible for the girls.[179] A stable, loving relationship is highly desirable, for men as well as women. For women, however, it is often what is most wanted. From 1997 to 2012, according to the Pew Research Centre,[180] the number of women aged 18 to 34 who said that a successful marriage is one of the most important things in life rose from 28 to 37 percent (an increase of more than 30 percent*). The number of young men who said the same thing declined 15 percent over the same period (from 35 to 29 percent†). During that time, the proportion of married people over 18

---

* $37\text{-}28/28 = 9/28 = 32$ percent.

† $35\text{-}29/35 = 6/35 = 17$ percent.

continued to decline, down from three-quarters in 1960 to half now.[181] Finally, among never-married adults aged 30 to 59, men are three times as likely as women to say they do not ever want to marry (27 vs 8 percent).

Who decided, anyway, that career is more important than love and family? Is working eighty hours a week at a high-end law firm truly worth the sacrifices required for that kind of success? And if it is worth it, why is it worth it? A minority of people (mostly men, who score low in the trait of agreeableness, again) are hyper-competitive, and want to win at any cost. A minority will find the work intrinsically fascinating. But most aren't, and most won't, and money doesn't seem to improve people's lives, once they have enough to avoid the bill collectors. Furthermore, most high-performing and high-earning females have high-performing and high-earning partners—and that matters more to women. The Pew data also indicate that a spouse with a desirable job is a high priority for almost 80 percent of never-married but marriage-seeking women (but for less than 50 percent of men).

When they hit their thirties, most of the top-rate female lawyers bail out of their high-pressure careers.[182] Only 15 percent of equity partners at the two hundred biggest US law firms are women.[183] This figure hasn't changed much in the last fifteen years, even though female associates and staff attorneys are plentiful. It also isn't because the law firms don't want the women to stay around and succeed. There is a chronic shortage of excellent people, regardless of sex, and law firms are desperate to retain them.

The women who leave want a job—and a life—that allows them some time. After law school and articling and the few first years of work, they develop other interests. This is common knowledge in the big firms (although it is not something that people are comfortable articulating in public, men and women alike). I recently watched a McGill University professor, female, lecture a room full of female law partners or near-partners about how lack of childcare facilities and "male definitions of success" impeded their career progress and caused women to leave. I knew most of the women in the room. We had talked at great length. I knew they knew that none of this was at all the problem. They had nannies, and they could afford them. They had already outsourced all their domestic obligations and necessities. They understood, as well—and perfectly well—that it was the market that defined success, not the men they worked with. If you are earning $650 an hour in Toronto as a top lawyer, and your client in Japan phones you at 4 a.m. on a Sunday, you answer. Now. You answer, now, even if you have just gone back to sleep after feeding the baby. You answer because some hyper-ambitious legal associate in New York would be happy to answer, if you don't—and that's why the market defines the work.

The increasingly short supply of university-educated men poses a problem of increasing severity for women who want to marry, as well as date. First, women have a strong proclivity to marry across or up the economic dominance hierarchy. They prefer a partner of equal or greater status. This holds true cross-culturally.[184] The same does not hold, by the way, for men, who are perfectly willing to marry across or down (as the Pew data indicate), although they show a preference for somewhat younger mates. The recent trend towards the hollowing-out of the middle class has also been increasing as resource-rich women tend more and more[185] to partner with resource-rich men. Because of this, and because of the decline in high-paying manufacturing jobs for men (one of six men of employable age is currently without work in the US), marriage is now something increasingly reserved for the rich. I can't help finding that amusing, in a blackly ironic manner. The oppressive patriarchal institution of marriage has now become a luxury. Why would the rich tyrannize themselves?

Why do women want an employed partner and, preferably, one of higher status? In no small part, it's because women become more vulnerable when they have children. They need someone competent to support mother and child when that becomes necessary. It's a perfectly rational compensatory act, although it may also have a biological basis. Why would a woman who decides to take responsibility for one or more infants want an adult to look after as well? So, the unemployed working man is an undesirable specimen—and single motherhood an undesirable alternative. Children in father-absent homes are four times as likely to be poor. That means their mothers are poor too. Fatherless children are at much greater risk for drug and alcohol abuse. Children living with married biological parents are less anxious, depressed and delinquent than children living with one or more non-biological parents. Children in single-parent families are also twice as likely to commit suicide.[186]

The strong turn towards political correctness in universities has exacerbated the problem. The voices shouting against oppression have become louder, it seems, in precise proportion to how equal— even now increasingly skewed against men—the schools have become. There are whole disciplines in universities forthrightly hostile towards men. These are the areas of study dominated by the postmodern/ neo-Marxist claim that Western culture, in particular, is an oppressive structure, created by white men to dominate and exclude women (and other select groups); successful only because of that domination and exclusion.[187]

The Patriarchy: Help or Hindrance?

Of course, culture *is* an oppressive structure. *It's always been that way.* It's a fundamental, universal existential reality. The tyrannical king is a symbolic truth; an archetypal constant. What we inherit from the past is willfully blind, and out of date. It's a ghost, a machine, and a monster. It must be rescued, repaired and kept at bay by the attention and effort of the living. It crushes, as it hammers us into socially acceptable shape, and it wastes great potential. But it offers great gain, too. Every word we speak is a gift from our ancestors. Every thought we think was thought previously by someone smarter. The highly functional infrastructure that surrounds us, particularly in the West, is a gift from our ancestors: the comparatively uncorrupt political and economic systems, the technology, the wealth, the lifespan, the freedom, the luxury, and the opportunity. Culture takes with one hand, but in some fortunate places it gives more with the other. To think about culture only as oppressive is ignorant and ungrateful, as well as dangerous. This is not to say (as I am hoping the content of this book has made abundantly clear, so far) that culture should not be subject to criticism.

Consider this, as well, in regard to oppression: *any hierarchy creates winners and losers*. The winners are, of course, more likely to justify the hierarchy and the losers to criticize it. But (1) the collective pursuit of any valued goal produces a hierarchy (as some will be better and some worse at that pursuit no matter what it is) and (2) it is the pursuit of goals that in large part lends life its sustaining meaning. We experience almost all the emotions that make life deep and engaging as a consequence of moving successfully towards something deeply desired and valued. The price we pay for that involvement is the inevitable creation of hierarchies of success, while the inevitable consequence is difference in outcome. Absolute equality would therefore require the sacrifice of value itself—and then there would be nothing worth living for. We might instead note with gratitude that a complex, sophisticated culture allows for many games and many successful players, and that a well-structured culture allows the individuals that compose it to play and to win, in many different fashions.

It is also *perverse* to consider culture the creation of men. Culture is symbolically, archetypally, mythically male. That's partly why the idea of "the patriarchy" is so easily swallowed. But it is certainly the creation of humankind, not the creation of men (let alone white men, who nonetheless contributed their fair share). European culture has only been dominant, to the degree that it is dominant at all, for about four hundred years. On the time scale of cultural evolution—which is to be measured, at minimum, in thousands of years—such a timespan barely registers. Furthermore, even if women contributed nothing substantial to art, literature and the sciences prior to the 1960s and the feminist revolution (which is not something I believe), then the role they played raising children and working on the farms was still instrumental in raising boys and freeing up men—a very few men—so that humanity could propagate itself and strive forward.

Here's an alternative theory: throughout history, men and women both struggled terribly for freedom from the overwhelming horrors of privation and necessity. Women were often at a disadvantage during that struggle, as they had all the vulnerabilities of men, with the extra reproductive burden, and less physical strength. In addition to the filth, misery, disease, starvation, cruelty and ignorance that characterized the lives of both sexes, back before the twentieth century (when even people in the Western world typically existed on less than a dollar a day in today's money) women also had to put up with the serious practical inconvenience of menstruation, the high probability of unwanted pregnancy, the chance of death or serious damage during childbirth, and the burden of too many young children. Perhaps that is sufficient reason for the different legal and practical treatment of men and women that characterized most societies prior to the recent technological revolutions, including the invention of the birth control pill. At least such things might be taken into account, before the assumption that men tyrannized women is accepted as a truism.

It looks to me like the so-called oppression of the patriarchy was instead an imperfect collective attempt by men and women, stretching over millennia, to free each other from privation, disease and drudgery. The recent case of Arunachalam Muruganantham provides a salutary example. This man, the "tampon king" of India, became unhappy because his wife had to use dirty rags during her menstrual period. She told him it was either expensive sanitary napkins, or milk for the family. He spent the next fourteen years in a state of insanity, by his neighbours' judgment, trying to rectify the problem. Even his wife and his mother abandoned him, briefly, terrified as they became of his obsession. When he ran out of female volunteers to test his product, he took to wearing a bladder of pig's blood as a replacement. I can't see how this behaviour would have improved his popularity or status. Now his low-cost and locally made napkins are distributed across India, manufactured by women-run self-help groups. His users have been provided with freedom they never previously experienced. In 2014, this high-school dropout was named one of *Time* magazine's 100 most influential people in the world. I am unwilling to consider personal gain Muruganantham's primary motivation. Is he part of the patriarchy?

In 1847, James Young Simpson used ether to help a woman who

had a deformed pelvis give birth. Afterwards, he switched to the better-performing chloroform. The first baby delivered under its influence was named "Anaesthesia." By 1853, chloroform was esteemed enough to be used by Queen Victoria, who delivered her seventh baby under its influence. Remarkably soon afterward, the option of painless childbirth was available everywhere. A few people warned of the danger of opposing God's pronouncement to women in Genesis 3:16: "I will greatly multiply thy sorrow and thy conception; in sorrow thou shalt bring forth children . . ." Some also opposed its use among males: young, healthy, courageous men simply did not need anaesthesia. Such opposition was ineffectual. Use of anaesthesia spread with extreme rapidity (and far faster than would be possible today). Even prominent churchmen supported its use.

The first practical tampon, Tampax, didn't arrive until the 1930s. It was invented by Dr. Earle Cleveland Haas. He made it of compressed cotton, and designed an applicator from paper tubes. This helped lessen resistance to the products by those who objected to the self-touching that might otherwise occur. By the early 1940s, 25 percent of women were using them. Thirty years later, it was 70 percent. Now it's four out of five, with the remainder relying on pads, which are now hyper-absorbent, and held in place by effective adhesives (opposed to the awkwardly placed, bulky, belted, diaper-like sanitary napkins of the 1970s). Did Muruganantham, Simpson and Haas oppress women, or free them? What about Gregory Goodwin Pincus, who invented the birth control pill? In what manner were these practical, enlightened, persistent men part of a constricting patriarchy?

Why do we teach our young people that our incredible culture is the result of male oppression? Blinded by this central assumption disciplines as diverse as education, social work, art history, gender studies, literature, sociology and, increasingly, law actively treat men as oppressors and men's activity as inherently destructive. They also often directly promote radical political action—radical by all the norms of the societies within which they are situated—which they do not distinguish from education. The Pauline Jewett Institute of Women's and Gender Studies at Ottawa's Carleton University, for example, encourages activism as part of their mandate. The Gender Studies Department at Queen's University in Kingston, Ontario, "teaches feminist, anti-racist, and queer theories and methods that centre activism for social change"—indicating support for the supposition that university education should above all foster political engagement of a particular kind.

Postmodernism and the Long Arm of Marx

These disciplines draw their philosophy from multiple sources. All are heavily influenced by the Marxist humanists. One such figure is Max Horkheimer, who developed critical theory in the 1930s. Any brief summary of his ideas is bound to be oversimplified, but Horkheimer regarded himself as a Marxist. He believed that Western principles of individual freedom or the free market were merely masks that served to disguise the true conditions of the West: inequality, domination and exploitation. He believed that intellectual activity should be devoted to social change, instead of mere understanding, and hoped to emancipate humanity from its enslavement. Horkheimer and his Frankfurt School of associated thinkers—first, in Germany and later, in the US—aimed at a full-scale critique and transformation of Western civilization.

More important in recent years has been the work of French philosopher Jacques Derrida, leader of the postmodernists, who came into vogue in the late 1970s. Derrida described his own ideas as a radicalized form of Marxism. Marx attempted to reduce history and society to economics, considering culture the oppression of the poor by the rich. When Marxism was put into practice in the Soviet Union, China, Vietnam, Cambodia and elsewhere, economic resources were brutally redistributed. Private property was eliminated, and rural people forcibly collectivized. The result? Tens of millions of people died. Hundreds of millions more were subject to oppression rivalling that still operative in North Korea, the last classic communist holdout. The resulting economic systems were corrupt and unsustainable. The world entered a prolonged and extremely dangerous cold war. The citizens of those societies lived the life of the lie, betraying their families, informing on their neighbours—existing in misery, without complaint (or else).

Marxist ideas were very attractive to intellectual utopians. One of the primary architects of the horrors of the Khmer Rouge, Khieu Samphan, received a doctorate at the Sorbonne before he became the nominal head of Cambodia in the mid-1970s. In his doctoral thesis, written in 1959, he argued that the work done by non-farmers in Cambodia's cities was unproductive: bankers, bureaucrats and businessmen added nothing to society. Instead, they parasitized the genuine value produced through agriculture, small industry and craft. Samphan's ideas were favourably looked upon by the French intellectuals who granted him his Ph.D. Back in Cambodia, he was provided with the opportunity to put his theories into practice. The Khmer Rouge evacuated Cambodia's cities, drove all the inhabitants into the countryside, closed the banks, banned the use of currency, and destroyed all the markets. A quarter of the Cambodian population were worked to death in the countryside, in the killing fields.

Lest We Forget: Ideas Have Consequences.

When the communists established the Soviet Union after the First World War, people could be forgiven for hoping that the utopian collectivist dreams their new leaders purveyed were possible. The decayed social order of the late nineteenth century produced the trenches and mass slaughters of the Great War. The gap between rich and poor was extreme, and most people slaved away in conditions worse than those later described by Orwell. Although the West received word of the horror perpetrated by Lenin after the Russian Revolution, it remained difficult to evaluate his actions from afar. Russia was in post-monarchical chaos, and the news of widespread industrial development and redistribution of property to those who had so recently been serfs provided reason for hope. To complicate things further, the USSR (and Mexico) supported the democratic Republicans when the Spanish Civil War broke out, in 1936. They were fighting against the essentially fascist Nationalists, who had overthrown the fragile democracy established only five years previously, and who found support with the Nazis and Italian fascists.

The intelligentsia in America, Great Britain and elsewhere were severely frustrated by their home countries' neutrality. Thousands of foreigners streamed into Spain to fight for the Republicans, serving in the International Brigades. George Orwell was one of them. Ernest Hemingway served there as a journalist, and was a supporter of the Republicans. Politically concerned young Americans, Canadians and Brits felt a moral obligation to stop talking and start fighting.

All of this drew attention away from concurrent events in the Soviet Union. In the 1930s, during the Great Depression, the Stalinist Soviets sent two million kulaks, their richest peasants, to Siberia (those with a small number of cows, a couple of hired hands, or a few acres more than was typical). From the communist viewpoint, these kulaks had gathered their wealth by plundering those around them, and deserved their fate. Wealth signified oppression, and private property was theft. It was time for some equity. More than thirty thousand kulaks were shot on the spot. Many more met their fate at the hands of their most jealous, resentful and unproductive neighbours, who used the high ideals of communist collectivization to mask their murderous intent.

The kulaks were "enemies of the people," apes, scum, vermin, filth and swine. "We will make soap out of the kulak," claimed one particularly brutal cadre of city-dwellers, mobilized by party and Soviet executive committees, and sent out into the countryside. The kulaks were driven, naked, into the streets, beaten, and forced to dig their own graves. The women were raped. Their belongings were "expropriated," which, in practice, meant that their houses were stripped down to the rafters and ceiling beams and everything was stolen. In many places, the non-kulak peasants resisted, particularly the women, who took to surrounding the persecuted families with their bodies. Such resistance proved futile. The kulaks who didn't die were exiled to Siberia, often in the middle of the night. The trains started in February, in the bitter Russian cold. Housing of the most substandard kind awaited them upon arrival on the desert taiga. Many died, particularly children, from typhoid, measles and scarlet fever.

The "parasitical" kulaks were, in general, the most skillful and hardworking farmers. A small minority of people are responsible for most of the production in any field, and farming proved no different. Agricultural output crashed. What little remained was taken by force out of the countryside and into the cities. Rural people who went out into the fields after the harvest to glean single grains of wheat for their hungry families risked execution. Six million people died of starvation in the Ukraine, the breadbasket of the Soviet Union, in the 1930s. "To eat your own children is a barbarian act," declared posters of the Soviet regime.

Despite more than mere rumours of such atrocities, attitudes towards communism remained consistently positive among many Western intellectuals. There were other things to worry about, and the Second World War allied the Soviet Union with the Western countries opposing Hitler, Mussolini and Hirohito. Certain watchful eyes remained open, nonetheless. Malcolm Muggeridge published a series of articles describing Soviet demolition of the peasantry as early as 1933, for the *Manchester Guardian*. George Orwell understood what was going on under Stalin, and he made it widely known. He published *Animal Farm*, a fable satirizing the Soviet Union, in 1945, despite encountering serious resistance to the book's release. Many who should have known better retained their blindness for long after this. Nowhere was this truer than France, and nowhere truer in France than among the intellectuals.

France's most famous mid-century philosopher, Jean-Paul Sartre, was a well-known communist, although not a card-carrier, until he denounced the Soviet incursion into Hungary in 1956. He remained an advocate for Marxism, nonetheless, and did not finally break with the Soviet Union until 1968, when the Soviets violently suppressed the Czechoslovakians during the Prague Spring.

Not long after came the publication of Aleksandr Solzhenitsyn's *The Gulag Archipelago*, which we have discussed rather extensively in previous chapters. As noted (and is worth noting again), this book utterly demolished communism's moral credibility—first in the West, and then in the Soviet System itself. It circulated in underground *samizdat* format. Russians had twenty-four hours to read their rare copy before handing it to the next waiting mind. A Russian-language reading was broadcast into the Soviet Union by Radio Liberty.

Solzhenitsyn argued that the Soviet system could have never survived without tyranny and slave labour; that the seeds of its worst excesses were definitively sowed in the time of Lenin (for whom the Western communists still served as apologists); and that it was propped up by endless lies, both individual and public. Its sins could not be blamed on a simple cult of personality, as its supporters continued to claim. Solzhenitsyn documented the Soviet Union's extensive mistreatment of political prisoners, its corrupt legal system, and its mass murders, and showed in painstaking detail how these were not aberrations but direct expressions of the underlying communist philosophy. No one could stand up for communism after *The Gulag Archipelago*—not even the communists themselves.

This did not mean that the fascination Marxist ideas had for intellectuals—particularly French intellectuals—disappeared. It merely transformed. Some refused outright to learn. Sartre denounced Solzhenitsyn as a "dangerous element." Derrida, more subtle, substituted the idea of power for the idea of money, and continued on his merry way. Such linguistic sleight-of-hand gave all the barely repentant Marxists still inhabiting the intellectual pinnacles of the West the means to retain their world-view. Society was no longer repression of the poor by the rich. It was oppression of everyone by the powerful.

According to Derrida, hierarchical structures emerged only to include (the beneficiaries of that structure) and to exclude (everyone else, who were therefore oppressed). Even that claim wasn't sufficiently radical. Derrida claimed that divisiveness and oppression were built right into language—built into the very categories we use to pragmatically simplify and negotiate the world. There are "women" only because men gain by excluding them. There are "males and females" only because members of that more heterogeneous group benefit by excluding the tiny minority of people whose biological sexuality is amorphous. Science only benefits the scientists. Politics only benefits the politicians. In Derrida's view, hierarchies exist because they gain from oppressing those who are omitted. It is this ill-gotten gain that allows them to flourish.

Derrida famously said (although he denied it, later): "Il n'y a pas de hors-texte"—often translated as "there is nothing outside the text." His supporters say that is a mistranslation, and that the English equivalent should have been "there is no outside-text." It remains difficult, either way, to read the statement as saying anything other than "everything is interpretation," and that is how Derrida's work has generally been interpreted.

It is almost impossible to over-estimate the nihilistic and destructive nature of this philosophy. It puts the act of categorization itself in doubt. It negates the idea that distinctions might be drawn between things for any reasons other than that of raw power. Biological distinctions between men and women? Despite the existence of an overwhelming, multi-disciplinary scientific literature indicating that sex differences are powerfully influenced by biological factors, science is just another game of power, for Derrida and his post-modern Marxist acolytes, making claims to benefit those at the pinnacle of the scientific world. There are no facts. Hierarchical position and reputation as a consequence of skill and competence? All definitions of skill and of competence are merely made up by those who benefit from them, to exclude others, and to benefit personally and selfishly.

There is sufficient truth to Derrida's claims to account, in part, for their insidious nature. Power is a fundamental motivational force ("a," not "the"). People compete to rise to the top, and they care where they are in dominance hierarchies. But (and this is where you separate the metaphorical boys from the men, philosophically) *the fact that power plays a role in human motivation does not mean that it plays the only role, or even the primary role.* Likewise, the fact that we can never know everything does make all our observations and utterances dependent on taking some things into account and leaving other things out (as we discussed extensively in Rule 10). That does not justify the claim that everything is interpretation, or that categorization is just exclusion. Beware of single-cause interpretations—and beware the people who purvey them.

Although the facts cannot speak for themselves (just as an expanse of land spread out before a voyager cannot tell him how to journey through it), and although there are myriad ways to interact with—even to perceive—even a small number of objects, that does not mean that all interpretations are equally valid. Some hurt—yourself and others. Others put you on a collision course with society. Some are not sustainable across time. Others do not get you where you want to go. Many of these constraints are built in to us, as a consequence of billions of years of evolutionary processes. Others emerge as we are socialized into cooperating and competing peacefully and productively with others. Still more interpretations emerge as we discard counter-productive strategies through learning. An endless number of inter-pretations, certainly: that is not different than saying an endless number of problems. *But a seriously bounded number of viable solutions.* Otherwise life would be easy. And it's not.

Now, I have some beliefs that might be regarded as left-leaning. I think, for example, that the tendency for valuable goods to distribute themselves with pronounced inequality constitutes an ever-present threat to the stability of society. I think there is good evidence for that. That does not mean that the solution to the problem is self-evident. We don't know how to redistribute wealth without introducing a whole host of other problems. Different Western societies have tried different approaches. The Swedes, for example, push equality to its limit. The US takes the opposite tack, assuming that the net wealth-creation of a more free-for-all capitalism constitutes the rising tide that lifts all boats. The results of these experiments are not all in, and countries differ very much in relevant ways. Differences in history, geographic area, population size and ethnic diversity make direct comparisons very difficult. But it certainly is the case that forced redistribution, in the name of utopian equality, is a cure to shame the disease.

I think, as well (on what might be considered the leftish side), that the incremental remake of university administrations into analogues of private corporations is a mistake. I think that the science of manage-ment is a pseudo-discipline. I believe that government can, sometimes, be a force for good, as well as the necessary arbiter of a small set of necessary rules. Nonetheless, I do not understand why our society is providing public funding to institutions and educators whose stated, conscious and explicit aim is the demolition of the culture that supports them. Such people have a perfect right to their opinions and actions, if they remain lawful. But they have no reasonable claim to public funding. If radical right-wingers were receiving state funding for political operations disguised as university courses, as the radical left-wingers clearly are, the uproar from progressives across North America would be deafening.

There are other serious problems lurking in the radical disciplines, apart from the falseness of their theories and methods, and their insistence that collective political activism is morally obligatory. There isn't a shred of hard evidence to support any of their central claims: that Western society is pathologically patriarchal; that the prime lesson of history is that men, rather than nature, were the primary source of the oppression of women (rather than, as in most cases, their partners and supporters); that all hierarchies are based on power and aimed at exclusion. Hierarchies exist for many reasons—some arguably valid, some not—and are incredibly ancient, evolutionarily speaking. Do male crustaceans oppress female crustaceans? Should their hierarchies be upended?

In societies that are well-functioning—not in comparison to a hypothetical utopia, but contrasted with other existing or historical cultures—*competence*, not power, is a prime determiner of status. Competence. Ability. Skill. Not *power*. This is obvious both anecdotally and factually. No one with brain cancer is equity-minded enough to refuse the service of the surgeon with the best education, the best reputation and, perhaps, the highest earnings. Furthermore, the most valid personality trait predictors of long-term success in Western countries are intelligence (as measured with cognitive ability or IQ tests) and conscientiousness (a trait characterized by industriousness and orderliness).[188] There are exceptions. Entrepreneurs and artists are higher in openness to experience,[189] another cardinal personality trait, than in conscientiousness. But openness is associated with verbal intelligence and creativity, so that exception is appropriate and understandable. The predictive power of these traits, mathematically and economically speaking, is exceptionally high—among the highest, in terms of power, of anything ever actually measured at the harder ends of the social sciences. A good battery of personality/cognitive tests can increase the probability of employing someone more competent than average from 50:50 to 85:15. These are the facts, as well supported as anything in the social sciences (and this is saying more than you might think, as the social sciences are more effective disciplines than their cynical critics appreciate). Thus, not only is the state supporting one-sided radicalism, it is also supporting indoctrination. We do not teach our children that the world is flat. Neither should we teach them unsupported ideologically-predicated theories about the nature of men and women—or the nature of hierarchy.

It is not unreasonable to note (if the deconstructionists would leave it at that) that science can be biased by the interests of power, and to warn against that—or to point out that evidence is too often what powerful people, including scientists, decide it is. After all, scientists are people too, and people like power, just like lobsters like power—just like deconstructionists like to be known for their ideas, and strive rightly to sit atop their academic hierarchies. But that doesn't mean that science—or even deconstructionism—is only about power. Why believe such a thing? Why insist upon it? Perhaps it's this: *if only power exists, then the use of power becomes fully justifiable.* There is no bounding such use by evidence, method, logic, or even the necessity for coherence. There is no bounding by anything "outside the text." That leaves opinion—and force—and the use of force is all too attractive, under such circumstances, just as its employment in the service of that opinion is all too certain. The insane and incomprehensible postmodern insistence that all gender differences are socially constructed, for example, becomes all too understandable when its moral imperative is grasped—when its justification for force is once and for all understood: *Society must be altered, or bias eliminated, until all outcomes are equitable.* But the bedrock of the social constructionist position is the wish for the latter, not belief in the justice of the former. Since all outcome inequalities must be eliminated (inequality being the heart of all evil), then all gender differences must be regarded as socially constructed. Otherwise the drive for equality would be too radical, and the doctrine too blatantly propagandistic. Thus, the order of logic is reversed, so that the ideology can be camouflaged. The fact that such statements lead immediately to internal inconsistencies within the ideology is never addressed. Gender is constructed, but an individual who desires gender re-assignment surgery is to be unarguably considered a man trapped in a woman's body (or vice versa). *The fact that both of these cannot logically be true, simultaneously, is just ignored* (or rationalized away with another appalling post-modern claim: that logic itself—along with the techniques of science—is merely part of the oppressive patriarchal system).

It is also the case, of course, that all outcomes cannot be equalized. First, outcomes must be measured. Comparing the salaries of people who occupy the same position is relatively straightforward (although complicated significantly by such things as date of hire, given the difference in demand for workers, for example, at different time periods). But there are other dimensions of comparison that are arguably equally relevant, such as tenure, promotion rate, and social influence. The introduction of the "equal pay for equal work" argument immediately complicates even salary comparison beyond practicality, for one simple reason: who decides what work is equal? It's not possible. That's why the marketplace exists. Worse is the problem of group comparison: women should make as much as men. OK. Black women should make as much as white women. OK. Should salary then be adjusted for all parameters of race? At what level of resolution? What racial categories are "real"?

The U.S. National Institute of Health, to take a single bureaucratic example, recognizes American Indian or Alaska Native, Asian, Black, Hispanic, Native Hawaiian or other Pacific Islander, and White. But there are more than five hundred separate American Indian tribes. By what possible logic should "American Indian" therefore stand as a canonical category? Osage tribal members have a yearly average income of $30K, while Tohono O'odham's make $11K. Are they equally oppressed? What about disabilities? Disabled people should make as much as non-disabled people. OK. On the surface, that's a noble, com-passionate, fair claim. But who is disabled? Is someone living with a parent with Alzheimer's disabled? If not, why not? What about some-one with a lower IQ? Someone less attractive? Someone overweight? Some people clearly move through life markedly overburdened with problems that are beyond their control, but it is a rare person indeed who isn't suffering from at least one serious catastrophe at any given time—particularly if you include their family in the equation. And why shouldn't you? Here's the fundamental problem: *group identity can be fractionated right down to the level of the individual.* That sentence should be written in capital letters. Every person is unique—and not just in a trivial manner: importantly, significantly, meaningfully unique. Group membership cannot capture that variability. Period.

None of this complexity is ever discussed by the postmodern/ Marxist thinkers. Instead, their ideological approach fixes a point of truth, like the North Star, and forces everything to rotate around it. The claim that all gender differences are a consequence of socializa-tion is neither provable, nor disprovable, in some sense, because culture can be brought to bear with such force on groups or individu-als that virtually any outcome is attainable, if we are willing to bear the cost. We know, for example, from studies of adopted-out identical twins,[190] that culture can produce a fifteen-point (or one standard deviation) increase in IQ (roughly the difference between the average high school student and the average state college student) at the cost of a three-standard-deviation increase in wealth.[191] What this means, approximately, is that two identical twins, separated at birth, will differ in IQ by fifteen points if the first twin is raised in a family that is poorer than 85 percent of families and the second is raised in a family richer than 95 percent of families. Something similar has recently been dem-onstrated with education, rather than wealth.[192] We don't know what it would cost in wealth or differential education to produce a more extreme transformation.

What such studies imply is that we could probably minimize the innate differences between boys and girls, if we were willing to exert enough pressure. This would in no way ensure that we were freeing people of either gender to make their own choices. But choice has no place in the ideological picture: if men and women act, voluntarily, to produce gender-unequal outcomes, those very choices must have been determined by cultural bias. In consequence, everyone is a brainwashed victim, wherever gender differences exist, and the rigorous critical theoretician is morally obligated to set them straight. This means that those already equity-minded Scandinavian males, who aren't much into nursing, require even more retraining. The same goes, in principle, for Scandinavian females, who aren't much into engineering.[193] What might such retraining look like? Where might its limits lie? Such things are often pushed past any reasonable limit before they are discontinued. Mao's murderous Cultural Revolution should have taught us that.

Boys into Girls

It has become a tenet of a certain kind of social constructionist theory that the world would be much improved if boys were socialized like girls. Those who put forward such theories assume, first, that aggression is a learned behaviour, and can therefore simply not be taught, and second (to take a particular example) that, "boys should be socialized the way girls have been traditionally socialized, and they should be encouraged to develop socially positive qualities such as tenderness, sensitivity to feelings, nurturance, cooperation and aesthetic appreciation." In the opinions of such thinkers, aggression will only be reduced when male adolescents and young adults "subscribe to the same standards of behavior as have been traditionally encouraged for women."[194]

There are so many things wrong with this idea that it is difficult to know where to start. First, it is not the case that aggression is merely learned. Aggression is there at the beginning. There are ancient biological circuits, so to speak, that underlie defensive and predatory aggression.[195] They are so fundamental that they still operate in what are known as decorticate cats, animals that have had the largest and most recently evolved parts of their brain—an overwhelmingly large percentage of the total structure—entirely removed. This suggests not only that aggression is innate, but that it is a consequence of activity in extremely fundamental, basic brain areas. If the brain is a tree, then aggression (along with hunger, thirst and sexual desire) is there in the very trunk.

And, in keeping with this, it appears that a subset of two-year-old boys (about 5 percent) are quite aggressive, by temperament. They take other kids' toys, kick, bite and hit. Most are nonetheless socialized effectively by the age of four.[196] This is not, however, because they have been encouraged to act like little girls. Instead, they are taught or otherwise learn in early childhood to integrate their aggressive tendencies into more sophisticated behavioural routines. Aggression underlies the drive to be outstanding, to be unstoppable, to compete, to win—to be actively virtuous, at least along one dimension. Determination is its admirable, pro-social face. Aggressive young children who don't manage to render their temperament sophisticated by the end of infancy are doomed to unpopularity, as their primordial antagonism no longer serves them socially at later ages. Rejected by their peers, they lack further socialization opportunities and tend towards outcast status. These are the individuals who remain much more inclined toward antisocial and criminal behavior when adolescent and adult. But this does not at all mean that the aggressive drive lacks either utility or value. At a minimum, it is necessary for self-protection.

Compassion as a Vice

Many of the female clients (perhaps even a majority) that I see in my clinical practice have trouble in their jobs and family lives not because they are too aggressive, but because they are not aggressive enough. Cognitive-behavioural therapists call the treatment of such people, generally characterized by the more feminine traits of agreeableness (politeness and compassion) and neuroticism (anxiety and emotional pain), "assertiveness training."[197] Insufficiently aggressive women—and men, although more rarely—do too much for others. They tend to treat those around them as if they were distressed children. They tend to be naïve. They assume that cooperation should be the basis of all social transactions, and they avoid conflict (which means they avoid confronting problems in their relationships as well as at work). They continually sacrifice for others. This may sound virtuous—and it is definitely an attitude that has certain social advantages—but it can and often does become counterproductively one-sided. Because too-agreeable people bend over backwards for other people, they do not stand up properly for themselves. Assuming that others think as they do, they expect—instead of ensuring—reciprocity for their thoughtful actions. When this does not happen, they don't speak up. They do not or cannot straightforwardly demand recognition. The dark side of their characters emerges, because of their subjugation, and they become resentful.

I teach excessively agreeable people to note the emergence of such resentment, which is a very important, although very toxic, emotion. There are only two major reasons for resentment: being taken advantage of (or allowing yourself to be taken advantage of), or whiny refusal to adopt responsibility and grow up. If you're resentful, look for the reasons. Perhaps discuss the issue with someone you trust. Are you feeling hard done by, in an immature manner? If, after some honest consideration, you don't think it's that, perhaps someone is taking advantage of you. This means that you now face a moral obligation to speak up for yourself. This might mean confronting your boss, or your husband, or your wife, or your child, or your parents. It might mean gathering some evidence, strategically, so that when you confront that person, you can give them several examples of their misbehaviour (at least three), so they can't easily weasel out of your accusations. It might mean failing to concede when they offer you their counterarguments. People rarely have more than four at hand. If you remain unmoved, they get angry, or cry, or run away. It's very useful to attend to tears in such situations. They can be used to motivate guilt on the part of the accuser due, theoretically, to having caused hurt feelings and pain. But tears are often shed in anger. A red face is a good cue. If you can push your point past the first four responses and stand fast against the consequent emotion, you will gain your target's attention—and, perhaps, their respect. This is genuine conflict, however, and it's neither pleasant nor easy.

You must also know clearly what you want out of the situation, and be prepared to clearly articulate your desire. It's a good idea to tell the person you are confronting exactly what you would like them to do instead of what they have done or currently are doing. You might think, "if they loved me, they would know what to do." That's the voice of resentment. Assume ignorance before malevolence. No one has a direct pipeline to your wants and needs—not even you. If you try to determine exactly what you want, you might find that it is more difficult than you think. The person oppressing you is likely no wiser than you, especially about you. Tell them directly what would be preferable, instead, after you have sorted it out. Make your request as small and reasonable as possible—but ensure that its fulfillment would satisfy you. In that manner, you come to the discussion with a solution, instead of just a problem.

Agreeable, compassionate, empathic, conflict-averse people (all those traits group together) let people walk on them, and they get bitter. They sacrifice themselves for others, sometimes excessively, and cannot comprehend why that is not reciprocated. Agreeable people are compliant, and this robs them of their independence. The danger associated with this can be amplified by high trait neuroticism. Agreeable people will go along with whoever makes a suggestion, instead of insisting, at least sometimes, on their own way. So, they lose their way, and become indecisive and too easily swayed. If they are, in addition, easily frightened and hurt, they have even less reason to strike out on their own, as doing so exposes them to threat and danger (at least in the short term). That's the pathway to dependent personality disorder, technically speaking.[198] It might be regarded as the polar opposite of antisocial personality disorder, the set of traits characteristic of delinquency in childhood and adolescence and criminality in adulthood. It would be lovely if the opposite of a criminal was a saint—but it's not the case. The opposite of a criminal is an Oedipal mother, which is its own type of criminal.

The Oedipal mother (and fathers can play this role too, but it's comparatively rare) says to her child, "I only live for you." She does everything for her children. She ties their shoes, and cuts up their food, and lets them crawl into bed with her and her partner far too often. That's a good and conflict-avoidant method for avoiding unwanted sexual attention, as well.

The Oedipal mother makes a pact with herself, her children, and the devil himself. The deal is this: "Above all, never leave me. In return, I will do everything for you. As you age without maturing, you will become worthless and bitter, but you will never have to take any responsibility, and everything you do that's wrong will always be someone else's fault." The children can accept or reject this—and they have some choice in the matter.

The Oedipal mother is the witch in the story of Hansel and Gretel. The two children in that fairy tale have a new step-mother. She orders her husband to abandon his children in the forest, as there is a famine and she thinks they eat too much. He obeys his wife, takes his children deep into the woods and leaves them to their fate. Wandering, starving and lonely, they come across a miracle. A house. And not just any house. A candy house. A gingerbread house. A person who had not been rendered too caring, empathic, sympathetic and cooperative might be skeptical, and ask, "Is this too good to be true?" But the children are too young, and too desperate.

Inside the house is a kind old woman, rescuer of distraught children, kind patter of heads and wiper of noses, all bosom and hips, ready to sacrifice herself to their every wish, at a moment's notice. She feeds the children anything they want, any time they want, and they never have to do anything. But provision of that kind of care makes her hungry. She puts Hansel into a cage, to fatten him up ever more efficiently. He fools her into thinking he's staying thin by offering her an old bone, when she tries to test his leg for the desired tenderness. She gets too desperate to wait, eventually, and stokes the oven, preparing to cook and eat the object of her doting. Gretel, who has apparently not been lulled into full submission, waits for a moment of carelessness, and pushes the kind old woman into the oven. The kids run away, and rejoin their father, who has thoroughly repented of his evil actions.

In a household like that, the choicest cut of child is the spirit, and it's always consumed first. Too much protection devastates the developing soul.

The witch in the Hansel and Gretel tale is the Terrible Mother, the dark half of the symbolically feminine. Deeply social as we are in our essence, we tend to view the world as a story, the characters of which are mother, father and child. The feminine, as a whole, is unknown nature outside the bounds of culture, creation and destruction: she is the protective arms of mother and the destructive element of time, the beautiful virgin-mother and the swamp-dwelling hag. This archetypal entity was confused with an objective, historical reality, back in the late 1800s, by a Swiss anthropologist named Johann Jakob Bachofen. Bachofen proposed that humanity had passed through a series of developmental stages in its history.

The first, roughly speaking (after a somewhat anarchic and chaotic beginning), was Das Mutterrecht[199]—a society where women held the dominant positions of power, respect and honour, where polyamory and promiscuity ruled, and where any certainty of paternity was absent. The second, the Dionysian, was a phase of transition, during which these original matriarchal foundations were overturned and power was taken by men. The third phase, the Apollonian, still reigns today. The patriarchy rules, and each woman belongs exclusively to one man. Bachofen's ideas became profoundly influential, in certain circles, despite the absence of any historical evidence to support them. One Marija Gimbutas, for example—an archaeologist—famously claimed in the 1980s and 1990s that a peaceful goddess-and-woman-centred culture once characterized Neolithic Europe.[200] She claimed that it was supplanted and suppressed by an invasive hierarchical warrior culture, which laid the basis for modern society. Art historian Merlin Stone made the same argument in his book *When God Was a Woman*.[201] This whole series of essentially archetypal/mythological ideas became touchstones for the theology of the women's movement and the matriarchal studies of 1970s feminism (Cynthia Eller, who wrote a book criticizing such ideas—*The Myth of Matriarchal Prehistory*—called this theology "an ennobling lie"). [202]

Carl Jung had encountered Bachofen's ideas of primordial matriarchy decades earlier. Jung soon realized, however, that the developmental progression described by the earlier Swiss thinker represented a psychological rather than a historical reality. He saw in Bachofen's thought the same processes of projection of imaginative fantasy on to the external world that had led to the population of the cosmos with constellations and gods. In *The Origins and History of Consciousness* [203] and *The Great Mother* [204], Jung's collaborator Erich Neumann extended his colleague's analysis. Neumann traced the emergence of consciousness, symbolically masculine, and contrasted it with its symbolically feminine, material (mother, matrix) origins, subsuming Freud's theory of Oedipal parenting into a broader archetypal model. For Neumann, and for Jung, consciousness—always symbolically masculine, even in women—struggles upwards toward the light. Its development is painful and anxiety-provoking, as it carries with it the realization of vulnerability and death. It is constantly tempted to sink back down into dependency and unconsciousness, and to shed its existential burden. It is aided in that pathological desire by anything that opposes enlightenment, articulation, rationality, self-determination, strength and competence—by anything that shelters too much, and therefore smothers and devours. Such overprotection is Freud's Oedipal familial nightmare, which we are rapidly transforming into social policy.

The Terrible Mother is an ancient symbol. It manifests itself, for example, in the form of Tiamat, in the earliest written story we have recovered, the Mesopotamian *Enuma Elish*. Tiamat is the mother of all things, gods and men alike. She is the unknown and chaos and the nature that gives rise to all forms. But she is also the female dragon-deity who moves to destroy her own children, when they carelessly kill their father and attempt to live on the corpse that remains. The Terrible Mother is the spirit of careless unconsciousness, tempting the ever-striving spirit of awareness and enlightenment down into the protective womb-like embrace of the underworld. It's the terror young men feel towards attractive women, who are nature itself, ever ready to reject them, intimately, at the deepest possible level. Nothing inspires self-consciousness, undermines courage, and fosters feelings of nihilism and hatred more than that—except, perhaps, the too-tight embrace of too-caring mom.

The Terrible Mother appears in many fairy tales, and in many stories for adults. In the *Sleeping Beauty*, she is the Evil Queen, dark nature herself—Maleficent, in the Disney version. The royal parents of Princess Aurora fail to invite this force of the night to their baby daughter's christening. Thus, they shelter her too much from the destructive and dangerous side of reality, preferring that she grow up untroubled by such things. Their reward? At puberty, she is still unconscious. The masculine spirit, her prince, is both a man who could save her, by tearing her from her parents, and her own consciousness, trapped in a dungeon by the machinations of the dark side of femininity. When that prince escapes, and presses the Evil Queen too hard, she turns into the Dragon of Chaos itself. The symbolic masculine defeats her with truth and faith, and finds the princess, whose eyes he opens with a kiss.

It might be objected (as it was, with Disney's more recent and deeply propagandistic *Frozen*) that a woman does not need a man to rescue her. That may be true, and it may not. It may be that only the woman who wants (or has) a child needs a man to rescue her—or at least to support and aid her. In any case, it is certain that a woman needs consciousness to be rescued, and, as noted above, consciousness is symbolically masculine and has been since the beginning of time (in the guise both of order and of the Logos, the mediating principle). The Prince could be a lover, but could also be a woman's own attentive wakefulness, clarity of vision, and tough-minded independence. Those are masculine traits—in actuality, as well as symbolically, as men are actually less tender-minded and agreeable than women, on average, and are less susceptible to anxiety and emotional pain. And, to say it again: (1) this is most true in those Scandinavian nations where the most steps towards gender equality have been taken—and (2) the differences are not small by the standards whereby such things are measured.

The relationship between the masculine and consciousness is also portrayed, symbolically, in the Disney movie *The Little Mermaid*. Ariel, the heroine, is quite feminine, but she also has a strong spirit of independence. For this reason, she is her father's favourite, although she also causes him the most trouble. Her father Triton is the king, representing the known, culture and order (with a hint of the oppressive rule-giver and tyrant). Because order is always opposed by chaos, Triton has an adversary, Ursula, a tentacled octopus—a serpent, a gorgon, a hydra. Thus, Ursula is in the same archetypal category as the dragon/queen Maleficent in *Sleeping Beauty* (or the jealous older queen in *Snow White*, Lady Tremaine in *Cinderella*, the Red Queen in *Alice in Wonderland*, Cruella de Vil in *101 Dalmations*, Miss Medusa in *The Rescuers* and Mother Gothel in *Tangled*).

Ariel wants to kindle a romance with Prince Eric, whom she previously rescued from a shipwreck. Ursula tricks Ariel into giving up her voice so that she can have three days as a human being. Ursula knows full well, however, that a voiceless Ariel will not be able to establish a relationship with the Prince. Without her capacity to speak—without the Logos; without the Divine Word—she will remain underwater, unconscious, forever.

When Ariel fails to form a union with Prince Eric, Ursula steals her soul, and places it in her large collection of shrivelled and warped semi-beings, well-protected by her feminine graces. When King Triton shows up to demand the return of his daughter, Ursula makes him a terrible offer: he can take Ariel's place. Of course, the elimination of the Wise King (who represents, to say it again, the benevolent side of the patriarchy) has been Ursula's nefarious plan all along. Ariel is released, but Triton is now reduced to a pathetic shadow of his former self. More importantly, Ursula now has Triton's magic trident, the source of his godlike power.

Fortunately for everyone concerned (except Ursula), Prince Eric returns, distracting the evil queen of the underworld with a harpoon. This opens an opportunity for Ariel to attack Ursula, who grows, in response, to monstrous proportions—in the same manner as Maleficent, *Sleeping Beauty*'s evil queen. Ursula creates a huge storm, and raises a whole navy of sunken ships from the ocean floor. As she prepares to kill Ariel, Eric commandeers a wrecked ship, and rams her with its broken bowsprit. Triton and the other captured souls are released. The rejuvenated Triton then transforms his daughter into a human being, so she can remain with Eric. For a woman to become complete, such stories claim, she must form a relationship with masculine consciousness and stand up to the terrible world (which sometimes manifests itself, primarily, in the form of her too-present mother). An actual man can help her do that, to some degree, but it is better for everyone concerned when no one is too dependent.

One day, when I was a kid, I was out playing softball with some friends. The teams were a mixture of boys and girls. We were all old enough so that the boys and girls were starting to be interested in one another in an unfamiliar way. Status was becoming more relevant and important. My friend Jake and I were about to come to blows, pushing each other around near the pitching mound, when my mom walked by. She was a fair distance away, about thirty yards, but I could immediately see by the change in her body language that she knew what was going on. Of course, the other kids saw her as well. She walked right by. I knew that hurt her. Part of her was worried that I would come home with a bloody nose and a black eye. It would have been easy enough for her just to yell, "Hey, you kids, quit that!" or even to come over and interfere. But she didn't. A few years later, when I was having teenage trouble with my dad, my mom said, "If it was too good at home, you'd never leave."

My mom is a tender-hearted person. She's empathetic, and cooperative, and agreeable. Sometimes she lets people push her around. When she went back to work after being at home with her young kids, she found it challenging to stand up to the men. Sometimes that made her resentful—something she also feels, sometimes, in relationship to my father, who is strongly inclined to do what he wants, when he wants to. Despite all that, she's no Oedipal mother. She fostered the independence of her children, even though doing so was often hard on her. She did the right thing, even though it caused her emotional distress.

Toughen Up, You Weasel

I spent one youthful summer on the prairie of central Saskatchewan working on a railway line crew. Every man in that all-male group was tested by the others during the first two weeks or so of their hiring. Many of the other workers were Northern Cree Indians, quiet guys for the most part, easygoing, until they drank too much, and the chips on their shoulders started to show. They had been in and out of jail, as had most of their relatives. They didn't attach much shame to that, considering it just another part of the white man's system. It was also warm in jail in the winter, and the food was regular and plentiful. I lent one of the Cree guys fifty bucks at one point. Instead of paying me back, he offered me a pair of bookends, cut from some of the original rail laid across western Canada, which I still own. That was better than the fifty bucks.

When a new guy first showed up, the other workers would inevitably provide him with an insulting nickname. They called me Howdy-Doody, after I was accepted as a crew member (something I am still slightly embarrassed to admit). When I asked the originator why he chose that moniker, he said, wittily and absurdly, "Because you look nothing like him." Working men are often extremely funny, in a caustic, biting, insulting manner (as discussed in Rule 9). They are always harassing each other, partly for amusement, partly to score points in the eternal dominance battle between them, but also partly to see what the other guy will do if he is subjected to social stress. It's part of the process of character evaluation, as well as camaraderie. When it works well (when everybody gets, and gives as good as they get, and can give and take) it's a big part of what allows men who work for a living to tolerate or even enjoy laying pipe and working on oil rigs and lumberjacking and working in restaurant kitchens and all the other hot, dirty, physically demanding and dangerous work that is still done almost totally by men.

Not too long after I started on the rail crew, my name was changed to Howdy. This was a great improvement, as it had a good Western connotation, and was not obviously linked to that stupid puppet. The next man hired was not so fortunate. He carried a fancy lunchbucket, which was a mistake, as brown paper bags were the proper, non-pretentious convention. It was a little too nice and too new. It looked like maybe his mother had bought it (and packed it) for him. Thus, it became his name. Lunchbucket was not a good-humored guy. He bitched about everything, and had a bad attitude. Everything was someone else's fault. He was touchy, and none too quick on the draw.

Lunchbucket couldn't accept his name, or settle into his job. He adopted an attitude of condescending irritation when addressed, and reacted to the work in the same manner. He was not fun to be around, and he couldn't take a joke. That's fatal, on a work crew. After about three days of carrying on with his ill-humour and general air of hard-done-by superiority, Lunchbucket started to experience harassment extending well beyond his nickname. He would be peevishly working away on the line, surrounded by about seventy men, spread out over a quarter mile. Suddenly a pebble would appear out of nowhere, flying through the air, aimed at his hardhat. A direct hit would produce a thunking sound, deeply satisfying to all the quietly attending onlookers. Even this failed to improve his humour. So, the pebbles got larger. Lunchbucket would involve himself in something and forget to pay attention. Then, "thunk!"—a well-aimed stone would nail him on the noggin, producing a burst of irritated and ineffectual fury. Quiet amusement would ripple down the rail line. After a few days of this, no wiser, and carrying a few bruises, Lunchbucket vanished.

Men enforce a code of behaviour on each other, when working together. Do your work. Pull your weight. Stay awake and pay attention. Don't whine or be touchy. Stand up for your friends. Don't suck up and don't snitch. Don't be a slave to stupid rules. Don't, in the immortal words of Arnold Schwarzenegger, be a girlie man. Don't be dependent. At all. Ever. Period. The harassment that is part of acceptance on a working crew is a test: are you tough, entertaining, competent and reliable? If not, go away. Simple as that. We don't need to feel sorry for you. We don't want to put up with your narcissism, and we don't want to do your work.

There was a famous advertisement in the form of a comic strip issued a few decades ago by the bodybuilder Charles Atlas. It was titled "The Insult that Made a Man out of Mac" and could be found in almost every comic book, most of which were read by boys. Mac, the protagonist, is sitting on a beach blanket with an attractive young woman. A bully runs by, and kicks sand in both their faces. Mac objects. The much larger man grabs him by the arm and says, "Listen here. I'd smash your face. . . . Only you're so skinny you might dry up and blow away." The bully departs. Mac says to the girl, "The big bully! I'll get even some day." She adopts a provocative pose, and says, "Oh, don't let it bother you, little boy." Mac goes home, considers his pathetic physique, and buys the Atlas program. Soon, he has a new body. The next time he goes to the beach, he punches the bully in the nose. The now-admiring girl clings to his arm. "Oh, Mac!" she says. "You're a real man after all."

That ad is famous for a reason. It summarizes human sexual psychology in seven straightforward panels. The too-weak young man is embarrassed and self-conscious, as he should be. What good is he? He gets put down by other men and, worse, by desirable women. Instead of drowning in resentment, and skulking off to his basement to play video games in his underwear, covered with Cheetos dust, he presents himself with what Alfred Adler, Freud's most practical colleague, called a "compensatory fantasy."[205] The goal of such a fantasy is not so much wish-fulfillment, as illumination of a genuine path forward. Mac takes serious note of his scarecrow-like build and decides that he should develop a stronger body. More importantly, he puts his plan into action. He identifies with the part of himself that could transcend his current state, and becomes the hero of his own adventure. He goes back to the beach, and punches the bully in the nose. Mac wins. So does his eventual girlfriend. So does everybody else.

It is to women's clear advantage that men do not happily put up with dependency among themselves. Part of the reason that many a working-class woman does not marry, now, as we have alluded to, is because she does not want to look after a man, struggling for employment, as well as her children. And fair enough. A woman should look after her children—although that is not all she should do. And a man should look after a woman and children—although that is not all he should do. But a woman should not look after a man, because she must look after children, and a man should not be a child. This means that he must not be dependent. This is one of the reasons that men have little patience for dependent men. And let us not forget: wicked women may produce dependent sons, may support and even marry dependent men, but awake and conscious women want an awake and conscious partner.

It is for this reason that Nelson Muntz of *The Simpsons* is so necessary to the small social group that surrounds Homer's antihero son, Bart. Without Nelson, King of the Bullies, the school would soon be overrun by resentful, touchy Milhouses, narcissistic, intellectual Martin Princes, soft, chocolate-gorging German children, and infantile Ralph Wiggums. Muntz is a corrective, a tough, self-sufficient kid who uses his own capacity for contempt to decide what line of immature and pathetic behaviour simply cannot be crossed. Part of the genius of *The Simpsons* is its writers' refusal to simply write Nelson off as an irredeemable bully. Abandoned by his worthless father, neglected, thankfully, by his thoughtless slut of a mother, Nelson does pretty well, everything considered. He's even of romantic interest to the thoroughly progressive Lisa, much to her dismay and confusion (for much the same reasons that *Fifty Shades of Grey* became a worldwide phenomenon).

When softness and harmlessness become the only consciously acceptable virtues, then hardness and dominance will start to exert an unconscious fascination. Partly what this means for the future is that if men are pushed too hard to feminize, they will become more and more interested in harsh, fascist political ideology. *Fight Club*, perhaps the most fascist popular film made in recent years by Hollywood, with the possible exception of the Iron Man series, provides a perfect example of such inevitable attraction. The populist groundswell of support for Donald Trump in the US is part of the same process, as is (in far more sinister form) the recent rise of far-right political parties even in such moderate and liberal places as Holland, Sweden and Norway.

Men have to toughen up. Men demand it, and women want it, even though they may not approve of the harsh and contemptuous attitude that is part and parcel of the socially demanding process that fosters and then enforces that toughness. Some women don't like losing their baby boys, so they keep them forever. Some women don't like men, and would rather have a submissive mate, even if he is useless. This also provides them with plenty to feel sorry for themselves about, as well. The pleasures of such self-pity should not be underestimated.

Men toughen up by pushing themselves, and by pushing each other. When I was a teenager, the boys were much more likely to get into car accidents than the girls (as they still are). This was because they were out spinning donuts at night in icy parking lots. They were drag racing and driving their cars over the roadless hills extending from the nearby river up to the level land hundreds of feet higher. They were more likely to fight physically, and to skip class, and to tell the teachers off, and to quit school because they were tired of raising their hands for permission to go to the bathroom when they were big and strong enough to work on the oil rigs. They were more likely to race their motorbikes on frozen lakes in the winter. Like the skateboarders, and crane climbers, and free runners, they were doing dangerous things, trying to make themselves useful. When this process goes too far, boys (and men) drift into the antisocial behavior which is far more prevalent in males than in females.[206] That does not mean that every manifestation of daring and courage is criminal.

When the boys were spinning donuts, they were also testing the limits of their cars, their ability as drivers, and their capacity for control, in an out-of-control situation. When they told off the teachers, they were pushing against authority, to see if there was any real authority there—the kind that could be relied on, in principle, in a crisis. When they quit school, they went to work as rig roughnecks when it was forty bloody degrees below zero. It wasn't weakness that propelled so many out of the classroom, where a better future arguably awaited. It was strength.

If they're healthy, women don't want boys. They want men. They want someone to contend with; someone to grapple with. If they're tough, they want someone tougher. If they're smart, they want someone smarter. They desire someone who brings to the table something they can't already provide. This often makes it hard for tough, smart, attractive women to find mates: there just aren't that many men around who can outclass them enough to be considered desirable (who are higher, as one research publication put it, in "income, education, self-confidence, intelligence, dominance and social position").[207] The spirit that interferes when boys are trying to become men is, therefore, no more friend to woman than it is to man. It will object, just as vociferously and self-righteously ("you can't do it, it's too dangerous") when little girls try to stand on their own two feet. It negates consciousness. It's antihuman, desirous of failure, jealous, resentful and destructive. No one truly on the side of humanity would ally him- or herself with such a thing. No one aiming at moving up would allow him or herself to become possessed by such a thing. And if you think tough men are dangerous, wait until you see what weak men are capable of.

Leave children alone when they are skateboarding.

PET A CAT WHEN YOU

ENCOUNTER ONE ON THE STREET

DOGS ARE OK TOO

I AM GOING TO START THIS CHAPTER by stating directly that I own a dog, an American Eskimo, one of the many variants of the basic spitz type. They were known as German spitzes until the First World War made it verboten to admit that anything good could come from Germany. American Eskimos are among the most beautiful of dogs, with a pointed, classic wolf face, upright ears, a long thick coat, and a curly tail. They are also very intelligent. Our dog, whose name is Sikko (which means "ice" in an Inuit language, according to my daughter, who named him), learns tricks very rapidly, and can do so even now that he's old. I taught him a new stunt, recently, when he turned thirteen. He already knew how to shake a paw, and to balance a treat on his nose. I taught him to do both at the same time. However, it's not at all clear he enjoys it.

We bought Sikko for my daughter, Mikhaila, when she was about ten years old. He was an unbearably cute pup. Small nose and ears, rounded face, big eyes, awkward movements—these features automatically elicit caretaking behaviour from humans, male and female alike.[208] This was certainly the case with Mikhaila, who was also occupied with the care of bearded dragons, gekkoes, ball pythons, chameleons, iguanas and a twenty-pound, thirty-two-inch-long Flemish Giant rabbit named George, who nibbled on everything in the house and frequently escaped (to the great consternation of those who then spied his improbably large form in their tiny mid-city gardens). She had all these animals because she was allergic to the more typical pets—excepting Sikko, who had the additional advantage of being hypo-allergenic.

Sikko garnered fifty nicknames (we counted) which varied broadly in their emotional tone, and reflected both the affection in which he was held and our occasional frustration with his beastly habits. Scumdog was probably my favorite, but I also held Rathound, Furball and Suck-dog in rather high esteem. The kids used Sneak and Squeak (sometimes with an appended o) most frequently, but accompanied it with Snooky, Ugdog, and Snorfalopogus (horrible though it is to admit). Snorbs is Mikhaila's current moniker of choice. She uses it to greet him after a prolonged absence. For full effect, it must be uttered in a high-pitched and surprised voice.

Sikko also happens to have his own Instagram hashtag: #JudgementalSikko.

I am describing my dog instead of writing directly about cats because I don't wish to run afoul of a phenomenon known as "minimal group identification," discovered by the social psychologist Henri Tajfel.[209] Tajfel brought his research subjects into his lab and sat them down in front of a screen, onto which he flashed a number of dots. The subjects were asked to estimate their quantity. Then he categorized his subjects as overestimators vs underestimators, as well as accurate vs inaccurate, and put them into groups corresponding to their performance. Then he asked them to divide money among the members of all the groups.

Tajfel found that his subjects displayed a marked preference for their own group members, rejecting an egalitarian distribution strategy and disproportionately rewarding those with whom they now identified. Other researchers have assigned people to different groups using ever more arbitrary strategies, such as flipping a coin. It didn't matter, even when the subjects were informed of the way the groups were composed. People still favoured the co-members of their personal group.

Tajfel's studies demonstrated two things: first, *that people are social*; second, *that people are antisocial*. People are social because they like the members of their own group. People are antisocial because they don't like the members of other groups. Exactly why this is so has been the subject of continual debate. I think it might be a solution to a complex problem of optimization. Such problems arise, for example, when two or more factors are important, but none can be maximized without diminishing the others. A problem of this sort emerges, for example, because of the antipathy between cooperation and competition, both of which are socially and psychologically desirable. Cooperation is for safety, security and companionship. Competition is for personal growth and status. However, if a given group is too small, it has no power or prestige, and cannot fend off other groups. In consequence, being one of its members is not that useful. If the group is too large, however, the probability of climbing near or to the top declines. So, it becomes too hard to get ahead. Perhaps people identify with groups at the flip of a coin because they deeply want to organize themselves, protect themselves, and still have some reasonable probability of climbing the dominance hierarchy. Then they favour their own group, because favouring it helps it thrive—and climbing something that is failing is not a useful strategy.

In any case, it is because of Tajfel's minimal-conditions discovery that I began this cat-related chapter with a description of my dog. Otherwise, the mere mention of a cat in the title would be enough to turn many dog people against me, just because I didn't include canines in the group of entities that should be petted. Since I also like dogs, there is no reason for me to suffer such a fate. So, if you like to pet dogs when you meet them on the street, don't feel obliged to hate me. Rest assured, instead, that this is also an activity of which I approve. I would also like to apologize to all the cat people who now feel slighted, because they were hoping for a cat story but had to read all this dog-related material. Perhaps they might be satisfied by some assurance that cats do illustrate the point I want to make better, and that I will eventually discuss them. First, however, to other things.

Suffering and the Limitations of Being

The idea that life is suffering is a tenet, in one form or another, of every major religious doctrine, as we have already discussed. Buddhists state it directly. Christians illustrate it with the cross. Jews commemorate the suffering endured over centuries. Such reasoning universally characterizes the great creeds, because human beings are intrinsically fragile. We can be damaged, even broken, emotionally and physically, and we are all subject to the depredations of aging and loss. This is a dismal set of facts, and it is reasonable to wonder how we can expect to thrive and be happy (or even to want to exist, sometimes) under such conditions.

I was speaking recently with a client whose husband had been engaging in a successful battle with cancer for an agonizing period of five years. They had both held up remarkably and courageously over this period. However, he fell prey to the tendency of that dread condition to metastasize and, in consequence, had been given very little time to live. It is perhaps hardest to hear terrible news like this when you are still in the fragile post-recovery state that occurs after dealing successfully with previous bad news. Tragedy at such a time seems particularly unfair. It is the sort of thing that can make you distrust even hope itself. It's frequently sufficient to cause genuine trauma. My client and I discussed a number of issues, some philosophical and abstract, some more concrete. I shared with her some of the thoughts that I had developed about the whys and wherefores of human vulnerability.

When my son, Julian, was about three, he was particularly cute. He's twenty years older than that now, but still quite cute (a compliment I'm sure he'll particularly enjoy reading). Because of him, I thought a lot about the fragility of small children. A three-year-old is easily damaged. Dogs can bite him. Cars can hit him. Mean kids can push him over. He can get sick (and sometimes did). Julian was prone to high fevers and the delirium they sometimes produce. Sometimes I had to take him into the shower with me and cool him off when he was hallucinating, or even fighting with me, in his feverish state. There are few things that make it harder to accept the fundamental limitations of human existence than a sick child.

Mikhaila, a year and a few months older than Julian, also had her problems. When she was two, I would lift her up on my shoulders and carry her around. Kids enjoy that. Afterwards, however, when I put her feet back on the ground, she would sit down and cry. So, I stopped doing it. That seemed to be the end of the problem—with a seemingly minor exception. My wife, Tammy, told me that something was wrong with Mikhaila's gait. I couldn't see it. Tammy thought it might be related to her reaction to being carried on my shoulders.

Mikhaila was a sunny child and very easy to get along with. One day when she was about fourteen months old I took her along with Tammy and her grandparents to Cape Cod, when we lived in Boston. When we got there, Tammy and her mom and dad walked ahead, and left me with Mikhaila in the car. We were in the front seat. She was lying there in the sun, babbling away. I leaned over to hear what she was saying.

"Happy, happy, happy, happy, happy."

That's what she was like.

When she turned six, however, she started to get mopey. It was hard to get her out of bed in the morning. She put on her clothes very slowly. When we walked somewhere, she lagged behind. She complained that her feet hurt and that her shoes didn't fit. We bought her ten different pairs, but it didn't help. She went to school, and held her head up, and behaved properly. But when she came home, and saw her Mom, she would break into tears.

We had recently moved from Boston to Toronto, and attributed these changes to the stress of the move. But it didn't get better. Mikhaila began to walk up and down stairs one step at a time. She began to move like someone much older. She complained if you held her hand. (One time, much later, she asked me, "Dad, when you played 'this little piggy,' with me when I was little, was it supposed to hurt?" Things you learn too late . . .).

A physician at our local medical clinic told us, "Sometimes children have growing pains. They're normal. But you could think about taking her to see a physiotherapist." So, we did. The physiotherapist tried to rotate Mikhaila's heel. It didn't move. That was not good. The physio told us, "Your daughter has juvenile rheumatoid arthritis." This was not what we wanted to hear. We did not like that physiotherapist. We went back to the medical clinic. Another physician there told us to take Mikhaila to the Hospital for Sick Children. The doctor said, "Take her to the emergency room. That way, you will be able to see a rheumatologist quickly." Mikhaila had arthritis, all right. The physio, bearer of unwelcome news, was correct. Thirty-seven affected joints. Severe polyarticular juvenile idiopathic arthritis (JIA). Cause? Unknown. Prognosis? Multiple early joint replacements.

What sort of God would make a world where such a thing could happen, at all?—much less to an innocent and happy little girl? It's a question of absolutely fundamental import, for believer and nonbeliever alike. It's an issue addressed (as are so many difficult matters) in *The Brothers Karamazov*, the great novel by Dostoevsky we began to discuss in Rule 7. Dostoevsky expresses his doubts about the propriety of Being through the character of Ivan who, if you remember, is the articulate, handsome, sophisticated brother (and greatest adversary) of the monastic novitiate Alyosha. "It's not God I don't accept. Understand this," says Ivan. "I do not accept the world that He created, this world of God's, and cannot agree with it."

Ivan tells Alyosha a story about a small girl whose parents punished her by locking her in a freezing outhouse overnight (a story Dostoevsky culled from a newspaper of the time). "Can you just see those two snoozing away while their daughter was crying all night?" says Ivan. "And imagine this little child: unable to understand what was happening to her, beating her frozen little chest and crying meek little tears, begging 'gentle Jesus' to get her out of that horrible place! . . . Alyosha:

if you were somehow promised that the world could finally have complete and total peace—but only on the condition that you tortured one little child to death—say, that girl who was freezing in the outhouse . . . would you do it?" Alyosha demurs. "No, I would not," he says, softly.[210] He would not do what God seems to freely allow.

I had realized something relevant to this, years before, about three-year-old Julian (remember him? :)). I thought, "I love my son. He's three, and cute and little and comical. But I am also afraid for him, because he could be hurt. If I had the power to change that, what might I do?" I thought, "He could be twenty feet tall instead of forty inches. Nobody could push him over then. He could be made of titanium, instead of flesh and bone. Then, if some brat bounced a toy truck off his noggin, he wouldn't care. He could have a computer-enhanced brain. And even if he was damaged, somehow, his parts could be immediately replaced. Problem solved!" But no—not problem solved—and not just because such things are currently impossible. Artificially fortifying Julian would have been the same as destroying him. Instead of his little three-year-old self, he would be a cold, steel-hard robot. That wouldn't be Julian. It would be a monster. I came to realize through such thoughts that what can be truly loved about a person is inseparable from their limitations. Julian wouldn't have been little and cute and lovable if he wasn't also prone to illness, and loss, and pain, and anxiety. Since I loved him a lot, I decided that he was all right the way he was, despite his fragility.

It's been harder with my daughter. As her disease progressed, I began to piggy-back her around (not on my shoulders) when we went for walks. She started taking oral naproxen and methotrexate, the latter a powerful chemotherapy agent. She had a number of cortisol injections (wrists, shoulders, ankles, elbows, knees, hips, fingers, toes and tendons), all under general anaesthetic. This helped temporarily, but her decline continued. One day Tammy took Mikhaila to the zoo. She pushed her around in a wheelchair.

That was not a good day.

Her rheumatologist suggested prednisone, a corticosteroid, long used to fight inflammation. But prednisone has many side effects, not the least of which is severe facial swelling. It wasn't clear that this was better than the arthritis, not for a little girl. Fortunately, if that is the right word, the rheumatologist told us of a new drug. It had been used previously, but only on adults. So Mikhaila became the first Canadian child to receive etanercept, a "biological" specifically designed for autoimmune diseases. Tammy accidentally administered ten times the recommended dose the first few injections. Poof! Mikhaila was fixed. A few weeks after the trip to the zoo, she was zipping around, playing little league soccer. Tammy spent all summer just watching her run.

We wanted Mikhaila to control as much of her life as she could. She had always been strongly motivated by money. One day we found her outside, surrounded by the books of her early childhood, selling them to passersby. I sat her down one evening and told her that I would give her fifty dollars if she could do the injection herself. She was eight. She struggled for thirty-five minutes, holding the needle close to her thigh. Then she did it. Next time I paid her twenty dollars, but only gave her ten minutes. Then it was ten dollars, and five minutes. We stayed at ten for quite a while. It was a bargain.

After a few years, Mikhaila became completely symptom-free. The rheumatologist suggested that we start weaning her off her medications. Some children grow out of JIA when they hit puberty. No one knows why. She began to take methotrexate in pill form, instead of injecting it. Things were good for four years. Then, one day, her elbow started to ache. We took her back to the hospital. "You only have one actively arthritic joint," said the rheumatologist's assistant. It wasn't "only." Two isn't much more than one, but one is a lot more than zero. One meant she hadn't grown out of her arthritis, despite the hiatus. The news demolished her for a month, but she was still in dance class and playing ball games with her friends on the street in front of our house.

The rheumatologist had some more unpleasant things to say the next September, when Mikhaila started grade eleven. An MRI revealed joint deterioration at the hip. She told Mikhaila, "Your hip will have to be replaced before you turn thirty." Perhaps the damage had been done, before the etanercept worked its miracle? We didn't know. It was ominous news. One day, a few weeks after, Mikhaila was playing ball hockey in her high school gym. Her hip locked up. She had to hobble off the court. It started to hurt more and more. The rheumatologist said, "Some of your femur appears to be dead. You don't need a hip replacement when you're thirty. You need one now."

As I sat with my client—as she discussed her husband's advancing illness—we discussed the fragility of life, the catastrophe of existence, and the sense of nihilism evoked by the spectre of death. I started with my thoughts about my son. She had asked, like everyone in her situation, "Why my husband? Why me? Why this?" My realization of the tight interlinking between vulnerability and Being was the best answer I had for her. I told her an old Jewish story, which I believe is part of the commentary on the Torah. It begins with a question, structured like a Zen koan. *Imagine a Being who is omniscient, omnipresent, and omnipotent. What does such a Being lack?*[211] The answer? *Limitation.*

If you are already everything, everywhere, always, there is nowhere to go and nothing to be. Everything that could be already is, and everything that could happen already has. And it is for this reason, so the story goes, that God created man. No limitation, no story. No story, no Being. That idea has helped me deal with the terrible fragility of Being. It helped my client, too. I don't want to overstate the significance of this. I don't want to claim that this somehow makes it all OK. She still faced the cancer afflicting her husband, just as I still faced my daughter's terrible illness. But there's something to be said for recognizing that existence and limitation are inextricably linked.

Though thirty spokes may form the wheel,
it is the hole within the hub
which gives the wheel utility.
It is not the clay the potter throws,
which gives the pot its usefulness,
but the space within the shape,
from which the pot is made.
Without a door, the room cannot be entered,
and without its windows it is dark
Such is the utility of non-existence.[212]

A realization of this sort emerged more recently, in the pop culture world, during the evolution of the DC Comics cultural icon Superman. Superman was created in 1938 by Jerry Siegel and Joe Shuster. In the beginning, he could move cars, trains and even ships. He could run faster than a locomotive. He could "leap over tall buildings in a single bound." As he developed over the next four decades, however, Superman's power began to expand. By the late sixties, he could fly faster than light. He had super-hearing and X-ray vision. He could blast heat-rays from his eyes. He could freeze objects and generate hurricanes with his breath. He could move entire planets. Nuclear blasts didn't faze him. And, if he did get hurt, somehow, he would immediately heal. Superman became invulnerable.

Then a strange thing happened. He got boring. The more amazing his abilities became, the harder it was to think up interesting things for him to do. DC first overcame this problem in the 1940s. Superman became vulnerable to the radiation produced by kryptonite, a material remnant of his shattered home planet. Eventually, more than two dozen variants emerged. Green kryptonite weakened Superman. In sufficient dosage, it could even kill him. Red caused him to behave strangely. Red-green caused him to mutate (he once grew a third eye in the back of his head).

Other techniques were necessary to keep Superman's story compelling. In 1976, he was scheduled to battle Spider-Man. It was the first superhero cross-over between Stan Lee's upstart Marvel Comics, with its less idealized characters, and DC, the owner of Superman and Batman. But Marvel had to augment Spider-Man's powers for the battle to remain plausible. That broke the rules of the game. Spider-Man is Spider-Man because he has the powers of a spider. If he is suddenly granted any old power, he's not Spider-Man. The plot falls apart.

By the 1980s, Superman was suffering from terminal deus ex machina—a Latin term meaning "god from a machine." The term described the rescue of the imperilled hero in ancient Greek and Roman plays by the sudden and miraculous appearance of an all-powerful god. In badly written stories, to this very day, a character in trouble can be saved or a failing plot redeemed by a bit of implausible magic or other chicanery not in keeping with the reader's reasonable expectations. Sometimes Marvel Comics, for example, saves a failing story in exactly this manner. Lifeguard, for example, is an X-Man character who can develop whatever power is necessary to save a life. He's very handy to have around. Other examples abound in popular culture. At the end of Stephen King's *The Stand*, for example (spoiler alert), God Himself destroys the novel's evil characters. The entire ninth season (1985–86) of the primetime soap *Dallas* was later revealed as a dream. Fans object to such things, and rightly so. They've been ripped off. People following a story are willing to suspend disbelief as long as the limitations making the story possible are coherent and consistent. Writers, for their part, agree to abide by their initial decisions. When writers cheat, fans get annoyed. They want to toss the book in the fireplace, and throw a brick through the TV.

And that became Superman's problem: he developed powers so extreme that he could "deus" himself out of anything, at any time. In consequence, in the 1980s, the franchise nearly died. Artist-writer John Byrne successfully rebooted it, rewriting Superman, retaining his biography, but depriving him of many of his new powers. He could no longer lift planets, or shrug off an H-bomb. He also became dependent on the sun for his power, like a reverse vampire. He gained some reasonable limitations. A superhero who can do anything turns out to be no hero at all. He's nothing specific, so he's nothing. He has nothing to strive against, so he can't be admirable. *Being of any reasonable sort appears to require limitation.* Perhaps this is because Being requires Becoming, as well as mere static existence—and to become is to become something more, or at least something different. That is only possible for something limited.

Fair enough.

But what about the suffering caused by such limits? Perhaps the limits required by Being are so extreme that the whole project should just be scrapped. Dostoevsky expresses this idea very clearly in the voice of the protagonist of *Notes from Underground*: "So you see, you can say anything about world history—anything and everything that the most morbid imagination can think up. Except one thing, that is.

It cannot be said that world history is reasonable. The word sticks in one's throat."[213] Goethe's Mephistopheles, the adversary of Being, announces his opposition explicitly to God's creation in *Faust*, as we have seen. Years later, Goethe wrote *Faust, Part II*. He has the Devil repeat his credo, in a slightly different form, just to hammer home the point:[214]

> *Gone, to sheer Nothing, past with null made one!*
> *What matters our creative endless toil,*
> *When, at a snatch, oblivion ends the coil?*
> *"It is by-gone"—How shall this riddle run?*
> *As good as if things never had begun,*
> *Yet circle back, existence to possess:*
> *I'd rather have Eternal Emptiness.*

Anyone can understand such words, when a dream collapses, a marriage ends, or a family member is struck down by a devastating disease. How can reality be structured so unbearably? How can this be?

Perhaps, as the Columbine boys suggested (see Rule 6), it would be better not to be at all. Perhaps it would be even better if there was no Being at all. But people who come to the former conclusion are flirting with suicide, and those who come to the latter with something worse, something truly monstrous. They're consorting with the idea of the destruction of everything. They are toying with genocide—and worse. Even the darkest regions have still darker corners. And what is truly horrifying is that such conclusions are understandable, maybe even inevitable—although not inevitably acted upon. What is a reasonable person to think when faced, for example, with a suffering child? Is it not precisely the reasonable person, the compassionate person, who would find such thoughts occupying his mind? How could a good God allow such a world as this to exist?

Logical they might be. Understandable, they might be. But there is a terrible catch to such conclusions. Acts undertaken in keeping with them (if not the thoughts themselves) inevitably serve to make a bad situation even worse. Hating life, despising life—even for the genuine pain that life inflicts—merely serves to make life itself worse, unbearably worse. There is no genuine protest in that. There is no goodness in that, only the desire to produce suffering, for the sake of suffering. That is the very essence of evil. People who come to that kind of thinking are one step from total mayhem. Sometimes they merely lack the tools. Sometimes, like Stalin, they have their finger on the nuclear button.

But is there any coherent alternative, given the self-evident horrors of existence? Can Being itself, with its malarial mosquitoes, child soldiers and degenerative neurological diseases, truly be justified? I'm not sure I could have formulated a proper answer to such a question in the nineteenth century, before the totalitarian horrors of the twentieth were monstrously perpetrated on millions of people. I don't know that it's possible to understand why such doubts are morally impermissible without the fact of the Holocaust and the Stalinist purges and Mao's catastrophic Great Leap Forward.[215] And I also don't think it is possible to answer the question by *thinking*. Thinking leads inexorably to the abyss. It did not work for Tolstoy. It might not even have worked for Nietzsche, who arguably thought more clearly about such things than anyone in history. But if it is not thinking that can be relied upon in the direst of situations, what is left? Thought, after all, is the highest of human achievements, is it not?

Perhaps not.

Something supersedes thinking, despite its truly awesome power. When existence reveals itself as existentially intolerable, thinking collapses in on itself. In such situations—in the depths—it's *noticing*, not thinking, that does the trick. Perhaps you might start by noticing this: when you love someone, *it's not despite their limitations. It's because of their limitations.* Of course, it's complicated. You don't have to be in love with every shortcoming, and merely accept. You shouldn't stop trying to make life better, or let suffering just be. But there appear to be limits on the path to improvement beyond which we might not want to go, lest we sacrifice our humanity itself. Of course, it's one thing to say, "Being requires limitation," and then to go about happily, when the sun is shining and your father is free of Alzheimer's disease and your kids are healthy and your marriage happy. But when things go wrong?

Disintegration and Pain

Mikhaila stayed awake many nights when she was in pain. When her grandfather came to visit, he gave her a few of his Tylenol 3s, which contain codeine. Then she could sleep. But not for long. Our rheumatologist, instrumental in producing Mikhaila's remission, hit the limit of her courage when dealing with our child's pain. She had once prescribed opiates to a young girl, who became addicted. She swore never to do so again. She said, "Have you tried ibuprofen?" Mikhaila learned then that doctors don't know everything. Ibuprofen for her was a crumb of bread for a starving man.

We talked to a new doctor. He listened carefully. Then he helped Mikhaila. First, he prescribed T3s, the same medication her grandfather had briefly shared. This was brave. Physicians face a lot of pressure to avoid the prescription of opiates—not least to children. But opiates *work*. Soon, however, the Tylenol was insufficient. She started taking oxycontin, an opioid known pejoratively as hillbilly heroin. This controlled her pain, but produced other problems. Tammy took Mikhaila out for lunch a week after the prescription started. She could have been drunk. Her speech was slurred. Her head nodded. This was not good.

My sister-in-law is a palliative care nurse. She thought we could add Ritalin, an amphetamine often used for hyperactive kids, to the oxycontin. The Ritalin restored Mikhaila's alertness and had some pain-suppressing qualities of its own (this is a very a good thing to know if you are ever faced with someone's intractable suffering). But her pain became increasingly excruciating. She started to fall. Then her hip seized up on her again, this time in the subway on a day when the escalator was not working. Her boyfriend carried her up the stairs. She took a cab home. The subway was no longer a reliable form of transportation. That March we bought Mikhaila a 50cc motor scooter. It was dangerous to let her ride it. It was also dangerous for her to lack all freedom. We chose the former danger. She passed her learner's exam, which allowed her to pilot the vehicle during the day. She was given a few months to progress towards her permanent licence.

In May her hip was replaced. The surgeon was even able to adjust for a pre-existent half centimetre difference in leg length. The bone hadn't died, either. That was only a shadow on the x-ray. Her aunt and her grandparents came to see her. We had some better days. Immediately after the surgery, however, Mikhaila was placed in an adult rehabilitation centre. She was the youngest person in the place, by about sixty years. Her aged roommate, very neurotic, wouldn't allow the lights to be off, even at night. The old woman couldn't make it to the toilet and had to use a bedpan. She couldn't stand to have the door to her room closed. But it was right beside the nurses' station, with its continual alarm bells and loud conversations. There was no sleeping there, where sleeping was required. No visitors were allowed after 7 p.m. The physio—the very reason for her placement—was on vacation. The only person who helped her was the janitor, who volunteered to move her to a multi-bed ward when she told the on-duty nurse that she couldn't sleep. This was the same nurse who had laughed when she'd found out which room Mikhaila had been assigned to.

She was supposed to be there for six weeks. She was there three days. When the vacationing physio returned, Mikhaila climbed the rehab-centre stairs and immediately mastered her additional required exercises. While she was doing that, we outfitted our home with the necessary handrails. Then we took her home. All that pain and surgery—she handled that fine. The appalling rehab centre? That produced post-traumatic stress symptoms.

Mikhaila enrolled in a full-fledged motorcycle course in June, so she could continue legally using her scooter. We were all terrified by this necessity. What if she fell? What if she had an accident? On the first day, Mikhaila trained on a real motorcycle. It was heavy. She dropped it several times. She saw another beginning rider tumble and roll across the parking lot where the course was held. On the morning of the second day of the course, she was afraid to return. She didn't want to leave her bed. We talked for a good while, and jointly decided that she should at least drive back with Tammy to the site where the training took place. If she couldn't manage it, she could stay in the car until the course finished. En route, her courage returned. When she received her certificate, everyone else enrolled stood and applauded.

Then her right ankle disintegrated. Her doctors wanted to fuse the large affected bones into one piece. But that would have caused the other, smaller bones in her foot—now facing additional pressure—to deteriorate. That's not so intolerable, perhaps, when you're eighty (although it's no picnic then either). But it's no solution when you're in your teens. We insisted upon an artificial replacement, although the technology was new. There was a three year-waiting list. This was simply not manageable. The damaged ankle produced much more pain than her previously failing hip. One bad night she became erratic and illogical. I couldn't calm her down. I knew she was at her breaking point. To call that stressful is to say almost nothing.

We spent weeks and then months desperately investigating all sorts of replacement devices, trying to assess their suitability. We looked everywhere for quicker surgery: India, China, Spain, the UK, Costa Rica, Florida. We contacted the Ontario Provincial Ministry of Health. They were very helpful. They located a specialist across the country, in Vancouver. Mikhaila's ankle was replaced in November. Post-surgery, she was in absolute agony. Her foot was mispositioned. The cast was compressing skin against bone. The clinic was unwilling to give her enough oxycontin to control her pain. She had built up a high level of tolerance because of her previous use.

When she returned home, in less pain, Mikhaila started to taper off the opiates. She hated oxycontin, despite its evident utility. She said it turned her life grey. Perhaps that was a good thing, under the circumstances. She stopped using it as soon as possible. She suffered through withdrawal for months, with night sweating and formication (the sensation of ants crawling upside down under her skin). She became unable to experience any pleasure. That was another effect of opiate withdrawal.

During much of this period, we were overwhelmed. The demands of everyday life don't stop, just because you have been laid low by a catastrophe. Everything that you always do still has to be done. So how do you manage? Here are some things we learned:

Set aside some time to talk and to think about the illness or other crisis and how it should be managed every day. *Do not* talk or think about it otherwise. If you do not limit its effect, you will become exhausted, and everything will spiral into the ground. This is not helpful. Conserve your strength. You're in a war, not a battle, and a war is composed of many battles. You must stay functional through all of them. When worries associated with the crisis arise at other times, remind yourself that you will think them through, during the scheduled period. This usually works. The parts of your brain that generate anxiety are more interested in the fact that there is a plan than in the details of the plan. Don't schedule your time to think in the evening or at night. Then you won't be able to sleep. If you can't sleep, then everything will go rapidly downhill.

Shift the unit of time you use to frame your life. When the sun is shining, and times are good, and the crops are bountiful, you can make your plans for the next month, and the next year, and the next five years. You can even dream a decade ahead. But you can't do that when your leg is clamped firmly in a crocodile's jaws. "Sufficient unto the day are the evils thereof"—that is Matthew 6:34. It is often interpreted as "live in the present, without a care for tomorrow." This is not what it means. That injunction must be interpreted in the context of the Sermon on the Mount, of which it is an integral part. That sermon distills the ten "Thou-shalt-nots" of the Commandments of Moses into a single prescriptive "Thou shalt." Christ enjoins His followers to place faith in God's Heavenly Kingdom, and the truth. That's a conscious decision to presume the primary goodness of Being. That's an act of courage. Aim high, like Pinocchio's Geppetto. Wish upon a star, and then act properly, in accordance with that aim. Once you are aligned with the heavens, you can concentrate on the day. Be careful. Put the things you can control in order. Repair what is in disorder, and make what is already good better. It is possible that you can manage, if you are careful. People are very tough. People can survive through much pain and loss. But to persevere they must see the good in Being. If they lose that, they are truly lost.

Dogs, Again—But Finally, Cats

Dogs are like people. They are the friends and allies of human beings. They are social, hierarchical, and domesticated. They are happy at the bottom of the family pyramid. They pay for the attention they receive with loyalty, admiration, and love. Dogs are great.

Cats, however, are their own creatures. They aren't social or hierarchical (except in passing). They are only semi-domesticated. They don't do tricks. They are friendly on their own terms. Dogs have been tamed, but cats have made a decision. They appear willing to interact with people, for some strange reasons of their own. To me, cats are a manifestation of nature, of Being, in an almost pure form. Furthermore, they are a form of Being that looks at human beings and approves.

When you meet a cat on a street, many things can happen. If I see a cat at a distance, for example, the evil part of me wants to startle it with a loud pfft! sound—front teeth over bottom lip. That will make a nervous cat puff up its fur and stand sideways so it looks larger. Maybe I shouldn't laugh at cats, but it's hard to resist. The fact that they can be startled is one of the best things about them (along with the fact that they are instantly disgruntled and embarrassed by their overreaction). But when I have myself under proper control, I'll bend down, and call the cat over, so I can pet it. Sometimes, it will run away. Sometimes, it will ignore me completely, because it's a cat. But sometimes the cat will come over to me, push its head against my waiting hand, and be pleased about it. Sometimes it will even roll over, and arch its back against the dusty concrete (although cats positioned in that manner will often bite and claw even a friendly hand).

Across the street on which I live is a cat named Ginger. Ginger is a Siamese, a beautiful cat, very calm and self-possessed. She is low in the Big Five personality trait of neuroticism, which is an index of anxiety, fear and emotional pain. Ginger is not at all bothered by dogs. Our dog, Sikko, is her friend. Sometimes when you call her—sometimes of her own accord—Ginger will trot across the street, tail held high, with a little kink at the end. Then she will roll on her back in front of Sikko, who wags his tail happily as a consequence. Afterward, if she feels like it, she might come visit you, for a half a minute. It's a nice break. It's a little extra light, on a good day, and a tiny respite, on a bad day.

If you pay careful attention, even on a bad day, you may be fortunate enough to be confronted with small opportunities of just that sort. Maybe you will see a little girl dancing on the street because she is all dressed up in a ballet costume. Maybe you will have a particularly good cup of coffee in a café that cares about their customers. Maybe you can steal ten or twenty minutes to do some little ridiculous thing that distracts you or reminds you that you can laugh at the absurdity of existence. Personally, I like to watch a *Simpsons* episode at 1.5 times regular speed: all the laughs; two-thirds the time.

And maybe when you are going for a walk and your head is spinning a cat will show up and if you pay attention to it then you will get a reminder for just fifteen seconds that the wonder of Being might make up for the ineradicable suffering that accompanies it.

Pet a cat when you encounter one on the street.

P.S. Soon after I wrote this chapter, Mikhaila's surgeon told her that her artificial ankle would have to be removed, and her ankle fused. Amputation waited down that road. She had been in pain for eight years, since the replacement surgery, and her mobility remained significantly impaired, although both were much better than before. Four days later she happened upon a new physiotherapist. He was a large, powerful, attentive person. He had specialized in ankle treatment in the UK, in London. He placed his hands around her ankle and compressed it for forty seconds, while Mikhaila moved her foot back and forth. A mispositioned bone slipped back where it belonged. Her pain disappeared. She never cries in front of medical personnel, but she burst into tears. Her knee straightened up. Now she can walk long distances, and traipse around in her bare feet. The calf muscle on her damaged leg is growing back. She has much more flexion in the artificial joint. This year, she got married and had a baby girl, Elizabeth, named after my wife's departed mother.

Things are good.

For now.

CODA

WHAT SHALL I DO WITH MY NEWFOUND PEN OF LIGHT?

IN LATE 2016 I travelled to northern California to meet a friend and business associate. We spent an evening together thinking and talking. At one point he took a pen from his jacket and took a few notes. It was LED-equipped and beamed light out its tip, so that writing in the dark was made easier. "Just another gadget," I thought. Later, however, in a more metaphorical frame of mind, I was struck quite deeply by the idea of a pen of light. There was something symbolic about it, something metaphysical. We're all in the dark, after all, much of the time. We could all use something written with light to guide us along our way. I told him I wanted to do some writing, while we sat and conversed, and I asked him if he would give me the pen, as a gift. When he handed it over, I found myself inordinately pleased. Now I could write illuminated words in the darkness! Obviously, it was important to do such a thing properly. So I said to myself, in all seriousness, "What shall I do with my newfound pen of light?" There are two verses in the New Testament that pertain to such things. I've thought about them a lot:

> Ask, and it shall be given to you; Seek, and ye shall find; Knock, and
> it shall be open unto you: For everyone who asks receives; the one who

seeks finds; and to the one who knocks, the door will be opened (Matthew 7:7-7:8)

At first glance, this seems like nothing but a testament to the magic of prayer, in the sense of entreating God to grant favours. But God, whatever or whoever He may be, is no simple granter of wishes. When tempted by the Devil himself, in the desert—as we saw in Rule 7 (Pursue what is meaningful [not what is expedient])—even Christ Himself was not willing to call upon his Father for a favour; furthermore, every day, the prayers of desperate people go unanswered. But maybe this is because the questions they contain are not phrased in the proper manner. Perhaps it's not reasonable to ask God to break the rules of physics every time we fall by the wayside or make a serious error. Perhaps, in such times, you can't put the cart before the horse and simply wish for your problem to be solved in some magical manner. Perhaps you could ask, instead, what you might have to do right now to increase your resolve, buttress your character, and find the strength to go on. Perhaps you could instead ask to see the truth.

On many occasions in our nearly thirty years of marriage my wife and I have had a disagreement—sometimes a deep disagreement. Our unity appeared to be broken, at some unknowably profound level, and we were not able to easily resolve the rupture by talking. We became trapped, instead, in emotional, angry and anxious argument. We agreed that when such circumstances arose we would separate, briefly: she to one room, me to another. This was often quite difficult, because it is hard to disengage in the heat of an argument, when anger generates the desire to defeat and win. But it seemed better than risking the consequences of a dispute that threatened to spiral out of control.

Alone, trying to calm down, we would each ask ourselves the same single question: *What had we each done to contribute to the situation we were arguing about? However small, however distant . . . we had each made some error.* Then we would reunite, and share the results of our questioning: *Here's how I was wrong. . . .*

The problem with asking yourself such a question is that you must truly want the answer. And the problem with doing that is that *you won't like the answer.* When you are arguing with someone, you want to be right, and you want the other person to be wrong. Then it's them that has to sacrifice something and change, not you, and that's much preferable. If it's you that's wrong and you that must change, then you have to reconsider yourself—your memories of the past, your manner of being in the present, and your plans for the future. Then you must resolve to improve and figure out how to do that. Then you actually have to do it. That's exhausting. It takes repeated practice, to instantiate the new perceptions and make the new actions habitual. It's much easier just not to realize, admit and engage. It's much easier to turn your attention away from the truth and remain wilfully blind.

But it's at such a point that you must decide whether you want to be right or you want to have peace.[216] You must decide whether to insist upon the absolute correctness of your view, or to listen and negotiate. You don't get peace by being right. You just get to be right, while your partner gets to be wrong—defeated and wrong. Do that ten thousand times and your marriage will be over (or you will wish it was). To choose the alternative—to seek peace—you have to decide that you want the answer, more than you want to be right. That's the way out of the prison of your stubborn preconceptions. That's the prerequisite for negotiation. That's to truly abide by principle of Rule 2 (Treat yourself like someone you are responsible for helping).

My wife and I learned that if you ask yourself such a question, and you genuinely desire the answer (no matter how disgraceful and terrible and shameful), then a memory of something you did that was stupid and wrong at some point in the generally not-distant-enough past will arise from the depths of your mind. Then you can go back to your partner and reveal why you're an idiot, and apologize (sincerely) and that person can do the same for you, and then apologize (sincerely), and then you two idiots will be able to talk again. Perhaps that is true prayer: the question, "What have I done wrong, and what can I do now to set things at least a little bit more right?" But your heart must be open to the terrible truth. You must be receptive to that which you do not want to hear. When you decide to learn about your faults, so that they can be rectified, you open a line of communication with the source of all revelatory thought. Maybe that's the same thing as consulting your conscience. Maybe that's the same thing, in some manner, as a discussion with God.

It was in that spirit, with some paper in front of me, that I asked my question: *What shall I do with my newfound pen of light?* I asked, as if I truly wanted the answer. I waited for a reply. I was holding a conversation between two different elements of myself. I was genuinely thinking—or listening, in the sense described in Rule 9 (Assume that the person you are listening to might know something you don't). That rule can apply as much to yourself as to others. It was me, of course, who asked the question—and it was me, of course, who replied. But those two me's were not the same. I did not know what the answer would be. I was waiting for it to appear in the theatre of my imagination. I was waiting for the words to spring out of the void. How can a person think up something that surprises him? How can he already not know what he thinks? Where do new thoughts come from? Who or what thinks them?

Since I had just been given, of all things, a Pen of Light, which could write Illuminated Words in the darkness, I wanted to do the best thing I could with it. So, I asked the appropriate question—and, almost immediately, an answer revealed itself: *Write down the words you want inscribed on your soul.* I wrote that down. That seemed pretty good—a little on the romantic side, granted—but that was in keeping with the game. Then I upped the ante. I decided to ask myself the hardest questions I could think up, and await their answers. If you have a Pen of Light, after all, you should use it to answer Difficult Questions. Here was the first: *What shall I do tomorrow?* The answer came: *The most good possible in the shortest period of time.* That was satisfying, as well—conjoining an ambitious aim with the demands of maximal efficiency. A worthy challenge. The second question was in the same vein: *What shall I do next year? Try to ensure that the good I do then will be exceeded only by the good I do the year after that.* That seemed solid, too—a nice extension of the ambitions detailed in the previous answer. I told my friend that I was trying a serious experiment in writing with the pen he had given to me. I asked if I could read aloud what I had composed so far. The questions—and the answers—struck a chord with him, too. That was good. That was impetus to continue.

The next question ended the first set: *What shall I do with my life? Aim for Paradise, and concentrate on today.* Hah! I knew what that meant. It's what Geppetto does in the Disney movie *Pinocchio,* when he wishes upon a star. The grandfatherly woodcarver lifts up his eyes to the twinkling diamond set high above the mundane world of day-to-day human concerns and articulates his deepest desire: that the marionette he created lose the strings by which he is manipulated by others and transform himself into a real boy. It's also the central message of the Sermon on the Mount, as we saw in Rule 4 (Compare yourself to who you were yesterday . . .), but which deserve repeating here:

> And why take ye thought for raiment? Consider the lilies of the field, how they grow; they toil not, neither do they spin: And yet I say unto you, That even Solomon in all his glory was not arrayed like one of these. Wherefore, if God so clothe the grass of the field, which to day is, and to morrow is cast into the oven, shall he not much more clothe you, O ye of little faith? Therefore take no thought, saying, What shall we eat? or, What shall we drink? or, Wherewithal shall we be clothed? For your heavenly Father knoweth that ye have need of all these things. But seek ye first the kingdom of God, and his righteousness; and all these things shall be added unto you (Matthew 6:28-6:33).

What does all that mean? Orient yourself properly. Then—and only then—concentrate on the day. Set your sights at the Good, the Beautiful, and the True, and then focus pointedly and carefully on the concerns of each moment. Aim continually at Heaven while you work diligently on Earth. Attend fully to the future, in that manner, while attending fully to the present. Then you have the best chance of perfecting both.

I turned, then, from the use of time to my relationships with people, and wrote down and then read these questions and answers to my friend: *What shall I do with my wife? Treat her as if she is the Holy Mother of God, so that she may give birth to the world-redeeming hero. What shall I do with my daughter? Stand behind her, listen to her, guard her, train her mind, and let her know it's OK if she wants to be a mother. What shall I do with my parents? Act such that your actions justify the suffering they endured. What shall I do with my son? Encourage him to be a true Son of God.*

To honour your wife as a Mother of God is to notice and support the sacred element of her role as mother (not just of your children, but as such). A society that forgets this cannot survive. Hitler's mother gave birth to Hitler, and Stalin's mother to Stalin. Was something amiss in their crucial relationships? It seems likely, given the importance of the maternal role in establishing trust[217]—to take a single vital example. Perhaps the importance of their motherly duties, and of their relationship with their children, was not properly stressed; perhaps what the women were doing in their maternal guise was not properly regarded by husband, father and society alike. Who instead might a woman produce if she was treated properly, honourably and carefully? After all, the fate of the world rests on each new infant—tiny, fragile and threatened but, in time, capable of uttering the words and doing the deeds that maintain the eternal, delicate balance between chaos and order.

To stand behind my daughter? That's to encourage her, in everything she wants courageously to do, but to include in that genuine appreciation the fact of her femininity: to recognize the importance of having a family and children and to forego the temptation to denigrate or devalue that in comparison to accomplishment of personal ambition or career. It's not for nothing that the Holy Mother and Infant is a divine image—as we just discussed. Societies that cease to honour that image—that cease to see that relationship as of transcendent and fundamental importance—also cease to be.

To act to justify the suffering of your parents is to remember all the sacrifices that all the others who lived before you (not least your parents) have made for you in all the course of the terrible past, to be grateful for all the progress that has been thereby made, and then to act in accordance with that remembrance and gratitude. People sacrificed immensely to bring about what we have now. In many cases, they literally died for it—and we should act with some respect for that fact.

To encourage my son to be a true Son of God? That is to want him above all *to do what is right*, and to strive to have his back while he is doing so. That is, I think, part of the sacrificial message: to value and support your son's commitment to transcendent good above all things (including his worldly progress, so to speak, and his safety—and, perhaps, even his life).

I continued asking questions. The answers came within seconds. *What shall I do with the stranger? Invite him into my house, and treat him like a brother, so that he may become one.* That's to extend the hand of trust to someone so that his or her best part can step forward and reciprocate. That's to manifest the sacred hospitality that makes life between those who do not yet know each other possible. *What shall I do with a fallen soul? Offer a genuine and cautious hand, but do not join it in the mire.* That's a good summary of what we covered in Rule 3 (Make friends with people who want the best for you). That's an injunction to refrain both from casting pearls before swine, and from camouflaging your vice with virtue. *What shall I do with the world? Conduct myself as if Being is more valuable than Non-Being.* Act so that you are not made bitter and corrupt by the tragedy of existence. That's the essence of Rule 1 (Stand up straight with your shoulders back): confront the uncertainty of the world voluntarily, and with faith and courage.

How shall I educate my people? Share with them those things I regard as truly important. That's Rule 8 (Tell the truth—or, at least, don't lie). That is to aim for wisdom, to distill that wisdom into words, and to speak forth those words as if they matter, with true concern and care. That's all relevant, as well, to the next question (and answer): *What shall I do with a torn nation? Stitch it back together with careful words of truth.* The importance of this injunction has, if anything, become clearer over the past few years: we are dividing, and polarizing, and drifting toward chaos. It is necessary, under such conditions, if we are to avoid catastrophe, for each of us to bring forward the truth, as we see it: not the arguments that justify our ideologies, not the machinations that further our ambitions, but the stark pure facts of our existence, revealed for others to see and contemplate, so that we can find common ground and proceed together.

What shall I do for God my Father? Sacrifice everything I hold dear to yet greater perfection. Let the deadwood burn off, so that new growth can prevail. That's the terrible lesson of Cain and Abel, detailed in the discussion of meaning surrounding Rule 7. *What shall I do with a lying man? Let him speak so that he may reveal himself.* Rule 9 (Listen . . .) is once again relevant here, as is another section of the New Testament:

> Ye shall know them by their fruits. Do men gather grapes of thorns, or figs of thistles? Even so every good tree bringeth forth good fruit; but a corrupt tree bringeth forth evil fruit. A good tree cannot bring forth evil fruit, neither can a corrupt tree bring forth good fruit. Every tree that bringeth not forth good fruit is hewn down, and cast into the fire. Wherefore by their fruits ye shall know them (Matthew 7:16-7:20).

The rot must be revealed before something sound can be put in its place, as was also indicated in Rule 7's elaboration—and all of this is pertinent to understanding the following question and answer: *How shall I deal with the enlightened one? Replace him with the true seeker of enlightenment.* There is no enlightened one. There is only the one who is seeking further enlightenment. Proper Being is process, not a state; a journey, not a destination. It's the continual transformation of what you know, through encounter with what you don't know, rather than the desperate clinging to the certainty that is eternally insufficient in any case. That accounts for the importance of Rule 4 (Compare yourself . . .). Always place your becoming above your current being. That means it is necessary to recognize and accept your insufficiency, so that it can be continually rectified. That's painful, certainly—but it's a good deal.

The next few Q & A's made another coherent group, focused this time on ingratitude: *What shall I do when I despise what I have? Remember those who have nothing and strive to be grateful.* Take stock of what is right in front of you. Consider Rule 12—somewhat tongue-in-cheek— (Pet a cat when you encounter one on the street). Consider, as well, that you may be blocked in your progress not because you lack opportunity, but because you have been too arrogant to make full use of what already lies in front of you. That's Rule 6 (Set your house in perfect order before you criticize the world).

I spoke recently with a young man about such things. He had barely ever left his family and never his home state—but he journeyed to Toronto to attend one of my lectures and to meet with me at my home. He had isolated himself far too severely in the short course of his life to date and was badly plagued by anxiety. When we first met, he could hardly speak. He had nonetheless determined in the last year to do something about all of that. He started by taking on the lowly job of dishwasher. He decided to do it well, when he could have treated it contemptuously. Intelligent enough to be embittered by a world that did not recognize his gifts, he decided instead to accept with the genuine humility that is the true precursor to wisdom whatever opportunity he could find. Now he lives on his own. That's better than living at home. Now he has some money. Not much. But more than none. And he earned it. Now he is confronting the social world, and benefitting from the ensuing conflict:

> *Knowledge frequently results*
> *from knowing others,*
> *but the man who is awakened,*
> *has seen the uncarved block.*
> *Others might be mastered by force,*
> *but to master one's self*
> *requires the Tao.*
> *He who has many material things,*
> *may be described as rich,*
> *but he who knows he has enough,*
> *and is at one with the Tao,*
> *might have enough of material things*
> *and have self-being as well.*[218]

As long as my still-anxious but self-transforming and determined visitor continues down his current path, he will become far more competent and accomplished, and it won't take long. But this will only be because he accepted his lowly state and was sufficiently grateful to take the first equally lowly step away from it. That's far preferable to waiting, endlessly, for the magical arrival of Godot. That's far preferable to arrogant, static, unchanging existence, while the demons of rage, resentment and unlived life gather around.

What shall I do when greed consumes me? Remember that it is truly better to give than to receive. The world is a forum of sharing and trading (that's Rule 7, again), not a treasure-house for the plundering. To give is to do what you can to make things better. The good in people will respond to that, and support it, and imitate it, and multiply it, and return it, and foster it, so that everything improves and moves forward.

What shall I do when I ruin my rivers? Seek for the living water and let it cleanse the Earth. I found this question, as well as its answer, particularly unexpected. It seems most associated with Rule 6 (Set your house . . .). Perhaps our environmental problems are not best construed technically. Maybe they're best considered psychologically. The more people sort themselves out, the more responsibility they will take for the world around them and the more problems they will solve.[219] It is better, proverbially, to rule your own spirit than to rule a city. It's easier to subdue an enemy without than one within. Maybe the environmental problem is ultimately spiritual. If we put ourselves in order, perhaps we will do the same for the world. Of course, what else would a psychologist think?

The next set were associated with proper response to crisis and exhaustion:

What shall I do when my enemy succeeds? Aim a little higher and be grateful for the lesson. Back to Matthew: "Ye have heard that it hath been said, Thou shalt love thy neighbour, and hate thine enemy. But I say unto you, Love your enemies, bless them that curse you, do good to them that hate you, and pray for them which despitefully use you, and persecute you; That ye may be the children of your Father which is in heaven" (5:43-5:45). What does this mean? Learn, from the success of your enemies; listen (Rule 9) to their critique, so that you can glean from their opposition whatever fragments of wisdom you might incorporate, to your betterment; adopt as your ambition the creation of a world in which those who work against you see the light and wake up and succeed, so that the better at which you are aiming can encompass them, too.

What shall I do when I'm tired and impatient? Gratefully accept an outstretched helping hand. This is something with a twofold meaning. It's an injunction, first, to note the reality of the limitations of individual being and, second, to accept and be thankful for the support of others—family, friends, acquaintances and strangers alike. Exhaustion and impatience are inevitable. There is too much to be done and too little time in which to do it. But we don't have to strive alone, and there is nothing but good in distributing the responsibilities, cooperating in the efforts, and sharing credit for the productive and meaningful work thereby undertaken.

What shall I do with the fact of aging? Replace the potential of my youth with the accomplishments of my maturity. This hearkens back to the discussion of friendship surrounding Rule 3, and the story of Socrates' trial and death—which might be summarized, as follows: *A life lived thoroughly justifies its own limitations.* The young man with nothing has his possibilities to set against the accomplishments of his elders. It's not clear that it's necessarily a bad deal, for either. "An aged man is but a paltry thing," wrote William Butler Yeats, "A tattered coat upon a stick, unless/Soul clap its hands and sing, and louder sing/For every tatter in its mortal dress. . . ."[220]

What shall I do with my infant's death? Hold my other loved ones and heal their pain. It is necessary to be strong in the face of death, because death is intrinsic to life. It is for this reason that I tell my students: aim to be the person at your father's funeral that everyone, in their grief and misery, can rely on. There's a worthy and noble ambition: strength in the face of adversity. That is very different from the wish for a life free of trouble.

What shall I do in the next dire moment? Focus my attention on the next right move. The flood is coming. The flood is always coming. The apocalypse is always upon us. That's why the story of Noah is archetypal. Things fall apart—we stressed that in the discussion surrounding

Rule 10 (Be precise in your speech)—and the centre cannot hold. When everything has become chaotic and uncertain, all that remains to guide you might be the character you constructed, previously, by aiming up and concentrating on the moment at hand. If you have failed in that, you will fail in the moment of crisis, and then God help you.

That last set contained what I thought were the most difficult of all the questions I asked that night. The death of a child is, perhaps, the worst of catastrophes. Many relationships fail in the aftermath of such a tragedy. But dissolution in the face of such horror is not inevitable, although it is understandable. I have seen people immensely strengthen their remaining family bonds when someone close to them has died. I have seen them turn to those who remained and redouble their efforts to connect with them and support them. Because of that, all regained at least some of what had been so terribly torn away by death. We must therefore commiserate in our grief. We must come together in the face of the tragedy of existence. Our families can be the living room with the fireplace that is cozy and welcoming and warm while the storms of winter rage outside.

The heightened knowledge of fragility and mortality produced by death can terrify, embitter and separate. It can also awaken. It can remind those who grieve not to take the people who love them for granted. Once I did some chilling calculations regarding my parents, who are in their eighties. It was an example of the hated arithmetic we encountered in the discussion of Rule 5 (Do not let your children do anything that makes you dislike them)—and I walked through the equations so that I would stay properly conscious. I see my Mom and Dad about twice a year. We generally spend several weeks together. We talk on the phone in the interim between visits. But the life expectancy of people in their eighties is under ten years. That means I am likely to see my parents, if I am fortunate, fewer than twenty more times. That's a terrible thing to know. But knowing it puts a stop to my taking those opportunities for granted.

The next set of questions—and answers—had to do with the development of character. *What shall I say to a faithless brother? The King of the Damned is a poor judge of Being.* It is my firm belief that the best way to fix the world—a handyman's dream, if ever there was one—is to fix yourself, as we discussed in Rule 6. Anything else is presumptuous. Anything else risks harm, stemming from your ignorance and lack of skill. But that's OK. There's plenty to do, right where you are. After all, your specific personal faults detrimentally affect the world. Your conscious, voluntary sins (because no other word really works) makes things worse than they have to be. Your inaction, inertia and cynicism removes from the world that part of you that could learn to quell suffering and make peace. That's not good. There are endless reasons to despair of the world, and to become angry and resentful and to seek revenge.

Failure to make the proper sacrifices, failure to reveal yourself, failure to live and tell the truth—all that weakens you. In that weakened state, you will be unable to thrive in the world, and you will be of no benefit to yourself or to others. You will fail and suffer, stupidly. That will corrupt your soul. How could it be otherwise? Life is hard enough when it is going well. But when it's going badly? And I have learned through painful experience that nothing is going so badly that it can't be made worse. This is why Hell is a bottomless pit. This is why Hell is associated with that aforementioned sin. In the most awful of cases, the terrible suffering of unfortunate souls becomes attributable, by their own judgment, to mistakes they made knowingly in the past: acts of betrayal, deception, cruelty, carelessness, cowardice and, most commonly of all, willful blindness. To suffer terribly and to know yourself as the cause: that is Hell. And once in Hell it is very easy to curse Being itself. And no wonder. But it's not justifiable. *And that's why the King of the Damned is a poor judge of Being.*

How do you build yourself into someone on whom you can rely, in the best of times and the worst—in peace and in war? How do you build for yourself the kind of character that will not ally itself, in its suffering and misery, with all who dwell in Hell? The questions and answers continued, all pertinent, in one way or another, to the rules I have outlined in this book:

What shall I do to strengthen my spirit? Do not tell lies, or do what you despise.

What shall I do to ennoble my body? Use it only in the service of my soul.

What shall I do with the most difficult of questions? Consider them the gateway to the path of life.

What shall I do with the poor man's plight? Strive through right example to lift his broken heart.

What shall I do when the great crowd beckons? Stand tall and utter my broken truths.

And that was that. I still have my Pen of Light. I haven't written anything with it since. Maybe I will again when the mood strikes and something wells up from deep below. But, even if I don't, it helped me find the words to properly close this book.

I hope that my writing has proved useful to you. I hope it revealed things you knew that you did not know you knew. I hope the ancient wisdom I discussed provides you with strength. I hope it brightened the spark within you. I hope you can straighten up, sort out your family, and bring peace and prosperity to your community. I hope, in accordance with Rule 11 (Do not bother children when they are skateboarding), that you strengthen and encourage those who are committed to your care instead of protecting them to the point of weakness.

I wish you all the best, and hope that you can wish the best for others.

What will you write with your pen of light?

ACKNOWLEDGEMENTS

I LIVED THROUGH A TUMULTUOUS time when I was writing this book, to say the least. I had more than my fair share of reliable, competent, trustworthy people standing with me, however, and thank God for that. I would particularly like to thank my wife, Tammy, my great and good friend for almost fifty years. She has been an absolute pillar of honesty, stability, support, practical help, organization and patience during the years of writing that continued during anything and everything else that has happened in our lives, no matter how pressing or important. My daughter, Mikhaila, and my son, Julian, as well as my parents, Walter and Beverley, were also right there beside me, paying careful attention, discussing complicated issues with me, and aiding me in the organization of my thoughts, words and actions. The same is true of my brother-in-law, Jim Keller, computer chip architect extraordinaire, and my always reliable and adventurous sister, Bonnie. The friendship of Wodek Szemberg and Estera Bekier has proved invaluable to me, in many ways, for many years, as has the behind-the-scenes and subtle support of Professor William Cunningham. Dr. Norman Doidge went beyond the call of duty writing and revising the foreword to this book, which took far more effort than I had originally estimated, and the friendship and warmth he and his wife, Karen, continually provide has been very much appreciated by my entire family. It was a pleasure to collaborate with Craig Pyette, my editor at Random House Canada. Craig's careful attention to detail and ability to diplomatically rein in excess bursts of passion (and sometimes irritation) in my many drafts made for a much more measured and balanced book.

Gregg Hurwitz, novelist, screen-writer and friend, used many of my rules for life in his bestseller *Orphan X*, well before my book was written, which was a great compliment and indicator of their potential value and public appeal. Gregg also volunteered as a dedicated, thorough, viciously incisive and comically cynical editor and commentator while I was writing and editing. He helped me cut unnecessary verbiage (some of it at least) and stay on the narrative track. Gregg also recommended Ethan van Sciver, who provided the fine illustrations that begin each chapter, and I would like to acknowledge him for that, as well as tipping my hat to Ethan himself, whose drawings add a necessary touch of lightness, whimsy and warmth to what might otherwise have been a too-dark and dramatic tome.

Finally, I would like to thank Sally Harding, my agent, and the fine people she works with at CookeMcDermid. Without Sally, this book would have never been written.

ENDNOTES

1. Solzhenitsyn, A.I. (1975). *The Gulag Archipelago 1918-1956: An experiment in literary investigation* (Vol. 2). (T.P. Whitney, Trans.). New York: Harper & Row, p. 626.

2. If you want to do some serious thinking about lobsters, this is a good place to start: Corson, T. (2005). *The secret life of lobsters: How fishermen and scientists are unraveling the mysteries of our favorite crustacean*. New York: Harper Perennial.

3. Schjelderup-Ebbe, & T. (1935). *Social behavior of birds*. Clark University Press. Retrieved from http://psycnet.apa.org/psycinfo/1935-19907-007; see also Price, J. S., & Sloman, L. (1987). "Depression as yielding behavior: An animal model based on Schjelderup-Ebbe's pecking order." *Ethology and Sociobiology*, 8, 85–98.

4. Sapolsky, R. M. (2004). "Social status and health in humans and other animals." *Annual Review of Anthropology, 33*, 393–418.

5. Rutishauser, R. L., Basu, A. C., Cromarty, S. I., & Kravitz, E. A. (2004). "Long-term consequences of agonistic interactions between socially naive juvenile American lobsters (Homarus americanus)." *The Biological Bulletin, 207*, 183–7.

6. Kravitz, E.A. (2000). "Serotonin and aggression: Insights gained from a lobster model system and speculations on the role of amine neurons in a complex behavior." *Journal of Comparative Physiology, 186*, 221-238.

7. Huber, R., & Kravitz, E. A. (1995). "A quantitative analysis of agonistic behavior in juvenile American lobsters (*Homarus americanus L.*)". *Brain, Behavior and Evolution, 46*, 72–83.

8. Yeh S-R, Fricke RA, Edwards DH (1996) "The effect of social experience on serotonergic modulation of the escape circuit of crayfish." *Science, 271,* 366–369.

9. Huber, R., Smith, K., Delago, A., Isaksson, K., & Kravitz, E. A. (1997). "Serotonin and aggressive motivation in crustaceans: Altering the decision to retreat." *Proceedings of the National Academy of Sciences of the United States of America, 94,* 5939–42.

10. Antonsen, B. L., & Paul, D. H. (1997). "Serotonin and octopamine elicit stereotypical agonistic behaviors in the squat lobster *Munida quadrispina (Anomura, Galatheidae)*." *Journal of Comparative Physiology A: Sensory, Neural, and Behavioral Physiology, 181,* 501–510.

11. Credit Suisse (2015, Oct). *Global Wealth Report 2015,* p. 11. Retrieved from https://publications.credit-suisse.com/tasks/render/file/?fileID=F2425415-DCA7-80B8-EAD989AF9341D47E

12. Fenner, T., Levene, M., & Loizou, G. (2010). "Predicting the long tail of book sales: Unearthing the power-law exponent." *Physica A: Statistical Mechanics and Its Applications, 389,* 2416–2421.

13. de Solla Price, D. J. (1963). *Little science, big science.* New York: Columbia University Press.

14. As theorized by Wolff, J.O. & Peterson, J.A. (1998). "An offspring-defense hypothesis for territoriality in female mammals." *Ethology, Ecology & Evolution, 10,* 227-239; Generalized to crustaceans by Figler, M.H., Blank, G.S. & Peek, H.V.S (2001). "Maternal territoriality as an offspring defense strategy in red swamp crayfish (*Procambarus clarkii, Girard*)." *Aggressive Behavior, 27,* 391-403.

15. Waal, F. B. M. de (2007). *Chimpanzee politics: Power and sex among apes.* Baltimore, MD: Johns Hopkins University Press; Waal, F. B. M. de (1996). *Good natured: The origins of right and wrong in humans and other animals.* Cambridge, MA: Harvard University Press.

16. Bracken-Grissom, H. D., Ahyong, S. T., Wilkinson, R. D., Feldmann, R. M., Schweitzer, C. E., Breinholt, J. W., Crandall, K. A. (2014). "The emergence of lobsters: Phylogenetic relationships, morphological evolution and divergence time comparisons of an ancient group." *Systematic Biology, 63,* 457–479.

17. A brief summary: Ziomkiewicz-Wichary, A. (2016). "Serotonin and dominance." In T.K. Shackelford & V.A. Weekes-Shackelford (Eds.). *Encyclopedia of evolutionary psychological science,* DOI 10.1007/978-3-319-16999-6_1440-1. Retrieved from https://www.researchgate.net/publication/310586509_Serotonin_and_Dominance

18. Janicke, T., Häderer, I. K., Lajeunesse, M. J., & Anthes, N. (2016). "Darwinian

sex roles confirmed across the animal kingdom." *Science Advances, 2,* e1500983. Retrieved from http://advances.sciencemag.org/content/2/2/e1500983

19. Steenland, K., Hu, S., & Walker, J. (2004). "All-cause and cause-specific mortality by socioeconomic status among employed persons in 27 US states, 1984–1997." *American Journal of Public Health, 94,* 1037–1042.

20. Crockett, M. J., Clark, L., Tabibnia, G., Lieberman, M. D., & Robbins, T. W. (2008). "Serotonin modulates behavioral reactions to unfairness." *Science, 320,* 1739.

21. McEwen, B. (2000). "Allostasis and allostatic load implications for neuropsychopharmacology." *Neuropsychopharmacology, 22,* 108–124.

22. Salzer, H. M. (1966). "Relative hypoglycemia as a cause of neuropsychiatric illness." *Journal of the National Medical Association, 58,* 12–17.

23. Peterson J.B., Pihl, R.O., Gianoulakis, C., Conrod, P., Finn, P.R., Stewart, S.H., LeMarquand, D.G. Bruce, K.R. (1996). "Ethanol-induced change in cardiac and endogenous opiate function and risk for alcoholism." *Alcoholism: Clinical & Experimental Research, 20,* 1542-1552.

24. Pynoos, R. S., Steinberg, A. M., & Piacentini, J. C. (1999). "A developmental psychopathology model of childhood traumatic stress and intersection with anxiety disorders." *Biological Psychiatry, 46,* 1542–1554.

25. Olweus, D. (1993). *Bullying at school: What we know and what we can do.* New York: Wiley-Blackwell.

26. Ibid.

27. Janoff-Bulman, R. (1992). *Shattered assumptions: Towards a new psychology of trauma.* New York: The Free Press.

28. Weisfeld, G. E., & Beresford, J. M. (1982). "Erectness of posture as an indicator of dominance or success in humans." *Motivation and Emotion, 6,* 113–131.

29. Kleinke, C. L., Peterson, T. R., & Rutledge, T. R. (1998). "Effects of self-generated facial expressions on mood." *Journal of Personality and Social Psychology, 74,* 272–279.

30. Tamblyn, R., Tewodros, E., Huang, A., Winslade, N. & Doran, P. (2014). "The incidence and determinants of primary nonadherence with prescribed medication in primary care: a cohort study." *Annals of Internal Medicine, 160,* 441-450.

31. I outlined this in some detail in Peterson, J.B. (1999). *Maps of meaning: The architecture of belief.* New York: Routledge.

32. Van Strien, J.W., Franken, I.H.A. & Huijding, J. (2014). "Testing the snake-detection hypothesis: Larger early posterior negativity in humans to

pictures of snakes than to pictures of other reptiles, spiders and slugs." *Frontiers in Human Neuroscience, 8,* 691-697. For a more general discussion, see Ledoux, J. (1998). *The emotional brain: The mysterious underpinnings of emotional life.* New York: Simon & Schuster.

33. For the classic treatise on this issue see Gibson, J.J. (1986). *An ecological approach to visual perception.* New York: Psychology Press. See also Floel, A., Ellger, T., Breitenstein, C. & Knecht, S. (2003). "Language perception activates the hand motor cortex: implications for motor theories of speech perception." *European Journal of Neuroscience, 18,* 704-708, for a discussion of the relationship between speech and action. For a more general review of the relationship between action and perception, see Pulvermüller, F., Moseley, R.L., Egorova, N., Shebani, Z. & Boulenger, V. (2014). "Motor cognition–motor semantics: Action perception theory of cognition and communication." *Neuropsychologia, 55,* 71-84.

34. Flöel, A., Ellger, T., Breitenstein, C. & Knecht, S. (2003). "Language perception activates the hand motor cortex: Implications for motor theories of speech perception." *European Journal of Neuroscience, 18,* 704-708; Fadiga, L., Craighero, L. & Olivier, E (2005). "Human motor cortex excitability during the perception of others' action." *Current Opinions in Neurobiology, 15,* 213-218; Palmer, C.E., Bunday, K.L., Davare, M. & Kilner, J.M. (2016). "A causal role for primary motor cortex in perception of observed actions." *Journal of Cognitive Neuroscience, 28,* 2021-2029.

35. Barrett, J.L. (2004). *Why would anyone believe in God?* Lanham, MD: Altamira Press.

36. For a decent review, see Barrett, J.L. & Johnson, A.H. (2003). "The role of control in attributing intentional agency to inanimate objects." *Journal of Cognition and Culture, 3,* 208-217.

37. I would also most highly recommend, in this regard, this book by C.G. Jung's most outstanding student/colleague, Neumann, E. (1955). *The Great Mother: An analysis of the archetype.* Princeton, NJ: Princeton University Press.

38. https://www.dol.gov/wb/stats/occ_gender_share_em_1020_txt.htm

39. Muller, M.N., Kalhenberg, S.M., Thompson, M.E. & Wrangham, R.W. (2007). "Male coercion and the costs of promiscuous mating for female chimpanzees." *Proceedings of the Royal Society (B), 274,* 1009-1014.

40. For a host of interesting statistics derived from the analysis of his dating site, OkCupid, see Rudder, C. (2015). *Dataclysm: Love, sex, race & identity.* New York: Broadway Books. It is also the case on such sites that a tiny minority of individuals get the vast majority of interested inquiries (another example of the Pareto distribution).

41. Wilder, J.A., Mobasher, Z. & Hammer, M.F. (2004). "Genetic evidence for

unequal effective population sizes of human females and males." *Molecular Biology and Evolution, 21,* 2047-2057.

42. Miller, G. (2001). *The mating mind: How sexual choice shaped the evolution of human nature.* New York: Anchor.

43. Pettis, J. B. (2010). "Androgyny BT." In D. A. Leeming, K. Madden, & S. Marlan (Eds.). *Encyclopedia of psychology and religion* (pp. 35-36). Boston, MA: Springer US.

44. Goldberg, E. (2003). *The executive brain: Frontal lobes and the civilized mind.* New York: Oxford University Press.

45. For the classic works, see Campbell, D.T. & Fiske, D.W. (1959). "Convergent and discriminant validation by the multitrait-multimethod matrix." *Psychological Bulletin, 56,* 81-105. A similar idea was developed in Wilson, E.O. (1998). *Consilience: The unity of knowledge.* New York: Knopf. It's also why we have five senses, so we can "pentangulate" our way through the world, with qualitatively separate modes of perception operating and cross-checking simultaneously.

46. Headland, T. N., & Greene, H. W. (2011). "Hunter-gatherers and other primates as prey, predators, and competitors of snakes." *Proceedings of the National Academy of Sciences USA, 108,* 1470–1474.

47. Keeley, L. H. (1996). *War before civilization: The myth of the peaceful savage.* New York: Oxford University Press.

48. "Gradually it was disclosed to me that the line separating good and evil passes not through states, nor between classes, nor between political parties either—but right through every human heart—and through all human hearts. This line shifts. Inside us, it oscillates with the years. And even within hearts overwhelmed by evil, one small bridgehead of good is retained. And even in the best of all hearts, there remains . . . an unuprooted small corner of evil. Since then I have come to understand the truth of all the religions of the world: They struggle with the evil inside a human being (inside every human being). It is impossible to expel evil from the world in its entirety, but it is possible to constrict it within each person." Solzhenitsyn, A.I. (1975). *The Gulag Archipelago 1918-1956: An experiment in literary investigation* (Vol. 2). (T.P. Whitney, Trans.). New York: Harper & Row, p. 615.

49. The best exploration of this I have ever encountered is to be found in the brilliant documentary about the underground cartoonist Robert Crumb, entitled *Crumb,* directed by Terry Zwigoff (1995), released by Sony Pictures Classic. This documentary will tell you more than you want to know about resentment, deceit, arrogance, hatred for mankind, sexual shame, the devouring mother and the tyrannical father.

50. Bill, V.T. (1986). *Chekhov: The silent voice of freedom.* Allied Books, Ltd.

51. Costa, P.T., Teracciano, A. & McCrae, R.R. (2001). "Gender differences in personality traits across cultures: robust and surprising findings." *Journal of Personality and Social Psychology, 81,* 322-331.

52. Isbell, L. (2011). *The fruit, the tree and the serpent: Why we see so well.* Cambridge, MA: Harvard University Press; see also Hayakawa, S., Kawai, N., Masataka, N., Luebker, A., Tomaiuolo, F., & Caramazza, A. (2011). "The influence of color on snake detection in visual search in human children." *Scientific Reports, 1,* 1-4.

53. Virgin and Child (c. 1480) by Geertgen tot Sint Jans (c. 1465- c. 1495) provides an outstanding example of this, with Mary, the Christ Child and the serpent additionally superimposed on a background of medieval musical instruments (and the infant Christ playing the role of conductor).

54. Osorio, D., Smith, A.C., Vorobyev, M. & Buchanan-Smieth, H.M. (2004). "Detection of fruit and the selection of primate visual pigments for color vision." *The American Naturalist, 164,* 696-708.

55. Macrae, N. (1992). *John von Neumann : The scientific genius who pioneered the modern computer, game theory, nuclear deterrence, and much more.* New York: Pantheon Books.

56. Wittman, A. B., & Wall, L. L. (2007). "The evolutionary origins of obstructed labor: bipedalism, encephalization, and the human obstetric dilemma." *Obstetrical & Gynecological Survey, 62,* 739–748.

57. Other explanations exist: Dunsworth, H. M., Warrener, A. G., Deacon, T., Ellison, P. T., & Pontzer, H. (2012). "Metabolic hypothesis for human altriciality." *Proceedings of the National Academy of Sciences of the United States of America, 109,* 15212–15216.

58. Heidel, A. (1963). *The Babylonian Genesis: The story of the creation.* Chicago: University of Chicago Press.

59. Salisbury, J. E. (1997). *Perpetua's passion: The death and memory of a young Roman woman.* New York: Routledge.

60. Pinker, S. (2011). *The better angels of our nature: Why violence has declined.* New York: Viking Books.

61. Nietzsche, F.W. & Kaufmann, W.A. (1982). *The portable Nietzsche.* New York: Penguin Classics (Maxims and Arrows 12).

62. Peterson, J.B. (1999). *Maps of meaning: The architecture of belief.* New York: Routledge, p. 264.

63. Miller, G. (2016, November 3). Could pot help solve the U.S. opioid epidemic? *Science.* Retrieved from http://www.sciencemag.org/news/2016/11/could-pot-help-solve-us-opioid-epidemic

64. Barrick, M. R., Stewart, G. L., Neubert, M. J., and Mount, M. K. (1998).

"Relating member ability and personality to work-team processes and team effectiveness." *Journal of Applied Psychology, 83,* 377-391; for a similar effect with children, see Dishion, T. J., McCord, J., & Poulin, F. (1999). "When interventions harm: Peer groups and problem behavior." *American Psychologist, 54,* 755-764.

65. McCord, J. & McCord, W. (1959). "A follow-up report on the Cambridge-Somerville youth study." *Annals of the American Academy of Political and Social Science, 32,* 89-96.

66. See https://www.youtube.com/watch?v=jQvvmT3ab8o (from *MoneyBART:* Episode 3, Season 23 of *The Simpsons*).

67. Rogers outlined six conditions for constructive personality change to occur. The second of these was the client's "state of incongruence," which is, roughly speaking, knowledge that something is wrong and has to change. See Rogers, C. R. (1957). "The necessary and sufficient conditions of therapeutic personality change." *Journal of Consulting Psychology, 21,* 95-103.

68. Poffenberger, A.T. (1930). "The development of men of science." *Journal of Social Psychology, 1,* 31-47.

69. Taylor, S.E. & Brown, J. (1988). "Illusion and well-being: A social psychological perspective on mental health." *Psychological Bulletin, 103,* 193-210.

70. The word *sin* is derived from the Greek ἁμαρτάνειν (*hamartánein*), which means to *miss the mark.* Connotations: error of judgment; fatal flaw. See http://biblehub.com/greek/264.htm

71. See Gibson, J. J. (1979). *The ecological approach to visual perception.* Boston: Houghton Mifflin.

72. Simons, D. J., & Chabris, C. F. (1999). "Gorillas in our midst: Sustained inattentional blindness for dynamic events." *Perception, 28,* 1059-1074.

73. http://www.dansimons.com/videos.html

74. Azzopardi, P. & Cowey, A. (1993). "Preferential representation of the fovea in the primary visual cortex." *Nature, 361,* 719-721.

75. see http://www.earlychristianwritings.com/thomas/gospelthomas113.html

76. Nietzsche, F. (2003). *Beyond good and evil.* Fairfield, IN: 1st World Library/Literary Society, p. 67.

77. http://www.nytimes.com/2010/02/21/nyregion/21yitta.html

78. Balaresque, P., Poulet, N., Cussat-Blanc, S., Gerard, P., Quintana-Murci, L., Heyer, E., & Jobling, M. A. (2015). "Y-chromosome descent clusters and male differential reproductive success: young lineage expansions dominate Asian pastoral nomadic populations." *European Journal of Human Genetics, 23,* 1413-1422.

79. Moore, L. T., McEvoy, B., Cape, E., Simms, K., & Bradley, D. G. (2006). "A Y-chromosome signature of hegemony in Gaelic Ireland." *American Journal of Human Genetics, 78,* 334–338.

80. Zerjal, T., Xue, Y., Bertorelle, G., Wells et al. (2003). "The genetic legacy of the Mongols." *American Journal of Human Genetics, 72,* 717–21.

81. Jones, E. (1953). *The life and work of Sigmund Freud* (Vol. I). New York: Basic Books. p. 5.

82. A decent brief summary of such ideas is provided here: https://www.britannica.com/art/noble-savage

83. Well reviewed in Roberts, B. W., & Mroczek, D. (2008). "Personality trait change in adulthood." *Current Directions in Psychological Science, 17,* 31–35.

84. For a thorough, empirically-grounded and reliable discussion of such matters, see Olweus, D. (1993). *Bullying at school: What we know and what we can do.* Malden, MA: Blackwell Publishing.

85. Goodall, J. (1990). *Through a window: My thirty years with the chimpanzees of Gombe.* Boston: Houghton Mifflin Harcourt.

86. Finch, G. (1943). "The bodily strength of chimpanzees." *Journal of Mammalogy, 24,* 224-228.

87. Goodall, J. (1972). *In the shadow of man.* New York: Dell.

88. Wilson, M.L. et al. (2014). "Lethal aggression in Pan is better explained by adaptive strategies than human impacts." *Nature, 513,* 414-417.

89. Goodall, J. (1990). *Through a window: My thirty years with the chimpanzees of Gombe.* Houghton Mifflin Harcourt, pp. 128–129.

90. Chang, I. (1990). *The rape of Nanking.* New York: Basic Books.

91. United Nations Office on Drugs and Crime (2013). *Global study on homicide.* Retrieved from https://www.unodc.org/documents/gsh/pdfs/2014_GLOBAL_HOMICIDE_BOOK_web.pdf

92. Thomas, E.M. (1959). *The harmless people.* New York: Knopf.

93. Roser, M. (2016). *Ethnographic and archaeological evidence on violent deaths.* Retrieved from https://ourworldindata.org/ethnographic-and-archaeological-evidence-on-violent-deaths/

94. Ibid; also Brown, A. (2000). *The Darwin wars: The scientific battle for the soul of man.* New York: Pocket Books.

95. Keeley, L.H. (1997). *War before civilization: The myth of the peaceful savage.* Oxford University Press, USA.

96. Carson, S.H., Peterson, J.B. & Higgins, D.M. (2005). "Reliability, validity and factor structure of the Creative Achievement Questionnaire." *Creativity Research Journal, 17,* 37-50.

97. Stokes, P.D. (2005). *Creativity from constraints: The psychology of breakthrough.* New York: Springer.

98. Wrangham, R. W., & Peterson, D. (1996). *Demonic males: Apes and the origins of human violence.* New York: Houghton Mifflin.

99. Peterson, J.B. & Flanders, J. (2005). Play and the regulation of aggression. In Tremblay, R.E., Hartup, W.H. & Archer, J. (Eds.). *Developmental origins of aggression.* (pp. 133-157). New York: Guilford Press; Nagin, D., & Tremblay, R. E. (1999). "Trajectories of boys' physical aggression, opposition, and hyperactivity on the path to physically violent and non-violent juvenile delinquency." *Child Development, 70,* 1181-1196.

100. Sullivan, M.W. (2003). "Emotional expression of young infants and children." *Infants and Young Children, 16,* 120-142.

101. See BF Skinner Foundation: https://www.youtube.com/watch?v=vGazyH6fQQ4

102. Glines, C.B. (2005). "Top secret World War II bat and bird bomber program." *Aviation History, 15,* 38-44.

103. Flasher, J. (1978). "Adultism." *Adolescence, 13,* 517-523; Fletcher, A. (2013). *Ending discrimination against young people.* Olympia, WA: CommonAction Publishing.

104. de Waal, F. (1998). *Chimpanzee politics: Power and sex among apes.* Baltimore: Johns Hopkins University Press.

105. Panksepp, J. (1998). *Affective neuroscience: The foundations of human and animal emotions.* New York: Oxford University Press.

106. Tremblay, R. E., Nagin, D. S., Séguin, J. R., Zoccolillo, M., Zelazo, P. D., Boivin, M., . . . Japel, C. (2004). "Physical aggression during early childhood: trajectories and predictors." *Pediatrics, 114,* 43-50.

107. Krein, S. F., & Beller, A. H. (1988). "Educational attainment of children from single-parent families: Differences by exposure, gender, and race." *Demography, 25,* 221; McLoyd, V. C. (1998). "Socioeconomic disadvantage and child development." *The American Psychologist, 53,* 185-204; Lin, Y.-C., & Seo, D.-C. (2017). "Cumulative family risks across income levels predict deterioration of children's general health during childhood and adolescence." *PLOS ONE, 12(5),* e0177531. https://doi.org/10.1371/journal.pone.0177531; Amato, P. R., & Keith, B. (1991). "Parental divorce and the well-being of children: A meta-analysis." *Psychological Bulletin, 110,* 26-46.

108. Eric Harris's diary: http://melikamp.com/features/eric.shtml

109. Goethe, J.W. (1979). *Faust, part one* (P. Wayne, Trans.). London: Penguin Books. p. 75.

110. Goethe, J.W. (1979). *Faust, part two* (P. Wayne, Trans.). London: Penguin Books. p. 270.

111. Tolstoy, L. (1887-1983). *Confessions* (D. Patterson, Trans.). New York: W.W. Norton, pp. 57-58.

112. The Guardian (2016, June 14). *1000 mass shootings in 1260 days: this is what America's gun crisis looks like.* Retrieved from https://www.theguardian.com/us-news/ng-interactive/2015/oct/02/mass-shootings-america-gun-violence

113. The words of Eric Harris: https://schoolshooters.info/sites/default/files/harris_journal_1.3.pdf

114. Cited in Kaufmann, W. (1975). *Existentialism from Dostoevsky to Sartre.* New York: Meridian, pp. 130-131.

115. See Solzhenitsyn, A.I. (1975). *The Gulag Archipelago 1918-1956: An experiment in literary investigation* (Vol. 2). (T.P. Whitney, Trans.). New York: Harper & Row.

116. Piaget, J. (1932). *The moral judgement of the child.* London: Kegan Paul, Trench, Trubner and Company; see also Piaget, J. (1962). *Play, dreams and imitation in childhood.* New York: W.W. Norton and Company.

117. Franklin, B. (1916). *Autobiography of Benjamin Franklin.* Rahway, New Jersey: The Quinn & Boden Company Press. Retrieved from https://www.gutenberg.org/files/20203/20203-h/20203-h.htm

118. See Xenophon's Apology of Socrates, section 23, retrieved at http://www.perseus.tufts.edu/hopper/text?doc=Perseus%3Atext%3A1999.01.0212%3Atext%3DApol.%3Asection%3D23

119. Ibid., section 2.

120. Ibid., section 3.

121. Ibid,, section 8.

122. Ibid., section 4.

123. Ibid., section 12.

124. Ibid., section 13.

125. Ibid., section 14.

126. Ibid., section 7.

127. Ibid.

128. Ibid., section 8.

129. Ibid.

130. Ibid., section 33.

131. Goethe, J.W. (1979b). *Faust, part two* (P. Wayne, Trans.). London: Penguin Books. p. 270.

132. There are very useful commentaries on every Biblical verse at http://biblehub.com/commentaries and specifically on this verse at http://biblehub.com/commentaries/genesis/4-7.htm

133. "For whence/ But from the author of all ill could spring/ So deep a malice, to confound the race/ Of mankind in one root, and Earth with Hell/ To mingle and involve, done all to spite /The great Creator?" Milton, J. (1667). *Paradise Lost*, Book 2, 381–385. Retrieved from https://www.dartmouth.edu/~milton/reading_room/pl/book_2/text.shtml

134. Jung, C.G. (1969). *Aion: Researches into the phenomenology of the self* (Vol. 9: Part II, Collected Works of C. G. Jung): Princeton, N.J.: Princeton University Press. (chapter 5).

135. http://www.acolumbinesite.com/dylan/writing.php

136. Schapiro, J.A., Glynn, S.M., Foy, D.W. & Yavorsky, M.A. (2002). "Participation in war-zone atrocities and trait dissociation among Vietnam veterans with combat-related PTSD." *Journal of Trauma and Dissociation, 3,* 107-114; Yehuda, R., Southwick, S.M. & Giller, E.L. (1992). "Exposure to atrocities and severity of chronic PTSD in Vietnam combat veterans." *American Journal of Psychiatry, 149,* 333-336.

137. See Harpur, T. (2004). *The pagan Christ: recovering the lost light.* Thomas Allen Publishers. There is also a discussion of this in Peterson, J.B. (1999). *Maps of meaning: The architecture of belief.* New York: Routledge.

138. Lao-Tse (1984). *The tao te ching.* (1984) (S. Rosenthal, Trans.). Verse 64: Staying with the mystery. Retrieved from https://terebess.hu/english/tao/rosenthal.html#Kap64.

139. Jung, C.G. (1969). *Aion: Researches into the phenomenology of the self* (Vol. 9: Part II, Collected Works of C. G. Jung): Princeton, N.J.: Princeton University Press.

140. Dobbs, B.J.T. (2008). *The foundations of Newton's alchemy.* New York: Cambridge University Press.

141. Ephesians 2:8–2:9 reads, for example (in the King James Version): For by grace are ye saved through faith; and that not of yourselves: it is the gift of God: Not of works, lest any man should boast. A similar sentiment is echoed in Romans 9:15–9:16: I will have mercy on whom I will have mercy, and I will have compassion on whom I will have compassion. So then it is not of him that willeth, nor of him that runneth, but of God that sheweth mercy.

The New International Version restates 9:16 this way: It does not, there-fore, depend on human desire or effort, but on God's mercy.

142. Nietzsche, F.W. & Kaufmann, W.A. (1982). *The portable Nietzsche*. New York: Penguin Classics. Contains, among others, Nietzsche's *Twilight of the idols and the anti-Christ: or how to philosophize with a hammer.*

143. Nietzsche, F. (1974). *The gay science* (Kaufmann, W., Trans.). New York: Vintage, pp. 181-182.

144. Nietzsche, F. (1968). *The will to power* (Kaufmann, W., Trans.). New York: Vintage, p. 343.

145. Dostoevsky, F.M. (2009). *The grand inquisitor*. Merchant Books.

146. Nietzsche, F. (1954). Beyond good and evil (Zimmern, H., Trans.). In W.H. Wright (Ed.), *The Philosophy of Nietzsche* (pp. 369-616). New York: Modern Library, p. 477.

147. "Let our conjectures, our theories, die in our stead! We may still learn to kill our theories instead of killing each other. . . . [It] is perhaps more than a uto-pian dream that one day may see the victory of the attitude (it is the rational or the scientific attitude) of eliminating our theories, our opinions, by rational criticism, instead of eliminating each other." From Popper, K. (1977). "Natural selection and the emergence of mind." Lecture delivered at Darwin College, Cambridge, UK. See http://www.informationphilosopher.com/solutions/philosophers/popper/natural_selection_and_the_emergence_of_mind.html

148. This is detailed in the introduction to Peterson, J.B. (1999). *Maps of meaning: the architecture of belief*. New York: Routledge.

149. Adler, A. (1973). "Life-lie and responsibility in neurosis and psychosis: a contribution to melancholia." In P. Radin (Trans.). *The practice and theory of Individual Psychology*. Totawa, N.J.: Littlefield, Adams & Company.

150. Milton, J. (1667). *Paradise Lost*. Book 1: 40-48. Retrieved from https://www.dartmouth.edu/~milton/reading_room/pl/book_1/text.shtml

151. Milton, J. (1667). *Paradise Lost*. Book 1: 249-253. Retrieved from https://www.dartmouth.edu/~milton/reading_room/pl/book_1/text.shtml

152. Milton, J. (1667). *Paradise Lost*. Book 1: 254-255. Retrieved from https://www.dartmouth.edu/~milton/reading_room/pl/book_1/text.shtml

153. Milton, J. (1667). *Paradise Lost*. Book 1: 261-263.Retrieved from https://www.dartmouth.edu/~milton/reading_room/pl/book_1/text.shtml

154. This is detailed in Peterson, J.B. (1999). *Maps of meaning: The architecture of belief*. New York: Routledge.

155. Hitler, A. (1925/2017). *Mein kampf* (M. Roberto, Trans.). Independently Published, pp. 172-173.

156. Finkelhor, D., Hotaling, G., Lewis, I.A. & Smith, C. (1990). "Sexual abuse in a national survey of adult men and women: prevalence, characteristics, and risk factors." *Child Abuse & Neglect, 14,* 19-28.

157. Rind, B., Tromovitch, P. & Bauserman, R. (1998). "A meta-analytic examination of assumed properties of child sexual abuse using college samples." *Psychological Bulletin, 124,* 22-53.

158. Loftus, E.F. (1997). "Creating false memories." *Scientific American, 277,* 70-75.

159. Taken from Rogers, C. R. (1952). "Communication: its blocking and its facilitation." *ETC: A Review of General Semantics, 9,* 83-88.

160. See Gibson, J.J. (1986). *An ecological approach to visual perception,* New York: Psychology Press, for the classic treatise on this issue. See also Floel, A., Ellger, T., Breitenstein, C. & Knecht, S. (2003). "Language perception activates the hand motor cortex: implications for motor theories of speech perception." *European Journal of Neuroscience, 18,* 704-708 for a discussion of the relationship between speech and action. For a more general review of the relationship between action and perception, see Pulvermüller, F., Moseley, R.L., Egorova, N., Shebani, Z. & Boulenger, V. (2014). "Motor cognition–motor semantics: Action perception theory of cognition and communication." *Neuropsychologia, 55,* 71-84.

161. Cardinali, L., Frassinetti, F., Brozzoli, C., Urquizar, C., Roy, A.C. & Farnè, A. (2009). "Tool-use induces morphological updating of the body schema." *Current Biology, 12,* 478-479.

162. Bernhardt, P.C., Dabbs, J.M. Jr., Fielden, J.A. & Lutter, C.D. (1998). "Testosterone changes during vicarious experiences of winning and losing among fans at sporting events." *Physiology & Behavior, 65,* 59-62.

163. Some, but not all of this, is detailed in Gray, J. & McNaughton, N. (2003). *The neuropsychology of anxiety: An enquiry into the functions of the septal-hippocampal system.* Oxford: Oxford University Press. See also Peterson, J.B. (2013). "Three forms of meaning and the management of complexity." In T. Proulx, K.D. Markman & M.J. Lindberg (Eds.). *The psychology of meaning* (pp. 17-48). Washington, D.C.: American Psychological Association; Peterson, J.B. & Flanders, J.L. (2002). "Complexity management theory: Motivation for ideological rigidity and social conflict." *Cortex, 38,* 429-458.

164. Yeats, W.B. (1933) The Second Coming. In R.J. Finneran (Ed.). *The poems of W.B. Yeats: A new edition.* New York: MacMillan, p. 158.

165. As reviewed in Vrolix, K. (2006). "Behavioral adaptation, risk compensation, risk homeostasis and moral hazard in traffic safety." *Steunpunt Verkeersveiligheid,* RA-2006-95. Retrieved from https://doclib.uhasselt.be/dspace/bitstream/1942/4002/1/behavioraladaptation.pdf

166. Nietzsche, F.W. & Kaufmann, W.A. (1982). *The portable Nietzsche*. New York: Penguin Classics, pp. 211-212.

167. Orwell, G. (1958). *The road to Wigan Pier*. New York: Harcourt, pp. 96-97.

168. Carson, R. (1962). *Silent spring*. Boston: Houghton Mifflin.

169. see http://reason.com/archives/2016/12/13/the-most-important-graph-in-the-world

170. http://www.telegraph.co.uk/news/earth/earthnews/9815862/Humans-are-plague-on-Earth-Attenborough.html

171. "The Earth has cancer, and the cancer is man." Mesarović, M.D. & Pestel, E. (1974). *Mankind at the turning point*. New York: Dutton, p. 1. The idea was first proposed (and the quote taken from) Gregg, A. (1955). "A medical aspect of the population problem." *Science, 121*, 681-682, p. 681 and further developed by Hern, W.M. (1993). "Has the human species become a cancer on the planet? A theoretical view of population growth as a sign of pathology." *Current World Leaders, 36*, 1089-1124. From the Club of Rome's King, A. & Schneider, B. (1991). *The first global revolution*. New York: Pantheon Books, p. 75: "The common enemy of humanity is man. In searching for a new enemy to unite us, we came up with the idea that pollution, the threat of global warming, water shortages, famine and the like would fit the bill. All these dangers are caused by human intervention, and it is only through changed attitudes and behavior that they can be overcome. The real enemy then, is humanity itself."

172. Costa, P. T., Terracciano, A., & McCrae, R. R. (2001). "Gender differences in personality traits across cultures: robust and surprising findings." *Journal of Personality and Social Psychology, 81*, 322–31; Weisberg, Y. J., DeYoung, C. G., & Hirsh, J. B. (2011). "Gender differences in personality across the ten aspects of the Big Five." *Frontiers in Psychology, 2*, 178; Schmitt, D. P., Realo, A., Voracek, M., & Allik, J. (2008). "Why can't a man be more like a woman? Sex differences in Big Five personality traits across 55 cultures." *Journal of Personality and Social Psychology, 94*, 168–182.

173. De Bolle, M., De Fruyt, F., McCrae, R. R., et al. (2015). "The emergence of sex differences in personality traits in early adolescence: A cross-sectional, cross-cultural study." *Journal of Personality and Social Psychology, 108*, 171–85.

174. Su, R., Rounds, J., & Armstrong, P. I. (2009). "Men and things, women and people: A meta-analysis of sex differences in interests." *Psychological Bulletin, 135*, 859–884. For a neuro-developmental view of such differences, see Beltz, A. M., Swanson, J. L., & Berenbaum, S. A. (2011). "Gendered occupational interests: prenatal androgen effects on psychological orientation to things versus people." *Hormones and Behavior, 60*, 313–7.

175. Bihagen, E. & Katz-Gerro, T. (2000). "Culture consumption in Sweden: the stability of gender differences." *Poetics, 27,* 327-3409; Costa, P., Terracciano, A. & McCrae, R.R. (2001). "Gender differences in personality traits across cultures: robust and surprising findings." *Journal of Personality and Social Psychology, 8,* 322-331; Schmitt, D., Realo. A., Voracek, M. & Alli, J. (2008). "Why can't a man be more like a woman? Sex differences in Big Five personality traits across 55 cultures." *Journal of Personality and Social Psychology, 94,* 168-182; Lippa, R.A. (2010). "Sex differences in personality traits and gender-related occupational preferences across 53 nations: Testing evolutionary and social-environmental theories." *Archives of Sexual Behavior, 39,* 619-636.

176. Gatto, J. N. (2000). *The underground history of American education: A school teacher's intimate investigation of the problem of modern schooling.* New York: Odysseus Group.

177. See *Why are the majority of university students women?* Statistics Canada: Retrieved from http://www.statcan.gc.ca/pub/81-004-x/2008001/article/ 10561-eng.htm

178. See, for example, Hango. D. (2015). "Gender differences in science, technology, engineering, mathematics and computer science (STEM) programs at university." *Statistics Canada,* 75-006-X: Retrieved from http://www. statcan.gc.ca/access_acces/alternative_alternatif.action?l=eng&loc=/pub/ 75-006-x/2013001/article/11874-eng.pdf

179. I'm not alone in this feeling. See, for example, Hymowitz, K.S. (2012). *Manning up: How the rise of women has turned men into boys.* New York: Basic Books.

180. see http://www.pewresearch.org/fact-tank/2012/04/26/young-men-and-women-differ-on-the-importance-of-a-successful-marriage/

181. see http://www.pewresearch.org/data-trend/society-and-demographics/ marriage/

182. This has been discussed extensively in the mainstream press: see https:// www.thestar.com/life/2011/02/25/women_lawyers_leaving_in_droves. html; http://www.cbc.ca/news/canada/women-criminal-law-1.3476637; http://www.huffingtonpost.ca/andrea-lekushoff/female-lawyers-canada_ b_5000415.html

183. Jaffe, A., Chediak, G., Douglas, E., Tudor, M., Gordon, R.W., Ricca, L. & Robinson, S. (2016) "Retaining and advancing women in national law firms." *Stanford Law and Policy Lab, White Paper*: Retrieved from https:// www-cdn.law.stanford.edu/wp-content/uploads/2016/05/Women-in-Law-White-Paper-FINAL-May-31-2016.pdf

184. Conroy-Beam, D., Buss, D. M., Pham, M. N., & Shackelford, T. K. (2015). "How sexually dimorphic are human mate preferences?" *Personality and*

Social Psychology Bulletin, 41, 1082–1093. For a discussion of how female mate preference changes as a consequence of purely biological (ovulatory) factors, see Gildersleeve, K., Haselton, M. G., & Fales, M. R. (2014). "Do women's mate preferences change across the ovulatory cycle? A meta-analytic review." *Psychological Bulletin, 140,* 1205–1259.

185. see Greenwood, J., Nezih, G., Kocharov, G & Santos, C. (2014)." Marry your like: Assortative mating and income inequality." *IZA discussion paper No. 7895.* Retrieved from http://hdl.handle.net/10419/93282

186. A good review of such dismal matters can be found in Suh, G.W., Fabricious, W.V., Parke, R.D., Cookston, J.T., Braver, S.L. & Saenz, D.S. "Effects of the interparental relationship on adolescents' emotional security and adjustment: The important role of fathers." *Developmental Psychology, 52,* 1666-1678.

187. Hicks, S. R. C. (2011). *Explaining postmodernism: Skepticism and socialism from Rousseau to Foucault.* Santa Barbara, CA: Ockham' Razor Multimedia Publishing. The pdf is available at http://www.stephenhicks.org/wp-content/uploads/2017/10/Hicks-EP-Full.pdf

188. Higgins, D.M., Peterson, J.B. & Pihl, R.O. "Prefrontal cognitive ability, intelligence, Big Five personality, and the prediction of advanced academic and workplace performance." *Journal of Personality and Social Psychology, 93,* 298-319.

189. Carson, S.H., Peterson, J.B. & Higgins, D.M. (2005). "Reliability, validity and factor structure of the Creative Achievement Questionnaire." *Creativity Research Journal, 17,* 37-50.

190. Bouchard, T.J. & McGue, M. (1981). "Familial studies of intelligence: a review." *Science, 212,* 1055-1059; Brody, N. (1992). *Intelligence.* New York: Gulf Professional Publishing; Plomin R. & Petrill S.A. (1997). "Genetics and intelligence. What's new?" *Intelligence, 24,* 41–65.

191. Schiff, M., Duyme, M., Dumaret, A., Stewart, J., Tomkiewicz, S. & Feingold, J. (1978). "Intellectual status of working-class children adopted early into upper-middle-class families." *Science, 200,* 1503–1504; Capron, C. & Duyme, M. (1989). "Assessment of effects of socio-economic status on IQ in a full cross-fostering study." *Nature, 340,* 552–554.

192. Kendler, K.S., Turkheimer, E., Ohlsson, H., Sundquist, J. & Sundquist, K. (2015). "Family environment and the malleability of cognitive ability: a Swedish national home-reared and adopted-away cosibling control study." *Proceedings of the National Academy of Science USA, 112,* 4612-4617.

193. For the OECD's take on this, see *Closing the gender gap: Sweden,* which starts by reviewing stats indicating that girls have an edge over boys with regards to education and that women are massively over-represented in

health care and then proceeds to decry the still extant advantage of men in computer science. Retrieved from https://www.oecd.org/sweden/Closing%20 the%20Gender%20Gap%20-%20Sweden%20FINAL.pdf

194. Eron, L. D. (1980). "Prescription for reduction of aggression." *The American Psychologist, 35*, 244–252 (p. 251).

195. Reviewed in Peterson, J.B. & Shane, M. (2004). "The functional neuro-anatomy and psychopharmacology of predatory and defensive aggression." In J. McCord (Ed.). *Beyond empiricism: Institutions and intentions in the study of crime.* (Advances in Criminological Theory, Vol. 13) (pp. 107-146). Piscataway, NJ: Transaction Books; see also Peterson, J.B. & Flanders, J. (2005). "Play and the regulation of aggression." In Tremblay, R.E., Hartup, W.H. & Archer, J. (Eds.). *Developmental origins of aggression.* (Chapter 12; pp. 133-157). New York: Guilford Press.

196. As reviewed in Tremblay, R. E., Nagin, D. S., Séguin, J. R., et al. (2004). "Physical aggression during early childhood: trajectories and predictors." *Pediatrics, 114*, 43-50.

197. Heimberg, R. G., Montgomery, D., Madsen, C. H., & Heimberg, J. S. (1977). "Assertion training: A review of the literature." *Behavior Therapy, 8*, 953–971; Boisvert, J.-M., Beaudry, M., & Bittar, J. (1985). "Assertiveness training and human communication processes." *Journal of Contemporary Psychotherapy, 15*, 58–73.

198. Trull, T. J., & Widiger, T. A. (2013). "Dimensional models of personality: The five-factor model and the DSM-5." *Dialogues in Clinical Neuroscience, 15*, 135–46; Vickers, K.E., Peterson, J.B., Hornig, C.D., Pihl, R.O., Séguin, J. & Tremblay, R.E. (1996). "Fighting as a function of personality and neuropsychological measures." *Annals of the New York Academy of Sciences. 794*, 411-412.

199. Bachofen, J.J. (1861). *Das Mutterrecht: Eine untersuchung über die gynaikokratie der alten welt nach ihrer religiösen und rechtlichen natur.* Stuttgart: Verlag von Krais und Hoffmann.

200. Gimbutas, M. (1991). *The civilization of the goddess.* San Francisco: Harper.

201. Stone, M. (1978). *When God was a woman.* New York: Harcourt Brace Jovanovich.

202. Eller, C. (2000). *The myth of matriarchal prehistory: Why an invented past won't give women a future.* Beacon Press.

203. Neumann, E. (1954). *The origins and history of consciousness.* Princeton, NJ: Princeton University Press.

204. Neumann, E. (1955). *The Great Mother: An analysis of the archetype.* New York: Routledge & Kegan Paul.

205. See, for example, Adler, A. (2002). Theoretical part I-III: The accentuated fiction as guiding idea in the neurosis. In H.T. Stein (Ed.). *The collected works of Alfred Adler volume 1: The neurotic character: Fundamentals of individual psychology and psychotherary (pp. 41-85).* Bellingham, WA: Alfred Adler Institute of Northern Washington, p. 71.

206. Moffitt, T.E., Caspi, A., Rutter, M. & Silva, P.A. (2001). *Sex differences in antisocial behavior: Conduct disorder, delinquency, and violence in the Dunedin Longitudinal Study.* London: Cambridge University Press.

207. Buunk, B.P., Dijkstra, P., Fetchenhauer, D. & Kenrick, D.T. (2002). "Age and gender differences in mate selection criteria for various involvement levels." *Personal Relationships, 9,* 271-278.

208. Lorenz, K. (1943). "Die angeborenen Formen moeglicher Erfahrung." *Ethology, 5,* 235-409.

209. Tajfel, H. (1970). "Experiments in intergroup discrimination." *Nature, 223,* 96-102.

210. Taken from Dostoevsky, F. (1995). *The brothers Karamazov* (dramatized by David Fishelson). Dramatists Play Service, Inc., pp. 54-55. Retrieved from http://bit.ly/2ifSkMn

211. And it's not the ability to microwave a burrito so hot that even He Himself could not eat it (as Homer asks, in *Weekend at Burnsie's* [episode 16, season 13, *The Simpsons*]).

212. Lao-Tse (1984). *The tao te ching.* (1984) (S. Rosenthal, Trans.). Verse 11: The Utility of Non-Existence. Retrieved from https://terebess.hu/english/tao/rosenthal.html#Kap11

213. Dostoevsky, F. (1994*). Notes from underground/White nights/The dream of a ridiculous man/The house of the dead* (A.R. MacAndrew, Trans.). New York: New American Library, p. 114.

214. Goethe, J.W. (1979). *Faust, part two* (P. Wayne, Trans.). London: Penguin Books. p. 270.

215. Dikotter, F. *Mao's great famine.* London: Bloomsbury.

216. See Peterson, J.B. (2006). Peacemaking among higher-order primates. In Fitzduff, M. & Stout, C.E. (Eds.). *The psychology of resolving global conflicts: From war to peace. In Volume III, Interventions (pp. 33-40).* New York: Praeger. Retrieved from https://www.researchgate.net/publication/235336060_Peacemaking_among_higher-order_primates

217. See Allen, L. (2011). Trust versus mistrust (Erikson's infant stages). In S. Goldstein & J. A. Naglieri (Eds.). *Encyclopedia of child behavior and development (pp. 1509–1510).* Boston, MA: Springer US.

218. Lao-Tse (1984). *The tao te ching.* (1984) (S. Rosenthal, Trans.). Verse 33: Without force: without perishing. Retrieved from https://terebess.hu/english/tao/rosenthal.html#Kap33

219. Consider, for example, the great and courageous Boyan Slaat. This young Dutch man, still in his early twenties, has developed a technology that could do exactly that, and profitably, and be employed in all the oceans of the world. There's a real environmentalist: See https://www.theoceancleanup.com/

220. Yeats, W.B. (1933). Sailing to Byzantium. In R.J. Finneran (Ed.). *The poems of W.B. Yeats: A new edition.* New York: MacMillan, p. 163.

INDEX

Abel, 150, 152, 164, 166–67, 175–76, 177–78, 184, 362

Abraham, 164, 170, 171

acting out
  experiences, 163
  of lies/lying, 228
  of understanding, 165

Adam, 45–46, 48, 50–52, 53–54, 120, 161–62, 163–64, 174–75

Adler, Alfred, 209, 215, 329

Adorno, Theodor, 179

advice, 233, 239–40

aggression
  in ancient world, 58
  in children, 139
  children and, 125–26
  and children's friends, 318
  compassionate/self-sacrificing people and, 23–25
  lack of, 318–19
  as learned behaviour, 317–18
  as morally wrong, 23
  See also bullying; conflict

agoraphobia, 20–22

agreeableness, 318–21

aim(s)/aiming
  and bargaining for self, 63
  and betterment of life, 101, 106
  chaos vs, 226–27
  character vs status and, 224
  as concentration on day/present vs future, 109–10
  and creation of hierarchies, 303
  current knowledge as sufficient and, 210
  at good, 110, 111, 358–59
  ideas and, 195
  importance of, 221
  and meaning, 63–64
  and navigation, 92
  at Paradise, 359
  precision in, 262
  in psychotherapy, 243–44
  pursuit of, and meaning, 303
  reliance on tradition for, 221–22
  and rise in baseline of self-comparison, 96
  seeing and, 92, 93, 96, 100, 101, 106
  Sermon on the Mount and, 109–10
  size of, 95–96
  small, and goal-setting, 95–96
  and value, xxv, 96
  willful blindness and, 225

alchemy, 185
alcohol, 19–20, 234
ambition(s). *See* aim(s)/aiming
anaesthesia, 305
Animal Farm (Orwell), 309
animals
    and Being, 55
    human beings vs, 194–95
    and self-consciousness, 54, 55
    and work, 164
anxiety
    disorders, 20–22
    hope vs, 131
    humility and, 363–64
Atlas, Charles, "The Insult that
        Made a Man out of Mac," 329
Attenborough, David, 297
Auschwitz, 179, 197

Bachofen, Johann Jakob, 322, 323
Bacon, Francis, 34
Baldung Grien, Hans, 49
Beatty, Warren, 115
Beethoven, Ludwig van, "Ode to Joy,"
        201
Being
    and animals, 55
    betterment of, 107, 109, 199
    chaos and, 38, 89, 230
    consciousness and, 60
    Descartes and, 194
    different ways of, 88
    good/goodness and, 56, 107, 351
    hatred/resentment of, 61
    identification and, 264
    importance of, xxvii
    inauthenticity of, 214
    irrelevance and, 87
    justification of, 90–91, 107, 110, 347
    and limitation, 343, 345
    limits of, 61
    in marriage, 272
    murder and, 147, 152, 346

order and, 38
posture and, 27, 28
and primordial desires, 101–2
as process, 362
questioning of, 55, 148–49
sacrifice and, 184–85
suffering and, xxv, 35, 152
vulnerability and, 343
Way and, 43
beliefs
    and actions, 103
    knowledge regarding, 103–4
    shared systems, xxiv–xxv
betrayal, xxiv–xxv, 269–78
Beyond Good and Evil (Nietzsche),
        105–6, 191–92
Bible, 57, 104
    creation stories, 33–34, 45–49
    Ephesians, 381n141
    Exodus, 164
    flood stories, 156, 176, 365–66
    Genesis, 33–34, 45–49, 56, 156, 161,
        176
    John, 43
    Luke, 110
    Matthew, 9, 43, 225–26, 351, 355–56,
        359, 362, 364
    Revelation, 105
    Romans, 381–82n141
    Wisdom, 162
birds, 2–4
boys
    achievements of, 297–98
    socialization of, 317–18, 330
    suffering of, 298
brain
    and chaos, 38
    and dominance, 14–15, 16
    neurochemistry of defeat and
        victory, 7–8
    and objective world, 40
    order/chaos duality in structure of,
        42

and self-consciousness, 52
as social, 39, 40
The Brothers Karamazov
  (Dostoevsky), 190–91, 340–41
Buddha/Buddhism, 226, 338
bullying, 22–23, 59, 120, 140–41, 153.
  See also aggression

Cain, 150, 152, 164, 166–67, 175–76,
  177–79, 184, 294, 362
Cambodia
  Khmer Rouge, 307
  Marxism in, 305, 306
  Pol Pot, 219
Carson, Rachel, *Silent Spring*, 296
cats, 337–38, 352–53
CBC Radio, *Just Say No to Happiness*,
  xx–xxi
Chamberlain, Wilt, 115
Chang, Iris, *The Rape of Nanking*,
  121
chaos
  about, xxii, 35–36, 37
  ambition vs, 226–27
  and Being, 38, 89, 230
  brain and, 38
  breakdowns and, 266–67, 268
  confrontation of, 275, 283
  as constituent element of world,
    xxi–xxii
  and development, 287
  development of, 271
  discipline of children vs, 144
  and emotions, 38
  error and, 279
  and excess of order, 114
  as feminine, xxii, 41
  ignored reality and, 281
  of immaturity vs responsible
    freedom, 119
  and marriage, 37
  and meaning, 199, 200, 268
  moving home and, 73

mutual exploration conversations
  and, 254
new information/learning and,
  223–24
order vs, 37–38, 56
parsing apart, 269, 279
precision in facing, 278
risk and, 287
and sexual selection, 41
and thinking, 38
toxic families and, 143
truth vs, 361
See also things falling apart
chaos/order duality
  as balance, 43–44
  Darwinian adaptation to, 43
  lived situations as composed of,
    44
  and meaning, 44
  posture and transformation of one
    into other, 27
  serpent and, 46
  in structure of brain, 42
  Word and, 223, 230, 254, 268, 281
  yin/yang and, xxii, 12, 42
Chekhov, Anton, 48
childbirth, 51–52, 161, 304–5
children
  abuse of, 153–54
  adultism/parent authority and,
    134–35
  aggressive, 125–26, 139
  autonomy, 114
  and bullying, 23, 140–41
  as damaged by omission vs
    commission, 122–23
  death of, 365, 366
  denial of love toward, 116–17
  divorce and, 119
  and eating, 116–17, 124, 126–27
  in father-absent homes, 301–2
  God and suffering of, 340–41
  honouring of mothers of, 360

liking of, 138
localization of problems in parents, 118
with married parents, 302
maximization of learning, 132
misbehaviour, 113–14
over-protection/sheltering of, 25, 47, 132, 133, 134
parents as friends of, 123
parents' terror of, 119
peer relations/friends, 122–23, 133, 135, 143–44, 318
and playgrounds, 286–87
preference for male, 114–17
problems, and resentment, 118
provocation of adults, 124–25
punishment of, 129–30, 134–35, 138–41, 144 (*see also* discipline of children)
reasons for crying, 128
in restaurants, 137–38
rewarding of, 127, 129, 130–31, 132, 135, 138
sexual abuse of, 237–38
shaping of behaviour, 132
and sharing, 133, 168
and sleep, 117–18, 124, 128–29
socialization of, 122–23, 124, 134–36, 143–44, 192, 250, 318
suffering of, 346, 348–50
tantrums, 113
and tyranny, 114
as unsullied/damaged by culture/society, 119–20
vulnerability of, 132, 338–41
See also discipline of children; parents
chimpanzees, 120–21, 124–25
China
Cultural Revolution, 295, 317
Marxism in, 306
one-child policy, 295
See also Mao Zedong

Christianity
achievements of, 186–87
and Christ's sacrifice as redemption of humanity, 189–90
church, 191
cross in, xxvi–xxvii
and development of science, 187–88
dogmatic belief in central axioms of, 189–90
Dostoevsky and, 189–91
emergence of, 58
and equality, 186–87
female/male dual unity in, 42
and freedom, 191–93
"I" as Word, 194
and life as suffering, 227
Nietzsche and, 188–89, 191–92
problems of, 187, 188, 191
and rationality, 219
science vs, 185
and self-sacrifice, 59–60
and slavery, 186–87
and suffering and cross, 338
and truth, 188, 192
See also Bible
Closing the Gender Gap: Sweden (OECD), 386–87n193
The Cocktail Party (Eliot), 154
Columbine High School killings, 147–48, 151, 180, 296–97, 346
common law, 136–37
communism, 154–55, 193, 197, 198, 215, 219, 307–10
comparison(s)
daily self-, 96, 362
of self vs others, 85–87, 89, 92, 111, 362
competition
cooperation vs, 337
gender differences in, 298–99
conflict
agreeableness and, 320
avoidance of, 91, 211, 319

desires and, 101
discipline of children and, 134
socialization and, 135
territory and, 4–7
thinking and, 241–42
truth and, 225–26
unaffordability of, xxvi
between value systems, xxv–xxvi
consciousness
animals and, 55
and Being, 60
as masculine, 323, 324–26
as mediating between order and
chaos, 35
as struggling upwards toward light,
323
See also self-consciousness
conversation(s)
definition of topics of, 282
dominance hierarchy in, 248–49,
252
and gender differences re specific
problems, 250–51
ideology in, 249
as lectures, 251–52
listening in, 248–50
in marriage, 273
mutual exploration during, 253–56
and organization of brains, 250
psychotherapy as, 233–34, 243–44
types of, 248–53
wit in, 252–53
cooperation
competition vs, 337
human capacity for, 60–61
corruption
of culture, 223
falsification of reality and, 212–13
Hebrews and, 156
of human species, 297
and lack of trust, 260
lies/lying and, 228–29
and New Orleans hurricane, 157

society and, 118, 120–21
and solution of individual problems
by cultural restructuring, 118–19
suffering and, 157
and things falling apart, 156
tyranny and, 24
untruth and, 215
Crime and Punishment (Dostoevsky),
103
Crumb, Robert, 375
culture(s)
corruption of, 223
individual problems and restructuring of, 118–19
and IQ, 316
and listening to crowd/public
opinion, 242–43
as male creation, 303
male oppression and, 305–6
as natural, 14
and oppression, 302, 306–7
Western withdrawal from, xxvi

Dallas (soap opera), 345
Darwin/Darwinianism, 14, 43, 194,
196, 295
David (Michelangelo), 83
Dawkins, Richard, 116
delay of gratification, 17, 164–65,
167–68, 169, 184–85. *See also*
future
depth psychology, 195, 288
Derrida, Jacques, 306, 310–11
Descartes, René, 34, 193–94, 196, 197
discipline of children
as careful/effective, 138
chaos vs, 144
clear principles for, 144
and conflict, 134
as correction, 122–24, 126, 366
as damaging, 124
and differences among children,
135–36

effective intervention in, 138
and effort, 124
and freedom, 192
happiness and shaping of
behaviour, 131
limitation of rules, 136, 137, 142
minimum necessary force in, 142
necessity for, 129–30
negative emotions and, 131–32
and neglect/mistreatment, 123
parent fear of, 129
parental strategy development,
143
and parents as proxies for real
world, 143
parents in pairs and, 142
as responsibility, 124
rewards and, 130–31, 135
saying no, 113–14, 139–40
dogs, 122, 335–36, 337, 352
dominance hierarchy/-ies
about, 14
birds and, 3–4
brain and, 14–15
in conversation, 248–49, 252
and emergencies, 16–17
high vs low status in, 15–17
historic nature of, 14
marriage and, 301
as permanent environmental
feature, 11
posture and, 25–27
power and, 313
serotonin and, 15
and stress, 16–17
and temptation of Christ, 183–84
Dostoevsky, Fyodor
The Brothers Karamazov, 190–91,
340–41
and Christianity, 189–91
Crime and Punishment, 103
and freedom requiring constraint,
192

Notes from Underground, 76–78,
345–46
and rise of Communism/Fascism,
193
doubt, 193–94
Douglas Hospital, Montreal, 203–5

Economist, "The Weaker Sex," 297
Eden (Paradise), 45–46, 50–52,
161–62, 163–64, 230
Eliot, T.S.
The Cocktail Party, 154
"Little Gidding," 57–58
Eller, Cynthia, *The Myth of
Matriarchal Prehistory*, 322–23
emergencies
dominance hierarchy and, 16–17
preparation for, 268
emotion(s)
body language and, 26
chaos and, 38
negative, 18, 23, 131–32
perception and, 268–69
Enuma Elish, 323
equality
of outcomes, 315–16
redistribution of wealth and, 312
and sacrifice of value, 303
social construction of gender
differences and, 314–15
and tyranny, 288
error, 219–20, 224–25, 279
Eve, 45–46, 48, 49, 50–52, 53–54,
161–62, 163–64, 174–75
evil
Christ and confrontation with, 180
expedience and, 185
in human beings, 120
human capacity for, 55, 197–98
motivation of, 177
perpetuation of, 153
and post-traumatic stress disorder,
176–77

and production of suffering for
sake of suffering, 347
sacrifice and, 174, 185
Satan and, 181, 217–18
self-consciousness and, 176
stopping of own, 157–58
and suffering, 174
See also good/evil duality
evolution, 11–12, 12–13
existence, questioning value of, 149–51
expedience, 162–63, 172, 173, 185,
199, 200–201

faith
about, 107
thinking and, 107–8
truth and act of, 226
Fall, the, 56, 57, 163–64, 174–75
fascism, 193, 197
Faust (Goethe), xxiv, 148, 346
Fight Club, 330
fitness, 12–13
fragility. *See* vulnerability/-ies
Frankfurt School, 306
Frankl, Viktor, *Man's Search for*
Meaning, 215
Franklin, Benjamin, 168
free association, 243
free choice, 56, 57–58
Freud, Sigmund
on dark side, 288
as depth psychologist, 195
and free association, 243
on mothers and sons, 115
Oedipal parenting theory, 47, 323
on psychoanalysis, 243, 245
and repetition compulsion, 75
on repression, 215
friends/friendship
aiming upward vs downward and
choice of, 82–83
children making, 133, 135, 143–44,
318

with healthy vs unhealthy people, 83
and hospitality, 361
human capacity for, 60–61
Jesus Christ and, 78
with people good for one, 82
pulling others down, 78–79
reasons for wrong choices of, 76
as reciprocal arrangement, 82–83
Rene Heck, 290–91
and sharing, 168
teenage, 70–75
Frozen (Disney), 324
future
aim, as concentration on day/
present vs, 109–10
expedience vs, 200
as judgmental father, 166
memory as past's guide to, 239
other human beings composing,
165–66
as resembling past, 94
sacrifices for, 52, 79, 164, 166, 167,
174, 195–96
self-care and, 62–63
vulnerability and, 164
See also delay of gratification

Gandhi, Mahatma, 155
Geertgen tot Sint Jans, *Virgin and*
Child, 376n53
gender differences
in achievement, 297–99
biological factors vs power, 311
in careers, 300
in competition, 298–99
division of life into sexes, 39, 40
feminine/masculine divide in brain
structure, 42
and gender re-assignment surgery,
315
in importance of marriage, 299–300
and individual choices, 316–17
in obedience, 298

in responding to specific problems, 250–51

social construction of, 314–15, 316, 317–18

Gender Studies Department, Queen's University, 306

Genghis Khan, 115, 116

Gimbutas, Marija, 322

Giocangga, 115

goals. *See* aim(s)/aiming

God

and Cain, 175–76

and childbirth, 51–52, 161

and circumcision, 171

death of, 188, 192, 193

and the Fall, 163–64

free choice and embodiment of image of, 57–58

Hebrew covenant with, 156

of New Testament, 105–6, 107

of Old Testament, 104–6, 107

and sacrifice, 166–67, 169–70, 175

sacrifice of selves to, 59

and sacrifice of son, 171–72

and serpent, 51

and suffering, 151

and suffering of children, 340–41, 346

and temptation of Christ, 182–83, 356

and vengeance, 60

walking with, 57

Goethe, Johann Wolfgang, 174

Faust, xxiv, 148, 346

Goldberg, Elkhonon, 42

Golden Rule, 59–60

Golding, William, *Lord of the Flies,* 120

Goodall, Jane, 120–21

good/evil duality

Adam/Eve and knowledge of, 53–54

human capacity for, 47, 120, 142–43, 194, 197–98

and infliction of suffering upon others, 54–55

serpent and, 47

good/goodness

as aims, 358–59

alleviation of suffering as, 198

Being and, 56, 107, 351

happiness and, 62

in human beings, 120

and justification of existence, 107

meaning as higher, 198–201

and obedience, 102

religion and, 102

sharing and, 168–69, 364

truth and, 226

The Great Mother (Neumann), 323, 374

The Gulag Archipelago (Solzhenitsyn), 155, 182, 197, 215, 309–10

Haas, Earle Cleveland, 305

Hansel and Gretel, 321–22

happiness

and goodness, 62

hope and, 94

and shaping of children's behaviour, 131

Harris, Eric, 180, 297

Havel, Václav, 155

Hebrews, 156, 157

Hell

as bottomless, 367

Christ in desert and, 179

confrontation of, 275

Heaven vs, 63

lies/lying and, 198, 220, 227, 229

revenge and, 229

warfare and, 180–81

Hemingway, Ernest, 308

Hermogenes, 172, 173

hierarchies

as masculine, 40

oppression and, 310–11

of success, 303
of value, 198–99
and winners vs losers, 303
See also dominance hierarchy/-ies
Hirohito, Emperor, 309
Hitler, Adolf, 154, 226, 309, 360
Hobbes, Thomas, 177
Holocaust, 200, 347
hope, 94, 131
Horkheimer, Max, 306
Horus, 181, 194, 222
humility, 158, 363–64
hurricanes, 157
Hurwitz, Gregg, xxviii
Orphan X, xxiii–xxiv
Huxley, Thomas, 295–96

identification, 263–64
ideology
    in conversation, 249
    and single axioms, 211
    truth telling vs, 230
"The Insult that Made a Man out of
    Mac" (Atlas), 329
internal critic, 85–87, 89, 93–95
Isaac, 170
Isbell, Lynn, 48–49
Isis, 42

Jesus Christ
    death of, 59
    in desert, 179, 180, 356
    feeling of abandonment on cross,
        151
    as friend of tax-collectors/
        prostitutes, 78
    imitation of, 189
    on Kingdom spread out upon
        earth, 103
    as Logos, 223
    and Matthew principle, 9
    portrayal with Mary and serpent,
        49

as sacrifice, 59, 171–72
sacrifice for truth, 223
Satan's temptations of, 178, 180,
    181–84, 356
as "second Adam," 45
Sermon on the Mount, 109–10
taking on sins of mankind,
    179–80
and truth as sword, 225–26
and Way, 43
Jews/Judaism, and life as suffering,
    227, 338
Job (prophet), 154
judgment
    judges of the human race, 294–95,
        296–97
    reliance on own standards, 158
Jung, Carl Gustav
    and Bachofen's ideas, 323
    on consequences and motivation,
        289–90
    on dark side, 288
    as depth psychologist, 195
    on Enlightenment and
        Christianity, 188
    on Golden Rule, 59–60
    and imitation of Christ, 189
    on invention of values, 193
    and moral hierarchy, 198–99
    on science vs Christianity, and
        suffering, 185
    on tree growing to Heaven with
        roots in Hell, 180
    and untruth and patients' moral
        problems, 215
Just Say No to Happiness (CBC
    Radio), xx–xxi

Kato people, 122
Kent, Jack, *There's No Such Thing as a
    Dragon,* 270–71
Kierkegaard, Søren, 214, 226
King, Stephen, *The Stand,* 345

Kingu (Mesopotamian monster), 55
!Kung bushmen, 121

Lamech (Biblical character), 176
Lenin, Vladimir Ilyich, 307, 310
lies/lying
    acting out, 228
    and aim/ambition, 221
    and corruption, 215, 228–29
    and Hell, 198, 220, 227, 229
    knowledge of, 214
    life-lies, 209–11
    listening to, 362
    and nobility, 173
    paying attention and, 224
    successful, 229
    and things falling apart, 228, 229
    truth as intolerable and, 92
    truth telling and avoidance of, 205
    and tyranny, 91
    and weakening of character, 212
    and willful blindness, 213
life
    betterment of, 100–101, 106
    cleaning up, 157–59, 367
    as suffering, 161, 227
    See also Being
limitation(s)
    Being and, 61, 343, 345
    change/improvement vs, 74–75
    Creation story and, 343
    difficulties pushing beyond, 216
    existence and, 343
    extent of human, 296
    and help, 365
    justification of, 365
    love and, 347
    of perceptions, 266–67
    science vs, 185
    and suffering, 345–46
    Superman and lack of, 344–45
listening
    advice vs, 240

    characteristics of persons, 242, 243
    in conversation, 248–50
    and counterfeit, 247–48
    to crowd/public opinion, 242–43
    to enemies, 364–65
    importance of, 255–56
    lies/lying and, 362
    as paying attention, 233–34
    in psychotherapy, 244–45
    Rogers on, 245–47
    to self, 358
    and straw-man arguments, 247
    and summarizing, 246–47
    and thinking, 242
    and transformation of people, 245–46
    without premature judgment, 248
"Little Gidding" (Eliot), 57–58
The Little Mermaid, 43, 325–26
lobsters, 1–2, 5–8, 9–11, 15, 25
Logos
    Christ as, 192, 194, 223
    consciousness and, 324
    "I" into, 194
    as Word of God, 223
    See also Word
Lord of the Flies/lying (Golding), 120
Luria, Alexander, 42
Luther, Martin, 189

malfunction. See things falling apart
manipulation
    and calculated ends, 209–10
    and expedience, 173
    rationality and capacity for, 217
    of reality, 210
    speech and, 209
    truth telling vs, 110
Man's Search for Meaning (Frankl), 215
Mao Zedong, 219, 221, 226, 295, 317, 347. See also China

Maps of Meaning (Peterson), xxi–xxiii, xxvi, 74

Marduk (Mesopotamian God), 194

Maroney, McKayla, 296

marriage

  betrayal/breakdown in, 266–67, 269–78

  careers and, 299–302

  chaos and, 37

  children with married parents, 302

  disagreements in, 356–57

  and dominance hierarchy, 301

  honouring of wife, 359–60

  and household division of labour, 271–72

  order and, 37

  precision in facing/specifiying problems in, 277–80

  socioeconomic circumstances and, 301

  women and, 299–300, 329–30

Marx, Karl, 189, 306

Marxism, 306–7

  neo-, 302

Mary

  as mother of Christ, 171

  portrayal with Christ Child and serpent, 49

matriarchy, 322–23

meaning

  about, 200–201

  aim and, 63–64

  and betterment of Being, 199

  better-worse standards and, 87

  chaos and, 199, 268

  chaos vs order and, 44, 200

  expedience vs, 172, 199, 200–201

  as higher good, 198–201

  in individual consciousness/ experience, xxvii

  mutual exploration conversations and, 255

  nihilism and lack of, 87

  obedient/self-obliterating person and elimination of, 211–12

  perception of, 261

  precision and, 283

  pursuit of goals and, 303

  Socrates and, 173

  suffering vs, 199

  value systems and, xxv

  as Way, 200

  yin/yang and, xxii

medication, 31–33, 53, 55

memory/-ies

  about, 237

  as past's guide to future, 239

  recovered, 236–39

  summarizing and, 246–47

men

  code of behaviour, 328–29, 331–32

  masculinity, xxii, 40, 42, 323, 324–26

  as oppressors, 305–6

  toughening up, 331–32

  women and self-consciousness of, 48, 51

mental illness, 19

Mephistopheles, 148

Michelangelo

  David, 83

  Pietà, 171

Milton, John, *Paradise Lost*, xxiv, 46–47, 178–79, 210, 217–18, 219–20

minimal group identification, 336–37

monkeys, catching, 170–71

mothers

  honouring of, 360

  of JP, 326

  Oedipal, 320–22, 323, 326

  and sacrifice, 171

  single, 142, 301–2

  and sons, 114–17, 216

Terrible, 322–24
vulnerability of, 301–2
motivation
    comparisons of self to others and, 89
    and consequences, 289–90
    for daily tasks, 108–9
    of evil, 177
    power and, 311
    for social reform, 289
Muggeridge, Malcolm, 309
murder/murderers, 120–22, 150, 152,
    175–76
    mass, 147–48, 150, 151, 297, 346
Muruganathan, Arunachalam, 304,
    305
Mussolini, Benito, 309
The Myth of Matriarchal Prehistory
    (Eller), 322–23

nakedness, 49–50, 54
natural selection, 11, 12–13, 39
nature
    about, 12–15
    and culture, 14
    environment, 12, 364
    evolution and, 11–12
Nazism, xxi, 109, 148, 194, 198, 215,
    221. *See also* Hitler, Adolf
negotiation
    in marriage, 272
    with self, 90, 94–95
Neumann, Erich
    The Great Mother, 323, 374n37
    The Origins and History of
        Consciousness, 323
Newton, Isaac, 34, 185
Nietzsche, Friedrich, 347
    Beyond Good and Evil, 105–6,
        191–92
    and Christianity, 188–89, 191–92
    on distress and nihilism, 153
    and invention of values after God's
        death, 193

and pale criminal, 239
on purpose in life, 63
on *ressentiment*, 288
on toleration of truth, and worth,
    223
nihilism
    Chris and, 75
    death and, 343
    God's death and, 193
    goodness and justification of Being
        vs, 107
    and hierarchies of accomplishment,
        87
    and meaninglessness, 87
    postmodernism and, 311
    and reality of suffering, 197
    shared belief systems vs, xxvii
    suffering and, xxv, 153
    truth telling vs, 230
Notes from Underground (Dostoevsky),
    76–78, 345–46
Nuremberg trials, 197

objectivity, 34–35, 38
octopamine, 7–8
"Ode to Joy" (Beethoven), 201
OECD, *Closing the Gender Gap:*
    Sweden, 386–87n193
omission vs commission
    damage of children by, 122
    of lies/lying, 214
    sins of, 211, 271
oppression
    among downtrodden, 76
    and culture, 305–6
    culture and, 302
    and hierarchies, 310–11
    and language, 310–11
    Marxism and, 306–7
    men and, 313
    of poor, 306
    postmodernism and, 310
    resistance to, 24, 25

and revenge, 91
wealth and, 308
order
about, xxii, 36–38, 40
and Being, 38
chaos breeding too much, 114
chaos vs, 37–38, 56
as constituent element of world,
xxi–xxii
conversational types and, 254
as destructive, 40
and marriage, 37
and masculinity, xxii, 40
meaning and, 200
precision and, 278, 279
revolution and, 12
yin/yang and, xxii, 12, 42
order/chaos duality. See chaos/order
duality
organ transplants, 32–33
Original Sin, 55, 164
The Origins and History of
Consciousness (Neumann), 323
Orphan X (Hurwitz), xxiii–xxiv
Orwell, George, 196, 307, 308
Animal Farm, 309
The Road to Wigan Pier, 288–89
Osiris, 42, 181, 222, 229

pain. See suffering
Panzram, Carl, 151–52
Paradise. See Eden (Paradise)
Paradise Lost (Milton), xxiv, 46–47,
178–79, 210, 217–18, 219–20
parents
adultism/authority over children,
134–35
denigration of adulthood and, 119
dislike of children, 144
friendship with children, 123
and human capacity for evil, 142–43
localization of children's problems
in, 118
married, 302
over-cautious/protective, 25, 47,
132, 133, 134
pairs of, 142
as proxies for real world, 143
resentment in, 142–43
sacrifices of, 360
spending time with, 366
terror of children, 119
understanding of own capacity,
142–43
See also children; mothers
Pareto, Vilfredo, 9, 26
past
conditions of present vs, 222–23
deterioration of wisdom of,
222–23
future compared to, 94
memory as guide to future, 239
patriarchy, 303, 304, 313, 315, 322
Paul (apostle), 189
Pauline Jewett Institute of Women's
and Gender Studies, Carleton
University, 305–6
paying attention
about, 108–11
and daily matters for fixing, 108–9
discrimination in, 98
and goal/ambition, 224–25
and lies/lying, 224
listening as, 233–34
and things falling apart, 156–57
See also seeing
perception
breakdowns and, 265–67, 268–69
and chaos of possibility, 270
and emotion, 268–69
of "enough"/sufficiency, 262, 267
extension of, 263–64
of hierarchical configurations, 39
and hyperactive agency detector,
39
limitations of, 266–67

of meaning, 261
of obstacles, 261
of order/chaos, 38–39
of other people, 262, 263–64
of ourselves, 262–63
of simplicity vs complexity of
reality, 264–66
of things as tools vs objects, 39
of tools/useful, 261, 263, 265–66
Peter Pan, 140, 192
Peterson, Jordan, *Maps of Meaning*,
xxi–xxiii, xxvi, 74
Peterson, Julian, 126–27, 217, 294,
297, 338–39, 341, 343
Peterson, Mikhaila, 125, 126, 138, 217,
292, 335, 336, 339–40, 341–43,
348–50, 353
Peterson, Tammy, 71, 116–17, 126–27,
207, 208, 292–94, 339, 341, 342,
348, 349
Pew Research Centre, 299–300
Pietà (Michelangelo), 171
Pincus, Gregory Goodwin, 305
Pinocchio, 43, 351, 359
Plato, 102
Popper, Karl, 194–95
positive feedback loops, 19–21, 26
postmodernism, 302, 306–7, 310–12
post-traumatic stress disorder, 25,
176–77, 180–81
posture, 26–28, 361
power
and bullying, 23
competence vs, 313–14
and gender differences, 311
and hierarchies, 313
and motivation, 311
science and, 311, 314
and temptation of Christ, 183–84
precision
in aim, 262
in conversation, 282
in facing incoherence, 277–78

and meaning, 283
as specifying, 280, 281–82
of speech, 277–78, 281, 282–83
suffering and, 280–81
and things as useful, 261
things falling apart and, 366
present
aim and concentration on, vs
future, 109–10
as flawed, 94
sacrifice for future vs, 52, 164,
195–96
sacrifice of future to, 79
See also expedience
Price's law, 8–9, 26
psychotherapy
advice vs, 233
as conversation, 233–34, 243–44
listening in, 244–45
and truth, 245
punishment
of children, 129–30, 134–35,
138–41, 144 (*see also* discipline of
children)
common law and, 136–37

Quora (website), xix–xx, xxiii–xxiv,
xxviii

The Rape of Nanking (Chang), 121
rationality/reason
about, 218–19
capacity for manipulation, 217
and Logos, 194–95
and self-love, 218
reality
falsification of, 212–13
imagination vs, 280–81
manipulation of, 210
willful blindness toward, 281
redistribution of wealth, 312
religion(s), 41–42, 102–3, 338. *See also*
Christianity

resentment
   agreeableness and, 319–20
   deceit/lies and, 221
   development in marriage, 271
   goodness and justification of Being
      vs, 107
   gratitude vs, 89
   immaturity and, 91
   malfunction and, 61
   mass murderers and, 297
   in parents, 142–43
   and problems with children, 118
   as revelatory, 91
   shame and, 50
   socialists and, 289
   for suffering, 153, 199
   tyranny vs, 24, 91
   and vengeance, 143, 288
revenge. *See* vengeance
revolution(s)
   changing values hierarchy and, 213
   Christianity and, 186–87
   as destabilizing/dangerous, 118–19
   and order, 12
   personal problems solved by,
      118–19
   of sixties, 71
   taking a stand and, 215
The Road to Wigan Pier (Orwell),
   288–89
Rogers, Carl, 81, 245–47
Rousseau, Jean-Jacques, 119–20

sacrifice(s)
   of Abel vs Cain, 166–67
   and alleviation of suffering, 174
   animal–human developmental
      progression and, 167–68
   and Being, 184–85
   of best-loved/valued, 170–71
   of Christ, for truth, 223
   circumcision, 171
   as delay of gratification, 164–65

error correction and, 213–14
and evil, 174, 185
and future, 166, 167, 174
God and, 59, 166–67, 169–70, 175
Jesus Christ as, 171–72
magnitude of, 166, 172
mother and, 171
for others, 319
and pain/suffering alleviation, 172
of parents/others, 360
of personal will to will of God, 226
and present vs future, 52, 79, 164,
   195–96
and pursuit of highest good, 110
self-, 59–60, 80–81, 82
and social contract, 168
Socrates and, 172–73
of sons, 170, 171–72
and success, 169
truth and, 213–14
as unequal in quality, 167
work and, 164, 166
Sailing to Byzantium (Yeats), 365
salvation, 76–82, 189–90
Samphan, Khieu, 307
Sandy Hook Elementary School, 147
Sartre, Jean-Paul, 309, 310
Satan, 46–47, 51, 178, 180, 181–84,
   210, 217–18, 219–20, 356
Schjelderup-Ebbe, Thorlief, 3
Schwartz, Yitta, 115
Schwarzenegger, Arnold, 328
science, 34, 35, 185, 187–88, 311, 314
"The Second Coming" (Yeats), 276,
   277
seeing
   about, 93
   and aim/aiming, 92, 93, 96, 100,
      101, 106
   blindness vs, 96–98
   complexity of world vs private
      concerns and, 98
   as expensive, 97–98

and focus, 93
and paying attention, 98
religious beliefs and, 103
as responsibility, 223
and taking stock, 93–94
triaging of, 97–98
wanting and, 99–100, 106
what is better, 100
world as *maya*, 98
See also paying attention; willful blindness
self-consciousness
of Adam and Eve, 45–46, 48, 51
alcohol and, 234
animals and, 54
brain and, 52
defined, 54
Eden and, 163
and evil, 176
excessive burdens of, 59
and moral knowledge, 57
nakedness and, 54
and suffering, 174
of women vs men, 48, 51
self-knowledge, 89–91, 109
self-respect, 58, 62
Sermon on the Mount, 109–10, 359
serotonin, 7–8, 15, 16, 17, 25, 85
serpent, 46–49, 51, 53, 163–64, 178
Set, 181, 222
sex differences. *See* gender differences
sharing
by children, 133, 168
and goodness, 168–69, 364
Silent Spring (Carson), 296
Simons, Daniel, 96–97
Simpson, James Young, 304–5
The Simpsons, 80, 330, 353
Skinner, B.F., 130, 131, 132
Slaat, Boyan, 389n219
slavery, 59, 89, 90, 186–87, 271–72, 310
sleep, 18, 117–18, 124, 128–29

Sleeping Beauty, 43, 132–33, 324, 325
social contract, xxiv–xxv, 168, 260
socialism, 196, 288–89
socialization
and aggression, 318
of boys/men like girls/women, 317–18, 330
of children, 122–23, 124, 134–36, 143–44, 192, 250, 318
and conflict, 135
of dogs, 122
and gender differences, 314–15, 316
Socrates, 172–73, 256, 365
Solzhenitsyn, Alexandr, xxi, 47, 154–55
The Gulag Archipelago, 155, 182, 197, 215, 309–10
Soviet Union, 154–55, 194, 306, 307, 308–10
Spanish Civil War, 307–8
speech
and chaos into Being, 230
and manipulation of reality, 209
precision of, 277–78, 281, 282–83
See also Word
Spiderman, 344
Stalin, Joseph, 154, 215, 219, 221, 226, 347, 360
The Stand (King), 345
standards, 86, 87, 89–91
standing up straight. *See* posture
Stone, Merlin, *When God Was a Woman*, 322–23
story telling, 163–64
stress, 16–17
success, 88–89, 92, 169, 301, 303
suffering
alleviation as good, 198
amplification to prove injustice, 76, 81
and behavioural changes, 149
Being and, xxv, 35, 152
blaming for, 151

of boys, 298
bullying and, 23
and change/death of convictions,
    195
and chaos, 37
of children, 340–41, 346, 348–50
cleaning up life and ability to bear,
    159
and corruption, 157
cross and, xxvii
daily tasks to reduce, 199–200
deceit and, 215–16, 216–17, 221
as defining world, 172
evil and, 174, 347
and expedience, 162–63, 174
fault-finding/blaming for, 149, 154
God and, 151, 340–41
and hatred of life, 346–47
infliction upon others, 54–55, 177,
    197
life as, 161, 227
limits and, 345–46
management of, 350–51
mass murderers and, 151
meaning vs, 199
and nihilism, xxv, 153
of others, 59
pleasure vs, 131
precision in, 280–81
reality of, 197
religions and, 338
resentment for, 153, 199
and ritual/myth, 163
sacrifice and alleviation of, 172, 174
salvation and reasons for, 80–81
science and, 187–88
self-consciousness and, 174
self-infliction of, 149
Solzhenitsyn and, 154–55
subjective reality of, 35
and sympathy for humanity, 61–62
thinking and, 347
and transformation, 152–53, 155

truth in bearing, 216–17
vengeance and, 177
vengeance for, 151–52, 154
wanting and, 100
suicide, 60, 150–51, 294, 297, 302, 346
Superman, 344–45

Tajfel, Henri, 336–37
taking stock, 93–94, 100, 362–63
talking
    forgetting vs remembering in, 247
    suffering, and setting aside time
        for, 350–51
    and thinking, 240
    See also conversation(s)
Taoism, 43, 104, 184, 255, 343, 363
    yin/yang, xxii, 12, 40, 42
teenagers, 70–75, 139
Terence, 180
There's No Such Thing as a Dragon
    (Kent), 270–71
things falling apart, 17–22, 61, 156–57,
    228, 229, 365–66. See also chaos
thinking
    and avatars, 241–42
    chaos and, 38
    and conflict, 241–42
    Darwinism and, 194–95
    and faith, 107–8
    forgetting vs remembering in, 247
    and ideas, 194–95
    listening and, 241, 242
    noticing vs, 347
    purpose of, 240
    self-criticism vs, 241
    suffering and, 347
    talking and, 240
Thomas, Elizabeth Marshall, 121
Thomas, Gospel of, 103
Tiamat (Mesopotamian mother
    figure), 323–24
Tolstoy, Leo, 149–51, 152, 347
tools, 75, 263, 265–66

totalitarianism
  and arbitrariness of adult dictates,
    135
  and betterment of life, 109
  concentration camps, 194
  and concentration camps, 179
  deceit/inauthenticity and, 215
  and error, 219–20, 224–25
  humility vs, 198
  production of horrors under, 347
  and reality of suffering, 197
  rebellion against, 193
  rebellion against "most High" as,
    218–19
  reliance on what is already known,
    218
tragedy/-ies. *See* suffering
transformation
  listening and, 245–46
  suffering and, 152–53
Trump, Donald, 330
trust
  corruption and, 260
  social contract of, 260
  in strangers, 361
truth
  advantages of telling, 230
  in bearing suffering, 216–17
  chaos vs, 361
  Christianity and, 188, 192
  Christ's sacrifice for, 223
  and conflict, 225–26
  deceit vs, 226
  and good, 226
  humour and, 252
  ideology vs, 230
  intolerability of, and lying, 92
  lack of, and corruption, 215
  manipulation of world vs, 110
  as meta-goal, 227
  moral/narrative vs objective, 188
  mutual exploration conversations
    and, 255

openness to, 356–58
personal, 230
psychotherapy and, 245
and sacrifice, 213–14
subjectivity vs objectivity in,
  34–35
as sword, 225–26
toleration of, and worth, 223
and values, 225
and wisdom, 361
truth telling
  avoidance of lies, 205
  life-lies vs., 208–9
  by saying no, 212
  self-knowledge and, 90–91
  Socrates and, 173
  Solzhenitsyn and, 215
  taking a stand and, 214–15
  vengeance vs, 230
Tubulcain (Biblical character), 176
Twain, Mark, 12
tyranny
  children and, 114
  communism and, 310
  and corruption, 24
  equality and, 288
  as expanding to fill space available,
    24
  lies/lying and, 91
  in marriage, 271–72
  resentment vs, 24, 91
  of self by self, 90
  self-sacrifice and, 59

unequal distribution, 8–9
universities
  administration, 312
  gender differences in, 299
  hostility toward men in disciplines,
    302
  postmodernism in, 302
  radical political action in, 305–6
utopianism, 109, 193, 210–11

value(s)
  aim/aiming and, 96
  beliefs and, 103
  and betterment of Being, 199
  conflict between, xxv–xxvi
  desires becoming, 102
  goals and, xxv
  hierarchies of, 198–99
  ideas and, 195
  judgments and action, 87
  and meaning, xxv
  truth and, 225
  wants and, 102, 103
vengeance
  deceit and, 221
  God and, 60
  and Hell, 229
  justice vs, 152
  oppression and, 91
  power and, 184
  resentment and, 143
  ressentiment and, 288
  and suffering, 151–52, 154, 177
  truth telling vs, 230
Victoria, Queen, 305
Vietnam, 181, 306
violence. *See* aggression
Virgin and Child (Geertgen tot Sint
  Jans), 376n53
Von Neumann, John, 50
vulnerability/-ies
  and Being, 343
  of children, 132
  death and, 366
  and future, 164
  of human beings, 338
  production in others, 174–75
  of small children, 338–41
  of women, 301–2, 303–5

Waal, Frans de, 10
wanting, 99–102, 103, 106

Way
  and Being, 43
  Christ and, 43
  meaning as, 200
  mutual exploration conversations
    and, 255
  Taoism and, 43
The Weaker Sex (Economist), 297
wealth
  oppression and, 308
  redistribution of, 312
When God Was a Woman (Stone),
  322–23
willful blindness
  about, 213
  culture/social organizations and,
    222, 223
  and goals, 225
  in marriage, 274–76
  and New Orleans hurricane, 157
  and sustained inattentional
    blindness, 96–98
  and things falling apart, 156
  toward reality, 281
  worthless feelings and, 86–87
  See also paying attention; seeing
women
  achievements, 297–98
  careers, 300–301
  and childbirth, 51–52, 304–5
  disadvantages/vulnerabilities, 303–5
  Eve-serpent relationship and, 48
  femininity, xxii, 41, 42
  and marriage, 299–300, 329–30
  men and oppression of, 313
  menstruation, 304, 305
  preferences in men, 301–2, 329–30,
    331–32
  and self-consciousness of men, 48,
    51
Word
  and Creation, 33–34, 56

"I" into, 194
and order vs chaos, 223, 230, 254,
    268, 281
See also Logos
wrongdoing. *See* evil

Yanomami people, 122
Yeats, William Butler, 365
    Sailing to Byzantium, 365
    "The Second Coming," 276, 277
yin/yang, xxii, 12, 40, 42

JORDAN B. PETERSON, raised and toughened in the frigid wastelands of Northern Alberta, has flown a hammerhead roll in a carbon fiber stunt plane, piloted a mahogany racing sailboat around Alcatraz Island, explored an Arizona meteorite crater with a group of astronauts, and built a Kwagu'l ceremonial bighouse on the upper floor of his Toronto home after being invited into and named by that Canadian First Nation. He's been a dishwasher, gas jockey, bartender, short-order cook, beekeeper, oil derrick bit re-tipper, plywood mill labourer and railway line worker. He's taught mythology to lawyers, doctors and business people, consulted for the UN Secretary General's High-level Panel on Sustainable Development, helped his clinical clients manage depression, obsessive-compulsive disorder, anxiety and schizophrenia, served as an advisor to senior partners of major Canadian law firms, identified thousands of promising entrepreneurs in sixty different countries, and lectured extensively in North America and Europe. Dr. Peterson has published more than a hundred scientific papers, advancing the modern understanding of personality and transforming the psychology of religion with his now-classic book, *Maps of Meaning: The Architecture of Belief.* As a Harvard professor, he was nominated for the prestigious Levenson Teaching Prize, and is regarded by his current University of Toronto students as one of three truly life-changing teachers. He's a Quora "Most Viewed Writer" in *Values and Principles* and *Parenting and Education,* and his classroom lectures on mythology were turned into a popular thirteen-part TV series on public television. Dr. Peterson's online mental-health improvement program, www.selfauthoring.com (featured in *O: The Oprah Magazine,* and on NPR's national website), has helped thousands of people address their past problems and improve their future, while the information provided by his new personality test at www.understandmyself.com aids its recipients in their quest to know themselves and others.

Follow @jordanbpeterson on Twitter, Dr Jordan B Peterson on Facebook and JordanPetersonVideos on YouTube.

Beyond Order

Beyond Order

12 MORE RULES
FOR LIFE

Jordan B. Peterson

ALLEN LANE
an imprint of
PENGUIN BOOKS

ALLEN LANE

UK | USA | Canada | Ireland | Australia
India | New Zealand | South Africa

Allen Lane is part of the Penguin Random House group of companies
whose addresses can be found at global.penguinrandomhouse.com.

First published in the United States of America by Portfolio Penguin,
an imprint of Penguin Random House LLC 2021
First published in Great Britain by Allen Lane 2021

009

Printed and bound in Great Britain by Clays Ltd, Elcograf S.p.A.

The authorized representative in the EEA is Penguin Random House Ireland,
Morrison Chambers, 32 Nassau Street, Dublin D02 YH68

A CIP catalogue record for this book is available from the British Library

Hardback ISBN: 978–0–241–40762–2
Trade paperback ISBN: 978–0–241–40763–9

www.greenpenguin.co.uk

Penguin Random House is committed to a
sustainable future for our business, our readers
and our planet. This book is made from Forest
Stewardship Council® certified paper.

To my wife, Tammy Maureen Roberts Peterson, whom I have loved deeply for fifty years, and who is admirable, in my estimation, in all regards, and beyond all reason.

Contents

Table of Illustrations xi

A Note from the Author in the Time of the Pandemic xiii

Overture xv

RULE I | Do not carelessly denigrate social institutions or creative achievement 1

RULE II | Imagine who you could be, and then aim single-mindedly at that 51

RULE III | Do not hide unwanted things in the fog 89

RULE IV | Notice that opportunity lurks where responsibility has been abdicated 111

RULE V | Do not do what you hate 141

RULE VI | Abandon ideology 157

RULE VII | Work as hard as you possibly can on at least one thing and see what happens 181

RULE VIII | Try to make one room in your home as beautiful as possible 201

RULE IX | If old memories still upset you, write them down carefully and completely 229

RULE X | Plan and work diligently to maintain the romance in your relationship 265

RULE XI | Do not allow yourself to become resentful, deceitful, or arrogant 303

RULE XII | Be grateful in spite of your suffering 355

Coda 377

Notes 383

Index 391

Table of Illustrations

1. The Fool: Inspired by Pamela Colman Smith, *The Fool*, from the Rider-Waite Tarot card deck, Rider & Son (1910).

2. Materia Prima: Inspired by Hermes Trismegistus, *Occulta philosophia* (1613). Also from H. Nollius, *Theoria philosophiae hermeticae* (Hanoviae: Apud P. Antonium, 1617).

3. St. George and the Dragon: Inspired by Paolo Uccello, *Saint George and the Dragon* (ca. 1458).

4. Atlas and the Hesperides: Inspired by John Singer Sargent, *Atlas and the Hesperides* (ca. 1922–1925).

5. Fallen Angel: Inspired by Alexandre Cabanel, *Fallen Angel* (1847).

6. In our Communal Farm: Inspired by B. Deykin, *In Our Communal Farm, There Is No Place for Priests and Kulaks* (1932).

7. Apprentice: Inspired by Louis-Emile Adan, *Apprentice* (1914).

8. Irises: Inspired by Vincent Van Gogh, *Irises* (1890).

9. The Temptation of St. Anthony: Inspired by Martin Schongauer, *The Temptation of Saint Anthony* (ca. 1470–1475).

10. The Love Drink: Inspired by Aubrey Beardsley, *How Sir Tristram Drank of the Love Drink* (1893).

11. Satan: Inspired by Gustave Doré, *Satan*, from John Milton, *Milton's Paradise Lost*, with illustrations by Gustave Doré (London: Cassell & Company, Ltd., 1905).

12. St. Sebastian: Inspired by Martin Schongauer, *Saint Sebastian* (ca. 1480).

A Note from the Author in the Time of the Pandemic

It is a perplexing task to produce a nonfiction book during the global crisis brought about by the spread of COVID-19. It seems absurd, in some sense, even to think about anything else but that illness during this trying time. Nonetheless, binding all the thoughts contained in any current work to the existence of the pandemic—which too shall pass—seems like an error, as the normal problems of life will return at some point (and thankfully) to the forefront. That all means that an author of the present day is inevitably going to make one mistake (concentrating too much on the pandemic, which has an uncertain life span, and producing a book that is instantly dated, in consequence) or another (ignoring the pandemic, which is very much like failing to attend to the proverbial elephant under the rug).

After considering this, as well as discussing the issues with my publishers, I decided to write *Beyond Order: 12 More Rules for Life* according to the plan laid out for it several years ago, and to concentrate on addressing issues not specific to the current time (thus, to risk the second error rather than the first). I suppose it may also be the case that those who have chosen to read this book or listen to the audio version might be relieved to turn their attention to something other than the coronavirus and the devastation it has wrought.

Overture

On the fifth of February 2020, I awoke in an intensive care ward in, of all places, Moscow. I had six-inch tethers attaching me to the sides of the bed because, in my unconscious state, I had been agitated enough to try to remove the catheters from my arm and leave the ICU. I was confused and frustrated not knowing where I was, surrounded by people speaking a foreign language, and in the absence of my daughter, Mikhaila, and her husband, Andrey, who were restricted to short visiting hours and did not have permission to be there with me at my moment of wakening. I was angry, too, about being there, and lunged at my daughter when she did visit several hours later. I felt betrayed, although that was the furthest from the truth. People had been attending to my various needs with great diligence, and in the wake of the tremendous logistic challenges that come about from seeking medical care in a truly foreign country. I do not have any memory of anything that happened to me during the most recent weeks preceding that, and very little between that moment and my having entered a hospital in

Toronto, in mid-December. One of the few things I could recall, looking back to the earliest days of the year, was the time I had spent writing this book.

I wrote much and edited almost all of *Beyond Order* during a time when my family was plagued by sequential and overlapping bouts of seriously impaired health, much of which was the subject of public discussion, and for that reason requires some detailed explanation. First, in January 2019, Mikhaila had to seek out a surgeon to replace much of her artificial ankle, implanted about a decade earlier, as the initial installation was never perfect, causing her serious pain and trouble with movement as a consequence, and then came near to failing. I spent a week with her at a hospital in Zurich, Switzerland, for the week of that procedure and her initial recovery.

At the beginning of March, my wife, Tammy, underwent routine surgery in Toronto for a common and eminently treatable kidney cancer. A month and a half after that surgery, which involved the removal of one third of the organ in question, we learned that she was actually suffering from an extremely rare malignancy, which had a one-year fatality rate of close to 100 percent.

Two weeks later, the surgeons involved in her care removed the remaining two thirds of her afflicted kidney, along with a substantial proportion of the related abdominal lymphatic system. The surgery appeared to bring the progression of the cancer to a halt, but produced leakage of fluid (up to four liters, or one gallon, a day) from her now-damaged lymphatic system—a condition known as chylous ascites—which rivaled the original condition in danger. We journeyed to see a medical team in Philadelphia, where within ninety-six hours of the initial injection of a poppy seed oil dye, whose practical purpose was the enhancement of images derived from CAT or MRI scans, the complete cessation of Tammy's fluid loss was achieved. This breakthrough occurred on the very day of our thirtieth wedding anniversary. She recovered rapidly and, to all appearances, completely—a testament to the luck without which none of us can live, and to her own admirable strength and resistance.

Unfortunately, while these events unfolded, my health fell apart. I had begun to take an antianxiety agent at the beginning of 2017, after suffering from what appeared to be an autoimmune reaction to something I had consumed during the Christmas holiday period of 2016.* The food reaction made me acutely and continually anxious, as well as freezing cold, no matter what clothes I was wearing or how many blankets I layered upon myself. Further, it lowered my blood pressure so dramatically that whenever I tried to stand I would gray out and be forced into a crouch half a dozen or more times before trying again. I also experienced insomnia that appeared near total. My family physician prescribed a benzodiazepine as well as a drug for sleeping. I took the latter a mere handful of times before ceasing its use entirely; the terrible symptoms I was experiencing, including the insomnia, were almost immediately and entirely eradicated by the benzodiazepine treatment, making the sleep agent unnecessary. I continued the benzodiazepine for almost exactly three years, because my life did seem unnaturally stressful during that time (the period when my life changed from the quiet existence of a university professor and clinician to the tumultuous reality of a public figure), and because I believed that this drug was—as is often claimed of benzodiazepines—a relatively harmless substance.

Things changed, however, in March 2019, at the onset of my wife's

---

*The illness that had destroyed Mikhaila's ankle, necessitating its replacement, as well as her hip, was also immune related, and my wife had some arthritic symptoms that were similar to hers. I am mentioning this to shed some light on why the assumption of an immune response program sprang to mind and made a certain sense.

medical battle. My anxiety spiked noticeably after Mikhaila's afore-mentioned hospitalization, surgery, and recovery. In consequence, I asked my family physician to increase my dose of benzodiazepine, so that I would not be preoccupied by nor preoccupy others with my anxiety. Unfortunately, I experienced a marked increase in negative emotion following the adjustment. I asked to have the dosage raised yet again (by this time, we were attempting to deal with the second of Tammy's surgeries and its complications, and I attributed my even more severe anxiety to that problem), but my anxiety increased even further. I attributed all of this not to a paradoxical reaction to the medication (which it was later diagnosed as), but to the recurrence of a tendency toward depression that had plagued me for years.* In any case, I ceased using the benzodiazepine entirely in May of that year, trying two doses of ketamine within a week, as suggested by a psychiatrist with whom I consulted. Ketamine, a nonstandard anesthetic/psychedelic, sometimes has overwhelming and sudden positive effects on depression. It produced nothing for me but two ninety-minute trips to hell. I felt to my bones as if I had everything to feel guilty and ashamed about, with nothing gained by my positive experiences.

A few days after the second ketamine experience, I began to suffer the effects of acute benzodiazepine withdrawal, which were truly intolerable—anxiety far beyond what I had ever experienced, an uncontrollable restlessness and need to move (formally known as akathisia), overwhelming thoughts of self-destruction, and the complete absence of any happiness whatsoever. A family friend—a physician—enlightened me as to the dangers of sudden benzodiazepine withdrawal. I therefore started to take a benzodiazepine once again—but a

---

*I had taken serotonin reuptake inhibitors such as Celexa for nearly two decades, greatly benefiting from their administration, before stopping in early 2016, because a dramatic dietary change seemed to render them unnecessary.

smaller dose than I had climbed to previously. Many, but not all, of my symptoms abated. To deal with those that remained, I also began to take an antidepressant that had been of great use to me in the past. All it did, however, was make me exhausted enough to require an additional four or more hours of sleep a day—which was not helpful in the midst of Tammy's serious health issues—as well as increase my appetite two- or threefold.

After about three months of terrible anxiety, uncontrollable hypersomnia, viciously torturous akathisia, and excessive appetite, I traveled to an American clinic that claimed to specialize in rapid benzodiazepine withdrawal. Despite the good intentions of many of its psychiatrists, the clinic managed only a slow cessation or tapering of my benzodiazepine dosage, the negative effects of which I was already experiencing and which were not and could not be controlled to any significant degree whatsoever by the inpatient treatment offered.

I resided at that clinic, nonetheless, from mid-August, a mere few days after Tammy had recovered from her postsurgical complications, to late November, when I returned home to Toronto, much the worse for wear. By this time, the akathisia (the disorder of uncontrollable movement alluded to earlier) had increased to the point where I could not sit or rest in any position for any length of time whatsoever without severe distress. In December I checked in to a local hospital, and it was at that point that my awareness of events prior to my awakening in Moscow ends. As I later learned, Mikhaila and Andrey removed me from the Toronto hospital in early January 2020, believing that the treatment I received there was doing me more harm than good (an opinion I concurred with entirely once I learned of it).

The situation I found myself in upon reattaining consciousness in Russia was complicated by the fact that I had also developed double pneumonia in Canada, although that was neither discovered nor

treated until I was in the Moscow ICU. However, I was there primarily so that the clinic could facilitate my withdrawal from benzodiazepines, using a procedure either unknown or regarded as too dangerous
in North America. Since I had not been able to tolerate any decrease in
dosage whatsoever—apart from the initial reduction, months before—
the clinic placed me in a medically induced coma so that I might remain unconscious during the very worst withdrawal symptoms. That
regimen started January 5 and lasted nine days, during which I was also
placed in a machine so that my breathing was mechanically regulated.
On January 14, I was taken off the anesthetic and the intubation. I
woke up for a few hours, and indicated during this time to Mikhaila
that I was no longer suffering from akathisia, although I remember
nothing of this.

On January 23, I was moved to another ICU specializing in neurological rehabilitation. I can recall waking up on the twenty-sixth for a
short period, until my more complete return to consciousness, as previously related, on February 5—ten days during which I passed through
a period of delirium of vivid intensity. Once that cleared, I moved to a
more homelike rehabilitation center in the outer suburbs of Moscow.
While there, I had to relearn how to walk and up and down stairs, button my clothes, lie down in bed on my own, place my hands in the
proper position on a computer keyboard, and type. I did not seem to
be able to see properly—or, more accurately, see how to use my limbs
to interact with what I perceived. A few weeks later, after the problems
in perception and coordination had essentially abated, Mikhaila, Andrey, their child, and I relocated to Florida for what we hoped would
be some peaceful time of recuperation in the sun (very much welcome
after the cold grayness of midwinter Moscow). This was immediately
before worldwide concern erupted over the COVID-19 pandemic.

In Florida, I attempted to wean off the medication prescribed by the Moscow clinic, although I was still experiencing numbness in my left hand and foot, trembling of those two extremities as well as the muscles in my forehead, seizure activity, and crippling anxiety. All these symptoms increased quite markedly as my intake of medication decreased, reaching the point where about two months later I returned to the dosages initially prescribed in Russia. This was a material defeat, as the process of lessening their use had been fueled by an optimism that was consequently shattered, as well as returning me to a state of medication usage that I had paid a heavy price for trying to eliminate. I had family members and friends stay with me during this time, thankfully, and their company helped me stay motivated to continue while the symptoms I was experiencing grew unbearable, particularly in the morning.

By the end of May, three months after leaving Russia, it had become obvious that I was worsening instead of improving, and relying on the people I loved and who reciprocated that emotion was both untenable and unfair. Mikhaila and Andrey had been in touch with a Serbian clinic that practiced a novel approach to the problem of benzodiazepine withdrawal, and they made arrangements to move me there, only two days after that country had reopened after the pandemic closure.

I am not going to make a claim that the events that befell my wife, me, and those who were closely involved in her care added up, in the final analysis, to some greater good. What happened to her was truly awful. She experienced a severe and near-fatal crisis of health every two or three days for more than half a year, and then had to cope with my illness and absence. I was plagued, for my part, with the likely loss of someone whom I had befriended for fifty years and been married to for thirty; the observation of the terrible consequences of that on her other family members, including our children; and the dire and dreadful consequences of a substance dependence I had unwittingly stumbled into. I am not going to cheapen any of that by claiming that we became better people for living through it. However, I can say that passing so near to death motivated my wife to attend to some issues regarding her own spiritual and creative development more immediately and assiduously than she might otherwise have, and me to write or to preserve while editing only those words in this book that retained their significance even under conditions characterized by extreme suffering. It is certainly thanks to family and friends (who are named specifically in the Coda of this book) that we are still alive, but it is also true that the meaningful immersion in what I was writing, which continued during the entire time I have related—excepting my unconscious month in Russia—provided me both with a reason to live and a means of testing the viability of the thoughts with which I wrestled.

I do not believe I have ever claimed—in my previous book or, indeed, this one—that it would be *necessarily* sufficient to live by the rules I have presented. I think what I claimed—what I hope I claimed—was this: When you are visited by chaos and swallowed up; when nature curses you or someone you love with illness; or when tyranny rends asunder something of value that you have built, it is salutary to know the rest of the story. All of that misfortune is only the bitter half of the tale of existence, without taking note of the heroic element of redemption or the nobility of the human spirit requiring a certain responsibility to shoulder. We ignore that addition to the story at our peril, because life is so difficult that losing sight of the heroic part of existence could cost us everything. We do not want that to happen. We need instead to take heart, and to take spirit, and to look at things carefully and properly, and to live the way that we could live.

You have sources of strength upon which you can draw, and even though they may not work well, they may be enough. You have what you can learn if you can accept your error. You have medications and hospitals, as well as physicians and nurses who genuinely and bravely care to lift you up and help you through every day. And then you have your own character and courage, and if those have been beat to a bloody pulp and you are ready to throw in the towel, you have the character and courage of those for whom you care and who care for you. And maybe, just maybe, with all that, you can get through. I can tell you what has saved me, so far—the love I have for my family; the love they have for me; the encouragement they have delivered, along with my friends; the fact that I still had meaningful work I could struggle through while in the abyss. I had to force myself to sit down at the computer. I had to force myself to concentrate, and to breathe, and to keep from saying and meaning "to hell with it" during the end-less months that I was possessed by dread and terror. And I was barely able to do it. More than half the time I believed that I was going to die in one of the many hospitals in which I resided. And I believe that if I had fallen prey to resentment, for example, I would have perished once and for all—and that I am fortunate to have avoided such a fate.

Is it not possible (even though it may not always deliver us from the terrible situation that we find ourselves in) that we would all be more able to deal with uncertainty, the horrors of nature, the tyranny of culture, and the malevolence of ourselves and others if we were better and more courageous people? If we strived toward higher values? If we were more truthful? Wouldn't the beneficial elements of experience be more likely to manifest themselves around us? Is it not possible, if your goals were noble enough, your courage adequate, your aim at the truth unerring, that the Good thereby produced would . . . well, not justify the horror? That is not exactly right, but it still comes close. Such attitudes and actions might at least provide us with meaning sufficient to stop our encounter with that terror and horror from corrupting us

and turning the surrounding world into something all too closely resembling hell.

Why *Beyond Order*? It is simple, in some regard. Order is explored
territory. We are in order when the actions we deem appropriate produce the results we aim at. We regard such outcomes positively, indicating as they do, first, that we have moved closer to what we desire, and
second, that our theory about how the world works remains acceptably
accurate. Nonetheless, all states of order, no matter how secure and
comfortable, have their flaws. Our knowledge of how to act in the
world remains eternally incomplete—partly because of our profound
ignorance of the vast unknown, partly because of our willful blindness, and partly because the world continues, in its entropic manner,
to transform itself unexpectedly. Furthermore, the order we strive to
impose on the world can rigidify as a consequence of ill-advised attempts to eradicate from consideration all that is unknown. When such
attempts go too far, totalitarianism threatens, driven by the desire to exercise full control where such control is not possible, even in principle.
This means risking a dangerous restriction of all the psychological and
social changes necessary to maintain adaptation to the ever-changing
world. And so we find ourselves inescapably faced with the need to
move beyond order, into its opposite: chaos.

If order is where what we want makes itself known—when we act
in accordance with our hard-won wisdom—chaos is where what we do
not expect or have remained blind to leaps forward from the potential
that surrounds us. The fact that something has occurred many times
in the past is no guarantee that it will continue to occur in the same
manner.[1] There exists, eternally, a domain beyond what we know and
can predict. Chaos is anomaly, novelty, unpredictability, transformation, disruption, and all too often, descent, as what we have come to
take for granted reveals itself as unreliable. Sometimes it manifests it-

self gently, revealing its mysteries in experience that makes us curious, compelled, and interested. This is particularly likely, although not inevitable, when we approach what we do not understand voluntarily, with careful preparation and discipline. Other times the unexpected makes itself known terribly, suddenly, accidentally, so we are undone, and fall apart, and can only put ourselves back together with great difficulty—if at all.

Neither the state of order nor the state of chaos is preferable, intrinsically, to the other. That is the wrong way to look at it. Nonetheless, in my previous book, *12 Rules for Life: An Antidote to Chaos*, I focused more on how the consequences of too much chaos might be remediated.[2] We respond to sudden and unpredictable change by preparing, physiologically and psychologically, for the worst. And because only God Himself knows what this worst might be, we must in our ignorance prepare for all eventualities. And the problem with that continual preparation is that, in excess, it exhausts us. But that does not imply in any manner that chaos should be eliminated (an impossibility, in any case), although what is unknown needs to be managed carefully, as my previous book repeatedly stressed. Whatever is not touched by the new stagnates, and it is certainly the case that a life without curiosity— that instinct pushing us out into the unknown—would be a much-diminished form of existence. What is new is also what is exciting, compelling, and provocative, assuming that the rate at which it is introduced does not intolerably undermine and destabilize our state of being.

Like *12 Rules for Life*, the current volume provides an explication of rules drawn from a longer list of 42, originally published and popularized on the Q and A website Quora. Unlike my previous book, *Beyond Order* explores as its overarching theme how the dangers of too much security and control might be profitably avoided. Because what we understand is insufficient (as we discover when things we are striving to control nonetheless go wrong around us), we need to keep one foot within order while stretching the other tentatively into the beyond. And so we are driven to explore and find the deepest of meanings in standing on the frontier, secure enough to keep our fear under control but learning, constantly learning, as we face what we have not yet made peace with or adapted to. It is this instinct of meaning—something far deeper than mere thought—that orients us properly in life, so that we do not become overwhelmed by what is beyond us, or equally dangerously, stultified and stunted by dated, too narrow, or too pridefully paraded systems of value and belief.

What have I written about, more specifically? Rule I describes the relationship between stable, predictable social structures and individual psychological health, and makes the case that such structures need to be updated by creative people if they are to retain their vitality. Rule II analyzes a centuries-old alchemical image, relying on several stories—ancient and modern—to illuminate the nature and development of the integrated human personality. Rule III warns of the dangers of avoiding the information (vital to the continual rejuvenation of the psyche) signaled by the emergence of negative emotions such as pain, anxiety, and fear.

Rule IV argues that the meaning that sustains people through difficult times is to be found not so much in happiness, which is fleeting, but in in the voluntary adoption of mature responsibility for the self and others. Rule V uses a single example, drawn from my experience as a clinical psychologist, to illustrate the personal and social necessity of attending to the dictates of conscience. Rule VI describes the danger of attributing the cause of complex individual and social problems to single variables such as sex, class, or power.

Rule VII outlines the crucial relationship between disciplined striving in a single direction and forging of the individual character capable of resilience in the face of adversity. Rule VIII focuses on the vital importance of aesthetic experience as a guide to what is true, good, and sustaining in the human world of experience. Rule IX makes the case that past experiences, whose current recall remains laden with pain and fear, can be stripped of their horror by voluntary verbal exploration and reconsideration.

Rule X notes the importance of explicit negotiation to maintenance of the good will, mutual regard, and heartfelt cooperation without which no true romance can be sustained. Rule XI opens by describing the world of human experience in a manner that explains what motivates three common but direly dangerous patterns of psychological response, delineates the catastrophic consequences of falling prey to any or all of them, and lays out an alternative route. Rule XII makes the case that thankfulness in the face of the inevitable tragedies of life should be regarded as a primary manifestation of the admirable moral courage required to continue our difficult march uphill.*

I hope that I am somewhat wiser in my explication of this second set of 12 rules than I was four years ago, when I wrote about the first dozen—not least because of the informative feedback I received in the course of my efforts to formulate my ideas for audiences around the world, in person, on YouTube, and through my podcast and blog.† I

---

*It may be of some interest to note that this book and its predecessor—although each stands on its own—were also designed jointly to represent the balance they both strive to describe. It is for this reason that (in the English-language versions, at least) the first is bound in white and the second in black. They constitute a matched set, like the Taoist yin and yang.
†My YouTube channel can be found at www.youtube.com/user/JordanPetersonVideos. My podcast and blog can be accessed at jordanbpeterson.com.

hope, in consequence, that I have managed to clarify some of the issues that were perhaps left less than optimally developed in my previous work, as well as presenting much that is original. Finally, I hope that people find this book as helpful personally as they seem to have found the first set of 12 Rules. It has been a source of immense gratification that so many people have reported drawing strength from the thoughts and the stories I have had the privilege of bringing forth and sharing.

THE FOOL.

RULE I

DO NOT CARELESSLY DENIGRATE
SOCIAL INSTITUTIONS OR
CREATIVE ACHIEVEMENT

LONELINESS AND CONFUSION

For years, I saw a client who lived by himself.* He was isolated in many other ways in addition to his living situation. He had extremely limited family ties. Both of his daughters had moved out of the country, and did not maintain much contact, and he had no other relatives except a father and sister from whom he was estranged. His wife and the mother of his children had passed away years ago, and the sole relationship he endeavored to establish while he saw me over the course of more than a decade and a half terminated tragically when his new partner was killed in an automobile accident.

When we began to work together, our conversations were decidedly awkward. He was not accustomed to the subtleties of social interaction,

---

*I have modified the accounts drawn from my clinical practice enough to ensure the continuing privacy of my clients while endeavoring to maintain the essential narrative truth of what I am relating.

so his behaviors, verbal and nonverbal, lacked the dance-like rhythm and harmony that characterize the socially fluent. As a child, he had been thoroughly ignored as well as actively discouraged by both parents. His father—mostly absent—was neglectful and sadistic in his inclinations, while his mother was chronically alcoholic. He had also been consistently tormented and harassed at school, and had not chanced upon a teacher in all his years of education who paid him any genuine attention. These experiences left my client with a proclivity toward depression, or at least worsened what might have been a biological tendency in that direction. He was, in consequence, abrupt, irritable, and somewhat volatile if he felt misunderstood or was unexpectedly interrupted during a conversation. Such reactions helped ensure that his targeting by bullies continued into his adult life, particularly in his place of work.

I soon noticed, however, that things worked out quite well during our sessions if I kept mostly quiet. He would drop in, weekly or biweekly, and talk about what had befallen and preoccupied him during the previous seven to fourteen days. If I maintained silence for the first fifty minutes of our one-hour sessions, listening intently, then we could converse, in a relatively normal, reciprocal manner, for the remaining ten minutes. This pattern continued for more than a decade, as I learned, increasingly, to hold my tongue (something that does not come easily to me). As the years passed, however, I noticed that the proportion of time he spent discussing negative issues with me decreased. Our conversation—his monologue, really—had always started with what was bothering him, and rarely progressed past that. But he worked hard outside our sessions, cultivating friends, attending artistic gatherings and music festivals, and resurrecting a long-dormant talent for composing songs and playing the guitar. As he became more social, he began to generate solutions to the problems he communicated

to me, and to discuss, in the latter portion of the hours we shared, some
of the more positive aspects of his existence. It was slow going, but he
made continual incremental progress. When he first came to see me,
we could not sit together at a table in a coffee shop—or, indeed, in any
public space—and practice anything resembling a real-world conversation without his being paralyzed into absolute silence. By the time
we finished, he was reading his original poetry in front of small groups,
and had even tried his hand at stand-up comedy.

He was the best personal and practical exemplar of something I
had come to realize over my more than twenty years of psychological practice: people depend on constant communication with others
to keep their minds organized. We all need to think to keep things
straight, but we mostly think by talking. We need to talk about the
past, so we can distinguish the trivial, overblown concerns that otherwise plague our thoughts from the experiences that are truly important. We need to talk about the nature of the present and our plans for
the future, so we know where we are, where we are going, and why we
are going there. We must submit the strategies and tactics we formulate to the judgments of others, to ensure their efficiency and resilience. We need to listen to ourselves as we talk, as well, so that we may
organize our otherwise inchoate bodily reactions, motivations, and
emotions into something articulate and organized, and dispense with
those concerns that are exaggerated and irrational. We need to talk—
both to remember and to forget.

My client desperately needed someone to listen to him. He also
needed to be fully part of additional, larger, and more complex social
groups—something he planned in our sessions together, and then carried out on his own. Had he fallen prey to the temptation to denigrate
the value of interpersonal interactions and relationships because of his
history of isolation and harsh treatment, he would have had very little

chance of regaining his health and well-being. Instead, he learned the ropes and joined the world.

SANITY AS A SOCIAL INSTITUTION

For Drs. Sigmund Freud and Carl Jung, the great depth psychologists, sanity was a characteristic of the individual mind. People were well-adjusted, in their views, when the subpersonalities existing within each of them were properly integrated and balanced in expression. The id, the instinctive part of the psyche (from the German "it," representing nature, in all its power and foreignness, inside us); the superego (the sometimes oppressive, internalized representative of social order); and the ego (the I, the personality proper, crushed between those two necessary tyrants)—all had their specialized functions for Freud, who first conceptualized their existence. Id, ego, and superego interacted with each other like the executive, legislative, and judicial branches of a modern government. Jung, although profoundly influenced by Freud, parsed the complexity of the psyche in a different manner. For him, the ego of the individual had to find its proper place in relationship to the shadow (the dark side of the personality), the anima or animus (the contrasexual and thus often repressed side of the personality), and the self (the internal being of ideal possibility). But all these different subentities, Jungian and Freudian alike, share one thing in common: they exist in the interior of the person, regardless of his or her surroundings. People are social beings, however—par excellence—and there is no shortage of wisdom and guidance outside of us, embedded in the social world. Why rely on our own limited resources to remember the road, or to orient ourselves in new territory, when we can rely on signs and guideposts placed there so effortfully by others? Freud and Jung, with their intense focus on the autonomous individual psyche, placed too little focus on the role of the community in the maintenance of personal mental health.

It is for such reasons that I assess the position of all my new clinical clients along a few dimensions largely dependent on the social world when I first start working with them: Have they been educated to the level of their intellectual ability or ambition? Is their use of free time engaging, meaningful, and productive? Have they formulated solid and well-articulated plans for the future? Are they (and those they are close to) free of any serious physical health or economic problems? Do they have friends and a social life? A stable and satisfying intimate partnership? Close and functional familial relationships? A career—or, at least, a job—that is financially sufficient, stable and, if possible, a source of satisfaction and opportunity? If the answer to any three or more of these questions is no, I consider that my new client is insufficiently embedded in the interpersonal world and is in danger of spiraling downward psychologically because of that. People exist among other people and not as purely individual minds. An individual does not have to be that well put together if he or she can remain at least minimally acceptable in behavior to others. Simply put: We outsource the problem of sanity. People remain mentally healthy not merely because of the integrity of their own minds, but because they are constantly being reminded how to think, act, and speak by those around them.

If you begin to deviate from the straight and narrow path—if you begin to act improperly—people will react to your errors before they become too great, and cajole, laugh, tap, and criticize you back into place. They will raise an eyebrow, or smile (or not), or pay attention (or not). If other people can tolerate having you around, in other words, they will constantly remind you not to misbehave, and just as constantly call on you to be at your best. All that is left for you to do is watch, listen, and respond appropriately to the cues. Then you might remain motivated, and able to stay together enough so that you will not begin the long journey downhill. This is reason enough to appreciate your immersion in the world of other people—friends, family members, and foes alike—despite the anxiety and frustration that social interactions so often produce.

But how did we develop the broad consensus regarding social behavior that serves to buttress our psychological stability? It seems a daunting task—if not impossible—in the face of the complexity that constantly confronts us. "Do we pursue this or that?" "How does the worth of this piece of work compare to the worth of that?" "Who is more competent, or more creative, or more assertive, and should therefore be ceded authority?" Answers to such questions are largely formulated in consequence of intensive negotiation—verbal and nonverbal—regulating individual action, cooperation, and competition. What we deem to be valuable and worthy of attention becomes part of the social contract; part of the rewards and punishments meted out respectively for compliance and noncompliance; part of what continually indicates and reminds: "Here is what is valued. Look at that (perceive that) and not something else. Pursue that (act toward that end) and not some other." Compliance with those indications and reminders is, in large measure, sanity itself—and is something required from every one of us right from the early stages of our lives. Without the intermediation of the social world, it would be impossible for us to organize our minds, and we would simply be overwhelmed by the world.

THE POINT OF POINTING

I have the great good fortune of a granddaughter, Elizabeth Scarlett Peterson Korikova, born in August 2017. I have watched her carefully while she develops, trying to understand what she is up to and playing along with it. When she was about a year and a half old, she engaged in all manner of unbearably endearing behaviors—giggling and laughing when she was poked, high-fiving, bumping heads, and rubbing noses. However, in my opinion, the most noteworthy of all the actions she undertook at that age was her pointing.

She had discovered her index finger, using it to specify all the objects in the world she found interesting. She delighted in doing so, particularly when her pointing called forth the attention of the adults surrounding her. This indicated, in a manner not duplicable in any other way, that her action and intention had *import*—definable at least in part as the tendency of a behavior or attitude to compel the attention of others. She thrived on that, and no wonder. We compete for attention, personally, socially, and economically. No currency has a value that exceeds it. Children, adults, and societies wither on the vine in its absence. To have others attend to what you find important or interesting is to validate, first, the importance of what you are attending to, but second, and more crucially, to validate you as a respected center of conscious experience and contributor to the collective world. Pointing is, as well, a crucial precursor to the development of language. To name something—to use the word for the thing—is essentially to point to it, to specify it against everything else, to isolate it for use individually and socially.

When my granddaughter pointed, she did it publicly. When she pointed to something, she could immediately observe how the people close to her reacted. There is just not that much point, so to speak, in pointing to something that no one else cares about. So, she aimed her index finger at something she found interesting and then looked around to see if anyone else cared. She was learning an important lesson at an early age: If you are not communicating about anything that engages other people, then the value of your communication—even the value of your very presence—risks falling to zero. It was in this manner that she began to more profoundly explore the complex hierarchy of value that made up her family and the broader society surrounding her.

Scarlett is now learning to talk—a more sophisticated form of pointing (and of exploration). Every word is a pointer, as well as a simplification or generalization. To name something is not only to make it shine forth against the infinite background of potentially nameable things, but to group or categorize it, simultaneously, with many other phenomena of its broad utility or significance. We use the word "floor," for example, but do not generally employ a separate word for all the floors we might encounter (concrete, wood, earth, glass), much less all the endless variations of color and texture and shade that make up the details of the floors that bear our weight. We use a low-resolution representation: If it holds us up, we can walk on it, and is situated inside a building, then it is a "floor," and that is precise enough. The word distinguishes floors, say, from walls, but also restricts the variability in all the floors that exist to a single concept—flat, stable, walkable indoor surfaces.

The words we employ are tools that structure our experience, subjectively and privately—but are, equally, socially determined. We would not all know and use the word "floor" unless we had all agreed that there was something sufficiently important about floors to justify a word for them. So, the mere fact of naming something (and, of course, agreeing on the name) is an important part of the process whereby the infinitely complex world of phenomena and fact is reduced to the functional world of value. And it is continual interaction with social institutions that makes this reduction—this specification—possible.

WHAT SHOULD WE POINT TO?

The social world narrows and specifies the world for us, marking out what is important. But what does "important" mean? How is it determined? The individual is molded by the social world. But social institutions are molded, too, by the requirements of the individuals who compose them. Arrangements must be made for our provisioning with the basic requirements of life. We cannot live without food, water, clean air, and shelter. Less self-evidently, we require companionship, play, touch, and intimacy. These are all biological as well as psychological necessities (and this is by no means a comprehensive list). We must signify and then utilize those elements of the world capable of providing us with these requirements. And the fact that we are deeply social adds another set of constraints to the situation: We must perceive and act in a manner that meets our biological and psychological needs—but, since none of us lives or can live in isolation, we must meet them in a manner approved of by others. This means that the solutions we apply to our fundamental biological problems must also be acceptable and implementable socially.

It is worth considering more deeply just how necessity limits the universe of viable solutions and implementable plans. First, as we alluded to, the plan must in principle solve some real problem. Second, it must appeal to others—often in the face of competing plans—or those others will not cooperate and might well object. If I value something, therefore, I must determine how to value it so that others potentially benefit. It cannot just be good for me: it must be good for me and for the people around me. And even that is not good enough—which means there are even more constraints on how the world must be perceived and acted upon. The manner in which I view and value the world, integrally associated with the plans I am making, has to work for me, my family, and the broader community. Furthermore, it needs to work today, in a manner that does not make a worse hash of tomorrow, next week, next month, and next year (even the next decade or century). A good solution to a problem involving suffering must be repeatable, without deterioration across repetitions—iterable, in a word—across people and across time.

These universal constraints, manifest biologically and imposed socially, reduce the complexity of the world to something approximating a universally understandable domain of value. That is exceptionally important, because there are unlimited problems and there are hypothetically unlimited potential solutions, but there are a comparatively limited number of solutions that work practically, psychologically, and socially simultaneously. The fact of limited solutions implies the existence of something like a natural ethic—variable, perhaps, as human languages are variable, but still characterized by something solid and universally recognizable at its base. It is the reality of this natural ethic that makes thoughtless denigration of social institutions both wrong and dangerous: wrong and dangerous because those institutions have evolved to solve problems that must be solved for life to continue. They are by no means perfect—but making them better, rather than worse, is a tricky problem indeed.

So, I must take the complexity of the world, reduce it to a single point so that I can act, and take everyone else and their future selves into consideration while I am doing so. How do I manage this? By communicating and negotiating. By outsourcing the terribly complex cognitive problem to the resources of the broader world. The individuals who compose every society cooperate and compete linguistically (although linguistic interaction by no means exhausts the means of cooperation and competition). Words are formulated collectively, and everyone must agree on their use. The verbal framework that helps us delimit the world is a consequence of the landscape of value that is constructed socially—but also bounded by the brute necessity of reality itself. This helps give that landscape shape, and not just any old shape. This is where hierarchies—functional, productive hierarchies— more clearly enter the picture.

Things of import must be done, or people starve or die of thirst or exposure—or of loneliness and absence of touch. What needs to be done must be specified and planned. The requisite skills for doing so must be developed. That specification, planning, and development of skills, as well as the implementation of the informed plan, must be conducted in social space, with the cooperation of others (and in the face of their competition). In consequence, some will be better at solving the problem at hand, and others worse. This variance in ability (as well as the multiplicity of extant problems and the impossibility of training everyone in all skilled domains) necessarily engenders a hierarchical structure—based ideally on genuine competence in relation to the goal. Such a hierarchy is in its essence a socially structured tool that must be employed for the effective accomplishment of necessary and worthwhile tasks. It is also a social institution that makes progress and peace possible at the same time.

BOTTOM UP

The consensus making up the spoken and unspoken assumptions of worth characterizing our societies has an ancient origin, developing over the course of hundreds of millions of years. After all, "How should you act?" is just the short-term, immediate version of the fundamental long-term question, "How should you survive?" It is therefore instructive to look into the distant past—far down the evolutionary chain, right to the basics—and contemplate the establishment of what is important. The most phylogenetically ancient multicellular organisms (that is far enough for our purposes) tend to be composed of relatively undifferentiated sensorimotor cells.[1] These cells map certain facts or features of the environment directly onto the motor output of the same cells, in an essentially one-to-one relationship. Stimulus A means response A, and nothing else, while stimulus B means response B. Among more differentiated and complex creatures—the larger and commonly recognizable denizens of the natural world—the sensory and motor functions separate and specialize, such that cells undertaking the former functions detect patterns in the world and cells in the latter produce patterns of motor output. This differentiation enables a broader range of patterns to be recognized and mapped, as well as a broader range of action and reaction to be undertaken. A third type of cell—neural—emerges sometimes, as well, serving as a computational intermediary between the first two. Among species that have established a neural level of operation, the "same" pattern of input can produce a different pattern of output (depending, for example, on changes in the animal's environment or internal psychophysical condition).

As nervous systems increase in sophistication, and more and more layers of neural intermediation emerge, the relationship between simple fact and motor output becomes increasingly complex, unpredictable, and sophisticated. What is putatively the same thing or situation can be perceived in multiple ways, and two things perceived in the same manner can still give rise to very different behaviors. It is very difficult to constrain even isolated laboratory animals, for example, so thoroughly that they will behave predictably across trials that have been made as similar as possible. As the layers of neural tissue mediating between sensation and action multiply, they also differentiate. Basic motivational systems, often known as drives, appear (hunger, thirst, aggression, etc.), adding additional sensory and behavioral specificity and variability. Superseding motivations, in turn—with no clear line of demarcation—are systems of emotion. Cognitive systems emerge much later, first taking form, arguably, as imagination, and later—and only among human beings—as full-fledged language. Thus, in the most complex of creatures, there is an internal hierarchy of structure, from reflex through drive to language-mediated action (in the particular case of human beings), that must be organized before it can function as a unity and be aimed at a point.[2]

How is this hierarchy organized—a structure that emerged in large part from the bottom up, over the vast spans of evolutionary time? We return to the same answer alluded to earlier: through the constant cooperation and competition—the constant jockeying for resources and position—defining the struggle for survival and reproduction. This happens over the unimaginably lengthy spans of time that characterize evolution, as well as the much shorter course of each individual life. Negotiation for position sorts organisms into the omnipresent hierarchies that govern access to vital resources such as shelter, nourishment, and mates. All creatures of reasonable complexity and even a minimally social nature have their particular place, and know it. All social creatures also learn what is deemed valuable by other group members, and derive from that, as well as from the understanding of their own position, a sophisticated implicit and explicit understanding of value itself. In a phrase: The internal hierarchy that translates facts into actions mirrors the external hierarchy of social organization. It is clear, for example, that chimpanzees in a troop understand their social world and its hierarchical strata at a fine level of detail. They know what is important, and who has privileged access to it. They understand such things as if their survival and reproduction depend upon it, as it does.[3]

A newborn infant is equipped with relatively deterministic reflexes: sucking, crying, startling. These nonetheless provide the starting point for the immense range of skills in action that develop with
human maturation. By the age of two (and often much earlier than
that, for many skills), children can orient with all their senses, walk
upright, use their opposable-thumb-equipped hands for all sorts of
purposes, and communicate their desires and needs both nonverbally
and verbally—and this is of course a partial list. This immense array
of behavioral abilities is integrated into a complex assortment of emotions and motivational drives (anger, sadness, fear, joy, surprise, and
more) and then organized to fulfill whatever specific, narrow purpose
inspires the child for the moment and, increasingly, over longer spans
of time.

The developing infant must also hone and perfect the operation of
his or her currently dominant motivational state in harmony with all
his or her other internal motivational states (as, for example, the separate desire to eat, sleep, and play must learn to coexist so each can manifest itself optimally), and in keeping with the demands, routines, and
opportunities of the social environment. This honing and perfecting
begin within the child's maternal relationship and the spontaneous
play behavior within that circumscribed but still social context. Then,
when the child has matured to the point where the internal hierarchy
of emotional and motivational functions can be subsumed, even temporarily, within a framework provided by a conscious, communicable
abstract goal ("let us play house"), the child is ready to play with
others—and to do so, over time, in an increasingly complex and sophisticated manner.[4]

Play with others depends (as the great developmental psychologist
Jean Piaget observed[5]) upon the collective establishment of a shared
goal with the child's play partners. The collective establishment of a

shared goal—the point of the game—conjoined with rules governing cooperation and competition in relationship to that goal or point, constitutes a true social microcosm. All societies might be regarded as variations upon this play/game theme—*E pluribus unum**—and in all functional and decent societies the basic rules of fair play, predicated upon reciprocity across situation and time, come inevitably to apply. Games, like solutions to problems, must be iterable to endure, and there are principles that apply to and undergird what constitutes that iterability. Piaget suspected, for example, that games undertaken voluntarily will outcompete games imposed and played under threat of force, given that some of the energy that could be expended on the game itself, whatever its nature, has to be wasted on enforcement. There is evidence indicating the emergence of such voluntary game-like arrangements even among our nonhuman kin.[6]

The universal rules of fair play include the ability to regulate emotion and motivation while cooperating and competing in pursuit of the goal during the game (that is part and parcel of being able to play at all), as well as the ability and will to establish reciprocally beneficial interactions across time and situation, as we already discussed. And life is not simply a game, but a series of games, each of which has something in common (whatever defines a game) and something unique (or there would be no reason for multiple games). At minimum, there is a starting point (kindergarten, a 0–0 score, a first date, an entry-level job) that needs to be improved upon; a procedure for enacting that improvement; and a desirable goal (graduation from high school, a winning score, a permanent romantic relationship, a prestigious career). Because of that commonality, there is an ethic—or more properly, a meta-ethic—that emerges, from the bottom up, across the set of

---

*"Out of many, one."

all games. The best player is therefore not the winner of any given game but, among many other things, he or she who is invited by the largest number of others to play the most extensive series of games. It is for this reason, which you may not understand explicitly at the time, that you tell your children: "It's not whether you win or lose. It's how you play the game!"* How should you play, to be that most desirable of

---

*Even rats understand this. Jaak Panksepp, one of the founders of the psychological sub-field called affective neuroscience and an extremely creative, courageous, and gifted researcher, spent many years analyzing the role of play in the development and social-ization of rats (see J. Panksepp, *Affective Neuroscience: The Foundations of Human and Animal Emotions* [New York: Oxford University Press, 1998], particularly the chapter on play, 280–99). Rats like to play. They particularly enjoy rough-and-tumble play, particularly if they are male juvenile rats. They enjoy it so much that they will voluntarily work—pulling a lever repeatedly, say—to gain the opportunity to enter an arena where another juvenile waits to play. When two juvenile strangers meet for the first time in this situa-tion, they size each other up and then establish dominance. If one rat is only 10 percent larger than the other, he can pretty much win every physical contest, every rat wrestling match—but they still wrestle to find out, and the larger rat almost inevitably pins the smaller. If you were inclined to view the establishment of hierarchy as equivalent to dominance by power, that would be game over. The larger, more powerful rat won. End of story. But that is by no means the end of the story, unless the rats meet only once. Rats live in social environments, and they interact with the same individuals over and over. Thus, the game, once started, continues—and the rules have to govern not so much the single game as the repeating one. Once dominance is established, the rats can play—something they do in a manner very different from genuine fighting (just like play fight-ing with a pet dog is very different from being attacked by a dog). Now, the larger rat could pin the smaller rat every time. However, that breaks the rules (really, the meta-rules: those that are observable only over the course of repeated games). The purpose of the repeated game is not dominance, but continuing play. This is not to say that the initial dominance is without significance. It matters, not least in the following manner: When the two rats meet a second time, they will both adopt a unique role. The smaller rat is now duty bound to invite his larger friend to play, and the larger rat is duty bound to accept the invitation. The former will jump around playfully, to indicate his intent. The larger rat might hang back and act cool and a bit dismissive (as is now his preroga-tive); but if he's a decent sort he will join in the fun, as in his heart of hearts he truly wants to play. However—and this is the critical issue—if the larger rat does not let the smaller rat win the repeated wrestling matches some substantial proportion of the time (Panksepp estimated 30 to 40 percent of the time), the smaller rat will stop exhibiting invitations to play. It is just not any fun for the little guy. Thus, if the larger rat dominates with power (like a bully), as he could, then he will lose at the highest level (the level players? What structure must take form within you so that such play is possible? And those two questions are interrelated, because the structure that will enable you to play properly (and with increasing and automated or habitual precision) will emerge only in the process of continually practicing the art of playing properly. Where might you learn how to play? Everywhere . . . if you are fortunate and awake.

THE UTILITY OF THE FOOL

It is useful to take your place at the bottom of a hierarchy. It can aid in the development of gratitude and humility. *Gratitude:* There are people whose expertise exceeds your own, and you should be wisely pleased about that. There are many valuable niches to fill, given the many complex and serious problems we must solve. The fact that there are people who fill those niches with trustworthy skill and experience is something for which to be truly thankful. *Humility:* It is better to presume ignorance and invite learning than to assume sufficient knowledge and risk the consequent blindness. It is much better to make friends with what you do not know than with what you do know, as there is an infinite supply of the former but a finite stock of the latter. When you are tightly boxed in or cornered—all too often by your own

---

where the fun continues for the longest possible time), even while he "wins" more frequently at the lower. What does this imply? Most important, that power is simply not a stable basis upon which to construct a hierarchy designed to optimally govern repeated interactions. And this is not just true for rats. Alpha males among at least certain primate groups are far more prosocial than their lesser comrades. Power doesn't work for them, either (see F. B. M. de Waal and M. Suchak, "Prosocial Primates: Selfish and Unselfish Motivations," *Philosophical Transactions of the Royal Society of London: Biological Science* 365 [2010]: 2711–22. See also F. de Waal, *The Surprising Science of Alpha Males*, TEDMED 2017, bit.ly/primate_ethic).

stubborn and fixed adherence to some unconsciously worshipped assumptions—all there is to help you is what you have not yet learned.

It is necessary and helpful to be, and in some ways to remain, a beginner. For this reason, the Tarot deck beloved by intuitives, romantics, fortune-tellers, and scoundrels alike contains within it the Fool as a positive card, an illustrated variant of which opens this chapter. The Fool is a young, handsome man, eyes lifted upward, journeying in the mountains, sun shining brightly upon him—about to carelessly step over a cliff (or is he?). His strength, however, is precisely his willingness to risk such a drop; to risk being once again at the bottom. No one unwilling to be a foolish beginner can learn. It was for this reason, among others, that Carl Jung regarded the Fool as the archetypal precursor to the figure of the equally archetypal Redeemer, the perfected individual.

The beginner, the fool, is continually required to be patient and tolerant—with himself and, equally, with others. His displays of ignorance, inexperience, and lack of skill may still sometimes be rightly attributed to irresponsibility and condemned, justly, by others. But the insufficiency of the fool is often better regarded as an inevitable consequence of each individual's essential vulnerability, rather than as a true moral failing. Much that is great starts small, ignorant, and useless. This lesson permeates popular as well as classical or traditional culture. Consider, for example, the Disney heroes Pinocchio and Simba, as well as J. K. Rowling's magical Harry Potter. Pinocchio begins as a wooden-headed marionette, the puppet of everyone's decisions but his own. The Lion King has his origin as a naive cub, the unwitting pawn of a treacherous and malevolent uncle. The student of wizarding is an unloved orphan, with a dusty cupboard for a bedroom, and Voldemort—who might as well be Satan himself—for his archenemy.

Great mythologized heroes often come into the world, likewise, in the most meager of circumstances (as the child of an Israelite slave, for example, or newborn in a lowly manger) and in great danger (consider the Pharaoh's decision to slay all the firstborn male babies of the Israelites, and Herod's comparable edict, much later). But today's beginner is tomorrow's master. Thus, it is necessary even for the most accomplished (but who wishes to accomplish still more) to retain identification with the as yet unsuccessful; to appreciate the striving toward competence; to carefully and with true humility subordinate him or herself to the current game; and to develop the knowledge, self-control, and discipline necessary to make the next move.

I visited a restaurant in Toronto with my wife, son, and daughter while writing this. As I made my way to my party's table, a young waiter asked if he might say a few words to me. He told me that he had been watching my videos, listening to my podcasts, and reading my book, and that he had, in consequence, changed his attitude toward his comparatively lower-status (but still useful and necessary) job. He had ceased criticizing what he was doing or himself for doing it, deciding instead to be grateful and seek out whatever opportunities presented themselves right there before him. He made up his mind to become more diligent and reliable and to see what would happen if he worked as hard at it as he could. He told me, with an uncontrived smile, that he had been promoted three times in six months.

The young man had come to realize that every place he might find himself in had more potential than he might first see (particularly when his vision was impaired by the resentment and cynicism he felt from being near the bottom). After all, it is not as if a restaurant is a simple place—and this was part of an extensive national organization, a large, high-quality chain. To do a good job in such a place, servers must get along with the cooks, who are by universal recognition a formidably troublesome and tricky lot. They must also be polite and engaging with customers. They have to pay attention constantly. They must adjust to highly varying workloads—the rushes and dead times that inevitably accompany the life of a server. They have to show up on time, sober and awake. They must treat their superiors with the proper respect and do the same for those—such as the dishwashers— below them in the structure of authority. And if they do all these things, and happen to be working in a functional institution, they will soon render themselves difficult to replace. Customers, colleagues, and superiors alike will begin to react to them in an increasingly positive manner. Doors that would otherwise remain closed to them— even invisible—will be opened. Furthermore, the skills they acquire will prove eminently portable, whether they continue to rise in the hierarchy of restaurateurs, decide instead to further their education, or change their career trajectory completely (in which case they will leave with laudatory praise from their previous employers and vastly increased chances of discovering the next opportunity).

As might be expected, the young man who had something to say to me was thrilled with what had happened to him. His status concerns had been solidly and realistically addressed by his rapid career advance, and the additional money he was making did not hurt, either. He had accepted, and therefore transcended, his role as a beginner. He had ceased being casually cynical about the place he occupied in the world and the people who surrounded him, and accepted the structure and the position he was offered. He started to see possibility and opportunity, where before he was blinded, essentially, by his pride. He stopped denigrating the social institution he found himself part of and began to play his part properly. And that increment in humility paid off in spades.

THE NECESSITY OF EQUALS

It is good to be a beginner, but it is a good of a different sort to be an equal among equals. It is said, with much truth, that genuine communication can take place only between peers. This is because it is very difficult to move information up a hierarchy. Those well positioned (and this is a great danger of moving up) have used their current competence—their cherished opinions, their present knowledge, their current skills—to stake a moral claim to their status. In consequence, they have little motivation to admit to error, to learn or change—and plenty of reason not to. If a subordinate exposes the ignorance of someone with greater status, he risks humiliating that person, questioning the validity of the latter's claim to influence and status, and revealing him as incompetent, outdated, or false. For this reason, it is very wise to approach your boss, for example, carefully and privately with a problem (and perhaps best to have a solution at hand—and not one proffered too incautiously).

Barriers exist to the flow of genuine information *down* a hierarchy, as well. For example, the resentment people lower in the chain of command might feel about their hypothetically lesser position can make them loath to act productively on information from above—or, in the worst case, can motivate them to work at counterpurposes to what they have learned, out of sheer spite. In addition, those who are inexperienced or less educated, or who newly occupy a subordinate position and therefore lack knowledge of their surroundings, can be more easily influenced by relative position and the exercise of power, instead of quality of argumentation and observation of competence. Peers, by contrast, must in the main be convinced. Their attention must be carefully reciprocated. To be surrounded by peers is to exist in a state of equality, and to manifest the give-and-take necessary to maintain that equality. It is therefore good to be in the middle of a hierarchy.

This is partly why friendships are so important, and why they form so early in life. A two-year-old, typically, is self-concerned, although also capable of simple reciprocal actions. The same Scarlett whom I talked about earlier—my granddaughter—would happily hand me one of her favorite stuffed toys, attached to a pacifier, when I asked her to. Then I would hand it, or toss it, back (sometimes she would toss it to me, too—or at least relatively near me). She loved this game. We played it with a spoon, as well—an implement she was just beginning to master. She played the same way with her mother and her grandmother—with anyone who happened to be within playing distance, if she was familiar enough with them not to be shy. This was the beginning of the behaviors that transform themselves into full-fledged sharing among older children.

My daughter, Mikhaila, Scarlett's mother, took her child to the outdoor recreational space on top of their downtown condo a few days before I wrote this. A number of other children were playing there, most of them older, and there were plenty of toys. Scarlett spent her time hoarding as many of the playthings as possible near her mother's chair, and was distinctly unimpressed if other children came along to purloin one for themselves. She even took a ball directly from another child to add to her collection. This is typical behavior for children two and younger. Their ability to reciprocate, while hardly absent (and able to manifest itself in truly endearing ways), is developmentally limited.

By three years of age, however, most children are capable of truly sharing. They can delay gratification long enough to take their turn while playing a game that everyone cannot play simultaneously. They can begin to understand the point of a game played by several people and follow the rules, although they may not be able to give a coherent verbal account of what those rules are. They start to form friendships upon repeated exposure to children with whom they have successfully negotiated reciprocal play relationships. Some of these friendships turn into the first intense relationships that children have outside their family. It is in the context of such relationships, which tend strongly to form between equals in age (or at least equals in developmental stage), that a child learns to bond tightly to a peer and starts to learn how to treat another person properly while requiring the same in return.

This mutual bonding is vitally important. A child without at least one special, close friend is much more likely to suffer later psychological problems, whether of the depressive/anxious or antisocial sort,[7] while children with fewer friends are also more likely to be unemployed and unmarried as adults.[8] There is no evidence that the importance of friendship declines in any manner with age.* All causes of mortality appear to be reduced among adults with high-quality social networks, even when general health status is taken into consideration. This remains true among the elderly in the case of diseases such as hypertension, diabetes, emphysema, and arthritis, and for younger and older adults alike in the case of heart attacks. Interestingly enough, there is some evidence that it is the provision of social support, as much or more than its receipt, that provides these protective benefits (and, somewhat unsurprisingly, that those who give more tend to receive more).[9] Thus, it truly seems that it is better to give than to receive.

Peers distribute both the burdens and joys of life. Recently, when my wife, Tammy, and I suffered serious health problems, we were fortunate enough to have family members (my in-laws, sister and brother;

---

*This makes the July 30, 2019, poll from YouGov, "Millennials Are the Loneliest Generation" (bit.ly/2TVVMLn), indicating that 25 percent have no acquaintances and 22 percent no friends, particularly ominous, if true.

my own mother and sister; our children) and close friends stay with us and help for substantial periods of time. They were willing to put their own lives on hold to aid us while we were in crisis. Before that, when my book *12 Rules for Life* became a success, and during the extensive speaking tour that followed, Tammy and I were close to people with whom we could share our good fortune. These were friends and family members genuinely pleased with what was happening and following the events of our lives avidly, and who were willing to discuss what could have been the overwhelming public response. This greatly heightened the significance and meaning of everything we were doing and reduced the isolation that such a dramatic shift in life circumstances, for better or worse, is likely to produce.

The relationships established with colleagues of similar status at work constitute another important source of peer regulation, in addition to friendship. To maintain good relationships with your colleagues means, among other things, to give credit where credit is due; to take your fair share of the jobs no one wants but still must be done; to deliver on time and in a high-quality manner when teamed with other people; to show up when expected; and, in general, to be trusted to do somewhat more than your job formally requires. The approval or disapproval of your colleagues rewards and enforces this continual reciprocity, and that—like the reciprocity that is necessarily part of friendship—helps maintain stable psychological function. It is much better to be someone who can be relied upon, not least so that during times of personal trouble the people you have worked beside are willing and able to step in and help.

Through friendship and collegial relationships we modify our selfish proclivities, learning not to always put ourselves first. Less obviously, but just as importantly, we may also learn to overcome our naive and too empathic proclivities (our tendency to sacrifice ourselves unsuitably and unjustly to predatory others) when our peers advise and encourage us to stand up for ourselves. In consequence, if we are fortunate, we begin to practice true reciprocity, and we gain at least some of the advantage spoken about so famously by the poet Robert Burns:

> O wad some Pow'r the giftie gie us
> To see oursels as ithers see us!
> It wad frae mony a blunder free us,
> An' foolish notion:
> What airs in dress an' gait wad lea'e us,
> An' ev'n devotion![10]

TOP DOG

It is a good thing to be an authority. People are fragile. Because of that, life is difficult and suffering common. Ameliorating that suffering— ensuring that everyone has food, clean water, sanitary facilities, and a place to take shelter, for starters—takes initiative, effort, and ability. If there is a problem to be solved, and many people involve themselves in the solution, then a hierarchy must and will arise, as those who *can* do, and those who *cannot* follow as best they can, often learning to be competent in the process. If the problem is real, then the people who are best at solving the problem at hand should rise to the top. That is not power. It is the authority that properly accompanies ability.

Now, it is self-evidently appropriate to grant power to competent authorities, if they are solving necessary problems; and it is equally appropriate to be one of those competent authorities, if possible, when there is a perplexing problem at hand. This might be regarded as a philosophy of responsibility. A responsible person decides to make a problem his or her problem, and then works diligently—even ambitiously—for its solution, with other people, in the most efficient manner possible (efficient, because there are other problems to solve, and efficiency allows for the conservation of resources that might then be devoted importantly elsewhere).

Ambition is often—and often purposefully—misidentified with the desire for power, and damned with faint praise, and denigrated, and punished. And ambition is sometimes exactly that wish for undue influence on others. But there is a crucial difference between *sometimes* and *always*. Authority is not mere power, and it is extremely unhelpful, even dangerous, to confuse the two. When people exert power over others, they compel them, forcefully. They apply the threat of privation or punishment so their subordinates have little choice but to act in a manner contrary to their personal needs, desires, and values. When people wield authority, by contrast, they do so because of their competence—a competence that is spontaneously recognized and appreciated by others, and generally followed willingly, with a certain relief, and with the sense that justice is being served.

Those who are power hungry—tyrannical and cruel, even psychopathic—desire control over others so that every selfish whim of hedonism can be immediately gratified; so that envy can destroy its target; so that resentment can find its expression. But good people are ambitious (and diligent, honest, and focused along with it) instead because they are possessed by the desire to solve genuine, serious problems. That variant of ambition needs to be encouraged in every possible manner. It is for this reason, among many others, that the increasingly reflexive identification of the striving of boys and men for victory with the "patriarchal tyranny" that hypothetically characterizes our modern, productive, and comparatively free societies is so stunningly counterproductive (and, it must be said, cruel: there is almost nothing worse than treating someone striving for competence as a tyrant in training). "Victory," in one of its primary and most socially important aspects, is the overcoming of obstacles for the broader public good. Someone who is sophisticated as a winner wins in a manner that improves the game itself, for all the players. To adopt an attitude of naive or willfully blind cynicism about this, or to deny outright that it is true, is to position yourself—perhaps purposefully, as people have many dark motives—as an enemy of the practical amelioration of suffering itself. I can think of few more sadistic attitudes.

Now, power may accompany authority, and perhaps it must. However, and more important, *genuine authority constrains the arbitrary exercise of power.* This constraint manifests itself when the authoritative agent cares, and takes responsibility, for those over whom the exertion of power is possible. The oldest child can take accountability for his younger siblings, instead of domineering over and teasing and torturing them, and can learn in that manner how to exercise authority and limit the misuse of power. Even the youngest can exercise appropriate authority over the family dog. To adopt authority is to learn that power requires concern and competence—and that it comes at a genuine cost. Someone newly promoted to a management position soon learns that managers are frequently more stressed by their multiple subordinates than subordinates are stressed by their single manager. Such experience moderates what might otherwise become romantic but dangerous fantasies about the attractiveness of power, and helps quell the desire for its infinite extension. And, in the real world, those who occupy positions of authority in functional hierarchies are generally struck to the core by the responsibility they bear for the people they supervise, employ, and mentor.

Not everyone feels this burden, of course. A person who has become established as an authority can forget his origins and come to develop a counterproductive contempt for the person who is just starting out.

This is a mistake, not least because it means that the established person cannot risk doing something new (as it would mean adopting the role of despised fool). It is also because arrogance bars the path to learning. Shortsighted, willfully blind, and narrowly selfish tyrants certainly exist, but they are by no means in the majority, at least in functional societies. Otherwise nothing would work.

The authority who remembers his or her sojourn as voluntary beginner, by contrast, can retain their identification with the newcomer and the promise of potential, and use that memory as the source of personal information necessary to constrain the hunger for power. One of the things that has constantly amazed me is the delight that decent people take in the ability to provide opportunities to those over whom they currently exercise authority. I have experienced this repeatedly: personally, as a university professor and researcher (and observed many other people in my situation doing the same); and in the business and other professional settings I have become familiar with. There is great intrinsic pleasure in helping already competent and admirable young people become highly skilled, socially valuable, autonomous, responsible professionals. It is not unlike the pleasure taken in raising children, and it is one of the primary motivators of valid ambition. Thus, the position of top dog, when occupied properly, has as one of its fundamental attractions the opportunity to identify deserving individuals at or near the beginning of their professional life, and provide them with the means of productive advancement.

SOCIAL INSTITUTIONS ARE NECESSARY— BUT INSUFFICIENT

Sanity is knowing the rules of the social game, internalizing them, and following them. Differences in status are therefore inevitable, as all worthwhile endeavors have a goal, and those who pursue them have different abilities in relationship to that goal. Accepting the fact of this disequilibrium and striving forward nonetheless—whether presently at the bottom, middle, or top—is an important element of mental health. But a paradox remains. The solutions of yesterday and today, upon which our current hierarchies depend, will not necessarily serve as solutions tomorrow. Thoughtless repetition of what sufficed in the past—or, worse, authoritarian insistence that all problems have been permanently solved—therefore means the introduction of great danger when changes in the broader world makes local change necessary. Respect for creative transformation must in consequence accompany appropriate regard for the problem-solving hierarchical structures bequeathed to us by the past. That is neither an arbitrary moral opinion nor a morally relative claim. It is something more akin to knowledge of twin natural laws built into the structure of our reality. Highly social creatures such as we are must abide by the rules, to remain sane and minimize unnecessary uncertainty, suffering, and strife. However, we must also transform those rules carefully, as circumstances change around us.

This implies, as well, that the ideal personality cannot remain an unquestioning reflection of the current social state. Under normal conditions, it may be nonetheless said that the *ability* to conform unquestioningly trumps the *inability* to conform. However, the *refusal* to conform when the social surround has become pathological—incomplete, archaic, willfully blind, or corrupt—is something of even higher value, as is the capacity to offer creative, valid alternatives. This leaves all of us with a permanent moral conundrum: When do we simply follow convention, doing what others request or demand; and when do we rely on our own individual judgment, with all its limitations and biases, and reject the requirements of the collective? In other words:

How do we establish a balance between reasonable conservatism and revitalizing creativity?

First and foremost on the psychological front is the issue of temperament. Some people are temperamentally predisposed to conservatism, and others to more liberal creative perception and action.[11] This does not mean that socialization has no ability to alter that predisposition; human beings are very plastic organisms, with a long period of preadult development, and the circumstances we find ourselves in can change us very drastically. That does not alter the fact, however, that there are relatively permanent niches in the human environment to which different modes of temperament have adapted to fill.

Those who tend toward the right, politically, are staunch defenders of all that has worked in the past. And much of the time, they are correct in being so, because of the limited number of pathways that produce personal success, social harmony, and long-term stability. But sometimes they are wrong: first, because the present and the future differ from the past; second, because even once-functional hierarchies typically (inevitably?) fall prey to internal machinations in a manner that produces their downfall. Those who rise to the top can do so through manipulation and the exercise of unjust power, acting in a manner that works only for them, at least in the short term; but that kind of ascendance undermines the proper function of the hierarchy they are nominally part of. Such people generally fail to understand or do not care what function the organization they have made their host was designed to fulfill. They extract what they can from the riches that lie before them and leave a trail of wreckage in their wake.

It is this corruption of power that is strongly objected to by those on the liberal/left side of the political spectrum, and rightly so. But it is critically important to distinguish between a hierarchy that is functional and productive (and the people who make it so) and the degenerate shell of a once-great institution. Making that distinction requires the capacity and the willingness to observe and differentiate, rather than mindless reliance on ideological proclivity. It requires knowing that there is a bright side to the social hierarchies we necessarily inhabit, as well as a dark (and the realization that concentrating on one to the exclusion of the other is dangerously biased). It also requires knowledge that on the more radical, creative side—the necessary source of revitalization for what has become immoral and outdated—there also lurks great danger. Part of the danger is that very tendency of those who think more liberally to see only the negative in well-founded institutions. The further danger stems from the counterpart to the corrupt but conservative processes that destabilize and destroy functional hierarchies: there are unethical radicals, just as there are crooked administrators, managers, and executives. These individuals tend to be profoundly ignorant of the complex realities of the status quo, unconscious of their own ignorance, and ungrateful for what the past has bequeathed to them. Such ignorance and ingratitude are often conjoined with the willingness to use tired clichés of cynicism to justify refusal to engage either in the dull but necessary rigors of convention or the risks and difficulties of truly generative endeavor. It is this corruption of creative transformation that renders the conservative—and not only the conservative—appropriately cautious of change.

A few years before writing this, I had a discussion with a young woman in her early twenties—the niece of someone who emailed me after watching some of my online lectures. She appeared severely unhappy, and said that she had spent much of the past six months lying in bed. She came to talk to me because she was becoming desperate. The only thing that stood between her and suicide, as far as she was concerned, was the responsibility she still maintained for an exotic pet, a serval cat. This was the last remaining manifestation of an interest in biology that once gripped her, but which she abandoned, much to her current regret, when she dropped out of high school. She had not been well attended to by her parents, who had allowed her to drift in the manner that had become disastrous over the span of several years.

Despite her decline, she had formulated a bit of a plan. She said she had thought about enrolling in a two-year program that would enable her to finish high school, as a prerequisite for applying to a veterinary college. But she had not made the necessary detailed inquiries into what would be required to carry out this ambition. She lacked a mentor. She had no good friends. It was far too easy for her to remain inactive and disappear into her isolation. We had a good conversation, for about three quarters of an hour. She was a nice kid. I offered to discuss her future in more detail if she would complete an online planning program designed by my professorial colleagues and me.*

All was going well until the discussion twisted toward the political. After discussing her personal situation, she began to voice her discontent with the state of the world at large—with the looming catastrophe, in her opinion, of the effects of human activity on the environment. Now, there is nothing wrong, in principle, with the expression of concern for planet-wide issues. That is not the point. There is something wrong, however, with overestimating your knowledge of such things—or perhaps even considering them—when you are a mid-twenty-year-old with nothing positive going on in your life and you are having great difficulty even getting out of bed. Under those condi-

---

*This is part of the Self-Authoring Suite, a set of individual programs designed to help people write about the troubles of their past (Past Authoring), the faults and virtues of their present personality (Present Authoring, in two parts), and their desires and wishes for the future (Future Authoring). I specifically recommended the latter.

tions, you need to get your priorities straight, and establishing the humility necessary to attend to and solve your own problems is a crucial part of doing just that.

As the verbal exchange continued, I found myself no longer engaged in a genuine conversation with a lost young woman who had come to speak with me. Instead, I became a hypothetically equal partner in a debate with an ideologue who knew what was wrong, globally speaking; who knew who was at fault for those global problems; who knew that participating in the continuing destruction by manifesting any personal desire whatsoever was immoral; and who believed, finally, that we were all both guilty and doomed. Continuing the conversation at that point meant I was (1) speaking not with this young woman so much as with whatever or whomever took possession of her while in the grip of generic, impersonal, and cynical ideas, and (2) implying that discussion of such topics under the circumstances was both acceptable and productive.

There was no point in either outcome. So, I stopped (which did not mean that the entire meeting had been a waste). It was impossible for me not to conclude that some of what had reduced her to her monthslong state of moral paralysis was not so much guilt about potentially contributing to the negative effects of human striving on the broader world, as it was the sense of moral superiority that concern about such things brought her (despite the exceptional psychological danger of embracing this dismal view of human possibility). Excuse the cliché, but it is necessary to walk before you can run. You may even have to crawl before you can walk. This is part of accepting your position as a beginner, at the bottom of the hierarchy you so casually, arrogantly, and self-servingly despise. Furthermore, the deeply anti-human attitude that often accompanies tears shed for environmental degradation and man's inhumanity to man cannot but help but have a marked effect on the psychological attitude that defines a person's relationship to him or herself.

It has taken since time immemorial for us to organize ourselves, biologically and socially, into the functional hierarchies that both specify our perceptions and actions, and define our interactions with the natural and social world. Profound gratitude for that gift is the only proper response. The structure that encompasses us all has its dark side—just as nature does, just as each individual does—but that does not mean careless, generic, and self-serving criticism of the status quo is appropriate (any more than knee-jerk objection to what might be necessary change).

THE NECESSITY OF BALANCE

Because doing what others do and have always done so often works, and because, sometimes, radical action can produce success beyond measure, the conservative and the creative attitudes and actions constantly propagate themselves. A functional social institution—a hierarchy devoted to producing something of value, beyond the mere insurance of its own survival—can utilize the conservative types to carefully implement processes of tried-and-true value, and the creative, liberal types to determine how what is old and out of date might be replaced by something new and more valuable. The balance between conservatism and originality might therefore be properly struck, socially, by bringing the two types of persons together. But someone must determine how best to do that, and that requires a wisdom that transcends mere temperamental proclivity. Because the traits associated with creativity, on the one hand, and comfort with the status quo, on the other, tend to be mutually exclusive, it is difficult to find a single person who has balanced both properly, who is therefore comfortable working with each type, and who can attend, in an unbiased manner, to the necessity for capitalizing on the respective forms of talent and proclivity. But the development of that ability can at least begin with an expansion of conscious wisdom: the articulated realization that conservatism is good (with a set of associated dangers), and that creative transformation—even of the radical sort—is also good (with a set of associated dangers). Learning this deeply—truly appreciating the need for both viewpoints—means at least the possibility of valuing what truly diverse people have to offer, and of being able to recognize when the balance has swung too far in one direction. The same is true of the knowledge of the shadow side of both. To manage complex affairs properly, it is necessary to be cold enough in vision to separate the power hungry and self-serving pseudoadvocate of the status quo from the genuine conservative; and the self-deceptive, irresponsible rebel without a cause from the truly creative. And to manage this means to separate those factors within the confines of one's own soul, as well as among other people.

And how might this be accomplished? First, we might come to understand consciously that these two modes of being are integrally interdependent. One cannot truly exist without the other, although they exist in genuine tension. This means, first, for example, that discipline—subordination to the status quo, in one form or another—needs to be understood as a necessary precursor to creative transformation, rather than its enemy. Thus, just as the hierarchy of assumptions that make up the structure that organizes society and individual perceptions is shaped by, and integrally dependent on, restrictions, so too is creative transformation. It must strain against limits. It has no use and cannot be called forth unless it is struggling against something. It is for this reason that the great genie, the granter of wishes—God, in a microcosm—is archetypally trapped in the tiny confines of a lamp and subject, as well, to the will of the lamp's current holder. Genie—genius—is the combination of possibility and potential, and extreme constraint.

Limitations, constraints, arbitrary boundaries—rules, dread rules, themselves—therefore not only ensure social harmony and psychological stability, they make the creativity that renews order possible. What lurks, therefore, under the explicitly stated desire for complete freedom—as expressed, say, by the anarchist, or the nihilist—is not a positive desire, striving for enhanced creative expression, as in the romanticized caricature of the artist. It is instead a negative desire—a desire for the complete absence of responsibility, which is simply not commensurate with genuine freedom. This is the lie of objections to the rules. But "Down with Responsibility" does not make for a compelling slogan—being sufficiently narcissistic to negate itself self-evidently—while the corresponding "Down with the Rules" can be dressed up like a heroic corpse.

Alongside the wisdom of true conservatism is the danger that the status quo might become corrupt and its corruption self-servingly exploited. Alongside the brilliance of creative endeavor is the false heroism of the resentful ideologue, who wears the clothes of the original rebel while undeservedly claiming the upper moral hand and rejecting all genuine responsibility. Intelligent and cautious conservatism and careful and incisive change keep the world in order. But each has its dark aspect, and it is crucial, once this has been realized, to pose the question to yourself: Are you the real thing, or its opposite? And the answer is, inevitably, that you are some of both—and perhaps far more of what is shadowy than you might like to realize. That is all part of understanding the complexity we each carry within us.

PERSONALITY AS HIERARCHY—AND CAPACITY FOR TRANSFORMATION

How, then, is the personality that balances respect for social institutions and, equally, creative transformation to be understood? It is not so easy to determine, given the complexity of the problem. For that reason, we turn to stories. Stories provide us with a broad template. They outline a pattern specific enough to be of tremendous value, if we can imitate it, but general enough (unlike a particular rule or set of rules) to apply even to new situations. In stories, we capture observations of the ideal personality. We tell tales about success and failure in adventure and romance. Across our narrative universes, success moves us forward to what is better, to the promised land; failure dooms us, and those who become entangled with us, to the abyss. The good moves us upward and ahead, and evil drags us backward and down. Great stories are about characters in action, and so they mirror the unconscious structures and processes that help us translate the intransigent world of facts into the sustainable, functional, reciprocal social world of values.*

The properly embodied hierarchy of values—including the value of conservatism and its twin, creative transformation—finds its expression as a personality, in narrative—an ideal personality. Every hierarchy has something at its pinnacle. It is for this reason that a story,

---

*You can see this played out, for example, in the proclivity of American evangelical Protestants to ask, when faced with a novel existential problem, "What would Jesus do?" It is an easy approach to parody, but indicates precisely the values of stories: Once a narrative has been internalized, it can be used as a template to generate new perceptions and behaviors. It might seem naive or presumptuous to imagine what actions the archetypal Savior Himself might undertake in the confines of a normal life, but the fundamental purpose of religious narratives is in fact to motivate imitation.

which is a description of the action of a personality, has a hero (and even if that someone is the antihero, it does not matter: the antihero serves the function of identifying the hero through contrast, as the hero is what the antihero is most decidedly not). The hero is the individual at the peak, the victor, the champion, the wit, the eventually successful and deserving underdog, the speaker of truth under perilous circumstances, and more. The stories we create, watch, listen to, and remember center themselves on actions and attitudes we find interesting, compelling, and worthy of communication as a consequence of our personal experience with both admirable and detestable people (or fragments of their specific attitudes and actions), or because of our proclivity to share what has gripped our attention with those who surround us. Sometimes we can draw compelling narratives directly from our personal experience with individual people; sometimes we create amalgams of multiple personalities, often in concert with those who compose our social groups.

The client whose story was told in part earlier had a life usefully employed as an example of the necessity of social engagement. That tale did not, however, exhaust the significance of his transformed attitudes and actions. While he was reconstructing his social life, becoming an active participant in a range of collective activities, he simultaneously developed a certain creative expertise that was equally unexpected. He had not benefited from formal education beyond the high school level, and did not have a personality that immediately struck the external observer as markedly creative. However, the personally novel social pursuits that attracted him were in the main oriented toward aesthetic endeavor.

He first developed his eye for form, symmetry, novelty, and beauty as a photographer. The social advantages of this pursuit were manifold: he joined a club that had its members attend biweekly photography walks, where they would sojourn as a group of twenty or so to parts of the city that were visually interesting, either for their natural beauty or uniqueness or for the attraction they held as industrial landscapes. He learned a fair bit about photographic equipment, technically, because of doing so. The group members also critiqued one another's work—and they did this constructively, which meant that all of them appeared to indicate what errors had been made but also what of value had been managed.

This all helped my client learn to communicate in a productive manner about topics that might otherwise have been psychologically difficult (touching as they did on criticisms that, because of their association with creative vision, could easily have generated counterproductively sensitive overreactions) and, as well, to increasingly distinguish between visual images that were trite or dull or conformist and those of genuine quality. After a few months, his perception had developed sufficiently so that he began to win local contests and generate small professional commissions. I had believed from the beginning that his participation in the photography club was well advised from the perspective of personality development, but I was genuinely struck by the rapid development of his visual and technical ability and very much enjoyed the times we spent in our sessions reviewing his work.

After a few months of work on the photography front, my client began to produce and to show me other images he had created, as well—which were in their first incarnation decidedly amateurish abstract line drawings done in pen. These essentially consisted of loops of various sizes, joined continuously, on a single page: scribbles, really, although more controlled and evidently purposeful than mere scribbles. As I had with the photographs (and the photography club), I regarded these as psychologically useful—as an extension of creative ability—but not as worthwhile artistic endeavors in their own right. He kept at it, however, generating several drawings a week, all the while bringing what he had created to our sessions. What he produced increased in sophistication and beauty with dramatic rapidity. Soon, he was drawing complex, symmetrical, and rather dramatic black-and-white pen-and-ink drawings of sufficient intrinsic beauty to serve as commercially viable T-shirt designs.

I had seen this sort of development clearly in the case of two other clients, both characterized by intrinsically creative temperaments (very well hidden in one of the cases; more developed, nurtured, and obvious in the other). In addition, I had read accounts of clinical cases and personal development by Carl Jung, who noted that the production of increasingly ordered and complex geometrical figures—often circles within squares, or the reverse—regularly accompanied an increase in organization of the personality. This certainly seemed true not only of my client, as evidenced by his burgeoning expertise at photography and the development of his skill as a graphic artist, but also of the two others I had the pleasure of serving as a clinical therapist. What I observed repeatedly was, therefore, not only the reconstruction of the psyche as a consequence of further socialization (and the valuation of social institutions) but the parallel transformation of primarily interior processes, indicated by a marked increase in the capacity to perceive and to create what was elegant, beautiful, and socially valued. My clients had learned not only to submit properly to the sometimes arbitrary but still necessary demands of the social world, but to offer to that world something it would not have had access to had it not been for their private creative work.

My granddaughter, Scarlett, also came to exhibit behaviors that were indicative of, if not her creative ability, then at least her appreciation for creative ability, in addition to her socialization as an agent of socially valued pointing. When people discuss a story—presented as a movie, or a play, or a book—they commonly attempt to come to a sophisticated consensus about its point (sophisticated because a group of people can generally offer more viewpoints than a single individual; consensus because the discussion usually continues until some broad agreement is reached as to the topic at hand). Now, the idea that a story is a form of communication—and entertainment—is one of those facts that appears self-evident upon first consideration, but that becomes more mysterious the longer it is pondered. If it is true that a story has a point, then it is clear that it is pointing to something. But what, and how? What constitutes pointing is obvious when it is an action specifying a particular thing, or a person by a particular person, but much less obvious when it is something typifying the cumulative behavior, shall we say, of a character in a story.

The actions and attitudes of J. K. Rowling's heroes and heroines once again provide popular examples of precisely this process. Harry Potter, Ron Weasley, and Hermione Granger are typified in large part by the willingness and ability to follow rules (indicating their expertise as apprentices) and, simultaneously, to break them. While those who supervise them are inclined, equally, to reward both apparently paradoxical forms of behavior. Even the technologies used by the young wizards during their apprenticeship are characterized by this duality. The Marauder's Map, for example (which provides its bearer with an accurate representation of explored territory in the form of the physical layout or geography of Hogwarts, the wizarding school, as well as the locale of all its living denizens), can be activated as a functional tool only by uttering a set of words that seem to indicate the very opposite of moral behavior: "I solemnly swear that I am up to no good," and deactivated, so that its function remains secret, with the phrase "Mischief managed."

It is no easy matter to understand how an artifact that requires such statements to make it usable could possibly be anything but "no good"—a tool of evil purpose, apparently. But, like the fact that Harry and his friends regularly but carefully break rules, and are equally regularly and carefully rewarded for doing so, the Marauder's Map varies in its ethical desirability with the intent of its users. There is a strong implication throughout the series that what is good cannot be simply encapsulated by mindless or rigid rule following, no matter how disciplined that following, or how vital the rules so followed. What this all means is that the Harry Potter series does not point to drone-like subservience to social order as the highest of moral virtues. What supersedes that obedience is not so obvious that it can be easily articulated, but it is something like "Follow rules except when doing so undermines the purpose of those selfsame rules—in which case take the risk of acting in a manner contrary to what has been agreed upon as moral." This is a lesson that seems more easily taught by representations of the behaviors that embody it than transmitted by, say, rote learning or a variant rule. Meta-rules (which might be regarded as rules about rules, rather than rules themselves) are not necessarily communicated in the same manner as simple rules themselves.

Scarlett, with her emphasis on pointing, learned soon after mastering the comparatively straightforward physical act, to grasp the more complex point of narratives. She could signify something with her index finger at the age of a year and a half. By two and a half years, however, she could understand and imitate the far more intricate point of a story. For a period of approximately six months, at the latter age, she would insist, when asked, that she was Pocahontas, rather than Ellie (the name preferred by her father) or Scarlett (preferred by her mother). This was a staggering act of sophisticated thought, as far as I was concerned. She had been given a Pocahontas doll, which became one of her favorite toys, along with a baby doll (also very well loved), who she named after her grandmother, my wife, Tammy. When she played with the infant doll, Ellie was the mother. With Pocahontas, however, the situation differed. That doll was not a baby, and Ellie was not its mother. My granddaughter regarded herself, instead, as the grown Pocahontas—mimicking the doll, which was fashioned like a young woman, as well as the character who served as the lead in the Disney movie of the same name, which she had raptly observed on two separate occasions.

The Disney Pocahontas bore marked similarities to the main protagonists of the Harry Potter series. She finds herself promised by her father to Kocoum, a brave warrior who embodies, in all seriousness, the virtues of his tribe, but whose behavior and attitudes are too rule bound for the more expansive personality of his bride-to-be. Pocahontas falls in love, instead, with John Smith, captain of a ship from Europe and representative of that which falls outside of known territory but is (potentially) of great value. Paradoxically, Pocahontas is pursuing a higher moral order in rejecting Kocoum for Smith—breaking a profoundly important rule (value what is most valued in the current culture's hierarchy of rules)—very much in the same manner as the primary Potter characters. That is the moral of both narratives: follow the rules until you are capable of being a shining exemplar of what they represent, but break them when those very rules now constitute the most dire impediment to the embodiment of their central virtues. And Elizabeth Scarlett, not yet three years of age, had the intrinsic wisdom to see this as the point of what she was watching (the Disney movie) and using as a role-playing aid (the doll Pocahontas). Her perspicacity in this regard bordered on the unfathomable.

The same set of ideas—respect for the rules, except when following those rules means disregarding or ignoring or remaining blind to
an even higher moral principle—is represented with stunning power in
two different Gospel narratives (which serve, regardless of your opinion about them, as central traditional or classical stories portraying a
personality for the purposes of evoking imitation). In the first, Christ
is presented, even as a child, as a master of the Jewish tradition. This
makes him fully informed as to the value of the past, and portrays him
as characterized by the respect typical, say, of the genuine conservative. According to the account in Luke 2:42–52,* Jesus's family journeyed to Jerusalem every year at the Jewish holiday of Passover:

> And when he was twelve years old, they went up to Jerusalem
> after the custom of the feast.
>
> And when they had fulfilled the days, as they returned, the
> child Jesus tarried behind in Jerusalem; and Joseph and his
> mother knew not of it.
>
> But they, supposing him to have been in the company, went
> a day's journey; and they sought him among their kinsfolk and
> acquaintance.
>
> And when they found him not, they turned back again to
> Jerusalem, seeking him.
>
> And it came to pass, that after three days they found him in
> the temple, sitting in the midst of the doctors, both hearing
> them, and asking them questions.
>
> And all that heard him were astonished at his understand-
> ing and answers.
>
> And when they saw him, they were amazed: and his mother

---

*All biblical citations are from the King James Version unless otherwise noted.

said unto him, Son, why hast thou thus dealt with us? behold, thy father and I have sought thee sorrowing.

And he said unto them, How is it that ye sought me? wist ye not that I must be about my Father's business?

And they understood not the saying which he spake unto them.

And he went down with them, and came to Nazareth, and was subject unto them: but his mother kept all these sayings in her heart.

And Jesus increased in wisdom and stature, and in favour with God and man.

A paradox emerges, however, as the entirety of the Gospel accounts are considered—one closely associated with the tension between respect for tradition and the necessity for creative transformation. Despite the evidence of His thorough and even precocious understanding and appreciation of the rules, the adult Christ repeatedly and scandalously violates the Sabbath traditions—at least from the standpoint of the traditionalists in His community, and much to His own peril. He leads His disciples through a cornfield, for example, plucking and eating the grains (Luke 6:1). He justifies this to the Pharisees who object by referring to an account of King David acting in a similar manner, feeding his people when necessity demanded it on bread that was reserved for the priests (Luke 6:4). Christ tells his interlocutors quite remarkably "that the Son of man is Lord also of the sabbath" (Luke 6:5).

An ancient document known as the Codex Bezae,* a noncanonical

---

*A codex is a book composed of sheets of vellum, papyrus, or most commonly, paper. The term is now generally reserved for manuscripts that have been handwritten, as in the case of the Codex Bezae. The Codex Bezae contains Greek and Latin versions of

variant of part of the New Testament, offers an interpolation just after the section of the Gospel of Luke presented above, shedding profound light on the same issue. It offers deeper insight into the complex and paradoxical relationship between respect for the rules and creative moral action that is necessary and desirable, despite manifesting itself in apparent opposition to those rules. It contains an account of Christ addressing someone who, like Him, has broken a sacred rule: "On that same day, observing one working on the Sabbath, [Jesus] said to him O Man, if indeed thou knowest what thou doest, thou art blest; but if thou knowest not, thou art accursed, and a transgressor of the Law."[12]

What does this statement mean? It sums up the meaning of Rule I perfectly. If you understand the rules—their necessity, their sacredness, the chaos they keep at bay, how they unite the communities that follow them, the price paid for their establishment, and the danger of breaking them—but you are willing to fully shoulder the responsibility of making an exception, because you see that as serving a higher good (and if you are a person with sufficient character to manage that distinction), then you have served the spirit, rather than the mere law, and that is an elevated moral act. But if you refuse to realize the importance of the rules you are violating and act out of self-centered convenience, then you are appropriately and inevitably damned. The carelessness you exhibit with regard to your own tradition will undo you and perhaps those around you fully and painfully across time.

This is in keeping with other sentiments and acts of Christ described in the Gospels. Matthew 12:11 states: "And he said unto them, What man shall there be among you, that shall have one sheep, and if it fall into a pit on the Sabbath day, will he not lay hold on it, and lift

---

Acts and most of the four Gospels that are unique in what they additionally include, what they omit, and often, the style in which they are written.

it out?" Luke chapter 6 describes Him healing a man with a withered hand on another Sabbath, stating "It is lawful on the Sabbath days to do good, or to do evil? to save life, or destroy it?" (Luke 6:9). This psychologically and conceptually painful juxtaposition of two moral stances (the keeping of the Sabbath versus the injunction to do good) is something else that constantly enrages the Pharisees, and is part of the series of events that eventually leads to Christ's arrest and Crucifixion. These stories portray the existential dilemma that eternally characterizes human life: it is necessary to conform, to be disciplined, and to follow the rules—to do humbly what others do; but it is also necessary to use judgment, vision, and the truth that guides conscience to tell what is right, when the rules suggest otherwise. It is the ability to manage this combination that truly characterizes the fully developed personality: the true hero.

A certain amount of arbitrary rule-ness must be tolerated—or welcomed, depending on your point of view—to keep the world and its inhabitants together. A certain amount of creativity and rebellion must be tolerated—or welcomed, depending on your point of view—to maintain the process of regeneration. Every rule was once a creative act, breaking other rules. Every creative act, genuine in its creativity, is likely to transform itself, with time, into a useful rule. It is the living interaction between social institutions and creative achievement that keeps the world balanced on the narrow line between too much order and too much chaos. This is a terrible conundrum, a true existential burden. We must support and value the past, and we need to do that with an attitude of gratitude and respect. At the same time, however, we must keep our eyes open—we, the visionary living—and repair the ancient mechanisms that stabilize and support us when they falter. Thus, we need to bear the paradox that is involved in simultaneously respecting the walls that keep us safe and allowing in enough of what is new and changing so that our institutions remain alive and healthy. The very world depends for its stability and its dynamism on the subsuming of all our endeavors under the perfection—the sacredness—of that dual ability.

Do not carelessly denigrate social institutions or creative achievement.

IMAGINE WHO YOU COULD BE, AND THEN AIM SINGLE-MINDEDLY AT THAT

WHO ARE YOU—AND WHO COULD YOU BE?

How do you know who you are? After all, you are complex beyond your own understanding; more complex than anything else that exists, excepting other people; complex beyond belief. And your ignorance is further complicated by the intermingling of who you are with who you could be. You are not only something that is. You are something that is becoming—and the potential extent of that becoming also transcends your understanding. Everyone has the sense, I believe, that there is more to them than they have yet allowed to be realized. That potential is often obscured by poor health, misfortune, and the general tragedies and mishaps of life. But it can also be hidden by an unwillingness to take full advantage of the opportunities that life offers—abetted by regrettable errors of all sorts, including failures of discipline, faith, imagination, and commitment. Who are you? And, more importantly, who could you be, if you were everything you could conceivably be?

Are such questions impossible to answer, or are there sources available to us from which guidance might be derived? After all, we have been observing ourselves behave—in our successes and failures—for tens (perhaps hundreds) of thousands of years. During that time, our shamans, prophets, mystics, artists, poets, and bards have distilled something vital from such observations—some concentrated essence of what makes us human in actuality and possibility. In doing so, they have provided us with representations of that vital essence, presenting itself to us as that which can be neither ignored nor forgotten. Those creative people write and act out the dramas and tell us the stories that capture our imagination, and they fill our dreams with visions of what might be. The deepest and most profound of these are remembered, discussed, and otherwise honed collectively, and made the focus of rituals that unite us across the centuries, forming the very basis of our cultures. These are the stories upon which the ritual, religious, and philosophical edifices characterizing sophisticated, populous, successful societies are built.

The stories we can neither ignore nor forget are unforgettable for this reason (among others): They speak to something we know, but do not know that we know. The ancient Greek philosopher Socrates believed that all learning was a form of remembering. Socrates posited that the soul, immortal in its essence, knew everything before it was born anew as an infant. However, at the point of birth all previous knowledge was forgotten and had to be recalled through the experiences of life. There is much to be said for this hypothesis, strange as it might now appear. There is much that we *could* do—much that our bodies and minds are capable of doing—that remains dormant, right down to the genetic level. Exposure to new experience activates this dormant potential, releasing abilities built into us over the vast span of our evolutionary history.[1] This is perhaps the most basic manner in which our bodies retain past wisdom and draw upon it when necessary. It is in this way, although not only in this way, that human possibility exists. Thus, there is something profound to be said for the concept of learning as remembering.

Obviously, as well as "remembering" (as in the turning on of innate but hidden possibilities), we can learn much that is new. This is one of the primary factors differentiating us from animals. Even complex and intelligent mammals such as chimpanzees and dolphins tend to repeat their species-typical behaviors generation after generation, with very little change. Humans, by contrast, can and continually do seek out and encounter what is new, investigate and adapt to it, and make it part of themselves. We can, as well, translate something we already know at one level of representation into knowledge at another. We can watch the actions of a living creature, animal or human, and then imitate them, translating our perceptions of their movement into new movements of our own. We can even generalize such imitative acts, catching the "spirit" of what or whom we are observing, and producing new ways of seeing and acting that are in some manner similar to that spirit.* This is part of what makes up the basis of the deeply embodied implicit knowledge that forms so much of the basis of our true understanding. We can also observe someone act or something occur and write down what we see, translating action into language that outlasts its utterance—and then communicate it later in the absence of what or whom is being described. Finally, and most mysteriously, we can imagine and then act

---

*Consider the professional impersonator. He or she doesn't necessarily copy the precise behaviors, movement for movement, of those being impersonated, but the spirit—what's common across all the behaviors of the target celebrity. The same is true when children play at being adults. It's the spirit they're after, not the individual behaviors.

out something that has simply not been seen before, something that is truly original. And we can code and represent all that ability—adaptive action and its transformation—in the stories we tell about those we admire, as well as those we hate. And that is how we determine who we are, and who we could perhaps become.

Stories become unforgettable when they communicate sophisticated modes of being—complex problems and equally complex solutions—that we perceive, consciously, in pieces, but cannot fully articulate. It was for this reason, for example, that the biblical story of Moses and the Israelites' exodus from Egypt became such a powerful touchstone for black slaves seeking emancipation in the United States:

> Go down, Moses, way down in Egypt land
>   Tell old Pharaoh
>   To let my people go.[2]

The biblical story of Exodus is properly regarded as archetypal (or paradigmatic or foundational) by psychoanalytic and religious thinkers alike, because it presents an example of psychological and social transformation that cannot be improved upon. It emerged as a product of imagination and has been transformed by constant collective retelling and reworking into an ultimately meaningful form that applies politically, economically, historically, personally, and spiritually, all at the same time. This is the very definition of literary depth—something that reaches its apogee in certain forms of ancient, traditional stories. The fact of that depth means that such accounts can be used diversely as a meaningful frame for any process of profound change experienced by any individual or society (stable state, descent into chaos, reestablishment of stability), and can lend that process multidimensional reality, context, powerful meaning, and motivation.

THE EMERGENCE OF THE UNFORGETTABLE

How might an unforgettable story come to be? What might precede its revelation? It is at the very least the consequence of a long period of observation. Imagine a scientist monitoring the behavior of a wolf pack, or a troop of chimps—indeed, any group of complex social animals. He or she attempts to identify regularities in the behavior of the individuals and the group (patterns, in a word) and to articulate those regularities—to encapsulate them in language. The scientist might first relate a series of anecdotes about animal actions emblematic of the general behavior of the species. He or she might then abstract even further, attempting to generalize across anecdotes with rule-like descriptions. I say "rule-like" because the animals are not following rules. Rules require language. Animals are merely acting out regularities. They cannot formulate, understand, or follow *rules*.

But human beings? We can observe ourselves acting, as a scientist might—more accurately, as a storyteller might. Then we can tell the stories to each other. The stories are already distillations of observed behavior (if they are not distillations, they will not be interesting; relating a sequence of everyday actions does not make for a good story). Once the story is established, we can analyze it, looking for deeper patterns and regularities. If that analysis is successful, we can generalize across anecdotes with the formulation of rules, and then we can learn, consciously, to follow those rules. Here is how this might happen. We all react judgmentally when a child or adult—or, indeed, a society—is acting improperly, unfairly, or badly. The error strikes us emotionally. We intuit that a pattern upon which individual and social adaptation depends has been disrupted and violated. We are annoyed, frustrated, hurt, or grief-stricken at the betrayal. This does not mean that each of us, reacting emotionally, has been successful at articulating a comprehensive philosophy of good and evil. We may never put our finger on what has gone wrong. However, like children unfamiliar with a new game but still able to play it, we know that the rules are being broken.

Something precisely like this is portrayed in the biblical story of Exodus, the ancient account of the flight of the Hebrew slaves from their Egyptian masters. Moses, who leads the escaping people, is continually called upon by his followers to draw very fine moral distinctions when they struggle with one another and seek his advice. In consequence, he spends a very long time observing and contemplating their behavior. It is as if the desert prophet had to discover what rules he and his Israelite followers were already struggling to act out, prior to his receipt of the explicit commandments from God. Remember: Every society is already characterized by patterned behavior; otherwise it would be pure conflict and no "society" at all. But the mere fact that social order reigns to some degree does not mean that a given society has come to explicitly understand its own behavior, its own moral code. It is therefore no accident that in this story Moses serves as a judge for his followers—and does so with sufficient duration and intensity to exhaust himself—before he receives the Ten Commandments:

> And it came to pass on the morrow, that Moses sat to judge the people: and the people stood by Moses from the morning unto the evening.
>
> And when Moses' father in law saw all that he did to the people, he said, What is this thing that thou doest to the people? why sittest thou thyself alone, and all the people stand by thee from morning unto even?

And Moses said unto his father in law, Because the people come unto me to inquire of God:

When they have a matter, they come unto me; and I judge between one and another, and I do make them know the statutes of God, and his laws.

And Moses' father in law said unto him, The thing that thou doest is not good.

Thou wilt surely wear away, both thou, and this people that is with thee: for this thing is too heavy for thee; thou art not able to perform it thyself alone. (Exodus 18: 13–18)

This difficult exercise in discrimination and judgment, observing and weighing, is an integral part of what prepared the biblical patriarch for the receipt of divine revelation. If there had been no behavioral base for those rules—no historical precedent codified in traditional ethics, no conventions, and no endless hours of observation of the moral patterns—the commandments simply could not have been understood and communicated, much less obeyed.

An unforgettable story captures the essence of humanity and distills, communicates, and clarifies it, bringing what we are and what we should be into focus. It speaks to us, motivating the attention that inspires us to imitate. We learn to see and act in the manner of the heroes of the stories that captivate us. These stories call to capacities that lie deep within our nature but might still never develop without that call. We are dormant adventurers, lovers, leaders, artists, and rebels, but need to discover that we are all those things by seeing the reflection of such patterns in dramatic and literary form. That is part of being a creature that is part nature and part culture. An unforgettable story advances our capacity to understand our behavior, beyond habit and expectation, toward an imaginative and then verbalized under-standing. Such a story presents us in the most compelling manner with the ultimate adventure, the divine romance, and the eternal battle be-tween good and evil. All this helps us clarify our understanding of moral and immoral attitude and action, personal and social. This can be seen everywhere, and always.

Question: Who are you—or, at least, who could you be? Answer: Part of the eternal force that constantly confronts the terrible un-known, voluntarily; part of the eternal force that transcends naivete and becomes dangerous enough, in a controlled manner, to understand evil and beard it in its lair; and part of the eternal force that faces chaos and turns it into productive order, or that takes order that has become too restrictive, reduces it to chaos, and renders it productive once again.

And all of this, being very difficult to understand consciously but vital to our survival, is transmitted in the form of the stories that we cannot help but attend to. And it is in this manner that we come to ap-prehend what is of value, what we should aim at, and what we could be.

MATERIA PRIMA: WHO YOU COULD BE (I)

I would like to try my hand at explaining the meaning of the illustra-tion, based on an ancient alchemical woodcut, that opens this chapter. Describing what it signifies reveals how much information can be con-tained within an image without the viewer possessing any explicit un-derstanding of its contents (such a picture is in fact better considered an early stage in the process by which such explicit understanding de-velops). The ancient alchemist* who produced the picture was dream-

*Alchemy—the search for the philosopher's stone, an artifact that would transform base ing, in a very real sense, while doing so—dreaming about what a person could be, and how that might come about.

At the very base of the image is a winged sphere. Atop that perches a dragon. Standing on the dragon is a two-headed human figure—one head male, the other female. The male head is associated with an image of the Sun; the female, with the Moon. In between but also above the two heads is the symbol for Mercury: god, planet, and metal, simultaneously. A variety of additional symbols round out the picture. Everything portrayed is enveloped in an egg-shaped container. This arrangement indicates that the image is of many things inside one thing—a multiplicity in a unity—just as an unhatched chick is encapsulated within a single container but is many increasingly differentiated and complex biological parts, particularly in its later stages of development. In its entirety, the image is labeled materia prima—Latin for the "primal element."

The alchemists regarded the materia prima as the fundamental substance from which everything else—matter and spirit included, equally—emerged, or was derived. You can profitably consider that primal element the potential we face when we confront the future, including our future selves—or the potential we cannot help upbraiding ourselves and others for wasting. It can also be usefully conceptualized as the information from which we build ourselves and the world, instead of the matter out of which we generally consider reality

---

metals into gold, as well as rewarding its bearer with health and immortality—was practiced for thousands of years by the misfits, mystics, magicians, and prescientific practitioners who took the first fantastical steps toward establishing what eventually became genuine science. As alchemy developed, however, the "stone" eventually became conceptualized as something more akin to a personality than a material object, as the alchemists increasingly realized that the development of the psyche was a more important pursuit than mere gold itself. I wrote about this in J. B. Peterson, *Maps of Meaning: The Architecture of Belief* (New York: Routledge, 1999), which contains the relevant references to the work on alchemy conducted by Jung and his students.

composed. Each interpretation—potential and information—has its advantages.

What does it mean that the world can be usefully considered as potential or information? Think about what happens, for example, when you stop by the mailbox and pick up your mail. Consider, as well, what that mail is "made of." Materially speaking, it is merely paper and ink. But that material substrate is essentially irrelevant. It would not matter if the message was delivered by email or voice—or in Morse code, for that matter. What is relevant is the content. And that means that each piece of mail is a container of content—of potential or information, positive, neutral, or negative. Maybe, for example, it is a notification of investigation from your country's tax department. This means that, despite its apparently harmless presence in your hand, the letter is tightly and inextricably connected to a gigantic, complex and oft-arbitrary structure that may well not have your best interests in mind. Alternatively, perhaps it is something joyful, such as an unexpected letter from someone loved or a long-awaited check. From such a perspective, an envelope is a container—a mysterious container, at least in potential—from which an entire new world might emerge.

Everyone understands this idea, even if they do not know it. If you have been having trouble with the tax authorities, for example, and you receive an official piece of mail from their agency, your blood pressure will increase (or drop precipitously), your heart will pound, your palms will sweat, and a feeling of intense fear, even doom, may sweep over you. That is the instinctive response, associated with preparation for action, that accompanies exposure to danger. And now you will have to decide: are you going to open the letter and face what is "inside"? And, having done so, are you going to think your way through the problem, terrible as that might be, and begin to address it? Or are you going to ignore what you now know, pretend that everything is all right (even though you know, emotionally—as a consequence of your anxiety—that it is not), and pay the inevitable psychological and physical price? It is the former route that will require you to voluntarily confront what you are afraid of—the terrible, abstract monster—and, hypothetically, to become stronger and more integrated as a result. It is the latter route that will leave the problem in its monstrous form and force you to suffer like a scared animal confronted by a predator's vicious eyes in the pitch of night.

A winged sphere, inscribed with a square, a triangle, and the numerals 3 and 4 occupies the bottom third of the image in question.* This singular entity or object was known by the alchemists as the "round chaos."[3] It is a container—the initial container of the primordial element—the container of what the world, and the psyche, consists of before it becomes differentiated. This is the potential, or information. This is what attracts your attention unconsciously and compels you to attend to something before you know why it has gripped your interest. This is when and where what is new makes its entrance into what is predictable and certain (for better or worse); what flits about you, with little voluntary control—as if it is something winged—as your imagination and your attention move unpredictably but meaningfully from association to association; and it is what you are looking at when you have no idea what it is you are

---

*We're going to approach the picture from the very bottom upward, as if each element were emerging from the lower. Images of this type (and they are a type) often represent a process of psychological or spiritual development or growth, and appear to employ the basic symbolism of a plant or a tree extending itself upward as it matures. Something similar can be observed in Eastern images of the Buddha, emerging from a lotus flower floating on the surface of placid water, with its stalk extending into the murky deep underneath and its roots grounded far, far below even that, into the mud that composes the lowest level of the depths.

confronting. Finally, it is what you cannot look away from when you are possessed by horror, even as such potential for horror simultaneously adds vital interest to life.

Strangely, the round chaos may be familiar to modern audiences (again, even if they do not know it), because of the Harry Potter series of books and films. J. K. Rowling, the series author, takes some pains to describe a sporting event, Quidditch, which helps to define and unify Hogwarts. The point of Quidditch is to drive a ball (the Quaffle) through one of the three hoops guarded by the opposing team, while flying about the playing pitch on enchanted brooms. Success in doing so gains the scorer's team 10 points. Simultaneously, two separate players (one from each team) play another game—a game within the game. Chosen for their exceptional skill in attention and flight, these two competitors—known as Seekers—attempt to locate, chase, and capture a winged ball, the Snitch, which is identical in appearance to the round chaos that sits at the bottom of the alchemist's image. The Snitch is golden—indicating its exceptional value and purity*—and zips around chaotically, at a very fast rate, darting, weaving, bobbing, and racing the Seekers as they pursue it astride their brooms. If a Seeker captures the Snitch, his or her team gains 150 points (typically enough to ensure victory) and the entire game comes to an end. This indicates that chasing and capturing whatever is represented by the Snitch—and, by implication, the round chaos—is a goal whose importance supersedes any other.† Why is Rowling's game, conjured up for

---

*As gold is both rare and unwilling, so to speak, to combine promiscuously with other elements or compounds.

†It is of some real interest to note—particularly in relationship to the discussion of the dangers of creativity presented in Rule I—that the Seekers chase the Snitch both inside and outside the playing field that provides boundaries for all the other players. While outside, they can career through the wooden foundation of the Quidditch stadium. This would not be a problem, if they weren't simultaneously being chased by a Bludger, a

us by her deep imagination, structured in that manner? What does her narrative idea signify? There are two ways of answering these questions (although both answers relate importantly to each other):

First: In Rule I, we discussed the idea that the true winner of any game is the person who plays fair. This is because playing fair, despite the particularities of any given game, is a higher-order accomplishment than mere victory. Striving to play fair, in the ultimate sense—following the spirit of the rules, as well as the letter—is an indication of true personality development, predicated as it is on concern for true reciprocity. The Seekers of the Snitch must ignore the details of the game of Quidditch, of which they are still a part, while attempting to find and seize the Snitch, just as the player of a real-world game must ignore the particularities of that game while attending to what constitutes truly ethical play, regardless of what is happening on the playing field. Thus, the ethical player, like the Seeker, indomitably pursues what is most valuable in the midst of complex, competing obligations.

Second: Among the alchemists, the round chaos was associated with the winged god Mercury, who served as messenger from the realm of the divine, guide of souls to the underworld, and bringer of good fortune. It is for this reason that the ancient symbol for Mercury is located at the very pinnacle (the most important location) of the image in question. It is an attempt to indicate what guides the process that the picture represents. Centuries ago, prior to the dawn of modern chemistry, the god Mercury represented what inspires or attracts interest involuntarily. He was the spirit who possessed a person when his or

---

solid, massive, flying ball capable not only of knocking them off their brooms, but of crashing through and seriously damaging that same structure. If they succeed in catching the Snitch, as we have indicated, they generally attain victory. But they risk damaging the very foundations of the game while doing so—just as creative people do when they pursue their innovative yet disruptive visions.

her attention was drawn irresistibly to some person, situation, or event. Imagine that there are very complex processes going on in your mind unconsciously, highlighting events of potential worth and distinguishing them from everything else constantly unfolding around you. Imagine that those processes that distinguish value are alive, which is certainly the case, and that they are complex and integrated enough to be conceptualized as a personality. That is Mercury. The draw he exerts on our attention reveals itself in a sense of significance—in the sense that something happening around you is worth attending to, or contains something of value. The Seeker—in real life, as well as in Rowling's Potter series and its Quidditch game—is he or she who takes that sense of significance more seriously than anything else. The Seeker is therefore the person who is playing the game that everyone else is playing (and who is disciplined and expert at the game), but who is also playing an additional, higher-order game: the pursuit of what is of primary significance. The Snitch (like the round chaos) can therefore be considered the "container" of that primary significance—that meaning—and, therefore, something revelatory when pursued and caught. We might in this context remember what has come to be known as the Golden Rule: "And as ye would that men should do to you, do ye also to them likewise" (Luke 6:31). There is nothing more important than learning to strive under difficult and frustrating circumstances to play fair. This is what should be chased, so to speak, during any game (even though it is also important to try to obtain victory in the game).*

---

*It is also of great interest to note, in this regard, that the metal mercury can be used in the mining and purification of gold. Gold dissolves in mercury, and mercury can, therefore, be used to draw out the small amounts of the precious metal typically found in ores. The mercury is then boiled off (it has a low boiling point) so that only the gold remains. The proclivity of mercury for gold has given rise to the symbolic idea that the liquid metal has an "affinity" for what is most precious: that mercury will seek what is noble

Each of us, when fortunate, is compelled forward by something that grips our attention—love of a person; a sport; a political, sociological, or economic problem, or a scientific question; a passion for art, literature, or drama—something that calls to us for reasons we can neither control nor understand (try to make yourself interested in something you just do not care about and see how well that works). The phenomena that grip us (*phenomena*: from the Greek word *phainesthai*, "to appear, or to be brought to light") are like lamps along a dark path: they are part of the unconscious processes devoted to integrating and furthering the development of our spirits, the furtherance of our psychological development. You do not choose what interests you. It chooses you. Something manifests itself out of the darkness as compelling, as worth living for; following that, something moves us further down the road, to the next meaningful manifestation—and so it goes, as we continue to seek, develop, grow, and thrive. It is a perilous journey, but it is also the adventure of our lives. Think of pursuing someone you love: catch them or not, you change in the process. Think, as well, of the traveling you have done, or of the work you have undertaken, whether for pleasure or necessity. In all these cases you experience what is new. Sometimes that is painful; sometimes it is better than anything else that has ever happened to you. Either way, it is deeply informative. It is all part of the potential of the world, calling you into Being, changing you forever—for better or worse—in consequence of your pursuit.

Atop the round chaos perches a dragon. This is because what is

---

and pure and incorruptible—like gold itself, speaking symbolically once again—and concentrate it in usable amounts. So, the fundamental idea is that the pursuit of meaning, guided by Mercury, messenger of the gods (the unconscious, as far as modern people are concerned), will enable the Seeker to collect what is, like gold, of the highest value. For the alchemists who created drawings like the one we are analyzing, that highest value came to be the ultimate development of the psyche, or spirit, or personality.

interesting and meaningful (and novel and unexpected, as those all go together) manifests itself in a form that is both dangerous and promising, particularly when its grip is intense and irresistible. The danger is, of course, signified by the presence of the immortal, predatory reptile; the promise is hinted at, as a dragon archetypally guards a great treasure. Thus, the drawing represents a psychological progression. First, you find yourself interested in something. That something (the round chaos) contains or is composed of potential, or information. If it is pursued and caught, it releases that information. Out of that information we build the world we perceive, and we build ourselves as perceivers. Thus, the round chaos is the container from which both matter (the world) and spirit (our psyches) emerge. There is some numerological indication of this on the spherical body of the round chaos itself: the number 3, accompanied by a triangle, which is traditionally associated with spirit (because of its association with the Holy Trinity), and the number 4, associated with the world of matter (because of its association with the four traditional elements: earth, water, wind, and fire). The dragon, in turn, perched on top of the round chaos, represents the danger and possibility of the information within.

Atop the dragon stands a figure known as a Rebis, a single body with two heads, one male, one female. The Rebis is a symbol of the fully developed personality that can emerge from forthright and courageous pursuit of what is meaningful (the round chaos) and dangerous and promising (the dragon). It has a symbolically masculine aspect, which typically stands for exploration, order, and rationality (indicated by the Sun, which can be seen to the left of the male head), and a symbolically feminine aspect, which stands for chaos, promise, care, renewal, and emotion (indicated by the Moon, to the right of the female). In the course of normal socialization, it is typical for one of these aspects to become more developed than the other (as males are

socialized in the male manner, to which they are also inclined biologically, and females in the female manner). Nonetheless, it is possible—
with enough exploration, enough exposure to the round chaos and the
dragon—to develop both elements. That constitutes an ideal—or so
goes the alchemical intuition.

Out of the unknown—the potential that makes up the world—
comes the terrible but promising form of the dragon, peril and promise united. It is an eternal dichotomy echoed by the presence of the
two remaining symbols to the right and above the dragon's tail: Jupiter,
representing the positive, and Saturn, the negative. Out of the confrontation with peril and promise emerges the masculine and feminine aspects of the psyche, working together in harmony. Guiding the
process is the spirit Mercurius, manifesting itself as meaning in the
world, working through unconscious means to attract exploration to
what will unite the various discordant and warring elements of the
personality. This can all be read, appropriately, as a story of the development of the ideal personality—an attempt, in image, to describe
what each of us could be.

POLYTHEISM INTO MONOTHEISM, AND
THE EMERGENCE OF THE VIRTUOUS HERO:
WHO YOU COULD BE (II)

Now we are going to attempt a description of "who you could be" from
another perspective, taken from one of the earliest stories we have been
fortunate enough to rediscover. In the ancient Mesopotamian *Enuma
Elish* (translation: When on High) we have the oldest near-complete
hero myth known, estimated at four thousand years of age in its written form and, no doubt, far older as an oral tradition. The story begins
when the primordial goddess Tiamat, embodiment of salt water (as

well as a monstrous aquatic dragon), enters into sexual union with her equally primordial male consort, Apsu, the embodiment of fresh water. This union gives rise to the initial realm of being, inhabited by the elder gods, the first children of Tiamat and Apsu.

To understand the beginning of this story, we need to know a few things the ancients held to be fundamentally true. These are markedly different from the truths of modern science. Before the dawn of the scientific worldview, a mere six hundred years ago, *reality* was construed as all that which human beings experience. That which we experience can be distinguished, conceptually, from *reality as objective world*—pure physical being—by its more comprehensive contents, which include subjective experiences such as emotions, dreams, visions, and motivational states such as hunger, thirst, and pain. That which we experience is better compared to a novel or a movie, which concentrates on the communication and sharing of subjective as well as objective states, than is reality as objective world, which we might liken to a scientific description of physical reality. It is the actual, particular, and unique demise of someone you love, for example, compared to the listing of that death in the hospital records. It is the drama of lived experience. It is because our own experience is genuinely literary, narrative, embodied, and storylike that we are so attracted to fictional representations. Movies, plays, operas, TV dramas—even the lyrics of songs—help us deal with our lived experiences, which are something different and broader than the mere material from which our experience hypothetically rises.

Engaging with the first part of the *Enuma Elish* requires us to understand a second fundamental realization of the ancients: the fundamentally social nature of our cognitive categories. That is why everything is personified in children's books: the Sun, the Moon, toys, animals— even machines. We see nothing strange in this, because it so profoundly mirrors our perceptual tendencies. We expect children to view and understand the world in this manner, and we can easily fall back into doing so ourselves. Something should be clarified here: It is not truly accurate to state that the reality portrayed in children's fiction is personified. It is the case, instead (and this is a genuine reversal of the presumption in question), that we directly and naturally perceive reality as personified, and then must work very diligently to strip that personification away, so that we can detect "objective reality."* We understand reality, therefore, as if it is constructed of personalities. That is because so much of what we encounter in our hypersocial reality, our complex societies, is in fact personality—and gendered personality, at that, reflecting the billion years or so since the emergence of sexual reproduction (ample time for its existence to have profoundly structured our perceptions). We understand male, and abstract from that the masculine. We understand female, and abstract from that the feminine. Finally, we understand the child, and abstract from that, most commonly, the son. These basic divisions are clearly reflected in the creation story of the *Enuma Elish*, just as they are reflected in, or more accurately underpin, our understanding of the stories we all know.

Tiamat, the primordial goddess, is chaos, a female monster, a dragon. She is the terror of nature, creative and destructive, mother and slayer of us all. Apsu, her husband, is the eternal father. He is the order that we depend upon for security, and by which we are simultaneously tyrannized.† These two most primal of deities come together in a produc-

---

*This is part of the reason science developed so long after religion and ritual—so incredibly recently, and by no means everywhere at once.
†Furthermore, in the mythological world, unlike the objective, logical world, things can be one thing and their opposite at the same time. And this representation in the mythological world is more accurate than the objective, in the experiential manner described previously: Nature, for example, is Creator and Destroyer, just as Culture is Protector and Tyrant. It might be objected: Nature and Culture are not singular things. They can

tive, sexual union, "mingling their waters," in the ancient words. In this fashion, they produce their first progeny, the elder gods of Mesopotamia. These gods represent elements of the world more differentiated than the primordial mother and father—such as heaven and earth, mud and silt, and war and fire.* However, they are also careless, noisy, and impulsive as two-year-old children (who are, after all, primal forces in their own right). Their continual ceaseless, thoughtless activity and general unconsciousness culminates in a catastrophe: their mutual decision to wage war upon and then slay Apsu, and consequent attempt to build a stable dwelling place on his corpse.

Tiamat—chaos itself—already irritated by the brainless racket of her children, is murderously enraged by the heedless slaughter of her husband. The Terrible Goddess builds an army of eleven monsters to deal with her wayward offspring, placing a demonic figure named Kingu, whom she takes as a second husband, at their head, and delivering to him the Tablet of Destinies (indicating his authority as ultimate ruler of the universe). The relationship between this brilliant dramatic representation and how we use, or misuse, the gifts of our culture is obvious: the careless demolition of tradition is the invitation to the (re)emergence of chaos. When ignorance destroys culture, monsters will emerge.

While Tiamat busily arranges her army, the elder gods continue

---

be differentiated, so that their paradoxical components are separated, understood, and dealt with. This is all true: but the paradoxical components are often experienced simultaneously and so unified. This occurs when anyone is betrayed, for example, in a love affair. Beast and man, Medusa and beloved woman are often united experientially in the same hypothetically unitary figure. This can be a terrible discovery when made in real life.

*The same idea is expressed in Taoist cosmogony, when the yin and the yang differentiate themselves into the five elements: wood, fire, earth, metal, and water. The ancient Greeks believed, similarly, that Earth and Sky (Gaia and Uranus) gave birth to the Titans, elemental deities of great strength and power.

their activity, pairing off, producing children, and then grandchildren, of their own. One of the latter, Marduk, appears particularly talented, powerful, and promising. He is born with eyes encircling his head. He can see everywhere. He can speak magic words. He is something entirely new—and this is noted early by his progenitors. While Marduk matures, the elder gods are compelled to confront Tiamat, with whom they are now at war. One after another they attempt to defeat her. All return in abject failure. Finally, someone suggests that Marduk, though still young, should be sent to confront his terrible grandmother. Approached with this idea, he agrees, but only on the condition that he is awarded the right, henceforth—if he is victorious—to hold the Tablet of Destinies, and sit atop the dominance hierarchy of the gods.

It is in this manner that this ancient story describes the emergence of monotheism out of polytheism. The *Enuma Elish* appears to be a dramatized account of the psychological or spiritual processes comprising this transformation. The ancient Mesopotamian civilization faced the necessity of incorporating and unifying many diverse tribes and peoples, each of whom had their own gods. The god who arose out of the conflict between all those gods ("Whose god is supreme?") was, therefore, a meta-god—a god composed of what was most important about all gods. It was for such a reason, for example, that fifty different names characterized Marduk. This emergence of one from many is a very common process, described by the scholar of myth Mircea Eliade as the war of the gods in heaven, a typical mythological motif, as well as alluded to earlier.* It is the psychological counterpart, in the world of imagination, to the genuine struggle of concepts of divinity and value on earth. Tribes unite. Each has its gods. The people comprising these multitudinous groups go to war, concretely and conceptually, for

---

E pluribus unum.

what they believe—sometimes for generations. It is as if the gods
they follow were battling for dominance over periods exceeding single
human lives, using their followers as proxies. That is reflected in the
ancient stories. If and when the gods come to an agreement about their
relative positions—more particularly, if they arrange themselves into
a hierarchy—it means that peace has genuinely been established, because peace is the establishment of a shared hierarchy of divinity, of
value. Thus, an eternal question emerges whenever people of different
backgrounds are required to deal with one another on a relatively permanent basis: What do all gods share that makes them gods? What is
God, in essence?

That is a very difficult question. It is, on the one hand, the question
of value: What is of the highest importance? It is, on the other hand,
the question of sovereignty: What principle should rule? These are
the questions posed by those pondering the ultimate source of divine
significance itself. Their difficulty meant that they, and by extension
the question of God, had to be answered over centuries, over millennia.
The answer emerged first in story form. The Mesopotamians brilliantly
intuited that the highest god—the highest good—involved careful attention (the multiple, head-circling eyes of Marduk) and effective language (the magic words of Marduk, capable of generating a cosmos), in
addition to the courage and strength to voluntarily confront and overcome chaos, the unknown. It could be argued that these are the defining features of the great central spirit of mankind, at least insofar as that
spirit is noble and admirable.

The ancient Egyptians formulated an idea similar in many important regards—which we will discuss later in detail—associating their
savior-god Horus, son of Osiris, with the sharp-eyed falcon, and identifying him with the vision willing to search out, detect, understand,

and defeat evil (symbolized with the famous Egyptian image of the single eye). Representing that reality—*pay attention, above all, even to what is monstrous and malevolent, and speak wisely and truthfully*—could be the single most important accomplishment of our species.[4] It allows us to apprehend in dramatic form the fundamental necessity of coming to grips with what our senses demonstrate to us, no matter how terrifying the reality revealed. It allows for the possibility of bringing our explicit understanding closer in line with our deepest being, making possible a truer union of body and spirit through the partial comprehension and imitation of the story. Most importantly, perhaps, it allows us to realize the immense importance of words in transforming potential into actuality, and helps us understand that the role we each play in that transformation is in some vital sense akin to the divine.

After his election to the highest of places, Marduk challenges Tiamat directly, encloses her, defeated, in a giant net, and cuts her into pieces, fashioning the heavens and the earth from her remains. One of Marduk's many names is, in fact, "he who makes ingenious things as a consequence of the conflict with Tiamat."[5] It might be noted, in this regard, that tens of thousands of years ago, men literally did construct the habitable world out of the pieces of monsters, making their early dwellings from the giant bones of animals they had so courageously speared.[6] Marduk simultaneously defeats his grandmother's monstrous army, including the leader, Kingu, from whom he takes the Tablet of Destinies, confirming his place as supreme leader of the cosmos. Then he returns home, enemies in tow. His compatriots celebrate his victory and accede yet more completely to his leadership, before he assigns them their various duties. Then, after consulting Ea, the god of wisdom, Marduk determines to create man, to aid the gods most fundamentally in the eternal task of maintaining the proper balance between order and chaos—to release those very gods from their service, and to transfer their burden onto our all-too-human shoulders.*

The basic story is this: when order (Apsu) is carelessly threatened or destroyed, the terrible forces of chaos from which the world was originally derived appear once again in their most destructive, monstrous, predatory guise. Then a hero, representing the highest of values, must arise or be elected to confront this chaotic force. He does so successfully, deriving or producing something of great worth. What the hero represents is the most important of the great forces that make up the human psyche. To think of it another way: the hero is the embodied principle of action and perception that must rule over all the primordial psychological elements of lust, rage, hunger, thirst, terror, and joy. For chaos to remain effectively at bay (or, even better, tamed and therefore harnessed), this heroic principle must be regarded as the most important of all things that can organize and motivate mankind. This means, at least, that it must be continually acted out, which is what "regarded as important" actually means. It is in this way that the spirit of Marduk still possesses each individual who engages courageously in the processes of encounter and confrontation that eternally create and renew society. It is this that happens when each small child learns to regulate and unite his emotions and motivations into a coherent personality, and then goes out to challenge the unknown world.

In slightly altered form, this is the story of St. George: The inhabitants of an ancient city must obtain water from a well beside the nest of a dragon. To do so, however, they have to offer the dragon some

---

*Ea makes man from the blood of Kingu, the most terrible of Tiamat's monsters. A bright graduate student and later colleague of mine once suggested that this was because of all God's creatures, only man could deceive; only man could voluntarily bring evil and discord into the world.

sacrifice—a sheep, under most circumstances, but a maiden, if no sheep can be found. The young women of the city draw lots when the supply of sheep is exhausted. One day it is the daughter of the king herself who loses. St. George appears, confronts the dragon with the sign of the cross—symbol of the eternal Redeemer, the archetypal hero— and frees the doomed princess. The city's inhabitants then convert to Christianity. Victory over the dragon—the predator, as such, the ruler of unexplored territory—is victory over all the forces that have threatened the individual and society, over evolutionary and historical spans of time, as well as the more abstract evil we all still face, without and within. The cross, for its part, is the burden of life. It is a place of betrayal, torture, and death. It is therefore a fundamental symbol of mortal vulnerability. In the Christian drama, it is also the place where vulnerability is transcended, as a consequence of its acceptance. This voluntary acceptance is also equivalent to victory over the dragon, representation of chaos, death, and the unknown. By accepting life's suffering, therefore, evil may be overcome. The alternative is hell, at least in its psychological form: rage, resentment, and the desire for revenge and destruction.

The same story is echoed in the tales of St. Patrick, who chases the snakes out of Ireland, and St. Michael, who defeats the Christian equivalent of Kingu, "that ancient serpent called the devil" (Revelation 12:9). This is the same story recounted by J. R. R. Tolkien in *The Hobbit*, which was in turn derived from the ancient poem *Beowulf*, the tale of a hero defeating a pair of intelligent monsters—son, and then worse, mother.[7] In *The Hobbit*, the hero develops character and wisdom (as a thief, strangely enough) during his quest to help discover the ancient treasure hoarded by the dragon. The story of Perseus and Medusa, whose visage was so terrible that it turned onlookers to stone, is another variant, as is Pinocchio, who rescues his father from a sub-aquatic monster, and dies and is reborn while doing so. Something similar is portrayed in the first of the recent Avengers movies, in which Iron Man—the man who has transformed himself into a partly golden superhero—defeats the alien dragon worms of the Chitauri (allied with the satanic Loki). He then dies, is reborn, and gets the maiden (in the nonswooning guise of Ms. Pepper Potts). It must be understood: Such stories would not even be comprehensible (not least to children, as well as adults) if our evolutionary history had importantly differed, and if our entire culture had not been shaped, implicitly and explicitly, by these ancient patterns.

All these heroes act out what was perhaps the greatest discovery ever made by man's primordial ancestors: if you have the vision and the courage (and a good stout stick, when necessary), you can chase away the worst of snakes. No doubt the greatest of our ancestors were beginning to threaten snakes with sticks when we still lived in trees. No doubt it was those voluntarily snake-chasing ancestors who reaped the benefits of their bravery in the form of nearby grateful maidens (or their ancestral arboreal equivalents)—and perhaps this is why dragons hoard virgins, as well as gold. What constitutes the worst of all snakes and the stoutest of all sticks, however, might be regarded as the central religious questions of humanity. It is interesting to note that in *The Hobbit*, the worst snake is "only" a dragon, but in *The Lord of the Rings*, the worst snake, so to speak, is the much more abstract evil of the wizard Sauron. As humanity became more sophisticated in its capacity to abstract, we increasingly appreciated the fact that predatory monsters can come in many guises, only some of which are animal in their form. Literature of an arguably more sophisticated form endlessly echoes this realization.

HERO, DRAGON, DEATH, AND REBIRTH: WHO YOU COULD BE (III)

In the second volume of J. K. Rowling's fantasy series, *Harry Potter and the Chamber of Secrets*, the castle of Hogwarts is threatened by strange, chaotic forces, due to the earlier and ongoing misbehavior of several powerful adult wizards (as established in volume one). Now, it is significant that Harry is orphaned: it is an integral part of the heroic pattern. He has his earthly parents, the thick and conventional Dursleys, willfully blind, shortsighted, and terribly overprotective of (and, therefore, tragically dangerous to) Dudley, their unfortunate but predictably self-centered and bullying natural son. But Harry has his heavenly parents, too, his true mother and father—symbolically, Nature and Culture (variants of chaos and order). They exist as part of his intrinsically magical potential—the magical potential of all of us, in fact, as we are all children of Nature and Culture, with the tremendous potential that implies, as well as the more mundane offspring of our particular parents.[8]

When Harry returns to Hogwarts after his summer vacation, he can detect strange and ominous noises emanating from somewhere in the building. At the same time, various students and residents of Hogwarts are found paralyzed—turned to stone—in diverse locations around the building. Turned to stone: What could that possibly mean? It certainly means to be unable to move—but it also signifies something deeper. It means to be *hunted*; to become a rabbit confronted by a wolf; to become the horrified and awestruck object of the predatory gaze. Many herbivores, comparatively defenseless, facing imminent and brutal death, freeze in place, paralyzed by fear, depending on camouflage and immobility to render them invisible to the terrible intentions

of nearby red-toothed and razor-clawed carnivores. Predatory, reptilian forms still particularly have that effect on human beings (hence our
awed fascination, for example, with dinosaurs). But to have no more
courage than a rabbit is definitely not to be everything you could be.

Eventually Harry learns that the force turning his friends into
stone is a gigantic snake, a basilisk, whose gaze exerts a paralyzing
force. He discovers that this serpent is continually slithering around
the very foundation of Hogwarts, in the immense waterworks that
serve the great castle. This basilisk is an analog to the great dragon
faced by Beowulf, hero of the thousand-year-old story that served as
pattern for Tolkien's adventures, perhaps the twentieth century's closest cousins to J. K. Rowling's extensive fantasy. It is, as well, the great
devouring shark of the movie *Jaws*, lurking in the black water of night,
ready at a moment's notice to pull the naked and unwary below; the
fragility of our homes and our institutions, which can collapse and leave
us stripped of their protective walls in a single terrible moment; and
more comprehensively, the underworld of the ancients, whose doors
gape open when everything predictable collapses. At the deepest of
levels, this is the chaos and potential that continually lurks under the
order of our familiar worlds, psychological and social.

After much searching, Harry gains entrance to this underworld
labyrinth of pipes and tunnels, and finds the central chamber. He does
this, significantly, through the sewer, acting out the ancient alchemical dictum, *in sterquilinis invenitur*: in filth it will be found.* What does

---

*It has been known for decades, explicitly (and forever, implicitly) that self-initiated
confrontation with what is frightening or unknown is frequently curative. The standard
treatment for phobias and anxiety is therefore exposure to what is feared. That treatment is effective—but the exposure must be voluntary. It is as if the anxiety systems of
the brain assume that anything that is advanced upon must not be a predator (or, if it is
a predator, it is the sort that can be easily kicked to the side and defeated). We now know
that even the emotional and bodily response to stress differs completely when that stress

this mean? That which you most need to find will be found where you least wish to look.* There, underground, Ginny (Virgin-ia), his best friend's sister and Harry's eventual serious romantic interest, lies unconscious. She is the maiden—or the *anima*, the soul—forever incarcerated by the dragon, as in the tale of St. George. It is up to Harry, orphaned hero, to wake and rescue her (just as Tolkien's Bilbo helps take the gold from the terrible Smaug; just as Disney's Prince Phillip rescues Sleeping Beauty—both rescuing what is most valuable from the clutches of a great dragon).†

---

is voluntarily faced rather than accidentally encountered. In the latter case, the threatened individual tenses up and readies him or herself defensively (see M. D. Seery, "Challenge or Threat? Cardiovascular Indexes of Resilience and Vulnerability to Potential Stress in Humans," *Neuroscience & Biobehavioral Reviews* 35 [2011]: 1603–4). That can become the chronically unhealthy posture of someone turned to stone. In the former case, the individual takes on the role of probable victor, and advances forthrightly. Such actions are indeed what has always saved humanity from the terrors of the night (and the evil lurking in the human heart). Our continual observation of that fact, over millennia, is what allowed us to represent it, abstractly, in our great religious stories, and then to imitate it, within the confines of our particular and unique life.

*This is at least in part because you are very unlikely to have already looked there, even though it would have been useful to do so.

†Something must be further clarified here. I made the case in the Overture, in Rule I, in *12 Rules for Life*, and in *Maps of Meaning* that chaos tends to find its representation in symbolic form as feminine—but here I am talking about chaos, in serpentine guise. I can explain this by elaborating on my explanation about the alchemical picture we discussed earlier—by reading it from the top down, however, this time. The more profound the threat—the deeper the chaos—the more likely that it will represent itself as mankind's most ancient enemy, the serpent. Perhaps it can be thought of like this: the unknown unknowns—those elements of being that are foreign and dangerous beyond imagination, and whose manifestation can kill or destroy psychologically—are those most likely to be represented in serpentine form. Out of this domain, which is in some important sense even more fundamental than sex itself, emerges the primordial feminine and masculine, although it seems that the feminine nonetheless retains a more primary connection with the fundamental unknowable itself. I think this has to do primarily with the absolute mystery of birth: with the relationship between the emergence of new forms from the feminine and the emergence of new forms from the absolutely unknown. It is perhaps something of this sort that accounts for the primacy of the relationship between the snake in the Garden of Eden and Eve, rather than between the snake and Adam. Perhaps, as well (and I am speculating wildly here, trying to move beyond my ignorance,

And of course, the unknown is a great predator—the basilisk Harry faces—and of course, that predator guards a great treasure, gold beyond measure or the sleeping virgin, because the individual brave enough to voluntarily beard the serpent in his lair is most likely to gain access to the untold riches that exist in potential, awaiting us in the adventure of our life, away from security and what is currently known. *Who dares wins**—if he does not perish. And who wins also makes himself irresistibly desirable and attractive, not least because of the development of character that adventure inevitably produces. And this is what makes us forever more than rabbits.

And Harry, like Bilbo, can only manage this—can only perceive the serpent, when it is invisible to everyone else—because he has a dark side. Tolkien's Bilbo must become a thief before he can become a hero. He must incorporate his monstrousness, so that he can supersede his naive harmlessness, before he is tough enough to face the terrors that confront him. Harry is touched by evil in another manner, as part of the incomparably dark wizard Voldemort's soul is embedded within him (although neither he nor Voldemort are initially aware of this). It is for this reason that the young wizard can speak with and hear

---

trying to account for the clear and omnipresent symbolic relationship), it has forever been the case that females attract snakes (as well as other dangerous predators), most particularly when they are taking care of their young, and that the heightened danger they therefore face has burned the danger of the feminine in relationship to the serpentine forever in our imagination. This would imply that the decision to take on a relationship with a female brings with it increased exposure to the terrible unknown (something that seems clearly true in the case of all the threats that are faced by children), as perhaps does the fact of being female itself. Now the female is also a rejecting force (particularly among humans, where the females are very choosy maters [see, for example, Y. Bokek-Cohen, Y. Peres, and S. Kanazawa, "Rational Choice and Evolutionary Psychology as Explanations for Mate Selectivity," *Journal of Social, Evolutionary, and Cultural Psychology* 2 (2008): 42–55]). That holding of the power of ultimate rejection makes Nature in all its cruelty (and, it must be said, wisdom). Perhaps that is also a nontrivial contributor to the feminine-serpent relationship.

*The motto of the British Special Air Service.

(that is, perceive) snakes. It is in keeping with this that he is disciplined and courageous, but also willing and ready to break the rules when necessary.

While in the bowels of Hogwarts, Harry comes under attack by the basilisk, which is under the control of Voldemort. Voldemort therefore bears the same relationship to the basilisk in Hogwarts as Satan does, strangely and incomprehensibly, to the vision-granting serpent in the Genesis story of the Garden of Eden. Why might this be? It could be said—and should be—that one form of serpentine chaos and danger is the threat of the reptilian predator itself. But another form, more abstract—more psychological, more spiritual—is human evil: the danger we pose to one another. At some point in our evolutionary and cultural history, we began to understand that human evil could rightly be considered the greatest of all snakes. So, the symbolic progression might be (1) snake as evil predator, then (2) external human enemy as snake/evil/predator, then (3) subjective, personal, or psychological darkness/vengefulness/deceit as snake/evil/predator. Each of these representations, which took untold centuries, perhaps millennia to conceptualize, constitute a tangible increase in the sophistication of the image of evil.[9]

All such manifestations of serpentine chaos and danger are apparently still first detected, processed, and symbolically interassociated by the ancient brain systems that evolved to protect us from predatory reptiles.[10] And freezing—prompted by those systems—solves the problem now, maybe, by hiding the individual who is currently being preyed upon, but it leaves the predator alive for tomorrow. Instead, the danger must be hunted down and destroyed—and even that is too concrete to constitute a permanent solution to the problem of evil itself (rather than a solution to any particular exemplar of evil). Most profoundly and abstractly (paralleling the idea that the greatest predator, the greatest snake, is the evil that lurks within), evil's destruction manifests as the life of virtue that constrains malevolence in its most abstracted and comprehensive form. It is for this reason, for example, that the Disney prince Phillip of *Sleeping Beauty* fame is armed for his conflict with the great Dragon of Chaos by benevolent Nature (in the form of the feminine fairies that accompany him and aid in his escape from Maleficent, the Evil Queen) with the Sword of Truth and Shield of Virtue.

Harry directly confronts the basilisk, down in the Chamber of Secrets, deep below the wizarding castle, but is cornered and in great peril. At that propitious moment, a phoenix kept by the wise headmaster of Hogwarts arrives, provides the young hero with a sword, and then attacks the giant snake, providing Harry with time to regroup. Harry slays the basilisk with the weapon, but is fatally bitten in the process. This is another deep mythological echo: In the story of Genesis, for example, the encounter with the snake proves fatal to man and woman alike, who become aware of their fragility and inevitable death soon after they awaken and gain vision. It is also a harsh truth: predators devour, dragons lay waste, chaos destroys. The threat is real. Even truth, virtue, and courage are not necessarily enough, but they are our best bet. And sometimes a little death is the medication necessary to forestall death itself. Fortunately, the phoenix has magical, revivifying tears, which it cries into Harry's wounds. Thus, the young wizard revives, defeats Voldemort (a much more challenging task than merely overcoming the gargantuan serpent), rescues Ginny, and saves the school.

It is with the introduction of the phoenix to the story of St. George that Rowling reveals another element of her intuitive genius. The phoenix is a fowl that can die and be reborn forever. It has, therefore, throughout the ages, been a symbol of Christ, with whom the magical bird shares many features. It is also, equally, that element of the individual human personality that must die and regenerate, as it learns, painfully, through the oft-tragic experience that destroys previous certainty, replacing it first with doubt, and then—when successfully confronted—with new and more complete knowledge. A voluntary death-and-rebirth transformation—the change necessary to adapt when terrible things emerge—is therefore a solution to the potentially fatal rigidity of erroneous certainty, excessive order, and stultification.

HOW TO ACT

People exchange information about how to act in many ways. They observe each other and imitate what they see. When they imitate, they use their bodies to represent the bodies of others. But this imitation is not mindless, automatized mimicry. It is instead the ability to identify regularities or patterns in the behavior of other people, and then to imitate those patterns. When a young girl plays at being a mother, for example, she does not duplicate, gesture for gesture, what she has previously observed of her mother's actions. Instead she acts "as if" she were a mother. If you ask the girl what she is doing, she will tell you that she is pretending to be a mother, but if you get her to describe what that means, particularly if she is a young child, her description will be far less complete than her actions would indicate. This means she can act out more than she can say—just as we all can. If you observed many little girls, acting out many mothers, you could derive a very good idea of what "mother" meant, in its purest form, even if you had never seen an actual mother. If you were good with words, then perhaps you could describe the essential elements of maternal behavior and transmit them. You might do that best in the form of a story.

It is easier and more direct to represent a behavioral pattern with behavior than with words. Outright mimicry does that directly, action for action. Imitation, which can produce new behaviors akin to those that motivated the mimicry, takes that one step further. Drama—formalized imitation, enacted upon a stage—is precisely behavior portraying behavior, but distilled ever closer to the essence. Literature takes that transmission one more difficult step, portraying action in the imagination of the writer and the reader, in the complete absence of both real actors and a material stage. It is only the greatest of storytellers who can manage that transformation, representing the greatest and most vitally necessary of acts in the most interesting, profound, and memorable words. Generations of great storytellers, retelling, modifying, and editing great stories, therefore end up jointly creating the greatest of stories. Once cultures become literate (something that has happened only recently, from the historical perspective), those stories can be written down. It is at this point, roughly, that myth and ritual might be said to transform themselves into religion.

The imitation and communication of the greatest, most memorable acts necessitates distillation and communication of the patterns of the deepest wisdom of mankind. If a great and memorable act is one undertaken by a particularly admirable individual, a local hero, then the greatest and most memorable acts possible would be those undertaken by the spirit (embodied in part by particular individuals) who exemplified what all local heroes everywhere have in common. That hero of heroes—that meta-hero—would have to exist, logically, in turn, *in a place that was common across all places requiring heroism.* That place might be regarded as a meta-world—even though it is real, even hyperreal (that is, more real in its abstraction across places than our direct perceptions of a given, singular time or place). It is precisely this hyperreal meta-world that consists of the continual interactions between chaos and order, which eternally serve as the battleground between good and evil characterizing the hero. The undying pattern that hero embodies, in turn—upon whose actions the individual and society both depend—is the highest of all Gods. He is both child of and mediator between those twin forces, transforming chaos into habitable order (as well as recasting order into chaos, so that it can be renewed, when it has become anachronistic and corrupt), as well as battling mightily so that good might prevail.

Everyone requires a story to structure their perceptions and actions in what would otherwise be the overwhelming chaos of being. Every story requires a starting place that is not good enough and an ending place that is better. Nothing can be judged in the absence of that end place, that higher value. Without it, everything sinks into meaninglessness and boredom or degenerates and spirals into terror, anxiety, and pain. But, as time changes all things inexorably, every specific, value-predicated story may fail, in its particular incarnation and locale, and need replacement by something newer, more complete, but different. In consequence, the actor of a given story (and, therefore, someone deeply affiliated with the plot and the characterization) still must bow to the spirit of creative transformation that originally created and may need to destroy and re-create that story. It is for this reason that spirit eternally transcends dogma, truth transcends presupposition, Marduk transcends the elder gods, creativity updates society, and Christ transcends the law (as does Harry Potter, along with his courageous but continually rule-breaking friends). But it is important to remember, as we discussed in Rule I: Those who break the rules ethically are those who have mastered them first and disciplined themselves to understand the necessity of those rules, and break them in keeping with the spirit rather than the letter of the law.

The second volume of Rowling's series proposes that predatory evil can be overcome by the soul willing to die and be reborn. The complete series ends with a creatively transformed repetition of the same message. The analogy with Christianity is obvious, and the message, in essence, the same: The soul willing to transform, as deeply as necessary, is the most effective enemy of the demonic serpents of ideology and totalitarianism, in their personal and social forms. The healthy, dynamic, and above all else truthful personality will admit to error. It will voluntarily shed—let die—outdated perceptions, thoughts, and habits, as impediments to its further success and growth. This is the soul that will let its old beliefs burn away, often painfully, so that it can live again, and move forward, renewed. This is also the soul that will transmit what it has learned during that process of death and rebirth, so that others can be reborn along with it.

Aim at something. Pick the best target you can currently conceptualize. Stumble toward it. Notice your errors and misconceptions along the way, face them, and correct them. Get your story straight. Past, present, future—they all matter. You need to map your path. You need to know where you were, so that you do not repeat the mistakes of the past. You need to know where you are, or you will not be able to draw a line from your starting point to your destination. You need to know where you are going, or you will drown in uncertainty, unpredictability, and chaos, and starve for hope and inspiration. For better or worse, you are on a journey. You are having an adventure—and your map better be accurate. Voluntarily confront what stands in your way. The way—that is the path of life, the meaningful path of life, the straight and narrow path that constitutes the very border between order and chaos, and the traversing of which brings them into balance.

Aim at something profound and noble and lofty. If you can find a better path along the way, once you have started moving forward, then switch course. Be careful, though; it is not easy to discriminate between changing paths and simply giving up. (One hint: if the new path you see forward, after learning what you needed to learn along your current way, appears more challenging, then you can be reasonably sure that you are not deluding or betraying yourself when you change your mind.) In this manner, you will zigzag forward. It is not the most efficient way to travel, but there is no real alternative, given that your goals will inevitably change while you pursue them, as you learn what you need to learn while you are disciplining yourself.

You will then find yourself turning across time, incrementally and gracefully, to aim ever more accurately at that tiny pinpoint, the X that marks the spot, the bull's-eye, and the center of the cross; to aim at the highest value of which you can conceive. You will pursue a target that is both moving and receding: moving, because you do not have the wisdom to aim in the proper direction when you first take aim; receding, because no matter how close you come to perfecting what you are currently practicing, new vistas of possible perfection will open up in front of you. Discipline and transformation will nonetheless lead you inexorably forward. With will and luck, you will find a story that is meaningful and productive, improves itself with time, and perhaps even provides you with more than a few moments of satisfaction and joy. With will and luck, you will be the hero of that story, the disciplined sojourner, the creative transformer, and the benefactor of your family and broader society.

Imagine who you could be, and then aim single-mindedly at that.

DO NOT HIDE UNWANTED THINGS IN THE FOG

THOSE DAMNED PLATES

I love my father-in-law. I respect him, too. He is extremely stable emotionally—one of those tough or fortunate people (perhaps a little of both) who can let the trials and tribulations of life roll off him and keep moving forward with little complaint and plenty of competence. He is an old guy now, Dell Roberts—eighty-eight. He has had a knee replaced, and is planning to get the remaining one done. He has had stents inserted into his coronary arteries and a heart valve replaced. He suffers from drop foot and sometimes slips and falls because of it. But he was still curling a year ago, pushing the heavy granite rock down the ice with a stick specifically designed for people who can no longer crouch down as easily as they once could.

When his wife, Beth, now deceased, developed dementia at a relatively young age, he took care of her in as uncomplaining and unresentful a manner as anyone could imagine. It was impressive. I am by no means convinced that I could have fared as well. He cared for her right to the point where it became impossible for him to lift her out of whatever chair she had settled into. This was long after she had lost the ability to speak. But it was obvious by the way her eyes lit up when he entered the room that she still loved him—and the feeling was mutual. I would not describe him as someone who is prone to avoidance when the going gets tough. Quite the contrary.

When Dell was a much younger man, he was for several decades a real estate dealer in Fairview, Alberta—the small town where I grew up (we lived right across the street from the Roberts family, in fact). During that time, he habitually went home for lunch, in accordance with the general custom. Beth typically prepared him soup (probably Campbell's, which everyone ate at that time—"M'm! M'm! Good!"), and a sandwich. One day, without warning, he snapped at his wife: "Why in the world do we always eat off these tiny plates? I hate eating off these tiny plates!"

She had been serving the sandwiches on bread-and-butter plates, which average about six or seven inches in diameter, instead of full-size dinner plates of ten to twelve inches. She related this story to her daughters, soon after, in a state of mild shock. This story has been re-told to much laughter at family gatherings many times since. After all, she had been serving him lunch on those plates for at least twenty years by the time he finally said anything. She had no idea that he was annoyed by her table settings. He had never objected. And there is something inexhaustibly amusing about that.

Now, it is possible that he was irritated by something else altogether that day and did not really care about the plates. And in one sense, it is a trivial issue. But seen another way, it is not trivial at all, for two reasons. First, if something happens every day, *it is important*, and lunch was happening every day. In consequence, if there was something about it that was chronically bothersome, even in a minor sort of way, it needed to be attended to. Second, it is very common to allow so-called minor irritations (which are not minor, as I said, if they happen constantly) to continue for years without comment or resolution.

Here is the problem: Collect a hundred, or a thousand, of those, and your life is miserable and your marriage doomed. Do not pretend you are happy with something if you are not, and if a reasonable solution might, in principle, be negotiated. Have the damn fight. Unpleasant as that might be in the moment, it is one less straw on the camel's back. And that is particularly true for those daily events that everyone is prone to regard as trivial—even the plates on which you eat your lunch. Life is what repeats, and it is worth getting what repeats right.

JUST NOT WORTH THE FIGHT

Here is a more serious story of the same type. I had a client who had come to see me about her plans to move to private practice after many years as an accountant with a large corporation. She was well respected in her profession, and was a competent, kind, and careful person. But she was also very unhappy. I presumed initially that her unhappiness stemmed from anxiety about her career transition. But she managed that move without a hitch during the time we continued our sessions, while other issues rose to the forefront.

Her problem was not her career change. It was her marriage. She described her husband as extraordinarily self-centered and simultaneously overly concerned with how he appeared in the eyes of others. It was a contradictory combination, in some manner, although it is common enough to see this touching of opposites in a personality: If you lean too far in one direction, something else in you leans equally far in the other. So, despite the husband's narcissism (at least from his wife's perspective), he was in thrall to the opinions of everyone he met—excepting the members of his own family. He also drank too much—a habit which exaggerated his temperamental defects.

My client was not comfortable in her own home. She did not feel there was anything truly of her within the apartment she shared with her husband (the couple had no children). Her situation provided a good example of how what is outside can profoundly reflect what is inside (which is why I suggest to people who are in psychological trouble that they might begin their recovery by cleaning up—and then beautifying, if possible—their rooms). All their household furnishings, which she described as showy, ornate, and uncomfortable, had been chosen by her husband. Furthermore, he avidly collected 1960s and 70s pop art, and the walls of the house were crowded with these items, which he had spent time seeking out in galleries and otherwise gathering for many years, often while she sat waiting outside in the car.

She told me that she did not care about the furnishings and the excess of decorative objects, but that was not really true. What was true was that she did not care *for* them—not a bit. Neither the showiness nor the furnishings nor the plethora of art works that made up her husband's collection appealed to her taste. She tended toward a minimalist aesthetic (or perhaps that preference was a consequence of her husband's decorative excesses). It was never quite clear what she might have preferred, and perhaps that was part of the problem: because she did not know what she liked (and was equally vague about her dislikes), she was not in the strongest position to put forward her own opinions. It is difficult to win an argument, or even begin one, if you have not carefully articulated what you want (or do not) and need (or do not).

However, she certainly did not enjoy feeling like a stranger in her own home. For that reason, she never had friends over to visit, which was also a nontrivial problem, contributing as it did to her feelings of isolation. But the furnishings and paintings continued to accrue, one shopping expedition at a time, in Canada and abroad, and with each purchase there was less of her in the house and in the marriage, and increasingly more of her husband. Nonetheless, my client never went to war. She never had a fit of anger. She never put her fist through a particularly objectionable canvas hanging on the living room wall. In all the decades of her married life, she never had an outburst of genuine rage; she never directly and conclusively confronted the fact that she hated her home and her subordination to her husband's taste. Instead, she let him have his way, repeatedly, increment by increment, because she claimed that such trivialities were not worth fighting for. And with each defeat, the next disagreement became more necessary—although less likely, because she understood that a serious discussion, once initiated, risked expanding to include all the things that were troublesome about her marriage, and that a real, no-holds-barred battle would therefore likely ensue. Then everything wrong might spill out and have to be faced and dealt with, by one means or another. So, she kept silent. But she was chronically repressed and constantly resentful, and felt that she had wasted much of the opportunity of her life.

It is a mistake to consider the furnishings and the pop art paintings as simple material objects. They were more truly and importantly containers of information, so to speak, about the state of the marriage, and were certainly experienced as such by my client. Every single object of art was the concrete realization of a victory (Pyrrhic though it may have been) and a defeat (or, at least, a negotiation that did not occur and, therefore, a fight that was over before it started). And there were dozens or perhaps hundreds of these: each a weapon in an unspoken, destructive, and decades-long war. Unsurprisingly, given the circumstances, the couple split up—after thirty years of marriage. I believe the husband retained all the furniture and art.

Here is a thought, a terrifying and dispiriting thought, to motivate improvement in your marriage—to scare you into the appalling difficulties of true negotiation. Every little problem you have every morning, afternoon, or evening with your spouse will be repeated for each of the fifteen thousand days that will make up a forty-year marriage. Every trivial but chronic disagreement about cooking, dishes, housecleaning, responsibility for finances, or frequency of intimate contact will be duplicated, over and over, unless you successfully address it. Perhaps you think (moment to moment, at least) that it is best to avoid confrontation and drift along in apparent but false peace. Make no mistake about it, however: you age as you drift, just as rapidly as you age as you strive. But you have no direction when you drift, and the probability that you will obtain what you need and want by drifting aimlessly is very low. Things fall apart of their own accord, but the sins of men speed their deterioration: that is wisdom from the ages. It may well be that conscious apprehension of the horror of the same small hell forever repeated is precisely what is necessary to force you to confront the problems in your marriage and negotiate in good and desperate faith to solve them. However, it is the easiest of matters, particularly in the short term, to ignore the prick of conscience and let the small defeats slide, day after day. This is not a good strategy. Only careful aim and wakeful striving and commitment can eliminate the oft-incremental calamity of willful blindness, stem the entropic tide, and keep catastrophe—familial and social alike—at bay.

CORRUPTION: COMMISSION AND OMISSION

Corruption of the form we are discussing is, in my opinion, integrally linked to deception—to lying, more bluntly—and more important, to self-deception. Now, strict logicians regard self-deception as an impossibility. They cannot understand how it is possible for a person to believe one thing and its opposite simultaneously. Logicians are not psychologists, however—and they obviously do not notice, or else fail to take into account, the fact that they themselves have family members, for example, for whom they at least occasionally feel love and hate at the same time. Furthermore, it is not obvious what "believe" means when discussing human belief, nor what is meant by "simultaneously." I can believe one thing today and another tomorrow and very often get away with it, at least in the short term. And on many occasions I have experienced what was very nearly simultaneous belief in one thing and its opposite while reading undergraduate university papers, in which the writer made a claim in one paragraph and a completely contradictory claim in the next. (Sometimes that happened within the span of a single sentence.)

There are many conditions or circumstances under which self-deception can theoretically occur. Psychoanalysts have explored many of these, with Freud leading the way. Freud believed that much of mental illness was due to repression, which is arguably and reasonably considered a form of self-deception. For him, memories of traumatically troubling events were unconsciously banished to perdition in the unconscious, where they rattled around and caused trouble, like poltergeists in a dungeon. Freud understood that the human personality was not unitary. Instead, it consists of a loose, fragmented cacophony of spirits, who do not always agree or even communicate. The truth of this claim is self-evident, at least in one simple manner: we can think about things—we can simulate potential or alternative actions or events—without immediately having to act them out. Dissociation of thought and action is necessary for abstract thought even to exist. Thus, we can clearly think or say one thing and do another. This is fine when merely thinking, prior to acting, but perhaps not so good when we promise or claim to believe something and then act in a manner indicating that we truly have faith in something else. This is a form of deception, a disjunction in character, a contradiction between modes of being. It has even been named: to claim one belief and then to act (or speak) in a different or even opposite manner constitutes a *performative contradiction*, according to certain modern philosophers:[1] an implicit lie, in my opinion. The holding of contradictory beliefs also becomes a problem when the holder attempts to act out both simultaneously and discovers, often to his or her great chagrin, the paradox that makes such an attempt impossible.

Freud catalogued an extensive list of phenomena akin to repression—the active rejection of potentially conscious psychological material from awareness—which he termed "defense mechanisms." These include denial ("the truth is not so bad"), reaction formation ("I really, really, really love my mother"), displacement ("the boss yells at me, I yell at my wife, my wife yells at the baby, the baby bites the cat"), identification ("I am bullied, so I am motivated to be a bully"), rationalization (a self-serving explanation for a low-quality action), intellectualization (a favorite of the early, funny, neurotic Woody Allen), sublimation ("I can always *paint* nude women"), and projection ("I am not touchy; you are just annoying"). Freud was an outstanding philosopher of deceit. He was not afraid to point out the relationship between dishonesty and psychopathology. Nonetheless, his ideas of self-deception suffer, in my opinion, from two major errors.

First error: Freud failed to notice that sins of omission contributed to mental illness as much as, or more than, the sins of commission, listed above, that constitute repression. In doing so, he merely thought in the typical manner. People generally believe that actively doing something bad (that is the sin of commission) is, on average, worse than passively not doing something good (that is the sin of omission). Perhaps this is because there are always good things we are not doing; some sins of omission are therefore inevitable. In any case, there are still times when willful blindness nonetheless produces more serious catastrophes, more easily rationalized away, than the active or the unconscious repression of something terrible but understood (the latter being a sin of commission, because it is known). The former problem— willful blindness—occurs when you *could* come to know something but cease exploring so that you fail to discover something that might cause you substantial discomfort. Spin doctors call this self-imposed ignorance "plausible deniability," which is a phrase that indicates intellectualized rationalization of the most pathological order. It should be noted that such blindness is often regarded as an outright crime. If you are a CEO, for example, and you suspect that your treasurer is cooking the books, and you do not investigate because you do not want to know, you may still be liable for your inaction—as is appropriate. Failing to look under the bed when you strongly suspect a monster is lurking there is not an advisable strategy.

Second error: Freud assumed that things experienced are things understood. In accordance with that assumption, he believed that a memory trace existed, somewhere in the mind, that accurately represented the past, like an objective video recording. These would be reasonable presumptions, if our experience was simply a series of objectively real and self-evident events transmitted through our senses, thought about, evaluated, and then acted upon. If this was all true, traumatic experience would be accurately represented in memory, even when pushed out of awareness by unconscious mechanisms (or conscious—but Freud presumed the former) because of its understood but terrible nature. However, neither reality nor our processing of reality is as objective or articulated as Freud presupposed.

Imagine, for example, that you have been ignored, romantically— more than you can tolerate—for several months by your wife or husband. Then you encounter him or her leaning over the fence, talking in a friendly manner (and perhaps no more than that) to an attractive neighbor. How we process such anomalous, novel, troublesome, or even traumatic experience is very rarely a matter of perception, followed by conscious understanding and thought, then emotion or motivation derived from that thought, then action. What happens instead is akin to what we discussed at length in Rule I and Rule II: We process the unknown world from the bottom up. We encounter containers of information, so to speak, whose full import is by no means self-evident. Upon witnessing your spouse talking to the neighbor, therefore, it is not as if you think, in an altogether articulated and fully developed philosophical form: "I have been lonesome and deprived physically for months by my spouse. Although I have not said anything in detail, this has caused me constant frustration and pain. Now he (or she) is rubbing it in, as far as I am concerned, by being so outgoing with a comparative stranger when I have experienced so little attention." It is much more likely that anger, grief, and loneliness have accumulated within you with each rejection, bit by bit, until you are filled to the brim—and, now, overflowing.

That sudden appearance of negative emotion does not necessarily mean that you are even now fully conscious of its accumulation. You may well (as in the case of my father-in-law, or my client) have experienced the frustration build up gradually enough so that you found yourself more irritable and unhappy, but that does not necessarily mean that you noticed the cause. And what *is* the cause? The range of possibilities is uncomfortably broad. Perhaps you are not being ignored at all. Instead, you have been having trouble at work, and that has produced a decrease in your overall confidence. In consequence, you have become sensitized to any signs of rejection, even imaginary, within your marriage. So, what you must determine is not so much why your wife or husband is no longer attentive to you, but what it is about your boss, colleagues, or career that is destabilizing you. That puts the true cause of your discomfort a long distance away from the symptoms (the feelings of rejection) that are making you irritable, sensitive, and hurt. There is nothing obvious about the relationship between cause and effect in such cases. Perhaps you really are being ignored, just as you suspect. Perhaps it is a sign of an impending affair and a manifestation of the trajectory that leads to divorce. Both of those, if true, are serious problems. It is no wonder you are upset. But you may remain stubbornly unwilling to consider that your career or marriage is in trouble. And that is no surprise. But it is not helpful.

On top of all that is the general complexity of life, complicating the search for clarity. Consider the question "What really happened?" say, in a failed marriage, divorce, and child-custody battle. The answer to that query is so complex that settling the disagreements frequently requires court evaluation and multi-party assessment. Even then, one or even both of the protagonists is unlikely to believe that the truth has been served. This is partly because events in general and interpersonal events specifically do not exist as simple, objective facts, independent of one another. Everything depends for its meaning—for the information it truly represents—on the context in which it is embedded, much of which is not available for perception or consideration when the event in question occurs. The meaning of what someone's wife says to him today is dependent on everything both have ever said to each other, everything they have ever done together, and the contents of their mutual imaginations—and that does not exhaust the complexity. Such meaning may even be importantly dependent on how, for example, the wife's mother treated her father (or her grandmother treated her grandfather), as well as the relationship between men and women in the broader culture. That is why domestic arguments so often spiral out of control, particularly when a pattern of continual and effective communication has never been established. One thing leads to a deeper thing, and that leads deeper yet, until an argument that started over what size plates are best used at lunchtime turns into a no-holds-barred war about whether the marriage in question would be better dissolved. And there is certainly fear of falling down a hole of that size (again, particularly when much has remained unspoken) that motivates the proclivity to keep things to yourself when they would be better, but dangerously, said.

WHAT IS THE FOG?

Imagine that you are afraid. You have reason to be. You are afraid of yourself. You are afraid of other people. You are afraid of the world. You are nostalgic for the innocence of the past; for the time before you learned the terrible things that shattered the trust characterizing your childhood. The knowledge you have gained of yourself, other people, and the world has embittered more than enlightened. You have been betrayed, hurt, and disappointed. You have become distrustful even of hope itself, as your hope has been repeatedly shattered (and that is the very definition of hopelessness). The last thing you want is to know more. Better to leave *what is* enshrouded in mystery. Better, as well, to avoid thinking too much (or at all) about *what could be*. When ignorance is bliss, after all, 'tis folly to be wise.

Imagine, more precisely, that you are so afraid that you will not allow yourself even to know what you want. Knowing would simultaneously mean hoping, and your hopes have been dashed. You have your reasons for maintaining your ignorance. You are afraid, perhaps, that there is nothing worth wanting; you are afraid that if you specify what you want precisely you will simultaneously discover (and all too clearly) what constitutes failure; you are afraid that failure is the most likely outcome; and, finally, you are afraid that if you define failure and then fail, you will know beyond a shadow of a doubt that it was you that failed, and that it was your fault.

So, you do not allow yourself to know what you want. You manage this by refusing to think it through. You are happy, satisfied, and engaged sometimes and unhappy, frustrated, and nihilistic other times, but you will not enquire deeply into why, because then you would know, and then you would encounter yet-again shattered hope and confirmed disappointment. You are also afraid, but for different reasons, to allow others to know what you want. First, if they were to find out just what you wanted, then they might tell you, and then you would know, even if you were fighting against gathering that very knowledge. Second, if they knew, they could then deny you what you truly wanted, even needed, and hurt you much more efficiently than they might if your deepest desires (and, therefore, your vulnerabilities) remained secret.

The fog that hides is the refusal to notice—to attend to—emotions and motivational states as they arise, and the refusal to communicate them both to yourself and to the people who are close to you. A bad mood signifies something. A state of anxiety or sadness signifies something, and not likely something that will please you to discover. The most probable outcome of successfully articulating an emotion that has accrued without expression over time is tears—an admission of vulnerability and pain (which are also feelings that people do not like to allow, particularly when they are feeling distrustful and angry). Who wants to dig down into the depths of pain and grief and guilt until the tears emerge? And voluntary refusal to take notice of our emotional states is not the only impediment to dealing with them. If your wife or husband (or whomever else you are tangled up with, unhappily, at the moment) says something that comes too close to the painful truth, for example, then a sharp and insulting remark will often shut them up—and is therefore very likely to be offered. This is partly a test: does the person being insulted care enough about you and your suffering to dig past a few obstacles and unearth the bitter truth? It is also partly, and more obviously, defensive: if you can chase someone away from something you yourself do not want to discover, that makes your life easier in the present. Sadly, it is also very disappointing if that defense succeeds, and is typically accompanied by a sense of abandonment, loneliness, and self-betrayal. You must nonetheless still live among other people, and they with you. And you have desires, wants, and needs, however unstated and unclear. And you are still motivated to pursue them, not least because it is impossible to live without desire, want, and need. Your strategy, under such conditions? Show your disappointment whenever someone close to you makes you unhappy; allow yourself the luxury and pleasure of resentment when something does not go your way; ensure that the person who has transgressed against you is frozen out by your disapproval; force them to discover with as much difficulty as possible exactly what they have done to disappoint you; and, finally, let them grope around blindly in the fog that you have generated around yourself until they stumble

into and injure themselves on the sharp hidden edges of your unrevealed preferences and dreams. And maybe these responses are tests,
too—tests deeply associated with the lack of courage to trust: "If you
really loved me, you would brave the terrible landscape that I have
arrayed around myself to discover the real me." And perhaps there is
even something to such claims, implicit though they may be. A certain
testing of commitment might have its utility. Everything does not have
to be given away for free. But even a little unnecessary mystery goes a
long way.

And you still must live with yourself. In the short term, perhaps
you are protected from the revelation of your insufficiency by your
refusal to make yourself clear. Every ideal is a judge, after all: the judge
who says, "You are not manifesting your true potential." No ideals?
No judge. But the price paid for that is purposelessness. This is a high
price. No purpose? Then, no positive emotion, as most of what drives
us forward with hope intact is the experience of approaching something we deeply need and want. And worse, when we are without purpose: chronic, overwhelming anxiety, as focused purpose constrains
what is otherwise likely to be the intolerable chaos of unexploited possibility and too much choice.

If you make what you want clear and commit yourself to its pursuit,
you may fail. But if you do not make what you want clear, then you
will certainly fail. You cannot hit a target that you refuse to see. You
cannot hit a target if you do not take aim. And, equally dangerously, in
both cases: you will not accrue the advantage of aiming, but missing.
You will not benefit from the learning that inevitably takes place when
things do not go your way. Success at a given endeavor often means
trying, falling short, recalibrating (with the new knowledge generated
painfully by the failure), and then trying again and falling short—
often repeated, *ad nauseam*. Sometimes all that learning, impossible

without the failure, leads you to see that aiming your ambition in a different direction would be better (not because it is easier; not because you have given up; not because you are avoiding—but because you have learned through the vicissitudes of your experience that what you seek is not to be found where you were looking, or is simply not attainable in the manner by which you chose to pursue it).

So, what might you do—what should you do—as an alternative to hiding things in the fog? *Admit to your feelings.* This is a very tricky matter (and it does not simply mean "give in" to them). First, noting, much less communicating, feelings of (petty) anger or pain due to lonesomeness, or anxiety about something that might be trivial, or jealousy that is likely unwarranted is embarrassing. The admission of such feelings is a revelation of ignorance, insufficiency, and vulnerability. Second, it is unsettling to allow for the possibility that your feelings, however overwhelming and convincing, might be misplaced and, in your ignorance, pointing you in the wrong direction. It is possible that you have misinterpreted the situation entirely, for reasons of which you remain fundamentally unconscious. It is for such reasons that trust is vital: but trust of the mature and tragic sort. A naive person trusts because he or she believes that people are essentially or even universally trustworthy. But any person who has truly lived has been—or has—betrayed.

Someone with experience knows that people are capable of deception and willing to deceive. That knowledge brings with it an arguably justified pessimism about human nature, personal and otherwise, but it also opens the door to another kind of faith in humanity: one based on courage, rather than naivete. I will trust you—I will extend my hand to you—despite the risk of betrayal, because it is possible, through trust, to bring out the best in you, and perhaps in me. So, I will accept substantial risk to open the door to cooperation and negotiation. And even if you do betray me, in a not-too unforgivable manner (assuming a certain degree, shall we say, of genuine apology and contrition on your part), I will continue to extend my hand. And part of the way I will do that is by telling you what I am feeling.

A certain necessary humility must accompany such raw revelations. I should not say—at least not ideally—"You have been ignoring me lately." I should say, instead, "I feel isolated and lonely and hurt, and cannot help but feel that you have not been as attentive to me over the last few months as I would have liked or that might have been best for us as a couple. But I am unsure if I am just imagining all this because I am upset or if I am genuinely seeing what is going on." The latter statement gets the point across, but avoids the accusatory stance that so often serves as the first defense against a serious, get-to-the-bottom-of-things conversation. And it is very possible that you are wrong about just what is causing you to feel the way you do. If you are, you need to know it, because there is no point in propagating errors that are causing you and others pain and interfering with your future. Best to find out what is true—best to disperse the fog—and find out if the sharp objects you feared were lurking there are real or fantastical. And there is always the danger that some of them are real. But it is better to see them than to keep them occluded by the fog, because you can at least sometimes avoid the danger that you are willing to see.

EVENTS AND MEMORIES

Events, as they lay themselves out in front of us, do not simply inform us of why they occur, and we do not remember the past in order to objectively record bounded, well-defined events and situations. The latter act is impossible, in any case. The information in our experience is latent, like gold in ore—the case we made in Rule II. It must be extracted and refined with great effort, and often in collaboration with other people, before it can be employed to improve the present and the future. We use our past effectively when it helps us repeat desirable—and avoid repeating undesirable—experiences. We want to know what happened but, more importantly, we want to know *why*. *Why* is wisdom. *Why* enables us to avoid making the same mistake again and again, and if we are fortunate helps us repeat our successes.

Extracting useful information from experience is difficult. It requires the purest of motivations ("things should be made better, not worse") to perform it properly. It requires the willingness to confront error, forthrightly, and to determine at what point and why departure from the proper path occurred. It requires the willingness to change, which is almost always indistinguishable from the decision to leave something (or someone, or some idea) behind. Therefore, the simplest response imaginable is to look away and refuse to think, while simultaneously erecting unsurmountable impediments to genuine communication.

Unfortunately, in the longer term, this willful blindness leaves life murky and foggy; leaves it void, unseen, without form, confused—and leaves you bewildered and astonished.[2] This is all a strange concatenation of the psychological and the real, the subjective and the objective. Is something frightening, or am I afraid? Is something beautiful, or am I imposing the idea of beauty upon it? When I become angry with someone, is it because of something they have done, or my lack of control? Such questions define the state of confusion you occupy chronically when the bottom has fallen out of your world. That state can have an objective element, because a fall is often caused by something real, such as a death, a serious illness, or a bout of unemployment; but it is also subjective, associated with a state composed of pain, doubt, confusion, and the inability to choose—or even perceive—a path forward.

The ground of Being is subject and object simultaneously—
motivation, emotion, and material thing all at once—before perception
is clarified, before the world is articulated. The wife remains uncomprehended. The context of her speech remains unexplored, for fear of
what that exploration might reveal. The situation cannot be described
because the word is left vague and unformed. Our own personal motivations begin in hidden form, and remain that way, because we do not
want to know what we are up to. The wheat remains unseparated from
the chaff. The gold remains in the clutches of the dragon, as does the
virgin. The philosopher's stone remains undiscovered in the gutter;
and the information hidden in the round chaos, beckoning, remains
unexplored. Such omission is the voluntary refusal of expanded consciousness. After all, the pathway to the Holy Grail has its beginnings
in the darkest part of the forest, and what you need remains hidden
where you least want to look.

If you pile up enough junk in your closet, one day, when you are
least prepared, the door will spring open, and all of what has been
packed inside, growing inexorably in the darkness, will bury you, and
you may not have enough time or energy left in your life to confront
it, sort through it, keep what you need, and discard the rest. This is
what it means to be crushed under excess baggage. This is the return
of Tiamat, the great Mesopotamian Goddess of Chaos, destroyer of
those who act improperly.

The world is full of hidden dangers and obstacles—and opportunities. Leaving everything hidden in the fog because you are afraid of
the danger you may find there will be of little help when fate forces
you to run headlong toward what you have refused to see. Impaling
yourself on sharp branches, stumbling over boulders, and rushing by
places of sanctuary, you will finally refuse to admit you could have
burned away the haze with the bright light of your consciousness, had

you not hidden it under a bushel. Then you will come to curse man, reality, and God himself for producing such an impenetrable maze of impediments and barriers. Corruption will beckon to you, led as you increasingly will be by dark, unexamined motivations—bred by failure, amplified by frustration—viciously culminating in the resentful belief that those who have transgressed against you are getting from you exactly what they deserve. This attitude and the actions and inactions it will inevitably produce will impoverish your life, your community, your nation, and the world. This will in turn impoverish Being itself (and that will be exactly what your darkest unexamined motivations desire).

With careful searching, with careful attention, you might tip the balance toward opportunity and against obstacle sufficiently so that life is clearly worth living, despite its fragility and suffering. If you truly wanted, perhaps you would receive, if you asked. If you truly sought, perhaps you would find what you seek. If you knocked, truly wanting to enter, perhaps the door would open. But there will be times in your life when it will take everything you have to face what is in front of you, instead of hiding away from a truth so terrible that the only thing worse is the falsehood you long to replace it with.

Do not hide unwanted things in the fog.

RULE IV

NOTICE THAT OPPORTUNITY LURKS WHERE RESPONSIBILITY HAS BEEN ABDICATED

MAKE YOURSELF INVALUABLE

In my dual role as clinical psychologist and professor, I have coached many people in the development of their careers. Sometimes those I am coaching consult me because their coworkers, subordinates, or bosses will not do their jobs properly. They are supervised by, working alongside, or managing people who are narcissistic, incompetent, malevolent, or tyrannical. Such things happen and must be dealt with in whatever reasonable manner will bring them to a halt. I do not encourage people to martyr themselves. It is a bad idea to sacrifice yourself uncomplainingly so that someone else can take the credit. Nonetheless, under such circumstances—if you are a wise and attentive person— you might still notice that your unproductive coworkers are leaving a plethora of valuable tasks undone. You might then ask yourself, "What would happen if I took responsibility for doing them?" It is a daunting question. What is left undone is often risky, difficult, and necessary. But that also means—does it not?—that it is worthwhile and significant. And you may have the eyes to see that there is a problem, despite your all-too-frequent blindness. How do you know that it is not, therefore, *your* problem? Why do you notice this issue and not some other? This is a question worth considering in depth.

If you want to become invaluable in a workplace—in any community—just do the useful things no one else is doing. Arrive earlier and leave later than your compatriots (but do not deny yourself your life).[1] Organize what you can see is dangerously disorganized. Work, when you are working, instead of looking like you are working. And finally, learn more about the business—or your competitors—than you already know. Doing so will make you invaluable—a veritable lynchpin. People will notice that and begin to appreciate your hard-earned merits.

You might object, "Well, I just could not manage to take on something that important." What if you began to build yourself into a person who could? You could start by trying to solve a small problem—something that is bothering you, that you think you could fix. You could start by confronting a dragon of just the size that you are likely to defeat. A tiny serpent might not have had the time to hoard a lot of gold, but there might still be some treasure to be won, along with a reasonable probability of succeeding in such a quest (and not too much chance of a fiery or toothsome death). Under reasonable circumstances, picking up the excess responsibility is an opportunity to become truly invaluable. And then, if you want to negotiate for a raise, or more autonomy—or more free time, for that matter—you can go to your boss and say, "Here are ten things that were crying out to be done, each of them vital, and I am now doing all of them. If you help me out a bit, I will continue. I might even improve. And everything, including your life, will improve along with me." And then, if your boss has any sense—

and sometimes bosses do—then your negotiation will be successful. That is how such things work. And do not forget that there is no shortage of genuinely good people who are thrilled if they can give someone useful and trustworthy a hand up. It is one of the truly altruistic pleasures of life, and its depth is not to be underestimated, or to be disregarded with the cheap cynicism that masks itself as world-weary wisdom.

It appears that the meaning that most effectively sustains life is to be found in the adoption of responsibility. When people look back on what they have accomplished, they think, if they are fortunate: "Well, I did that, and it was valuable. It was not easy. But it was worth it." It is a strange and paradoxical fact that there is a reciprocal relationship between the worth of something and the difficulty of accomplishing it. Imagine the following conversation: "Do you want difficulty?" "No, I want ease." "In your experience, has doing something easy been worthwhile?" "Well, no, not very often." "Then perhaps you really want something difficult." I think that is the secret to the reason for Being itself: *difficult is necessary.*

It is for this reason that we voluntarily and happily place limitations on ourselves. Every time we play a game, for example, we accept a set of arbitrary restrictions. We narrow and limit ourselves, and explore the possibilities thereby revealed. That is what makes the game. But it does not work without the arbitrary rules. You take them on voluntarily, absurdly, as in chess: "I can only move this knight in an L. How ridiculous. But how fun!" Because it is not fun, oddly enough, if you can move any piece anywhere. It is not a game anymore if you can make any old move at all. Accept some limitations, however, and the game begins. Accept them, more broadly speaking, as a necessary part of Being and a desirable part of life. Assume you can transcend them by accepting them. And then you can play the limited game properly.

And this is all not merely of psychological import, and it is by no means just a game. People need meaning, but problems also need solving. It is very salutary, from the psychological perspective, to find something of significance—something worth sacrificing for (or to), something worth confronting and taking on. But the suffering and malevolence that characterize life are real, with the terrible consequences of the real—and our ability to solve problems, by confronting them and taking them on, is also real. By taking responsibility, we can find a meaningful path, improve our personal lot psychologically, and make what is intolerably wrong genuinely better. Thus, we can have our cake and eat it, too.

RESPONSIBILITY AND MEANING

The idea that life is suffering is a relatively universal truism of religious thinking. This is the first of the Four Noble Truths of Buddhism as well as a key Hindu concept. There is a tradition that the ancient Indian word for suffering—*dukkha* (from the Pali language) or *duhka* (from Sanskrit)—is derived from *dus* (bad) and *kha* (hole)—particularly the hole in a horse-drawn cart wheel, through which the axle passes. The proper place for such a hole is dead center, right on target. The ride is likely to be very bumpy, otherwise—with the bumps directly proportional in magnitude to the degree of offset. This is quite reminiscent, to me, of the Greek term *hamartia*, which is frequently translated as "sin," in the context of Christian thought.

Hamartia was originally an archery term, and it meant to miss the mark or target. There are many ways that a target can be missed. Frequently, in my clinical practice—and in my personal life—I observed that people did not get what they needed (or, equally importantly perhaps, what they wanted) because they never made it clear to themselves or others what that was. It is impossible to hit a target, after all, unless you aim at it. In keeping with this: People are more commonly upset by what they did not even try to do than by the errors they actively committed while engaging with the world.[2] At least if you misstep while doing something, you can learn from doing it wrong. But to remain passive in the face of life, even if you excuse your inaction as a means of avoiding error—that is a major mistake. As the great blues musician Tom Waits insists (in his song "A Little Rain"): "You must risk something that matters."

This is the colossal blunder made, for example, by the fictional Peter Pan. "Pan"—a name echoing the Greek god of the wilds—means "encompassing everything." Peter Pan, the magical boy, is capable of everything. He is potential itself, like every child, and that makes him magical, in the same way that every child is magical. But time whittles that magic away, transforming the fascinating potentiality of childhood into the oft-apparently more mundane but genuine actuality of adulthood. The trick, so to speak, is to trade that early possibility for something meaningful, productive, long term, and sustainable. Peter Pan refuses to do so. This is at least in part because his major role model is Captain Hook. Captain Hook is the archetypal Tyrannical King, the pathology of order—a parasite and a tyrant, terrified of death. He has his reasons. Death stalks Hook in the form of a crocodile with a clock in his stomach. That is time: ticktock, ticktock. That is life vanishing, as the seconds march by. The crocodile has had a taste of Hook, too, and liked it. That is life, as well. It is not only cowards who are terrified by what lurks down in the chaotic depths. It is a rare person who has not suffered through disappointment, disease, and the death of a loved one by the time childhood ends. Such experiences can leave those who have had them bitter, resentful, predatory, and tyrannical—just like Hook. With a role model like the captain, it is no wonder Peter Pan does not want to grow up. Better to remain king of the Lost Boys. Better to remain lost in fantasy with Tinkerbell, who provides everything a female partner can provide—except that she does not exist.

Wendy, the great love of Pan's life, chooses to grow up, despite her admiration for her friend Peter. She takes a husband, facing—even welcoming—her maturation, and its lurking hints of mortality and death. She consciously chooses to sacrifice her childhood for the realities of adulthood, but gains real life in return. Peter remains a child: magical, to be sure, but still a child—and life, limited, finite, and unique, passes him by. In the J. M. Barrie play *Peter Pan or The Boy Who Would Not Grow Up*, Pan is portrayed as unafraid of death, which he faces on Marooners' Rock. His attitude might be misunderstood by inattentive viewers as courage. After all, Pan says, "To die will be an awfully big adventure."* But the psychologically insightful unseen narrator objects: "To live would be an awfully big adventure" (truly, a statement about what might have happened had the Boy King chosen Wendy), noting, immediately afterward, "but he can never quite get the hang of it."† Pan's hypothetical lack of fear of death is not courage, but the manifestation of his basically suicidal nature, the sickness of life (which he is constantly manifesting by his very refusal to mature).

It is by no means a good thing to be the oldest person at the frat party. It is desperation, masquerading as cool rebelliousness—and there is a touchy despondence and arrogance that goes along with it. It smacks of Neverland. In the same manner, the attractive potential of a directionless but talented twenty-five-year-old starts to look hopeless and pathetic at thirty, and downright past its expiration date at forty.

Peter Pan, Act III, gutenberg.net.au/ebooks03/0300081h.html.
†*Peter Pan*, Act V, scene 2 (closing paragraph), gutenberg.net.au/ebooks03/0300081h.html.

You must sacrifice something of your manifold potential in exchange for something real in life. Aim at something. Discipline yourself. Or suffer the consequence. And what is that consequence? All the suffering of life, with none of the meaning. Is there a better description of hell?

Life is *duhka* for the Buddhists—equally, perhaps, although less explicitly, for the Hindus. The Hebrew Scriptures, for their part, chronicle the history of the suffering of the Jewish people, individually and as a nation, although the triumphs are not ignored. Even those who are called on by YHWH Himself to move into the adventure of life by no means escape catastrophe. Perhaps Abraham, the archetypal Patriarch, had an intuition of this. He was clearly something of a Peter Pan himself. The biblical account insists that Abraham stayed safely ensconced within his father's tent until he was seventy-five years old (a late start, even by today's standards). Then, called by God—inspired by the voice within, let us say, to leave family and country—he journeys forward into life. And what does he encounter, after heeding the divine call to adventure? First, famine. Then tyranny in Egypt; the potential loss of his beautiful wife to more powerful men; exile from his adopted country; conflicts over territory with his kinsmen; war, and the kidnapping of his nephew; extended childlessness (despite God's promise to make him the progenitor of a great nation); and finally, terrible conflict between his spouses.

The Abrahamic story made a great impact on me when I began to study and appreciate it more deeply. It has at its core a strange combination of pessimism and realistic, genuine encouragement. The pessimism? Even if you are called by God Himself to venture out into the world, as Abraham was, life is going to be exceptionally difficult. Even under the best of all conceivable circumstances, almost insuperable obstacles will emerge and obstruct your path. The encouragement? You will have the opportunity to reveal yourself as much stronger and more competent than you might imagine. There is a potential within you (some of that magic so evident in childhood) that will emerge when circumstances demand and transform you—God willing—into someone who can prevail.

There is a very old idea, which I have only recently come to comprehend, at least in part. It is something you see manifested in many literary, imagistic, and dramatic forms, ancient and modern. It has to do with responsibility and meaning, but its true significance appears hidden, in precisely the same way that the wisdom dreams can bring forth is so often hidden. It is associated with the labyrinthine myth of the hero: He who speaks magic words, sees what others cannot (or refuse to see), overcomes the giant, leads his people, slays the dragon, finds the treasure hard to attain, and rescues the virgin. These are all variants of the same perceptual and behavioral pattern, which is an outline of the universally adaptive pattern of being. The hero is also he who rescues his father from the belly of the beast. What could this idea, expressed so commonly in narrative form, possibly mean?

RESCUE YOUR FATHER: OSIRIS AND HORUS

Consider the ancient Egyptian story of Osiris, Set, Isis, and Horus.* The Egyptians regarded Osiris as the founding deity of the state. You can profitably consider him to be an amalgam of all the personality characteristics of all the people who established the astonishing civilization on the Nile River. Osiris was worshipped as the culture-establishing hero, whose world-creating exploits as a young,

---

*I provided an extensive analysis in my first book, *Maps of Meaning*, as well as mentioning it in *12 Rules for Life*, Rule 7: Pursue what is meaningful (not what is expedient).

vibrant god produced one of the first great and enduring civilizations. But he aged, as all things do, and became willfully blind. The Egyptians insisted that this crucially important figure in their mythology possessed both of these attributes—and that insistence constituted a great truth. The great founder-god became anachronistic but, more importantly, he began to close his eyes when he knew full well he should have kept them open. Osiris stopped paying attention to how his kingdom was being run. That was willful blindness, and there is no blaming that on mere age. It is a terrible temptation, as it allows for the sequestration into the future the trouble we could face today. That would be fine if trouble did not compound, like interest—but we all know that it does.

Osiris's decision to close his eyes when he should have kept them open exacted a brutally heavy price: subjugation to his evil brother, Set. The idea that the state had a malevolent brother was an axiom, we might say, of the Egyptian worldview—no doubt the consequence of a complex, long-standing civilization observing its own flaws—and something that has retained its relevance to the current day. Once a properly functional hierarchy has been established, an opportunity opens for its positions of authority to be usurped, not by people who have the competence demanded by the task at hand, but by those willing to use manipulation, deceit, and compulsion to gain status and control. It was all those counterproductive forces that the Egyptians were attempting to conceptualize in the figure of Set, the enemy of illumination, enlightenment, vision, and consciousness.[3] It was Set's greatest ambition to rule Egypt, to take the place of the rightful Pharaoh. By turning a blind eye to his evil brother's machinations—by refusing to see—Osiris allowed Set to gain strength. This proved fatal (or as fatal as an error can be to an immortal). Set bided his time, until he caught Osiris in a moment of weakness. Then he dismembered him and scattered the pieces over the Egyptian countryside. It was not (is not) possible to finally kill Osiris, the eternal human impulse toward social organization. That is a force that will not die. But it is possible to break him into pieces—to make it difficult for him to get his act together—and that is exactly what Set managed.

Osiris, god of order, falls apart. This happens all the time, in people's individual lives, and equally in the history of families, cities, and states. Things fall apart when love affairs collapse, careers deteriorate, or cherished dreams die; when despair, anxiety, uncertainty, and hopelessness manifest themselves in the place of habitable order; and when nihilism and the abyss make their dread appearance, destroying the desirable and stable values of current life. Under such circumstances, chaos emerges. And that is why the goddess Isis, Queen of the Underworld and consort of Osiris, makes her appearance when Osiris is destroyed by Set. Isis scours the countryside, searching for the vital essence of Osiris. She finds it in the form of his dismembered phallus—vessel of the seminal idea, the spermatic word, the fructifying principle—and makes herself pregnant. What does this mean? The queen of the underworld, the goddess of chaos, is also the force that eternally renews. All the potential constrained by the previous system of apprehension, of category, of assumption—all the invisible limitation imposed upon the inhabitants of that orderly state—is released, for better and worse, when that system breaks into pieces. Thus, when the center will no longer hold—even at the darkest hour—new possibility makes itself manifest. It is for this reason that the archetypal Hero is born when things are at their worst.

The now pregnant Isis returns to her home in the underworld and gives birth, in due time, to Horus, rightful son of the long-lost king, alienated as he matures from his now corrupted kingdom (something we all experience during our maturation). His primary attribute is the eye—the famous Egyptian single eye—while his avatar is the falcon, a bird that takes precise aim at its prey, strikes the target with deadly accuracy, and possesses an acuity of vision unparalleled in the kingdom of living things. More importantly, however, Horus has the *will* to see, along with the ability. This is courage itself: the refusal to shrink from what makes itself known, no matter how terrible it seems. Horus is the great god of attention, and the Egyptians determined, in their strange narrative manner—in a form of imaginative thinking that stretched over thousands of years—that the faculty of attention should rule over all others. Horus differs from Osiris, his father, in his willingness to see. He sees his uncle Set, for example, precisely for what he is. Set is pure malevolence; evil itself. Nonetheless, upon his maturity, Horus returns to the kingdom usurped from his father and confronts his uncle. They engage in an epic battle. The young god and rightful heir to the throne sees the opportunity lurking where responsibility has been abdicated, and is unwilling to look away. This is no feat for the faint of heart—not when it is taken all the way to its logical conclusion; not when the corruption and the willful blindness is exposed, all the way to the bottom. To look upon evil with eyes unshielded is dangerous beyond belief, regardless of how necessary it is to look. This is represented by Horus's initial partial defeat: During their confrontation, Set tears out one of his courageous nephew's eyes.

Despite the damage he sustains, Horus emerges victorious. It is of vital importance to reiterate, in light of this victory, the fact that he enters the battle voluntarily. It is a maxim of clinical intervention—a consequence of observation of improvement in mental health across many schools of practical psychological thought—that voluntary confrontation with a feared, hated, or despised obstacle is curative. We become stronger by voluntarily facing what impedes our necessary progress. This does not mean "bite off more than you can chew" (any more than "voluntarily enter battle" means "seek conflict carelessly"). We are well advised to take on challenges at precisely the rate that engages and compels alertness, and forces the development of courage, skill, and talent, and to avoid foolhardy confrontation with that which lies beyond current comprehension.

How is it possible to gauge the rate at which challenges should be sought? It is the instinct for meaning—something far deeper and older than mere thought—that holds the answer. Does what you are attempting compel you forward, without being too frightening? Does it grip your interest, without crushing you? Does it eliminate the burden of time passing? Does it serve those you love and, perhaps, even bring some good to your enemies? That is responsibility. Constrain evil. Reduce suffering. Confront the possibility that manifests in front of you every second of your life with the desire to make things better, regardless of the burden you bear, regardless of life's often apparently arbitrary unfairness and cruelty. All other approaches merely deepen the pit, increase its heat, and doom those who inhabit it to continual worsening of their already serious problems. Everyone knows it. Everyone's conscience proclaims it. Everyone's true friend or loved one observes it and despairs when they see someone for whom they care failing to do what needs to be done.

Horus takes his eye back from the defeated Set and banishes him beyond the borders of the kingdom. There is no killing Set. He is eternal as Osiris, eternal as Isis and Horus. The evil that threatens at all levels of experience is something—or someone—that everyone has to contend with always, psychologically and socially. But for a time evil can be overcome, banished, and defeated. Then peace and harmony can prevail for as long as people do not forget what brought them both about.

Horus recovers his eye. A sensible person, in such a situation, would thank his lucky stars, place his eye back into its empty socket, and get on with his life. But that is not what Horus does. He returns, instead, to the underworld, to the belly of the beast, to the kingdom of the dead, where he knows he will find the spirit of Osiris. Dismembered though he may be, near death—even dead, in a sense—Osiris inhabits the underworld domain of chaos itself. That is the dead father in the belly of the beast. Horus finds the once-great king and grants to him the eye torn out by Set. Once again—because of the sacrifice and vision of his son—the ancient of days can see. Horus then takes his father, vision restored, and returns with him to the kingdom, so they can rule in tandem. The Egyptians insisted that it was this combination of vision, courage, and regenerated tradition that constituted the proper sovereign of the kingdom. It was this juxtaposition of wisdom and youth that comprised the essence of the power of the Pharaoh, his immortal soul, the source of his authority.

When you face a challenge, you grapple with the world and inform yourself. This makes you more than you are. It makes you increasingly into who you could be. Who could you be? You could be all that a man or woman might be. You could be the newest avatar, in your own unique manner, of the great ancestral heroes of the past. What is the upper limit to that? We do not know. Our religious structures hint at it. What would a human being who was completely turned on, so to speak, be like? How would someone who determined to take full responsibility for the tragedy and malevolence of the world manifest himself? The ultimate question of Man is not who we are, but who we could be.

When you peer into an abyss, you see a monster. If it is a small abyss, then it is a small monster. But if it is the ultimate abyss, then it is the ultimate monster. That is certainly a dragon—perhaps even the dragon of evil itself. The conceptualization of the monster in the abyss is the eternal predator lurking in the night, ready and able to devour its unsuspecting prey. That is an image that is tens of millions of years old, something coded as deeply in the recesses of our biological structure as anything conceptual can be coded. And it is not just the monsters of nature, but the tyrants of culture and the malevolence of individuals. It is all of that, with the latter dominant, terrible as that is to consider. And it is in the nature of mankind not to cower and freeze as helpless prey animals, nor to become a turncoat and serve evil itself, but to confront the lions in their lairs. That is the nature of our ancestors: immensely courageous hunters, defenders, shepherds, voyagers, inventors, warriors, and founders of cities and states. That is the father you could rescue; the ancestor you could become. And he is to be discovered in the deepest possible place, as that is where you must go if you wish to take full responsibility and become who you could be.

AND WHO MIGHT THAT BE?

Let us agree, to begin with, that you have a minimum moral obligation to take care of yourself. Maybe you are just selfishly interested in taking care of yourself. But then the questions arise: What do you mean by "care"? Which "yourself" are you talking about? We will just consider pure selfishness to begin with, uncontaminated self-interest. That keeps it simple. That means, for starters, that you are free do anything you want—because you do not have to care about anyone else. But then something in you might well object: "Wait just a moment. That will not work." Why not? Well, which self are you taking care of? Are you taking care of the you that specifically exists this minute? What will happen, then, in the next? Because the future is coming, as certainly, for all intents and purposes, as the sun rises in the morning. And you are best advised to be ready for it.

You know the risks if you choose to maximize now at the expense of later. Imagine that you are about to utter something thoughtless and angry. You think, "Take no prisoners," and say whatever comes to mind, no matter how unjust and cruel. You experience a release of positive emotion and enthusiasm along with that, as well as the satisfying venting of resentment. Immediately thereafter, however, you are in trouble, and that trouble might stick around for a very long time. You have clearly not acted in your best interests, even though you did just what you selfishly wanted to. And no one with any sense tells their beloved son or daughter, "Look, kid, just do exactly what feels good in the moment, and to hell with everything else. It does not matter." You do not say that, because you know full well that the future is coming for your child as surely as it comes for you. The mere fact that something makes you happy in the moment does not mean that it is in your best interest, everything considered. Life would be simple if that were the case. But there is the you now, and the you tomorrow, and the you next week, and next year, and in five years, and in a decade—and you are required by harsh necessity to take all of those "yous" into account. That is the curse associated with the human discovery of the future and, with it, the necessity of work—because to work means to sacrifice the hypothetical delights of the present for the potential improvement of what lies ahead.

Now, there is some utility in discounting the importance of the "yous" who exist far enough into the future, because the future is uncertain. It is not the case that you should be as concerned about the effects of your current actions twenty years down the road as you are now, because there is a very high probability that you are here right now (if you are reading this) and somewhat less of a chance that you will be around then. And then there are the errors of prediction you will make when looking so far ahead. But the mounting uncertainty of distance in time does not stop sensible people from preparing for their later years. Here is what the future means: If you are going to take care of yourself, you are already burdened (or privileged) with a social responsibility. The you for whom you are caring is a community that exists across time. The necessity for considering this society of the individual, so to speak, is a burden and an opportunity that seems uniquely characteristic of human beings.

Animals do not seem to consider the future in the same manner as we do. If you visit the African veldt, and you observe a herd of zebras, you will often see lions lazing about around them. And as long as the lions are lying around relaxing, the zebras really do not mind. This attitude seems a little thoughtless, from the human perspective. The zebras should instead be biding their time until the lions go to sleep. Then they should run off to a corner of the field in a herd and conspire a bit. And then several dozen of them should rush the sleeping lions and stomp them to death. That would be the end of the lion problem. But that is not what zebras do. They think, "Ah, look at those relaxed lions! Relaxed lions are never a problem!" Zebras do not seem to have any real sense of time. They cannot conceptualize themselves across the temporal expanse. But human beings not only manage such conceptualization, they cannot shake it. We discovered the future, some long time ago—and now the future is where we each live, in potential. We treat that as *reality*. It is a reality that only *might be*—but it is one with a high probability of becoming *now*, eventually, and we are driven to take that into account.

You are stuck with yourself. You are burdened with who you are right now and who you are going to be in the future. That means that if you are treating yourself properly, you must consider your repetition across time. You are destined to play a game with yourself today that must not interfere with the game you play tomorrow, next month, next year, and so on. Thus, narrow selfishness is destined to be non-productive. It is for this reason, among others, that a strictly individualist ethic is a contradiction in terms. There is in fact little difference between how you should treat yourself—once you realize that you are a community that extends across time—and how you should treat other people.

In a marriage, for example, you face the same problem with your marital partner as you do with yourself: You are stuck with the consequences of an iterating game. You can treat your husband or wife any old way right now, this moment, no matter how horrid and thoughtless that way might be, but you are going to wake up with him or her tomorrow, and next month, and a decade from now (and, if not that person, then someone else equally unfortunate). If you treat the person you are committed to in a manner that does not work when it is repeated across time, then you are playing a degenerating game, and you are both going to suffer terribly for it. This problem is not materially different from failing to make peace with your future self. The consequences are identical.

HAPPINESS AND RESPONSIBILITY

People want to be happy, and no wonder. I have longed deeply, many times, for the return of happiness—hoping for its current presence—and I am certainly not alone in that. However, I do not believe you should *pursue* happiness. If you do so, you will run right into the iteration problem, because "happy" is a right-now thing. If you place people in situations where they are feeling a lot of positive emotion, they get present-focused and impulsive.[4] This means "make hay while the sun shines"—take your opportunities while things are good and act now. But *now* is by no means everything, and unfortunately, everything must be considered, at least insofar as you are able. In consequence, it is unlikely that whatever optimizes your life across time is happiness. I am not denying its desirability, by the way. If happiness comes to you, welcome it with gratitude and open arms (but be careful, because it does make you impetuous).

What might serve as a more sophisticated alternative to happiness? Imagine it is living in accordance with the sense of responsibility, because that sets things right in the future. Imagine, as well, that you must act reliably, honestly, nobly, and in relationship to a higher good, in order to manifest the sense of responsibility properly. The higher good would be the simultaneous optimization of your function and the function of the people around you, across time, as we have discussed previously. That is the highest good. Imagine that you make that aim conscious, that you articulate that aim as an explicit goal. Then a question arises: "What is the consequence of that psychologically?"

First, consider that most of the positive emotion people experience does not come from attaining something. There is the simple pleasure (more accurately, the satisfaction) that comes from having a good meal when hungry, and there is the more complex but similar satisfaction that is associated with accomplishing something difficult and worthwhile. Imagine, for example, that you graduate from grade 12. Graduation Day marks the event. It is a celebration. But the next day that is over, and you immediately face a new set of problems (just as you are hungry again only a few hours after a satisfying meal). You are no longer king of the high school: you are bottom dog in the work force, or a freshman at a postsecondary institution. You are in the position of Sisyphus. You strove and struggled to push your boulder to the pinnacle, and you find yourself, instead, at the foot of the mountain.

There is a near-instantaneous transformation that comes as a consequence of attainment. Like impulsive pleasure, attainment will produce positive emotion. But, also like pleasure, attainment is unreliable. Another question thus emerges: "What is a truly reliable source of positive emotion?" The answer is that people experience positive emotion in relationship to the *pursuit* of a valuable goal. Imagine you have a goal. You aim at something. You develop a strategy in relationship to that aim, and then you implement it. And then, as you implement the strategy, you observe that it is working. *That is* what produces the most reliable positive emotion.[5] Imagine over time that the attitudes and actions that manage this most effectively (in a competition that is very Darwinian) come, eventually, to dominate over all others.[6] Imagine that is true psychologically and socially, simultaneously. Imagine that this occurs in your own life, but also across the centuries, as everyone interacts and talks and raises a particular mode of being to primary status.

This implies something crucial: no happiness in the absence of responsibility. No valuable and valued goal, no positive emotion. You might object, "Well, what exactly constitutes a valid goal?" Imagine that you are pursuing something pleasurable, but short term and trivial. The wise part of you will be comparing that pursuit to the possible goal of acting in the best interest of your community of future selves and your community of other people. Perhaps you are unwilling to allow yourself to realize that wisdom: You do not wish to bear the responsibility—not in place of an immediate, impulsive focus on pleasure. You are fooling yourself, however, especially at the deeper levels of your being, if you believe such avoidance will prove successful. The wise and ancient parts of you, seriously concerned with your survival, are neither easy to deceive nor to set aside. But you take aim at a trivial goal anyway, and develop a rather shallow strategy to attain it, only to find it is not satisfying because you do not care enough. It does not matter to you—not deeply. Furthermore, the fact that you are not pursuing the goal you should rightly be pursuing means that you are feeling guilty, ashamed, and lesser at the same time.

This is not a helpful strategy. It is not going to work. I have never met anyone who was satisfied when they knew they were not doing everything they should be doing. We are temporally aware creatures: We know that we are continually and inescapably playing an iterated game from which we cannot easily hide. No matter how much we wish to discount the future completely, it is part of the price we paid for being acutely self-conscious and able to conceptualize ourselves across the entire span of our lives. We are stuck with it. There is no escaping from the future—and when you are stuck with something and there is no escaping from it, the right attitude is to turn around voluntarily and confront it. That works. And so, instead of your short-term impulsive goal, you lay out a much larger-scale goal, which is to act properly in relationship to the long term for everyone.

PICK UP THE EXTRA WEIGHT

There is a proper way to behave—an ethic—and you are destined to contend with it. You cannot help but calculate yourself across time, and everyone else across time, and you are reporting back to yourself, inevitably, on your own behavior and misbehavior. What works across multiple time frames and multiple places for multiple people (including yourself)—that is the goal. It is an emergent ethic, hard to formulate explicitly, but inescapable in its existence and its consequences, and an ineradicably deep part of the game of Being. Great players are attractive. Attractive people attract mates. The closer we match the pattern—the emergent pattern—the more likely we are to survive and protect our families. The playing field selects the players on the basis of their ethical behavior. And we are therefore biologically prepared to

respond positively to and to imitate the Great Player—and to disapprove, even violently, of the deceiver, the cheat, and the fraud. And it
is your conscience—your instinct for moral virtue—that indicates deviation from the path. When your child purposefully trips an opponent during a soccer game, or fails to pass to an open teammate with a
great opportunity to score, you frown. You feel shame, as you should,
because you are witnessing the betrayal of someone you love, by someone you love—and that is your child's self-betrayal. Something similar
occurs when you violate your own sense of propriety. It is the same
instinct, and it is best attended to. If you do not follow the right path,
you will wander off a cliff and suffer miserably—and there is simply
no way that the most profound parts of yourself are going to allow that
without protest.

You might rationalize: "There is no cliff here now. There is no cliff
I can see nearby. And a cliff I will not tumble off for ten years is a long
way away." But the part of your psyche that is most profound invariably objects: "Such thinking is not appropriate. It will not do. What is
ten years away is still real, despite its distance (allowing for unavoidable errors of prediction). If there is a catastrophe waiting there, we are
not going to aim at it now. Not without objection." If your behavior
suggests that you are tilting in that direction, then you are going to
feel guilty and horrible about it, if you are lucky and even minimally
awake. And thank God for that. If the cost of betraying yourself, in the
deepest sense, is guilt, shame, and anxiety, the benefit of not betraying yourself is meaning—the meaning that sustains. That is the most
valuable of opportunities that lurks where responsibility has been abdicated.

If you attend to your conscience, you will begin to determine that
some of the things you are doing are wrong. More precisely: if you are
alerted to the possibility of your own wrongdoing by your conscience,

and you then begin to engage in a true dialogue with that same agent, you will begin to develop a clear picture of what is wrong—and, by implication, of what is right. Right is not least the opposite of wrong—and wrong is in some clear sense more blatant and obvious. A sense of right can therefore be developed and honed through careful attention to what is wrong. You act and betray yourself, and you feel bad about that. You do not know exactly why. You try to avoid thinking about it, because it is less painful and easier in the short term not to think about it. You try with all your might to ignore it, but all that does is increase your sense of self-betrayal and further divide you against yourself.

So, you reconsider, perhaps, and you confront your discomfort. You note your disunity and the chaos that comes with it. You ask yourself—you pray to discover—what you did wrong. And the answer arrives. And it is not what you want. And part of you must therefore die, so that you can change. And the part that must die struggles for its existence, puts forward its rationale, and pleads its case. And it will do so with every trick in its possession—employing the most egregious lies, the bitterest, most resentment-eliciting memories of the past, and the most hopelessly cynical attitudes about the future (indeed, about the value of life itself). But you persevere, and discriminate, judge, and decide exactly why what you did was wrong, and you start to understand, by contrast, what might have been right. And then you determine to start acting in accordance with your conscience. You decide that it is a partner, despite its adversarial form. You put all that you have discovered to be right into action, and you begin your ascent. You start to monitor yourself, ever more careful to ensure you are doing the right thing—listening to what you say, watching yourself act, trying not to deviate from the straight and narrow path. That becomes your goal.

An idea begins to take shape: "I am going to live my life properly. I am going to aim at the good. I am going to aim at the highest good I can possible manage." Now, all the parts of you taking care of your future self are on board. You are all aimed in one direction. You are no longer a house divided against itself. You are standing solidly on a firm foundation. You are no longer so easy to dissuade or discourage. Your resolution trumps your nihilism and despair. The struggle you have had with your own tendency to doubt and dissimulate protects you against the unwarranted and cynical criticisms of others. There is a high goal, a mountain peak, a star that shines in the darkness, beckoning above the horizon. Its mere existence gives you hope—and that is the meaning without which you cannot live.

Remember Pinocchio? When Geppetto wants to transform the wooden-headed puppet he created into something real, he first raises his eyes above the horizon and wishes on a star. It is the same star that announces Pinocchio's birth at the beginning of the movie and whose light is reflected in the golden badge granted to Jiminy Cricket at the close. It is the same star, symbolically speaking, that announces the birth of Christ in the depths of the darkness. Geppetto focuses on the star and makes a wish. The wish is that his marionette with strings controlled by someone or something else will become real. The story of the puppet and his temptations and trials is a psychological drama. We all understand it, even though we cannot necessarily articulate that understanding. It is necessary to lift your eyes above the horizon, to establish a transcendent goal, if you wish to cease being a puppet, under the control of things you do not understand and perhaps do not want to understand. Then all the subsystems or subpersonalities that might otherwise be pursing their own limited fulfillment will join together under the aegis of the truly ideal, and the consequence of that will be an engagement that approximates the ultimate or total. Under such conditions, all the parts of you are going to be on board. That is the psychological equivalent of monotheism. That is the emergence of the higher self that might be the true servant of God, in whatever metaphysical reality potentially underlies what is obvious to our blind and limited mortal selves.

What is the antidote to the suffering and malevolence of life? The highest possible goal. What is the prerequisite to pursuit of the highest possible goal? Willingness to adopt the maximum degree of responsibility—and this includes the responsibilities that others disregard or neglect. You might object: "Why should I shoulder all that burden? It is nothing but sacrifice, hardship, and trouble." But what makes you so sure you do not want something heavy to carry? You positively need to be occupied with something weighty, deep, profound, and difficult. Then, when you wake up in the middle of the night and the doubts crowd in, you have some defense: "For all my flaws, which are manifold, at least I am doing *this*. At least I am taking care of myself. At least I am of use to my family, and to the other people around me. At least I am moving, stumbling upward, under the load I have determined to carry." You can attain some genuine self-respect that way—but it is not a mere shallow psychological construct that has to do with how you are construing yourself in the moment. It is far deeper than that—and it is not only psychological. It is *real*, as well as psychological.

Your life becomes meaningful in precise proportion to the depths of the responsibility you are willing to shoulder. That is because you are now genuinely involved in making things better. You are minimizing the unnecessary suffering. You are encouraging those around you, by example and word. You are constraining the malevolence in your own heart and the hearts of others. A bricklayer may question the utility of laying his bricks, monotonously, one after another. But perhaps he is not merely laying bricks. Maybe he is building a wall. And the wall is part of a building. And the building is a cathedral. And the purpose of the cathedral is the glorification of the Highest Good. And under such circumstances, every brick laid is an act that partakes of the divine. And if what you are doing in your day-to-day activity is not enough, then you are not aiming at the construction of a proper cathedral. And that is because you are not aiming high enough. Because if you were, then you would experience the sense of meaning in relationship to your sufficiently high goal, and it would justify the misery and limitations of your life. If you have something meaningful to pursue, then you are engrossed in life. You are on a meaningful path. The most profound and reliable instinct for meaning—if not perverted by self-deceit and sin (there is no other way to state it)— manifests itself when you are on the path of maximum virtue.

The sense of meaning is an indicator that you are on that path. It is an indication that all the complexity that composes you is lined up within you, and aimed at something worth pursuing—something that balances the world, something that produces harmony. It is something you hear made manifest in music, and the profound sense of meaning that music intrinsically produces. Maybe you are a nihilistic death-metal punk. You are deeply skeptical and pessimistic. You find meaning nowhere. You hate everything, just on principle. But then your favorite nihilistic death-metal punk band lead guitarist and his bandmates start to blast out their patterned harmonies—each in alignment with the other—and you are caught! "Ah, I do not believe in anything— but, God, that music!" And the lyrics are destructive and nihilistic and cynical and bitter and hopeless but it does not matter, because the music beckons and calls to your spirit, and fills it with the intimation of meaning, and moves you, so that you align yourself with the patterns, and you nod your head and tap your feet to the beat, participating despite yourself. It is those patterns of sound, layered one on top of another, harmoniously, moving in the same direction, predictably and unpredictably, in perfect balance: order and chaos, in their eternal dance. And you dance with it, no matter how scornful you are. You align yourself with that patterned, directional harmony. And in that you find the meaning that sustains.

You are possessed of an instinct—a spirit—that orients you toward the highest good. It calls your soul away from hell and toward heaven. And because it is there, you find yourself frequently disillusioned. People disappoint you. You betray yourself; you lose a meaningful connection to your workplace, boss, or partner. You think, "The world is not set right. It is deeply troubling to me." That very disenchantment, however, can serve as the indicator of destiny. It speaks of abdicated responsibility—of things left undone, of things that still *need to be done.* You are irritated about that need. You are annoyed with the government, you are embittered and resentful about your job, you are unhappy with your parents, and you are frustrated with all these people around you who will not take on responsibility. There are, after all, things that are crying out to be accomplished. You are outraged that what needs to be done *is not being done.* That anger—that outrage—is, however, a *doorway.* That observation of abdicated responsibility is the indication of destiny and meaning. The part of you that is oriented toward the highest good is pointing out the disjunction between the ideal you can imagine—the ideal that is possessing you—and the reality you are experiencing. There is a gap there, and it is communicating its need to be filled. You can give way to fury, in consequence, and blame it on someone else—and it is not as if other people are not contributing to the problems. Or you can come to understand that your very disappointment is an indication to you from the most fundamental levels of your being that there is something wrong that needs to be set right—and, perhaps, *by you.* What is it, that concern, that care, that irritation, that distraction? It is not the call to happiness. It is the call to the action and adventure that make up a real life. Consider, once again, the biblical story of Abraham. God comes to Abraham, and says,

> Go from your country, your people and your father's household to the land I will show you.
>
> I will make you into a great nation, and I will bless you; I will make your name great, and you will be a blessing.
>
> I will bless those who bless you, and whoever curses you I will curse; and all peoples on earth will be blessed through you. (Genesis 12:1–3)

That late bloomer Abraham has been hanging around his father's tent for far too many years, to put it mildly. But if God's call comes, it is better to heed it, no matter how late (and in that, there is real hope, for those who believe that they have delayed too long). Abraham leaves his country, and his people, and his father's household, and journeys out into the world, following the still small voice; following God's call. And it is no call to happiness. It is the complete bloody catastrophe we previously described: famine, war, and domestic strife. All this might make the reasonable individual (not to mention Abraham himself) doubt the wisdom of listening to God and conscience, and of adopting the responsibility of autonomy and the burden of adventure. Better to be lying in a hammock, devouring peeled grapes in the security of Dad's tent. What calls you out into the world, however—to your destiny—is not ease. It is struggle and strife. It is bitter contention and the deadly play of the opposites. It is probable—inevitable—that the adventure of your life will frustrate and disappoint and unsettle you, as you heed the call of conscience and shoulder your responsibility and endeavor to set yourself and the world right. But that is where the deep meaning that orients you and shelters you is to be found. That is where things will line up for you; where things that have been scattered apart and broken will come together; where purpose will manifest itself; where what is proper and good will be supported and what is weak and resentful and arrogant and destructive will be defeated. That is where the life that is worth living is to be eternally found—and where you can find it, personally, if only you are willing.

Notice that opportunity lurks where responsibility has been abdicated.

DO NOT DO WHAT YOU HATE

PATHOLOGICAL ORDER IN ITS DAY-TO-DAY GUISE

I once had a client who was subject to a barrage of constant idiocy as part of her work in a giant corporation. She was a sensible, honest person who had withstood and managed a difficult life and who genuinely wished to contribute and work in a manner commensurate with her good sense and honesty. She became subject while employed in the corporate environment to a long, in-person and email-mediated dispute about whether the term "flip chart" (a common phrase, referring to a large pad of paper sheets, typically supported by a tripod) was in fact a term of abuse. For those of you who still find it difficult to believe that conversations such as this occupy the hours of corporate workers, try a quick Google search. "Flip chart derogatory" will suffice. You will see immediately that concern about this issue genuinely and rather widely exists. Many meetings were held by her superiors at work to discuss this issue.

"Flip" was apparently at one time a derogatory term for Filipino (I could find little evidence for its use now). Even though the former slur has nothing whatsoever to do with "flip chart," the administrators of her firm felt that their time was well spent discussing the hypothetically prejudicial nature of the phrase and formulating a replacement term, the use of which eventually became mandatory among employees. This was all despite the fact that no employee of Filipino nationality or descent had ever complained about the corporation's use of the term. According to the Global Language Monitor (languagemonitor .com), which monitors but does not approve politically correct word usage, the proper term is now "writing block," despite the fact that a flip chart is in no way a "block."

In any case, the corporation in question settled on "easel pad," which seems somewhat more descriptively accurate—not that this comparatively elegant solution detracts from the foolishness in question. After all, we are still left with "flip-flopped," "flippant," "flip-flops," "flippers," and so on, and at least the first two of those sound more derogatory on first exposure than "flip chart," if we are going to concern ourselves with such things. Now, you might wonder: "What difference does this minor change in terminology really make? It is a trivial problem. Why would someone become concerned about the fact that such change is being discussed? Why not ignore it, as it is best to ignore so much folly, and concentrate on something of more importance?" Because, of course, you could claim that paying attention to someone attending to such issues is as much a waste of time as attending to the discussion in the first place. And I would say that is precisely the conundrum Rule V is trying to address. When do you stop participating in a worrisome process that you see, or think you see, unfolding in front of you?

My client first wrote me about the fact that not only was the string of communication discussing the use of "flip chart" well received by her coworkers, but that a contest of sorts immediately emerged to identify and communicate additional words that might also be offensive.* "Blackboard" was mentioned, as was "master key" (the former perhaps because referring to anything as "black"—even if it is black—is somehow racist in our hypersensitive times; the latter because of its hypothetical relationship to terminology historically associated with slavery). My client tried to make sense of what she was witnessing: "Such discussions give people the superficial sense of being good, noble, compassionate, openhearted, and wise. So, if for the sake of argument anyone disagrees, how could that person join the discussion without being considered anticompassionate, narrow minded, racist and wicked?"

She was also perturbed because no one at her workplace was apparently bothered that any given group of people might endow themselves with the authority to ban words (and to disdain or even discipline those who continued to use them) without perceiving any ethical overreach on their part, and without perceiving the danger of such censorship, which could easily extend, say, to personal opinions, topics of conversation—or, for that matter, books. Finally, she believed that the entire discussion constituted a prime example of "diversity," "inclusivity," and "equity"—terms that had become veritable mantras for the departments of Human Resources or Learning and Development (the latter of which she worked for). She regarded them as "engines of corporate indoctrination and ideological propaganda" and as part of the manner in which the political correctness that characterizes, above all, many university programs extends its reach into the broader culture. More importantly, however, she asked me in one of her letters, "Is this a case where enough is enough?" When and where do we stop?

---

*I have obtained direct express permission from my client to communicate all this information in this manner.

If a tiny minority of people even hypothetically finds some words offensive, then what? Do we continue to ban words endlessly?"

What my client was perceiving—at least as far as she was concerned—was *not* a single event, hypothetically capable of heading those involved in it down a dangerous path, but a clearly identifiable and causally related variety or sequence of events, all heading in the same direction. Those events seemed to form a coherent pattern, associated with an ideology that was directional in its intent, explicitly and implicitly. Furthermore, the effect of that directionality had been manifesting itself, by all appearances, for a reasonable amount of time, not only in the corporate world my client inhabited, but in the broader world of social and political institutions surrounding the corporation for which she worked. Although rather isolated in the department she happened to work in (the very epicenter of the ideological blitz of the corporation in question), she could see around her evidence that the processes disturbing her were also having a detrimental effect on other people. And then there was the effect on her conscience. It is important to understand that these issues were not minor philosophical concepts to her. They were bothering her deeply and upsetting her life.

It is, of course, the case that being required to do stupid, hateful things is demoralizing. Someone assigned a pointless or even counterproductive task will deflate, if they have any sense, and find within themselves very little motivation to carry out the assignment. Why? Because every fiber of their genuine being fights against that necessity. We do the things we do because we think those things important, compared to all the other things that could be important. We regard what we value as worthy of sacrifice and pursuit. That worthiness motivates us to act, despite the fact that action is difficult and dangerous. When we are called upon to do things that we find hateful and stupid, we are simultaneously forced to act contrary to the structure of values motivating us to move forward stalwartly and protecting us from dissolution into confusion and terror. "To thine own self be true,"[1] as Polonius has it, in Shakespeare's *Hamlet*. That "self"—that integrated psyche—is in truth the ark that shelters us when the storms gather and the water rises. To act in violation of its precepts—its fundamental beliefs—is to run our own ship onto the shoals of destruction. To act in violation of the precepts of that fundamental self is to cheat in the game we play with ourselves, to suffer the emptiness of betrayal, and to perceive abstractly and then experience in embodied form the loss that is inevitably to come.

What price did my client pay for her initial subjugation to the arbitrary dictates of her managers? She was an immigrant from a former Soviet bloc country and had experienced more than a sufficient taste of authoritarian ideology. In consequence, her inability to determine how she might object to what was happening left her feeling both weak and complicit. Furthermore, no sensible person could possibly remain motivated to put forth effort anywhere such as her workplace had become, where absurdities of a conceptual sort were not only continually occurring but encouraged or, even worse, required. Such "action" makes a mockery of productive work itself—even the very idea of productive work (and that is in fact part of the true motivation for such behavior: those jealous of genuine competence and productivity have every reason to undermine and denigrate even the concept of both). So, what did she do about the demoralizing state in which she found herself?

My client did not feel sufficiently confident in her position or in the ability of her managers to engage in a genuine conversation with them about her objections, although it was clear from my conversations with her that she wished very much to escape from the situation.

In consequence, she began to develop what might be considered a rear-guard action. She was already involved in developing in-house education projects for the company, as we mentioned. It was possible for her, therefore, to begin to branch out, offering her services as a speaker at a variety of corporate conferences. Although she never directly confronted the flip chart issue (and may have been wise to avoid doing so), she began to speak out against the kind of pseudoscience that characterizes many of the ideas that corporate managers, particularly in Human Resources departments, regard as valid. She presented a number of talks, for example, criticizing the widespread fad of "learning styles"—a theory predicated on the idea that there are between four and eight different modalities that individuals prefer and that aid them if used when they are trying to master new ideas. These include, for example, visual, auditory, verbal, physical, and logical, among others.

The problem with the learning styles theory? Most basically: there is simply no evidence whatsoever for its validity. First, although students may express a preference for information being delivered in one form over another, practically delivering it in that form does not improve their academic performance.[2] Second (and this makes sense, given the first problem), there is no evidence that teachers can accurately assess the "learning style" of their students.[3] So, although it was not possible for my client to directly confront the particular foolishness that was disturbing her, after long strategizing and much work she did manage to push back very effectively against the ignorance that characterized what passed for psychological knowledge among a substantial subset of her coworkers (as well as those who worked in other companies, where the same things were taking place). She had also done some work as a journalist for one of the major newspapers in Albania, her country of origin, and began to make continuing to do so a higher priority. This did not pay well, but she developed a stellar professional reputation there, and fought hard in print for what she believed in, warning the citizens of her once-Communist-dominated state of the move toward totalitarian opinion beginning to make itself attractive to people in the West.

What price did she pay for her decision to stand up and fight? To begin with, she had to face her fear of reprisal, as well as the fact that such fear—in combination with the profound distaste she felt for the ideological maneuvers characterizing her workplace—was destroying her interest in her office profession, as well as making her feel inadequate and cowardly. Then, she had to broaden her professional activities: first, taking the risk of offering herself as a speaker at corporate conventions (and people are generally very loath to talk publicly—it is a common fear, often severe enough to interfere with career progression[4]); second, mastering the literature, enabling her to speak in a credible and informed manner; and third, presenting material that, given its critical nature, was bound to offend a reasonable proportion of those in the audience (precisely those who had accepted and who were propagating the theories that she was now discrediting). This all meant the facing of her fear—of inaction, as well as action. These moves challenged her deeply—but the consequence was an expansion of personality and competence, as well as the knowledge that she was making a genuine social contribution.

I believe that the good that people do, small though it may appear, has more to do with the good that manifests broadly in the world than people think, and I believe the same about evil. We are each more responsible for the state of the world than we believe, or would feel comfortable believing. Without careful attention, culture itself tilts toward corruption. Tyranny grows slowly, and asks us to retreat in comparatively tiny steps. But each retreat increases the possibility of the next retreat. Each betrayal of conscience, each act of silence (despite the resentment we feel when silenced), and each rationalization weakens resistance and increases the probability of the next restrictive move forward. This is particularly the case when those pushing forward delight in the power they have now acquired—and such people are always to be found. Better to stand forward, awake, when the costs are relatively low—and, perhaps, when the potential rewards have not yet vanished. Better to stand forward before the ability to do so has been irretrievably compromised. Unfortunately, people often act in spite of their conscience—even if they know it—and hell tends to arrive step by step, one betrayal after another. And it should be remembered that it is rare for people to stand up against what they know to be wrong even when the consequences for doing so are comparatively slight. And this is something to deeply consider, if you are concerned with leading a moral and careful life: if you do not object when the transgressions against your conscience are minor, why presume that you will not willfully participate when the transgressions get truly out of hand?

Part of moving Beyond Order is knowing when you have such a reason. Part of moving Beyond Order is understanding that your conscience has a primary claim on your action, which supersedes your conventional social duty. If you decide to stand up and refuse a command, if you do something of which others disapprove but you firmly believe to be correct, you must be in a position to trust yourself. This means that you must have attempted to live an honest, meaningful, productive life (of precisely the sort that might characterize someone else you would tend to trust). If you have acted honorably, so that you are a trustworthy person, it will be your decision to refuse to comply or to act in a manner contrary to public expectation that will help society itself maintain its footing. By doing so you can be part of the force of truth that brings corruption and tyranny to a halt. The sovereign individual, awake and attending to his or her conscience, is the force that prevents the group, as the necessary structure guiding normative social relations, from becoming blind and deadly.

I do not want to end this section on a falsely optimistic note. I know from further correspondence with my client that she shifted her employment from one large organization to another several times in the years that followed. In one case, she found a good position, where it was possible to engage in productive, sensible, meaningful work. However, although successful there, she was laid off during a corporate reorganization, and has since found the other companies she has worked for as thoroughly possessed by the current linguistic and identity-politics fads as her original place of employment. Some dragons are everywhere, and they are not easy to defeat. But her attempts to fight back—her work debunking pseudoscientific theories; her work as a journalist—helped buttress her against depression and bolster her self-regard.

FORTIFY YOUR POSITION

When culture disintegrates—because it refuses to be aware of its own pathology; because the visionary hero is absent—it descends into the chaos that underlies everything. Under such conditions, the individual can dive voluntarily as deeply as he or she dares into the depths and rediscover the eternal principles renewing vision and life. The alternative is despair, corruption, and nihilism—thoughtless subjugation to the false words of totalitarian utopianism and life as a miserable, lying, and resentful slave.

If you wish instead to be engaged in a great enterprise—even if you regard yourself as a mere cog—you are required not to do things you hate. You must fortify your position, regardless of its meanness and littleness, confront the organizational mendacity undermining your spirit, face the chaos that ensues, rescue your near-dead father from the depths, and live a genuine and truthful life. Otherwise, nature hides her face, society stultifies, and you remain a marionette, with your strings pulled by demonic forces operating behind the scenes—and one more thing: it is your fault. No one is destined in the deterministic sense to remain a puppet.

We are not helpless. Even in the rubble of the most broken-down lives, useful weapons might still be found. Likewise, even the giant most formidable in appearance may not be as omnipotent as it proclaims or appears. Allow for the possibility that you may be able to fight back; that you may be able to resist and maintain your soul—and perhaps even your job. (But a better job may also beckon if you can tolerate the idea of the transformation.) If you are willing to conceptualize yourself as someone who could—and, perhaps more importantly, should—stand fast, you may begin to perceive the weapons at your disposal. If what you are doing is causing you to lash out at others impulsively; if what you are doing is destroying your motivation to move forward; if your actions and inactions are making you contemptuous of yourself and, worse, of the world; if the manner in which you conduct your life is making it difficult for you to wake happily in the morning; if you are plagued by a deep sense of self-betrayal—perhaps you are choosing to ignore that still small voice, inclined as you may be to consider it something only attended to by the weak and naive.

If you are at work, and called upon to do what makes you contemptuous of yourself—weak and ashamed, likely to lash out at those you love, unwilling to perform productively, and sick of your life—it is possible that it is time to meditate, consider, strategize, and place yourself in a position where you are capable of saying no.* Perhaps you will garner additional respect from the people you are opposing on moral grounds, even though you may still pay a high price for your actions. Perhaps they will even come to rethink their stance—if not now, with time (as their own consciences might be plaguing them in that same still small manner).

PRACTICALITIES

Perhaps you should also be positioning yourself for a lateral move—into another job, for example, noting as you may, "This occupation is deadening my soul, and that is truly not for me. It is time to take the painstaking steps necessary to organize my CV, and to engage in the difficult, demanding, and often unrewarding search for a new job" (but you have to be successful only once). Maybe you can find something that pays better and is more interesting, and where you are working with people who not only fail to kill your spirit, but positively rejuvenate it. Maybe following the dictates of conscience is in fact the best possible plan that you have—at minimum, otherwise you have to live with your sense of self-betrayal and the knowledge that you put up with what you truly could not tolerate. Nothing about that is good.

I might get fired. Well, prepare now to seek out and ready yourself for another job, hopefully better (or prepare yourself to go over your manager's head with a well-prepared and articulate argument). And do not begin by presuming that leaving your job, even involuntarily, is necessarily for the worst.

---

*Perhaps not just once, because that makes your reaction too impulsive; perhaps not just twice, because that still may not constitute sufficient evidence to risk undertaking what might be a genuine war; but definitively three times, when a pattern has been clearly established.

I am afraid to move. Well, of course you are, but afraid compared to what? Afraid in comparison to continuing in a job where the center of your being is at stake; where you become weaker, more contemptible, more bitter, and more prone to pressure and tyranny over the years? There are few choices in life where there is no risk on either side, and it is often necessary to contemplate the risks of staying as thoroughly as the risks of moving. I have seen many people move, sometimes after several years of strategizing, and end up in better shape, psychologically and pragmatically, after their time in the desert.

Perhaps no one else would want me. Well, the rejection rate for new job applications is extraordinarily high. I tell my clients to assume 50:1, so their expectations are set properly. You are going to be passed over, in many cases, for many positions for which you are qualified. But that is rarely *personal.* It is, instead, a condition of existence, an inevitable consequence of somewhat arbitrary subjection to the ambivalent conditions of worth characterizing society. It is the consequence of the fact that CVs are easy to disseminate and difficult to process; that many jobs have unannounced internal candidates (and so are just going through the motions); and that some companies keep a rolling stock of applicants, in case they need to hire quickly. That is an actuarial problem, a statistical problem, a baseline problem—and not necessarily an indication that there is something specifically flawed about you. You must incorporate all that sustainingly pessimistic realism into your expectations, so that you do not become unreasonably downhearted. One hundred and fifty applications, carefully chosen; three to five interviews thereby acquired. That could be a mission of a year or more. That is much less than a lifetime of misery and downward trajectory. But it is not nothing. You need to fortify yourself for it, plan, and garner support from people who understand what you are up to and are realistically appraised of the difficulty and the options.

Now it may also be that you are lagging in the development of your skills and could improve your performance at work so that your chances of being hired elsewhere are heightened. But there is no loss in that. You cannot effectively pronounce "no" in the presence of corrupt power when your options to move are nonexistent. In consequence, you have a moral obligation to place yourself in a position of comparative strength, and to do then what is necessary to capitalize on that strength. You may also have to think through worst-case situations and to discuss them with those who will be affected by your decisions. But it is once again worth realizing that staying where you should not be may be the true worst-case situation: one that drags you out and kills you slowly over decades. That is not a good death, even though it is slow, and there is very little in it that does not speak of the hopelessness that makes people age quickly and long for the cessation of career and, worse, life. That is no improvement. As the old and cruel cliché goes: If you must cut off a cat's tail, do not do it half an inch at a time. You may well be in for a few painful years of belated recognition of insufficiency, and required to send out four or five or ten job applications a week, knowing full well that the majority will be rejected with less than a second look. But you need to win the lottery only once, and a few years of difficulty with hope beat an entire dejected lifetime of a degenerating and oppressed career.

And let us be clear: It is not a simple matter of hating your job because it requires you to wake up too early in the morning, or to drag yourself to work when it is too hot or cold or windy or dry or when you are feeling low and want to curl up in bed. It is not a matter of frustration generated when you are called on to do things that are menial or necessary such as emptying garbage cans, sweeping floors, cleaning bathrooms, or in any other manner taking your lowly but well-deserved place at the bottom of the hierarchy of competence—even of seniority. Resentment generated by such necessary work is most often merely ingratitude, inability to accept a lowly place at the beginning, unwillingness to adopt the position of the fool, or arrogance and lack of discipline. Refusal of the call of conscience is by no means the same thing as irritation about undesirably low status.

That rejection—that betrayal of soul—is truly the requirement to perform demonstrably counterproductive, absurd, or pointless work; to treat others unjustly and to lie about it; to engage in deceit, to betray your future self; to put up with unnecessary torture and abuse (and to silently watch others suffer the same treatment). That rejection is the turning of a blind eye, and the agreement to say and do things that betray your deepest values and make you a cheat at your own game. And there is no doubt that the road to hell, personally and socially, is paved not so much with good intentions as with the adoption of attitudes and undertaking of actions that inescapably disturb your conscience.

Do not do what you hate.

RULE VI

ABANDON IDEOLOGY

THE WRONG PLACES

After I published my last book, my wife, Tammy, and I embarked on a lengthy speaking tour throughout the English-speaking world and a good part of Europe, particularly in the north. Most of the theaters I spoke at were old and beautiful, and it was a delight to be in buildings with such rich architectural and cultural histories, where so many of the bands we loved had played, and where other performing artists had had their great moments. We booked 160 theaters—generally with a capacity of about 2,500 to 3,000 people (although there were smaller venues in Europe, and larger in Australia). I was—and am—struck to the core by the fact that there was such an extensive audience for my lectures—and that we found that audience seemingly everywhere. The same surprise extends to my YouTube and podcast appearances—on my own channels, in interviews on others, and in the innumerable clips that people have voluntarily cut from my longer talks and discussions with journalists. These have been watched or listened to hundreds of millions of times. And finally, there is the afore-mentioned book, which will have sold something like four million copies in English by the time the present volume is published, and which will be translated into fifty additional languages, assuming matters continue as they are now. It is not at all easy to know what to think about finding myself with an audience like that.

What is going on? Any sensible person would be taken aback—to put it mildly—by all of this. It seems that my work must be addressing something that is missing in many people's lives. Now, as I mentioned previously, I am relying for much of my content on the ideas of great psychologists and other thinkers, and that should count for something. But I have also been continually considering what else more specific (if anything) might be attracting people's attention, and have been relying on two sources of information to try to determine exactly that. The first is the response I get directly from individuals themselves, when I meet them in the immediate aftermath of one of my lectures or when they stop me on the street, in airports, cafés, or other public places.

In one midwestern American city (I think it might have been Louisville), a young man met me after my lecture and said, "Quick story. Two years ago, I was released from prison. Homeless. Broke. I started listening to your lectures. Now I have a full-time job, and I own my apartment, and my wife and I just had our first child—a daughter. Thank you." And the "thank you" was accompanied with direct eye contact and a firm handshake, and the story was told in the voice of conviction. And people tell me very similar stories on the street, often in tears, although the one I just related was perhaps a bit more extreme than the average tale. They share very private good news (the kind you share only with people to whom you can safely tell such things). And I feel greatly privileged to be one of those people, although it is emotionally demanding to be the recipient of continual personal revelations, regardless (or maybe even because) of the fact that they are so positive. I find it heart-wrenching to see how little encouragement and guidance so many people have received, and how much good can emerge when just a little more is provided. "I knew you could do it" is a good start, and goes a long way toward ameliorating some of the unnecessary pain in the world.

So, that is one form of story that I hear, continually, in many variants. When we meet, one on one, people also tell me that they enjoy my lectures and what I have written because what I say and write provides them with the words they need to express things they already know, but are unable to articulate. It is helpful for everyone to be able to represent explicitly what they already implicitly understand. I am frequently plagued with doubts about the role that I am playing, so the fact that people find my words exist in accordance with their deep but heretofore unrealized or unexpressed beliefs is reassuring, helping me maintain faith in what I have learned and thought about and have now shared so publicly. Helping people bridge the gap between what they profoundly intuit but cannot articulate seems to be a reasonable and valuable function for a public intellectual. And then there is the final piece of information bearing on whatever it is that I am accomplishing. I have garnered it as a direct consequence of the live lectures that I have had so many opportunities to deliver. It is a privilege and a gift to be able to talk repeatedly to large groups of people. It provides a real-time opportunity to judge the zeitgeist, the spirit of the times. It also allows me to formulate and immediately test new ideas for their communicability and their ability to grip attention and, thereby, to judge their quality—at least in part. This occurs during the talk when I attend to how the audience responds.

In *12 Rules for Life*, Rule 9: Assume that the person you are listening to might know something you do not, I suggest that when speaking to a large group you should nonetheless always be attending to specific individuals—the crowd is somewhat of an illusion. However, you can augment your individual-focused visual attention by simultaneously listening to the entire group, so that you hear them rustling around, laughing, coughing, or whatever they happen to be doing, while you concentrate on perceiving specific individuals. What you want to see from the person you are facing is rapt attention. What you want to hear from the crowd is dead silence. You want to hear *nothing.* Achieving that means your listeners are not distracted by everything they could be thinking about while in attendance. If you are an audience member at a performance, and you are not completely enthralled by the content, you become preoccupied by some slight physical discomforts, and shift from place to place. You become aware of your own thoughts. You begin to think about what you need to do tomorrow. You whisper something to the person beside you. That all adds up to discontent in the audience, and audible noise. But if you, as speaker, are positioned properly on stage, physically and spiritually, then everybody's attention will be focused with laser-like intensity on whatever you are saying, and no one will make a sound. In this manner, you can tell what ideas have power.

While watching and listening in the way I just described to all the gatherings I have spoken to, I became increasingly aware that the mention of one topic in particular brought every audience (and I mean that without exception) to a dead-quiet halt: responsibility—the very topic we made central in this book in Rule IV: Notice that opportunity lurks where responsibility has been abdicated. That response was fascinating—and not at all predictable. Responsibility is not an easy sell. Parents have been striving forever to make their kids responsible.

Society attempts the same thing, with its educational institutions, apprenticeships, volunteer organizations, and clubs. You might even consider the inculcation of responsibility the fundamental purpose of society. But something has gone wrong. We have committed an error, or a series of errors. We have spent too much time, for example (much of the last fifty years), clamoring about rights, and we are no longer asking enough of the young people we are socializing. We have been telling them for decades to demand what they are owed by society. We have been implying that the important meanings of their lives will be given to them because of such demands, when we should have been doing the opposite: letting them know that the meaning that sustains life in all its tragedy and disappointment is to be found in shouldering a noble burden. Because we have not been doing this, they have grown up looking in the wrong places. And this has left them vulnerable: vulnerable to easy answers and susceptible to the deadening force of resentment. What about the unfolding of history has left us in this position? How has this vulnerability, this susceptibility, come about?

PERHAPS HE IS ONLY SLEEPING

In the last quarter of the nineteenth century, the German philosopher Friedrich Nietzsche famously announced "God is dead." This utterance has become so famous that you can even see it scribbled on the walls of public bathrooms, where it often takes the following form: "God is dead" —Nietzsche. "Nietzsche is dead" —God. Nietzsche did not make this claim in a narcissistic or triumphant manner. The great thinker's opinion stemmed from his fear that all the Judeo-Christian values serving as the foundation of Western civilization had been made dangerously subject to casual rational criticism, and that the most important axiom upon which they were predicated—the existence of a transcendent, all-powerful deity—had been fatally challenged. Nietzsche concluded from this that everything would soon fall apart, in a manner catastrophic both psychologically and socially.

It does not require a particularly careful reader to note that Nietzsche described God, in *The Gay Science*, as the "holiest and mightiest of all that the world has yet owned," and modern human beings as "the murderers of all murderers."[1] These are not the sorts of descriptions you might expect from a triumphant rationalist celebrating the demise of superstition. It was instead a statement of absolute despair. In his other works, particularly in *The Will to Power*, Nietzsche describes what would occur in the next century and beyond because of this murderous act.[2] He prophesied (and that is the correct word for it) that two major consequences would arise—apparent opposites, although each linked inextricably and causally together—and both associated with the death of traditional ritual, story, and belief.

As the purpose of human life became uncertain outside the purposeful structure of monotheistic thought and the meaningful world it proposed, we would experience an existentially devastating rise in nihilism, Nietzsche believed. Alternatively, he suggested, people would turn to identification with rigid, totalitarian ideology: the substitute of human ideas for the transcendent Father of All Creation. The doubt that undermines and the certainty that crushes: Nietzsche's prognostication for the two alternatives that would arise in the aftermath of the death of God.

The incomparable Russian novelist Fyodor Dostoyevsky addressed the same question as Nietzsche—at about the same time—in his masterwork *The Possessed* (alternatively known as *Demons* or *The Devils*).[3] The protagonist in that novel, Nikolai Stavrogin, is wed to the same ideals that eventually birthed revolutionary communism, although he lives his fictional life decades before the full-fledged turmoil began in what became the Soviet Union. The appearance of these ideals was not a positive development, in Dostoevsky's view. He could see that the adoption of a rigid, comprehensive utopian ideology, predicated on a few apparently self-evident axioms, presented a political and spiritual danger with the potential to far exceed in brutality all that had occurred in the religious, monarchical, or even pagan past. Dostoyevsky, like Nietzsche, foresaw that all of this was coming almost fifty years (!) before the Leninist Revolution in Russia. That incomprehensible level of prophetic capacity remains a stellar example of how the artist and his intuition brings to light the future far before others see it.

Nietzsche and Dostoevsky both foresaw that communism would appear dreadfully attractive—an apparently rational, coherent, and moral alternative to religion or nihilism—and that the consequences would be lethal. The former wrote, in his inimitably harsh, ironic, and brilliant manner, "In fact, I even wish a few experiments might be made to show that in socialistic society life denies itself, and itself cuts away its own roots. The earth is big enough and man is still unexhausted enough for a practical lesson of this sort and *demonstratio ad absurdum*—even if it were accomplished only by a vast expenditure of lives—to seem worthwhile to me."[4] The socialism Nietzsche referred to was not the relatively mild version later popular in Britain, Scandinavia, and Canada, with its sometimes genuine emphasis on the improvement of working-class life, but the full-blown collectivism of Russia, China, and a host of smaller countries. Whether we have truly learned the "practical lesson"—the demonstration of the absurdity of the doctrine—as a consequence of Nietzsche's predicted "vast expenditure of lives" remains to be seen.

Nietzsche appears to have unquestioningly adopted the idea that the world was both objective and valueless in the manner posited by the emergent physical sciences. This left him with a single remaining escape from nihilism and totalitarianism: the emergence of the individual strong enough to create his own values, project them onto valueless reality, and then abide by them. He posited that a new kind of man—the Übermensch (the higher person or superman)—would be necessary in the aftermath of the death of God, so that society would not drift toward the opposing rocky shoals of despair and oversystematized political theorizing. Individuals who take this route, this alternative to nihilism and totalitarianism, must therefore produce their own cosmology of values.

However, the psychoanalysts Freud and Jung put paid to that notion, demonstrating that we are not sufficiently in possession of ourselves to create values by conscious choice. Furthermore, there is little evidence that any of us have the genius to create ourselves *ex nihilo*— from nothing—particularly given the extreme limitations of our experience, the biases of our perceptions, and the short span of our lives. We have a nature—or, too often, it has us—and only a fool would now dare to claim that we have sufficient mastery of ourselves to create, rather than discover, what we value. We have the capacity for spontaneous revelatory experience—artistic, inventive, and religious. We discover new things about ourselves constantly, to our delight—and also to our dismay, as we are so often overcome by our emotions and motivations. We contend with our nature. We negotiate with it. But it is not at all obvious that the individual will ever be capable of bringing the new values that Nietzsche so fervently longed for into being.

There are other problems with Nietzsche's argument, as well. If each of us lives by our own created and projected values, what remains to unite us? This is a philosophical problem of central importance. How could a society of Übermenschen possibly avoid being at constant odds with one another, unless there was something comparable about their created values? Finally, it is by no means obvious that any such supermen have ever come into existence. Instead, over the last century and a half, with the modern crisis of meaning and the rise of totalitarian states such as Nazi Germany, the USSR, and Communist China, we appear to have found ourselves in exactly the nihilistic or ideologically possessed state that Nietzsche and Dostoevsky feared, accompanied by precisely the catastrophic sociological and psychological consequences they foretold.

It is also by no means self-evident that value, subjective though it appears to be, is not an integral part of reality, despite the undeniable utility of the scientific method. The central scientific axiom left to us by the Enlightenment—that reality is the exclusive domain of the objective—poses a fatal challenge to the reality of religious experience, if the latter experience is fundamentally subjective (and it appears to be exactly that). But there is something complicating the situation that seems to lie between the subjective and the objective: What if there are experiences that typically manifest themselves to one person at a time (as seems to be the case with much of revelation), but appear to form a meaningful pattern when considered collectively? That indicates something is occurring that is not merely subjective, even though it cannot be easily pinned down with the existing methods of science. It could be, instead, that the value of something is sufficiently idiosyncratic—sufficiently dependent on the particularities of time, place, and the individual experiencing that thing— that it cannot be fixed and replicated in the manner required for it to exist as a scientific object. This does not mean, however, that value is not *real*: It means only that it is so complex that it cannot yet and may never fit itself within the scientific worldview. The world is a very strange place, and there are times when the metaphorical or narrative description characteristic of culture and the material representation so integral to science appear to touch, when everything comes together—when life and art reflect each other equally.

The psyche—the soul—that produces or is the recipient of such experiences appears incontrovertibly real: the proof lying not least in our actions. We all axiomatically assume the reality of our individual existences and conscious experiences, and we extend the same courtesy to others (or else). It is by no means unreasonable to suggest that such existence and experience has a deep underlying biological and physical structure. Those with a psychoanalytic bent certainly assume so, as do many who study biological psychology, particularly if they focus on motivation and emotion.[5] That structure, accepted as a given by scientists and by the general population in equal measure, appears to manifest religious experience as part of its basic function—and that religious function has enough commonality across people to make us at least understand what "religious experience" means—particularly if we have had a taste of it at some point in life.

What does that imply? It might be that the true meaning of life is available for discovery, if it can be discovered at all, by each individual, alone—although in communication with others, past and present. It may well be, therefore, that the true meaning of life is not to be found in what is objective, but in what is subjective (but still universal). The existence of conscience, for example, provides some evidence for that, as does the fact that religious experiences can reliably be induced chemically, as well as through practices such as dancing, chanting, fasting, and meditating. Additionally, the fact that religious ideas are capable of uniting vast numbers of people under a single moral umbrella (although such ideas can divide across sects, as well) also indicates something universal calling from within. Why do we so easily assume that nothing about that is real, given its apparent commonality and necessity—given, as well, the near certainty that the capacity for valuing is an ancient evolved function, selected for by the very reality we are attempting to define and understand?

We have seen the consequences of the totalitarian alternatives in which the collective is supposed to bear the burdens of life, lay out the proper pathway, and transform the terrible world into the promised utopia. The communists produced a worldview that was attractive to fair-minded people, as well as those who were envious and cruel. Perhaps communism may even have been a viable solution to the problems of the unequal distribution of wealth that characterized the industrial age, if all of the hypothetically oppressed were good people and all of the evil was to be found, as hypothesized, in their bourgeoisie overlords. Unfortunately for the communists, a substantial proportion of the oppressed were incapable, unconscientious, unintelligent, licentious, power mad, violent, resentful, and jealous, while a substantial proportion of the oppressors were educated, able, creative, intelligent, honest, and caring. When the frenzy of dekulakization swept through the newly established Soviet Union, it was vengeful and jealous murderers who were redistributing property, while it was competent and reliable farmers, for the most part, from whom it was violently taken. One unintended consequence of that "redistribution" of good fortune was the starvation of six million Ukrainians in the 1930s, in the midst of some of the most fertile land in the world.

The other major villains of the twentieth century, Germany's National Socialists, were, of course, also powerful and dangerous ideologues. It has been suggested that Hitler's acolytes were inspired by Nietzsche's philosophy. This claim may hold some truth in a perverse manner, as they were certainly trying to create their own values, although not as the individuals whose development the philosopher promoted. It is more reasonable to say that Nietzsche identified the cultural and historical conditions that made the rise to influence of ideas akin to those promoted by the Nazis extremely likely. The Nazis were trying to create a post-Christian, postreligious perfect man, the ideal Aryan, and certainly formulated that ideal in a manner not in accordance with the dictates of either Judaism or Christianity. Thus, the perfect Aryan could be and certainly was conceptualized by the Nazis as a "higher man." This does not mean that the Nazi ideal as postulated bore any resemblance to the Nietzschean ideal. Quite the contrary: Nietzsche was a fervent admirer of individuality and would have considered the idea of the higher man as state creation both absurd and abhorrent.

THE FATAL ATTRACTION OF THE FALSE IDOL

Consider those who have not gone so far as to adopt the discredited ideologies of the Marxist-Leninists and the Nazis, but who still maintain faith in the commonplace isms characterizing the modern world: conservatism, socialism, feminism (and all manner of ethnic- and gender-study isms), postmodernism, and environmentalism, among others. They are all monotheists, practically speaking—or polytheistic worshippers of a very small number of gods. These gods are the axioms and foundational beliefs that must be accepted, a priori, rather than proven, before the belief system can be adopted, and when accepted and applied to the world allow the illusion to prevail that knowledge has been produced.

The process by which an ism system can be generated is simple in its initial stages but baroque enough in its application to mimic (and replace) actual productive theorizing. The ideologue begins by selecting a few abstractions in whose low-resolution representations hide large, undifferentiated chunks of the world. Some examples include "the economy," "the nation," "the environment," "the patriarchy," "the people," "the rich," "the poor," "the oppressed," and "the oppressors." The use of single terms implicitly hypersimplifies what are in fact extraordinarily diverse and complex phenomena (that masked complexity is part of the reason that the terms come to carry so much emotional weight). There are many reasons, for example, why people are poor. Lack of money is the obvious cause—but that hypothetical obviousness is part of the problem with ideology. Lack of education, broken families, crime-ridden neighborhoods, alcoholism, drug abuse, criminality and corruption (and the political and economic exploitation that accompanies it), mental illness, lack of a life plan (or even failure to realize that formulating such a plan is possible or necessary), low conscientiousness, unfortunate geographical locale, shift in the economic landscape and the consequent disappearance of entire fields of endeavor, the marked proclivity for those who are rich to get richer still and the poor to get poorer, low creativity/entrepreneurial interest, lack of encouragement—these are but a few of the manifold problems that generate poverty, and the solution to each (assuming that a solution exists) is by no means obviously the same. Nor are the villains hiding behind each putative and differentiable cause the same villains (assuming that there are even villains to be found).

All such problems require careful, particularized analysis, followed by the generation of multiple potential solutions, followed by the careful assessment of those solutions to ensure that they are having their desired effect. It is uncommon to see any serious social problem addressed so methodically. It is also rare that the solutions generated, even by methodical process, produce the intended outcome. The great difficulty of assessing problems in sufficient detail to understand what is causing them, followed by the equally great difficulty of generating and testing particularized solutions, is sufficient to deter even the stouthearted, let us say, from daring to tackle a true plague of mankind. Since the ideologue can place him or herself on the morally correct side of the equation without the genuine effort necessary to do so validly, it is much easier and more immediately gratifying to reduce the problem to something simple and accompany it with an evildoer, who can then be morally opposed.

After breaking the world into large, undifferentiated pieces, describing the problem(s) that characterize each division, and identifying the appropriate villains, the ism theorist then generates a small number of explanatory principles or forces (which may indeed contribute in some part to the understanding or existence of those abstracted entities). Then he or she grants to that small number primary causal power, while ignoring others of equal or greater importance. It is most effective to utilize a major motivational system or large-scale sociological fact or conjecture for such purposes. It is also good to select those explanatory principles for an unstated negative, resentful, and destructive reason, and then make discussion of the latter and the reason for their existence taboo for the ideologue and his or her followers (to say nothing of the critics). Next, the faux theorist spins a post-hoc theory about how every phenomenon, no matter how complex, can be considered a secondary consequence of the new, totalizing system. Finally, a school of thought emerges to propagate the methods of this algorithmic reduction (particularly when the thinker is hoping to attain dominance in the conceptual and the real worlds), and those who refuse to adopt the algorithm or who criticize its use are tacitly or explicitly demonized.

Incompetent and corrupt intellectuals thrive on such activity, such games. The first players of a given game of this sort are generally the brightest of the participants. They weave a story around their causal principle of choice, demonstrating how that hypothetically primary motivational force profoundly contributed to any given domain of human activity. Sometimes this is even helpful, as such activity may shed light on how a motivation heretofore taboo to discuss or consider might play a larger role in affecting human behavior and perception than was previously deemed acceptable (this is what happened, for example, with Freud, and his emphasis on sex). Their followers, desperate to join a potentially masterable new dominance hierarchy (the old one being cluttered by its current occupants), become enamored of that story. While doing so, being less bright than those they follow, they subtly shift "contributed to" or "affected" to "caused." The originator(s), gratified by the emergence of followers, start to shift their story in that direction as well. Or they object, but it does not matter. The cult has already begun.

This kind of theorizing is particularly attractive to people who are smart but lazy. Cynicism serves as an aid, too, as does arrogance. The new adherents will be taught that mastering such a game constitutes education, and will learn to criticize alternative theories, different methods, and increasingly, even the idea of fact itself. If an impenetrable vocabulary accompanies the theory, so much the better. It will then take potential critics some valuable time even to learn to decode the arguments. And there is a conspiratorial aspect that rapidly comes to pervade the school where such "education" occurs, and where such activity is increasingly all that is permitted: Do not criticize the theory— and do not get singled out. Do not become unpopular. Even: Do not receive a bad grade, or a poor review, for expressing a taboo opinion (and even when this does not occur in practice, the fear that it might keeps many students and professors, or employees and employers, in check).

Freud, as we noted, attempted to reduce motivation to sexuality, to libido. The same can be done quite effectively by anyone sufficiently literate, intelligent, and verbally fluent. This is because "sexuality" (like any multifaceted single term) can be defined as tightly or as loosely as necessary by those who use it for comprehensively explanatory purposes. No matter how defined, sex is a crucially important biological phenomenon—key to complex life itself—and its influence may therefore be genuinely detected or plausibly invented in any important field of endeavor and then exaggerated (while other factors of significant import are diminished in importance). In this manner, the single explanatory principle can be expanded indefinitely, in keeping with the demands placed upon it.

Marx did the same thing when he described man in a fundamentally economic, class-based manner, and history as the eternal battleground of bourgeoisie and proletariat. Everything can be explained by running it through a Marxist algorithm. The wealthy are wealthy because they exploit the poor. The poor are poor because they are exploited by the wealthy. All economic inequality is undesirable, unproductive, and a consequence of fundamental unfairness and corruption. There is, of course—as in the case of Freud—some value in Marx's observations. Class is an important element of social hierarchies, and tends to maintain itself with a certain stability across time. Economic well-being, or the lack thereof, is of crucial significance. And the damnable fact of the Pareto distribution[6]—the tendency of those who have more to get more (which seems to apply in any economic system)—does mean that wealth accumulates in the hands of a minority of people. The people who make up that minority do change substantively, regardless of the aforementioned class stability,[7] and that is a crucial point, but the fact that the comparatively rich are always a minority—and a small one, at that—seems dismally immutable.

Regardless of its hypothetical virtues, however, the implementation of Marxism was a disaster everywhere it was attempted—and that has motivated attempts by its unrepentant would-be present-day adherents to clothe its ideas in new garb and continue forward, as if nothing of significance has changed. Thinkers powerfully influenced by Marx and overwhelmingly influential in much of the academy today (such as Michel Foucault and Jacques Derrida) modified the Marxist simplification essentially by replacing "economics" with "power"—as if power were the single motivating force behind all human behavior (as opposed, say, to competent authority, or reciprocity of attitude and action).

Ideological reduction of that form is the hallmark of the most dangerous of pseudo-intellectuals. Ideologues are the intellectual equivalent of fundamentalists, unyielding and rigid. Their self-righteousness and moral claim to social engineering is every bit as deep and dangerous. It might even be worse: ideologues lay claim to rationality itself. So, they try to justify their claims as logical and thoughtful. At least the fundamentalists admit devotion to something they just believe arbitrarily. They are a lot more honest. Furthermore, fundamentalists are bound by a relationship with the transcendent. What this means is that God, the center of their moral universe, remains outside and above complete understanding, according to the fundamentalist's own creed. Right-wing Jews, Islamic hard-liners, and ultra-conservative Christians must admit, if pushed, that God is essentially mysterious. This concession provides at least some boundary for their claims, as individuals, to righteousness and power (as the genuine fundamentalist at least remains subordinate to Something he cannot claim to totally understand, let alone master). For the ideologue, however, nothing remains outside understanding or mastery. An ideological theory explains everything: all the past, all the present, and all the future. This means that an ideologue can consider him or herself in possession of the complete truth (something forbidden to the self-consistent fundamentalist). There is no claim more totalitarian and no situation in which the worst excesses of pride are more likely to manifest themselves (and not only pride, but then deceit, once the ideology has failed to explain the world or predict its future).

The moral of the story? Beware of intellectuals who make a monotheism out of their theories of motivation. Beware, in more technical terms, of blanket univariate (single variable) causes for diverse, complex problems. Of course, power plays a role in history, as does economics. But the same can be said of jealousy, love, hunger, sex, cooperation, revelation, anger, disgust, sadness, anxiety, religion, compassion, disease, technology, hatred, and chance—none of which can definitively be reduced to another. The attraction of doing so is, however, obvious: simplicity, ease, and the illusion of mastery (which can have exceptionally useful psychological and social consequences, particularly in the short term)—and, let us not forget, the frequent discovery of a villain, or set of villains, upon which the hidden motivations for the ideology can be vented.

RESSENTIMENT

Ressentiment[8]—hostile resentment—occurs when individual failure or insufficient status is blamed both on the system within which that failure or lowly status occurs and then, most particularly, on the people who have achieved success and high status within that system. The former, the system, is deemed by fiat to be unjust. The successful are deemed exploitative and corrupt, as they can be logically read as undeserving beneficiaries, as well as the voluntary, conscious, self-serving, and immoral supporters, if the system is unjust. Once this causal chain of thought has been accepted, all attacks on the successful can be construed as morally justified attempts at establishing justice—rather than, say, manifestations of envy and covetousness that might have traditionally been defined as shameful.

There is another typical feature of ideological pursuit: the victims supported by ideologues are always innocent (and it is sometimes true that victims *are* innocent), and the perpetrators are always evil (evil perpetrators are also not in short supply). But the fact that there exist genuine victims and perpetrators provides no excuse to make low-resolution, blanket statements about the global locale of blameless victimization and evil perpetration—particularly of the type that does not take the presumed innocence of the accused firmly into account. *No group guilt should be assumed*—and certainly not of the multigenerational kind.[9] It is a certain sign of the accuser's evil intent, and a harbinger of social catastrophe. But the advantage is that the ideologue, at little practical costs, can construe him or herself both as nemesis of the oppressor and defender of the oppressed. Who needs the fine distinctions that determination of individual guilt or innocence demands when a prize such as that beckons?

To take the path of ressentiment is to risk tremendous bitterness. This is in no small part a consequence of identifying the enemy without rather than within. If wealth is the problem at issue, for example, and the wealthy perceived as the reason for poverty and all the other problems of the world, then the wealthy become the enemy—indistinguishable, in some profound sense, from a degree of evil positively demonic in its psychological and social significance. If power is the problem, then those who have established any authority at all are the singular cause of the world's suffering. If masculinity is the problem, then all males (or even the concept of male) must be attacked and vilified.* Such division of the world into the devil without and the saint within justifies self-righteous hatred—necessitated by the morality of the ideological system itself. This is a terrible trap: Once the source of evil has been identified, it becomes the duty of the righteous to eradicate it. This is an invitation to both paranoia and persecution. A world where only you and people who think like you are good is also a world where you are surrounded by enemies bent on your destruction, who must be fought.

It is much safer morally to look to yourself for the errors of the world, at least to the degree to which someone honest and free of willful blindness might consider. You are likely to be much more clear minded about what is what and who is who and where blame lies once you contemplate the log in your own eye, rather than the speck in your brother's. It is probable that your own imperfections are evident and plentiful, and could profitably be addressed, as step one in your Redeemer's quest to improve the world. To take the world's sins onto yourself—to assume responsibility for the fact that things have not been set right in your own life and elsewhere—is part of the messianic

---

*And don't think the game can't be played (isn't played) in the opposite manner. The same applies for femininity, for example, in too many places in the world: in Arabic, for example, the word *awrah* denotes the body's intimate parts, which must be clothed. The term's root *awr* means something approximating "weakness," "imperfection," or "defectiveness." "Nakedness" is the most common English translation. Other meanings include "falseness," "artificiality," or "blindness." According to the dictionary compiled by Mohammad Moin, a well-known Iranian scholar of Persian literature and Iranian studies, *awrah* means both "nakedness" or "shame" and "young woman." In keeping with this network of ideas, the word *awrat*, derived from *awrah*, has been used widely in various Arabic-influenced cultures to signify "woman." It is for such reasons that women are viewed by those who follow the Wahhabi strand of Islam, for example—ultraconservative, austere, and puritanical—as sufficiently responsible for the evil and temptation of the world that their movements must be drastically and severely restricted, even that they are not allowed to show themselves in any important manner in the public sphere.

path: part of the imitation of the hero, in the most profound of senses. This is a psychological or spiritual rather than a sociological or political issue. Consider the characters fabricated by second-rate crafters of fiction: they are simply divided into those who are good and those who are evil. By contrast, sophisticated writers put the divide inside the characters they create, so that each person becomes the locus of the eternal struggle between light and darkness. It is much more psychologically appropriate (and much less dangerous socially) to assume that you are the enemy—that it is your weaknesses and insufficiencies that are damaging the world—than to assume saintlike goodness on the part of you and your party, and to pursue the enemy you will then be inclined to see everywhere.

It is impossible to fight patriarchy, reduce oppression, promote equality, transform capitalism, save the environment, eliminate competitiveness, reduce government, or to run every organization like a business. Such concepts are simply too low-resolution. The Monty Python comedy crew once offered satirical lessons for playing the flute: blow over one end and move your fingers up and down on the holes.[10] True. But useless. The necessary detail is simply not there. Similarly, sophisticated large-scale processes and systems do not exist in a manner sufficiently real to render their comprehensive unitary transformation possible. The idea that they do is the product of twentieth-century cults. The beliefs of these cults are simultaneously naive and narcissistic, and the activism they promote is the resentful and lazy person's substitute for actual accomplishment. The single axioms of the ideologically possessed are gods, served blindly by their proselytizers.

Like God, however, ideology is dead. The bloody excesses of the twentieth century killed it. We should let it go, and begin to address and consider smaller, more precisely defined problems. We should conceptualize them at the scale at which we might begin to solve them, not by blaming others, but by trying to address them personally while simultaneously taking responsibility for the outcome.

Have some humility. Clean up your bedroom. Take care of your family. Follow your conscience. Straighten up your life. Find something productive and interesting to do and commit to it. When you can do all that, find a bigger problem and try to solve that if you dare. If that works, too, move on to even more ambitious projects. And, as the necessary beginning to that process . . . abandon ideology.

WORK AS HARD AS YOU POSSIBLY CAN ON AT LEAST ONE THING AND SEE WHAT HAPPENS

THE VALUE OF HEAT AND PRESSURE

When coal is subjected to intense heat and pressure, far below the Earth's surface, its atoms rearrange themselves into the perfect repeating crystalline alignment characterizing a diamond. The carbon that makes up coal also becomes maximally durable in its diamond form (as diamond is the hardest of all substances). Finally, it becomes capable of reflecting light. This combination of durability and glitter gives a diamond the qualities that justify its use as a symbol of value. That which is valuable is pure, properly aligned, and glitters with light— and this is true for the person just as it is for the gem. Light, of course, signifies the shining brilliance of heightened and focused consciousness. Human beings are conscious during the day, when it is light. Much of that consciousness is visual and therefore dependent on light. To be illumined or enlightened is to be exceptionally awake and aware—to attain a state of being commonly associated with divinity. To wear a diamond is to become associated with the radiance of the Sun, like the king or queen whose profile is stamped on the sunlike disc of the gold coin, a near-universal standard of worth.

Heat and pressure transform the base matter of common coal into the crystalline perfection and rare value of the diamond. The same can be said of a person. We know that the multiple forces operating in the human soul are often not aligned with one another. We do the things we wish we would not do and do not do the things we know we should do. We want to be thin, but we sit on the couch eating Cheetos and despairing. We are directionless, confused, and paralyzed by indecision. We are pulled in all directions by temptations, despite our stated will, and we waste time, procrastinate, and feel terrible about it, but we do not change.

It was for such reasons that archaic people found it easy to believe that the human soul was haunted by ghosts—possessed by ancestral spirits, demons, and gods—none of whom necessarily had the best interests of the person at heart. Since the time of the psychoanalysts, these contrary forces, these obsessive and sometimes malevolent spirits, have been conceptualized psychologically as impulses, emotions, or motivational states—or as complexes, which act like partial personalities united within the person by memory but not by intent. Our neurological structure is indeed hierarchical. The powerful instinctual servants at the bottom, governing thirst, hunger, rage, sadness, elation, and lust, can easily ascend and become our masters, and just as easily wage war with one another. The resilience and strength of a united spirit is not easy to attain.

A house divided against itself, proverbially, cannot stand. Likewise, a poorly integrated person cannot hold himself together when challenged. He loses union at the highest level of psychological organization. He loses the properly balanced admixture of properties that is another feature of the well-tempered soul, and cannot hold his self together. We know this when we say "He lost it" or "He just fell apart." Before he picks up the pieces and rearranges them, such a person is likely to fall prey to domination by one or more partial personalities. This might be a spirit of rage, or anxiety, or pain, leaping in to occupy the person when his temper is lost. You can see this occurring most clearly in the case of a two-year-old having a tantrum. He has lost himself temporarily, and is for the moment pure emotion. This is an occurrence that is often deeply upsetting to the two-year-old himself, and one of an intensity that would be terrifying to beholders if manifested by an adult. The archaic motivational systems governing anger merely push the toddler's developing personality aside, and have their way with his mind and actions. This is a true and unfortunate defeat for the still-fragile centralizing ego, struggling against powerful forces toward psychological and social integration.

Lack of internal union also makes itself known in the increased suffering, magnification of anxiety, absence of motivation, and lack of pleasure that accompany indecision and uncertainty. The inability to decide among ten things, even when they are desirable, is equivalent to torment by all of them. Without clear, well-defined, and non-contradictory goals, the sense of positive engagement that makes life worthwhile is very difficult to obtain. Clear goals limit and simplify the world, as well, reducing uncertainty, anxiety, shame, and the self-devouring physiological forces unleashed by stress. The poorly integrated person is thus volatile and directionless—and this is only the beginning. Sufficient volatility and lack of direction can rapidly conspire to produce the helplessness and depression characteristic of prolonged futility. This is not merely a psychological state. The physical consequences of depression, often preceded by excess secretion of the stress hormone cortisol, are essentially indistinguishable from rapid aging (weight gain, cardiovascular problems, diabetes, cancer, and Alzheimer's).[1]

The social consequences are just as serious as the biological. A person who is not well put together overreacts to the slightest hint of frustration or failure. He cannot enter into productive negotiations, even with himself, because he cannot tolerate the uncertainty of discussing potential alternative futures. He cannot be pleased, because he cannot get what he wants, and he cannot get what he wants because he will not choose one thing instead of another. He can also be brought to a halt by the weakest of arguments. One of his multiple, warring subpersonalities will latch on to such arguments, often contrary to his best interest, and use them, in the form of doubts, to buttress its contrarian position. A deeply conflicted person can therefore be stopped, metaphorically, with the pressure of a single finger exerted on his chest (even though he may lash out against such an obstacle). To move forward with resolve, it is necessary to be organized—to be directed toward something singular and identifiable.

Aim. Point. All this is part of maturation and discipline, and something to be properly valued. If you aim at nothing, you become plagued by everything. If you aim at nothing, you have nowhere to go, nothing to do, and nothing of high value in your life, as value requires the ranking of options and sacrifice of the lower to the higher. Do you really want to be anything you could be? Is that not too much? Might it not be better to be something specific (and then, perhaps, to add to that)? Would that not come as a relief—even though it is also a sacrifice?

THE WORST DECISION OF ALL

When I was in graduate school at McGill University in Montreal studying for my clinical PhD, I noticed a pronounced improvement in character in everyone who continued in the progressively more difficult five- to six-year program. Their social skills improved. They became more articulate. They found a profound sense of personal purpose. They served a useful function in relation to others. They became more disciplined and organized. They had more fun. This was all despite the facts that the graduate courses were often of lower quality than they might have been, the clinical placements unpaid and difficult to come by, and the relationships with graduate supervisors sometimes (but by no means always) subpar. Those beginning graduate work were often still immature and confused. But the discipline imposed upon them by the necessity of research—and more particularly, thesis preparation—soon improved their characters. To write something long, sophisticated, and coherent means, at least in part, to become more complex, articulate, and deeper in personality.

When I became a professor and started mentoring undergraduate and graduate students, I observed the same thing. The undergrad psychology students who allied themselves with a lab (and therefore took on additional work) obtained better grades than those who burdened themselves less. Taking on the functions of junior researchers helped them establish a place and a community, while requiring them to discipline themselves, not least by necessitating more efficient use of their time. I observed a similar process when working as a clinical psychologist. I typically encouraged my clients to choose the best path currently available to them, even if it was far from their ideal. This sometimes meant tolerating at least a temporary decrease in ambition, or in pride, but had the advantage of substituting something real for something available only in fantasy. Improvements in mental health almost invariably followed.

Is there anything worth committing to? I am now old enough to have seen what happens when the various manners in which this question

might be answered manifest themselves. In my career as undergraduate, graduate student, professor, clinical psychologist, researcher, and
in my various additional forays, I have seen the same twin paths of
development manifest themselves repeatedly. Both are available, in
principle, to everyone—to each of the half-developed, wandering, prematurely cynical, questioning, doubtful, and hopeful fools that we all
are to varying degrees when young and on the brink of adulthood. It
has become self-evident to me that many commitments have enduring value: those of character, love, family, friendship, and career foremost among them (and perhaps in that order). Those who remain
unable or unwilling to establish a well-tended garden, so to speak, in
any or all those domains inevitably suffer because of it. However, commitment requires its pound of flesh. To pursue an undergraduate degree means sacrifice and study, and the choice of a given discipline
means forgoing the possibility of other pathways of study. The same
goes for selecting a partner or group of friends. Cynicism about such
things, or mere indecision or doubt, finds an easy but truly adversarial ally in the mindlessly nihilistic rationality that undermines everything: Why bother? What difference is it going to make in a thousand
years? What makes one pathway preferable to another—or to none—
anyway?

It is possible to be content, or even happy, with one partner or another, or with one group of friends or another, or with one career or
another. In some sense, the satisfaction that these arrangements bring
could have been generated by different choices. They are also each
deeply flawed: romantic partners can be fickle and complex, as can
friends, and every career or job is characterized by frustration, disappointment, corruption, arbitrary hierarchy, internal politics, and sheer
idiocy of decision making. We could conclude from that lack of spe-

cific or ideal value that nothing matters more than anything else—or
to draw the even more hopeless allied conclusion that nothing therefore matters at all. But those who draw such conclusions, no matter
how well armed they are with rationally coherent arguments, pay a
high price. People suffer for it if they quit before completing an undergraduate degree or the study of a trade. And this means "quit," not fail,
although the two can be difficult to distinguish. Sometimes people fail
because they just cannot manage the job, despite good intentions and
necessary discipline. It takes a certain verbal capacity to operate effectively as a lawyer, and a certain degree of facility with mechanical
objects, for example, to become a carpenter. Sometimes the match between person and choice is so poor that even commitment will not
suffice to bring about the desired end. But very often failure is a consequence of insufficient single-mindedness, elaborate but pointless
rationalization, and rejection of responsibility. And little good comes
of that.

People who do not choose a job or a career commonly become un-
moored and drift. They may attempt to justify that drifting with a
facade of romantic rebelliousness or prematurely world-weary cynicism. They may turn to casual identification with avant-garde artistic
exploration or treat the attendant despair and aimlessness with the
pursuit of hard-core alcohol and drug use and their instant gratifica-
tions. But none of that makes for a successful thirty-year-old (let alone
someone a decade older). The same holds true for people who cannot
choose and then commit to a single romantic partner, or are unable or
unwilling to be loyal to their friends. They become lonely, isolated,
and miserable, and all that merely adds the additional depth of bitterness to the cynicism that spurred the isolation in the first place. That
is not the sort of vicious circle that you want to characterize your life.

The people I knew who finished their undergraduate degrees or trade programs were better for it. Not "good," necessarily. Not functioning optimally. Not necessarily thrilled with their choices, or devoid of doubt and misgiving. Not even certain to continue in pursuit of what they had studied. But far better than those who withdrew and drifted. The commitments and the sacrifices thereby entailed matured those who endured and made them better people. So, what is the conclusion? There are many things to which we might commit ourselves. A case can be made for the arbitrary and even meaningless nature of any given commitment, given the plethora of alternatives, given the corruption of the systems demanding that commitment. But the same case cannot be made for the fact of commitment itself: Those who do not choose a direction are lost. It is far better to become something than to remain anything but become nothing. This is despite all the genuine limitations and disappointments that becoming something entails. Everywhere, the cynic despairs, are bad decisions. But someone who has transcended that cynicism (or more accurately, replaced it with an even more profound doubt—that is, the doubt that doubt itself is an ultimately reliable guide) objects: the worst decision of all is none.

DISCIPLINE AND UNITY

The discipline that enables concentration on one thing begins young. At a very early age, children begin to order the multiplicity of emotions and motivations that constitute their basic instincts of survival into the strategies of cooperation and competition that involve others, voluntarily—and children who are well constituted and fortunate manage this in a manner that is simultaneously socially desirable and psychologically healthy. When a child's self-directed experience is interrupted by the emergence of an instinctual system (when the child is hungry, angry, tired, or cold), the good parent steps in, solving the problem disrupting the child's fragile unity or, better yet, teaching the child to solve the problem himself. When the latter process has been completed with sufficient thoroughness, the child is ready to join the social world. This must happen by the age of four, or it may never happen.[2] A child must be sufficiently self-organizing to be desirable to his or her peers by the age of four or risk permanent social ostracism. A child who is still having temper tantrums by that age runs precisely that risk.

The process of integration is furthered by peers—friends—for the child well trained or fortunate enough to be accepted. When a child plays a game with others, she is disciplining herself. She is learning to subordinate all her competing impulses to the dictates of that game— one thing, despite the potential multiplicity of rules; learning to subjugate herself voluntarily to its rules and well-defined goals. To play in such a manner, she must transform herself into a functional subunit of a larger social machine. This can be interpreted as a sacrifice of individuality, if individuality is defined as limitless choice of impulsive gratification. But it is much more accurately *development* of individuality, considered at a higher level: the properly functioning and integrated individual tempers the desires of the present with the necessities of the future (including the necessity of playing well with others). It is in this manner that the multifarious games of childhood temper the screaming cacophony of late infancy. The payoff for such development is, of course, the security of social inclusion, and the pleasure of the game.

This, it should be noted, is not *repression*. This point must be made clear, as people believe that the things discipline imposed by choice prevents us from doing will somehow be lost forever. It is this belief, in large part—often expressed with regard to creativity—that makes so many parents afraid of damaging their children by disciplining them. But proper discipline organizes rather than destroys. A child terrified into obedience or shielded from every possible chance of misbehavior is not disciplined, but abused. A child who has been disciplined properly, by contrast—by parents, other adults, and most significantly, by other children—does not battle with, defeat, and then permanently *inhibit* her aggression. Such a child does not even sublimate that aggression, or transform it into something different. Instead, she integrates it into her increasingly sophisticated game-playing ability, allowing it to feed her competitiveness and heighten her attention, and making it serve the higher purposes of her developing psyche. A well-socialized child does not therefore lack aggression. *She just becomes extremely good at being aggressive*, transmuting what might otherwise be a disruptive drive into the focused perseverance and controlled competitiveness that make for a successful player. By the dawn of adolescence, such a child can organize herself into ever more complex games—joint, goal-directed activities that everyone plays voluntarily, and that everyone enjoys and benefits from, even if only one person or one team can win at a time. This ability is civilization itself in its nascent form, at the level of the individual player and group. This is where both cooperation and the opportunity to compete and win make themselves simultaneously manifest. This is all necessary preparation for the more permanent choices that must be made for a successful adulthood.

It is certainly possible—and reasonable—to have some doubt and to argue about which game might best be played here and now; but it is not reasonable to state that all games are therefore unnecessary.

Likewise, although it may be possible to argue about which morality is the *necessary* morality, it is not possible to argue that morality itself is thus unnecessary. Doubt about which game is appropriate right now is not relativism. It is the intelligent consideration of context. The fact that happiness is not appropriate, for example, at a funeral, does not mean that happiness itself lacks value. Likewise, the claim that morality is both necessary and inevitable is not totalitarian. It is merely the observation that basic, primitive unidimensional values must be subsumed under socially organized structures for peace and harmony to exist and be maintained. It was the bringing together of a warring multiplicity under the unifying doctrines of Christianity that civilized Europe. It could, perhaps, have been Buddhism, Confucianism, or Hinduism, insofar as the East is also both broadly civilized and unified. But it could not have been the absence of any doctrine whatsoever. Without a game, there is no peace, only chaos. Furthermore, the game that exists must be playable (as we discussed in Rule IV: Notice that opportunity lurks where responsibility has been abdicated). This means that it must be structured by a communally acceptable set of rules—by only those constraints that many people are willing to abide by, for a long time. It is possible that many such games exist, theoretically, but it is at least equally possible that there are only a few. In any case, the rules of Christianity and the rules of Buddhism are by no means arbitrary, by no means nonsensical superstition, any more than the rules of a playable game are merely arbitrary or nonsensically superstitious. To think that peace can exist without the overarching and voluntarily accepted game is to misunderstand the ever-present danger of the fragmented tribalism to which we can so easily and devastatingly regress.

Once the social world has forced the child to integrate his multiple subpersonalities, he can play with others. After that, he should be ready to engage in the more serious games that make up jobs or professions, with their highly structured expectations, skills, and rules. He must learn those, as well as—when older—the dance of the sexes. He must integrate his socialized personality with that of another, so that the couple he makes with that other can exist together peacefully, productively, within society, over the long term—while maintaining voluntary willingness to do so. This is the dual process of psychological and social integration that accompanies apprenticeship, all associated with the outsourcing of sanity. Adherence to this process will make him a socially sophisticated, productive, and psychologically healthy adult, capable of true reciprocity (and, perhaps, the temporary suspension of the demand of reciprocity necessary to raise children).

But the story of integration and socialization does not end here. This is because two things are happening at once, during an apprenticeship worthy of the name (just as learning to play a game and learning to be a good sport happen at the same time, while playing). Initially, the apprentice must become a servant of tradition, of structure, and of dogma, just as the child who wants to play must follow the rules of the game. At its best, this servitude means grateful alliance, in one form or another, with the institutions typically considered patriarchal. Apprenticeship means heat and pressure (as new workmen are tried by their peers, as articling law students are tried by their employers, as medical residents are tried by physicians, nurses, and patients). The goal of this heat and pressure is subordination of an undeveloped personality (by no means "individual" at this point) to a single path, for the purposes of transformation from undisciplined beginner to accomplished master.

The master, who is the rightful product of apprenticeship, is, however, no longer the servant of dogma. Instead, he is now himself served by dogma, which he has the responsibility to maintain as well as the right to change, when change is necessary. This makes the master, who once allowed himself to be enslaved, an emergent follower of spirit—the wind (spirit) that bloweth where it listeth (John 3:8). The master can allow himself his intuitions, as the knowledge obtained by the discipline he has acquired will enable him to criticize his own ideas and assess their true value. He may therefore more clearly perceive the fundamental patterns or principles that underlie the dogmas of his discipline, and draw inspiration from those, instead of blindly adhering to the rules as currently articulated or embodied. He may even rely on the integrated union of his personality and his training to modify or transform even those more fundamental, deeply intuited principles, in the service of an even higher union.

DOGMA AND SPIRIT

The limiting disciplines that serve both as precondition for a game and for the development of a unity of being can usefully be considered Thou Shalt Nots—rules that highlight what is definitely not to be done, while whatever is supposed to be done is taking place. Abiding by these rules produces a development of character—character with a particular nature or essence (we have already discussed this as, say, the development of personal desirability as a player of many games, or sequences of games). As is the case in many other situations, it appears that this idea is already implicit in the stories that make up the bedrock of our culture. This is particularly evident in the Gospel of Mark, which is a commentary on what are among the most influential Rules of the Game ever formulated—the Mosaic Ten Commandments (and, even more broadly, a commentary on rules themselves). The commandments follow:

1. Though shalt have no other gods before me.
2. Though shalt not make unto thee any graven image.
3. Thou shalt not take the name of the Lord thy God in vain.
4. Remember the sabbath day, to keep it holy.
5. Honor thy father and thy mother.
6. Thou shalt not kill.
7. Thou shalt not commit adultery.
8. Thou shalt not steal.
9. Thou shalt not bear false witness against thy neighbor.
10. Thou shalt not covet.

The first speaks to the necessity of aiming at the highest possible unity; the second to the danger of worshipping false idols (by confusing the representation, or the image, with the ineffable it is supposed to represent); the third means that it is wrong to claim moral inspiration from God while knowingly committing sinful acts; the fourth means that it is necessary to leave time to regularly consider what is truly valuable or sacred; the fifth keeps families together, mandating honor, respect, and gratitude from children as just reward for the sacrifices made by parents; the sixth prevents murder (obviously) but, by doing so, also protects the community from potential descent into constant and potentially multigenerational feuding; the seventh mandates the sacredness of the marriage vow, predicated on the assumption (like the fifth) that the stability and value of the family is of paramount importance; the eighth allows for honest, hardworking people to reap the benefits of their efforts without fear that what they have produced will be taken from them arbitrarily (and, thereby, makes civilized society a possibility); the ninth maintains the integrity of the law, reducing or eliminating its use as a weapon; and the tenth is a reminder that envy and the resentment it breeds is a destructive force of the highest power.

It is worthwhile thinking of these Commandments as a minimum set of rules for a stable society—an iterable social game. The Commandments are rules established in the book of Exodus, and part of that unforgettable story. But they are also pointers to something else—something that simultaneously emerges from and transcends the rules and constitutes their essence. The core idea is this: subjugate yourself voluntarily to a set of socially determined rules—those with some tradition in their formulation—and a unity that transcends the rules will emerge. That unity constitutes what you could be, if you concentrate on a particular goal and see it through.

There is a story relevant to this idea in the Gospel of Mark. The pertinent section begins with Christ journeying to the temple of Jerusalem, where He casts out the moneychangers and merchants and addresses the crowd with an irresistible charisma. And, as the tale goes, "the scribes and chief priests heard it, and sought how they might destroy him: for they feared him, because all the people was astonished at his doctrine" (Mark 11:18). In consequence, they begin to conspire, questioning this strange prophet, hoping to entice Him into a heretical and therefore potentially fatal statement, sending to Him "certain of the Pharisees and of the Herodians, to catch him in his words" (Mark 12:13). Christ deals masterfully, to say the least, with the questioners, reducing them to an aggrieved and resentful silence. The section ends with what is arguably the most difficult and treacherous of questions, posed by a particularly cunning but also perhaps begrudgingly admiring interlocutor (Mark 12:28–34):

> And one of the scribes came, and having heard them reasoning together, and perceiving that he had answered them well, asked him, Which is the first commandment of all?
>
> And Jesus answered him, The first of all the commandments is, Hear, O Israel; The Lord our God is one Lord:
>
> And thou shalt love the Lord thy God with all thy heart, and with all thy soul, and with all thy mind, and with all thy strength: this is the first commandment.
>
> And the second is like, namely this, Thou shalt love thy neighbor as thyself. There is none other commandment greater than these.
>
> And the scribe said unto him, Well, Master, thou hast said the truth: for there is one God; and there is none other but he:
>
> And to love him with all the heart, and with all the understanding, and with all the soul, and with all the strength, and to love his neighbor as himself, is more than all whole burnt offerings and sacrifices.
>
> And when Jesus saw that he answered discreetly, he said unto him, Thou art not far from the kingdom of God. And no man after that durst ask him any question.

What does this all mean? The personality integrated by disciplined adherence to a set of appropriate rules is simultaneously (although perhaps unknowingly) guided by or imitating the highest possible ideal—precisely that ideal that constitutes whatever common element of "moral" makes all the rules good, just, and necessary. That ideal, according to Christ's answer, is something singular (the "one Lord"), thoroughly embodied (loved with "all thy heart," "soul," "understanding," and "strength"), and then manifested as a love that is identical for self and all mankind.

Western culture is "unconsciously" underpinned by a very profound drama, reflecting all this, because of its origin in Judeo-Christian conceptualization. Psychologically speaking, Christ is a representation, or an embodiment, of the mastery of dogma and the (consequent) emergence of spirit. Spirit is the creative force that gives rise to what becomes dogma, with time. Spirit is also that which constantly transcends such time-honored tradition, when possible. It is for this reason that an apprenticeship ends with a masterpiece, the creation of which signifies not only the acquisition of the requisite skill, but the acquisition of the ability to create new skills.

Although Christ commits many acts that might be considered revolutionary, as we discussed in Rule I, He is nonetheless explicitly portrayed in the Gospels as the master of tradition, and says of Himself, "Think not that I am come to destroy the law, or the prophets: I am not come to destroy, but to fulfill" (Matthew 5:17, KJV). The New International Version of the Bible perhaps puts it more comprehensibly: "Do not think that I have come to abolish the Law or the Prophets; I have not come to abolish them but to fulfill them." Christ therefore presents Himself as both the product of tradition, and the very thing that creates and transforms it. The same pattern of creative conflict pervades the Old Testament, which is in large part a series of stories about the spirit in prophetic opposition to the inevitable corruption of dogma harnessed to serve power. It is the personality who mimics that model who might be regarded as truly Western, in the deepest of psychological senses.

If you work as hard as you can on one thing, you will change. You will start to also become one thing, instead of the clamoring multitude you once were. That one thing, developed properly, is not only the disciplined entity formed by sacrifice, commitment, and concentration. It is that which creates, destroys, and transforms discipline itself—civilization itself—by expressing its unity of personality and society. It is the very Word of truth, upon whose function all habitable order, wrenched out of chaos, eternally depends.

Work as hard as you possibly can on at least one thing and see what happens.

TRY TO MAKE ONE ROOM IN YOUR HOME AS BEAUTIFUL AS POSSIBLE

CLEANING YOUR ROOM IS NOT ENOUGH

I have become known for encouraging people to clean up their rooms. Perhaps that is because I am serious about that prosaic piece of advice, and because I know that it is a much more difficult task than it appears. I have been unsuccessfully cleaning up my room, by the way—my home office (which I generally keep in relatively pristine condition)—for about three years now. My life was thrown into such chaos over that period by the multitude of changes I experienced—political controversies, transformation of career, endless travel, mountains of mail, the sequence of illnesses—that I simply became overwhelmed. The disorganization was heightened by the fact that my wife and I had just finished having much of our house renovated, and everything we could not find a proper place for ended up in my office.

There is a meme floating around the internet, accusing me of hypocrisy on account of this: a still taken from a video I shot in my office, with a fair bit of mess in the background (and I cannot say that I look much better myself). Who am I to tell people to clean up their rooms before attempting to fix the rest of the world when, apparently, I cannot do it myself? And there is something directly synchronistic and meaningful about that objection, because I am not in proper order at that moment myself, and my condition undoubtedly found its reflection in the state of my office. More piled up every day, as I traveled, and everything collected around me. I plead exceptional circumstances, and I put many other things in order during the time my office was degenerating, but I still have a moral obligation to get back in there and put it right. And the problem is not just that I want to clean up the mess. I also want to make it beautiful: my room, my house, and then, perhaps, in whatever way I can manage, the community. God knows it is crying out for it.

Making something beautiful is difficult, but it is amazingly worthwhile. If you learn to make something in your life truly beautiful—even one thing—then you have established a relationship with beauty. From there you can begin to expand that relationship out into other elements of your life and the world. That is an invitation to the divine. That is the reconnection with the immortality of childhood, and the true beauty and majesty of the Being you can no longer see. You must be daring to try that.

If you study art (and literature and the humanities), you do it so that you can familiarize yourself with the collected wisdom of our civilization. This is a very good idea—a veritable necessity—because people have been working out how to live for a long time. What they have produced is strange but also rich beyond comparison, so why not use it as a guide? Your vision will be grander and your plans more comprehensive. You will consider other people more intelligently and completely. You will take care of yourself more effectively. You will understand the present more profoundly, rooted as it is in the past, and you will come to conclusions much more carefully. You will come to treat the future, as well, as a more concrete reality (because you will have developed some true sense of time) and be less likely to sacrifice it to impulsive pleasure. You will develop some depth, gravitas, and true thoughtfulness. You will speak more precisely, and other people will become more likely to listen to and cooperate productively with you, as you will with them. You will become more your own person, and less a dull and hapless tool of peer pressure, vogue, fad, and ideology.

Buy a piece of art. Find one that speaks to you and make the purchase. If it is a genuine artistic production, it will invade your life and change it. A real piece of art is a window into the transcendent, and you need that in your life, because you are finite and limited and bounded by your ignorance. Unless you can make a connection to the transcendent, you will not have the strength to prevail when the challenges of life become daunting. You need to establish a link with what is beyond you, like a man overboard in high seas requires a life preserver, and the invitation of beauty into your life is one means by which that may be accomplished.

It is for such reasons that we need to understand the role of art, and stop thinking about it as an option, or a luxury, or worse, an affectation. Art is the bedrock of culture itself. It is the foundation of the process by which we unite ourselves psychologically, and come to establish productive peace with others. As it is said, "Man shall not live by bread alone" (Matthew 4:4). That is exactly right. We live by beauty. We live by literature. We live by art. We cannot live without some connection to the divine—and beauty is divine—because in its absence life is too short, too dismal, and too tragic. And we must be sharp and awake and prepared so that we can survive properly, and

orient the world properly, and not destroy things, including ourselves—
and beauty can help us appreciate the wonder of Being and motivate
us to seek gratitude when we might otherwise be prone to destructive
resentment.

MEMORY AND VISION

The pride of the peacock is the glory of God.
The lust of the goat is the bounty of God.
The wrath of the lion is the wisdom of God.
The nakedness of woman is the work of God.
Excess of sorrow laughs. Excess of joy weeps.
The roaring of lions, the howling of wolves, the raging of the
    stormy sea, and the destructive sword, are portions of
    eternity too great for the eye of man.

—WILLIAM BLAKE, FROM "PROVERBS OF HELL,"
The Marriage of Heaven and Hell

When I was a child, I knew the contours and details of all the houses
in my immediate neighborhood. I knew the back alleys, the places behind the fences, the location of each crack in the pavement, and the
shortcuts that could be taken from one place to another. My geographical locale was not large, but I had explored it thoroughly and my
knowledge of it was very detailed. Now that I am an adult, the same is
not true. I lived in Fairview, the town I grew up in for most of my
childhood and adolescence, for only nine years, but I am still able to
picture in high resolution the street I lived on. I have lived in Toronto,
on the same street, for more than twice as long, but I still have only a
vague sense of the houses that surround mine.

I do not think that is a good thing. I feel far less at home because of it.

It is as if when I walk down the street and glance at a local house, I think of "house" as an icon (because, really, what practical difference does it make to me what particularities characterize each house?), and then my attention is turned to something else. I do not see the house, with its specific shingles, colors, flowers, and architectural details, despite the interest that might have been elicited in me had I paid careful attention. By this point in my life, I have seen so many houses in so many places that I know what a house is likely to do when I walk by it—which is very little. Thus, I ignore the engaging idiosyncrasies and beauties of its details—its unique character, for better or worse—and see just enough to stay oriented as I walk past and continue to think and be elsewhere as I do so. There is real loss in that. I am simply *not there* in my adult neighborhood the same way I was as a child in my home-town. I am separated from the reality of the world. And a very deep feeling of belonging is missing in some important way because of that.

Perception has been replaced for me with functional, pragmatic memory. This has made me more efficient, in some ways, but the cost is an impoverished experience of the richness of the world. I remember when I started working as a junior professor in Boston, when my kids were about two and three years old. I was very preoccupied with my work, trying to keep up, trying to advance my career, trying to make enough money to support my family on a single income. I would come home and take a walk with Tammy and our children, Mikhaila and Julian. I found it very difficult to remain patient with them. I had too much work to do, always—or believed I did—and had disciplined myself through years of effort to focus continually on that. If we went for a walk, I wanted to know exactly where we were going, just how long it would take to get there, and precisely when we were going back. This is no attitude to adopt when trying to have a pleasant and reasonable time with toddlers. Not if you want to immerse yourself in the experience. Not if you want to watch and participate in the pleasure they take in their timeless discovery. Not unless you want to risk missing something of crucial import.

It was very difficult for me to relax and focus on the present and watch my little kids pursue their meandering route through the neighborhood, with no particular destination, purpose, or schedule in mind, engaging themselves deeply in an encounter with a local dog, bug, or earthworm, or in some game they invented on the way. Now and then, however, I could snap briefly into that same frame of reference (that is one of the wonderful gifts provided by young children) and see the pristine world they inhabited, still untrammeled by practiced and efficient memory, capable of producing pure joy in the newness of everything. But I was still possessed enough by my future concerns to be involuntarily pulled back into intense preoccupation with getting the next thing done.

I knew perfectly well that I was missing out on beauty and meaning and engagement, regardless of whatever advantages in efficiency my impatience brought. I was narrow, sharp, and focused, and did not waste time, but the price I paid for that was the blindness demanded by efficiency, accomplishment, and order. I was no longer seeing the world. I was seeing only the little I needed to navigate it with maximum speed and lowest cost. None of that was surprising. I had the responsibilities of an adult. I had a demanding job. I had to take care of my family, and that meant sacrificing the present and attending to the future. But having little children around and noticing their intense preoccupation with the present, and their fascination with what was directly around them, made me very conscious of the loss that accompanied maturity. Great poets are expressly aware of this, and they do what they can to remind the rest of us:

There was a time when meadow, grove, and stream,
The earth, and every common sight,
To me did seem
Apparelled in celestial light,
The glory and the freshness of a dream.
It is not now as it hath been of yore;—
Turn wheresoe'er I may,
By night or day.
The things which I have seen I now can see no more. . . .
Ye blessèd creatures, I have heard the call
Ye to each other make; I see
The heavens laugh with you in your jubilee;
My heart is at your festival,
My head hath its coronal,
The fulness of your bliss, I feel—I feel it all.
Oh evil day! if I were sullen
While Earth herself is adorning,
This sweet May-morning,
And the Children are culling
On every side,
In a thousand valleys far and wide,
Fresh flowers; while the sun shines warm,
And the Babe leaps up on his Mother's arm:—
I hear, I hear, with joy I hear!
—But there's a Tree, of many, one,
A single field which I have looked upon,
Both of them speak of something that is gone;
The Pansy at my feet
Doth the same tale repeat:

Whither is fled the visionary gleam?
Where is it now, the glory and the dream?

—WILLIAM WORDSWORTH, "ODE: INTIMATIONS OF IMMORTALITY
FROM RECOLLECTIONS OF EARLY CHILDHOOD"

Some, in fact, never lose the glorious vision of childhood. This is particularly true of artists (and, indeed, seems a vital part of what makes them artists). William Blake, the English painter, printmaker, and poet, appears to have been one such person. He inhabited a uniquely visionary world. Blake perceived something closer to what the philosopher Immanuel Kant termed "the thing in itself"[1] than do most mortals, left as we are with the pale reflection of our surroundings that our increasingly restricted mature perceptions deliver to us. Blake was also exquisitely sensitive to the metaphoric or dramatic significance of each apparently isolated event—the manner in which each event is rife with endless poetically echoing connotations:

Every Farmer Understands
Every Tear from Every Eye
Becomes a Babe in Eternity
This is caught by Females bright
And returnd to its own delight
The Bleat the Bark Bellow & Roar
Are Waves that Beat on Heavens Shore
The Babe that weeps the Rod beneath
Writes Revenge in realms of Death
The Beggars Rags fluttering in Air
Does to Rags the Heavens tear
The Soldier armd with Sword & Gun

Palsied strikes the Summers Sun
The poor Mans Farthing is worth more
Than all the Gold on Africs Shore
One Mite wrung from the Labrers hands
Shall buy & sell the Misers Lands
Or if protected from on high
Does that whole Nation sell & buy
He who mocks the Infants Faith
Shall be mockd in Age & Death
He who shall teach the Child to Doubt
The rotting Grave shall neer get out
He who respects the Infants faith
Triumphs over Hell & Death

—WILLIAM BLAKE, "AUGURIES OF INNOCENCE" (LINES 67–90)

The vision of a true artist such as Blake is truly too much, because what is beyond our memory-restricted perceptions is too much. It is the unfathomable totality of the world, past, present, and future bound up together: every level connected to every other level, nothing existing in isolation, everything implying something vital but beyond our comprehension, and all of it speaking of the overwhelming mystery of Being. The visionary concentrates on something we all see, hypothetically: a vase of flowers, perhaps, in all its complexity and beauty, each bloom springing forth out of nothingness, before its dissolution and return; a haystack in the spring, and its appearance in the summer, autumn, and winter, observing and portraying the absolute mystery of its existence, with its different shades of light and color, as well as the underlying commonality of form, which we can easily confuse with the full and incomprehensible actuality of what is there.

How do you know but ev'ry Bird that cuts the airy way, Is an immense world of delight, clos'd by your senses five?

—WILLIAM BLAKE, FROM "A MEMORABLE FANCY,"
The Marriage of Heaven and Hell

To perceive Van Gogh's painting *Irises*—from which the illustration that begins this chapter is derived—is, for example, to gaze through a window back into the eternity that our perceptions once revealed, so that we can remember how awe inspiring and miraculous the world really is, under the mundane familiarity to which we have reduced it. To share in the artist's perception reunites us with the source of inspiration that can rekindle our delight in the world, even if the drudgery and repetition of daily life has reduced what we see to the narrowest and most pragmatic of visions.

> But for those first affections,
> Those shadowy recollections,
> Which, be they what they may
> Are yet the fountain-light of all our day,
> Are yet a master-light of all our seeing;
> Uphold us, cherish, and have power to make
> Our noisy years seem moments in the being
> Of the eternal Silence: truths that wake,
> To perish never;
> Which neither listlessness, nor mad endeavour,
> Nor Man nor Boy,
> Nor all that is at enmity with joy,
> Can utterly abolish or destroy!

—WILLIAM WORDSWORTH, "ODE: INTIMATIONS OF IMMORTALITY
FROM RECOLLECTIONS OF EARLY CHILDHOOD"

All of this is very frightening. It is frightening to perceive the shells of ourselves that we have become. It is frightening to glimpse, even for a moment, the transcendent reality that exists beyond. We think we border our great paintings with luxurious, elaborate frames to glorify them, but we do it at least as much to insist to ourselves that the glory of the painting itself ends at the frame. That bounding, that bordering, leaves the world we are familiar with comfortably intact and unchanged. We do not want that beauty reaching out past the limitations imposed on it and disturbing everything that is familiar.

We do the same with museums, those asylums for genius: we isolate everything that is great—everything that could in principle be distributed throughout the world. Why cannot every small town have a shrine devoted to one great piece of art, instead of having every piece collected in a manner impossible for anyone ever to take in at once? Is not one masterpiece enough for a room, or even for a building? Ten great works of art, or a hundred, in a single room is absurd, given that each is a world in and of itself. Such mass collection is a degrading of the unique singular particularity and worth of what is priceless and irreplaceable. It is fear that entices us to imprison art. And no wonder.

> Have you reckon'd a thousand acres much? have you reckon'd
>   the earth much?
> Have you practis'd so long to learn to read?
> Have you felt so proud to get at the meaning of poems?
> Stop this day and night with me and you shall possess the
>   origin of all poems,
> You shall possess the good of the earth and sun, (there are
>   millions of suns left,)
> You shall no longer take things at second or third hand, nor

look through the eyes of the dead, nor feed on the
    spectres in books,
You shall not look through my eyes either, nor take things
    from me,
You shall listen to all sides and filter them from your self.

—WALT WHITMAN, "SONG OF MYSELF"

It can be overwhelming to open ourselves up to the beauty in the world that we as adults have painted over with simplicity. In not doing so, however—in not taking a proper walk with a young child, for example—we lose track of the grandeur and the awe the untrammeled world is constantly capable of producing, and reduce our lives to bleak necessity.

THE LAND YOU KNOW, THE LAND YOU DO NOT KNOW, AND THE LAND YOU CANNOT EVEN IMAGINE

You inhabit the land you know, pragmatically and conceptually. But imagine what lies just outside of that. There exists an immense space of things you do not know, but which other people might comprehend, at least in part. Then, outside of what anyone knows, there is the space of things that no one at all knows. Your world is known territory, surrounded by the relatively unknown, surrounded by the absolutely unknown—surrounded, even more distantly, by the absolutely unknowable. Together, that is the canonical, archetypal landscape. The unknown manifests itself to you in the midst of the known. That revelation—sometimes exciting, but often quite painful—is the source of new knowledge. But a fundamental question remains: How is that knowledge generated? What is comprehended and understandable does not just leap in one fell swoop from the absolutely unknown to the thoroughly and self-evidently articulated. Knowledge must pass through many stages of analysis—a multitude of transformations—before it becomes, let us say, commonplace.

The first stage is that of pure action—reflex action, at the most basic of levels.[2] If something surprises you, you react to it first with your body. You crouch defensively, or freeze, or run away in panic. Those are all forms of representation and categorization, in nascent form. Crouch means predatory attack. Freeze means predatory threat. Panic means terror necessitating escape. The world of possibility begins to actualize itself with such instinctual, embodied action, unconscious and uncontrollable. The first realization of possibility, of potential, is not conceptual. It is embodied, but it is still representational. (It is no longer the thing in itself we referred to earlier, but the transmutation of that thing into a commensurate physical response. That is a *representation*.)

Maybe you are at home, at night. Assume you are alone. It is dark and late. An unexpected noise startles you, and you freeze. That is the first transmutation: unknown noise (a pattern) to frozen position. Then your heart rate rises, in preparation for (unspecified) action.[3] That is the second transmutation. You are preparing to move. Next, your imagination populates the darkness with whatever might be making the noise.[4] That is the third transmutation, part of a complete and practical sequence: embodied responses (freezing and heart-rate increase) and then imagistic, imaginative representation. The latter is part of exploration, which you might extend by overcoming your terror and the freezing associated with it (assuming nothing else too unexpected happens) and investigating the locale, once a part of your friendly house, from where the noise appeared to emanate. You have now engaged in active exploration—a precursor to direct perception (hopefully nothing too dramatic); then to explicit knowledge of the source; and then back to routine and complacent peace, if the noise proves to be nothing of significance. That is how information moves from the unknown to the known. (Except that sometimes the noise does not prove insignificant. Then there is trouble.)

Artists are the people who stand on the frontier of the transformation of the unknown into knowledge. They make their voluntary foray out into the unknown, and they take a piece of it and transform it into an image. Maybe they do it through choreography and dance—by representing the manifestation of the world in physical display, communicable, although not in words, to others. Maybe they do it by acting, which is a sophisticated form of embodiment and imitation, or by painting or sculpting. Perhaps they manage it through screenwriting, or by penning a novel. After all that come the intellectuals, with philosophy and criticism, abstracting and articulating the work's representations and rules.

Consider the role that creative people play in cities. They are typically starving a bit, because it is virtually impossible to be commercially successful as an artist, and that hunger is partly what motivates them (do not underestimate the utility of necessity). In their poverty, they explore the city, and they discover some ratty, quasi-criminal area that has seen better days. They visit, look, and poke about, and they think, "You know, with a little work, this area could be cool." Then they move in, piece together some galleries, and put up some art. They do not make any money, but they civilize the space a bit. In doing so, they elevate and transform what is too dangerous into something cutting edge. Then a coffee shop pops up, and maybe an unconventional clothing store. The next thing you know, the gentrifiers move in. They are creative types, too, but more conservative (less desperate, perhaps; more risk averse, at least—so they are not the first ones on the edge of the frontier). Then the developers show up. And then the chain stores appear, and the middle or upper class establishes itself. Then the artists have to move, because they can no longer afford the rent. That is a loss for the avant-garde, but it is okay, even though it is harsh, because with all that stability and predictability the artists should not be there anymore. They need to rejuvenate some other area. They need another vista to conquer. That is their natural environment.

That edge, where artists are always transforming chaos into order, can be a very rough and dangerous place. Living there, an artist constantly risks falling fully into the chaos, instead of transforming it. But artists have always lived there, on the border of human understanding. Art bears the same relationship to society that the dream bears to mental life. You are very creative when you are dreaming. That is why, when you remember a dream, you think, "Where in the world did that come from?" It is very strange and incomprehensible that something can happen in your head, and you have no idea how it got there or what it means. It is a miracle: nature's voice manifesting itself in your psyche. And it happens every night. Like art, the dream mediates between order and chaos. So, it is half chaos. That is why it is not comprehensible. It is a vision, not a fully fledged articulated production. Those who actualize those half-born visions into artistic productions are those who begin to transform what we do not understand into what we can at least start to see. That is the role of the artist, occupying the vanguard. That is their biological niche. They are the initial civilizing agents.

The artists do not understand full well what they are doing. They cannot, if they are doing something genuinely new. Otherwise, they could just say what they mean and have done with it. They would not require expression in dance, music, and image. But they are guided by feel, by intuition—by their facility with the detection of patterns—and that is all embodied, rather than articulated, at least in its initial stages. When creating, the artists are struggling, contending, and wrestling with a problem—maybe even a problem they do not fully understand—and striving to bring something new into clear focus. Otherwise they are mere propagandists, reversing the artistic process, attempting to transform something they can already articulate into image and art for the purpose of rhetorical and ideological victory. That is a great sin, harnessing the higher for the purposes of the lower. It is a totalitarian tactic, the subordination of art and literature to politics (or the purposeful blurring of the distinction between them).

Artists must be contending with something they do not understand, or they are not artists. Instead, they are posers, or romantics (often romantic failures), or narcissists, or actors (and not in the creative sense). They are likely, when genuine, to be idiosyncratically and peculiarly obsessed by their intuition—possessed by it, willing to pursue it even in the face of opposition and the overwhelming likelihood of rejection, criticism, and practical and financial failure. When they are successful they make the world more understandable (sometimes replacing something more "understood," but now anachronistic, with something new and better). They move the unknown closer to the conscious, social, and articulated world. And then people gaze at those artworks, watch the dramas, and listen to the stories, and they start to become informed by them, but they do not know how or why. And people find great value in it—more value, perhaps, than in anything else. There is good reason that the most expensive artifacts in the world—those that are literally, or close to literally, priceless—are great works of art.

I once visited the Metropolitan Museum of Art in New York. It contained a collection of great and famous Renaissance paintings—each worth hundreds of millions of dollars, assuming they were ever made available for purchase. The area containing them was a shrine, a place of the divine—for believers and atheists alike. It was in the most expensive and prestigious of museums, located on real estate of the highest quality and desirability, in what might well be the most active and exciting city in the world. The collection had been put together over a great expanse of time, and with much difficulty. The gallery was packed with people, many of whom had voyaged there as part of what must be most properly regarded as a pilgrimage.

I asked myself, "What are these people up to, coming to this place, so carefully curated, traveling these great distances, looking at these paintings? And what do they believe they are up to?" One painting featured the Immaculate Conception of Mary, brilliantly composed. The Mother of God was rising to heaven, in a beatific state, encapsulated in a mandorla of clouds, embedded with the faces of putti. Many of the people gathered were gazing, enraptured, at the work. I thought, "They do not know what that painting means. They do not understand the symbolic meaning of the mandorla, or the significance of the putti, or the idea of the glorification of the Mother of God. And God, after all, is dead—or, so goes the story. Why does the painting nonetheless retain its value? Why is it in this room, in this building, with these other paintings, in this city—carefully guarded, not to be touched? Why is this painting—and all these others—beyond price and desired by those who already have everything? Why are these creations stored so carefully in a modern shrine, and visited by people from all over the world, as if it were a duty—even as if it were desirable or necessary?"

We treat these objects as if they are sacred. At least that is what our actions in their vicinity suggest. We gaze at them in ignorance and wonder, and remember what we have forgotten; perceiving, ever so dimly, what we can no longer see (what we are perhaps no longer willing to see). The unknown shines through the productions of great artists in partially articulated form. The awe-inspiring ineffable begins to be realized but retains a terrifying abundance of its transcendent power. That is the role of art, and that is the role of artists. It is no wonder we keep their dangerous, magical productions locked up, framed, and apart from everything else. And if a great piece is damaged anywhere, the news spreads worldwide. We feel a tremor run through the bedrock of our culture. The dream upon which our reality depends shakes and moves. We find ourselves unnerved.

ONE ROOM

I live with my wife in a small semidetached house, with a living room that cannot be larger than 12' x 12'. But we worked to make that room extremely beautiful, while endeavoring to do the same with the rest of the house. In the living room hung some large paintings (not to everyone's taste, certainly: they were Soviet realist/impressionist pieces, some illustrating the Second World War, some representing the triumph of communism), as well as a variety of cubist miniatures and South American pieces heavily influenced by the native tradition. Prior to our recent renovations the room had held at least twenty-five paintings, including about fifteen smaller pieces (12" x 12"). There was even one—reminiscent of a medieval etching, although painted on canvas—on the ceiling, where I had attached it with magnets. It was from a Romanian church. The largest was 6' high and about 8' wide. (I know perfectly well that aggregating all these paintings together in such a small space contradicts my earlier point about devoting a room or even a building to a single work of art, but I have only a single house, so I plead necessity: If I wanted to collect paintings, they had to be put where I was able to put them.) In the rest of the house, we used thirty-six different colors, and a variety of different glosses on the walls and the trim throughout the building—all from a palette that matched a large realist painting of a railway yard in Chicago in the 1950s, created by the same artist who helped us plan and then renovate our home.

I bought the Soviet pieces on eBay from Ukrainian junk dealers specializing in Soviet-era artifacts. At one point, I had a network of about twenty people in the Ukraine sending me photographs of whatever paintings they had scrounged from the ruins of the Soviet bureaucracy. Most were awful. But some were amazing. I have a great painting, for example, of Yuri Gagarin, the first man in space, standing in front of a rocket and a radar installation, and another from the 1970s of a lonesome soldier writing his mother in front of a large radio. It is really something to see relatively modern events memorialized in oil by talented artists. (The Soviets kept their academies functioning continuously from the nineteenth century onward and, although tremendous restrictions were placed on what could be produced, those who passed through them became highly skilled painters.)

The Soviet paintings eventually took over our house. Most of them were small and insanely inexpensive, and I bought dozens of them. The Soviet era produced its own impressionism, often depicting landscapes, rougher and harsher than the classic French versions but much to my taste and reminiscent of where I grew up in western Canada. While seeking them out, I exposed myself to a larger number of paintings, I like to think, than anyone else in history. For at least four years, starting in 2001, I searched eBay, looking at roughly a thousand paintings a day,* seeking the one or two in that number that were of genuine

---

*So that's 1,000 pictures of paintings x 300 days per year x 4 = 1,200,000 paintings. That has to be some sort of record (not that it matters, but it's comical to consider), mostly because I do not think it would have been possible to see that many paintings before internet technology made massive databases possible.

quality. It was most often a Russian or Soviet landscape selling for a song—better paintings than I had ever seen in galleries or museum collections in Toronto. I would place them in a list of items I was interested in—an eBay feature—print them out, lay them on the floor, and then ask my wife, Tammy, to help me narrow my choices. She has a good eye and a fair bit of training as an artist. We would discard anything we found to be flawed and purchase what remained. Because of this, my kids grew up surrounded by art, and it certainly left an impression. Many of my paintings now hang in their respective dwellings. (They tended to avoid the more political Soviet propaganda, which I was interested in because of its historical significance and because of the ongoing war on the canvases between art—a consequence of the painter's undeniable talent—and the propaganda that art was doomed to serve. I can tell you that the art shines through the propaganda as the years pass by. That is something very interesting to observe.)

I also tried, at about that time, to make my university office beautiful. After I was transferred from an office I had already put some work into, the same artist who helped redesign the interior of our house (and from whom I also purchased many large paintings, which also hang in our house) tried to help me transform my new factory-like, fluorescent-lit catastrophe of a 1970s sealed-windows hellhole office into something that someone with some sense could sit in for thirty years without wanting to die. Faculty members were forbidden to undertake any major modifications to these spaces, due to union requirements (or administration interpretations of those requirements). So, my artist friend and I devised an alternate plan.

We decided to insert some heavy, nickel-plated hooks into the cinderblock, in pairs about four feet apart and seven feet above the ground, and then to hang from those hooks good three-quarter-inch sanded and stained wood sheets with cherry veneer on one side. Voila:

wood-paneled office, for the cost of about eight seventy-five-dollar pieces of plywood, plus some labor. We were going to install these on a weekend, when there was no one else around. Then we planned to paint the drop ceilings (carefully, as asbestos lurked above the tiles). Hell is a place of drop ceilings, rusted ventilation grates, and fluorescent lights; the dismal ugliness and dreariness and general depression of spirit that results from these cost-saving features no doubt suppresses productivity far more than the cheapest of architectural tricks and the most deadening of lights saves money. Everyone looks like a corpse under fluorescents. Penny-wise and pound-foolish indeed.

We were going to paint the ceiling with a paint called Hammerite, which looks like beaten metal once it dries. That would have transformed the unavoidable industrial aesthetic, which can be attractive if handled wisely, into something thoughtful and unique. This could also have been done for minimal cost. A good carpet, perhaps Persian (also very inexpensive on eBay), some reasonably high-quality curtains, and a decent industrial desk: one weekend of secretive work, and an office that a civilized person could inhabit without resentment and self-contempt.

But I made a fatal error. I spoke to one of the senior administrators of the psychology department about my plans. She and I had previously discussed the sheer ugliness of the floor our area inhabited and the dismal state of all the offices, and I thought we had established consensus that improvement was warranted. I assumed she was on board. We had even talked about transforming her corner office. I began to excitedly share my intentions. She looked displeased instead of happy, and said unexpectedly, "You cannot do that." I shook my head in disbelief and thought: "What? I am planning to make something exceedingly ugly better, quickly, with no trouble, for no money to speak of—and your response is, 'You cannot do that!?'" I said, "What do you mean?"

She said, "Well, if you do it, everyone else will want to do it." Four responses flashed through my mind: One: "No, they would not." Two: "Everyone *could* do it, because it would be dirt cheap." Three: "I thought we were sane adults, having a productive conversation about improving something important in a university, but we are actually children squabbling in a kindergarten playground." Four: "I thought I was speaking with someone sane and reasonable, but I was clearly wrong." She finished the conversation with a direct threat: "Do not push me on this." Stupid me. I asked for permission. (Not really: I was trying to communicate something motivating, beautiful, and exciting. But it boiled down to a power game.) I shared none of my four responses, however—although I was sorely tempted to voice all of them—and immediately recalibrated my strategy.

My artist friend and I were already more than conversant with the essential insanity and intransigence of mid-level bureaucracies, so we had already dreamed up a less expansive plan B. This involved the careful choosing of paint for the walls (rather than the much preferable wood), with some accent painting where that was possible, and matching carpets and drapery. I still had to fight the administration to get the precise colors I had chosen (which suited the industrial feel of the office), but won that battle. Plan B was not as good as plan A, but it was still much better than the status quo. Later, I added a dropped copper ceiling, using lightweight adhesive plastic tiles that mimic decorative metal quite accurately, hung a few paintings, and added a couple of suitable statues. Students, colleagues, and visitors come in and do a double take. My office is a place of creativity and beauty, and not a bloody horrible fluorescent-lit factory. Visitors are surprised, therefore—surprised, relieved, and pleased.

Not long after, I discovered that the department was now bringing potential new hires into my office to show them what kind of creative freedom was possible at the University of Toronto. I thought that was insanely comical. I thought about all of that for a long time. The resistance I encountered was somewhat incomprehensible in its strength. I wondered, "God, people seem to be afraid of what I am doing in this office. Perhaps there is a reason—an important reason—I do not understand." Then I came across a story by the biologist Robert Sapolsky. It was about wildebeest.[5] Wildebeest are herd animals and very difficult to distinguish from one another (maybe not for other wildebeest, but certainly for those who wish to study them). They blend together. At one point in the past, this presented a serious problem to biologists needing to observe individual animals for enough time to derive some conclusions about their behavior. They would watch a wildebeest, look away for a moment to make notes, and be unable to locate the same animal when they glanced back up.

Eventually, they settled on a potential solution. The biologists drove up adjacent to the herd in a Jeep, armed with a bucket of red paint and a stick with a rag on it. They dabbed a red spot on one of the wildebeest's haunches. Now they could track the activities of that particular animal, and hopefully learn something new about wildebeest behavior. But guess what happened to the wildebeest, now differentiated from the herd? The predators, always lurking around the herd, took it down. Lions—a major wildebeest threat—cannot easily bring a single wildebeest down unless they can identify it. They cannot hunt a blur of indistinguishable herd animals. They cannot track down four wildebeest at a time. They must organize their hunt around an identifiable individual. Thus, when lions go after the little ones or the ones that limp, they are not culling the weak, in some natural display of beneficial altruism. They would rather dine on a nice, healthy, delicious, juicy wildebeest than one that is tiny, old, or ill. But they must be able to identify their prey. What is the moral of the story? Make yourself colorful, stand out, and the lions will take you down. And the lions are always there.

If you stick your neck out, then the sword will come. Many, many cultures have a saying like that. The English version? "The poppy that grows higher than the rest is the first one to have its head removed by the scythe." In Japan: "The nail that sticks up above the rest is the first to get hit by the hammer." This is a nontrivial observation: hence its commonality. Artistic, creative endeavor is high risk, while the probability of return is low. But the probability of exceptionally high return does exist, and creative endeavor, while dangerous and unlikely to be successful, is also absolutely vital to the transformation that enables us to keep our footing. Everything changes. Pure traditionalism is doomed for that very reason. We need the new, merely to maintain our position. And we need to see what we have become blinded to, by our very expertise and specialization, so that we do not lose touch with the Kingdom of God and die in our boredom, ennui, arrogance, blindness to beauty, and soul-deadening cynicism. Plus, are we helpless prey animals, cowering and protecting ourselves, hiding and camouflaging, or are we human beings?

NOT DECORATION

People are often upset by abstract art, or by art that appears to devote itself to producing negative reactions such as disgust or horror merely for the shock value. I have a tremendous respect for ideals of traditional beauty and, therefore, some sympathy for that response, and there is little doubt that many who merely disdain tradition mask the sentiment with artistic pretension. However, the passage of time differentiates truly inspired work from the fraudulent sort, even if imperfectly, and what is not crucial is generally left behind. It is easy to make the opposite error, as well: that art should be pretty and easily appreciated, without work or challenge: it should be decorative; it should match the living-room furniture. But art is not decoration. That is the attitude of a naive beginner, or of someone who will not let their terror of art allow them to progress and learn.

Art is exploration. Artists train people to see. Most people with any exposure to art now regard the work of the impressionists, for example, as both self-evidently beautiful and relatively traditional. This is in no small part because we all perceive the world now, at least in part, in the manner that only impressionists could manage in the latter half of the nineteenth century. We cannot help doing so, because the impressionist aesthetic has saturated everything: advertisements, movies, popular posters, comic books, photographs—all forms of visual art. Now we all see the beauty of light that only the impressionists could once apprehend. They taught us this. But when the impressionists first displayed their paintings—in the Salon des Refusés of 1863, as the traditional Paris Salon had rejected them—the pieces were met with laughter and contempt. The idea of perceiving that way (paying particular attention to light, essentially, rather than form) was so radical that it caused people to have emotional fits.

I am often struck by how common even the tropes of cubism, much more extreme and strange in some ways than impressionism, have become part and parcel of our visual vernacular. I have seen the multidimensional but flattened faces of the genre even in comic books. The same is true of surrealism, which has become popularly integrated almost to the point of cliché. It is worth repeating: Artists teach people to see. It is very hard to perceive the world, and we are so fortunate to have geniuses to teach us how to do it, to reconnect us with what we have lost, and to enlighten us to the world. It is for such psychological reasons that lines such as Christ's can be profitably considered:

> At that time the disciples came to Jesus and asked, "Who, then, is the greatest in the kingdom of heaven?"
>
> He called a little child to him, and placed the child among them.
>
> And he said: "Truly I tell you, unless you change and become like little children, you will never enter the kingdom of heaven. (Matthew 18:1–3)

Beauty leads you back to what you have lost. Beauty reminds you of what remains forever immune to cynicism. Beauty beckons in a manner that straightens your aim. Beauty reminds you that there is lesser and greater value. Many things make life worth living: love, play, courage, gratitude, work, friendship, truth, grace, hope, virtue, and responsibility. But beauty is among the greatest of these.

> What though the radiance which was once so bright
> Be now for ever taken from my sight,
> Though nothing can bring back the hour
> Of splendour in the grass, of glory in the flower;
> We will grieve not, rather find
> Strength in what remains behind;
> In the primal sympathy
> Which having been must ever be;
> In the soothing thoughts that spring

Out of human suffering;
In the faith that looks through death,
In years that bring the philosophic mind.

> —WILLIAM WORDSWORTH, "ODE: INTIMATIONS OF IMMORTALITY
> FROM RECOLLECTIONS OF EARLY CHILDHOOD"

Try to make one room in your home as beautiful as possible.

IF OLD MEMORIES STILL UPSET YOU, WRITE THEM DOWN CAREFULLY AND COMPLETELY

BUT IS YESTERDAY FINISHED WITH YOU?

Imagine you undertook some truly terrible actions in the past. You betrayed or hurt people in a genuinely damaging manner. You damaged their reputation with gossip and innuendo. You took credit for their work. You robbed them materially or spiritually. You cheated on them. Or imagine, instead, that you have been the target of some such events—and let us also assume you have become wise enough to try to avoid repeating the experience. In both circumstances (as perpetrator or victim) the actual events and the associated memories evoke fear, guilt, and shame. Why?

In the first case, you have betrayed yourself. You did not play the medium- to long-term game properly, and are suffering the consequences. You are not the sort of person other people choose to have around. You might not even be the sort of person you want to have around. In the second case, you were badly mistreated by someone else. In some real sense, however, it does not matter whether you were suffering because of self-betrayal or at the hands of others. What does matter is that you do not desire any recurrence.

Now, if you recall the memory, or if it comes back unbidden, complete with terror, shame, and guilt, this means something specific. It means that you fell into a hole—a pit, more accurately—or were pushed there. And that is not good. But what is worse is that you do not know why. Perhaps you trusted other people too easily. Perhaps you were too naive. Perhaps you were willfully blind. Perhaps you encountered genuine malevolence, on the part of another or yourself (and that is the worst situation, and the one most difficult to overcome). But at one level of analysis, whether you fell or were pushed makes little difference—not to the emotional systems that have emerged over the course of evolution and now serve to protect you. They care about one thing and one thing only: that you do not repeat a mistake.

The alarms those systems activate are fear-based (that is too weak a phrase—terror-based is more accurate, the kind of terror limited to neither time nor place), and all they care about is reminding you of the still-extant danger. A part of reality, and a perilous part, has remained unmapped, low resolution, lacking sufficient detail—and so has a part of you. You are not sharp, alert, dangerous, wary, wise, or kind enough—who knows?—so that the terror systems protecting you are confident in your ability to wend your way successfully through the same maze if it once again manifests itself in front of you.

Learn from the past. Or repeat its horrors, in imagination, endlessly.

Frequently, people do not so much repress the terrible things that happened in the past as refuse to think them through, pushing them out of their mind or occupying themselves with other activities. They have their reasons. And sometimes traumatized people appear literally unable to understand what befell them. It can be prohibitively difficult for abused children, for example, to generate a worldview philosophically sophisticated enough to span the full spectrum of human motivation. They simply cannot understand why someone might torment them physically or abuse them sexually. If they are young enough, it is likely that they do not even explicitly comprehend what is happening. Comprehending such matters is exceptionally challenging, even for adults. But in some unfortunate and arguably unjust sense, it does not matter. Refusal or inability both leave a geographic area in memory— unexplored, active, and rife with danger. It is a psychological truism that anything sufficiently threatening or harmful once encountered can never be forgotten if it has never been understood.[1]

To orient ourselves in the world, we need to know where we are and where we are going. Where we are: that concept must optimally include a full account of our experience of the world to date. If you do not know what roads you have traversed, it is difficult to calculate where you are. Where we are going: that is the projection of our ultimate ideal—by no means simply a question, say, of accomplishment, love, wealth, or power, but development of the character that makes all fortunate outcomes more likely and all unfortunate outcomes less likely. We map the world so that we can make the move from where we are—from point A—to where we are going—to point B. We use our map to guide our movement, and we encounter successes and obstacles along the way.

The successes are both confidence building and exhilarating. Not only are we moving toward our ultimate desire, we appear to be doing so properly (and are therefore not only moving ahead but validating our map). The obstacles and failures are, by contrast, anxiety provoking, depressing, and painful. They indicate our profound ignorance. They indicate that we do not understand with sufficient depth where we have been, where we are, or where we are going. They indicate that something we have built with great difficulty and wish above all to protect is flawed—to a degree both serious and not fully understood.

We must recollect our experiences and derive from them their moral. Otherwise, we remain in the past, plagued by reminiscences, tormented by conscience, cynical for the loss of what might have been, unforgiving of ourselves, and unable to accept the challenges and tragedies facing us. We must recollect ourselves or suffer in direct proportion to our ignorance and avoidance. We must gather everything from the past that we avoided. We must rekindle every lost opportunity. We must repent for missing the mark, meditate on our errors, acquire now what we should have acquired then, and put ourselves back together. And I am not saying this is always possible. I have seen people so lost that there was not enough spark left to survive. The person in the present had been rendered too insignificant to confront, in his or her current condition, what was avoided even by a once-healthier self in the past. And cynicism about the future rationalizes the avoidance and deception. That is hell, and there is no limit to its depth. The humility required to clamber out of such hell exists in precise proportion to the magnitude of the unrequited errors of the past. And that is enough to send a shudder of true terror down the spine of anyone even partly awakened. We are not allowed, it seems, to avoid the responsibility of actualizing potential. And if we have made a mistake in the past, and left what could be unmanifest—regardless of the reason—then we pay the price for that in the inability to forget, and in the emotion that constitutes the pangs of conscience for past misbehavior.

Imagine that when you are very young, the map of the world you use to guide your immature self is correspondingly underdeveloped, like a child's drawing of a house: always straight and centered, portraying only the front; always (or close enough) with a door and two windows; always with a square for the outside wall and a triangle for the roof; always with a chimney and smoke (which is a surprise, because smoking chimneys are not all that common now). The sun is shining irrepressibly—a circle with rays emanating from it. There are a few flowers—single lines with the schematic of a bloom at the top, and two leaves halfway up the "stems." It is a very low-resolution representation of a house. It is more hieroglyph than drawing; more concept than sketch. It is something that represents the idea of house, or perhaps home, generically, like the words "house" or "home" themselves. However, it is almost always enough: The child who drew the picture knows it is a house, and the other children and the adults who see the picture know it is a house. The drawing does the trick. It fulfills its purpose. It is a good-enough map.

But all too often appalling events occur within houses. These are not so easy to represent. Maybe the house has adults in it—parents, grandparents, uncles, or aunts—who say such things as "Never—and I mean never—speak to anyone about what happens here." A few squares, a triangle, a smattering of flowers, and a benevolent solar orb offer only an inadequate representation of the horrors characterizing such a dwelling place. Maybe what is happening inside the house is beyond both tolerability and understanding. But how can what is terrifying be beyond understanding? How can trauma even exist without comprehension? Is not understanding in some sense a prerequisite to experience itself? These are all great mysteries. But everything is not experienced at the same level of conception. We have all been petrified by the unknown, even though that seems a contradiction in terms. But the body knows what the mind does not yet grasp. And it remembers. And it demands that understanding be established. And there is simply no escaping that demand. If something befalls us—or, perhaps worse, we engage in some act—that freezes us in terror and nauseates us to recall, we are bound by implacable fate to transform raw horror into understanding, or suffer the consequences.

DO NOT FALL TWICE INTO THE SAME PIT

I had a client who began speaking to me almost immediately after we met of the sexual abuse she suffered in childhood at the hands of of an older cousin, with whom she lived. She became markedly tearful and upset when she recounted her experiences. I asked her how old she was when the abuse occurred. She told me she was four. She described her attacker as much larger, stronger, and older than her. I allowed my imagination to roam freely as she spoke, making the assumptions I believed (or my fantasy presumed) were justified by the nature of her description. I envisioned the nefarious, sadistic, and criminal machinations of a late adolescent or young adult. Then I asked her how much difference in age there was between her and her victimizer. She replied, "Two years. He was two years older than me." This came as a genuine surprise. It changed the picture in my mind almost completely.

I told her what I had been imagining, because I wanted her to know what assumptions I had been formulating as she related her story. Then I said, "You know, you are all grown up now, and have been for a long time. But you told me your story in the same way that you might have told it when you were four, when the molestation was still occurring—or at least with many of the same emotions. And there is no doubt that you remember your cousin as much larger and stronger and older than you. A six-year-old is, after all, half again as old as a four-year-old, and from that younger child's perspective, perhaps more akin to an adult. But your cousin was six—almost as much a child as you. So, here is another way you might consider thinking about what happened. First, recall the six-year-olds with whom you are now familiar. You know that they are still immature and cannot be held accountable as adults might be for their actions, even though they might also not be altogether innocent. I am not trying to minimize the seriousness of what happened to you, and I am not questioning the intensity of your emotions. But I am asking you to consider the situation as if you became aware of its occurrence among two children you presently know. Kids are curious. They play doctor. And if the adults around them are not paying attention properly, such games can get out of hand. Would it be possible to consider that you were not molested by an overpowering and malevolent force—the way you might be if you were raped now? Maybe, instead, you and your cousin were very poorly supervised children."

In some important way, the memories she retained of her childhood experiences had not altered as she matured. She was still experiencing the terror of a four-year-old, helpless in the hands of someone old enough to be perceived as grown-up. But her twenty-seven-year-old self needed to update that memory. She was no longer at risk for such treatment, in any obvious manner. And it came as a great relief to her to reframe what had happened. She could now consider it as a potential consequence of curiosity untrammeled by adult attention. This shifted her view of her cousin, the situation, and herself. She could now see the event from the perspective of an adult. This freed her from much of the terror and shame still associated with the memories, and it did so with remarkable rapidity. She confronted the horrors of the past voluntarily, finding a causal explanation that was much less traumatic—lacking, as it did, the vision of her cousin as a malevolent, powerful perpetrator and her as the inevitably hapless victim of such a force. All this transformation occurred in a single session. Such can be the power of the story surrounding the terrible events of our pasts.

This experience left me with a profound philosophical quandary. The memories my client brought into my office had remained unchanged for decades. The memories she walked out with were markedly altered. Which, then, were real? It could easily be argued that her original story was more accurate. It was, after all, as direct an imprint as might be left on the open book of a four-year-old's mind. It had not been altered (and therefore changed) by any previous therapeutic intervention. Was it not, then, the genuine article? But it is also the case that an event that means one thing one day might come to mean something quite different another. Is it so unusual for us to better understand what motivated the otherwise inexplicable behavior of our parents, for example, as we ourselves enter parenthood? And which memory is more accurate: the partial picture of adult motivation we have as children, or the revised recollections made possible by maturity? If it is the latter—and that does not seem unreasonable (and certainly seemed true in the case of my client)—how is it that an altered memory can become more accurate than one retaining its original configuration?

POSSESSED BY GHOSTS

I recall another client who remembered, in a striking sense, and changed. His memories were shrouded much more profoundly in mystery, and his remembrance was of a slower, more surprising, and unlikelier sort. He was a young, gay African American man who was suffering from a set of incomprehensible mental and physical symptoms. A psychiatrist had recently diagnosed him with schizophrenia, but his aunt, who had taken him to the hospital for evaluation, believed that insufficient time had been spent on her nephew's evaluation. She contacted me for a second opinion and brought him to my office. I saw him alone.

He was shy and reserved, but neatly and carefully dressed, and appeared fully oriented when I started to gather his history. Furthermore, he wore eyeglasses—and they were well taken care of, lacking tape on the bridge or arms, and with lenses that were perfectly clean. These observations were all relevant, as far as I was concerned. Schizophrenics lose the ability to monitor themselves effectively, so unkempt clothing and damaged eyeglasses—particularly with badly smudged lenses—are telling features (not invariably: so those of you with subpar eyewear are not required to consider yourself classified). In any case, he also had a full-time job of reasonable complexity (another rarity for someone with schizophrenia), and he could carry on a conversation with no problem, apart from his tendency toward shyness. I accepted him as a client, and we began to meet regularly.

I had to see him a few times before I could determine why the psychiatrist had diagnosed him with such a serious disorder. He began by telling me that for the last four years he had been depressed and anxious. There was nothing markedly uncommon in that. His symptoms followed on the heels of a serious fight with his boyfriend and the permanent cessation of their relationship, which had lasted several years. Nothing in that was unusual, either. The two had been living together. Their partnership was important to him, emotionally and practically—and the dissolution of an intimate relationship produces unhappiness and confusion in most everyone, and can trigger more severe and lasting anxiety and depression in people who are so predisposed. The duration was out of the ordinary, however. People typically pick up the pieces and move on in under a year. That is not a hard-and-fast rule, but four years is a long time. That piqued my curiosity. He also revealed something else very much out of the ordinary. He told me that he experienced strange, convulsive bodily movements—every night—while attempting to sleep. His body would contort into a fetal position, and his arms would cross over his face. Then he would relax, only to find himself repeating the movements. So it went, for hours. Apart from being concerning because of its incomprehensibility, it was interfering badly with his sleep. This had been going on for about the same amount of time as the anxiety and depression, and the poor sleep, if not the movements themselves, was certainly a contributing factor. I asked him what he thought was happening. He said, with a laugh, "My family thinks I am possessed, and I am not sure they are wrong."

My client's familial background was somewhat unusual. His parents, immigrants to Canada from the southern United States, were uneducated to a marked degree, very superstitious and religious, and apparently serious in the belief that spirits inhabited their son. I asked him, "Did you by chance tell the psychiatrist about being possessed?" He said, "Yes." I thought, "Well, that explains why he diagnosed you with schizophrenia." That explanation, in tandem with the strange physical symptoms, would have been sufficient, in my experience.* However,

---

*A word of advice for anyone seeking mental health help in a large city clinic, where the psychiatrist seeing you might take fifteen minutes to assess your life and determine the nature of your illness: do not casually mention any odd experiences or beliefs. You may well live to regret it. It takes very little to accrue a diagnosis of schizophrenia in the conditions that prevail in an overloaded mental health system—and once the diagnosis has been established, it is very hard to shake. It is difficult, personally, not to take a medical description seriously. It is harder than you might think to disbelieve a qualified psychiatrist (who should, after all, know what he or she is talking about), particularly if you are experiencing strange symptoms. It is difficult practically, as well, because once such a diagnosis becomes part of your permanent medical record, it is very difficult to have it modified. Anything out of the ordinary about you will, from then on, attract undue attention (even from yourself), and any displays of normality will be downplayed. Now, I say all that knowing full well that some people who have odd beliefs are in fact schizophrenic—but a fair bit of digging is usually in order to establish that diagnosis, and busy psychiatrists in public hospitals seldom have the time for careful excavation.

after meeting with this man for several sessions, it was clear to me that whatever was plaguing him was not schizophrenia. He was perfectly rational and lucid. But what in the world could be causing these strange, nightly, seizure-like convulsions? I had never encountered anything of the sort. My first hypothesis was that he suffered from a very severe form of sleep paralysis. This is a reasonably common condition. It generally occurs when people are sleeping on their backs (which he tended to do). A person with sleep paralysis semi-awakens, but not enough to stop dreaming, nor to escape from the inability to move that characterizes the rapid-eye-movement (REM) phase of sleeping. When you are dreaming, the same brain areas that govern active movement when you are awake are often stimulated (you experience this as the sense of moving while in your dream). You do not move around in sync with that brain activation because your voluntary musculature is switched off, physiologically, by a specialized neurochemical mechanism that has exactly that function.[2] Otherwise you would get out of bed and act out your dream and get yourself into trouble very quickly.

During a sleep paralysis episode, the sufferer wakes up enough to be semi-aware of the real world, but is still in REM paralysis and dreaming. All sorts of strange experiences can occur in such a state. Many people have, for example, claimed to have been abducted and medically examined by aliens.[3] This otherwise inexplicable nighttime phenomenon (barring the existence of curious and surgically inclined extraterrestrials) has been blamed on this condition of immobility and the often bizarre and frightening fantasies that accompany it.[4] He was quite bright, literate, and curious, so I gave him a book called *The Terror That Comes in the Night*,[5] which illuminates the strange phenomena that can accompany sleep paralysis. The author, David Hufford, describes the night terror his title refers to as a variant of the "Old Hag" experience (a term from folklore). Those who have had such an experience (up to

15 percent of the population) describe fear and paralysis, sensations of suffocation, and encounters with malign entities. My client read the book, but told me that he did not believe what Hufford described accurately characterized her experience. He felt the same way about the sleep paralysis hypothesis more generally. For one thing, the convulsions occurred before he fell asleep; second, he did not experience the inability to move.

I learned much more about him as we continued to get to know one another. I learned, for example, that he had studied history as an undergraduate, and had completed his degree. I learned that his parents had been exceptionally strict with him through his childhood and teenage years. They never allowed him to stay overnight at his friends' houses, and they monitored his behavior very closely until he escaped to university. He also related a fair bit more about the fight that occurred immediately before the breakup of his last relationship. He had returned with his boyfriend to their shared apartment after having a few drinks and arguing in public. At home, the fight escalated to physical conflict. They began pushing each other around, with increasing violence. After one particularly aggressive shove, my client fell to the living room floor. While lying there, he swept his boyfriend's feet out from underneath him. Then my client picked himself up off the floor and headed for the door. He returned several days later when he knew he would not be at home to pack up his belongings and move. That was the end of their existence as a couple.

But there was an element of his personality at play in this conflict that was not obvious. In consequence, he was struck very deeply by his boyfriend's assault. He told me while discussing this sequence of events that he did not believe people were capable of violence. I said, "What do you mean by that? You earned a history degree. You have obviously read about the horrors and atrocities of the human past. You watch the news . . ." He said that, as a matter of fact, he did not watch the news. "Fair enough," I replied, "but what about everything you learned in university? Did not that teach you that human aggression is both real and exceptionally common?" He said, "I read the books, but I just put everything I had learned into a compartment and did not think any further about it." I thought that was a striking answer, particularly in combination with something else he told me. "When I was a child," he said, "I picked up the idea that people were only good. My parents taught me that adults were angels." I asked, "What do you mean by that? That adults never did anything bad or wrong?" He said, "No, you do not understand. My parents taught me and my sister and brother that adults were literally God's angels, and that they were only good." I said, "You believed this?" He said that he had believed it deeply, partly because he had been so sheltered, partly because his parents had been so insistent, and partly, of course, because it was comforting.

I suggested that something had to be done about his naivete. It was not doing him any good. He was far too old and intelligent to maintain faith in such a childish dream. We discussed this in detail, speaking about the horrific events of the twentieth century and the mass shootings and other terrors of the more recent past. I asked him to explain such occurrences, and to pay more attention to any examples of his own anger and hostility. However, he denied the very existence of the latter and could not generate any convincing explanations for the former.

So, I assigned him a book called *Ordinary Men*.[6] That book excruciatingly details how a group of ordinary policemen from Germany were turned into cold-blooded executioners in Poland during the Nazi occupation. To call the account chilling is to say almost nothing. I told him with all due seriousness that he had to read the book as if it really happened, and more, as if he and the people he knew were capable of the same heinous acts. It was time for him to grow up. We had established a very solid rapport by this time, and when I told him that his rose-colored view of the world was presenting him with danger sufficient to destroy his life he took me seriously. The next time I saw him, a week later, he had finished the book. His face had hardened. He looked older and wiser. I had seen this happen frequently in my clinical practice when people incorporated the darker parts of themselves, instead of—let us say—compartmentalizing them. They no longer had the habitual look of deer caught in the headlights. They looked like people from whom decisions emanated, rather than people to whom things merely happened. Then I asked him to read *The Rape of Nanking*,[7] about Japanese atrocities in China in 1937. It is a horrifying book. The woman who wrote it committed suicide. My client read that, too, and we talked about it. He emerged sadder, but wiser. His nighttime symptoms, however, did not abate.

Nonetheless, his comments about adults-as-angels, claims to have compartmentalized his knowledge of evil, and the presence of the inexplicable convulsions had started some wheels turning in the far recesses of my brain. Many years earlier, I had another client (a young woman, as is more typically the case) who had hysterical epilepsy—a classic case of Freudian hysteria, where bodily symptoms were expressing psychological problems. She had been raised in the rural Midwest, in a very repressed, Victorian-like Christian fundamentalist atmosphere. She had one of her "seizures" in my office—full grand mal. The sight of it left me cold. I watched impassively as she thrashed and convulsed violently for several minutes, eyes rolled back. I did not worry. I did not feel sorry for her. I did not feel anything. I thought, "Why is this not affecting me? My client is having, by all evidence, a serious convulsive episode." I did not call an ambulance. When she came out of it and sat back down, dazed, I told her that I had responded to her seizure neither physically nor emotionally as if it were real, despite its otherwise fully credible manifestation. Previously, after pulling similar stunts (consciously? unconsciously? some mixture of the two?), she had barely skirted consignment to a psychiatric ward. She had also risked a diagnosis of psychosis and prescription for the medication accompanying that. We had some very serious talks about what she was doing. I let her know that I did not buy her epilepsy—that I had experienced it as false, even though it seemed quite real to her. (She had been tested, by the way, for epilepsy, and the results had come back equivocal.)

So, she was plausibly someone who "somatized," or physically represented their psychological symptoms. Freud noted that such somatization was often symbolic—that the manner in which the physical disability or oddity manifested had some meaningful relationship with the trauma that had precipitated it. Her hysterical epilepsy appeared to originate in her ambivalence and ignorance about sex, a substantial degree of childish immaturity, and some dangerous game-playing on her part. We made a lot of progress in our discussions. She was far from unintelligent, and the wiser part of her prevailed. Her seizures came to an end, along with the equally dangerous drama. Even better, she avoided the psych ward and continued with her university career. In any case, I learned then that Freudian hysterics existed, because I had just worked with one.

I began to hypothesize that my current client was suffering, in a similar manner, from a somatization disorder. I knew about the fight that had terminated his last relationship, just before the onset of his symptoms. Perhaps his strange movements were somehow associated with that event? I also knew from his own account that he compartmentalized—that he put things in a corner of his mind where he would not think about them again. I did not have much experience with hypnosis but knew both that people capable of compartmentalization tended to be highly hypnotizable, and that hypnosis had been used with some success (albeit many years ago) with somatization disorders. Freud used hypnosis to treat his hysterical clients, who were apparently quite numerous during the Victorian period, at least in the upper class, fixated as they were on the sexual, the theatrical, and the dramatic.[8] So, I thought I might try hypnosis to treat my client.

Now, I often used guided relaxation techniques on my clients, sitting them comfortably in their armchair in my office, asking them to focus on different parts of their body, from the soles of their feet, step by step up their legs and torso, with a brief detour down their arms, to the top of their head, focusing on their breathing and relaxing. After seven or eight minutes of the relaxation instructions, I would count back from ten to one, requesting after each count or two that they relax more deeply. It was a reasonably good, quick treatment for agitation, anxiety, and insomnia. I decided to start this way, because hypnosis employs essentially the same technique, adding questions about past trauma or other relevant issues once relaxation had been established. Its effectiveness varies substantially from person to person.[9] (That is why stage performers who use hypnosis on audience members will bring twenty people to the front of the theater, run through the initial hypnotic suggestions, and then retain only the few who are obviously responsive.) In any case, I told my client that I thought hypnotizing him and talking about the night he fought with his boyfriend might be useful. I told him why (suggesting that his nighttime movements might be associated with that event). Then I told him exactly how we were going to do it, and that he was free to refuse or agree. I would stop whenever he asked me to, if he asked; and he would remember everything when we were finished.

He agreed to try, so I began: "Sit comfortably in your chair. Place your hands on the arms of the chair or in your lap—wherever you are most comfortable. Close your eyes. Listen carefully to the noises that you hear in the world around you, and then turn your attention inward to your breathing. Breathe in deeply. . . . Hold it. . . . Breathe out. Move your attention down your body from your breathing to your thighs, and lower legs, and feet. Let your feet rest heavily on the floor. Pay attention to your toes, and the soles of your feet, and your ankles, and remember to breathe slowly, regularly, and deeply. Let all the tension flow out of your feet. Do not forget to breathe slowly, regularly, and deeply. Pay attention to your calves, and your shins . . ." and so on, up the whole body. Usually.

My client fell spontaneously into a deep hypnotic trance before I got past his feet. His head lolled heavily. I asked if he could hear me. "Yes," he said, barely audibly. I had to advance my chair and put my ear within inches of his mouth to make out what he was saying. I asked him if he knew where he was. "In your office," he said. That was good. I said, "We are returning to the time when you had a fight with your boyfriend, before you moved out. Tell me what happened." He said, "We had just returned to our apartment. We had both been drinking. We were fighting about finances and our future at the bar. We both got angry. We walked through the doorway of our house—there." He half gestured with his arm, although it was still mostly limp, like the rest of his body. I was watching his eyes dart back and forth, like those of someone in REM sleep, under three-quarter-closed lids. "I was walking backward. We were moving toward the living room. I pushed him. Then he pushed me back. I pushed him again. He pushed me backward over our coffee table and onto the floor. He picked up our floor lamp and held it over his head. I looked directly into his eyes. I had never seen an expression so hostile. I curled into a ball and crossed my hands over my face to protect myself." He said all this very slowly, gesturing awkwardly and minimally all the while, pointing as if toward the area in the apartment he was imagining. It was uncannily as if he were reliving the experience in real time. I glanced at the clock. The explanation, preparation, relaxation, and the slow recounting had taken us up to the one-hour mark—our normal session duration. I said, "I do not want to push you too far. We are running out of time. When you are ready, and comfortable, you might open your eyes and wake up fully. We could continue next week." But he did not respond. His head continued to loll forward, and his eyes kept moving. I called his name. No change.

This worried me, quite frankly. I had never heard of someone failing to emerge from a trance when requested. I was not sure what to do. Fortunately, however, he was the last client I was seeing that evening, so I had some time. I thought, "Well, he is in a deep trance and truly immersed in this account. Maybe he needs to tell the whole story. Let us continue and see what happens. When he is finished with his account, I will try to bring him around again." I went out to the hallway to speak with his waiting aunt, and informed her that we required a bit more time. I returned to my office and sat back down, near him as before. I said, "What happened then?" He replied, "The expression on his face—I had never seen someone look like that before. I was forced to realize then that my boyfriend could want to hurt me; that one person—even if adult—could truly desire to bring harm to another. It was the first time I truly learned that such events were possible." He began to weep, but continued his account: "I knocked his feet from under him, got up, and started running. He chased me out of the living room, down the hallway of our house, and through the front door. I could run faster, and got ahead of him. It was about four in the morning. It was still dark. I was terrified. I got far enough ahead of him to hide behind some nearby cars. He could not find me. I watched him looking for a long while. Then he gave up and turned around." He was sobbing openly by this point. "When I was sure he was gone, I went to my mother's place and stayed there. I could not believe what had happened. He might have killed me, and he was going to do it on purpose. I couldn't stand it. I pushed it from my mind and tried never to think about it again."

He fell silent. I called his name. He responded. I asked him, "Do you know that you are in my office and sitting in the chair you usually occupy?" He nodded. "Are you finished telling me your story?" He replied in the affirmative. I said, "You did well. It was very brave of you to go through all that. Are you ready to open your eyes?" He said that he was. I said, "Take your time. When you are ready, come back fully awake, slowly. You are going to feel relaxed and well. You will remember everything you just told me and everything that happened here." He nodded. A few moments later he opened his eyes. I asked him what had happened—what he remembered. He briefly recounted the evening's events, including our initial discussion about hypnosis. I then called in his aunt and told her that he needed to rest at home, with someone in attendance, because the session had been intense. Adults were not angels, and people could not only hurt each other— they could desire that hurt with all their heart. But my client did not know what to do with such knowledge, sheltered as he was, deluded as he was by his parents—blind as he allowed himself to remain with his "compartmentalization." This did not stop the inarticulate elements of his being from endeavoring to dramatically represent and bring toward consciousness both the fact of intended harm and everything more broadly evil such intent implied. He found himself compelled to duplicate precisely the defensive bodily movements he had made to during the fight with his boyfriend.

The next week, my client did not show up for his session. I thought "Oh, God. Maybe I did him some serious damage." However, he arrived on time the next week. He apologized for missing the last session, but said that he had become extremely upset and was in consequence too scrambled to attend or even to contact me. I asked why. He said, "The day after we last met, I was sitting in a restaurant downtown, and I saw my old boyfriend!" It was an uncanny coincidence. "It really rattled me, you know," he continued, "but nothing came of it, and I calmed down in a day or two. And guess what?" "What?" I said. "I only had convulsions one night this week! And they only lasted a few minutes!" I said, "That is great! That is really great! What a relief! What do you think changed?" He said, "What really got to me in that fight was not our disagreement about what future we wanted. It was not the physical contact—the pushing and shoving. It was the fact that he truly wished me harm. I could see it in his face. His look truly terrified me. I could not handle it. But I can understand it better now."

I asked him if I could hypnotize him again. "You are obviously better," I said, "but I want to make sure that we got everything." He agreed, and we began. He fell into a trance just as easily. But this time, he condensed the story. He got through the whole account in fifteen minutes, as opposed to the ninety required previously. He had extracted what was important: the fact that he was in danger; the fact that someone wanted to hurt him; the fact that he had defended himself successfully—the fact that the world was a place inhabited by demons, so to speak, as well as angels. When I asked him to come out of the trance, in the same way I had before, he opened his eyes almost immediately, and was calm and fully aware.

The change in his condition was remarkable. The next week, he said that his symptoms had disappeared completely. No more convulsions— and no more belief in the untarnished goodness of mankind. He had grown up and faced the reality of his own experience, as well as the nature of the world. It was something to see. Conscious acceptance of the presence of malevolence cured him of years of suffering. He now understood and admitted enough of the potential dangers that surrounded him to make his way in reasonable safety through the world. It was no longer necessary for what he had learned but refused to acknowledge to force itself upon him in its dramatic, embodied manner. He made what he now knew part of his personality—part of the map that would guide him henceforth in his actions—and freed himself from the ghosts that possessed him.

UNCOMPREHENDED MALEVOLENCE

I had another client, a young man who was terribly bullied in his first year of vocational college. When he first came to see me, he could barely talk, and was taking a high dose of antipsychotic medication. When he sat in the chair in front of the desk in my office, he would twist his head and shoulders back and forth in a very abnormal and mechanical manner. When I asked him what he was doing, he told me that he was trying to make the shapes go away. Apparently, he could perceive geometric images of some kind in front of him, and felt compelled to manipulate them. I never did understand exactly what that signified, except that he was in a world of his own.

I spent several months working with him, and did it in a more structured manner than previously—having, in the interim, developed the tools to do so. This client could only communicate a little at the beginning of our work together, but that was enough to start the ball rolling. Some girl at the college had developed a crush on him. He informed her that her romantic interest was not reciprocated. She became exceedingly vindictive, and set out to make his life hell. She spread rumors about his sexual habits. She encouraged some of her male friends to physically threaten him at school. She had people on hand to humiliate him constantly and unmercifully in transit to and from campus. Noting his distress, his parents alerted the school, but nothing was done to stop the ongoing torment. Unable or unwilling to tolerate the mounting peer pressure, the friends he had only recently made began to avoid and then entirely abandoned him. He began to break down, and as his behavior became stranger, his outcast status was cemented into place. And he broke.

I asked him to let me know exactly what happened—and to reach a long way back while formulating his answer. I wanted to understand what, if anything, made him vulnerable to the situation he found himself in, and what exactly had happened when he was being tormented by his spurned admirer. And I structured this so that he could write, as well as talk (more accurately, so that he could talk about what he was writing). My colleagues and I had developed an online writing exercise* to provide some helpful structure for those delving into and

---

*The Past Authoring Program at www.selfauthoring.com. Dr. James W. Pennebaker of the University of Texas at Austin, and a host of colleagues working directly with him and independently, have demonstrated that writing that reduces existential uncertainty (there's no simpler general way of putting it) reduces anxiety, improves mental health, and boosts immunological function. All of these effects appear associated with a general decrease in complexity-induced stress and the hormones—harmful in excess—consequentially produced. Pennebaker demonstrated, for example, that students who wrote for three days, consecutively, about the worst events in their lives experienced, first, a decline in mood (no doubt elicited by calling forth such memories) but significant improvement in their lot over the period of the following months. Other researchers showed similar effects when students wrote about their future. Pennebaker initially assumed that it was something akin to emotional expression, or catharsis (following Freud), that produced these positive effects—the opportunity to express anger or regret or sorrow—but found, as the result of a careful semantic analysis, that it was the development of a cognitive and causal understanding of the reason for the events and their significance that was curative. The effects of writing about the future seemed similar, in that the plans thereby generated reduced uncertainty and put forward a simpler and more well-defined structure around what might otherwise have been the intol-

making sense of their past. I asked my young client to try it. Because he was too impaired in his motivation and his thoughts to complete the process at home, I had him do his writing in my office. I set him at my computer and asked him to read each question in the exercise aloud to me before writing his answer, and then to read that aloud as well. If I failed to understand something he had written or felt that more detail was required, I suggested he clarify the issues at hand with more writing and read me his revisions.

The exercise opened by asking him to break his life into key epochs—sections of his autobiographical past that lent themselves naturally to categorization as a unit or theme. That might be, say, age two through kindergarten, elementary school, junior high, high school, college, etc.—although some people are inclined, particularly as they get older, to group their experiences according to the various relationships of which they were a member. After he subdivided his past in the manner he chose, the exercise then asked him to identify key experiences during each of those epochs: events that he believed, in retrospect, shaped him as a person, for better or worse. Obviously, events of the latter type are likely to be marked in memory by negative emotions such as anxiety, anger, or the desire for revenge—and, perhaps, by a strong tendency to avoid remembering and considering altogether.

My client broke his life into the epochs that seemed relevant to him, and then identified the key events, both positive and negative, characterizing each period. Next, he analyzed them causally, coming to understand why some things had gone well, while others had deteriorated so terribly. He concentrated most intensely on what gave rise to the most disturbing events of the past—assessing particulars of his

---

erably unspecified looming weeks and months ahead. For a review, see J. W. Pennebaker and J. F. Evans, *Expressive Writing: Words That Heal* (Enumclaw, Wash.: Idyll Arbor Inc., 2014).

own behavior, motivations of other people, and characteristics of time and place. He considered what effects those produced, for better and worse (because we can learn things from difficult experiences), and thought through what might have happened or been done differently. The consequence of all this, at least in principle, was the mining of past experiences for their true perceptual and behavioral significance, and an update of his autobiographical map.

As his account progressed from day care through public schooling—he had divided his life into sections defined by school grade—he became increasingly articulate. Recollecting his life was putting him back together. As he wrote, read what he wrote, and answered the questions I put to him while listening, his account of the past became more detailed and his understanding of it deeper. We discussed the undesirable things that children do to each other, and that led us to the topic of malevolence and evil—in the adult world, as well. He was very naive about this. He expressed the belief that people were universally good (even though he had experience to the contrary). He had no theory of motivation for destruction, cruelty, and the desire for mayhem.

We walked through his life, developing a particularly detailed account of everything he had suffered at the hands of his tormentor. He became sophisticated enough to articulate some initial understanding of her motivations. She had been spurned and was, in consequence, hurt, embarrassed, and angry. He had not realized either how much impact his rejection might produce or how much impact rejection can have on people in general. He did not seem to understand, furthermore, that he had the right to defend himself. We talked about what he could have done differently, or might do differently in the future, to protect himself. He realized that he had taken far too much insult at school without reaching out for help. He could have let the appropriate administrative staff at the college know what was going on. He could have confronted his tormentor directly, publicly, earlier in the abuse, and demanded that she stop. He could have let his classmates know that the only reason he was being tormented was because he had refused a date, and that she was so fragile and brittle that she could not handle the rejection and was inventing lies for revenge. In the extreme, he could have had her charged with criminal harassment and defamatory libel. None of these strategies would have been sure to work, but they would have been worth trying, and were certainly justified and necessary under the circumstances.

As he worked through the memories of his recent month at college, his psychotic symptoms receded dramatically. At every session he attended, he was more clearheaded. He stopped manifesting his strange behaviors. He enrolled in summer school and finished his remaining coursework. It was a near-miraculous recovery.

POTENTIAL INTO ACTUALITY

It is far from uncommon for people to worry, sometimes unbearably, about what lies ahead of them. That worry is a both a consequence of and an investigation into the multiple pathways extending from now into the future. Concerns line themselves up, often involuntarily, for consideration: troublesome issues at work, problems with friends and loved ones, practical issues of economic and material survival. Each concern requires multiple decisions: What problems should be solved? In what order should action proceed? What strategy should be employed? All of this requires something like choice—free choice, free will. And the choice to act seems voluntary; it is a simple thing (although very psychologically unsatisfying) to succumb to paralysis of will.

To decide, by contrast, voluntarily and freely, is difficult and demanding. It feels nothing like the automatic processes of reflexive or habitual pathways moving us thoughtlessly forward. We do not appear to ourselves to be driven by the past, in some fundamentally deterministic manner, like a mechanical clock in which the spring drives the gears that turn the hands and tell the time. Instead, when we decide, we actively confront the future. We seem destined to face something akin to unformed potential and to determine what will emerge as the present—and then the past.

We literally make the world what it is, from the many things we perceive it could be. Doing so is perhaps the primary fact of our being, and perhaps of Being itself. We face a multitude of prospects—of manifold realities, each almost tangible—and by choosing one pathway rather than another, reduce that multitude to the singular actuality of reality. In doing so, we bring the world from becoming into Being. This is the most profound of mysteries. What is that potential that confronts us? And what constitutes our strange ability to shape that possibility, and to make what is real and concrete from what begins, in some sense, as the merely imaginary?

There is something else of perhaps equal import allied with this, impossible as that might seem, given the very unlikeliness of the role we appear to play in the shaping of reality. Not only do our choices play a determining role in transforming the multiplicity of the future into the actuality of the present, but—more specifically—the ethics of our choices play that role. Actions based upon the desire to take responsibility; to make things better; to avoid temptation and face what we would rather avoid; to act voluntarily, courageously, and truthfully— these make what comes into Being much better, in all ways, for ourselves and for others, than what arises as a consequence of avoidance, resentment, the search for revenge, or the desire for mayhem. This means that if we act ethically, in the deepest and most universal of senses, then the tangible reality that emerges from the potential we face will be good instead of dreadful—or at least as good as we can make it.

Everyone seems to know this. We are universally tormented by our consciences for what we know we should have done yet did not do. We are tormented equally by what we did but know we should not have done. Is this not a universal experience? Can anyone escape the pangs of conscience at four o'clock in the morning after acting immorally or destructively, or failing to act when action was necessary? And what is the source for that inescapable conscience? If we were the source of our own values and masters of our own houses, then we could act or fail to act as we choose and not suffer the pangs of regret, sorrow, and shame. But I have never met anyone who could manage that. Even the most psychopathic of people seemed motivated at least to mask their malfeasance with a layer of lies (with the depth of that layer precisely proportionate to the severity of the impropriety in question). Even the most malevolent, it appears, must find justification for his or her evil.

If we fail to hold ourselves to that standard of responsibility, then other people regard us as lacking in ethics and integrity. And it does not end there. Just as we hold people (including ourselves) accountable for the wrongs they have done, or the good they have failed to do, we also believe (or at least act out the proposition) that someone who has made a good decision freely, deserves whatever benefit might come of that decision. It is for that reason that we believe each person should justly receive the fruit of their honest and voluntary labor. There seems something natural and inevitable about such judgments; something at work within them that is universal and inescapable, psychologically and socially. What all this means is that everyone—child, adult, self, others—will rebel against being treated as a cog in a wheel, incapable of choice and devoid of freedom, and (similarly) that it is practically impossible to establish a positive relationship with any other (or even our private selves) without that attribution of personal agency, free will, and responsibility.

THE WORD AS SAVIOR

The twin ideas that we all are, as sovereign individuals, first, voluntarily participating in the act of creation itself and, second, determining the quality of that creation with the ethics of our choices finds reflection in myriad manners within our relationships, private and public. These ideas are also encapsulated and represented in the narratives, the fundamental narratives, that sit at the base of our culture. These stories—whatever their ultimate metaphysical significance— are at least in part a consequence of our watching ourselves act across eons of human history, and distilling from that watching the essential patterns of our actions. We are cartographers, makers of maps; geographers, concerned with the layout of the land. But we are also, more precisely and accurately, charters of courses, sailors and explorers. We recall the places we started from, the positions we occupied when our stories began. We remember the pitfalls and successes of the past so that we can avoid the former and repeat the latter. To do so, we need to know where we have been, where we currently are, and in what direction we are headed. We reduce that account to its causal structure: we need to know what happened and why, and we need to know it as simply and practically as possible.

It is for such reasons we are so captivated by people who can tell a story—who can share their experiences concisely and precisely, and who get to the point. That point—the moral of the story—is what

they learned about who and where they were or are, and where they
are going and why. Such information is irresistible to us all. It is how
(and why) we derive wisdom from the risks taken by those before us,
and who lived to tell the story: "This is what life was like then. This is
what we wanted, and why. This is what we envisioned, and how we
strategized, planned, and then acted. Sometimes, we succeeded and
realized our aims. But too often (and this is what is crucial to a great
story): here is how what we did not expect occurred, here is how we
were knocked off the path, here are the tragedies we encountered and
the mistakes we made—and here is how we put the world back together (or failed to do so)." We value such stories particularly if they
have attained the pinnacle of generalizability, representing heroic battles with the unknown, as such, or the dissolution of tyrannical order
into revivifying chaos and the (re)establishment of benevolent society.[10] This can be seen everywhere that people tell and listen avidly to
stories: and that is literally everywhere.[11]

The most fundamental stories of the West are to be found, for
better or worse, in the biblical corpus. That collection of ancient and
eminently influential books opens with God Himself, in His Fatherly
guise, portrayed as the ordered entity who confronts chaos and creates
habitable order in consequence:

> And the earth was without form, and void; and darkness was
> upon the face of the deep. And the Spirit of God moved upon
> the face of the waters. (Genesis 1:2)

This formlessness, void, darkness, and water (a confusing conglom-
eration of attributes) is a consequence of the translation of a biblical
Hebrew phrase, *tohu wa-bohu* (תֹהוּ־רָבֹ֔הוּ), made up of two words, *tohuw*
and *bohuw*. *Tohuw* is even more complicated than mere formlessness,

etc.; it also means "that which is laid waste," "vanity" (which might be something likely to be laid to waste, psychologically speaking), and "desert" (which is uninhabitable and void).[12] It is also associated with another Hebrew word, *tehom* (תְּהוֹם), which is the source of the phrase "the deep." *Tehom*, in turn, means "the abyss," and is associated with an earlier Sumerian term, Tiamat,[13] who is the great mother goddess/dragon (and denizen of salt water) who creates the world with her consort, Apsu, in the Mesopotamian creation myth *Enuma Elish*.

According to the Genesis account, there exists something—a potential, let us say, associated symbolically with the abyss, with the oceanic depths—but also with desert, dragons, maternality/matriarchy, emptiness, formlessness, and darkness.[14] This is all the attempt of poetry and metaphor to give initial, ordered, conceptual form to the formless. The abyss is what terrifies, what is at the end of the earth, what we gaze upon when contemplating our mortality and fragility, and what devours hope. Water is depth and the source of life itself. The desert is a place of abandonment, isolation, and loneliness, as well as the interregnum between tyranny and the promised land. The dragon is the ancient image of the predator as such—the fire-breathing tree-cat-snake-bird[15]—eternally lurking in the forest beyond the familiar confines of tribe and village. It is as well the Leviathan hidden in the salt water, the depths—the terrible monster Jehovah refers to overcoming in Job 41:25–34 and in many other places in the Old Testament accounts.[16]

God has an attribute, or an alternative Person, or a faculty, or a tool that aids Him or that He relies on when confronting possibility and the void. That is the Word, from the Christian perspective—but certainly the capacity for speech, regardless of religious framework, Jewish or Christian. There is a continual insistence in Genesis on the importance of speech. The act of creation on each day begins with the phrase "and God said" (with additional emphasis on the act of naming: "and God called"). The seven days of creation begin:

> And God said, Let there be light: and there was light.
>
> And God saw the light, that it was good: and God divided the light from the darkness.
>
> And God called the light Day, and the darkness he called Night. And the evening and the morning were the first day. (Genesis 1:3–5)

Almost immediately after God first reveals Himself, His creative actions, and the initial creation (thus, almost instantly after we are introduced to Him), He creates human beings. Three features of that creation stand forth, in addition to its immediacy: the insistence that mankind is to have dominion* over the rest of creation; the shocking and incomprehensibly modern and egalitarian insistence that God created man and woman equally in His own image (stated twice; Genesis 1:27); and the equally unlikely and miraculous insistence that the creation of humanity was, like the rest of the Creation, good. If God is, above all, as He is initially described, that implies that the men and women created in His image share with Him something of import—or, more to the point, they share an analogous destiny, necessity, or responsibility.

The Word—the tool God uses to transform the depths of potential—is truthful speech. It appears necessarily allied, however, with the courage to confront unrealized possibility in all its awful potential, so that reality itself may be brought forth. Perhaps both this

---

*Responsibility, stewardship, service; not from physical strength (Cambridge Bible for Schools and Colleges); the power of governing and controlling; but most important, the same dominion as God has over or for man.

Truth and Courage must finally be subsumed, in turn, under the broader principle of Love—love for Being itself, despite its fragility, tyranny, and betrayal; love that has as its aim what is best for the best in everything. It is that combination of Truth, Courage, and Love comprising the Ideal, whose active incarnation in each individual does in fact take the potential of the future and make the best of it. And who would deny this? No one teaches a beloved son to cringe in terror and cowardice from what confronts him. No one teaches a beloved daughter that deceit will set the world right, and that whatever works expediently is to be practiced, honored, and mimicked. And no one tells anyone he or she cares for that the proper response to Being is hatred and the desire to produce pain, suffering, mayhem, and catastrophe. Thus, it can be assumed from analysis of our own behavior that we know the difference between the pathway of good and the pathway of evil, and that we believe above all (despite our conscious resistance and prideful argument) in the existence of both. But there is yet more: the insistence of God on the goodness of creation reflected the fact that Truth, Courage, and Love were united in His creative action. Thus, there is an ethical claim deeply embedded in the Genesis account of creation: everything that emerges from the realm of possibility in the act of creation (arguably, either divine or human) is good insofar as the motive for its creation is good. I do not believe there is a more daring argument in all of philosophy or in theology than this: To believe this, to act it out, is the fundamental act of faith.

There is an argument presented much later in the biblical narrative, in the New Testament. Christ says the following words to His followers. It is a commentary on the potential for completing your life, for reclaiming what you have lost—or even discovering what you did not know was there:

And I say unto you, Ask, and it shall be given you; seek, and ye shall find; knock, and it shall be opened unto you.

For every one that asketh receiveth; and he that seeketh findeth; and to him that knocketh it shall be opened.

If a son shall ask bread of any of you that is a father, will he give him a stone? or if he ask a fish, will he for a fish give him a serpent?

Or if he shall ask an egg, will he offer him a scorpion?

If ye then, being evil, know how to give good gifts unto your children: how much more shall your heavenly Father give the Holy Spirit to them that ask him? (Luke 11:9–13)

This is not a casual statement. It is not naive. It is not a matter of asking for a present, unearned. God is no granter of casual wishes.* It is a matter, first, of truly Asking. This means being willing to let go of anything and everything that is not in keeping with the desire. Otherwise there is no Asking. There is only an immature and too-often resentful whim and wish: "Oh, that I could have what I want, without doing what is necessary." That will not suffice. So, to ask, seek, and knock is to do everything required to gather what has been left unfinished and to complete it, now. And to ask, seek, and knock is, as well, to determine what must be asked for. And that has to be something that is worthy of God. Why else would it be granted? How else could it possibly be granted?

Imagine for a moment you have been given all you need. There is possibility within you, waiting for the proper demand to release itself. There is all that is outside of you, waiting to inform and teach you.

---

*Perhaps it is for this reason that Christ insists "it is also written: 'Do not put the Lord your God to the test.'" (In this instance I prefer Matthew 4:7 of the New International Version to the same verse in the King James Version.)

But all of it is necessary—the good, bad, and unbearable. You know that when something does not go well, you should analyze the problem, resolve it, apologize, repent, and transform. An unsolved problem seldom sits there, in stasis. It grows new heads, like a hydra. One lie— one act of avoidance—breeds the necessity for more. One act of self-deception generates the requirement to buttress that self-deceptive belief with new delusions. One devastated relationship, unaddressed, damages your reputation—damages your faith in yourself, equally— and decreases the probability of a new and better relationship. Thus, your refusal or even inability to come to terms with the errors of the past expands the source of such error—expands the unknown that surrounds you, transforms that unknown into something increasingly predatory.

And, while that is happening, you get weaker. You are less than you could be because you did not change. You did not become who you could have become as a consequence of that change—and worse: you have now taught yourself, by your own example, that such turning away is acceptable, and you are therefore more likely to commit the same error in the future. And what you failed to face is now larger. This is not the kind of causal process, the kind of positive feedback loop, that you want to find yourself trapped within. So, you must confess, at least to yourself, and repent, at least within yourself, and you must change, because you were wrong. And you must humbly ask, and knock, and seek. And that is the great barrier to the enlightenment of which we are all capable in principle. This is not to claim that the courage necessary to confront the full horrors of life is easy to muster. But the alternative is worse.

It is our destiny to transform chaos into order. If the past has not been ordered, the chaos it still constitutes haunts us. There is information—vital information—resting in the memories that affect us negatively. It is as if part of the personality is still lying latent, out in the world, making itself manifest only in emotional disruption. What is traumatic but remains inexplicable indicates that the map of the world that guides our navigation is insufficient in some vital manner. It is necessary to understand the negative well enough so that it can be circumvented as we move into the future if we do not wish to remain tormented by the past. And it is not the expression of emotion associated with unpleasant events that has curative power. It is the development of a sophisticated causal theory: Why was I at risk? What was it about the world that made it dangerous? What was I doing or not doing to contribute to my vulnerability? How can I change the value hierarchy I inhabit to take the negative into account so that I can see and understand it? How much of my old map do I have to let crumble and burn—with all the pain dying tissue produces—before I can change enough to take my full range of experience into account? Do I have the faith to step beyond what should and must die and let my new and wiser personality emerge? To some great degree, we are our assumptions. They structure the world for us. When basic axioms of faith are challenged ("People are basically good"), the foundation shakes and the walls crumble. We have every reason to avoid facing the bitter truth. But making what is—and what was—clear and fully comprehended can only protect us. If you are suffering from memories that will not stop tormenting you, there is possibility—possibility that could be your very salvation—waiting there to be discovered.

If old memories still upset you, write them down carefully and completely.

RULE X

PLAN AND WORK DILIGENTLY
TO MAINTAIN THE ROMANCE
IN YOUR RELATIONSHIP

THE UNBEARABLE DATE

I am not a couples' therapist. But sometimes, when I see a client, it becomes necessary to include his or her intimate partner in one or more sessions. I do that only when directly asked. I also make it clear that the couple should seek out a marital counseling specialist if that is their central goal. However, if one of the primary problems my client is addressing is dissatisfaction in the marriage, it is often counter-productive to speak with only one member of the couple. Finally, it is often the case (and no wonder, really) that the partner in question does not trust his or her better half's therapist—me—and a meeting with all three of us can go a long way toward rectifying that.

Prior to meeting with a couple, I will have discussed some basic rules for relationship improvement with my client. Let us say he or she has decided to make some time for romance: four hours a week or something like that (I am speaking here of adults, with their full share of responsibilities). Maybe that much can be managed. Maybe even more is possible. But there is not that much time in seven days, and the situation must be set up correctly and carefully. And when all this is first practiced—all this conscious negotiation and enactment—it is going to be done badly and stupidly, with all the attendant pain, resentment, and vengefulness. And then such negative emotion can be nursed and the relationship damaged—sometimes permanently.

Perhaps my client and his or her partner have become estranged from one another over several years when we first start to discuss their situation. They are not happy, and they hate me—maybe even more than they hate each other. They sit there, distant, arms crossed and eyes rolling (hopefully not the latter: that is a bad sign[1]). Neither will give an inch. I ask them when they last did something romantic together; when they last went out together for a date. They laugh ruefully, if things have not gone too far, or scoff outright. I suggest, nonetheless, that they try going out with each other; or more, that they start making dates a regular practice. The former suggestion is bad enough; the second, intolerable. They indicate: "We are not going on any damn dates. We dated before we got married, when it was appropriate. Besides, all we will do is fight."

And here is my take on that angry, bitter, and shallow response: "This is the theory you are putting forth: You are never going to accompany each other on another date in your entire married life. (So much for romance and intimacy.) Instead, you are just going to give that up. Why not, instead, risk the time? Take each other somewhere nice. Dare to put your arm around your partner, or your hand on a knee (and not your own, either). I know you are angry with each other, and probably for good reason. I have met both of you: I understand why you both feel that way :-). But just try it. You do not have to like it. You do not have to expect to be good at it, or give up your anger, or have a good time. You just have to tolerate it."

They both leave incensed at me for suggesting such an irritating idea. But they agree grudgingly, and at their next session inform me: "It happened just as we told you: we had an absolutely wretched time. We fought before we went out, while we were out, and again, when we returned home. We are certainly not going to risk a date again." They often evince a certain pride at reaching such a conclusion, as both had generally decided ahead of time that the whole idea was pointless. So, I ask: "That is the plan, is it? You are going to be married for sixty years. You put a small amount of begrudging effort into having one date. You were already not getting along, so there was a negligible probability you were going to take any pleasure in it. Besides that, irritated at me as you were for my childish suggestion, you were both motivated to make it go horribly, just as it did. So, you are done with it. And now you have decided that this is how you are going to conduct yourselves across the decades you have promised each other: with spite and bitterness instead of mutual regard?

"Let us try thinking about it this way, instead: Neither of you have any skill at dating. One attempt is therefore going to be insufficient. Maybe you need fifteen dates—or forty—because you have lost the knack, need the practice, and must develop the habit and goodwill. Perhaps neither of you are very romantic to begin with; or if you were once, those days have long gone. This is a skill you must learn, not an unearned gift from Cupid."

Assume you are married—or the equivalent. Assume, as well, that you have, or could have, a romantic interlude twice a week. It may be less; it may be more: but we will do the arithmetic for twice weekly. That is a hundred times a year. Let us imagine that you are going to be married thirty more years. Thirty times one hundred is three thousand times. Is there not some possibility that you could devote a fraction of all that time to perfecting your technique, seduction, communication, and lovemaking? What does it matter, therefore, if you have fifteen miserable dates before managing one that verges on acceptable? That is fifteen times out of a possible three thousand. That is half a percent of the romantic time you could possibly spend together. Maybe you could dare even more to determine if things could be set right between you. Why would you possibly assume that something as complex as maintaining a marriage could be managed without commitment, practice, and effort?

"So maybe the first date is wretched and horrible. You never want to repeat it but you do, because you would rather save your marriage than quit outright. And maybe the next one is five percent better. And maybe after some repeated attempts you remember for at least a brief moment why you once liked the person you married. Perhaps you manage something a little more exciting than putting your arm around him or her, and perhaps receive a bit of a response from someone who actually cares for you somewhere in their now cold and shriveled heart. And if you are in it for the long run, as indicated by the original marital vows, perhaps you will put in the time to get it right."

And maybe the couple has enough sense to do the arithmetic and contemplate all that wasted time, as well as the bitterness, resentment, and deadness of life without romance, and they agree to go on another date, or two, or three, or ten—and by the tenth session they come to see me, smiling, and tell me they had a pretty good time. And then we have an even more serious discussion about just what it takes to maintain love and respect, and invoke desire and response. How do you find the mystery in the other person over the long run? Can you muster up the will and the romantic imagination and the playfulness to manage that, each time you are together intimately, for the next three thousand occasions? That is going to require some thoughtful effort.

For each person is in truth an unfathomable enigma. With care, you might keep rediscovering, in the person you have chosen, enough residual mystery to maintain the spirit that first brought you together. With care, you can avoid stowing each other away in a conveniently sized box, punishment at hand should either of you dare to emerge, and contempt for the consequent predictability you both now face lurking not so far beneath the surface. If you are fortunate, you might rekindle that glimpse you had when you first were attracted to each other, of what your life could be like if you were better people than you are. That is what happens two people fall under the spell of love. For a while, both become better than they were, and see that, but then that magic fades away. Both receive that experience as a gift. Both have their eyes open and can see what is visible to no one else. Such love is a glimpse of what could be, if the relationship remained true. It is delivered as a gift initially, from fate, but requires tremendous effort to realize and maintain. And once that is understood, the goal is clear.

BEDROCK

The sexual aspect of a relationship can often tell us a great deal about the whole, but not always. I have known couples who fought like proverbial cats and dogs and who had a wildly successful sex life (at least in the short term), and other couples who were well suited to each other temperamentally but one or the other could not find the spark. People and their relationships are too complex to reduce to a single aspect—but it is still reasonable to note that a good marriage is accompanied by mutual desire, mutually requited. Unfortunately, desire is not something that can be managed in isolation: "Let us fix our sex life" is a resolution too narrow in ambition to fulfill its aim.

There must be a broader, relationship-wide strategy in place to maintain romance with your partner across time. Regardless of what that strategy might be, its success is going to depend on your ability to negotiate. To negotiate, you and the person you are negotiating with must first know what you each need (and want)—and second, be willing to discuss both forthrightly. There are many serious obstacles both to knowing what you need and want, and to discussing it. If you allow yourself to know what you want, then you will also know precisely when you are failing to get it. You will benefit, of course, because you will also know when you have succeeded. But you might also fail, and you could well be frightened enough by the possibility of not getting what you need (and want) that you keep your desires vague and unspecified. And the chance that you will get what you want if you fail to aim for it is vanishingly small.

Aim is likely a problem for you. If you have a partner, the problem may be compounded. The person you have chosen is unlikely to be any smarter about you than you are, except in minor instances (and is in fact likely to be even more in the dark with regard to your innermost desires). Your failure to specify your desires means your unfortunate lover will have to guess what would please and displease you, and is likely to be punished in some manner for getting it wrong. Furthermore, given all the things you could want—and do not want—it is virtually certain that your lover will get it wrong. In consequence, you will be motivated to blame them, at least implicitly, or nonverbally, or unconsciously, for not caring enough to notice what you are unwilling even to notice yourself. "If you really loved me," you will think—or feel, without thinking—"I would not have to tell you what would make me happy." This is not a practical approach to a happy marriage.

That is all bad enough, but there is a second and equally severe problem lurking in the byways. If you have solved the problem of knowing what you want, admitted it to yourself in a verbalizable form, and let someone else know your wishes, you have then granted them a dangerous source of power. The person whom you have made your confidant is now in a position to fulfill your desires, but could equally deprive you of what you want, embarrass you for wanting it, or hurt you in some other manner, because you have now made yourself vulnerable. Naive people are possessed of the delusion that everyone is good, and that no one—particularly someone loved—would be motivated to cause pain and misery, either for revenge, as a consequence of blindness, or merely for the pleasure of doing so. But people who have matured enough to transcend their naivete have learned that they can be hurt and betrayed both by themselves and at the hands of others. So why increase the odds of being hurt by letting someone in? It is to defend against such betrayal that naivete is often replaced by cynicism, and it must be said in all truth that the latter is an improvement over the former. But such substitution is not the final word in wisdom, and thank God for that. Trust in turn trumps cynicism, and true trust is not naivete. Trust between people who are not naive is a form of courage, because betrayal is always a possibility, and because this is consciously understood. This applies with particular force within the confines of an intimate relationship. To trust is to invite the best in your partner to manifest itself, with yourself and your freely given trust as the enticement. This is a risky business, but the alternative is the impossibility of true intimacy, and the sacrifice of what could have been two minds in dialogue working in tandem to address the difficult problems of life for a single mind striving in solitude.

Romance requires trust—and the deeper the trust, the deeper the possibility for romance. But trust has its requirements, as well, apart from the courage required of the individuals wise enough to distrust but brave enough to risk putting their faith in a partner. The first of those requirements is truth. You cannot maintain trust in yourself if you lie. You cannot maintain trust in yourself, likewise, if you act in a manner that would require a lie if it was discovered. Similarly, you cannot maintain trust in your partner if he or she lies, or betrays you in action or in silence. So, the vow that makes a marriage capable of preserving its romantic component is first and foremost the decision not to lie to your partner.

There are also immense practical advantages to this, if practiced properly. There will come a time in your life when you have done something you should not have done or failed to do something that you should have done. You may need advice. You may need support. You may need exactly what your partner could provide, if only you dared to allow them to help. And at some time they are going to find themselves in exactly the same position. Life is too difficult to negotiate alone. If you tell your partner the truth, and you strive to act so that you can tell the truth about how you act, then you have someone to rely on when the seas become high and your ship threatens to founder. This can literally be a matter of life or death. In a relationship where romance remains intact, truth must be king.

CHRIST IN THE CANDLE

I have a friend of Scandinavian descent, although he is Canadian. He married a Canadian woman, also of Scandinavian descent. They decided to get married in Sweden, as a tribute to their joint ancestry. They were both at least nominally Christian, so they were married in a ceremony reflecting that. During their exchange of vows, the bride and groom held a lit candle aloft between them. I spent a long time thinking about the significance of that ritual.

There is an ancient conceit in the book of Genesis (2:21–22) that Eve was taken out of Adam—created from his rib. Woman from man: this presents something of a mystery, reversing, as it does, the normative biological sequence, where males emerge from females at birth. It also gave rise to a line of mythological speculation, attempting to account for the strangeness of this creative act, predicated on the supposition that Adam, the original man produced by God, was hermaphroditic— half masculine and half feminine—and only later separated into the two sexes. This implies not only the partition of a divinely produced unity, but the incompleteness of man and woman until each is brought together with the other.[2] The fact that the candle is held jointly indicates the binding of the two celebrants. The fact that the candle is held aloft, lit, implies that something higher—something superordinate—is representing or performing the union. Light, light in the heavens, light in the darkness, illumination, enlightenment. Prior to the invention of modern electric lights, candles were often used for this purpose. Evergreens, the standard choice for Christmas trees, represent life unending, as they do not "die" annually in the same manner as their deciduous counterparts. Such trees therefore symbolize the Tree of Life, which serves as the very foundation of the cosmos.[3] So, we illuminate the Tree of Life, at or near December 21, the darkest time of year, at least in the Northern Hemisphere.[4] That is why Christmas is located where it is on the calendar; the reappearance of the light is associated with the birth of the Universal Savior—signifying the eternal reemergence of light in the Stygian blackness.

Christ has long been regarded as the second (perfected) Adam and, just as there was speculation about the hermaphroditic nature of the first Adam prior to God's creation of the independent sexes, there is a line of speculation about Christ's spiritual perfection being a consequence of the ideal balance of masculine and feminine elements.*[5] It is very difficult for individuals joining themselves together to become desperate enough to cease their hiding and avoidance, live in truth, and repair themselves in the light cast by their joint existence. It is for this reason that both swear the dread vow of permanence ("What God has joined together, let not man put asunder" [Matthew 19:6]). "I am bound to you," claims one party to the agreement. "And I to you," says the other, and both think, if they have any sense, that they should each transform themselves and one another, to forestall any unnecessary suffering. So, what is the superordinate principle to which both marital partners must bow? It is not illumination as mere verbal abstraction. It is not that they are only supposed to think and speak the truth. It is that they are supposed to act it out. And that is the ancient idea that the Word should be made flesh.

The individuals who make up a married couple might well engage in a lifelong struggle concerning a single inappropriately conceptualized question: "Who is subordinate to whom in a marriage?" After all, each might reason, as people commonly do, that such an arrangement is a zero-sum game, with one winner and one loser. But a relationship does not have to be and should not be a question of one or the other as winner, or even each alternating in that status, in an approximation of fairness. Instead, the couple can decide that each and both are subordinate to a principle, a higher-order principle, which constitutes

---

*The same idea emerged constantly in the centuries of alchemical literature, which tended overwhelmingly to represent the perfect person (the possessor, in a spiritual or psychological sense, of the philosopher's stone) as a consequence of the mystical marriage between the feminine and masculine elements of the psyche. We discussed this in some detail in Rule II: Imagine who you could be and aim single-mindedly at that, with regard to the figure of the Rebis.

their union in the spirit of illumination and truth. That ghostly figure, the ideal union of what is best in both personalities, should be constantly regarded as the ruler of the marriage—and, indeed, as something as close to divine as might be practically approached by fallible individuals. That is what the ceremony of the candle represents: Neither participant rules the other. Instead, both bow to the principle of illumination. In that circumstance, it is not that one must abide by what the other wants (or vice versa). Instead, it is that both should be oriented toward the most positive future possible, and agree that speaking the truth is the best pathway forward. That orientation and truthfulness will engender a transformative dialogue, verbal and nonverbal, if the partners in the arrangement commit to abiding by the consequence of that dialogue. Voluntary subordination to this higher-order principle of illumination both unifies and revitalizes.

Imagine that you have just participated in such a ceremony. What does your participation signify? Do you *believe* in the ideas that you have just acted out? Do you believe that man and woman were once together, as a single being, were then separated, and must be restored as a unity? You can believe it dramatically, poetically, and metaphorically instead of merely rationally and mechanically, and that can lead you to deep truths. Do you want to find your soul mate? It is a romantic trope, obviously, but there are deep reasons for the existence of romantic fictions. Maybe you take someone on a date to a romantic movie. You both watch the movie hero and heroine find their soul mates. If you are fortunate, while you are watching you are thinking, "Well, maybe this person I am sitting with is the one for me, too." In the best of all situations, that is also what your date is hoping for. Maybe that is too much to hope for in real life. But the romantic part of you is longing for it regardless.

There is an inevitable yearning in our natures for the completion that someone else might provide. There is a sense that you are missing something, otherwise, and that only the proper romantic union will provide it. It is true, too—you are indeed missing something. If you were not, sex would never have evolved. The entire biological course of our destiny, since reproduction progressed past the mere division of cells, appears driven by the fact that it was better for two dissimilar creatures to come together to produce a comparatively novel version of themselves than to merely clone their current embodiment. You have your idiosyncrasies, your blind spots, your biases. Some of these are implicit. They are often paired inextricably with your unique talents: you seldom gain an advantage without a corresponding disadvantage, and you are a particular person, with particular attributes. If you are on your own, you are inevitably lopsided, one-sided. That is often not for the best.

There is unrealized utility in the marital institution about which we have become cynical—a consequence of our immaturity and naivete. A marriage is a vow, and there is a reason for it. You announce jointly, publicly: "I am not going to leave you, in sickness or health, in poverty or wealth—and you are not going to leave me." It is actually a threat: "We are not getting rid of each other, no matter what." You are shackled together, like two angry cats at the bottom of a barrel with the lid on. In principle, there is no escape. If you have any sense (besides the optimism of new love) you also think, "Oh, God. That is a horrifying possibility." The part of you that claims to desire freedom (but really wants to avoid any permanent and therefore terrifying responsibility) desires a trapdoor through which escape might be made, if and when it is necessary. That seems convenient—and it is true that there are unbearable marriages—but it is an option with extreme perils. Do you really want to keep asking yourself for the rest of your life—because you would always have the option to leave—if you made the right choice? In all likelihood, you did not. There are seven billion people in the world. At least a hundred million (let us say) might have made good partners for you. You certainly did not have time to try them out, and the probability that you found the theoretically optimal person approaches zero. But you do not *find* so much as *make*, and if you do not know that you are in real trouble. Furthermore, if you have an escape route, there will not be enough heat generated in the chamber you find yourself jointly trapped in to catalyze the change necessary in both of you—the maturation, the development of wisdom—because maturation and the development of wisdom require a certain degree of suffering, and suffering is escapable as long as there is an out.

You are not going to get along with your partner—not easily, unless you agree to be tyrannized and silent (and even then you will take your revenge)—because you are different people. No one just simply gets along, precisely because of that. And not only are you different from your partner, but you are rife with inadequacies and so is he—or she. And that is not bad enough. There is also the fact that even people of good will and character locked together in matrimony will face the mundane, quotidian, dull, tragic, and terrible together, because life can be—and certainly will be at some point—difficult to the point of impossibility. It is going to be tough. Even if you strive to pull yourselves together, and succeed at that admirably, there are going to be brutal times, and they are not necessarily going to be brief. Maybe life will be better if you stay together—that is the hope, and the likelihood, as far as I can tell—but the brutal times will still be there. What is going to make you voluntarily deal with your differences and establish a genuine agreement, a true consensus? You are going to have to negotiate in good faith, continually, to come to some sort of peaceful and productive accommodation. And if you do not? You are going to have your hands around each other's throats for sixty years.

In clinical practice, I have seen whole families in that situation. Imagine five people in a circle. Imagine further that each has their hands around the neck of the person in front of them. All are squeezing with just enough force to kill in a few decades. This is a decision, formulated over years of unspoken argument and refusal to negotiate: "I am going to kill you. It is just going to take me a lifetime." It is very possible that you have someone you might like to slowly throttle in your family, or who is currently doing it to you. Perhaps not, hopefully not (perhaps you would not admit it even if you knew it was true)— but it is common enough. If you do not negotiate peace with your partner, that is the situation you will find yourself in. There are three fundamental states of social being: tyranny (you do what I want), slavery (I do what you want), or negotiation. Tyranny is obviously not so good for the person enslaved, but it is also not good for the tyrant— because he or she becomes a tyrant, and there is nothing ennobling about that. There is nothing but cynicism, cruelty, and the hell of unregulated anger and impulsivity. Slavery is not good either, likewise for the slave and the tyrant. Slaves are miserable, wretched, angry, and resentful. They will take any and all chances whatsoever available to them to take revenge on their tyrants, who will in consequence find themselves cursed and damaged by their slaves. It is not easy to get the best out of someone by arbitrarily brandishing a stick at them, particularly when they try to do something good (and that diminution of spirit is the cruelest trick of the tyrant). But you can be certain, you want-to-be tyrants, that your slaves will take their revenge where they can, even if that means merely being much less than they could be.

My wife told me a terrible story once, about a couple she observed while volunteering in a palliative care ward. The husband was dying, and his wife was trimming his nails—a little too close. With each clip, there was blood, as she trimmed close enough to damage the quick. You see something like that, and wisdom speaks its terrible truth: "I know *exactly* what is going on there." That is the end stage of an unbelievably deceitful and brutal relationship. It is subtle. It does not announce itself loudly as murderous. No one knows, except the couple (even though they are perhaps striving with all their might, under the circumstances, not to know) and the careful observer, who sees a dying man and a wife who has determined, for whatever reasons, to make his death a little worse. That is not a desirable outcome. You do not want to end up in that situation, or anything like it. You want to negotiate. The question is, "What is going to make you desperate enough to negotiate?" And that is one of the mysteries that must be addressed if you wish to keep the romance alive in your relationship.

NEGOTIATION, TYRANNY, OR SLAVERY

Negotiation is exceptionally difficult. We already discussed the problems associated with determining what you want and then mustering up the courage to tell someone exactly that. And there are the tricks that people use, too, to avoid negotiation. Perhaps you ask your partner what he or she wants—perhaps during a difficult situation. "I don't know" is a common answer (you get that from children, too, and even more often from adolescents). It is not acceptable, however, in a discussion that cannot in good faith be avoided. Sometimes "I don't know" truly means what it is supposed to mean—the person who utters the phrase is at a genuine loss—but often it means, instead: "I don't want to talk about it, so go away and leave me alone." Irritation or outright anger, sufficient to deter the questioner, often accompanies this response. That brings the discussion to a halt, and it can stay halted forever. Maybe that has happened once or twice or a dozen times too often, so you—the questioner, in this instance—have had enough of your partner's refusal, or you have decided that you are done being cowardly or a victim of your own misplaced compassion and you are not about to take "I don't know" for an answer. In consequence, you persist in pursuing your target. "Well, *guess*," you might say. "Throw something on the table, for God's sake. I do not care what it is. Even if it is wrong, it is at least a start." "I don't know" means not only "Go away and leave me alone." It also frequently means "Why don't you go away, do all the work necessary to figure out what is wrong, and come back and tell me—if you're so smart," or "It is intolerably rude of you to refuse to allow me to remain in my willful or dangerous ignorance, given that it obviously bothers me so much to think about my problems." It is not rude, though—or even if it is, you still need to know what your partner wants, and so does he or she, and how in the world are either or both of you going to figure it out if you cannot even get the conversation off the ground? It is not rude. It is a cruel act of love.

Persistence under such conditions is a necessity, a terrible necessity, akin to surgery. It is difficult and painful because it takes courage and even some foolhardiness to continue a discussion when you have been told in no uncertain terms by your partner to go the hell away (or worse). It is a good thing, however—an admirable act—because a person bothered by something they do not wish to talk about is very likely to be split internally over the issue at hand. The part that wants to avoid is the part that gets angry. There is a part that wants to talk, too, and to settle the issue. But doing so is going to be cognitively demanding, ethically challenging, and emotionally stressful. In addition, it is going to require trust, and people test trust, not least by manifesting anger when approached about something touchy just to determine if the person daring the approach cares sufficiently to overcome a serious barrier or two or three or ten to get to the horrible bottom of things. And avoidance followed by anger is not the only trick in the book.

The next serious hurdle is tears. Tears are easily mistaken for the distress due to sadness, and they are very effective at bringing tender-hearted people to a dead halt as a consequence of their misplaced compassion. (Why misplaced? Because if you leave the person alone because of their tears, they quit suffering right then, but continue with their unresolved problem until they solve it, which might be never.) Tears, however, are just as often anger (perhaps more often) as they are sadness or distress. If the person you are chasing down and corner-ing is red-faced, for example, in addition to their tears, then he or she is probably angry, not hurt (that is not inevitably the case, but it is a reasonably common sign). Tears are an effective defense mechanism, as it takes a heart of stone to withstand them, but they tend to be the last-ditch attempt at avoidance. If you can get past tears, you can have a real conversation, but it takes a very determined interlocutor to avoid the insult and hurt generated by anger (defense one) and the pity and compassion evoked by tears (defense two). It requires someone who has integrated their shadow (their stubbornness, harshness, and capac-ity for necessary emotionless implacability) and can use it for long-term benefit. Do not foolishly confuse "nice" with "good."

Remember the options previously discussed: negotiation, tyranny, or slavery. Of those, negotiation is the least awful, even though it is no joke to negotiate, and it is perhaps the most difficult of the three, in the short term, because you have to fight it out, now, and God only knows how deep you are going to have to go, how much diseased tis-sue you will have to remove. For all you know, you are fighting with the spirit of your wife's grandmother, who was treated terribly by her alcoholic husband, and the consequences of that unresolved abuse and distrust between the sexes are echoing down the generations. Children are amazing mimics. They learn much of what they know implicitly long before they can use language, and they imitate the bad along with the good. It is for this reason that it has been said that the sins of the fathers will be visited on the children to the third and fourth generation (Numbers 14:18).

Hope, of course, can drive us through the pain of negotiation, but hope is not enough. You need desperation, as well, and that is part of the utility of "till death do us part." You are stuck with each other, if you are serious—and if you are not serious, you are still a child. That is the point of the vow: the possibility of mutual salvation, or the closest you can manage here on Earth. In a truly mature marriage, if your health holds out, you are there for the aforementioned sixty years, like Moses in the desert searching for the Promised Land, and there is plenty of trouble that must be worked through—all of it—before peace might be established. So, you grow up when you marry, and you aim for peace as if your soul depends upon it (and perhaps that is more serious than your life depending on it), and you make it work or you suffer miserably. You will be tempted by avoidance, anger, and tears, or enticed to employ the trapdoor of divorce so that you will not have to face what must be faced. But your failure will haunt you while you are enraged, weeping, or in the process of separating, as it will in the next relationship you stumble into, with all your unsolved problems intact and your negotiating skills not improved a whit.

You can keep the possibility of escape in the back of your mind. You can avoid the commitment of permanence. But then you cannot achieve the transformation, which might well demand everything you can possibly muster. The difficulty, however, that is implicit in the negotiation carries with it a tremendous promise, which is part of a radically successful life: *You could have a marriage that works.* You could make it work. That is an achievement—a tangible, challenging, exceptional, and unlikely achievement. There are not many genuine achievements of that magnitude in life; a number as small as four is a reasonable estimate. Maybe, if you strive for it, you have established a solid marriage. That is achievement *one*. Because of that, you have founded a solid and reliable, honest and playful home into which you could dare bring children. Then you can have kids, and with a solid marriage that can work out for you. That is achievement *two*. Then you have brought upon yourself more of the responsibility that will demand the best from you. Then you will have new relationships of the highest quality, if you are fortunate and careful. Then you will have grandchildren so that you are surrounded by new life when yours begins to slip away. In our culture, we live as if we are going to die at thirty. But we do not. We live a very long time, but it is also all over in a flash, and it should be that you have accomplished what human beings accomplish when they live a full life, and marriage and children and grandchildren and all the trouble and heartbreak that accompanies all of that is far more than half of life. Miss it at your great peril.

You meet people, usually young, unwise but laden with the unearned cynicism that substitutes for wisdom in youth, and they say, categorically—even pridefully—"I do not want children." Plenty of nineteen-year-olds say that, and that is acceptable, in some sense, because they are nineteen, and they have time, and what do they know at nineteen, anyway? And some twenty-seven-year-olds say that, but not so many, particularly if they are female and the least bit honest with themselves. And some forty-five-year-olds say the same thing, in the past tense, and some of them, perhaps, are telling the truth; but most are celebrating closing the barn door after the cattle have bolted. No one will speak the truth about this. To note outright that we lie to young women, in particular, about what they are most likely to want in life is taboo in our culture, with its incomprehensibly strange insistence that the primary satisfaction in the typical person's life is to be found in career (a rarity in itself, as most people have jobs, not careers). But it is an uncommon woman, in my clinical and general professional experience, regardless of brilliance or talent, training, discipline, parental desire, youthful delusion, or cultural brainwashing who would not perform whatever sacrifice necessary to bring a child into the world by the time she is twenty-nine, or thirty-five, or worse, forty.

Here is a pathway to misery I would strongly recommend avoiding, aimed primarily at the women who read this book (although wise boyfriends and husbands should take equal note). Decide that you want children when you are twenty-nine or thirty, and then be unable to have them: I would not recommend that. You will not recover. We are too fragile to play around with what life might offer us. Everyone thinks, when they are young and do not know any better, "Well, pregnancy can be taken for granted." That is only true if you absolutely do not want and should not have a child, and you have sex in the backseat of a car when you are fifteen. Then, for sure, you will find yourself in trouble. But a successful pregnancy is not a foregone conclusion, not by any stretch of the imagination. You can push trying for children to the older end of that spectrum—and many people are encouraged or encourage themselves to do exactly that—but up to 30 percent of couples experience trouble becoming pregnant.[6]

You encounter something similar—that is, the incaution about what life will and will not offer—when people whose marriages have stagnated begin to develop the delusion that a romantic affair will address their unmet needs. When I had clients considering such a move—or perhaps involved in an affair, currently—I tried to bring them back down to earth. "Let us think it through, all the way. Not just for this week, or this month. You are fifty. You have this twenty-four-year-old, and she is willing to break up your marriage. What is she thinking? Who must she be? What does she know?" "Well, I am really attracted to her." "Yes, but she has a personality disorder. Seriously, because what the hell is she doing with you, and why is she willing to break up this marriage?" "Well, she does not care if I stay married." "Oh, I see. So, she does not want to have an actual relationship with someone, with any degree of long-term permanency. Somehow that is going to work out well for you, is it? Just think about that. It is going to be a little rough on your wife. A lot of lies are going to go along with that. You have children—how are they going to respond when all this comes out, as it most certainly will? And what do you think about the ten years in court that are now beckoning, that are going to cost you a third of a million dollars and put you in a custody battle that will occupy all your time and attention?"

I have seen people who were in custody battles who would seriously have preferred cancer. It is no joke to have your arm caught in the dangerous machinery of the courts. You spend much of the time truly wishing you were dead. So that is your "affair," for God's sake. It is even more delusional than that, because, of course, if you are married to someone, you often see them at their worst, because you have to share the genuine difficulties of life with them. You save the easy parts for your adulterous partner: no responsibility, just expensive restaurants, exciting nights of rule breaking, careful preparation for romance, and the general absence of reality that accompanies the privilege of making one person pay for the real troubles of existence while the other benefits unrealistically from their absence. You do not have a life with someone when you have an affair with them. You have an endless array of desserts (at least in the beginning), and all you have to do is scoop the whipped cream off the top of each of them and devour it. That is it. You see each other under the best possible

conditions, with nothing but sex in your minds and nothing else interfering with your lives. As soon as it transforms from that into a relationship that has any permanency, a huge part of the affair immediately
turns right back into whatever it was that was bothering you about your
marriage. An affair is not helpful, and people end up horribly hurt.
Particularly children—and it is to them you owe primary allegiance.

I am not trying to be unreasonably categorical about marriage and
family. You cannot expect every social institution to work out for everyone. Sometimes, you have married someone who is a psychopathic
brute, a congenital and incorrigible liar, a criminal, an alcoholic, a sa-
dist (and maybe all five at once). Then you must escape. But that is not
a trapdoor. That is a catastrophe, like a hurricane, and you should
move out of its path. You might be tempted to conclude: "Well, how
about we live together, instead of getting married? We will try each
other out. It is the sensible thing to do." But what exactly does it mean,
when you invite someone to live with you, instead of committing
yourself to each other? And let us be appropriately harsh and realistic
about our appraisal, instead of pretending we are taking a used car for
a test jaunt. Here is what it means: "You will do, for now, and I presume you feel the same way about me. Otherwise we would just get
married. But in the name of a common sense that neither of us possesses we are going to reserve the right to swap each other out for a
better option at any point." And if you do not think that is what living
together means—as a fully articulated ethical statement—see if you
can formulate something more plausible.

You might think, "Look, Doc, that is pretty cynical." So why not we
consider the stats, instead of the opinion of arguably but not truly old-
fashioned me? The breakup rate among people who are not married
but are living together—so, married in everything but the formal
sense—is substantially higher than the divorce rate among married

couples.[7] And even if you do get married and make an honest person, so to speak, of the individual with whom you cohabited, you are still much more rather than less likely to get divorced than you would be had you never lived together initially.[8] So the idea of trying each other out? Sounds enticing, but does not work.

It is of course possible that people who are more likely to get divorced, for reasons of temperament, are also more likely to live together, before or without marriage, rather or in addition to the possibility that living together just does not work. It is no simple matter to disentangle the two causal factors. But it does not matter, practically. Cohabitation without the promise of permanent commitment, socially announced, ceremonially established, seriously considered, does not produce more robust marriages. And there is nothing good about that—particularly for children, who do much worse in single parent (generally male-absent) families.[9] Period. So, I just do not see it as a justifiable social alternative. And I say that as someone who lived with my wife before I married her. I am not innocent in this regard. But that does not mean I was right. And there is something else, and it is far from trivial. You just do not have that many chances in life to have an intimate relationship work out properly. Maybe it takes you two or three years to meet the potential Mr. or Ms. Right, and another two or three to determine if they are in fact who you think they are. That is five years. You get old a lot faster than you think you will, no matter how old you are now, and most of what you could do with your family—with marriage, children, and so forth—is from twentysomething to about thirty-five. How many good five-year chances do you therefore have? Three? Four, if you are fortunate?

This means that your options decrease as you wait, rather than increase. If you are a widower, or a widow, and you must hit the dating scene when you are forty or fifty, so be it. You have been struck by tragedy, and that is life. But I have watched friends do it, and it is not a fate I would casually wish on anyone I loved. Let us continue to be reasonable about this: All sixteen- to eighteen-year-olds have much in common. They are unformed. They are malleable. That is not an insult. It is just a fact. It is also why they can go off to college and make a lifelong friend (no cynicism whatsoever intended) from a roommate within a single semester. By the time you are in your midforties, however—if you have lived at all—you have become somewhat of a singular and unique person. I have known people I met at that time of my life for a decade or more whom I still seem to consider new acquaintances. That is a pure function of the complexity of increasing age. And that is mere friendship, not love—not a joint life and perhaps even the bringing together of two disparate families.

And so you have your marriage and your children, and that is working out well because you are stubborn and sufficiently terrified of the hell that awaits anyone who fails to negotiate for peace and make the sacrifices necessary to establish it. You are undoubtedly more prepared now for your career—or more likely, your job. That is the *third* of the four achievements you might manage, with good fortune and an undaunted spirit, in the brief flash of your existence. You have learned how to establish productive harmony in the close confines of your most intimate and private relationships, and some of that wisdom spills over into your workplace. You are a mentor for younger people, a helpful peer and reliable subordinate, and instead of the hash you could so easily make of the place you inhabit, you improve it. And if everyone did that the world would be a much less tragic and unhappy place. Maybe it would even be a self-evidently good place. And perhaps you learn how to make good use of your time away from family and work— your leisure—and you make that meaningful and productive. And that is the *fourth* of the four achievements—and one, like the others, that can grow. Perhaps you get better and better at such things so that you can work on solving more and more difficult problems, and become a credit, in your own way, to the spirit of humanity itself. And that is life.

Back to marriage. How do you plan and diligently maintain the romance in your relationship? Well, you have to decide: "Do you want some romance in your life or not?" If you really think about it, without resentment—without the joy of depriving your partner, now alienated, of the pleasure that might come with such an attempt—the answer is generally yes. Sexual romance: the adventure, pleasure, intimacy, and excitement people fantasize about experiencing, when they are feeling in need of a touch of the divine. You want that. The joys of life are rare and precious, and you do not want to forsake them without due cause. How are you going to accomplish that? With luck, it will happen between you and someone you like; with better luck, and sufficient commitment, it will happen between you and someone you love. Little about this is easy. If you set up a household with someone, you are going to have to do an awful lot of negotiation to keep both "like" and "love" alive.

THE DOMESTIC ECONOMY

Here are some practical considerations. They may seem far from the topic of romance. The discussion is necessary, however, because we transcended—or lost—our traditional roles, and have not formulated replacements for them. Before that—perhaps before the invention of the birth control pill, which was a biological revolution—men did male things, whatever they were, and women did female things, whatever they were. Traditional roles are far more helpful than modern people, who vastly overestimate their tolerance for freedom and choice, tend to realize. In a less rapidly mutable society, everyone has some sense of their respective duties. That does not eliminate the tension (nothing eliminates the tension), but at least there is a template. If there is no template for what either of you should be doing when you live together with someone, then you are required to argue about it—or negotiate about it, if you are good at that, which you are probably not. Few people are.

If you are going to set up a household in peace with someone you love and hopefully like, and wish to continue loving and liking, you are going to have to determine in some manner who is going to do what. That is the replacement for roles. Who makes the bed? When should it be made? At what level of perfection does the bed have to be made to be mutually acceptable? And if this is not handled well, the conversation becomes counterproductive rapidly: "I made the bed." "Well, you did not do a very good job." "Nothing's ever good enough for you. If you do not think I did a good enough job making the bed, maybe I will just stop, and you can make it yourself!" "Well, maybe you should raise your standards a bit, and maybe not just about the bed!" It is going to take days to sort that out—if it ever does get sorted out—and that is just the bed. That is just the first ten minutes of the morning. So maybe it remains unmade or made badly and bitterly for the next sixty years (there is that time span again), and there are many more domestic issues to address than just the bed. But if that is not sorted out, then it is a problem every morning of every day and every day of every week and month and year and everyone is angry at least under the surface as soon as they awaken or every time they enter the bedroom and other things begin to fall out of order. There is nothing good about that.

Whose career is going to take priority? When and why? How will the children be educated and disciplined, and by whom? Who does the cleaning? Who sets the table? Takes out the garbage? Cleans up the bathroom? How are the bank accounts set up and managed? Who shops for groceries? Clothes? Furniture? Who pays for what? Who adopts responsibility for the taxes? Et cetera, et cetera, et cetera. Two hundred things, perhaps, to run a household properly—as complex a problem as running a business, with the additional difficulty of trying to manage it with a family member, much of it repeated daily. Your life is, after all, mostly composed of what is repeated routinely. You either negotiate responsibility for every single one of these duties or you play push and pull forever, while you battle it out nonverbally, with stubbornness, silence, and half-hearted attempts at "cooperation." That is not going to do your romantic situation any good. It is of vital necessity, in consequence, to place the domestic part of the household economy on firm ground.

It is an incredibly difficult set of problems to solve, because it means you must consciously sort the hierarchy of responsibilities between the partners in the household. You are required to negotiate every damned and apparently trivial detail (but the apparent triviality is a delusion): Who prepares the meals? When do they prepare the meals? What is that worth in terms of trade-off for other tasks? How do you thank someone for conducting themselves properly in the kitchen? Who loads the dishwasher? Who does the dishes? How fast do the dishes have to be cleared off the table after you eat? Which dishes are going to be used? What are we going to eat? What role are the kids going to play? Do we sit down together? Do we have regular mealtimes? Each of these questions can become a bloody war. One person thinks one thing, and the other person thinks another thing, and who knows who's right? So, you have to have a struggle with it, and you have to come to a consensus. Doing so is difficult. Maybe it means hundreds of fights. It certainly means dozens. But they are fights with a purpose, and that purpose is to fight it out until a solution arises, so that fights about that issue are no longer necessary. That makes peace the goal, and it cannot be established except through negotiation, and that requires a commitment strong enough to withstand serious and deep conflict.

The next thing you have to do—I know this from both my clinical and marital experience (thirty years of each)—is actually talk to your partner for about ninety minutes a week, purely about practical and personal matters. "What is happening to you at work?" "What is going on, as far as you are concerned, with the kids?" "What needs to be done around the house?" "Is there anything bothering you that we can address?" "What do we have to do that is necessary to keep the wolf from the door next week?" Just pure, practical communication: partly because you have a story, your partner has a story, and you have a joint story. To know your story, you must tell it, and, for your partner to know it, he or she must hear it. It is necessary for that communication to happen on an ongoing basis. It does not have to be ninety minutes all at once. Maybe it can be fifteen minutes a day. But you keep those lines of pragmatic communication open, so you know where the other person is, and vice versa. If you dip below ninety minutes a week, you generate a backlog, and your mutual story begins to unwind. At some point, that backlog is so large that you do not know who you are yourself, and you certainly do not know who your partner is, and you become mutually alienated. Your relationship loses its coherence. That is a bad situation.

When I am helping someone straighten out their marriage, let us say, we do very mundane things. I am not interested in vacations, special occasions, or anything that happens that is out of the ordinary. It is not that those things are unimportant, but they are not vital in the same sense that daily routines are vital. It is the latter that must be set right. I want to know what interrelationships constitute the bulk of your typical day. You wake up together, perhaps; you eat together. You do such things every day. Maybe waking up, preparing for the day, and eating make up five hours a day. That is a third of your waking time and, therefore, a third of your life. It is thirty-five hours every seven days—a whole workweek; an entire career. Get it right. Ask yourself and each other: How do we want these times to be structured? How can we make the morning awakening pleasant? Can we attend to each other politely and with interest and perhaps without electronic distractions while we eat? Could we make our meals delicious and the atmosphere welcoming? Consider coming home in the evening. Let us say that routine takes ten minutes. So that is another hour plus per week; fifty hours a year—one and a half workweeks. You spend one and a half workweeks a year being greeted as you come in the door. It is a sizable fraction of your existence. Does somebody meet you at the door and indicate a certain degree of happiness to see you, or are you ignored because everyone is using their smartphones, or met with a litany of complaints? How would you like to organize that, so you do not dread the moment you arrive at home? There are things you do together that are mundane things; those things you do every day. But they are your whole life. You get those things right and you have established yourself much more effectively than you might realize. If you can successfully fight the war that establishes harmony in the domestic economy, you have both won a major victory. And then you can concentrate on what might happen during a romantic vacation to a boutique hotel, or your parents' cottage, or an all-inclusive resort, or an adventure holiday—or just during that twice-weekly date we discussed earlier that you are both so reluctant to attempt.

Start by getting these things straight, and see what happens. Then you will have peaceful mealtimes, for example, and you will not die of frustration or high blood pressure. You will have to fight for such an accomplishment. What matters, however, is not whether you fight (because you have to fight), but whether you make peace as a consequence. To make peace is to manage a negotiated solution. And you want and need to come to a negotiated solution about every responsibility and opportunity you share as a couple—and about every obstacle you encounter. At least then you will have someone to talk things through with when your life gets complex, as it inevitably will. And you have the advantage of two heads, even though they will not see eye to eye. What all this means is that the problems of knowing what you want and discussing it with your partner must be solved before the romance in your relationship can be maintained.

Other people keep you sane. That is partly why it is a good idea to get married. Why? Well, you are half insane, and so is your spouse (well, maybe not half—but plenty). Hopefully, however, it is not generally the same half. Now and then you meet couples who have the same weakness, and they compound that failing in each other. Maybe they are both too fond of wine, for example, and they drift together toward alcoholism. What you might want, to avoid such a fate, is that one person in the couple is fond of alcohol, but not both. This will cause a certain amount of short-term conflict, in situations where drinking is occurring or likely to occur, but the long-term consequences (avoiding either of you becoming an alcoholic) are likely to be beneficial. The one who does not drink will have a drink or two on a social occasion, just to avoid being too rigid and horrible, and the one who likes to drink will get what is hopefully a salutary reprimand if he or she does not exercise proper control.

It is a fortunate happenstance, generally speaking, that your idiosyncrasies are likely to be somewhat randomly distributed, and that if you unite with someone else you are likely to find some strength where you are weak and vice versa. When you unite the two of you to recreate that original being—that is the symbolic idea—then you have a chance of producing one reasonable, sane being. That is good for you both, even better for your children (who now have a fighting chance of adapting to what constitutes generally sane behavior), and it is good for friendship and the broader world, too.

A lot of that movement toward functional unity is a consequence of dialogue and communication. If you are old enough, you know that people are badly broken. When you are young and not very experienced, you are likely to make two assumptions, in a rather unquestioning and implicit manner, that are simply not true. The first is that there is someone out there who is perfect. You are likely even to encounter this hypothetically perfect person, whom you view through your delusion, and to fall desperately and foolishly in love with them (foolishly because you are in love with your projection of perfection, rather than the person—which is very confusing to the target of your affection). The second assumption is that there is someone out there who is perfect *for you*. From these assumptions, you are making at least three errors, which is quite an accomplishment, given you have made only two assumptions.

To begin with, there is not anyone out there who is perfect. There are just people out there who are damaged—quite severely, although not always irreparably, and with a fair bit of individual idiosyncrasy. Apart from that, if there was someone out there who was perfect, they would take one look at you and run away screaming. Unless you are deceiving someone, why would you end up with anyone better than you? You should be truly terrified if you have been accepted as a date. A sensible person would think of their new potential romantic partner: "Oh, my God! You are either blind, desperate, or as damaged as me!" That is a horrifying idea—signing up with someone who is as at least as much trouble as you. It is by no means as bad as being alone with yourself, but it is still out of the frying pan and into the fire—and at least the fire might transform you. Thus, you get married, if you have any courage—if you have any long-term vision and ability to vow and adopt responsibility; if you have any maturity—and you start to transform the two of you into one reasonable person. And it is even the case that participating in such a dubious process makes the two of you into one reasonable person with the possibility of some growth. So, you talk. About everything. No matter how painful. And you make peace. And you thank providence if you manage it, because strife is the default condition.

FINALLY: ROMANCE

There was not much point in this chapter in talking about romance immediately—at least not about its maintenance. Romance is play, and play does not take place easily when problems of any sort arise. Play requires peace, and peace requires negotiation. And you are lucky even then if you get to play.

The issue of marital romance—intimacy and sex—is a complex one, with a dragon lurking under every question. For example: What do you owe each other sexually if you are entangled in a marriage? The answer is not "no sex." That is not the answer, because part of the contractual arrangement is to organize your romantic life in a mutually satisfactory manner. It is an implicit precondition for the stability of the marriage. It is probably not sex fifteen times a day, and it is probably not sex begrudgingly once a year. It is somewhere between extremes, and that is where you must begin to negotiate.

My observation has been that the typical adult couple—when they have a job, children, and the domestic economy we just discussed, and all that worry and responsibility and concern—might manage once or twice a week, or even three times a week (not likely), for a reasonable romantic interlude. That frequency, if handled well, seems to work out acceptably for both partners. I have observed that twice is better than once, but once is much better than zero. Zero is bad. If you go to zero, then one of you is tyrannizing the other, and the other is submitting. If you go to zero, then one of you is going to have an affair—physical, emotional, fantastical, or some combination of the three. I do not say that lightly. Something has to give, and there has to be a *no* there, somewhere, when the romance disappears and the frequency of sexual intimacy hits rock bottom; there has to be a strong indication that "that is not good enough." I am not recommending the affair, but that is what you are setting yourself up for if your sex life vanishes. Maybe you want to take that pathway and facilitate the affair because you want to play the martyr: "My wife left me to have an affair, and poor me." And why did she do such a thing? "Well, perhaps our sex life was not all it could have been" (and this is an answer that may require a fair bit of digging). "What exactly do you mean by 'was not all it could have been'?" "Well, we had not made love for two years, and she went and had an affair."

That is not a shock. You should begin by assuming that your partner is a relatively normal human being, and that there is a certain amount of sexual satisfaction that is a reasonable requirement—let us say twice a week, or once a week, under conditions of intense busyness. In the early days of marriage it might be no problem to express romantic interest in your partner, but there is so much that must be done to live. Dating is a pain, even if you are single. I am perfectly aware that there is adventure there, too, but a lot of that occurs in movies, and not on internet dating sites, in text exchanges, coffee shops, restaurants, and bars, where the first awkward encounters occur.

You really have to work at it, and you will, if you are single, because you are lonesome, starved for attention, and desperate for physical intimacy. (Single people have far less sex, on average, than married people, although I suppose that a small percentage are making out like bandits. But I cannot see that even those successful in that manner are doing themselves any favors.)

So, as a single person, you will work at dating, because you are lonesome and deprived, but it is no simple matter. You must make space in your life for it. You have to plan. You must use your imagination, spend money, find an acceptable dating partner, and, as they say, kiss a lot of frogs to find a prince (or to find a princess, as well). People are often relieved when they get married, because they do not have to make all that so often counterproductive effort anymore. But that does not at all mean that you are now off the hook; that you can just lay back in your worn white underwear and socks and assume that all the hypothetical pleasures of Hugh Hefner are going to automatically manifest themselves in your household. There is still plenty of effort required, unless you want the romance to vanish. You have to talk about it. You have to have the difficult and embarrassing conversation: "What is it going be, dear? Tuesday and Thursday? Wednesday and Friday? Monday and Saturday?" You think, "Oh, God. That is so cut and dried. That is so mundane and planned. That is so scheduled, predictable, bourgeois, antiromantic, and robotic. It is demeaning and constricting, and it just turns sex into a duty. Where is the fun? Where is the spontaneity, the light jazz, cocktails, and excitement of sudden unexpected attraction? Where is the tuxedo and the little black dress?" That is what you expect? Even unconsciously, in your foolish fantasies? How often did you manage that when you were dating? Ever? And (remember, we are adults talking here) you want two jobs (two careers, two incomes), two kids, a reasonable standard of living—and spontaneity? And you are not about to "settle" for anything less?

Good luck with that. It is not going to happen—not in my clinical (and personal) experience—not without a lot of effort. What will happen is that the absolute necessities of life will inexorably start to take priority over the desirable necessities. Maybe there is a list of ten things you will do in a day, and sex is number eleven. It is not that you do not think sex is important, but you do not ever get past number five on the list of ten. You must make space and time, and, as far as I can tell, you have to do it consciously. You might think, "What would it be like to spend some time with this person I was once romantically attracted to?" You have to think that through. Maybe you only have time to watch half an hour of a TV show before you hop into bed. Maybe you have an hour and a half, or an hour, because life is too hectic. It would not be too bad an idea to have a shower. A little lipstick—that could be good. Some perfume. Some clothing that is attractive and erotic. Buy some lingerie for your wife, if you are a man, and wear it, with some courage, if you are a woman. Maybe you, if you are a man, can find something to wear that is reasonably sexy in a men's shop or a place that sells erotic clothing that is not too extreme and does not scream of poor taste and produce intense and counterproductive self-consciousness. And a compliment or two when all that courage is manifested is not such a bad idea. Maybe each time it happens for a year. You are trying to build some confidence. Try some nice soft lighting—maybe some candles (and someone has to buy the candles, and should be encouraged to do so; and the cynicism should be kept to an absolute minimum, if you do not want to banish what is fragile out of existence altogether). Here is a rule: do not ever punish your partner for doing something you want them to continue doing. Particularly if it took some real courage—some real going above and beyond the call of duty—to manage.

How about trying to set up the whole situation in the romantic manner that you might imagine, if you were imagining having an affair, because that is the sort of thing that people imagine when they imagine an affair (if they have any imagination). Try having an affair with your wife or husband. Maybe the latter can set up the bedroom while the former is preparing in the bathroom. We already mentioned candles. How about some music? How about making sure that the room is clean and—God willing—aesthetically attractive? That might be a start. And maybe, the two you of will not get old and fat, unhealthy and hypochondriacal as fast as possible just to spite each other, which many couples certainly do. And then, maybe, you could both have what you need, and maybe even what you want. But you would have to admit your desires, and you would have to negotiate with your partner. What do you like? What does she like? And are you going to let each other know? Are you going to risk practicing badly? Are you going to learn some new tricks, even if you feel like a fool when you first try?

None of this is easy. People will do things with or to each other that they will not talk about with each other, which is not helpful if they are married. It could be, maybe, if you were in a trading mood and approaching this with goodwill, that you could decide what you need and want, and arrange exactly the right trade. You might ask yourself, "Look, how do I have to set this up so I am likely to continue being romantically interested in my wife or my husband for the next twenty years, so that I do not wander off and do something stupid, like so many people do? What is my minimal precondition for erotic satisfaction?" You might try to convince yourself that it is not necessary; that you can put up with what you have, even if it is nothing. But you cannot. Not if you have any self-respect or sense. There is something that you are going to want and need. It is possible that, if you communicate openly what that something is, and at the same time leave yourself open to the same communication coming from your partner, that you both could get not only what you want from each other, but even more than you expect.

Arrange some dates, and then practice making those dates and going on them until you are expert at it. Negotiate, and practice that, too. Allow yourself to become aware of what you want and need, and have the decency to let your partner in on the secret. After all, who else are you going to tell? Devote yourself to the higher ideal upon which an honest and courageous relationship is necessarily dependent, and do that with the seriousness that will keep your soul intact. Maintain your marital vows, so that you are desperate enough to negotiate honestly. Do not let your partner brush you off with protestations of ignorance or refusal to communicate. Do not be naive, and do not expect the beauty of love to maintain itself without all-out effort on your part. Distribute the requirements of your household in a manner you both find acceptable, and do not tyrannize or subject yourself to slavery. Decide what you need to keep yourself satisfied both in bed and out of it. And maybe—just maybe—you will maintain the love of your life and you will have a friend and confidant, and this cold rock we live on at the far end of the cosmos will be a little warmer and more comforting than it would otherwise be. And you are going to need that, because rough times are always on their way, and you better have something to set against them or despair will visit and will not depart.

Plan and work diligently to maintain the romance in your relationship.

DO NOT ALLOW YOURSELF TO BECOME RESENTFUL, DECEITFUL, OR ARROGANT

THE STORY IS THE THING

You have your reasons for being resentful, deceitful, and arrogant. You face, or will face, terrible, chaotic forces, and you will sometimes be outmatched. Anxiety, doubt, shame, pain, and illness, the agony of conscience, the soul-shattering pit of grief, dashed dreams and disappointment, the reality of betrayal, subjection to the tyranny of social being, and the ignominy of aging unto death—how could you not degenerate, and rage, and sin, and come to hate even hope itself? I want you to know how you might resist that decline, that degeneration into evil. To do so—to understand your own personality and its temptation by darkness—you need to know what you are up against. You need to understand your motivations for evil—and the triad of resentment, deceit, and arrogance is as good a decomposition of what constitutes evil as I have been able to formulate.

Is it possible to understand the world in a manner that provides protection against the temptation to traverse that lowest of roads? It is an axiom of human wisdom that clearer formulation and deeper comprehension of a problem is salutary. We will begin just that attempt with a conceptual shift—one that is difficult and perplexing for the committed materialists we moderns are. First, a question: *What is the world made of?* To answer this, we will need to consider reality—the world—as it is fully experienced by someone alive and awake, with all the richness of subjective being left intact—dreams, sensory experiences, feelings, drives, and fantasies. This is the world that manifests itself to—or, better, that you meet head-on with—your unique individual consciousness.

Consider the act of awakening in the morning. If you were asked what you perceive, at that moment, you might well mention the same concrete objects that anyone else might see, if they woke up in bed beside you. You might describe all that you have gathered around you in your bedroom—the desk, the chairs, the clothes (messy or neatly arrayed, depending on your temperament and preference and, perhaps, your condition last night). You are likely to answer in this very objective, realistic manner, claiming, essentially, to see the furniture of the stage. There is, of course, some truth to your answer, although you may pay less attention to the familiar things around you than you think. Why waste time and energy perceiving what you can simply remember?

However, the furniture and other contents of your bedroom are *not* truly what you perceive when you first wake up. You are already familiar with the place where you sleep, and what it contains. There is no reason to continue to effortfully and consciously apprehend what you already understand. Instead, you are liable to perceive your surroundings *psychologically*. You begin to consider how you are going to conduct yourself on the stage you will inevitably occupy, and what is going to happen in consequence. What you see upon waking is an array of possibilities, many of them concerning the day at hand, and others associated with the weeks, months, and years to come. What you are truly concerned with upon waking is the answer to a question: "What shall I make of the possibilities that I see in play in front of me, complex, worrisome, exciting, dull, restricted, unlimited, fortunate, or catastrophic as they may be?"

Out there in the potential is everything you could have. It is the realm of unrealized possibility, and no one knows its full extent. There appears to be no limit, in principle, to what can be made from what has not yet manifested itself. Everything that might yet be makes its home there. You could well consider what remains to be encountered as an eternal treasure house—a horn of plenty (which are in fact two of its representations). But that is only half the story (and there is the rub). If the potential you confront manifests improperly (because of a mistake on your part; because of the sheer arbitrariness of the world), then you can find yourself in terrible trouble. Out there, in the unknown— in the future, which is what you truly contend with, when your consciousness reawakens—awaits everything good, but also everything terrible, painful, hellish, and deadly. Whatever *potential* might be, therefore, it does not follow the simple rules of material logic. Objects that play by the rules of the game we consider real (when we assume that what is real is also logical) can only be one thing at a time, and certainly not themselves and their opposite, simultaneously. Potential, however, is not like that. It is not categorizable in that manner. It is tragedy, comedy, good and evil, and everything in between at the same time. It is also not tangible, in the sense that the things we consider must be tangible. It does not even exist—except as *what could be* exists. Perhaps it is best considered as the structure of reality, before reality manifests itself concretely in the present, where reality appears to most self-evidently exist. But creatures such as us do not contend with the present. It may therefore be that it is not the present that is most real—at least as far as our consciousness is concerned. We have to fight to "be here now," the advice of the sages. Left to our own devices, we turn our minds instead to investigating the future: *What could be?* Attempting to answer that question—that is life. That is the true encounter with reality. *What is?* That is the dead past, already accomplished. *What could be?* That is the emergence of new being, new adventure, brought about by the conjunction of living consciousness with the great expanse of paradoxical possibility.

And if it is possibility that is most real, rather than actuality (as evidenced by the fact that it is possibility we are destined to contend with), then it is the investigation into possibility that is the most important of all investigations. But how do we investigate something that is not here, or there, or anywhere? How do we examine what has not yet manifested itself; explore what only could be but is not yet? And how can we possibly communicate with each other intelligibly about that attempt, trade information about the most effective conceptualizations, approaches, and strategies? The answer to that, as far as I can tell, is by communicating through stories about what is and, equally, what could be. And what that implies is that if possibility is the ultimate element of reality with which we contend, then it is stories that hold the wisdom that we most need to know.

We naturally think of our lives as stories, and communicate about our experience in that same manner. We tell people automatically where we are (to set the stage) and where we are going, so that we can create the present out of the possibility that springs forth as we journey toward our destination. No one finds such an account out of the ordinary. But we are doing more than portraying our lives, and those of others, as a sequence of events. It is something deeper than that.

When you depict a person's actions in the world, you describe how they perceive, evaluate, think, and act—and, when you do so, a story unfolds (and the better you are at such descriptions, the more storylike your accounts are). Furthermore, we experience the world as populated by figures that represent exactly what we must contend with. The unknown, unexpected, and novel—the world of possibility—is represented in dramatic form, as is the world that we expect and strive to bring into being, and ourselves, as actors faced with the unknown and the predictable alike. We use the story to represent all of this.

Could it be that we communicate in stories (and everyone else understands them) because what everyone is doing in the world *is* fundamentally a story? Could that mean that the world of experience is, in truth, indistinguishable from a story—that it cannot be represented in a manner more accurate than that of the story? We are, in principle, adapted to the world—adapted to its realities. Thus, if we naturally construe the world as a story, then perhaps the world is most accurately, or at least most practically, construed as a story (and *accurate* and *practical* are not so easy to distinguish). You might argue, contrarily, that the scientific view of the world is more accurate, in some sense, and that the scientific view is not fundamentally a story. But, as far as I can tell, it is still *nested inside* a story: one that goes something like "careful and unbiased pursuit of the truth will make the world a better place for all people, reducing suffering, extending life, and producing wealth." Why practice science otherwise? Why would anyone take on the difficulties and rigors of scientific training without that motivation? There are more effective ways of making money, for example, if you have the intelligence and discipline to become a genuine researcher. And in terms of intrinsic motivation, the love of science is not precisely disinterested learning. The great experimenters and scientific writers I have known are passionate about their pursuit. Something emotional drives them.

They hope that their learning (disinterested though it may be, as at present it has no specific aim except that of learning) will have some genuinely positive outcome: making the world a better place. That provides the entire pursuit with a narrative element, the motive that accompanies any good plot, and the transformation of character that makes up the best of stories.

We conceptualize what we experience as a story. That story is, roughly speaking, the description of the place we are at right now, as well as the place that we are going to, the strategies and adventures that we implement and experience along the way, and our downfalls and reconstitutions during that journey. You perceive and act inside a structure like that all the time, because you are always somewhere, going somewhere else, and you are always evaluating where you are and what is going on in relation to your goal. Part of this thinking in stories is our tendency to see the world as a selection of characters, each of which represents either where we are or are going, the unexpected occurrences we may encounter, or ourselves as actors. We see animated intent everywhere[1]—and we certainly present the world that way to our children. That is why Thomas the Tank Engine has a face and a smile, and the sun has a face and a smile. That is why—even among adults—there is a man in the moon, and deities scattered across the stars. Everything is animated. That is a reflection of our proclivity to treat things as if they are personalities with intent, regardless of what they are, regardless of whether they are animate or inanimate. That is why it is okay with you that your car has a face (on the front, where faces belong), which it most certainly does.

We act (perceive, think, react) that way because each member of the human species does almost everything he or she does in the presence, for better or worse, of other people. And that has been the case forever. Virtually everything we encountered in the long biological rise to our current form was social. If we were not interacting with people, then it was with animals. Maybe we were hunting them, or herding them, or playing with them, once they had been domesticated—or maybe they were hunting us, and we had to understand them to escape them or defend ourselves. All that tribal, intertribal, and cross-species interaction molded our brains, shaped our fundamental categories, rendering them social, not objective—not like the categories of science. It is not as if we are born with an instinct for the periodic table of the elements. No. We only managed to get that straight a few hundred years ago, and it took a lot of conscious time and effort to formulate. Furthermore, even though it was other people who did the terribly hard work necessary to establish that remarkable chemical category system, it is difficult to learn. It is not that interesting, intrinsically (at least for most people), because there is no story associated with it. It is an accurate and useful representation of the objective reality of what is, beyond the shadow of a doubt, but it is a struggle to master perception of that abstracted sort.

Conversely, if someone is telling you a story, it attracts your attention immediately. It can be a complicated and cognitively difficult story—something requiring hours of concentration. It might even be the story of how the periodic table of the elements was discovered, and the triumphs and difficulties that accompanied the process. It does not matter. If it is well told, it is gripping, and likely to be remembered. If you want to teach a child something and get them to attend, tell them a story. They will repeatedly ask you to do that. They do not grab your pant leg and beg, "Dad, one more line from the periodic table of the elements before bed!" But they are highly motivated to hear a story—sometimes even the same one every night. That is an indication of the depth and importance of stories. You might think the story is simple, but your child, listening intently, is processing the multiple levels of meaning represented in any decent tale—meanings of which you are very unlikely to be aware, if the story you are telling is traditional and deep.

We are all human. That means there is something about our experience that is the same. Otherwise, we would not all be human. We would not even be able to communicate. To communicate, paradoxically, there must be things about you and others that can go without saying. Imagine telling someone, "I got really angry this morning." If there is any indication you want the conversation to continue and they are agreeable, they might ask you why; but they are not likely to ask you, "What do you mean, 'angry'?" They do not ask the latter question because they already know, from their own experience, what "angry" means. It can be assumed, rather than explained. In fact, the only reason you can talk about anything at all is because there are some things you do not ever have to talk about. You can just take them for granted. We know, worldwide, for example, that there are basic sets of emotions shared by all humans—and by many animals.[2] Everyone understands a growling mother bear standing in front of her cubs, teeth bared for all to see. It is those things that you do not have to talk about that most precisely make us human, that constitute the essence, mutable though it remains through the actions of society and environment.

So, on to the story—to the story of the story, in fact. We will begin by meeting the characters whose existence universally structures our understanding of the potential of the world. And, with luck, as you meet them, you will begin to understand their relationship to resentment, arrogance, and deceit well enough so that understanding will offer you some protection.

THE ETERNAL CHARACTERS
OF THE HUMAN DRAMA

THE DRAGON OF CHAOS

When my son, Julian, was about four years old, he watched the movie *Pinocchio* obsessively—particularly the sequence that portrays the whale, Monstro, transforming into a fire-breathing dragon. He must have seen it fifty times. And it was not obvious that he enjoyed it. He was clearly afraid of the climactic scene. I could see it on his face. He had good reason for his fear. The characters he had come to identify with had laid it all on the line. There was a strong motif of danger and sacrifice. Nonetheless, it was the scene that fascinated him the most.

What in the world was he doing, watching the film repeatedly? Particularly if the emotion it produced was fear? Why would a child voluntarily subject himself to that? Julian was using all the faculties of his newly forming mind, rational and unconscious alike, to process the relationships in such a tale. *Pinocchio* and tales like it are dense, layered, and complex in ways that seize the imagination of children and will not let go. That is not accidental. Kids are small and young and, in some ways, they do not know anything, because they have very little personal experience. But they are also very ancient creatures, in another manner, and by no means stupid or inattentive. The fact that they are gripped by fairy tales and stories like *Pinocchio* is an indication of just how much depth children perceive in those stories, even if you, as an adult observer, do not notice it anymore.

That whale is the Dragon of Chaos. This is the symbolic representation of potential, of possibility, for better and for worse. Representations of this figure appear everywhere, and children see them, even if they have no idea what those figures mean. In the Disney classic *Sleeping*

Beauty, for example, the Evil Queen, Maleficent, entraps Prince Phillip. She chains him in her castle dungeon and tells him a charming fairy tale of sorts. She delights in describing to him the ruined and ancient man he will be, six or seven decades in the future, when she deigns to release him from his cell. She portrays him as nothing but the parody of a hero, and has a fine time doing so, locking the door to his prison cell on her departure, climbing the stairs back to her palace, laughing evilly all the while. She is the classic devouring Oedipal mother, preventing her son from manifesting his destiny by refusing to allow him to leave home.

The prince escapes from the dungeon, with the help of the positive feminine: three helpful fairies, who are clearly the mythical counterparts to Maleficent. The Evil Queen sees him mount his horse and make his dangerous way through her army, across her crumbling, quickly closing drawbridges, and down the road leading outside the would-be death trap of her castle. With ever-increasing dismay, she leaps from turret to turret, until she makes her way to the uppermost place. There she stands, enraged, calling up the fires of hell themselves, and transforms herself into a gigantic, fire-breathing dragon. Everyone viewing the movie accepts that as a given: "Of course the Evil Queen turns into a dragon. There is no problem with that." Why, exactly, is that universally acceptable? On the face of it, the transformation makes no sense at all. One moment, she is standing, a perfectly understandable although exceedingly irritated Evil Queen. Next, she spins around a few times and—poof!—she is a gigantic fire-breathing reptile. Perhaps you are all thinking as you read this, "Why are you making an issue of this? Even my four-year-old understands that!" I do not have a problem with an Evil Queen turning into a dragon. It is so self-evident that it can happen even in the middle of a popular movie and be accepted at face value—so self-evident that it is very difficult to draw people's attention to the idea that something very strange has happened.

However, if Queen Elizabeth II suddenly turned into a giant fire-breathing lizard in the midst of one of her endless galas, a certain amount of consternation would be both appropriate and expected. People—even monarchs of a great kingdom—do not just transform into dangerous reptiles and attack their guests (well, not at most parties). But if it happens within the context of a story, then we accept it. That does not explain the mystery, however. Not just any old transformation can happen within a story. It would not have made any sense if Maleficent had donned a sparkly pink outfit and begun to cast roses on the pathway Prince Phillip galloped down to escape his confinement. That was not in Maleficent's nature, nor in the set of narrative expectations that every audience implicitly brings to every movie (and is unlikely to appreciate having disrupted, unless done with exceptional finesse and higher-order purpose). But it is no problem for her to become a dragon. Why? It is partly because nature can and constantly does revert from her dangerous but still understandable guise into total chaos. This happens, for example, when the campfire we just built to cook our hot dogs and sit around singing campfire songs catches a sudden gust of hot, dry air and the long-parched forest hypothetically sheltering our tents ignites into a raging inferno. Dangers we can handle can suddenly turn themselves into dangers we cannot handle. That is why it is no surprise to anyone when the Evil Queen becomes the Dragon of Chaos.

Imagine, for a moment, that you are a prehistoric protohuman being. You are camped for the night, and that site is defined territory—safety and predictability, for the time. Your friends are there, your tribal kin. You have your spears. You have your fire. It is safe—or at least what passes for safe under such conditions. But if you carelessly wander a mere two hundred feet away from the campfire, then something horrible with teeth and scales eats you. That is what is out there in the terrible unknown. That idea is deeply embedded inside of us. We know that human beings are innately afraid of reptilian predators, for example—and that there is good reason for that. It is not merely that we are prepared to learn fear of them (which we certainly are): the fear itself is innate.[3] For all intents and purposes, there is an image that exists inside of us of the terrible hunter that lurks in the night. That is why children become afraid of the dark once they are old enough to move around by themselves.[4] "There is a monster in the dark, Dad!" they insist, at nighttime. And Dad assures his son or daughter that there is no such thing as a monster. Well, the adult is wrong, and the child is exactly right. There might not be a monster in that particular section of the dark, right now, but that is of small comfort when you are three feet high and tasty, and there could be—will be—a monster there in the future. That is why it might be of more use to let your child know directly and through your own actions that there is always something sinister and dangerous in the dark, and that it is the job of the well-prepared individual to confront it and take the treasure it archetypally guards. It is something that an adult and child can act out with great results.

About a year and a half before his encounter with Pinocchio, I took Julian to the Boston Science Museum. There was a Tyrannosaurus rex skeleton there. It was impressively large, as far as I was concerned. But it was even larger, from his perspective. He would not get closer than 100 feet. At 150 feet, his curiosity drove him forward. But things came to a stop when we got closer. That was a neurological phenomenon, too. His curiosity drove him forward, toward the monster, so he could collect some useful information—until the fear froze him. I could see exactly where that boundary lay. Maybe it defined how far away he would need to be to remain safe if that thing suddenly whipped its head around to grab him.

There is an idea embedded deep within the human psyche that potential can be a place of maximal horror, home to an infinite predator—or an infinite variety of predators. Practically speaking, it is true, as human beings have been prey animals since the beginning of time, although we made it very difficult for the predators once we effectively armed and banded together. (Personally, I am happy about that. I have camped where the grizzly bears were plentiful. It is nice that they are on the planet and all that, but I prefer my grizzlies shy, not too hungry, and far enough away to be picturesque.) But there are spiritual and psychological forces operating in a predatory manner that can destroy you, as well—and they can present an even greater danger. The malevolence in the heart of people that makes them criminal falls into that category, as does the evil that drives the totalitarian war of revenge, rapine, greed, or sheer love of blood and destruction. And that malevolence also exists in your heart, and that is the greatest dragon of all—just as mastering that malevolence constitutes the greatest and unlikeliest of individual achievements.

You are built, neurologically, to interpret the world in this dramatic manner, at a very deep level. An ancient part of your brain known as the hypothalamus[5]—a small region, sitting atop the spinal cord—regulates many of the fundamental responses that find their expression in the conceptualization of danger and potential. One of its two modules is responsible for self-preservation (hunger, thirst, and, most important for our purposes, defensive aggression in the face of threat) as well as reproduction (sexual arousal and basic sexual behavior). The second is responsible for exploration.* Half of the hypothalamus

---

*It is possible, in fact, to remove the entire brain of a female cat—to take a common

drives our use of what has been explored previously to quell and satisfy the basic demands of life, including our capability to protect ourselves in the case of attack. The other half is always asking, What is out there? What could it be used for? How might it be dangerous? What are its habits? So, what is the story? Eat, drink, and be merry, until the provisions run out—but watch out, always, for the monsters. Then venture out into the dangerous but promising unknown world and discover what is there. Why? Well, you already know a lot of things you need to know, although you do not know nearly enough. You understand that, because life is not as good as it could be, and because you are going to die. Obviously, under such conditions, you should learn more. So, you are driven to explore. The fundamental representation of reality, as an eternal treasure house guarded by an eternal predator, is therefore a perfect representation of the way you are wired to react to the world at the most fundamental depths of your Being.

NATURE: CREATION AND DESTRUCTION

We all have an image of nature. It might be an image akin to a beautiful landscape—nature as benevolent and renewing. It is an image of that kind that grounds the sentimental environmentalist view of the world. Being from Northern Alberta, I do not share exactly the same view of nature, since up in my hometown of Fairview nature was constantly conspiring either to freeze its inhabitants to death for six months of the year, and to devour them with insects for at least two

---

example from the scientific literature—excepting the hypothalamus and the spinal cord, and the cat can still maintain itself in relative normality, as long as its environment is reasonably constrained. Furthermore, it becomes hyperexploratory. That's truly staggering, in my estimation. Think about it: if you surgically remove 95 percent of a cat's brain, it cannot stop exploring. You would think an essentially brainless cat would just sit there, but that's not what happens. The curious part of its brain is still there.

more. So that is the less romantic part of nature, which is red in tooth and claw. That is the part of nature that is associated with injury, disease, death, insanity, and everything else that can and will befall you, as a biological creature, on the negative end of the continuum.

There is the potential of the future that has not yet been transformed into reality (represented, as we have seen, by the Dragon of Chaos). But then there is the nature you encounter directly in your life, and which cannot be considered absolutely unknown. There is the benevolence of nature: the fact that you are here, alive—and sometimes happy; the fact that there is delicious food to eat, and attractive, interesting people to interact with, and no shortage of fascinating things to see and do. There are amazing vistas of landscape. There is the beauty and immortality and immensity of the ocean. There is all the bountiful, wondrous element of natural Being. But there is also the absolute horror that goes along with that: destruction, disease, suffering, and death. Those two elements of experience exist side by side. It is even the case that the former could not exist without the latter: even within your own body, healthy as it may be, a very delicate balance between the death of every cell that has outlasted its utility and the new life that springs forward to replace it is a prerequisite for your continued existence.

Both these elements of existence manifest themselves in our imagination in personified form. One is the Evil Queen, the Goddess of Destruction and Death; the other is her positive counterpart, the Fairy Godmother, the benevolent monarch, the young and loving mother watching with infinite care over her helpless charge. To live properly, you need to be acquainted with both these figures. If you are a child, abused by your mother, familiar only with the Evil Queen, then you are damaged by the absence of love, stunted by lack of attention, and arbitrarily subject to fear and pain and aggression. That is no way to

live, and it is very difficult to grow up functional and capable and void
of distrust, hate, and the desire, say, for revenge. You need to find
someone to act the part of the Benevolent Queen: a friend, a family
member, a fictional character—or a part of your own psyche, motivated by knowing that your mistreatment is wrong, swearing to take
any opportunity that comes your way to escape your misfortunate circumstances, leave them behind, and balance your life appropriately.
Maybe the first step in this direction is to posit, despite your mistreatment, that you are in fact worthy of care; and the second step is to give
it, where you can, despite receiving tragically little yourself.

If you understand the polarity of nature, its terror and benevolence,
you recognize two fundamental elements of experience, permanent,
eternal, and unavoidable, and you can begin to understand, for example, the profound pull toward sacrifice. It is a religious trope that sacrifices keep the gods happy, and coming to understand just who the
unhappy gods are, so to speak, and just how terrible they are when
they are unhappy is a genuine step toward wisdom—a genuine and
humbling step. Modern people have a hard time understanding what
sacrifice means, because they think, for example, of a burnt offering
on an altar, which is an archaic way of acting out the idea. But we have
no problem at all when we conceptualize sacrifice psychologically, because we all know you must forgo gratification in the present to keep
the wolf from the door in the future. So, you offer something to the
negative goddess, so that the positive one shows up. You train long,
difficult hours to be a nurse or a physician or a social worker. That
sacrificial attitude is in fact the great discovery of the future, conjoined with the ability to negotiate and bargain and cope with that
future—abandon impulsive gratification; let go of something you need
and want; obtain something valuable in the long run in consequence
(and keep the horror at bay). You forgo the partying and the easy hours.

You immerse yourself, instead, in the difficulties of life. You do that so that fewer of those difficulties will manifest themselves—for yourself, employed gainfully as you will become, and for all the others you will help as the strength you developed through proper sacrifice makes itself manifest. We are always bargaining in that manner. We act out the belief that we can strike a bargain with the structure of reality. Strangely enough, we often can. If you are sensible, you do that all the time. You prepare for the worst. You prepare for the arrival of the Evil Queen. You do what you have to do, knowing about her existence, and you keep her at bay—in proportion to your wisdom and in accordance with your luck. And if you succeed, Benevolent Nature smiles upon you—until she does not. But at least you have some control over the situation. You are not a sitting duck, or a babe in the woods, or a rube at the amusement park—or at least no more so than you have to be.

Nature is chaos, too, because it is always wreaking havoc with culture, its existential opposite—and the next subject of our investigation. After all, as Robert Burns has it, "The best laid schemes o' Mice an' Men / Gang aft a-gley." And it is often nature in positive and negative guise that does precisely that. It is no easy matter to balance the fragility of life and the necessity for procreation (and all the uncertainty of pregnancy and birth and child-rearing) with the desire for certainty, predictability, and order. And this is to say nothing of death (and even cancer is, after all, just another form of life). But all that is not to say, ever, that chaos is of less value than order. There is nothing but sterility without unpredictability, even though a bit less unpredictability often seems eminently desirable.

This nature/chaos combination is often seen in pop culture representations. As we mentioned, in the Disney movie *Sleeping Beauty*, for example, there is an Evil Queen—just as there is in *The Little Mermaid* (Ursula), *Snow White* (Grimhilde), *One Hundred and One Dalmatians*

(Cruella de Vil), *Cinderella* (Lady Tremaine), *Tangled* (Mother Gothel), and *Alice in Wonderland* (the Queen of Hearts). She represents the harsh element of the natural world. The example of *Sleeping Beauty* is, once again, particularly germane. Remember what happens at the movie's opening. The king and queen have waited long, and are now desperate to have a baby. The blessing arrives; the baby is born and they call her Aurora, the dawn. They are all thrilled, and so is the whole kingdom— properly so, because new life has arrived. They plan a great christening party. It is a fine idea, but they fail to invite Maleficent, the Evil Queen, to the celebrations. And it is not ignorance that prevents them. They know of her existence, and they are well acquainted with her power. It is willful blindness, and it is a bad move. They desire to shield their new and precious daughter from the negative element of the world, instead of determining how to provide her with the strength and wisdom to prevail, despite the reality of the negative. All this does is keep Aurora naive and vulnerable. Maleficent shows up anyway, as she most certainly will, and there is a message in that: invite the Evil Queen to your child's life. If you fail to do so, your children will grow up weak and in need of protection, and the Evil Queen is going to make herself known no matter what steps you take to stop her. At the christening, in fact, not only does she arrive, well behaved but uninvited, but she offers a present (in the form of a curse): the death of Aurora at the age of sixteen, brought about by the prick of the spindle of a spinning wheel. And all that because she was not invited to celebrate the young princess's christening. Only because a compassionate and powerful guest intercedes—one of the three aforementioned fairies, representative of the positive feminine—is the curse transmuted from death into profound unconsciousness, a state barely less fatal.

That is what happens to those beauties, so to speak, who remain far too unawakened when they hit sixteen: They do not want to be conscious, because they have not developed the courage and ability to face the negative element of the natural world. Instead of being encouraged, they have been sheltered. And if you shelter young people, you destroy them. You did not invite the Evil Queen, even for short visits. What are your children going to do when she shows up in full force, if they are entirely unprepared? They are not going to want to live. They are going to long for unconsciousness. And it gets worse. If you overprotect your kids, you become the very thing from which you are trying to shelter them. Depriving them of their young lives' necessary adventures, you weaken their characters. You become the Destroying Agent itself—the very witch that devours their autonomous consciousness.

I had a client many years ago who was a real-life version of Sleeping Beauty. She was tall, blonde haired, razor thin (as the saying goes), and profoundly unhappy. She was enrolled in a local junior college, attempting to upgrade so that she could attend university. She came to see me because she did not want to live. She also did not want to die, really—at least not actively. Instead, she attempted to keep herself unconscious with the use of Valium and its variants, including sleeping pills, which she procured in sufficient quantities from her (several) physicians, who were no doubt overworked enough not to keep track of exactly what she was doing. She managed to keep herself asleep fifteen or sixteen hours a day. She was smart and literate, and showed me a philosophy essay she had written on the pointlessness not only of her life but life in general. She was unable to tolerate the responsibility, by all appearances, but also could not deal with the cruelty she saw everywhere around her. She was a vegan, for example, and that was directly associated with her acute physical terror of life. She was unable even to enter the aisles of a supermarket where meat was displayed. Where others saw the cuts they were going to prepare for their family, she saw rows of dead body parts. That vision only served to confirm her belief that life was, in essence, unbearable.

Her biological mother had died in childbirth, and she was raised by her father and her stepmother. The latter was a holy terror. I met her only once, in my office, during what would have ordinarily been a clinical session with her stepdaughter. She spent the entire hour actively tearing strips off me: first for being of little use as a clinician, and second for "no doubt" blaming everything that was wrong with my client on her (step)mothering. I do not think I got more than a dozen words in edgewise. It was a remarkable performance, brought on, I believe, by my insistence that the phone calls she made two or three times a day to my client while the latter was away at school—some of which I heard in recordings—had to be reduced by a factor of ten, and certainly needed to be more pleasant. I am not saying and did not believe then that all this was the stepmother's fault. I am sure she had her reasons to be frustrated. Her stepdaughter was not fully engaged in life, by any means, and was an expensive four underperforming years into what should have been a two-year certificate. But it was clear that thrice-daily phone calls consisting mostly of anger and insults were not adding to my client's desire to be alive. I suggested that weekly phone calls should become the norm, and encouraged her to hang up if the conversation took a wicked turn. She started to put that into practice, and I presumed all that contributed to her stepmother's demand to meet and confront me.

Sleeping Beauty described her childhood as idyllic. She said that she lived the life of a fairy-tale princess; an only child, the darling of both parents. But that all changed when she hit adolescence. Her stepmother's attitude changed from trust to deep distrust, and they began the fights that continually characterized their relationship from then on (she was in her early thirties when I met her). The problem of sex had reared its ugly head. The stepmother responded by acting as if her innocent child had been replaced by a corrupt impostor; the step-daughter responded by dating a series of ne'er-do-wells whom at one level she probably thought she deserved (having lost the perfect innocence of the child princess) and at another constituted the perfect punishment for her mother.

Together, we designed an exposure-training program to help her overcome her fear of life. We first undertook to visit a nearby butcher shop. The shop owner and I had become friendly acquaintances over the years. After I explained my client's situation to him (with her permission), I asked if I could bring her into his store, show her the meat counter, and then—when she was ready—bring her to the back to watch as his team cut up the carcasses that were delivered through the alleyway loading dock. He quickly agreed. Our initial goal was merely to get to the store together. I assured her that we could pause at any time, or stop altogether, and that under no conditions would I trick, entice, or even cajole her into pushing her beyond what she could tolerate. During the first session, she managed to enter the store and place her hand on the display case. She did it shaking and in visible tears (also no easy thing to manage in public), but she did it. By the fourth session, she was able to watch the butchers use their knives and saws on the large and still animal-like carcasses they were slicing into the standard cuts they sold. There was no doubt that this was good for her. She was less inclined, for example, to medicate herself into unconsciousness and more likely to attend classes. She became tougher, harder, harsher—adjectives that are not always meant as compliments but are sometimes the precise antidote to too much sentimentality, which is dangerously infantilizing. We also made arrangements for her to spend a weekend at a local farm where a few common barnyard animals were kept (pigs, horses, chickens, goats). I asked the farmer, who had also been a client of mine, to allow her to accompany him while he attended to his livestock.

A city girl to the core, my client knew nothing whatsoever about animals, and tended, in consequence, to romanticize them, in exactly the fairy-tale manner appropriate to the conditions of her childhood. Her two-day sojourn in the country and her decision to observe the animals carefully helped her develop a much less romanticized perception of the true nature of the animals we raise and dine upon. They are sentient beings, in part, and we have a responsibility not to inflict any more suffering upon them than necessary, but they are not human beings, and they are certainly not children. This needs to be understood at an embodied level. Excess sentimentality is an illness, a developmental failure, and a curse to children and others who need our care (but not too much of it).

Sleeping Beauty was a remarkable dreamer. I have had clients who would commonly remember two or three dreams a night, though not always in great detail. She not only remembered many dreams, but remembered them fully, and she also often became lucid—conscious of dreaming—while she slept. She was the only person I ever met who could ask her dream characters what they meant—symbolically speaking—or what message they had for her, and they would tell her outright. One day she came to me with one of her many dreams: She had journeyed alone deep into the depths of an old-growth forest and met a dwarf dressed like a harlequin in the darkness and gloom. The dwarf offered to answer a question, if my client had one to ask. She asked the strange figure what she would have to do to finish her college certificate, a task that had taken her the four aforementioned years and plenty of negotiation with the requisite university authorities for permission to continue. The answer she received? "You will have to learn to work in a slaughterhouse."

Now, as far as I am concerned, dreams are statements from nature. It is not so much that we create them. They manifest themselves to us. I have never seen a dream present something I believed to be untrue. I also do not believe—contra Freud—that dreams attempt to disguise what they mean. They are, instead, an earlier part of the process by which fully developed thoughts come to be born, as they certainly do not just appear magically out of nowhere. We must confront the unknown, as such—the great Dragon of Chaos or the Terrible Queen—and we do not know how to do it, to begin with. The dream serves as the first cognitive step—in the wake of basic emotional, motivational, and bodily reactions such as fear or curiosity or freezing—in transforming that unknown into actionable and even articulable knowledge. The dream is the birthplace of the thought, and often of the thought that does not come easily to the conscious mind. It is not hiding anything; it is just not very good at being clear (although that certainly does not mean that it cannot be profound).

In any case, this dream was not difficult to interpret, particularly because its main character, the dwarf, simply spoke his mind. So, I listened carefully to my client's account (remember, this was after the butcher shop and the farm) and asked her what we might do about that. I had no idea how I might arrange a visit to an actual slaughterhouse. I did not even know if they existed in the city we inhabited, and if they did, I could not imagine they would appreciate visitors, regardless of motivation. She was convinced, however, that she had been told the truth, and that something of the sort had to be done. So we discussed the consequences of her toughening up, and the fact that she had successfully put her hypercritical stepmother on the back burner, and left it at that for the remainder of the session, although she was tasked (as was I) with determining something that might serve as a reasonable substitute for a slaughterhouse.

A week later, she returned for her scheduled session. She announced the last thing, perhaps, that I could have possibly imagined from her—or anyone else, for that matter: "I think I need to see an embalming." I did not know what to say. I did not want to see an embalming, personally—not at all. I had seen body sections in science museums, and there was something about them that refused to leave my memory. I had also gone to see one of the displays of plasticized, sculptured bodies that were so popular about a decade ago, and I was horrified by it. I became a psychologist, not a surgeon—or, for that matter, a coroner—for a reason. However, this was not about me. It was about my client, Sleeping Beauty, and her desire to awaken, and there was no way I was going to let my wishes or lack thereof interfere with whatever wisdom the dwarf who inhabited the deep forest of her unconscious mind was about to impart. I told her I would see what I could do. It all turned out to be much simpler to arrange than I expected. I simply picked up the phone and called a local mortician's office. To my great surprise, he immediately agreed. I suppose he had seen his fair share of people grieving and frightened, and was accustomed to dealing with them calmly and wisely. So that was that. I was stuck with the visit, and my client wanted to go through with it.

Two weeks later, we went to the funeral home. My client had asked me if a friend could attend with her, and I said yes. The mortician offered the three of us a tour first. He showed us the chapel and the display room for the caskets. We asked him how he managed his job, given its endless concentration on death and suffering and grief. He said that it was his heartfelt responsibility to make his clients' most terrible of times the least painful they could be, and that he took heart from that. That made sense to both of us, and helped us understand how he could continue with his work, day in and out. After the tour, we went to the embalming room. It was a small space, perhaps a hundred feet square. The naked body of an aged man was lying motionless, gray, and mottled on a stainless-steel table. Because there was not space in the small room, and to provide us both with some distance, my client, her friend, and I took our places in the hallway immediately outside the door and observed the proceedings, which were entirely unimpeded by our trivial separation from the mortician's operations. He drained the blood and other liquids from the body. They ran undramatically but in some sense all the more horribly for that, because of their mundane mode of disposal, I suppose. It seemed like something that precious and vital deserved better. He made his surgical alterations, and sewed together the eyelids, and made up the face, and injected the embalming fluid. I watched. And I watched my client. To begin with, she looked down the hallway, avoiding the scene unfolding in front of her. But as the minutes ticked by, she started to glance at the proceedings, and by the time a quarter of an hour had passed, she was spending far more time observing than looking away. I could see, however, that she had taken her friend's hand, and was gripping it tightly.

She was seeing firsthand that something she had believed would terrify her (and reasonably so) was not in fact doing so. She could manage the experience. She did not panic, become ill, run away, or even cry. She asked the mortician if she could put a hand on the body. He offered her a rubber glove, which she pulled on. She walked directly into the operating station, in a quiet and meditative state, and placed her gloved hand on the ribs of the body, and she kept it there, as if it was a comfort both to her and the poor departed soul. The procedure terminated soon after that, and we left quietly together, after offering the mortician our genuine and heartfelt thanks.

The three of us expressed our shared astonishment that we had managed such a visit. My client had learned something vitally important about her tolerance for the terrors of life. Equally importantly, she had a reference point for her fears: from that point onward (and I am by no means claiming complete success in her treatment) she had

something truly awe inspiring—something truly serious and horrifying and graphic and real—to compare with the other, almost inevitably lesser, horrors of life. Were the mundane miseries of existence as
challenging as the experience she had put herself through voluntarily?
Was the butcher shop more frightening than human death, in all its
reality, at such close proximity? Had she not demonstrated to herself
that she could encounter the worst that Terrible Nature could throw
at her and face it courageously? And that was to her a paradoxical and
ineradicable source of comfort.

As with the Sleeping Beauty of fairy tales, my client's family had
failed to invite the Evil Queen, the terrible aspect of nature, into their
child's life. This left her completely unprepared for life's essential
harshness—the complications of sexuality and the requirement for everything that lives to devour other lives (and to be eventually subjected
to the same fate). The Evil Queen made her reappearance at puberty—
in the form of my client's stepmother, whose character apparently turned
180 degrees—as well as in her own personal inability to deal with the
responsibilities of maturity and stark obligations of biological survival.
Like Sleeping Beauty, as well—as that tale is multistoried and deep in
the way of ancient fairy tales, which can be thousands of years old—
she needed to be awakened by the forces of exploration, courage, and
fortitude (often represented by the redeeming prince, but which she
found within herself).

CULTURE: SECURITY AND TYRANNY

If the Dragon of Chaos and the paired Benevolent and Evil Queen are
representatives of potential and of the unknown, the Wise King and
the Authoritarian Tyrant are representatives of the structures, social
and psychological, that enable us to overlay structure on that poten-

tial. We interpret the present through the lens of culture. We plan for the future by attempting to bring into being what we have been taught and what we have determined, personally, to value. All of that seems good, but a too-rigid approach to understanding what is currently in front of us and what we should pursue can blind us to the value of novelty, creativity, and change. When the structures that guide us are merely secure, rather than inflexible, we leaven our desire for routine and predictability with the curiosity that makes us attracted to and appreciative of what remains outside our conceptual schemes. When those same structures degenerate into stasis, we run from and deny the existence of what we do not yet understand and what we have not yet encountered, and this means that we make ourselves unable to change when change is required. Understanding that both possibilities exist is of crucial importance to establish the balance that is required in life.

We could use a poetic metaphor to represent the elements of experience that we have so far discussed (this is in fact how the world I am describing is usually considered). Imagine the realm of the Dragon of Chaos as the night sky, stretching infinitely above you on a clear night, representing what will remain forever outside your domain of understanding. Maybe you are standing on a beach, looking up, lost in contemplation and imagination. Then you turn your attention to the ocean—as grand in its way as the starry cosmos, but tangible and manifest and knowable, comparatively speaking. That is nature. It is not mere potential. It is there, in its unknowability, instead of removed from comprehension entirely. It is not yet tamed, however; not brought into the domain of order. And it is beautiful in its mystery. The moon reflects on its surface; the waves crash eternally and lull you to sleep; you can swim in its welcoming waters. But that beauty has a price. You better keep an eye out for sharks. And poisonous jellyfish. And the riptide that can pull you or your children under. And the storms that could destroy your warm and welcoming beach house.

Imagine, further, that the beach on which you stand is the shore of an island. The island is culture. People live there—perhaps in harmony and peace, under a benevolent ruler; perhaps in a war-torn hell of oppression, hunger, and privation. And that is culture: Wise King or Authoritarian Tyrant. It is of vital necessity to become acquainted with both characters, just as in the case of Evil Queen and Benevolent Goddess, to ensure the appropriate balance in attitude required to adapt properly to the vicissitudes of life. Too much emphasis on the Wise King blinds those who hold that attitude to the injustice and unnecessary suffering that is a consequence of the inevitable flaws in our all-too-human social structures. Too much insistence on the Authoritarian Tyrant means lack of appreciation for the often fragile structures that bind us together and protect us from the chaos that would otherwise certainly reign.

The ideological systems we are prone to adopting—the systems that so polarize us, politically and personally, can be profitably understood in light of the present conceptualization. They are cultural narratives usefully considered as parasites upon a more fundamental religious, mythological, or dramatic substructure—ancient, evolved, and deeply biological in its nature. Ideologies take on the structure of a story that is essentially religious, but they do so incompletely, including certain elements of experience or eternal characters while ignoring others. The power remains in the representation, nonetheless, because what is included retains its fundamentally mythological/biological nature— its instinctual meaning—but the missing elements mean that what remains, however powerful in its expression, is biased in a way that restricts its utility. That bias is desirable subjectively, as it simplifies what would otherwise be too complex to understand, but dangerous because of its one-sidedness. If the map you are using is missing part of the world, you are going to be utterly unprepared when that absent element makes itself manifest. How is it possible for us to retain the advantages of simplification, without falling prey to the accompanying blindness? The answer is to be found in the constant dialogue between genuinely different types of people.

Much of what people believe politically—ideologically, let us say— is based on their inborn temperament. If their emotions or motivations tend to tilt one way (and much of that is a consequence of biology), then they tend to adopt, say, a conservative or liberal tendency. It is not a matter of opinion. Imagine, instead, that animals have a niche—a place or space that suits them. Their biology is matched to that place. Lions are not found in the open ocean, and killer whales do not roam the African veldt. The animal and its environment are of a piece.

Human beings are similar, at least in the realm of abstraction. We are nonetheless capable of making ourselves at home almost every-where, geographically, because we change the geography, as neces-sary, as well as modify our own behavior. But we have perceptual or cognitive niches. Liberals, for example, are positively enthralled by new ideas. The advantages to being attracted by new ideas are obvious. Sometimes problems require new solutions, and it is people who take pleasure in novel conceptions who find them. Such people also tend not to be particularly orderly.[6] Perhaps this is because if you are gripped and driven by new ideas, and are also inclined to test or implement them, you need to be able to tolerate the intermediary chaos produced between the time the old idea disintegrates and the new idea takes control. If you are a conservative, you have the opposite advantage and problem. You are wary of new ideas, and not particularly attracted to them, and that is in part because you are less sensitive to their possi-bilities and more concerned about their unpredicted consequences.

Just because a new idea fixes one problem, after all, does not mean that it will fail to generate another, or several others. If you are conservative, you like things to be where they are supposed to be, when they are supposed to be there. You are in the place you want to be when people act conventionally, responsibly, and predictably.

Conservatives are necessary for maintaining things the way they are when everything is working and change might be dangerous. Liberals, by contrast, are necessary for changing things when they are no longer working. It is no easy task, however, to determine when something needs to be preserved or when it needs to be transformed. That is why we have politics, if we are fortunate, and the dialogue that accompanies it, instead of war, tyranny, or submission. It is necessary for us to argue vociferously and passionately about the relative value of stability versus change, so that we can determine when each is appropriate and in what doses.

It is of great interest to note that difference in fundamental political belief appears to determine which of the twinned Great Fathers are considered of fundamental reality. The liberal tends strongly to see the world as the Authoritarian Tyrant suppressing the Benevolent Goddess—as the arbitrary strictures of dead culture corrupting and oppressing citizen and foreigner alike, or as the military-industrial structure of modern society threatening Gaia, the living planet, with pollution, mass extinction, or climate change. Such a viewpoint is obviously useful when culture has become truly tyrannical—and that is by no means uncommon. The conservative tends, conversely, to see the world as Wise King—security of place, order, and predictability—bringing to heel, taming and disciplining the Evil Queen—nature as disorder and chaos. That is obviously necessary as well. No matter how beautiful the natural world, we should remember that it is always conspiring to starve, sicken, and kill us, and that if we lacked the protective shield constituted by Culture as Security we would be devoured by wild animals, frozen by blizzards, prostrated by the heat of the desert, and starved by the fact that food does not simply manifest itself for our delectation. So there are two different ideologies—both of which are "correct," but each of which tell only half the story.*

To develop a properly balanced view of the world of experience, it is necessary to accept the reality of both elements of culture. Those with a conservative bent, drawn temperamentally to regard the status quo as protective, must to come to understand that mere order is insufficient. Because the future and the present differ from the past, what worked before will not necessarily work now, and it is necessary to understand that the line between the stability bequeathed to us by our ancestors and the tyranny that can so easily become shifts and moves with the transformations of existence. Equally, however, the more liberal types, prone to see the Authoritarian Tyrant everywhere, must work to develop gratitude for the social and psychological structures of interpretation that continually shield us from the terrors of nature and the absolute unknown. It is difficult for any of us to see what we are blinded to by the nature of our personalities. It is for this reason that we must continually listen to people who differ from us, and who, because of that difference, have the ability to see and to react appropriately to what we cannot detect.

---

*I am aware, of course, that conservatives also have a proclivity to object to big government, which seems to contradict the fundamental point I am making. But, in Western democracies, that's primarily because the faith that conservatives manifest in culture is predicated more on the eternal verities of the Constitution and the more permanent elements of government (so Culture with a capital "C") than on the too variable and too unpredictable whims of whomever might be elected presently, conservative or liberal. Likewise, in the same democracies, the liberals tend to look to government for the solution to the problems that concern them, but that's because they believe more in the dynamism of the current crop of politicians (particularly, but not only, if they are liberal themselves) and less in the eternal verities of the underlying structure.

THE INDIVIDUAL: HERO AND ADVERSARY

If the night sky is chaos, the ocean nature, and the island culture, then the individual—hero and adversary—is one brother locked in combat with his twin in the middle of the isle. Chaos, treasure and dragon, have their negative and positive element, as do Nature—Evil Queen and Benevolent Mother—and Culture—Authoritarian Tyrant and Wise King. No less the individual. The positive element is the heroic aspect: the person who can sacrifice properly to nature and strike a bargain with fate such that benevolence reigns; the person who is awake, alert, attentive, communicative, and bears responsibility, so that the tyrannical part of the state remains at bay; and the person who is aware of his or her own faults and proclivity for malevolence and deceit, so that proper orientation is maintained. The negative element is everything despicable and contemptible—particularly evident in yourself, if you have any sense, but also manifested to some degree by other people and (more clearly) in stories. Those are the hostile brothers, a very old mythological idea: the hero and the adversary. The archetypal representations of those two forces, those two personified figures, are Cain and Abel. That is one level of representation. Christ and Satan are a pair representing an even more fundamental duality. Cain and Abel, after all, are human (the first humans, born in the human manner, as Adam and Eve were created directly by God). Christ and Satan are elements of personified (deified?) eternity itself.

So, there exists a hero and an adversary; a wise king and a tyrant; a positive and negative maternal figure; and chaos itself. That is the structure of the world in six characters (with the strange seventh of chaos in some sense the ultimate birthplace of all the others). It is necessary to understand that all seven exist, and that they are all existential permanents—elements of experience with which every soul, rich, poor, blessed, cursed, talented, dull, male, and female must inevitably contend. That is life—*they* are life. Partial knowledge of the cast, conscious or unconscious, leaves you undefended; leaves you naive, unprepared, and likely to become possessed by deceit, resentment, and arrogance. If you do not know that the treasure is guarded by a dragon, or that nature, beautiful nature, can turn its teeth on you in an instant, or that the peaceful society you take for granted is threatened constantly by authoritarianism and tyranny, or that you contain within yourself the adversary who might wish that all those negative transformations occur, then you are, first, a needy acolyte for an ideology that will provide you with a partial and insufficient representation of reality; and, second, someone blind in a manner dangerous to themselves and others alike. If you are wise, your political philosophy encompasses a representation of all seven, even if you could not articulate it in those terms. We should always have enough sense to keep in mind, for example, that a great predator lurks beneath the thin ice of our constructed realities. I remember a vision I once had about my then very young daughter, portraying exactly that reality. In the winter, in Northern Alberta—where, as I said, I grew up—there were years where the snow stayed at bay for weeks after the lakes themselves had frozen, smooth, perfectly clear, rock hard, barren, and not without beauty and mystery. (A stone skipped across their expanse would chime and echo melodically as it skidded across the slippery surface.) I imagined my daughter Mikhaila—a toddler dressed only in a diaper—sitting at some distance from me, directly on the ice. Underneath her, I could see a huge fish, a whale shark (although carnivorous, in this incarnation)—hanging motionless below her, waiting, upright in the water underneath the ice, mouth gaping. That is life, and death, and the pure chaos that destroys our hard-won certainties, but it is also the prophet-swallowing whale who grants wisdom and rebirth, if it does not kill.

And what is the proper attitude of the hero, let us say, with respect to the remaining six characters (assuming we have dealt sufficiently with chaos with that last anecdote)? Obviously, we must endeavor to preserve Nature, upon whose benevolence we are finally dependent for everything that life requires. But it is also perfectly worthwhile for us to note and take seriously the fact that the same Nature is doing her best to kill us, and that we have every reason to erect the structures we do, despite their often unfortunate environmental costs.* Something similar applies to culture. We all have reason to be grateful, in the main, for the wisdom and the structure that our forebears bequeathed to us, to their great cost. That does not mean that those benefits are distributed equally, because they are not and never will be, no more than the benefits of Nature are distributed equally. That gratitude also does not justify any willfully blind optimism with regard to the nature of society. As individuals—struggling, let us say, against the adversarial tendency and the Authoritarian Tyrant simultaneously—we need to be awake to the fact that our functional hierarchical structures can become unproductive, tyrannical, and blind in the blink of an eye. We have a responsibility to ensure that they do not become radically unfair and corrupt and begin to distribute their rewards on the basis of power or unmeritocratic privilege instead of competence. We must attend to them constantly and adjust them carefully so they remain suf-

----

*There is little doubt that we create a fair bit of "unnatural" mess while we are doing so (another ideological idea, based as it is on the one-sided view of Nature as the victim of our rapine and greed), but it's not as if we are doing it for trivial reasons. That's why I have some sympathy for humanity, as well as for the individuals who compose the mass of humanity, and why I cannot find it in my heart to forgive those who say foolish things such as "the planet would be better off if there were no people on it." That's the genocidal element of the radical environmentalist ethos, and it's a consequence of an ideology that sees only the Adversary, the Authoritarian Tyrant, and the Benevolent Mother as the prime actors of being. It's something horrible to behold, if you think it through with any degree of depth.

ficiently stable and appropriately dynamic. That is a fundamental part of our roles and responsibilities as persons aiming courageously at the good. We manage that partly in democratic systems by throwing out the people in charge on a regular basis, and replacing them with their ideological opposites. That capability and opportunity constitutes one of the fundamental achievements of a democratic society. In the absence of the ability to regularly choose only the wise and good as leaders (and good luck finding them), it is worthwhile to elect a pack blind to half of reality in one cycle and another blind to the other half the next. Then at least most of society's concerns are attended to in some reasonable measure over the course of something approximating a decade.

I think that somewhat pessimistic but also eminently realistic strategy is in keeping with the vision of the people who founded the American system (and the actions and attitudes of the English and other early democrats and parliamentarians whose gradually evolving systems laid the groundwork for the explicit claims those founders made). They were not utopian in their essential viewpoint. They believed that the people who were inevitably to be their successors were going to be just as flawed as they were, and just as flawed as people before them. What do you do about that, when you are not blinded by ideology, and you see the world and all its dramatic characters clearly? Well, you do not hope for the infinite perfectibility of humanity and aim your system at some unattainable utopia. You try to design a system that sinners such as you cannot damage too badly—too permanently—even when they are half blind and resentful. To the degree that I am conservative in orientation, I believe in the wisdom of that vision. I believe that is a more appropriate way of looking at things. Let us not get too grandiose. We can design systems that allow us a modicum of peace, security, and freedom and, perhaps, the possibility of incremental improvement.

That is a miracle in and of itself. We should have the wisdom to doubt that we will produce some positive transformation of individual, society, and nature simultaneously, particularly if those improvements are to be brought about in consequence of our own intrinsic, personal goodwill, which is often in too short supply (despite our protestations to the contrary).

RESENTMENT

Why do you and others fall prey to resentment—that terrible hybrid emotional state, an admixture of anger and self-pity, tinged, to various degrees, with narcissism and the desire for revenge? Once you understand the world as a dramatic forum, and you have identified the major players, the reasons become clear. You are resentful because of the absolute unknown and its terrors, because nature conspires against you, because you are a victim of the tyrannical element of culture, and because of the malevolence of yourself and other individuals. That is reason enough. It does not make your resentment appropriate, but it certainly makes the emotion understandable. None of these existential problems are trivial. In fact, they are serious enough to make the real question not "Why are you resentful?" but "Why is not everyone resentful about everything all the time?" We are the focus of unbelievably powerful and often malevolent transpersonal forces. There is a terrible reptilian predator, metaphorically speaking, pursuing you all the time, just like the crocodile with the ticktock of time emanating from the clock he swallowed chasing the tyrannical coward Captain Hook. And there is nature herself. She is hell-bent on doing you in, in a million horrible ways. Then there is the tyrannical element of the social structure, which has molded you—taught you, so to speak—and made you into the quasi-civilized, semi-useful creature that you are, but crushed a tremendous amount of life force out of you at the same time, pounding you like the proverbial square peg into the round hole. There were many things you could have been. Maybe some of them were more than you have become. But you were lessened and reduced by the demand for social existence.

And you are stuck with yourself, too, and that is no picnic. You procrastinate, you are lazy, you lie, and you do vicious things to yourself and others. It is no wonder you feel like a victim, given what is arrayed against you: chaos, the brute force of nature, the tyranny of culture, and the malevolence of your own nature. It is no wonder you might feel resentful. And it is certainly the case that these forces are arrayed against some of you in a manner that seems far more serious, unjust, arbitrary, continuous, and unpredictable than it seems for others. How could you fail to feel victimized and resentful under those conditions? Life contains no shortage of fundamental brutality.

There is a problem with this logic, however, inexorable though it may seem. The first is that not everyone does in fact construe him or herself as a victim and fall prey, in consequence, to resentment—and that includes a large proportion of people who have had a very hard time in their lives. In fact, I think it is reasonable to posit that it is often the people who have had too easy a time—who have been pampered and elevated falsely in their self-esteem—who adopt the role of victim and the mien of resentment. You can encounter people, contrarily, who have been hurt virtually beyond all hope of repair who are not resentful and who would never deign to present themselves as victims. They are not that common, but they are not so very rare either. Thus, resentment does not appear to be an inevitable consequence of suffering itself. Other factors are at play, in addition to the undeniable tragedy of life.

Maybe you—or just as tragically, someone close to you—contracts

a serious illness. It is typical in such circumstances to ask the question
(of whom? God?) "Why did this have to happen to me?" Well, what
do you mean? Would you wish it instead upon a friend, neighbor, or
even a random stranger? You certainly might be tempted to spread your
misery, but such a response does not seem either reasonable or a choice
that a good person, thinking clearly, would ever make, and it certainly
would not make the situation more just. To be fair, the question "Why
me?" constitutes, in part, a psychologically appropriate response. It is
often the case that if something bad happens to you, you should ask
yourself if there is something that you have done in the past that has
increased the probability of the terrible event—as we have discussed
at length—because it is possible that you have something to learn that
would decrease the chances of its recurrence. But often that is not at
all what we are doing. The question "Why did this have to happen to
me?" frequently contains a reproachful element, based on a sense of
injustice: "There are all these bad people in the world, and they seem
to be getting away unpunished for this misbehavior," or "There are all
these people in the world who are enjoying good health, and it seems
singularly unfair for them to be in that fortunate position when I am
not." That means that "Why me?" is in this manner generally con-
taminated with a sense of victimization, signifying injustice. This
false misapprehension that the terrible experience that has befallen
you somehow singularly characterizes you—is aimed, particularly, at
you—is part of what turns exposure to tragedy into the very resentment we are discussing.

   The fact that unfortunate things are happening or are going to happen to you is built into the structure of reality itself. There is no doubt
that awful things happen, but there is an element of true randomness
about them. You might think, "That is trivial compensation, and of
little help." But some appreciation for the random element can be

helpful, by distancing the personal element, and that can help you erect some barriers to developing that intense egotistical resentment. Furthermore, it can be of great utility to realize that each of the negatives that characterize human existence are balanced, in principle, by their positive counterpart.

Here is something I have learned in my years as a clinical psychologist. I constantly saw people who were hurt by life. They had their reasons for feeling resentful, and those reasons were often far from trivial. I would propose: "Let us take your problems apart, even though many of them are real. We will try to figure out which ones are your fault, because some of them are going to be. Some of them, alternatively, are just the catastrophe of life. We will delineate that very carefully. Then we will start having you practice overcoming whatever it is that you are bringing to the situation that is making it worse. We will start to make some strategic plans about how you might confront the parts of your life that are truly just tragic, and we will get you to do that in a truthful, open, and courageous manner. Then we will watch what happens."

People got better. Not always. Some of my clients even died. We would be halfway through their clinical issues, and they would be carried off by a sudden cancer or killed in a traffic accident. There is no certain path, even with the noblest of actions. The arbitrariness of the world is always at the ready, preparing to manifest itself. There is no reason or excuse to be stupidly naive or optimistic. But most people did get better. Encouragement prepared them to confront their problems head-on, and that voluntary confrontation dispelled some of their fear. This was not because things around them became less dangerous, but because the people facing the danger became braver. It is unbelievable how strong and courageous people can become. It is miraculous what sort of load people can bear when they take it on voluntarily. I know we cannot have an infinite capacity for that, but I also believe that it is in some sense unlimited. I think the more voluntary confrontation is practiced, the more can be borne. I do not know what the upper limit is for that.*

People not only become encouraged, so they can stave off the horror and resentment from a psychological perspective, but they also become more able. Not only are they contending with the existential burden of life more effectively from a spiritual perspective, say, but they start to be better people in the world. They start to constrain the malevolence and resentment in their own hearts that makes the horror of the world even more dismal than it must be. They become more honest. They make better friends. They make more productive and meaningful career choices. They start aiming higher. Thus, they can cope better, psychologically, but they also reduce the volume of what they and the others around them must cope with. Then they suffer less unnecessarily, and so do their families. Then, maybe, the same thing starts to happen with their communities. And then there is the other half of the story: the treasure that the dragon hoards, the benevolent element of nature, the security and shelter provided by society and culture, and the strength of the individual. Those are your weapons in times of trouble. And they are just as real, and perhaps of sufficient power, that their full use will provide you with the means to cope when your life falls apart. The issue is: can you organize the structure of reality so that you find the treasure, the positive aspect of nature smiles upon you, you are ruled by the wise king, and you play

---

*If I didn't say it before, I can certainly say it now: I was and remain in constant awe as a consequence of the absolute courage and grace that my wife, for example, manifested in the face of her trials in the first six months of 2019, after she was diagnosed with terminal cancer (and perhaps cured). Shame, too . . . because I am not at all convinced that I could have done the same.

the role of hero? The hope is that you can conduct yourself in such a manner that it tilts things in that direction. That it is all we have—and it is much better than nothing. If you confront the suffering and malevolence, and if you do that truthfully and courageously, you are stronger, your family is stronger, and the world is a better place. The alternative is resentment, and that makes everything worse.

DECEIT AND ARROGANCE

There appear to be two broad forms of deceit: sins of commission, the things you do knowing full well they are wrong; and sins of omission, which are things you merely let slide—you know you should look at, do, or say something, but you do not. Maybe your business partner is a little bit crooked with the books, and you decide that you are just not going to audit them; or you turn a blind eye to your own misbehavior; or you fail to investigate the misdeeds of a child, adolescent, or your partner in your household. Instead, you just let it go.

What motivates these kinds of deceit? We lie, outright—the sin of commission—knowing full well that we are doing so, to make things easier for us, in theory, regardless of the effect upon other people. We try to tip the world in our own personal favor. We try to gain an edge. We endeavor to avoid a just punishment that is coming our way—often by passing it to others. We commit the sin of omission, alternatively (and perhaps more subtly), in the belief that what we are avoiding will just go away, which it seldom does. We sacrifice the future to the present, frequently suffering the slings and arrows of outraged conscience for doing so, but continuing, rigidly and stubbornly, in any case.

So, what do people use to justify bending and twisting the structure of reality, at the cost of others or even their future selves, to benefit themselves now? It is a motivation clearly embedded in resentment.

Lies are justified by the belief lurking at the bottom of the resentful soul that the terrors of the world have been aimed specifically at the sufferer attempting to justify his lying. But we need to bring arrogance into the conversation, along with resentment, to truly understand why we practice to deceive. It is not obvious that these states of mind can exist in the absence of each other, anyway. They are coconspirators, so to speak.

COMMISSIONS

The first conspiracy between deceit and arrogance might be regarded as a denial or rejection of the relationship between divinity, truth, and goodness. In the early chapters of Genesis, God creates habitable chaos out of order with the Word, with the Logos: courage, love, and truth. Courage, we might say, is the willingness of God to confront the nothingness that preceded Being, which is perhaps of the same form we manage when we rise up from poverty and nothingness to thrive, or rebuild our lives when they have been reduced to chaos by disaster and catastrophe. Love is the ultimate aim—the desire to create the very best that can be created. It provides the same kind of superstructure for Being, perhaps, as the desire for a peaceful and harmonious home provides when such desire allows the truth to be spoken. The Word God uses to confront the nothingness we spoke of is the Truth, and that truth creates. But it does not just create: it appears to create the Good—the very best that love would demand. It is not for nothing that God is so insistent that what has been created is Good. Arrogance and deceit unite to oppose the idea that courageous truth aimed at love creates the Good, and replace it with the idea that any whim, large or small, has the right and opportunity to reveal itself for purposes that are instead narrow and self-serving.

The second form of arrogance that enables deceit has something to do with the assumption of the power of divinity itself. Someone who lies, through action, inaction, words, or silence, has made a choice about what element of becoming (what element of still-unformed but potential chaos) is or is not going to manifest itself. This means that the deceitful individual has taken it upon him or herself to alter the very structure of reality. And for what? For a wish based on the idea that whatever egotistical falsehood conjured up by the act of deceit will be better than the reality that would have transpired had the truth been enacted or spoken. The liar acts out the belief that the false world he brings into being, however temporarily, will serve at least his own interests better than the alternative. That is the arrogance of someone who believes that he can alter the structure of reality through pretense, and that he can get away with it. It is not clear how either of these beliefs could be sustained, if they are thought through carefully (which implies, of course, that they are generally not). First, the transgressor himself is going to know that he is not to be trusted in word or action, and then, to the degree that genuine self-regard relies on such truth, the deceitful words and acts are inevitably going to undermine the personality of the liar. At minimum, he will not be living in the real world, or in the same world as other people, and so he will be weaker than he would have been had he learned what was true instead of having substituted for it what is false. Second, for the liar to genuinely believe that he is "going to get away with it," carries with it the belief that he is smarter than everyone else—that is, the everyone who will not notice (and perhaps that belief comes to encompass God, the Creator, whether explicitly or implicitly). Perhaps he will get away with one, two, or ten lies, of increasing severity, as he is emboldened by success. Each time he succeeds, however, his arrogance will increase, as success is rewarding and will inspire efforts to duplicate and even increase that reward. This cannot help but motivate larger and riskier lies, each associated with a longer fall from the heights of pride. The strategy seems unworkable—a positive feedback loop designed to drag those who entrap themselves within it lower and lower, faster and faster.

The third form of arrogance that underlies deceit has to do with the belief that the deceitful act (which, as we already discussed, has bent or warped the structure of reality) will stand on its own powerfully, without being revealed and destroyed as reality itself straightens and reforms, as it inevitably will. That is the arrogance behind the liar's belief that the lie has somehow permanently altered the form of the world, so that now life in the world can be conducted as if that lie is somehow real. But reality is very complicated and almost every-thing, it seems, touches on everything else. It is very difficult, for ex-ample, to make the consequences of an adulterous affair stop spreading. People are seen. Tongues start to wag. More lies are generated and must be validated to account for the time spent on the affair. Scents linger. Affection within the relationship starts to be replaced by hatred or contempt (particularly if the betrayed person is a genuinely good person, providing no excuse for the sinful actions taken against him or her).

The fourth form of arrogance that justifies deceit has to do with a warped sense of justice, often brought about by resentment. People employ deception in this fourth set of circumstances because they are resentful and angry about their victimized positions in the hell and tragedy of the world. This response is entirely understandable, al-though no less dangerous because of that. The logic is simple and even compelling, particularly in the case of people who have been truly hurt: "I can do what I want because I have been unfairly treated." This reasoning can be seen as simple justice, although it is seldom the case that the people who are now being lied to or deceived are the same individuals who produced the unfair treatment used to justify the falsehood. The arrogance is in believing that the unfair treatment was specifically personal, existentially speaking, rather than being an expected part of existence itself, given its unknown natural, social, and individual dangers. If you have been the victim of what appears to be some malevolent cosmic joke, then why should not you do whatever is in your power to set things a little bit right for yourself? All that line of reasoning does, however, is make life worse. If your justification for misbehaving was that life was bad, then the rationale for continuing to misbehave cannot reasonably be that you should embark on a pattern of action that does nothing but make it more so.

OMISSIONS

There are a variety of reasons why you stand idly by when something you know to be terrible and wrong is occurring, and do nothing (including what you know you should have done) to interfere. The first of these is nihilism. It might not be immediately obvious what nihilism and pride have to do with each other (and even less what both have to do with sins of omission). But the nihilistic attitude is one of certainty: everything is meaningless, or even negative. It is a judgment, a conclusion—and it is a sin of pride, in my estimation. I think we are properly bounded in humility by a reasonable sense of our own ignorance not to take the terrible risk of damning the structure of existence itself.

Another motive for a sin of omission? The claim that it is justifiable to take the easy path. This means living life so that true responsibility for anything important never falls on your shoulders. And you might think that is perfectly acceptable: "Why should I expend extra effort and risk when someone else is lining up for it; pushing actively for it;

or just not sophisticated enough to slip away from it when it seeks them out?" But everyone should take their turn—both at receiving the benefits of social interaction and of bearing the responsibility for en- suring that such interaction remains possible. Children who do not learn that at three do not make any friends, and there are good rea- sons for that. They do not know how to play a game that can sustain itself across time, which is exactly what a friendship is (as well as the attitude that makes for good superiors, peers, and subordinates in a business organization).

Critically consider, as well, the assumption that it is somehow ac- ceptable or even wise to slip by without paying your bills in full. This is another variant of the judgment of existence. "It does not matter if I take the easy path" begins with "It does not matter," and that is Being, judged and damned, with a twist. The second part of the statement, "if I take the easy path," is a self-imposed curse. If you take your turn at the difficult tasks, people learn to trust you, you learn to trust your- self, and you get better at doing difficult things. All of that is good. If you leave all that undone, you will find yourself in the same position as the child whose parents insisted upon doing everything for him or her: bereft of the capacity to thrive in the face of the difficulties/ challenges of life. "It does not matter if I take the easy path," is true only if there is no personality element of the speaker that could be called out by a true adventure. And those who avoid their destiny by standing back when asked to step forward also deprive everyone else of the advantages that may have come their way had the person who took the easy way instead determined to be all they could be.

The final form of sins of omission is associated with lack of faith in yourself—perhaps in humanity in general—because of the fundamen- tal nature of human vulnerability. There is a scene in the book of Gen- esis in which the scales fall from the eyes of Adam and Eve, and they realize they are vulnerable and naked—both part and parcel of self-consciousness. At the same time, they develop the knowledge of good and evil. These two developments coincide because it is not possible to hurt other people with true effectiveness until you know how you can be hurt yourself. And you do not know that you can be hurt until you are, more or less, fully self-conscious; until you know that you can suffer excruciating pain; until you know that you can be killed; until you realize the limits of your being. And as soon as you know all that, you have knowledge of your own nakedness, and you can apply knowledge of that vulnerability with malevolent intent to other people. And then you understand and are capable of Good and Evil.

When called upon later to account for his behavior—for eating of the forbidden fruit—Adam blames the woman for the development of his painful self-knowledge, and God for making her, saying as he does, "The woman whom thou gavest to be with me, she gave me of the tree, and I did eat" (Genesis 3:12). The first man's refusal to take responsibility for his actions is associated with resentment (for his acquisition of painful knowledge), deceit (as he knows he made a free choice, regardless of his wife's behavior), and arrogance (he dares to blame God and the woman the divinity created). Adam takes the easy way out—just as you might, when you say to yourself, "I do not need to have this fight with my wife. I do not have to stand up to my tyrannical boss. I do not have to live by what I believe to be true. I can get away with avoiding my responsibilities." Some of that is inertia and cowardice, but some of it is also motivated by a deep sense of disbelief in your own personal ability. Like Adam, you know you are naked. You are intimately aware of your flaws and vulnerabilities, and the faith in yourself dissolves. This is understandable, but neither helpful nor, in the final analysis, excusable.

THE EXISTENTIAL DANGER OF
ARROGANCE AND DECEIT

As Proverbs 9:10 has it: "The fear of the Lord is the beginning of wisdom." The connection between deception and the deepest of orient-
ing instincts can be profitably comprehended in light of that. If you
understand that deception corrupts and distorts the function of the
most fundamental instinct that guides you through the difficulties of
life, that prospect should scare you enough so that you remain careful
in what you say and do. A truthful person can rely on his or her innate sense of meaning and truth as a reliable guide to the choices that
must be made through life's days, weeks, and years. But there is a rule
that applies—the same rule that computer programmers well know:
"garbage in, garbage out." If you deceive (particularly yourself), if you
lie, then you begin to warp the mechanisms guiding the instinct that
orients you. That instinct is an unconscious guide, so it works underneath your cognitive apparatus, especially once it has become habitual. If you rewire the unconscious mechanisms that maintain you with
assumptions derived from something you know to be unreal, then
your meaningful instinct will take you places you should not go, in
proportion to its corruption. There is little more terrifying than the
possibility that you could come to a crisis point in your life when you
need every faculty you possess, at that moment, to make the decision
properly, only to find you have pathologized yourself with deceit and
can no longer rely on your own judgment. Good luck to you, because
nothing but luck will then serve to save you.

There is a sin somewhat mysteriously defined by Christ as unforgivable: "Whosoever speaketh against the Holy Ghost, it shall not be
forgiven him, neither in this world, neither in the world to come"
(Matthew 12:32). St. Paul, one of Christianity's founders, shed some

light on this statement, when he associated that Third Person of the Trinity with conscience: "I say the truth in Christ, I lie not, my conscience also bearing me witness in the Holy Ghost" (Romans 9:1). Conscience is no less than the sharing of moral knowledge with the self. Deceit necessitates voluntary refusal to abide by the dictate of conscience, and risks pathologizing that very vital function. There is no walking away from that corruption unscathed. This is true even in a neurological sense. Drugs of addiction are generally characterized by their effects upon the neurotransmitter dopamine, increasing its effects in some manner. Dopamine essentially produces the pleasure associated with hope or possibility. Furthermore, your brain is wired so that if you do something that feels good (and therefore produces a dopamine kick) then the parts of you that played a role in the action under question become stronger, more dominant, more able to inhibit the function of other parts of your being. Continued use of an addictive drug therefore feeds the growth of what can be accurately conceptualized as a living monster in the user's psyche—and the attention and intention of that monster is single-mindedly devoted to the drug's effect. It wants one thing, and it comes armed with an entire philosophy about why that one thing must be considered of primary import.

Imagine you are recovering, fragilely, from addiction. Something goes wrong in your life. Resentment emerges. You think, "Oh, to hell with it!" as the initial event leading to reuse of the drug, and the experience of the subsequent dopamine hit. In consequence, the little circuits that formulate the thought "to hell with it" grow more powerful than the parts of the addict's psyche that might be motivating refusal to use the drug. "To hell with it" is a multifaceted philosophy. It means "This is worth sacrificing anything for." It means "Who cares about my life. It is not worth anything, anyway." It means "I do not care if I have to lie to those who love me—my parents, my wife and children—because what difference does it make, anyway? What I want is the drug." There is no easy coming back from that.

When you habitually engage in deceit, you build a structure much like the one that perpetuates addiction, especially if you get away with it, however briefly. The success of the lie is rewarding—and if the risks were high, and you are not caught out, that successful reward might well be intense. This reinforces the development of the neural mechanism in your brain comprising the structure of the entire system of deception. With continued success, at least in the short term, this mechanism begins to work with increasing automaticity—and comes to act, in its arrogant manner, knowing that it can get away with it. That is more obvious for sins of commission; but it is equally and more dangerously and subtly true for what you could know but refuse to—sins of omission. That is the arrogance of believing that what you know is sufficient (regardless of the evidence that accumulates around you, in the form of suffering, which is all too easily and archetypally, let us say, blamed on the structure of reality and the apparent insufficiency of God).

THE PLACE YOU SHOULD BE

It is in our individual capacity to confront the potential of the future and to transform it into the actuality of the present. The way we determine what it is that the world transforms into is a consequence of our ethical, conscious choices. We wake up in the morning and confront the day, with all its possibilities and terrors. We chart a course, making decisions for better or worse. We understand full well that we can do evil and bring terrible things into Being. But we also know that we can do good, if not great, things. We have the best chance of doing the latter if we act properly, as a consequence of being truthful, responsible, grateful, and humble.

The right attitude to the horror of existence—the alternative to resentment, deceit, and arrogance—is the assumption that there is enough of you, society, and the world to justify existence. That is faith in yourself, your fellow man, and the structure of existence itself: the belief that there is enough to you to contend with existence and transform your life into the best it could be. Perhaps you could live in a manner whose nobility, grandeur, and intrinsic meaning would be of sufficient import that you could tolerate the negative elements of existence without becoming so bitter as to transform everything around you into something resembling hell.

Of course, we are oppressed by the fundamental uncertainty of Being. Of course, nature does us in, in unjust and painful ways. Of course, our societies tend toward tyranny, and our individual psyches toward evil. But that does not mean we cannot be good, that our societies cannot be just, and that the natural world cannot array itself in our favor. What if we could constrain our malevolence a bit more, serve and transform our institutions more responsibly, and be less resentful? God only knows what the ultimate limit to that might be. How much better could things become if we all avoided the temptation to actively or passively warp the structure of existence; if we replaced anger with the vicissitudes of Being with gratitude and truth? And if we all did that, with diligent and continual purpose, would we not have the best chance of keeping at bay those elements of self, state, and nature that manifest themselves so destructively and cruelly, and that motivate our turning against the world?

Do not allow yourself to become resentful, deceitful, or arrogant.

RULE XII

BE GRATEFUL IN SPITE OF
YOUR SUFFERING

DOWN CAN DEFINE UP

I have been searching for decades for certainty. It has not been solely a matter of thinking, in the creative sense, but of thinking and then attempting to undermine and destroy those thoughts, followed by careful consideration and conservation of those that survive. It is identification of a path forward through a swampy passage, searching for stones to stand on safely below the murky surface. However, even though I regard the inevitability of suffering and its exaggeration by malevolence as unshakable existential truths, I believe even more deeply that people have the ability to transcend their suffering, psychologically and practically, and to constrain their own malevolence, as well as the evils that characterize the social and the natural worlds.

Human beings have the capacity to courageously confront their suffering—to transcend it psychologically, as well as to ameliorate it practically. This is the most fundamental twin axiom of psychotherapy, regardless of school of thought, as well as key to the mystery of human success and progress across history itself. If you confront the limitations of life courageously, that provides you with a certain psychological purpose that serves as an antidote to the suffering. The fact of your voluntary focus on the abyss, so to speak, indicates to yourself at the deepest of levels that you are capable of taking on without avoidance the difficulties of existence and the responsibility attendant upon that. That mere act of courage is deeply reassuring at the most fundamental levels of psychological being. It indicates your capability and competence to those deep, ancient, and somewhat independent biological and psychological alarm systems that register the danger of the world.

But the utility of such confrontation is by no means merely psychological, as important as that is. It is the appropriate pragmatic approach as well: If you act nobly—a word that is very rarely used now, unfortunately—in the face of suffering, you can work practically and effectively to ameliorate and rectify your own and other people's misery, as such. You can make the material world—the real world—better (or at least stop it from getting worse). The same goes for malevolence: you can constrain that within yourself. When you are about to say something, your conscience might (often does) inform you, noting, "That is not true." It might present itself as an actual voice (internal, of course) or a feeling of shame, guilt, weakness, or other inner disunity—the physiological consequence of the duality of psyche you are manifesting. You then have the opportunity to cease uttering those words. If you cannot tell the truth, you can at least not consciously lie.[1] That is part of the constraint of malevolence. That is something within our grasp. Beginning to cease knowingly lying is a major step in the right direction.

We can constrain our suffering, and we can face it psychologically. That makes us courageous. Then we can ameliorate it practically, because that is what we do when we care for ourselves and other people. There seems to be almost no limit to that. You can genuinely and competently come to care for yourself and your family. You can then extend that out into the broader community. Some people become unbelievably good at that. People who work in palliative care constitute a prime example. They work continually, caring for people who are suffering and dying, and they lose some of those people every day. But they manage to get out of bed every morning, go to work, and face all that pain, tragedy, and death. They make a difference under virtually impossible circumstances. It is for such reasons and because of such examples—watching people confront the existential catastrophe of life forthrightly and effectively—that I am more optimistic than pessimistic, and that I believe that optimism is, fundamentally, more reliable than pessimism. To come to such a conclusion, and then to find it unshakable, is a good example of how and why it may be necessary to encounter the darkness before you can see the light. It is easy to be optimistic and naive. It is easy for optimism to be undermined and demolished, however, if it is naive, and for cynicism to arise in its place. But the act of peering into the darkness as deeply as possible reveals a light that appears unquenchable, and that is a profound surprise, as well as a great relief.

The same holds true for the issue of gratitude. I do not believe you can be appropriately grateful or thankful for what good you have and for what evil has not befallen you until you have some profound and even terrifying sense of the weight of existence. You cannot properly appreciate what you have unless you have some sense not only of how terrible things could be, but of how terrible it is likely for things to be, given how easy it is for things to be so. This is something that is very much worth knowing. Otherwise you might find yourself tempted to ask, "Why would I ever look into the darkness?" But we seem positively

drawn to look. We are fascinated by evil. We watch dramatic representations of serial killers, psychopaths, and the kings of organized
crime, gang members, rapists, contract killers, and spies. We voluntarily frighten and disgust ourselves with thrillers and horror films—
and it is more than prurient curiosity. It is the development of some
understanding of the essentially moral structure of human existence,
of our suspension between the poles of good and evil. The development of that understanding is necessary; it places a *down* below us and
an *up* above us, and orients us in perception, motivation, and action. It
protects us, as well. If you fail to understand evil, then you have laid
yourself bare to it. You are susceptible to its effects, or to its will. If you
ever encounter someone who is malevolent, they have control over you
in precise proportion to the extent that you are unwilling or unable to
understand them. Thus, you look in dark places to protect yourself, in
case the darkness ever appears, as well as to find the light. There is
real utility in that.

THE MEPHISTOPHELIAN SPIRIT

The great German writer Goethe, who is to Germanic culture what
Shakespeare is to English, wrote a famous play, *Faust*, the story of a
man who sells his soul to the devil for knowledge.[2] Mephistopheles is
the devil in Goethe's play—the adversary. The adversary is a mythical
figure; the spirit who eternally works against our positive intent (or,
perhaps, against positive intent generally). You can understand that
psychologically, as well as metaphysically or religiously. We all see
within ourselves the emergence of good intentions and the repeated
instructions to ourselves to act accordingly, yet we note distressingly
often that we leave undone what we know we should do, and do instead what we know we should not. There is something in all of us that

works in counterposition to our voluntarily expressed desires. There are in fact many such somethings—a chorus of demons, so to speak—working at cross-purposes even to each other; many dark and unarticulated motivations and systems of belief, all manifesting themselves as partial personalities (but with all the essential features of personality, despite their partial nature).

To realize this is uncanny. That realization is the great contribution of the psychoanalysts, who insisted above all, perhaps, that we were inhabited by spirits that were beyond not only our control but even our conscious knowledge. And that realization brings up great and paralyzing questions: If you are not in control of yourself, who or what is? If you are not, a challenge has been posed to the very idea of the centrality, unity, and even reality of the "you" whose existence seems so immediately certain. And what is that *who* or *what* that is not you up to? And toward what end is it acting? We all hope we are the sorts of creatures who can tell ourselves what to do, and who will then do exactly that, in accordance with our will. You are you, after all, and you should—virtually by definition—be in control of yourself. But things often do not work that way, and the reason or reasons they do not are deeply mysterious.

Sometimes, of course, it is simply much easier just not to do the things we should. Good actions can be and often are difficult to undertake, and there is danger—exhaustion not the least of it—in difficulty. Inertia is also a powerful reason for stasis and can provide a certain immediate safety. But there is more to the problem. It is not just that you are lazy: it is also that you are bad—and declared so by your own judgment. That is a very unpleasant realization, but there is no hope of becoming good without it. You will upbraid yourself (or your conscience will do so) for your shortcomings. You will treat yourself as if you were or are at least in part an immoral agent. That is all deeply unpleasant too, and you might well be motivated to avoid your own judgment. But no simple rationalizations will allow for your escape.

You will see, if you are willing to look, the adversarial force at work within you, working to undermine your best intentions. The exact nature of that force is grounds for endless speculation—philosophical, literary, psychological, and above all, religious or theological. The Christian conception of the great figure of evil—Mephistopheles, Satan, Lucifer, the devil himself—is, for example, a profound imaginative personification of that spirit. But the adversary is not merely something that exists in the imagination—certainly not only in the individual imagination. It is also something that manifests itself through something that is still aptly described as "possession" in the motivation for malevolent actions, as well as in the acts themselves. Everyone who has thought or said something akin to "I do not understand what came over me" after acting in a particularly unseemly manner notes the existence of such possession, even if they cannot or do not articulate that noting. In consequence, we may ask ourselves, in utter dismay, "Why would such a spirit exist? Why would it be part of each of us?"

The answer appears to be partly associated with the powerful sense that each of us shares of our own intrinsic mortal limitations, our subjugation to the suffering inflicted upon us by ourselves, society, and nature. That embitters and produces a certain self-contempt or disgust, inspired by our own weaknesses and inadequacies (and I am not speaking here yet of immorality, merely of our intrinsic and terrible fragility), and also by the apparent unfairness, unpredictability, and arbitrariness of our failings. Given all these disappointing realizations, there is no reason to assume that you are going to be satisfied or happy with yourself, or with Being itself. Such dissatisfaction—such unhappiness—can easily come to reinforce and magnify itself in a vicious circle. With each step you take against yourself or others as a consequence of your unhappiness and resentment, there is more to be ashamed of, and more reason for self-directed antagonism. It is not for nothing that approximately one person in five engages in some form of serious physical self-harm in their lifetime.[3] And this does not include the most serious act—suicide itself (or the more common tendency toward suicidal ideation). If you are unhappy with yourself, why would you work in your best interest? Maybe something vengeful would emerge from you, instead; maybe something capable of justifying itself while it metes out hypothetically deserved suffering, designed to interfere with your movement forward. If you conceptually aggregate and unite into a single personality all that opposes you in you, all that opposes your friendships, and all that opposes your wife or husband, the adversary emerges. That is precisely Mephistopheles in Goethe's play—the devil himself. That is the spirit who works *against*—and that is exactly how he describes himself: "I am the spirit that denies."[4] Why? Because everything in the world is so limited and imperfect—and causes itself so much trouble and terror because of that—that its annihilation is not only justified but ethically demanded. So goes, at least, the rationalization.

This is no mere lifeless abstraction. People struggle in a deadly fashion with such ideas. Women wrestle with them when they consider having a baby, inquiring of themselves: "Should I really bring an infant into a world like this? Is that an ethical decision?" The followers of the philosophical school of antinatalism, of whom the South African philosopher David Benatar is perhaps the leading advocate,[5] would decisively answer no to both of those questions. I debated his views with him a few years back.[6] It was not as if I failed to understand his position. There is no doubt that the world is steeped in suffering. A few years later, I debated another philosopher, Slavoj Žižek—known much more widely for his Marxist predilections than his religious convictions. He said something during our discussion that might be theologically debatable, but that I found of great interest. In the Christian tradition, even God Himself, in the form of Christ, despairs of the meaning of life and the goodness of His Father in the agony of His Crucifixion. At the peak of his suffering, just before death, He utters the words "*Eli Eli lama sabachthani*"[7]—"My God, my God, why has thou forsaken me?" (Matthew 27:46). This appears to strongly imply, in its narrative way, that the burden of life can become so great that even God Himself can lose faith when confronted with the unbearable reality of injustice, betrayal, suffering, and death.

It is hard to imagine a story more sympathetic to mere mortals. If God Himself experiences doubts in the midst of His self-imposed agony, how could we mere humans not fall prey to the same failing? And it is possible that it was compassion that was driving the antinatalist Benatar's position. I saw no evidence that Benatar was malevolent in any obvious manner. He appeared to truly believe—in a manner I found reminiscent of Goethe's Mephistopheles—that the combination of consciousness, vulnerability, and mortality is so dire that there is simply no moral excuse for its continuance. Now, it is entirely possible that Mephistopheles's opinion is not to be trusted. Since he is Satan himself, there is no reason to assume that the argument he puts forward to justify his adversarial stance toward Being is valid, or even that he himself truly believes it. And perhaps the same was true of Benatar, who was and is no doubt prey to the frailties that characterize each of us (and that certainly includes me, despite the stance I took in opposition to him). But I believed then and still firmly believe now that the consequences of his self-negating position are simply too dire. It leads directly to an antilife or even an anti-Being nihilism so profound that its manifestation could not help but exaggerate and amplify the destructive consequences of existence that are already the focus of the hypothetically compassionate antinatalists themselves (and I am not being sarcastic or cynical about the existence of that compassion, misplaced though I believe it to be).

Benatar's hypothesis was that life is so rife with suffering that it is, actually, a sin—for all intents and purposes—to bring any new conscious beings into existence, and that the most appropriate ethical action for human beings to take would be to simply stop doing so: to render ourselves voluntarily extinct. Such a viewpoint is more widespread, in my opinion, than you might think, although perhaps rarely held for long. Whenever you are cut off at the knees by one of life's many catastrophes, whenever a dream collapses, or someone close to you is hurt in some fundamental way—especially a child or another loved one—then you can easily find yourself thinking, "Perhaps it would be better if the whole mess was just brought to a halt."

That is certainly what people think when they contemplate suicide. Such thoughts are generated in their most extreme variant by the serial killers, by high school shooters, by all generally homicidal and genocidal actors. They are acting out the adversarial attitude as fully as they might. They are truly possessed, in a manner that exceeds the merely metaphorical. They have decided not only that life is unbearable and the malevolence of existence is inexcusable, but that everything should be punished for the mere sin of its Being. If we want to have any hope of dealing with the existence of evil, and working toward its minimization, we must understand these sorts of impulses. It is in no small part the consciousness of suffering and malevolence that embitters people. And it is toward this embitterment that I believe the antinatalist position would, if widely adopted, inevitably drift. First, it might be the mere refusal to reproduce. But I cannot believe that it would be long until that impulse to cease production of new life was transformed into a similar impulse to destroy life that currently exists, in consequence of the "compassionate" judgment that some lives are so terrible that it is merciful to bring them to an end. That philosophy emerged relatively early in the Nazi era, for example, when individuals judged unbearably damaged by life were euthanized for purposes deemed "morally merciful." The question this line of thinking leads to is where does such "mercy" stop? How sick, old, intellectually impaired, crippled, unhappy, unproductive, or politically inappropriate do you have to be before dispensing with you is a moral imperative? And why would you believe, once the eradication or even merely the limitation of life became your guiding star, that you would not continue down that road to its hellish end?

I found the Columbine High School killers' writings particularly instructive in that regard. They are scrawled out, and are careless, incoherent, and narcissistic, but there is definitely a philosophy at the base of them: that things deserve to suffer for the crime of their existence. The consequence of that belief is the creative elaboration and extension of that suffering. One of the killers wrote that he considered himself the judge of all that exists—a judge that found Being, particularly of the human form, wanting—and that it would be better if the entire human race was eradicated. That defined the scope of his horrific vision. He and his partner shot their classmates in their local high school, but that was only a tiny fraction of what they were planning. They had incendiary devices laid out across the community, and had fantasized together about trying to take out the entire city. Such plans are just a step on the way to the ultimate genocidal vision.

You do not have those sorts of visions unless you are deeply possessed by something very much resembling the adversarial spirit. That is Mephistopheles, whose essential viewpoint might be paraphrased as follows: "Life is so terrible, because of its limitations and malevolence, that it would be better if it did not exist at all." That is the central doctrine of the spirit that works at counterpurposes to you. It is an arguable case and not surprising that it should emerge, and it seems terribly credible at moments of crisis, even though I believe it is deeply wrong. I think the reason that it is wrong, in part, is because, when it is realized, all it does is exacerbate an already admittedly bad situation. If you set about making things worse, they are likely, in fact, to get worse. I cannot see how this constitutes an improvement, if your original objection was motivated by the essential terror of our existential situation itself. It does not seem to be a pathway that a conscious creature, with a bit of gratitude, might walk down. There is an incoherency to it that is logically untenable, and that therefore seems to make the argument fundamentally specious, and cannot help but make the listener think, "There are things going on here behind the scenes that are both unspoken and unspeakable, despite the surface logic."

The failings in the adversary's logic do not mean that constructing an unshakable viewpoint to counter it is a simple matter. In the most straightforward sense, identifying that vision of objection and vengefulness is useful, in the way that negative space in a painting is useful: it defines the positive, by contrast. Good can be conceptualized—however vaguely in its initial formulation—as the opposite of whatever constitutes evil, which is usually more readily identifiable in the world than goodness. I have been trying to find touchstones on that pathway of opposition to evil, so that people can identify what that good might be. Some of these are very practical, if difficult. I have been suggesting to my viewers and listeners,[8] for example—particularly those currently burdened by the mortal illness of a parent—that it is useful to consciously take on the task of being the most reliable person in the aftermath of the death, during the grief-stricken preparations for the funeral and the funeral itself, and for the care of family members during and after the catastrophe. There is a call to your potential in doing that. There is a call to the strength of Being itself—the Being that could manifest itself in you. The human race has been dealing with loss and death forever. We are the descendants of those who could manage it. That capability is within us, grim as the task might seem.

If you truly love someone, it can seem a deep form of betrayal to stay integrated and healthy, in essence, in their absence or sadly waning presence. What does that ability indicate, after all, about the true depths of your love? If you can witness their demise and survive the loss, does that not imply that the bond was shallow and temporary, and even replaceable? If you were truly bonded, should not it destroy you (as it sometimes does)? But we cannot wish that every inevitable loss leads to the destruction of everyone affected, because we would then all be doomed, far more immediately than we currently are. And it certainly is not the case that the last wish of the dying is or should be the interminable suffering of those they love. My impression has been, instead, that people tend to feel guilty on their deathbeds (because of their immediate uselessness and the burden that causes, but even more because of their apprehension about the grief and trouble they will cause those left behind). Thus, their most fervent wish, I believe, is that those whom they love will be able to move forward and live happily, after a reasonable time of mourning.

To collapse in the aftermath of a tragic loss is therefore more accurately a betrayal of the person who has died, instead of a tribute, as it multiplies the effect of that mortal catastrophe. It takes a dying person of narcissistic selfishness to wish endless grief on their loved ones. Strength in the face of death is better for the person who is dying and for those who remain living alike. There are family members who are suffering because of their loss who need taking care of, and who may be too old and infirm and otherwise troubled to cope with the situation properly. And so someone strong has to step in and exercise the terrible authority that makes even of death something to face and over-come. To understand clearly that you are morally obliged under such circumstances to manifest strength in the face of adversity is to indicate to yourself—and, perhaps, to other people—that there is something in you of sufficient grandeur and power to face the worst forthrightly and to yet prevail. That is certainly what people need to encounter at a funeral. There is little to say, explicitly, in the face of death. Everyone is rendered speechless when they encounter the infinite expanse of emptiness surrounding our too-brief existence. But uprightness and courage in such a situation is truly heartening and sustaining.

I have suggested that strength at the funeral of someone dear and close is a worthy goal more than once during a lecture (where people might encounter it live, or on YouTube or a podcast). In consequence, a not insignificant number of people have indicated to me that they took heart in desperate times as a consequence. They set reliability and strength in a crisis as a conscious goal and were able to manage exactly that, so that the devastated people around them had someone to lean on and see as an example in the face of genuine trouble. That, at the very least, made a bad situation much less dreadful than it might have been. And that is something. If you can observe someone rising above the catastrophe, loss, bitterness, and despair, then you see evidence that such a response to catastrophe is possible. In consequence, you might mimic that, even under dire circumstances. Courage and nobility in the face of tragedy is the reverse of the destructive, nihilistic cynicism apparently justified under just such circumstances.

Again, I understand the negative attitude. I have had thousands hours of clinical experience. I have been deeply involved in some very difficult situations, along with those I was listening to and strategizing with, as well as within the confines of my private life. People have arduous lives. You think your life is hard (and it probably is, at least at times), then you meet someone and your life is so much better than theirs that, no matter what your hardships are, you cannot even conceive of how they might continue to exist in their current misery. And you find out, not infrequently, that those same unfortunate people know someone else whose life is so hard that they feel the same way about them. And even they are often left feeling guilty that they believe what they have is a hard lot, because they know just how much worse it could be.

It is not as if the suffering and betrayal, the catastrophes, are of insufficient gravity to make bitterness a real option. But there is just no good whatsoever in that option, and plenty of evident harm. So, what constitutes the alternative? I began to seriously contemplate the topic of this rule just before Thanksgiving, in 2018, when I was touring the United States. That holiday has become, arguably, the biggest shared celebration in America (and is also a major event in Canada, approximately a month earlier). The only competitor, particularly since Easter has largely faded away, is Christmas, which is also in some sense a holiday of thanksgiving, concentrating as it does on the arrival of the eternal Redeemer in the midst of the darkness and cold of winter, and so reflects the endless birth and rebirth of hope itself. The giving of thanks is an alternative to bitterness—perhaps *the* alternative. My observation of American holidays—I lived in the States for seven years, and I have spent time there on countless other occasions—is that the prominence of Thanksgiving among holidays seems to be a good thing, practically and symbolically. The fact that the primary feast of celebration characterizing a country would be one of explicitly "giving thanks" appears, in principle, as a positive commentary on the fundamental ethic of the state. It means that the individual is striving to have his or her heart in the right place, and that the group is supporting and encouraging that endeavor. Why is that, given the trouble that constitutes life? It is because you can be courageous. You can be alert, awake, attentive. You can see how demanding life is and can be, and you can see it clearly. Despite this, you can remain grateful, because that is the intrepid attitude toward life and its difficulties. You are grateful not because you are naive, but because you have decided to put a hand forward to encourage the best in yourself, and the state, and the world. You are grateful, in the same manner, not because suffering is absent, but because it is valiant to remember what you have and what you may still be offered—and because the proper thankful attitude toward that existence and possibility positions you better than any other attitude toward the vicissitudes of existence.

To be grateful for your family is to remember to treat them better. They could cease to exist at any moment. To be grateful for your friends is to awaken yourself to the necessity of treating them properly, given the comparative unlikelihood of friendship itself. To be grateful to your society is to remind yourself that you are the beneficiary of tremendous effort on the part of those who predeceased us, and left this amazing framework of social structure, ritual, culture, art, technology, power, water, and sanitation so that our lives could be better than theirs.

The temptation to become embittered is great and real. It requires a genuine moral effort not to take that path, assuming that you are not—or are no longer—naive. The gratitude associated with that state of Being is predicated on ignorance and inexperience. That is not virtue. Thus, if you are attentive and awake, and you can see the structure of the world, bitterness and resentment beckon as a viable response. Then you might well ask yourself, "Well, why not walk down that dark path?" It seems to me that the answer to that, to state it again, is courage: the courage to decide "No, that is not for me, despite the reasons I may have for being tempted in that direction," and to decide, instead, "Despite the burden of my awake mortality, I am going to work for the good of the world."

COURAGE—BUT SUPERORDINATE, LOVE

That decision seems to me to be courage subsumed to love. If it is resentment and bitterness and the consequent hatred that emerges from that tempting us toward the torment and destruction of everything that lives and suffers, then perhaps it is active love that aims at its betterment. And that seems to me to be the fundamental decision of life, and that it is correct to identify it, at least in a vital part, as an act of voluntary will. The reasons for acrimony, anger, resentment, and malevolence are strong and plentiful. Thus, it must be a leap of faith—a decision about a mode of being not so clearly justified by the evidence, particularly in hard times—that Being should be strengthened and supported by your aims and your acts. That is something done in some deep sense despite *"Eli Eli lama sabachthani"*—something that says "despite it all, no matter what *it* is, onward and upward"—and that is precisely the impossible moral undertaking that is demanded from each of us for the world to function properly (even for it to avoid degeneration into hell).

It is within the frame of that impossible undertaking—that decision to love—that courage manifests itself, enabling each person who adopts the courageous pathway to do the difficult things that are necessary to act for the good in even the worst of times. If you determine to manifest the two virtues of love and courage—simultaneously, consciously— you decide that you are going to work to make things better and not worse, even for yourself, even though you know that because of all your errors and omissions you are already three-quarters lost.

You are going to work to make things better for yourself, as if you are someone you are responsible for helping. You are going to do the same thing for your family and the broader community. You are going to strive toward the harmony that could manifest itself at all those levels, despite the fact that you can see the flawed and damaged substructure of things, and have had your vision damaged in consequence. That is the proper and courageous pathway forward. Maybe that is the definition of gratitude, of thankfulness, and I cannot see how that is separate from courage and love.

You might well ask, "Do people actually perceive and act in this manner?"—even—"Can they?" One of the most compelling pieces of evidence I have come across is the fact of grief over the loss of someone close. Even if you are ambivalent about life itself—and maybe even if you are ambivalent, to some degree, about the person that you lost, because that can certainly be the case—your likely response to a death is grief. That response is not exactly conscious. Grief is a strange experience. It seizes you unexpectedly. You feel shock and confusion. You are not at all sure how to respond. What is it that you are supposed to do? But if it is conscious grieving—the voluntary acting out of the supposedly appropriate response—it is not real; not in the manner that genuine grief grips you of its own accord. And if you do not feel yourself seized, unwittingly, in the latter sense, you might think, "I am not feeling the way I am supposed to feel. I am not crying. I am not overwhelmed by sorrow. I am going far too normally about my day-to-day business" (something particularly likely to occur if you receive the news of a death from a distant locale). But then, as you engage in something trivial, as if things are normal, the grief will strike you like a rogue wave. That happens repeatedly, God only knows for how long. It is something that arises from the depths, and it takes you irresistibly in its grasp.

Grief must be a reflection of love. It is perhaps the ultimate proof of love. Grief is an uncontrollable manifestation of your belief that the lost person's existence, limited and flawed as it might have been, was worthwhile, despite the limitations and flaws even of life itself. Otherwise, why would you feel the loss? Otherwise, why would you feel, involuntarily, sorrowful and bereft (and that from a source self-deception cannot reach)? You grieve because something that you valued is no longer in existence. Thus, in the core of your Being, you have decided that the person's life was valuable, despite whatever trouble they caused you—and themselves. In my experience, that happens even when people die who were quite monstrous. It is a rare person whose life has gone so catastrophically wrong that their death brings no sorrow.

There is a deep part of us that makes the decision, when we grieve for someone we have lost, that their existence was worthwhile, despite it all. Maybe that is a reflection of an even more fundamental decision: Being itself is worth having, despite it all. Gratitude is therefore the process of consciously and courageously attempting thankfulness in the face of the catastrophe of life. Maybe that is what we are trying to do when we meet with our families during a holiday, wedding, or funeral. Those are often contentious and difficult affairs. We face a paradoxical, demanding tension. We bring people that we know and love close to us; we are pleased at their existence and their proximity, but also wish they could be more. We are inevitably disappointed in each other, and in ourselves, as well.

In any familial gathering, there is tension between the warmth you feel and the bonding of memory and shared experience, and the sorrow inevitably accompanying that. You see some relatives who are in a counterproductive stasis, or wandering down a path that is not good for them. You see others aging, losing their vitality and health (and that sight interferes with and disrupts your memories of their more powerful and youthful selves: a dual loss, then, of present and past). That is all painful to perceive. But the fundamental conclusion, despite all of that, is that "It is good that we are all together and able to share a meal, and to see and talk to each other, and to note that we are all here and facing this celebration or difficulty together." And everyone hopes that "perhaps if we pull together, we can manage this properly." And so you make the same fundamental decision, when you join communally with your people, that you make when you grieve: "Despite everything, it is good that we are together, and that we have one another." That is something truly positive.

The same is true of your relationship with your children. My grief at life in recent decades was exaggerated in the case of my daughter, because she was very ill for many years as a child, adolescent, and young adult. A child is a being of tremendous potential, capable of developing an admirable, productive, and ever-increasing autonomy and ability. But there is also something truly fragile about their three- or four- or five- (or even fifteen- or twenty-five-) year-old forms (because that fragility never truly disappears from a parent's perception, once it has been experienced deeply, as it certainly will be with the experience of caring for young children). All that is part of the joy of having them, but also part of the pain. The pain is the absolute certainty that the fragility will be exploited. And yet I thought that whatever steps I might take to eradicate that fragility in my children would also destroy that for which I was thankful. I remember thinking this quite distinctly with my son when he was three, because he was super-cute and fun. But he was three, so he was little. He would collapse, bang his head on tables, fall down the stairs, and get into little scraps with other kids. Maybe he would be playing in the supermarket parking lot and, distracted, run off briefly. This is not a wise move in a place ruled by cars. There is an undeniable vulnerability around children that wakes you up and makes you very conscious of the desire to protect them, but also of the desire to foster their autonomy and push them out in the world, because that is how you strengthen them. It is also a vulnerability that can make you angry at life because of its fragility, and lead you to curse the fate that joins the two together.

When I think about my parents, the same thing comes to mind. They are getting old. As people get older, in some sense, you see them crystallize into the people that they are. My father and my mother both have a decided character. They were who they were in their fifties, and now they are perhaps even more so. They have their limitations and their advantages (and it is even the case that the latter are often integrally necessary to the former). They are in their eighties now and are very particularized. Sometimes it is frustrating to deal with people and their particularities. You think, "Would not it be better if they could be some other way?" I am not saying I think that about my parents more than people generally think that about each other. It is by no means a criticism of them. In addition, there is no doubt that they (and others—many others) feel the same way about me. But it is necessary to understand that, just as in the case of children, all those particularities, fragilities, and limitations are part and parcel of what it is that you come to love.

So, you might love people despite their limitations, but you also love them *because* of their limitations. That is something very much worth understanding. Doing so may help you see how gratitude remains possible. Despite the fact that the world is a very dark place, and that each of us has our black elements of soul, we see in each other a unique blend of actuality and possibility that is a kind of miracle: one that can manifest itself, truly, in the world, in the relationships we have that are grounded in trust and love. That is something for which you can be courageously thankful. That is something in which you can discover part of the antidote to the abyss and the darkness.

Be grateful in spite of your suffering.

Coda

As I indicated in the overture, much of this book was written during long
months spent in hospitals—first, visiting or staying with my daughter,
Mikhaila, then doing the same over a longer period with my wife, Tammy,
and finally—when it became necessary—during my repeated admis-
sions. I do not think it appropriate to write about those personal trials in
any more detail than I already have in the Overture—partly because the
common circumstances of the COVID-19 pandemic have rendered everyone's life tragic in an unimaginable manner, so that it seems superfluous, in some sense, to provide a detailed account of familial or individual
suffering on top of that, and partly because the current book is not about
my daughter's troubles, or my wife's, or mine, directed as it is to topics
of general psychological import. What I truly find necessary to relate,
however, is our appreciation to all those many people who supported us
during this trying time. So, some additional discussion of our various mal-
adies appears unavoidable at this point.

On the public front, we received an outpouring of good wishes from thousands of people who had become familiar with my work. Some of this was delivered in person, when people met Tammy or me in public; some was sent by email and social media; and some of it came in YouTube comments on my videos. This was exceptionally heartening. My sister, Bonnie, gathered and printed out particularly thoughtful messages to Tammy from around the world, and posted them in bright colors on the walls of the hospital room where they could be easily seen. The messages later addressed to me helped bolster my oft-wavering conviction that I could and should prevail in the face of the difficulties I was experiencing, and that the book you are reading or listening to would maintain its relevance, even in the face of the terrible pandemic that currently envelops the world. We were also the beneficiaries of medical care, much of it extreme, but most often provided with optimism, care, and competence. Tammy's dual cancer surgeries were courageously performed by Dr. Nathan Perlis of the Princess Margaret Cancer Centre, and when the complications arising thereof became too extreme, was treated by Dr. Maxim Itkin, director of Philadelphia's Penn Center for Lymphatic Disorders.

More privately, Tammy and I were individually and jointly the grateful beneficiaries of constant support from family and friends, who interrupted their lives to spend days, weeks, or months of time with us while we were undergoing our trials. I can only hope, in the face of serious doubts about the matter, that I would have chosen to be as generous with my time and attention as they were if the tables were turned. It is particularly necessary to thank my family members—my daughter, Mikhaila Peterson, and her husband, Andrey Korikov; my son, Julian Peterson, and daughter-in-law, Jillian Vardy; my brother-in law and sister Jim and Bonnie Keller; my brother and sister-in-law Joel and Kathleen Peterson; my parents, Beverley and Walter Peterson; my brother- and sister-in-law Dale and Maureen Roberts, and their daughter, Tasha; my sister-in-law Della Roberts and her husband, Daniel Grant; as well as our friends Wayne

Meretsky, Myriam Mongrain, Queenie Yu, Morgan and Ava Abbott, Wodek Szemberg and Estera Bekier, Wil Cunningham and Shona Tritt, Jim Balsillie and Neve Peric, Dr. Norman and Karen Doidge, Gregg and Dr. Delinah Hurwitz (the former of whom also profoundly helped me edit and improve *12 Rules for Life: An Antidote to Chaos*), Dr. Cory and Nadine Torgerson, Sonia and Marshall Tully, Dr. Robert O. and Sandra Pihl, Dr. Daniel Higgins and Dr. Alice Lee, Dr. Mehmet and Lisa Oz, and Dr. Stephen and Dr. Nicole Blackwood, all of whom went above and beyond the call of duty in the attention they paid to Tammy and me over the last two years. There are, finally, three men of God who were of service, particularly to Tammy: Fathers Eric Nicolai, Fred Dolan, and Walter Hannam.

My family made arrangements to have me treated in Moscow for the consequence of a paradoxical reaction and then a dependence on the hypothetically safe but truly dangerous benzodiazepine antianxiety medication. This was arranged with exceptional efficiency, despite the time of year (the Christmas and New Year holidays in 2019–20), by Kirill Sergeevich Mikhailov, the consul general of the Russian Federation in Toronto, and the consular staff who provided an urgent visa in a matter of days. Many people, including Kelly and Joe Craft, Anish Dwivedi, Jamil Javani, Zach Lahn, Chris Halverson, Metropolitan Jonah, and the V. Rev. Victor Potapov and Dimitir Ivanov, helped expedite what was a very complex, multidimensional process. While in Russia, my safety was ensured by Alexander Usov, and my sense of isolation diminished by daily visits by Mikhaila and her husband, Andrey, who truly cannot be thanked enough. The Russian medical teams included IMC Addiction by Roman Yuzapolski, who agreed to supervise my case despite being advised by assorted experts that it was too dangerous to do so, and his staff members, Herman Stepnov, administrative directors, and Alexandr, therapist, who translated for me constantly for a two-week period, without even a change of clothes. The team of the Russian Academy of Medical Sciences took me in with undiagnosed double pneumonia and in a state of catatonia and delirium, and restored my ability to ambulate. Dr. Marina Petrova, the deputy director, and Dr. Michael, the head doctor of what was known as the Reanimatology Ward, were of particular and notable aid. Uliana Efros, nanny to my granddaughter, Elizabeth Scarlett, always had our backs and traveled with Mikhaila, Andrey, and me for eight months from Russia to Florida and Serbia, caring for Scarlett, including spending a month in quarantine. Thanks as well to Uli's daughter Liza Romanova, who helped take care of Scarlett in Russia, so that my daughter and son-in-law could visit me in the hospital. Finally, on the Russian end, I would like to thank Mikhail Avdeev, who helped us extensively with provision of medication and translation of medical information—both on very short notice.

Later, in June 2020, I sought admission at the IM Clinic for Internal Medicine in Belgrade, an institution dedicated to benzodiazepine withdrawal, and fell directly under the competent and caring treatment provided by Dr. Igor Bolbukh and his staff. Dr. Bolbukh had flown to Russia previously to consult there while I was in a state of delirium, provided months of pro bono medical guidance, moved me to a more stable condition when I arrived in Serbia, and managed my care thereafter. The IM Clinic was founded by Dr. Nikolai Vorobiev, and his staff were very patient, without resentment—a difficult feat to manage in these days of COVID and the inevitable accompanying and sudden quarantines.

There are also those who profoundly deserve credit, recognition, and gratitude on the professional front. Thank you to my agents, Mollie Glick of Creative Artists Agency, as well as Sally Harding of CookeMcDermid (Canada) and her colleagues Suzanne Brandreth and Hana El Niwairi of Cooke Agency International Canada. Thank you to the editors and publishers of *12 Rules for Life: An Antidote to Chaos*: Penguin Random House

Canada senior editor Craig Pyette, who played a diligent and instrumental role in quality control and enhancement; former CEO Brad Martin; current CEO Kristin Cochrane; publisher of the Knopf Random House Canada Publishing Group Anne Collins; vice president, associate publisher, and director of marketing strategy Scott Sellers; Penguin Random House UK editor Laura Stickney and her colleague Penelope Vogler, and CEO Tom Weldon; and Penguin Random House International CEO Markus Dohle. Thanks to the editors and publishers of the current book, a group that includes the immediately aforementioned individuals, as well as additional Penguin Random House US personnel, including publisher of the Portfolio and Sentinel imprints Adrian Zackheim and editor Helen Healey. Finally, thank you to Professor Bruce Pardy and lawyer Jared Brown for their active support of my ideas during a time when doing so could be truly hazardous to one's professional reputation and security.

The worldwide tour of 160 cities that Tammy and I undertook during the incubation period of this book as well as its preliminary formulation was organized with exceptional efficiency and good nature by Creative Artists Agency representatives Justin Edbrooke (assisted by Daniel Smith) and Ari Levin (assisted by Colette Silver), as well as Live Nation's Andrew Levitt. The Australian and New Zealand tour benefited from the attention of Australian producer TEG Dainty's Brad Drummond, tour manager Simon Christian, and security man Scott Nicholson. Gunnlaugur Jónsson and his crew were exceptionally hospitable to Tammy and me (as well as to my mother and aunt, who accompanied us for the days we were in Iceland). John O'Connell served as primary tour manager, and was extremely professional, great at problem solving, and consistently upbeat and supportive over the months of travel and organization.

Dave Rubin of *The Rubin Report* traveled with us, introduced my lectures, and emceed the question-and-answer periods that followed, adding a necessary bit of levity to what might otherwise have been a too-serious endeavor. Rob Greenwald of Rogers & Cowan helped ensure appropriate media coverage. Joe Rogan, Ben Shapiro, Douglas Murray, Gad Saad, and Steven Crowder extended their friendship and shared their extensive media presence. Zachary Lahn was there many times as needed, and Jeff Sandefer opened up his extensive connection network. Bill Vardy, Dennis Thigpen, Duncan Maisels, and Melanie Paquette served as drivers for the tour leg in North America when we used motor homes. Tammy and I would also like to thank designer Shelley Kirsch and the crew at SJOC Construction for completing the renovation of our house during these trying times with minimal supervision on our part. So much has happened in the last three years I am sure that I have missed key people, and for that I sincerely apologize.

Thanks is due, finally, to all of you who have read or listened to my books—*Maps of Meaning: The Architecture of Belief,* as well as the two 12 Rules volumes—and/or tuned in to my YouTube videos and podcasts. I have been profoundly struck, as have the people close to me, by the exceptional loyalty and care you have demonstrated over the last half decade. May all of you reading or listening to this book wend your way successfully through these difficult times. I hope you are surrounded by people you love and who love you in turn. I hope that you can rise to the challenge presented by our current circumstances, and that we all might have the good fortune to eventually turn our attention to rebuilding the world after the deluge.

Notes

OVERTURE

1. This is the philosopher David Hume's famous "scandal of induction." For further reading, see D. Humes and P. Millican, *An Enquiry Concerning Human Understanding* (New York: Oxford University Press, 1748/2008).
2. J. B. Peterson, *12 Rules for Life: An Antidote to Chaos* (Toronto: Random House Canada, 2018).

RULE I: DO NOT CARELESSLY DENIGRATE SOCIAL INSTITUTIONS OR CREATIVE ACHIEVEMENT

1. S. Hughes and T. Celikel, "Prominent Inhibitory Projections Guide Sensorimotor Communication: An Invertebrate Perspective," *BioEssays* 41 (2019): 190088.
2. L. W. Swanson "Cerebral Hemisphere Regulation of Motivated Behavior." *Brain Research* 886 (2000): 113–64.
3. F. B. M. de Waal and M. Suchak, "Prosocial Primates: Selfish and Unselfish Motivations," *Philosophical Transactions of the Royal Society of London: Biological Science* 365 (2010): 2711–22.
4. J. B. Peterson and J. Flanders, "Play and the Regulation of Aggression," in *Developmental Origins of Aggression*, eds. R. E. Tremblay, W. H. Hartup, and J. Archer (New York: Guilford Press, 2005), 133–57.
5. J. Piaget, *Play, Dreams and Imitation in Childhood* (New York: W. W. Norton & Company, 1962).

6. F. de Waal, *Good Natured: The Origins of Right and Wrong in Humans and Other Animals* (Cambridge, Mass.: Harvard University Press, 1997).

7. K. S. Sakyi et al., "Childhood Friendships and Psychological Difficulties in Young Adulthood: An 18-Year Follow-Up Study," *European Child & Adolescent Psychiatry* 24 (2012): 815–26.

8. Y. M. Almquist, "Childhood Friendships and Adult Health: Findings from the Aberdeen Children of the 1950s Cohort Study," *European Journal of Public Health* 22 (2012): 378–83.

9. All of the adult data here is derived from M. Reblin and B. N. Uchino, "Social and Emotional Support and Its Implications for Health," *Current Opinions in Psychiatry* 21 (2009): 201–2.

10. R. Burns, "To a Louse: On Seeing One on a Lady's Bonnet at Church," *The Collected Poems of Robert Burns* (Hertfordshire, UK: Wordsworth Poetry Library, 1786 /1988), 138.

11. J. B. Hirsh et al., "Compassionate Liberals and Polite Conservatives: Associations of Agreeableness with Political Ideology and Moral Values," *Personality and Social Psychology Bulletin* 36 (2010): 655–64.

12. J. F. Fenlon, "Bible Encyclopedias, The Catholic Encyclopedia, Codex Bezae," Study Light.org, www.studylight.org/encyclopedias/tce/c/codex-bezae.html. See also *The Catholic Encyclopedia*, "Codex Bezae" (New York: Robert Appleton Company, 1913).

RULE II: IMAGINE WHO YOU COULD BE, AND THEN AIM SINGLE-MINDEDLY AT THAT

1. We have recently discovered, for example, that new experiences turn on new genes, which code for new proteins, which build new structures of mind and body. Novel demands therefore appear to activate biological switches, allowing thoughts and actions once latent to make themselves manifest. For a review, see D. J. Sweatt, "The Emerging Field of Neuroepigenetics," *Neuron* 80 (2013): 624–32.

2. From the traditional spiritual "Go Down Moses," ca. 1850.

3. C. G. Jung, *Psychology and Alchemy*, vol. 12 of *Collected Works of C. G. Jung* (Princeton, N.J.: Princeton University Press, 1968), 323.

4. This set of ideas, as well as the Mesopotamian creation myth, are discussed in detail in my first book, J. B. Peterson, *Maps of Meaning: The Architecture of Belief* (New York: Routledge, 1999).

5. Tablet 7:112, 7:115; A. Heidel, *The Babylonian Genesis* (Chicago: Chicago University Press/Phoenix Books, 1965), 58.

6. I. H. Pidoplichko, *Upper Palaeolithic Dwellings of Mammoth Bones in the Ukraine: Kiev-Kirillovskii, Gontsy, Dobranichevka, Mezin and Mezhirich*, trans. P. Allsworth-Jones (Oxford, UK: J. and E. Hedges, 1998).

7. J. R. R. Tolkien, H. Carpenter, and C. Tolkien, *The Letters of J. R. R. Tolkien* (Boston: Houghton Mifflin, 1981), letter 25.

8. See Peterson, *Maps of Meaning*, for an extended discussion of this symbolic world and the reasons for the various equivalencies.
9. I covered this in much more detail in J. B. Peterson, *12 Rules for Life: An Antidote to Chaos* (Toronto: Random House Canada, 2018), Rule 2: Treat yourself like someone you are responsible for helping.
10. Some of the neuropsychology of this ancient predator-detection system, whose dis-inhibition produces fight or flight, fear or panic, is detailed in Peterson, *Maps of Meaning*.

RULE III: DO NOT HIDE UNWANTED THINGS IN THE FOG

1. J. Habermas, *Discourse Ethics: Notes on a Program of Philosophical Justification*, in *Moral Consciousness and Communicative Action*, ed. J. Habermas, trans. C. Lenhardt and S. W. Nicholsen (Cambridge, Mass.: MIT Press, 1990).
2. It is of some interest to note that these are all variant meanings or the *tohu wa bohu*, the chaos out of which God made order, according to the initial verses of the book of Genesis. Rabbi Dr. H. Freedman and M. Simon, eds., *The Midrash Rabbah: Genesis*, vol. 1 (London: Soncino Press, 1983), 15.

RULE IV: NOTICE THAT OPPORTUNITY LURKS WHERE RESPONSIBILITY HAS BEEN ABDICATED

1. Those who work forty-five hours a week instead of forty (that's an increase of 13 percent in time) make, on average, 44 percent more money. W. Farrell, *Why Men Earn More* (New York: AMACOM Books, 2005), xviii.
2. J. Feldman, J. Miyamoto, and E. B. Loftus, "Are Actions Regretted More Than Inactions?," *Organizational Behavior and Human Decision Processes* 78 (1999): 232–55.
3. It is for this reason, among others, that the figure of Satan, the Christian represen-tation of evil itself, is in fact a later development of the personality of Set. J. B. Pe-terson, *Maps of Meaning: The Architecture of Belief* (New York: Routledge, 1999).
4. J. B. Hirsh, D. Morisano, and J. B. Peterson, "Delay Discounting: Interactions Between Personality and Cognitive Ability," *Journal of Research in Personality* 42 (2018): 1646–50.
5. J. Gray, *The Neuropsychology of Anxiety: An Enquiry into the Functions of the Septal-hippocampal System* (New York: Oxford University Press, 1982).
6. N. M. White, "Reward or Reinforcement: What's the Difference?," *Neuroscience & Biobehavioral Reviews* 13 (1989): 181–86.

RULE V: DO NOT DO WHAT YOU HATE

1. W. G. Clark and W. A. Wright, eds., *Hamlet: Prince of Denmark* (Oxford: Clarendon Press, 1880), 1.3.78, 17.

2. For a critical review, see H. Pashler et al., "Learning Styles: Concepts and Evidence," *Psychological Science in the Public Interest* 9 (2008): 105–99.
3. M. Papadatou-Pastou, M. Gritzali, and A. Barrable, "The Learning Styles Educational Neuromyth: Lack of Agreement Between Teachers' Judgments, Self-Assessment, and Students' Intelligence," article 105, *Frontiers in Education* 3 (2018).
4. V. Tejwani, "Observations: Public Speaking Anxiety in Graduate Medical Education—A Matter of interpersonal and Communication Skills?," *Journal of Graduate Medical Education* 8 (2016): 111.

RULE VI: ABANDON IDEOLOGY

1. F. Nietzsche, *The Gay Science*, trans. W. Kaufmann, section 125 (New York: Vintage Books, 1880/1974), 181.
2. F. Nietzsche, *The Will to Power*, trans. W. Kaufmann and R. J. Hollingdale (New York: Vintage, 1880/2011).
3. F. Dostoevsky, *The Devils* (*The Possessed*), trans. D. Magarshack (New York: Penguin Classics, 1872/1954).
4. F. Nietzsche, *The Will to Power: An Attempted Transvaluation of All Values*, trans. A. M. Ludovici, vol. 14 of *The Complete Works of Friedrich Nietzsche*, ed. Oscar Levy (London: T. N. Foulis, 1914), 102–3.
5. See J. Panksepp, *Affective Neuroscience* (New York: Oxford University Press, 1998).
6. A very interesting variant of this "Pareto principle" was identified by D. J. de Solla Price, *Little Science, Big Science* (New York: Columbia University Press, 1963), who indicated that half the work was done—or half the value accrued—by the square root of the number of people involved.
7. T. A. Hirschel and M. R. Rank, "The Life Course Dynamics of Affluence," *PLoS One* 10, no. 1 (2015): e0116370, doi:10.1371/journal.pone.0116370. eCollection 2015.
8. F. Nietzsche, *On the Genealogy of Morals*, trans. W. Kaufman and R. J. Hollingdale, and *Ecce Homo*, trans. W. Kaufman, ed. W. Kaufman (New York: Vintage, 1989), 36–39.
9. In the USSR, for example, deadly action was taken against those whose parents or grandparents were deemed "class enemies" because of their relative economic prosperity. See A. Solzhenitsyn, *The Gulag Archipelago*, abridged ed. (New York: Vintage, 1973/2018).
10. *Monty Python's Flying Circus*, season 3, episode 2, "How to Play the Flute," October 26, 1972, BBC.

RULE VII: WORK AS HARD AS YOU POSSIBLY CAN ON AT LEAST ONE THING AND SEE WHAT HAPPENS

1. B. E. Leonard, "The Concept of Depression as a Dysfunction of the Immune System," *Current Immunology Reviews* 6 (2010): 205–12; B. E. Cohen, D. Edmonson, and I. M. Kronish, "State of the Art Review: Depression, Stress, Anxiety and the Cardio-

vascular System," *American Journal of Hypertension* 28 (2015): 1295–1302; P. Karling et al., "Hypothalamus-Pituitary-Adrenal Axis Hypersuppression Is Associated with Gastrointestinal Symptoms in Major Depression," *Journal of Neurogastroenterology and Motility* 22 (April 2016): 292–303.

2. Failure to inhibit aggression properly from an early age appears to characterize about 15 percent of children. S. M. Côté et al., "The Development of Physical Aggression from Toddlerhood to Pre-Adolescence: A Nation Wide Longitudinal Study of Canadian Children," *Journal of Abnormal Child Psychology* 34 (2006): 71–85.

RULE VIII: TRY TO MAKE ONE ROOM IN YOUR HOME AS BEAUTIFUL AS POSSIBLE

1. N. F. Stang, "Kant's Transcendental Idealism," *Stanford Encyclopedia of Philosophy* (Winter 2018), ed. E. N. Zalta, plato.stanford.edu/archives/win2018/entries/kant -transcendental-idealism.

2. E. Comoli et al., "Segregated Anatomical Input to Sub-Regions of the Rodent Superior Colliculus Associated with Approach and Defense," *Frontiers in Neuroanatomy* 6 (2012): 9, doi.org/10.3389/fnana.2012.00009.

3. D. C. Fowles, "Motivation Effects on Heart Rate and Electrodermal Activity: Implications for Research on Personality and Psychopathology," *Journal of Research in Personality* 17 (1983): 48–71. Fowles actually argued that the heart beats to reward, but also that the safety that beckons in escape from a looming predator was just such a reward.

4. E. Goldberg, and K. Podell, "Lateralization in the Frontal Lobes," in *Epilepsy and the Functional Anatomy of the Frontal Lobe*, vol. 66 of *Advances in Neurology*, eds. H. H. Jasper, S. Riggio, and P. S. Goldman-Rakic (Newark, Del.: Raven Press/University of Delaware, 1995), 85–96.

5. R. Sapolsky, Personal communication with the author, September 11, 2019. I've told this story to a few audiences, erroneously substituting zebras for wildebeest. Such are the vagaries of memory. But wildebeest is the correct animal.

RULE IX: IF OLD MEMORIES STILL UPSET YOU, WRITE THEM DOWN CAREFULLY AND COMPLETELY

1. J. B. Peterson and M. Djikic, "You Can Neither Remember nor Forget What You Do Not Understand," *Religion and Public Life* 33 (2017): 85–118.

2. P. L. Brooks and J. H. Peever, "Identification of the Transmitter and Receptor Mechanisms Responsible for REM Sleep Paralysis," *Journal of Neuroscience* 32 (2012): 9785–95.

3. J. E. Mack, *Abduction: Human Encounters with Aliens* (New York: Scribner, 2007).

4. R. E. McNally and S. A. Clancy, "Sleep Paralysis, Sexual Abuse and Space Alien Abduction," *Transcultural Psychiatry* 42 (2005): 113–22.

5. D. J. Hufford, *The Terror that Comes in the Night: An Experience-centered Study of Super-natural Assault Traditions* (Philadelphia: University of Pennsylvania Press, 1989).
6. C. Browning, *Ordinary Men: Reserve Police Battalion 101 and the Final Solution in Poland* (New York: Harper Perennial, 1998).
7. I. Chang, *The Rape of Nanking* (New York: Basic Books, 1990).
8. H. Ellenberger, *The Discovery of the Unconscious: The History and Evolution of Dynamic Psychiatry* (New York: Basic Books, 1981).
9. H. Spiegel and D. Spiegel, *Trance and Treatment* (New York: Basic Books, 1978).
10. J. B. Peterson, *Maps of Meaning: The Architecture of Belief* (New York: Routledge, 1999).
11. M. Eliade, *A History of Religious Ideas*, trans. W. Trask, vols. 1–3 (Chicago: University of Chicago Press, 1981).
12. See Strong's Hebrew concordance for the King James Version—a tool that lists all the occurrences of a given word (twenty in nineteen verses in the case of *tohuw*).
13. H. Zimmern, *The Ancient East*, vol. 3 of *The Babylonian and Hebrew Genesis*, trans. J. Hutchison (London: David Nutt, 1901).
14. E. Neumann, *The Great Mother: An Analysis of the Archetype*, trans. R. Manheim (New York: Pantheon Books, 1955); E. Neumann, *The Origins and History of Consciousness*, trans. R. F. C. Hull (Princeton, N.J.: Princeton University Press/Bollingen, 1969).
15. D. E. Jones, *An Instinct for Dragons* (New York: Psychology Press, 2002).
16. See, for example, Psalm 74, Psalm 104:24–26, and Isaiah 27:1.

RULE X: PLAN AND WORK DILIGENTLY TO MAINTAIN THE ROMANCE IN YOUR RELATIONSHIP

1. J. Gottman, *What Predicts Divorce? The Relationship Between Marital Processes and Marital Outcomes* (Hillsdale, N.J.: Erlbaum, 1994).
2. C. G. Jung, *Mysterium Coniunctionis*, vol. 14 of *Collected Works of C. G. Jung*, trans. G. Adler and R. F. C. Hull (Princeton, N.J.: Princeton University Press, 1970), 407, doi:10.2307/j.ctt5hhr0d.
3. M. Eliade, *Shamanism: Archaic Techniques of Ecstasy*, trans. W. R. Trask (Princeton, N.J.: Princeton University Press, 1951).
4. C. G. Jung, "The Philosophical Tree" in *Alchemical Studies*, vol. 13 of *The Collected Works of C. G. Jung*, trans. G. Adler and R. F. C. Hull (Princeton, N.J.: Princeton University Press, 1954/1967), 251–349.
5. C. G. Jung, "Gnosticism as Dealing with the Feminine," in *The Gnostic Jung: Including Seven Sermons to the Dead*, ed. S. A. Hoeller (New York: Quest Books, 1982), 114–18.
6. Defined as inability to conceive within one year of trying: W. Himmel et al., "Voluntary Childlessness and Being Childfree," *British Journal of General Practice* 47 (1997): 111–18.
7. Statistics Canada, "Common-Law Couples Are More Likely to Break Up," www150 .statcan.gc.ca/n1/pub/11-402-x/2011000/chap/fam/fam02-eng.htm.
8. Excepting, perhaps, in the first year. M. J. Rosenfeld and K. Roesler, "Cohabitation

Experience and Cohabitation's Association with Marital Dissolution," *Journal of Marriage and Family* 81 (2018): 42–58.

9. US Census Bureau, 2017. Data represent children living without a biological, step, or adoptive father. Also see E. Leah, D. Jackson, and L. O'Brien, "Father Absence and Adolescent Development: A Review of the Literature," *Journal of Child Health Care* 10 (2006): 283–95.

RULE XI: DO NOT ALLOW YOURSELF TO BECOME RESENTFUL, DECEITFUL, OR ARROGANT

1. J. L. Barrett, *Why Would Anyone Believe in God?* (Lanham, Md.: AltaMira Press, 2004).
2. P. Ekman, *Emotions Revealed*, 2nd ed. (New York: Holt Paperback, 2007).
3. A. Öhman and S. Mineka, "The Malicious Serpent: Snakes as a Prototypical Stimulus for an Evolved Module of Fear," *Current Directions in Psychological Science* 12 (2003): 5–9.
4. J. Gray and N. McNaughton, *The Neuropsychology of Anxiety: An Enquiry into the Function of the Septo-Hippocampal System* (New York: Oxford University Press, 2000).
5. L. W. Swanson, "Cerebral Hemisphere Regulation of Motivated Behavior," *Brain Research* 886 (2000): 113–64.
6. All these ideas find their empirical demonstration in J. B. Hirsh et al., "Compassionate Liberals and Polite Conservatives: Associations of Agreeableness with Political Ideology and Moral Values," *Personality and Social Psychology Bulletin* 36 (December 2010): 655–64.

RULE XII: BE GRATEFUL IN SPITE OF YOUR SUFFERING

1. This was covered in detail in Rule 8: Tell the truth—or, at least, don't lie, in J. B. Peterson, *12 Rules for Life: An Antidote to Chaos* (Toronto: Random House Canada, 2018).
2. I discussed this play previously, both in J. B. Peterson, *Maps of Meaning: The Architecture of Belief* (New York: Routledge, 1999), 319–20, and Peterson, *12 Rules for Life*, 148.
3. J. J. Muehlenkamp et al., "International Prevalence of Adolescent Non-Suicidal Self-Injury and Deliberate Self-harm," *Child and Adolescent Psychiatry and Mental Health* 6 (2012): 10–18.
4. J. W. Von Goethe, *Faust*, trans. George Madison Priest (1806).
5. D. Benatar, *Better Never to Have Been: The Harm of Coming into Existence* (New York: Oxford University Press, 2008).
6. Jordan B. Peterson and David Benatar, *The Renegade Report*, January 9, 2018, podtail.com/en/podcast/the-renegade-report/jordan-b-peterson-david-benatar.
7. Jesus, on the Cross, quoting the opening words of Psalm 22.
8. I mention this briefly in the Coda to *12 Rules for Life*.

Index

ability as related to authority, 25
Abraham (biblical), 117–18, 137
abyss, 123, 258, 375
achievements in life, four, 283, 288–89
Adam and Eve, 79n, 334, 348–49
addictions, 351–52
adolescents, 190, 322–23, 328
the adversary
   about, 358–59, 361
   and genocidal vision, 364
   within individuals, 334, 335, 360
   logical failings of, 365
aesthetic experience, 91–94. *See also* beauty
affairs, extramarital, 284–86, 296, 297
agency, personal, 255–56, 342
aggression
   of children, 190
   human capacity for, 240–41, 252
   vulnerability to, 317
aging and old age, 23, 374
aims/aiming
   beauty's influence on, 226
   and confrontation of problems, 342
   consequences associated with lack of, 117, 184
   in democratic systems, 337
   at the highest good, 128, 133, 194
   and hitting targets, 103, 115
   in intimate/domestic relationships, 270, 282
   love as ultimate, 344

   and mapping your path, 86
   and positive emotions, 129
   and sense of meaning, 135
   strengthening Being with, 370
   at trivial goals, 129–30
   value accrued by missing, 103–4
   at a worthy target, 86–87
alchemists and alchemy, 58–59n, 59–60, 274n
alien abductions, 239
ambition, 26
American system of democracy, 337
anima/animus, 4
animals, 126, 323–24
antinatalism, 361, 362–64
anxiety, 183, 250n
apprenticeship, 192–93, 197
Apsu (Mesopotamian god), 68, 69–70, 74, 258
arguments/fights, domestic, 91–94, 98–100, 291–92, 294
arrogance, 28, 343–47, 349, 352–53
art and artists
   abstract art, 224–25
   art collection of author, 218–20
   buying art, 203
   civilizing influence of, 215
   cubism, 225
   distribution of, 211
   and frames bordering paintings, 211
   as high risk endeavor, 224

art and artists (*cont.*)
  impressionists, 225
  influence of, on individuals, 202–3
  and museums, 211
  non-decorative function of, 225
  and politics, 216
  and propaganda, 220
  role of, 217–18
  surrealism, 225
  transformation of unknown to knowledge,
      214, 216
  transformation of urban environments, 214–15
  vanguard position occupied by, 215–16
  vision/perception of, 208, 209, 210, 225–26
  and wisdom of civilization, 202–3
asking, power of, 261
assumptions, 263
attainment, transformation as consequence of,
      128–29
attention, 7, 121, 190
audiences at author's lectures, 157–60
"Auguries of Innocence" (Blake), 208–9
Authoritarian Tyrant persona, 328–29, 332, 333,
      334, 336
authority, 19–20, 25–28
Avengers movie franchise, 76
avoidance, 232, 254, 262, 281, 282

beauty
  and author's home, 218–20
  and author's university office, 220–23
  central importance of, 226
  and the divine, 203–4
  establishing a relationship with, 202–4
  failure to be present for, 206
  and frames bordering paintings, 211
  opening oneself up to, 212
  See also art and artists
beginner mindset, 18–20, 33, 154, 192
Being
  ability to bring evil into, 352
  and accepting limitations, 113
  adversarial attitudes toward, 362–63, 364
  and artists' visions, 209
  and avoiding becoming embittered, 369
  bringing the future into, 254
  call to strength of, 366
  dissatisfaction with, 360
  and ethics of our behaviors/choices, 130,
      254–55
  ground of, as subject and object, 107
  love for, 260
  and Mephistopheles, 362
  and nature, 317

  and necessity of the difficult, 113
  role of beauty in, 202, 204
  strengthening with aims and acts, 370
  and superstructure provided by love, 344
  uncertainty of, 353
  value of, 372
Benatar, David, 361, 362–63
Benevolent Queen/Mother personification, 317,
      318, 332, 334
benzodiazepine, xvii–xx, xxi
Beowulf, 75
betrayal of self, 131, 132, 136, 150, 154, 229
bitterness, 368, 369
Blake, William
  "Auguries of Innocence," 208–9
  "A Memorable Fancy," 209–10
  "Proverbs of Hell," 204
boys, ambition of, 26–27
Buddha/Buddhism, 61n, 114, 117, 191
Burns, Robert, 25, 319

Cain and Abel, 334
Captain Hook, 115–16
careers, 284, 288. *See also* employment and
      workplace
certainty, search for, 355
change, failure to embrace, 262
chaos
  about, xxiv–xxv
  Dragon of Chaos, 82, 311–16, 317, 325, 328, 329
  heroic confrontation of, 74
  and hyperreal meta-world, 84–85
  in nature (Evil Queen personification), 313,
      317, 319–20, 321, 328, 332, 334
  and new ideas, 331
  and order, xxiv, xxv, 84–85, 262, 319
  and perils of carelessly destroying culture, 70
  in pop culture, 319–20
  round, 61–64, 66–67 107
  serpents as symbolic of, 79n
  and six characters comprising the world/life,
      334–35
  and Tiamat, 69, 70
character, development of, 193
children
  abused, 230
  as achievements in life, 283
  aggression management in, 190
  custody battles over, 285
  discipline in, 188–92
  fear of the dark, 314
  focus on the present, 206
  friendships of, 23
  innate fear of monsters, 314–15

mimicry ability of, 282
parents' relationship with, 373–74
play of, 14–17, 22–23
poets' visions of childhood, 207–9, 210, 226–27
and preparing for family life, 192
and process of integration, 189, 191–92
and sharing/reciprocation, 22–23
sheltered/overprotected, 320–21
and stories, 309–10, 311–12
vulnerability of, 373–74
women who don't want to have, 283–84
chimpanzees, 13, 53
choices, ethics of, 254–55, 256
Christianity
    civilizing influence of, 191
    and creation story, 257–59
    and cross's symbolism, 75
    and overcoming evil, 86
    and Ten Commandments, 56–57, 193–96
    and tension with tradition illustrated in
        Gospels, 44–47
    See also Jesus Christ
Christmas, 273, 368
cities, artists' transformations of, 214–15
class, 172
cleaning and beautifying one's home, 92, 201–2,
    218–20
Codex Bezae, 45–46, 45–46n
cohabitation, 286–87
colleagues, 24
Columbine High School shootings, 364
commission, sins of, 97, 343, 344–47, 352
commitment
    benefits of, 184–88
    consequences associated with lack of, 186–88
    to marriage, 276–77, 286, 292
    sacrifices made for, 184, 186, 188
    transformative power of, 192–93, 197–98
communication
    cognitive function of, 3
    of desires, wants, and needs, 101–3
    of feelings, 104–5
    in hierarchical structures, 8, 21
    imperative of, 3
    in marriage, 270, 292, 301
    between peers, 21
    with those different from ourselves, 331
communism, 163, 167
compartmentalization, 241, 242, 243–44, 247
competence, 26, 27
competitiveness, 190
conforming to social norms, 29–30
confrontation
    avoiding, 91–94

of challenges/difficulties, 341–42, 352
of suffering, 355–56
Confucianism, 191
conscience
    alerted by wrongdoing, 131–32
    challenges associated with heeding call of, 137
    and Holy Ghost, 351
    and standing against corruption and tyranny,
        148–49
    and subjectivity of meaning of life, 166
    torments of, 255
consciousness, 181, 304
conservatism and conservatives
    and achieving balanced view of world, 333
    balancing creative transformation with, 30,
        34–36, 37, 47–48
    and big government, 333n
    caution toward change, 31
    and danger of corruption, 36
    faith placed in, 168
    and maintaining status quo, 332
    and new ideas, 331–32
    temperamental predispositions to, 30, 331
    wisdom of, 337–38
    and Wise King perspective of world, 332
containers and their contents, 59, 60–61, 64, 66
corruption, 36, 107, 147–49, 351
courage
    act of, as reassuring, 356
    in confronting suffering, 355–56
    and creation story, 344
    exercised in marriage, 271–72, 296, 299–300
    faith in humanity based in, 104
    of gratitude, 369–70
    of heroes and leaders, 76
    lacked by overprotected children, 321
    and love, 370–71
    and Peter Pan, 116
    potential for, 341–42
    trust as form of, 104, 271
    and truthful speech, 259–60
COVID-19 pandemic, xiii–xiv, xx, 377
creation story, biblical, 257–59
creative transformation and revitalization
    balancing conservatism with, 30, 34–36, 37,
        47–48
    danger lurking in, 31, 36
    discipline as precursor to, 35
    essential role played by, 47
    in Gospel accounts, 45–46
    and necessity of social constraints,
        35–36
    and respect for social institutions, 29
    and social engagement, 38–41

creative transformation and revitalization (*cont.*)
    temperamental predispositions to, 30
    See also liberalism and liberals
creativity, 190, 224
crowds, addressing, 160
cubism, 225
culture
    art's central function in, 203
    gratitude for, 336
    and ideological systems, 330–33
    pathology in, 141–49
    perils of carelessly destroying, 70
    Wise King and Authoritarian Tyrant personas,
        328–30
curiosity, xxv, 316n
cynicism, 186, 188, 271

daily routines in marriage, 289–94, 301
damaged people, 295–96
danger, responding to, 60–61
darkness
    fear of, 314
    relationships as antidote to, 375
    understanding of, 357–58
dating
    challenges of, 297–98
    date nights in marriages, 264–69, 301
    by widows/widowers, 287–88
death
    and destructive potential of nature, 317
    exercising strength in face of, 365–67
    and grief, 371–72
    overcoming evil through, 85–86
    and regeneration of personality, 83
deception, 95–98, 104, 272, 343–50
defense mechanisms, 96
democratic systems, 337
depression, 183–84
Derrida, Jacques, 173
desires, 101–3, 261, 270
destiny, disenchantment as indicator of, 136
diamonds, creation of, 181–82
difficulties in life
    avoidance of, 232, 262, 281, 282
    developing causal theories for
        understanding, 263
    gratitude in the face of, 372
    importance of recollecting and understanding,
        229–34
    voluntarily confronting sources of, 121–22
difficult tasks, 113
discipline
    in children, 188–92
    organizing function of, 190

as precursor to creative revitalization and
    transformation, 35
disease, 317
Disney heroes and stories, 18, 43, 76, 82, 133,
    311–12, 319–20
diversity, 143
divinity, 203–4, 345
dogma, 192, 193, 197
dolphins, 53
dopamine, 351
Dostoevsky, Fyodor, 162–63, 165
    The Possessed, 162–63
dragons and monsters
    in the abyss, 123, 258
    as the ancient predator, 258
    basilisk in Harry Potter book series, 77, 78–79,
        80–81, 82
    children's innate fear of, 314–15
    confronting conquerable, 112
    Dragon of Chaos, 82, 311–16, 317, 325, 328, 329
    and hero archetype, 118
    Leviathan, 258
    in modern films and books, 75–76, 79, 82
    in *Pinocchio*, 311
    as representation of chaos and death, 75
    slain by St. George, 74–75
    in *Sleeping Beauty*, 312–13
    and snake-chasing ancestors, 76
    symbolism of, in woodcut, 59, 65–67
    threat posed by, 82
    Tiamat (Mesopotamian goddess), 69, 258
    treasure guarded by, 66, 80, 112, 314, 316,
        335, 342
dramas on stage, 84
dreaming, 215, 324–25
drives, 12–13
drugs of addiction, 351–52

easy path, taking, 347–48, 349
economic inequality, 169, 172
education, 184–85, 187–88
ego, 4
Egyptians, ancient, 72–73, 118–23
elderly population, 23, 374
Eliade, Mircea, 71
embalming, witnessing, 326–28
emotions, 15, 104–5, 309–10
employment and workplace
    and achievements in life, 288
    assuming additional responsibility in, 111–14
    and changing jobs, 151–53
    expectations for finding satisfaction in, 284
    pathological culture in, 141–44, 146
    positioning for lateral moves in, 151

and responsibility to not do things you hate,
    150–51
risks associated with not choosing, 187
stupid things required in, 144–45
termination from, 151
encouragement, dearth of, 159
enlightenment, 262
Enuma Elish narrative from Mesopotamia, 67–74
environmental concerns/environmentalism, 32,
    33–34, 168, 316, 332, 336, 336n
epilepsy, hysterical, 242–43
equality among peers, 21–25
errors, admitting to, 86
ethic
    in games and play, 15–16
    natural, 10
    of our choices, 254–55, 256
euthanization, "merciful," 364
evangelical Protestants, 37n
Eve and the serpent, 79n
evil
    and acceptance of life's suffering, 75
    and conceptualization of Good, 365
    constraint of, by life of virtue, 82
    knowledge of, in Garden of Eden, 349
    motivations for, 303
    overcoming, through death/rebirth, 85–86
    as personified in Christianity, 360
    snakes' symbolism of, 81
    understanding of, 357–58, 363
Evil Queen persona, 312–13, 317–18, 319–21, 328,
    332, 334
evolution, 13
Exodus, book of, 56–57, 195
Exodus from Egypt, 54, 56
exploration, 315–16, 315–16n

failures
    as lack of single-mindedness, 187
    as prerequisite of success, 103–4
    and self-contempt, 360–61
faith
    in humanity, 104
    in oneself, 348–49, 353
families and family life
    as achievement in life, 283
    and custody battles over children, 285
    and familial gatherings, 372–73
    gratitude for, 369
    value of, 194
    See also marriage
Faust (Goethe), 358, 361
fear
    of employment termination, 151

as innate, 314–15
of life, 321–28
paralysis/freezing in place from, 77–78, 81, 83
voluntarily confronting sources of, 60–61,
    78–79n, 121
and willful ignorance, 100–101
feminism, 168
fights/arguments, domestic, 91–94, 98–100,
    291–92, 294
"flip chart" controversy, 141–44, 146
fool, persona of, 18, 154
Foucault, Michel, 173
Freud, Sigmund, 4–5, 95, 164, 171, 243, 244
friendships
    of children, 23
    critical importance of, 23
    in early vs. later life, 288
    lack of loyalty exercised in, 187
    reciprocation practiced in, 22–25
    role of responsibility in, 348
fundamentalists, religious, 173
funerals, exercising strength at, 367
future
    bringing into Being, 254
    preparing for, 124–27, 131
    sacrificing the present for, 206
    worrying about, 253
    writing about, 250–51n

games, 14–17, 63, 189, 191
Garden of Eden, 79n, 81, 82, 348–49
The Gay Science (Nietzsche), 162
gender roles, traditional, 289–90
Genesis story, 79n, 81, 82, 257–59, 260, 273, 344,
    348–49
genocidal actors, 363, 364
ghosts, souls haunted by, 182
Global Language Monitor, 142
goals
    changing course with, 86–87
    collective determination of, 14–15
    establishing a transcendent, 133–34
    ethic of behavior in relationships, 130–31
    and *hamartia* (missing the mark), 114–15
    and meaning, 133, 134–38
    and personal potential, 51–54
    in play, 14–15
    positive emotions in pursuit of, 129
    trivial, 129–30
    and value of subjugation to rules, 195
God
    and creation story, 257–59
    following call of, 137
    Mesopotamians' expectations of, 72

God (*cont.*)
  Nietzsche on death of, 161–62
  and the Word, 258–59, 344
gold, 62, 62n, 64–65n
Golden Rule, 64
the Good, 344
grandchildren, 283
gratitude
  about, 17
  as alternative to bitterness, 368
  beauty's ability to promote, 204
  courage of, 369–70
  in the face of life's catastrophes, 372
  for family, 369
  and knowledge of darkness, 357–58
  and relationships, 374–75
  for social institutions, 34
  and Thanksgiving holidays, 368–69
Greeks, ancient, 70n
grief, 371–72

hamartia (missing the mark), 114–15
happiness, 127–29, 137
Harry Potter book series
  basilisk in, 77, 78–79, 80–81, 82
  dark side of Potter in, 80
  and Quidditch, 62, 62–63n, 63, 64
  rule breaking illustrated in, 41–42, 80, 85
  Voldemort in, 18, 80–81, 82
helplessness, 183
heroes
  and beginner mindset, 18–19
  and confrontation of problems, 343
  dark side of, 80–81
  emergence of virtuous, 67–76
  and following/breaking rules, 41–42, 43, 47
  and hyperreal meta-world, 84–85
  individuals' heroic aspects, 334, 335
  Marduk's heroism, 71–74
  and responsibility, 118
  St. George's heroism, 74–75
  St. Michael's heroism, 75
  St. Patrick's heroism, 75
  in stories, 38
  and understanding of seven characters of the
      world/life, 336
  vision and courage in, 76
hierarchical structures
  addressing suffering, 25
  and beginner mindset, 18–20, 33
  class, 172
  communication challenges in, 21
  function of, 11
  in human development, 13

  and humility's role in success, 19–20
  negotiation for positions in, 13
  in restaurant industry, 19–20
  social institutions as, 11
  unjust power exercised in, 30
high school shooters, 363, 364
Hinduism, 114, 191
Hitler, Adolf, 167
The Hobbit (Tolkien), 75, 76, 80
Holy Ghost, 350–51
home
  aesthetic experience of, 91–94
  beautifying one's, 218–20
  cleaning up one's, 92, 201–2
homicidal actors, 363
hope, distrust in, 100
Horus, 72–73, 120–23
Hufford, David, 239–40
humility
  about, 17
  as catalyst for personal growth, 19–20
  and communication of feelings, 105
  and discontent expressed by ideologues, 33
  and facing the errors of one's past, 232
  of heroes and leaders, 19
hypothalamus, 315–16, 316n
hysterical epilepsy, 242–43

id, 4
Ideal (comprised of Truth, Courage, and
      Love), 260
ideals, absence of, 103
identity politics, 149
ideology and ideologues
  and assuming personal responsibility, 176–77
  and blanket statements about victims and
      perpetrators, 175
  communism, 163, 167
  death of, 177–78
  and democratic system, 337
  and Dostoevsky, 162–63, 165
  and generation of ism systems, 168–72
  and identification of enemies, 175–76
  ideologues' claim to rationality, 173
  and Nietzsche, 162, 163–65, 167–68
  overcoming evil of, 86
  and ressentiment, 174–75
  self-righteous hatred generated by, 176
  systems of, 330
  temperamental predispositions to, 30, 331–32
  and understanding of seven characters of the
      world/life, 335
  and univariate causes ascribed to complex
      problems, 174

willingness to transform as guard against, 86
    and Wise King/Authoritarian Tyrant
        personas, 332
idiosyncrasies balanced in marriage, 294–95
"I don't know" phrase, 279–80
ignorance, willful, 100–101
imagination, 53–54
imitation, 53, 83–84
impersonators, 53n
impressionists, 225
inclusivity, 143
indecision, 183, 186
individuality, development of, 189
individuals, heroic and adversarial aspects in,
        334, 335
infants, 14
injustice, sense of, 330, 340
instincts, 350
interests, 65, 66
Irises (Van Gogh), 210
Iron Man, 76
irritations, addressing, 90–91
ism systems, generation of, 168–72
Israelites' exodus from Egypt, 54, 56

Jesus Christ
    on asking/seeking, 260–61
    on becoming like children, 226
    despair during Crucifixion, 362
    exchange with scribe about Commandments,
        195–96
    as ideal balance of masculine/feminine
        elements, 274
    law transcended by, 85
    meager circumstances of birth, 19
    and phoenix symbolism, 82
    relationship with tradition, 44–47, 197
    as representation of mastery of dogma, 197
    and Satan (duality), 334
    star announcing birth of, 133
    on unforgivable sin, 350–51
Jewish people, suffering of, 117
Job, book of, 258
John, Gospel of, 193
Jung, Carl, 4–5, 18, 40, 164
justice, sense of, 346–47
justifications, 343–44

Kant, Immanuel, 208
knowledge, unknown as source of,
        212–14
Korikov, Andrey, xv, xix, xxi
Korikova, Elizabeth Scarlett Peterson, 6–7, 22,
        40–41, 42–43

language
    collective determination of, 8, 10–11
    creative power of, 258–59
    and linguistic fads, 149
    and pathological culture, 141–44, 146
    pointing as precursor to, 7
    and social institutions, 8
    transformative potential of, 73
    and truthful speech, 259–60
learning
    arrogance as barrier to, 28
    humility required for, 17
    from the past, 229, 340
    as remembering, 52–53
learning styles theory, 146
leisure time, 288–89
Leviathan, 258
liberalism and liberals
    and achieving balanced view of world, 333
    anti-human attitudes of, 33–34
    and Authoritarian Tyrant perspective of
        world, 332, 333
    balancing conservatism with, 30, 34–36, 37,
        47–48
    and changing the status quo, 332
    danger lurking in, 31
    and environmentalism, 32, 33–34, 168, 316,
        332, 336, 336n
    and functioning vs. non-functioning
        institutions, 30–31
    and government's role, 333n
    moral superiority assumed by, 32–33
    and new ideas, 331–32
    self-serving criticism of the status quo, 32–34
    temperamental predispositions to, 30, 331
    unethical radicals among, 31
    See also creative transformation and
        revitalization
light and illumination, 273, 275
limitations
    accepting and transcending, 113
    loving others because of their, 374
literature, 84
loneliness, 1–4, 23n, 187
The Lord of the Rings (Tolkien), 76
love
    and courage, 370–71
    grief as a reflection of, 372
    as ultimate aim, 344
Luke, Gospel of, 44–47, 64, 261

Maleficent, 312–13
malevolence
    compartmentalization of, 243–49

malevolence (*cont.*)
  confrontation of, 343
  consciousness of, as embittering, 363
  in oneself, 315, 356
  uncomprehended, 249–53
  vulnerability to, 358
Marduk, 71, 72, 73, 74, 85
Mark, Gospel of, 193, 195–96
marriage
  achievement of, 283
  and affairs, 284–86, 297
  avoidance in, 91–94, 281, 282
  challenges in, 277
  commitment to, 276–77, 286, 292
  communication in, 270, 292, 301
  courage exercised in, 271–72, 296, 299–300
  daily routines in, 289–94, 301
  and date nights, 264–69, 301
  effort required in, 268
  ending, 282, 286, 287
  and failure to communicate desires, 270
  fighting/arguing in, 91–94, 98–100,
      291–92, 294
  idiosyncrasies balanced in, 294–95
  living together prior to, 286–87
  making peace in, 278, 282, 288, 292, 294, 296
  negotiation in, 270, 277–82, 289–94, 301
  repetitive experiences in, 94
  and sexual intimacy, 269–70, 296–301
  subordination in, 274–75
  and Ten Commandments, 194
  and treatment of one's partner, 127
  trust exercised in, 271–72, 280
  vows of, 276–77, 282, 301
  and widows/widowers, 287–88
Marx, Karl, 172–73
Marxism, 173
master, transformation of beginner to, 192–93
materia prima, 59–60
Matthew, Gospel of, 46, 197, 203, 226, 261n, 274,
      350, 362
meaning
  and goals, 133, 134–38
  life-orienting function of, xxvi
  and music, 135–36
  as reliable guide, 350
  and responsibility, xxvi, 114–18, 131,
      134–38, 161
  as subjective, 166
  suffering without, 117
"A Memorable Fancy" (Blake), 209–10
memories
  accuracy of, 97–98, 236
  compartmentalization of, 242, 243–44, 247

developing causal theories for
      understanding, 263
  of events, 105–8
  inability to forget poorly understood, 229–34
  of malevolence, 236–42, 243–49
  protective function of uncomfortable,
      229–30
  reframing, 235–36
  of sexual abuse, 234–36
  and therapeutic writing exercises, 250–51n,
      250–52
  vital information in negative, 262–63
men
  ambition of, 26–27
  and demonization of masculinity, 175–76
mental health
  and committing to a path, 185
  and conforming to social norms, 29
  and diagnoses made in busy city clinics,
      238–39n
  Freudian and Jungian theories on, 4–5,
      95–98
  role of community in, 5–6
  and rules of social games, 28
  social feedback loop in, 5–6
  and status differences, 28–29
  and writing exercises, 32n, 250–51n, 250–52
Mephistopheles, 358–59, 360, 361, 362, 364–65
Mercurius, 67
Mercury, 63–64, 64–65n
Mesopotamian *Enuma Elish*, 67–74
Metropolitan Museum of Art in New York,
      216–17
millennials, 23n
mimicry, 83–84
mistakes and misbehavior
  and failure to embrace change, 262
  importance of recollecting and understanding,
      229–34
  justifications created for, 255
  and torments of conscience, 255
monotheism, 71
monsters. *See* dragons and monsters
morality, 191
Moses (biblical), 19, 54, 56–57
mothers, girls' imitation of, 83
motivations
  hidden, 107
  and motivational systems (drives), 12–13, 15
  of poorly integrated people, 183
  unexamined, 108
murderers, 363
museums, 211
music, meaning produced by, 135–36

nakedness of Adam and Eve, 349
nature
    Benevolent Queen/Mother personification,
        317, 318, 319
    destructive aspects of, 316–17, 332–33, 335, 336
    disorder/chaos in (Evil Queen
        personification), 313, 317, 319–20, 321,
        328, 332, 334
    dreams as statements from, 324–25
    and environmentalism, 168, 316, 332, 336, 336n
    and fear of life, 321–28
    polarity of, 317–18
    reversion to chaos, 313
Nazi Germany, 167–68, 241–42, 364
negotiation in marriage, 270, 277–82,
    289–94, 301
nervous system, 12–13
new experiences, exposure to, 52–53, 65
new ideas, 331–32
Nietzsche, Friedrich, 161–62, 163–65, 167–68
    The Gay Science, 162
    The Will to Power, 162
nihilism, 162, 164, 186, 347, 362
Numbers, book of, 282

"Ode: Intimations of Immortality from
    Recollections of Early Childhood"
    (Wordsworth), 207–8, 210, 226–27
omission, sins of, 97, 107, 347–49, 352
opportunity
    assuming additional responsibility as, 112
    cultivation of, for subordinates, 28
    searching for, 108
    unwillingness to pursue, 51
    where responsibility has been abdicated, 121,
        131, 138, 160, 191
    See also responsibility
optimism, 357
order
    and chaos, xxiv, xxv, 84–85, 262, 319
    and conservative outlook, 332, 333
    and hyperreal meta-world, 84–85
    and liberals, 331
    pathology in, 141–49
    perils of carelessly destroying, 74
Ordinary Men (Browning), 241–42
Osiris, 118–23
outrage as indicator of destiny, 136

palliative care workers, 357
pandemic of 2020, xiii–xiv, xx, 377
Panksepp, Jaak, 16n
paranoia, 176
parents, aging, 374

Pareto distribution, 172
"patriarchal tyranny" claims, 26–27
Paul (biblical), 350–51
peers and equality, 21–25
Pennebaker, James W., 250n
performative contradiction, 96
perpetrators, evil, 175
persecution, 176
Perseus, 75–76
personal growth, role of humility in, 19–20
personality
    death and regeneration of, 83, 86, 132
    ideal, 29–30, 37, 67
    incorporation of darker aspects of, 242
    masculine and feminine aspects of, 66–67
    of poorly integrated people, 182–84
    Rebis symbol for fully developed, 66–67
    and value of subjugation to rules, 196
personification, 68–69, 308
pessimism, 357
Peter Pan, 115–16
Peterson, Jordan
    art collection of, 218–20
    audiences at lectures of, 157–60
    depression tendency of, xviii
    health issues in 2020, xv–xvi, xvii–xxii, xxiii
    home of, 201–2, 218–20
    university office of, 220–23
Peterson, Julian, 205–6, 311, 314–15, 373–74
Peterson, Mikhaila, xv, xvi, xviii, xix, xxi, 22,
    205–6, 335, 373, 377
Peterson, Tammy
    and family walks, 205
    health crisis of, xvi–xviii, xix, xxi–xxii,
        23–24, 342n
phoenix, 82–83
Piaget, Jean, 14, 15
Pinocchio (Disney), 18, 76, 133, 311
plausible deniability, 97
play
    of children, 14–17
    of rats, 16–17n
    rules of fair play, 15–17, 16–17n, 63–64
pleasure, lack of, 183
Pocahontas (Disney), 43
pointing and pointers, 6–8
political correctness, 141–44, 146
polytheism, 71
The Possessed (Dostoevsky), 162–63
possession, 360, 363, 364
postmodernism, 168
potential and possibility
    and Dragon of Chaos, 311
    failure to achieve, 339

potential and possibility (*cont.*)
  Jesus' guidance on, 260–61
  nature of, 305–6
  and new experiences, 52–53
  of predators, 315
  sense of, 51
  as ultimate question of man, 123
  unwillingness to pursue, 51
poverty and the poor, 169, 172
power
  ambition misidentified as desire for, 26
  and authority, 25–28
  corruption of, 30
  demonized by ideologues, 173, 174, 175
  hunger for, 26
  and providing opportunities to others, 28
  unjust exercise of, 30
predators, 314–15, 316. *See also* dragons and
     monsters
pregnancies, 284, 319
present, focusing on, 204–6
pride, 20, 347
problem solving, 9–11, 114
propaganda, art's ability to shine through, 220
Proverbs, book of, 350
"Proverbs of Hell" (Blake), 204
pseudoscientific theories, speaking out against,
    146, 149
psychotherapy, 355–56
purpose, 103, 185

quitting, consequences of, 187, 188
Quora, xxv

The Rape of Nanking (Chang), 242
rationality, ideologues' claim to, 173
rats, 16–17n
reality, 68–69, 306
Rebis, 66–67
reciprocation, 21–25
relationships
  and arguments, 98–100
  communication of desires, wants, and needs
    in, 101–3
  ethic of behavior in, 130–31
  and gratitude, 374–75
  inability to commit to, 187
  lack of loyalty exercised in, 187
  and particularities of people, 374
  termination of, 237
  See also friendships; marriage
religion
  and emergence of monotheism, 71
  and fundamentalists, 173

myth and ritual transformed into, 84
  and religious experiences, 166
  religious narratives, 37n
  and sacrifice trope, 318
remembering, learning as, 52–53
repetitive experiences, 90–91, 94
repression, 95, 96, 97, 189–90, 229
reproduction, 276, 315, 319, 362–64
resentment, 161, 338–44, 346–47,
    349, 351
responsibility
  abdicated, 131, 136, 138, 160
  and accepting challenges, 122
  Adam's refusal of, 349
  as antidote to suffering, 134
  assigned to humanity by God, 259, 259n
  assuming additional, 111–14
  and considering the future, 124–27
  and ethics of our choices, 254–55
  and friendships, 348
  and happiness, 127–29
  inculcation of, as purpose of society, 161
  and meaning, xxvi, 114–18, 131,
    134–38, 161
  to not do things you hate, 150–51
  resonance of idea, 160–61
  and sins of omission, 347–48
  to stand against corruption and tyranny,
    147–49
  and taking the easy path, 347–48
ressentiment, 174–75
restaurant industry, 19–20
risk taking, 18, 224
Roberts, Beth, 89–90
Roberts, Dell, 89–90
round chaos, 61–64, 66–67, 107
Rowling, J. K., 18, 41–42, 62–64, 77–83. *See also*
    Harry Potter book series
rules
  breaking, 41–42, 43, 46, 47, 81, 85
  of children's games, 189
  of Christianity, 191
  communicated through stories, 55–57
  and conforming to social norms, 29
  and creative transformation, 29, 36, 47
  of fair play, 15–17, 16–17n, 63–64
  following, 28, 41, 42, 43–44, 46, 47
  Gospel narratives discussing, 44–47
  and Harry Potter book series, 41–42,
    80, 85
  heroes' negotiation of, 41–42, 43, 47
  meta-rules, 42
  respect for, 43–44, 85
  Ten Commandments, 56–57, 193–96

unity that transcends, 195
value of subjugation to, 195–96

sacrifice, 116–17, 186, 318–19
St. George's heroism, 74–75, 79
St. Michael's heroism, 75
St. Patrick's heroism, 75
sanity. *See* mental health
Sapolsky, Robert, 223
Sauron, 76
schizophrenia diagnoses, 237, 238–39,
      238–39n
science, 307–8
self, Jungian concept of, 4
Self-Authoring Suite, 32n, 250, 250–51n
self-care, moral obligation of, 124–27
self-consciousness, 349
self-contempt, 360–61
self-deception, 95–98, 262, 350
self-harm, 361
self-preservation, 315
self-respect, 134
sensorimotor cells, 12
sentimentality, excessive, 323–24
serial killers, 363
sexual abuse, 234–36
sexuality
    of adolescents, 322–23, 328
    and sexual intimacy in married life, 269–70,
      296–301
shadow, 4, 281
shame, 360–61
sharing, 22
Simba (Disney), 18
sin, 350–51. *See also* commission, sins of; omission,
      sins of
slavery, 278, 281
Sleeping Beauty (Disney), 82, 311–12, 319, 320
sleep paralysis, 239–40
snakes
    basilisk in Harry Potter book series, 77, 78–79,
      80–81, 82
    feminine-serpent relationship, 79–80n
    in Garden of Eden, 79n
    St. Patrick's banishment of, 75
    as symbolic of human evil, 81
    See also dragons and monsters
social contract, 6
social institutions
    balancing creative transformation with, 47–48
    and conforming to social norms, 29–30
    distinguishing between functioning and
      non-functioning, 30–31
    gratitude for, 34, 47

as hierarchical structures, 11
and language, 8
problem solving function of, 9–11
self-serving criticism of, 32–34
thoughtless denigration of, 10
socialism, 163, 168
social problems, 169–70, 176–77
Socrates, 52
somatization, 243
"Song of Myself" (Whitman), 211–12
Soviet Union, 163, 167, 219, 220
spirit, 197
status, differences in, 28–29
stories
    behavioral norms shared through,
      55–58
    and children, 309–10, 311–12
    communication through, 41, 306–10
    as distillations of observed behavior, 55,
      57, 84
    and emergence of religion, 84
    generalizability of, 257
    memorable, 309
    and personalities, 37–38
    reframing, 235–36
    unforgettable, 52, 54, 55–58
    value of, 37n
    wisdom derived from, 257
strength
    drawing on, xxii–xxiii
    potential for, 341
    while facing death, 365–67
subordination in marriage, 274–75
success
    demonization of, 174–75
    and prerequisite failures, 103–4
suffering
    ability and authority required to
      address, 25
    acceptance of life's, 75
    acting nobly in the face of, 356
    ameliorating, 356–57
    and antinatalism, 361, 362–64
    of Christ during Crucifixion, 362
    confrontation of, 343, 355–56
    consciousness of, as embittering, 363
    and destructive potential of nature, 317
    and family health crises, xv–xxii
    inevitability of, 355
    of poorly integrated people, 183
    and resentment, 339
    as truism in religious thinking, 114
    without meaning, 117
    worthy goals as antidote to, 134

suicide, 363
superego, 4
surrealism, 225
systems deemed unjust, 174–75

Taoist cosmogony, 70n
Tarot and the Fool, 18, 154
tears, emotions underlying, 281
temperaments, inborn, 30, 331
Ten Commandments given to Moses, 56–57,
    193–96
The Terror That Comes in the Night (Hufford),
    239–40
Thanksgiving holidays, 368–69
Tiamat (Mesopotamian goddess), 67–68, 69–70,
    73, 107, 258
"to hell with it" philosophy, 351–52
Tolkien, J. R. R.
    The Hobbit, 75, 76, 80
    The Lord of the Rings, 76
totalitarianism
    fortifying your position against, 149–51
    historical outcomes of, 167
    and imbalance of chaos and order, xxiv
    move toward, in the West, 147
    and Nietzsche, 162, 164
    willingness to transform as guard against, 86
tradition
    and apprenticeship, 192
    Jesus' relationship with, 44–47, 197
    and necessity of the new, 224
    and perils of carelessly destroying culture, 70
tragedies of life, 339–40, 341, 367
traumas
    developing causal theories for
        understanding, 263
    experiencing malevolence, 236–42, 243–49
    inability to forget poorly understood,
        229–34
    refusal to think through past, 229
    sexual abuse, 234–36
    somatization following, 243
Tree of Life, 273
tribalism, 191
trust
    courage to, 104, 271
    in marriage, 271–72
    people's testing of, 280
    requirements of, 271–72
    willingness to extend, 104–5
truth, 259–60, 272, 344, 350

12 Rules for Life (Peterson), xxv, xxvii, 24, 157–60
tyranny, 147–49, 278, 281

Übermensch of Nietzsche, 164–65, 168
univariate causes ascribed to complex
        problems, 174
unknown
    deeply embedded fear of, 314
    as predator, 80
    serpents as symbolic of, 79n
    as source of knowledge, 212–14
    voluntarily confronting sources of, 78n

values
    attacked by casual rational criticism, 161–62
    communicated through stories, 37
    and Nietzsche, 161–65
Van Gogh, Vincent, 210
veganism, 321, 323–24
victimization, sense of, 338–40
victims, innocent, 175
violence, human capacity for, 240–41, 252
Voldemort, 18, 80–81, 82
vulnerability, 348–49

wealth and the wealthy, 172, 175
whales, 311, 335
Whitman, Walt, "Song of Myself," 211–12
widows/widowers, 287–88
wildebeest, 223–24
willful blindness, 94, 97, 106–7, 119, 121, 320
The Will to Power (Nietzsche), 162
wisdom, 350
Wise King persona, 328–29, 334, 342
women
    and careers, 284
    and creation story, 273
    feminine-serpent relationship, 79–80n
    power of rejection held by, 80n
    and pregnancies, 284, 319
    Wahhabism's views of, 176n
    who don't want children, 283–84
the Word (Logos), 258, 344
Wordsworth, William, "Ode: Intimations of
        Immortality from Recollections of Early
        Childhood," 207–8, 210, 226–27
workplace. *See* employment and workplace
writing exercises, therapeutic, 32n, 250–51n,
        250–52

Žižek, Slavoj, 361–62